REAL ESTATE FINANCE

REAL ESTATE
FINANCE

SHERMAN J. MAISEL

University of California, Berkeley

Harcourt Brace Jovanovich, Publishers

San Diego   New York   Chicago   Austin   Washington, D.C.

London   Sydney   Tokyo   Toronto

PREFACE

Real estate finance has emerged as one of the most dynamic fields in our economy, experiencing rapid progress in both analysis and practice. The recent developments incorporated in this book include advances in the application of new concepts from the general field of finance, the important changes in analytical emphasis resulting from the Tax Reform Act of 1986, and the rapid change in lenders' behavior following the inflationary and deregulatory buffeting they absorbed in the early 1980s.

This volume presents an initial exposure to real estate finance for students with diverse needs and interests who are taking their first course in this field. Some may be active real estate professionals; others plan careers in the field after college. Many students may be taking the course because real estate is so critical to the operations of financial institutions. Others are interested in real estate because it is one of the largest areas for investment. Still other students want financing information because of the significant role the purchase of a home plays in a family's success in saving and investing.

Although this book was planned primarily for introductory courses in real estate finance or investment, it may be used successfully, with supplementary readings, with students who plan to take only a single real estate course. Instructors teaching such general courses should find that this volume includes the topics students feel are the most interesting and relevant.

Innovation, Progress, and Change

During the past decade, progress and innovation in real estate finance have been fully as great as the rapid pace of real estate development itself, and of the growth of new products in such fields as chemicals and electronics. In its preparation, I found that I could use unchanged less than ten percent of my previous work in the field. First, the Tax Reform Act of 1986 made much of the previous literature obsolete. Approaches to financing that featured tax considerations had to be replaced by those emphasizing the underlying economic feasibility of the investment. Second, the rise of the secondary market and the deregulation of financial institutions led to significant innovations in the way most private, long-term borrowing takes place. Third, inflation, deflation, and wide swings in interest rates caused major reactions in credit costs and availability, as well as in real estate prices and the volume of building. Finally, new concepts of finance and investment helped move real estate analysis forward. The types of mortgages proliferated, making it more difficult for both borrowers and lenders to figure the costs, yields, advantages, and disadvantages of the different instruments without these new techniques.

Even a partial listing of the many approaches revised or given greater emphasis in *Real Estate Finance* must be long in comparison with many earlier texts. Featured here are such concepts as these:

- The application of the modern theory of finance to basic lending, borrowing, and investing decisions.
- The secondary market and how mortgage-backed securities work; the increased role of the investment community.
- The important interaction between the general market for credit and the mortgage market.
- Analyzing the costs, benefits, and risks of the new types of mortgages.
- Making decisions about whether to borrow or lend on the new types of income property mortgages.
- The factors that determine what interest rates are charged on mortgages.
- Changes in sources of mortgage money and the future role of the thrift industry.
- The importance of prepayments and buy-downs in determining the rate and yield on mortgages.
- The impact of inflation and deflation on affordability and the costs of home ownership or of other investments in real estate.
- Shopping for mortgages using the new computer-assisted services.
- Analyzing and structuring loans on income properties so that borrowers and lenders share risks and profit possibilities.

An Overview of This Book

The aim of *Real Estate Finance* is to offer students the background and analytical concepts needed to answer the many questions they will face when making decisions to borrow, lend, or invest in real property.

Part 1 of the book supplies necessary background, an overview of upcoming issues, and the basic concepts needed for real estate financing analysis. It discusses what a mortgage is and how it works; the costs and premiums that determine a mortgage's interest rate; and valuation concepts, including discounted cash flows, rates of return, and leverage.

Part 2 describes the sources of mortgage money and the reasons they fluctuate. Shifts in the sources and uses of funds, and actions taken by the Federal Reserve, cause changes in interest rates and the availability of funds. Such changes dominate much of real estate activity. The organization of real estate lending and sources of funds are also changing. The most significant development has been the greatly expanded secondary market.

Part 3 examines closely the financing of individual homes from the viewpoints of both the buyer and the lender. In addition to analyzing standard and creative financing mortgages, it shows how students can develop answers to the questions paramount in most buyers' minds: "How much should I pay and borrow in buying a home?" and "What will my real costs be?"

Part 4 examines in detail the analysis necessary for financing and investing in income properties. It emphasizes the fact that similar considerations enter into decision analysis whether one is a borrower or a lender. Several basic case examples that span entire chapters illustrate the analysis of standard loans and investments, the impact of tax reform, and the great variety of possible lending and investing arrangements.

Each part is nearly self-sufficient as an instructional unit; therefore, instructors may assign the parts in any order they desire. Although Chapters 1–4 (Part 1) and Chapter 5 form a necessary introduction, instructors can then move directly to the analysis of income properties in Part 4, or to the discussion of home ownership in Part 3. The sources of funds and the secondary market (Part 2) can be studied first, last, or along with other material.

Each chapter contains pedagogical aids designed to help students master the material in the text. An *Objectives* section outlines what students should grasp upon completing the chapter. For review purpose, a *Summary* section focuses neatly on the chapter's main points and a *Key Terms* list includes the boldfaced major terms from the chapter. (Other important terms are italicized where they are mentioned.) A *Questions* section asks that students apply concepts presented in the chapter to solve analytical problems; it was designed as well to promote retention of important ideas and to stimulate independent thought about background issues.

Key concepts that require practical illustration are followed by *Examples,* which provide students with analyses of financing situations they may encounter beyond the classroom.

Two of the chapters contain *appendixes* for instructors who wish to use them. Chapter 7, "The Government and Housing Finance," concludes with an appendix on direct federal housing assistance. Chapter 9, "Change and the Mortgage Market of the Future," contains an appendix on calculating duration.

A useful *Glossary* at the end of the book contains the boldfaced key terms from the chapters. Concluding each definition is the chapter number in which the term is discussed.

An *Instructor's Manual,* designed to be most useful in the preparation of quizzes and tests, contains answers to end-of-chapter questions, discussion of points worth special emphasis, and true-or-false and multiple-choice questions and answers.

Acknowledgments

I am indebted to a large number of individuals who helped make this work possible. My students at the University of California, Berkeley, who used the text in preliminary form, caught many errors and showed me where simplifications or further elaborations were desirable. Alan Cerf, Ned Eichler, David Hartzell, Kenneth Lusht, Mary McDonald, John Opperman, Kenneth Rosen, and Wallace

Smith provided helpful criticism of early drafts of the manuscript. I am also grateful for research support through my chair as California Professor of Real Estate and Urban Economics, funded by the California Department of Real Estate, and from the Center for Real Estate Research at the University of California, Berkeley.

My able research assistants were Watson Chan and Charles Martin. An excellent editing and production job was done at Harcourt Brace Jovanovich by Kenneth Rethmeier, Craig Avery, and Karen Lenardi, editors, and by Diane Pella, the book's designer. As always, this effort would not have been possible without the constant aid and support of my wife, Lucy, who was the book's primary editor.

Sherman J. Maisel

CONTENTS

3 Interest Rates, Discount Rates, and Present Values 48

4 Debt Service, Rates of Return, and Leverage

11 Creative Financing and Alternative Mortgage Instruments

PART 4 ANALYSIS FOR FINANCING INCOME PROPERTIES

14 Decisions to Invest and Lend on Income Properties

15 The Lender's Evaluation

A Background for Real Estate Financing

1 Introduction to Real Estate Finance

OBJECTIVES

When you finish this chapter, you should be able to:

- recognize the major participants in real estate finance.

- understand the relationship between mortgage availability and real estate activity.

- describe the main sources of mortgage funds.

- discuss some of the forces changing the mortgage market.

SOONER OR LATER most Americans invest in some kind of real estate—a house, income property, or real estate securities. Many such investments have been spectacularly successful; others have been failures. The fluctuating supply and cost of mortgage money are critical in determining success or failure. When mortgages are obtainable at reasonable rates, real estate sales and prices rise. In credit crunches, sales fall drastically while prices adjust more slowly.

Mortgage loans account for the greatest share of all private borrowing, and real estate lending is a major function of most financial institutions. Their profits or losses depend heavily on how well they do in this market. Recently real estate loans have caused the bankruptcy or near failure of some of our largest financial institutions.

Since credit is of crucial importance in most real estate deals, knowledge of how the loan market operates is fundamental for all real estate professionals. Successful investments, property development, and sales depend on obtaining proper financing at the right price. Given the many ways in which financing can be structured, professionals must understand how the many alternatives differ in their ability to increase potential gains and raise or lower the risks of failure.

New pressures have altered traditional mortgage lending. Fifty years ago, most mortgage money came from local lenders. Every loan was treated differently and, once made, loans were held until the debt was paid off. Today, mortgages are traded in a national market. The ability to sell mortgages over a wider area has increased competition and lowered costs. But even while many features have become more standardized, the types and terms of mortgages have become more diverse.

THE FLOW OF CAPITAL FOR REAL ESTATE FINANCE

The study of real estate finance analyzes the decisions by which money resources are raised for the purpose of owning or developing real property. Although all decisions could be, and sometimes are, made by a single person, two or three separate parties are usually active in a financing transaction (see Figure 1-1):

1. As users of capital, potential developers and owners of real estate must obtain financing in order to build, own, and operate properties. Very different financial analyses lie behind decisions made by the largest group of users, those who wish to own homes, compared to the decisions made in buying income properties or land.
2. Funds are supplied by a variety of individuals, firms, institutions, and governments. Some of these institutions are discussed in detail in Chapter 6.

3

Figure 1-1
The Flow of Real Estate Financial Capital

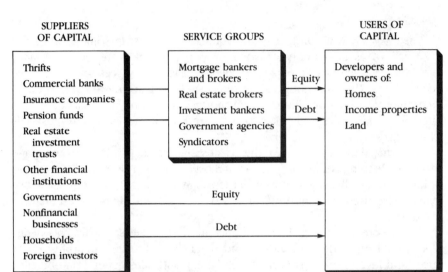

Federal, state, and local governments and their agencies have become increasingly important sources of funds, as have foreign investors.

3. Between the users and the sources of funds are a number of service organizations that make raising capital easier and more efficient. Some funds do go directly from suppliers to users, as many institutions and non-institutional investors operate directly with the final users. However, the importance of service groups has been growing. Mortgage and real estate brokers help locate funds and advise users about the best sources of funds. Mortgage and investment bankers have grown in importance as more funds are raised in securities markets. The government agencies have also expanded their role. **Syndicators***—promoters who sell shares in properties—have built up nationwide sales organizations and have utilized the stockbroker community to raise large amounts of equity capital.

Debts and Equities

Financial capital flows from suppliers to users in the form of both debt and equity. Lenders furnish funds in return for debt instruments. A **debt** is an obligation of a borrower to make payments in accordance with the terms of a specific agreement. In real estate finance, debt obligations are usually secured

---

*Words printed in boldface are key terms. A list of key terms appears at the end of each chapter. These terms are also collected and defined in the Glossary at the end of the book. Words in italics are less significant but still important terms, or terms that appear elsewhere in boldface.

by a *mortgage,* an instrument that pledges property as collateral to insure repayment.

Other funds are supplied by investors who own **equity.** They have the residual claim against the revenues from the operation or sale of a property. Equity owners are obligated to pay off the debt, but they then have the right to all the remaining income.

The Financing Revolution

Mortgages have always played a key role in modern economies. Major industries such as construction, real estate, savings banks, insurance, and banking are heavily influenced by the mortgage market. Following World War II, the **thrift industry,** consisting of savings and loan associations and savings banks, and government-insured loans dominated lending on residential properties. The markets were protected by government regulations and subsidies. Most loans were made on fixed-rate mortgages.

The past decade witnessed great changes. Inflation and fluctuating interest rates shook the foundations of the market. New technology, international markets, more information, developments in financial theory, and deregulation emphasizing freer markets meant that business as usual was no longer possible. As a result of deregulation, financial institutions entered new markets. They could lend in different ways and to a wider circle of customers. New forms of mortgages and new sources of funds came to dominate the market. An increasing share of home mortgages has been funded in the general markets for capital instead of in separate, isolated, local markets.

The equity market for income properties has also become more national and international. Formerly, lenders such as large insurance companies made loans nationwide, but ownership was mainly in the hands of either corporate users or local investors. Now syndications, insurance companies, pension funds, and real estate investment trusts invest and raise money throughout the nation.

The changes in both lending and investing have had significant effects on how real estate is financed, on the cost of funds and the expected returns, and on the level of new construction.

THE CHALLENGE OF REAL ESTATE FINANCE

All of the participants in real estate finance—whether it is a would-be homeowner seeking a loan, someone planning to sell or invest in real property, an employee of a financial institution active in lending and building a mortgage portfolio, or a mortgage or investment banker developing new ways to raise money on securities—require certain basic knowledge to function well. This book is planned to present the background and analytical concepts they need and can use. Each of its four parts examines a separate set of ideas and institutions basic to real estate financing decisions.

Part 1 provides the necessary background to the study of real estate finance: what mortgages are, what interest rates cover, and how loans and investments are valued. Part 2 examines the availability, cost, and sources of mortgage funds. It explains how interest rates are determined, both in the general financial markets and in the housing market in particular. It examines the main sources of funds and shows how and why they have been shifting. Especially important is the growth of the secondary mortgage market, in which existing mortgages are bought and sold (discussed in Chapter 8).

Part 3 examines borrowing on individual homes. It explains the lending criteria set by lending agencies and shows how they evaluate loan applicants. And it points out how the problem of affordability has led to "creative financing" and a variety of new types of mortgages. Part 4 is concerned with decisions to finance income properties and new construction. It explains the key factors in making decisions to lend and invest. It gives examples of how complex lending and investing have become. And it describes the techniques and analysis used by both sources and users of financial capital.

What Determines Interest Rate Levels?

How much it costs to borrow and the terms of repayment determine whether real estate purchases are financially possible and, to a great extent, profitable. Some lucky people still pay only 5 percent interest on their mortgages; those who borrowed in 1981 had to pay 19 percent or higher.

Major swings in rates primarily reflect movements in overall interest rates. However, special factors in the mortgage market also enter. At times, government regulations and subsidies have brought about low mortgage rates. Rates have also been low because lenders badly underestimated the risks of inflation and mispriced key features of their loans.

Mortgages must carry rates high enough to make them competitive in deregulated markets. However, there is no guarantee that current rates are at an equilibrium. In the short run, underlying supply and demand may not match. Special institutional features in the mortgage market cause rates to vary considerably around the competitive norm. If we understand why interest rates change, we can understand the effect they are likely to have on prices, rents, and sales in real estate markets.

Who Lends on Mortgages?

Where to obtain money is a basic problem in real estate finance. Thrift institutions—the major source of mortgage loans—were among those hardest hit by inflation and rising interest rates. They had borrowed from short-term lenders to lend on long-term mortgages. The imbalance in the maturity of their borrowing and lending and the lack of diversity in their portfolios (they were concentrated geographically and by type of loan) led to an erosion of their net worth and forced them to change their operations. Their share of mortgage lending and their competitive position in the market have fluctuated widely.

Partly as a result of their problems, but for other reasons as well, a massive expansion has occurred in the secondary mortgage market, where existing mortgages are traded among investors. In the mid-1980s, the number of mortgages sold by lenders to new holders equaled 70 percent of all mortgages originated. The biggest change was due to the large-scale entry of government agencies into the secondary market. Their purchases of mortgages and the sales of securities which depend on their guarantees have ranged between 40 percent and 80 percent of all residential mortgage loans.*

In real estate finance, shifts occur constantly in where best to borrow and in available terms. Knowledge of the sources of funds, and why they operate as they do, can lead to more profitable operations. In addition, investors must be able to recognize and take advantage of the fact that the new techniques of buying, selling, and pledging mortgages have generated a major new security market which is a source not only of funds, but also of jobs and profits.

How Can Home Buyers Obtain Affordable Financing?

If mortgage interest rates rise, many would-be borrowers are knocked out of the market because they cannot qualify for a loan at the high rates. That is, lenders will not give them money because they believe the borrower's income that is available for repaying the loans is too small. In the early 1980s, this inability of borrowers to qualify for credit brought about the rise of **"creative financing"**—the use of nontraditional techniques that allow people to buy properties even when interest rates are high. The problem facing the mortgage market is not hard to understand. Houses are a very large durable item. They are expensive and cost several times the normal family income. Given limited income and wealth, how can borrowers make the necessary payments in periods of high interest?

The procedures lenders follow determine how difficult it is for borrowers to qualify for a loan and what loan seekers can do to improve their chances. Anyone selling or buying homes needs to understand the basic rules in order to make possible adjustments that would permit a sale to go through.

The types of mortgages available and methods of borrowing on them have proliferated. In housing markets in many recent years, less than half of the loans were made with fixed rates. The other half were nontraditional loans carrying varying interest rates and payments that are combined in hundreds of possible ways. The new instruments reflect major changes in the way the mortgage market functions and in the needs and desires of those in the market. The advantages and disadvantages peculiar to each loan differ greatly depending on what occurs

*Federal Home Loan Mortgage Corporation, *Secondary Mortgage Markets* (quarterly) carries detailed information on this market.

in the economy after the loan is made. Unexpected events can bring about large economic gains and losses.

Those engaged in financing should understand the major innovations and be aware of their risks and advantages. In the recent past, many home buyers suddenly found themselves with unexpectedly high payments because they did not understand what they had signed. Many institutions found themselves in similar distress. When they made new types of loans, they entered into expensive contracts because they failed to recognize the effects of "creative" new clauses and conditions.

Investments and Loans for Income Properties: A New Sophistication

Large as the changes in the single-family market have been, those for income properties are probably greater. New sources of equity capital and new lending techniques have become extremely significant. Many new and more complex loans have come into existence. Lenders became investors, just as sellers of equities became lenders.

Traditional methods of evaluating loans and investments have come under attack as more sophisticated techniques have developed. Players in the markets need to understand why the changes have occurred and how to use the new techniques to analyze opportunities. Perhaps even more important, they must recognize the possible analytical weaknesses in order to understand how and why the techniques may go wrong.

Changes in the ability to afford purchases and to qualify for loans occur because movements in financing terms cause major reactions in the prices and profitability of buying and holding property. The study of real estate finance enables us to understand such changes. It shows us how to take the potential impact of financing into account in order to determine which loans and investments are sound and which are not.

THE MORTGAGE MARKET AND THE ECONOMY

Daily newspapers carry pages filled with stock prices and news of the stock market. Sharp ups and downs in the stock market often hit the front page and become the lead stories on the evening television news. In contrast, you have to search hard in the *Wall Street Journal* or the financial section of most newspapers to find brief items about what is happening to prices and interest rates in the mortgage market. Yet the dollar amount of mortgages outstanding roughly equals that of common stock.* Although mortgage prices do not fluctuate as much in a day as stock prices do, they still experience major ups and downs.

Prospects for Financial Markets in 1986 (New York: Salomon Brothers, 1985), Tables 2, 3c.

Furthermore, the changes in the mortgage market may cause an individual's wealth to vary as much as or more than do the movements in stock prices. To buy real property, most people need financing. Shifts in the mortgage market cause large swings in the value of properties nationally and in the number of construction starts. The major bursts of speculation and overdevelopment experienced by the real estate market have almost always been financed by an excess availability of mortgage funds.

In 1986, outstanding mortgage debt was over $2.3 trillion. This total was nearly three times as large as all outstanding corporate and foreign bonds. More than a third of all private funds borrowed in the United States come through the mortgage market.

The large size of the mortgage market reflects the importance of real estate to the rest of our economy. Total private investment in real property in the United States is well over $9 trillion, or more than 75 percent of all private wealth in the country.* Even through business equipment and inventories and holdings of consumer goods are more frequently analyzed and discussed, their combined share of our wealth is less than one-quarter of that of real property.

Mortgages and Housing Starts

Housing production is one of the most important and volatile segments of our economy. Fluctuations in the level of house building exert a multiplied effect on production and the gross national product. Figure 1-2 reflects the instability of housing starts from 1947 to 1985. The number of units started bounced up and down, declining 50 percent, rising 100 percent every few years. Few sectors of the economy fluctuate more than house building. It is a major cause of cycles of national prosperity and depression.

Mortgage interest rates are also unstable. More important for the economy, however, has been the apparent upward shift in their level (see Figure 1-3). From 1955 to 1965, mortgage interest rates averaged under 5.5 percent. Between 1965 and 1969, they rose more than 40 percent, to over 8.5 percent. In 1973 they jumped again and then continued to rise. Between 1977 and 1981, they doubled before coming part of the way back down. One of the questions for the future is whether they are likely to be more stable.

The relationship among the factors of ample or tight credit, mortgages, housing production, and sales is clear. When the demand for credit exceeds supply at the previous rates, mortgage interest rises. But higher rates *cut* the demand for new houses. Simultaneously, the availability of mortgage funds to builders and home purchasers is curtailed. Almost all studies of housing show that these two factors—mortgage availability and rates—are the driving forces causing the fluctuations in housing starts.

---

*Board of Governors of the Federal Reserve System, *Flow of Funds Accounts* and *Balance Sheets for the U.S. Economy,* 1985.

Figure 1-2

The Number of U.S. Housing Starts Quarterly from 1947 to 1985

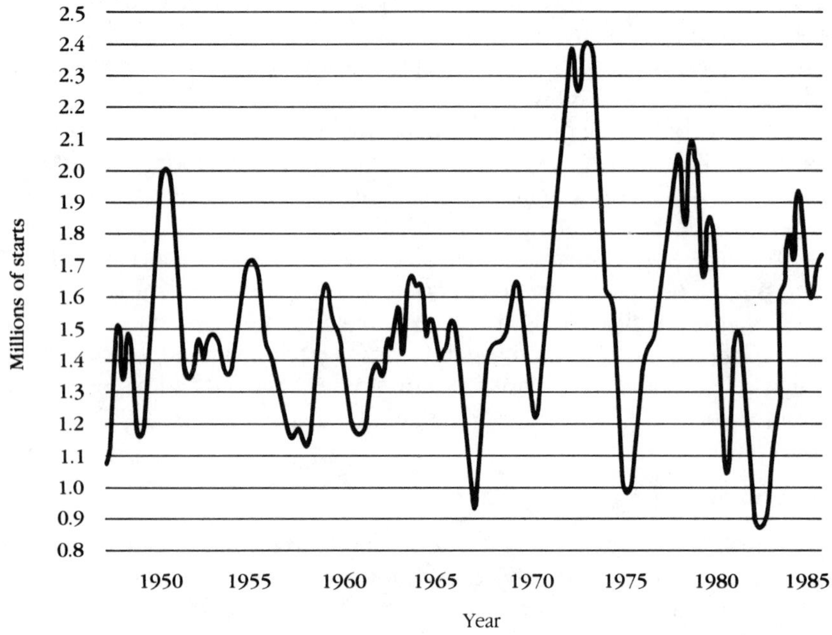

Source: U.S. Bureau of the Census, *Housing Starts, Construction Reports,* Series C-20 (Washington, D.C.: U.S. Government Printing Office) (various years).

Mortgages, Wealth, and Welfare

Interest rates have a direct impact on the welfare and wealth of everyone in the economy. When interest rates rise, fewer families can afford to buy houses. Property values fall because less financing is available. Higher interest rates lower the amount and quality of housing space demanded. The income of creditors rises, as do the expenses of those with new or adjustable-rate loans.

It is easy to see why prices and demand fall. If interest rates are 10 percent, a standard-payment $75,000 25-year mortgage requires a monthly payment of $681. If interest rates rise to 14 percent, the monthly payment on this same mortgage goes up to $908, or about one-third higher. Fewer families can afford the larger payments. Home buyers must accept less space with fewer amenities. Some would-be buyers double up with family or friends, or live in mobile homes or other types of less expensive housing.

For commercial properties, the depressing effect of higher payments and less available credit is reinforced by the fact that higher interest rates directly lower a property's value. The value of a capital asset is equal to the present value of the discounted future income expected from it. A rise in interest rates increases

Figure 1-3
Average Mortgage Interest Rates
Yield, Including Fees, Monthly from 1963 to 1985

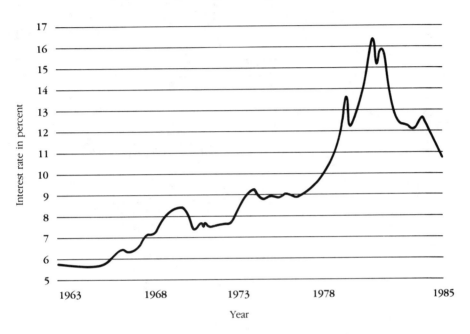

Source: U.S. Federal Home Loan Bank Board, *Federal Reserve Bulletin,* Table 1.53, "Mortgage Markets."

the amount of discount. This lowers the value of future income and, therefore, the price of the property.

SOURCES OF MORTGAGE MONEY

Table 1-1 gives an overview of the mortgage market. It shows the total amount of money lent in this market, the main types of loans made, and the major lenders. The years 1979, 1982, 1984, and 1985 were chosen to demonstrate the variations in amounts lent by lenders in the course of a credit cycle. When interest rates rise, certain lenders almost disappear from the market. Since variations in lending tend to level out over the course of cycles, the total amount outstanding, shown here for 1986, gives a better picture of the average participation in the market than does the amount due in any single year.

Over $227 billion was lent in the mortgage market in 1985. Of this amount about two-thirds went to one- to four-family houses and the remainder to income properties. The total amount of outstanding loans was over $2.3 trillion in 1986—an amount far surpassing that of any other type of private debt. A comparison of the amount mortgage loans grow in a given year with the total amount out-

Table 1-1
Mortgage Holding and Lending
(in billions of dollars)

	Net Mortgage Lending (Increases in Outstandings)				Total Outstanding Mortgage Holdings	
						Percent of
	1979	1982	1984	1985	1986	Total
All holders, total	166.2	86.2	211.2	227.6	2,365	100.0
By Type of Property:						
For one- to four-family dwellings	121.7	50.4	129.6	149.6	1,550	65.6
For multifamily dwellings	8.3	5.3	20.1	24.8	215	9.1
For commercial property	24.4	25.2	62.5	58.1	500	21.1
For farm property	11.8	5.3	(1.0)	(4.9)	100	4.2
By Type of Lender:						
A. Financial institutions						
Commercial banks	32.0	21.6	44.3	48.2	447	18.9
Thrifts	49.1	(25.6)	83.0	55.9	795	33.6
Life insurance companies	12.6	4.2	5.7	11.2	173	7.3
Other financial institutions	2.9	4.0	9.9	10.6	160	6.8
B. Government agencies and mortgage pools	50.4	71.5	57.6	89.1	625	26.4
C. Individuals	19.2	16.2	10.7	12.6	165	7.0

Source: Adapted from U.S. Federal Home Loan Bank Board, *Federal Reserve Bulletin* (various issues), Table 1.54, "Mortgage Debt Outstanding."

standing indicates that the average mortgage loan remains in existence for between 8 and 11 years.

Types of Lenders

It is important to distinguish between those who originate mortgages— that is, those who make the initial loan—and those who actually put up the money, the ultimate lenders who hold the mortgages in their portfolios. The latter are shown in Table 1-1. Chapter 8, which discusses the secondary mortgage market, explains the significant differences between originators and ultimate lenders.

Thrift Institutions Savings and loans and savings banks hold the largest share of mortgage loans. They account for about 34 percent of all outstanding mortgages and have a slightly higher share of the residential mortgage market. However, note that the amount lent by thrifts can vary greatly from year to year, as Table 1-1 reflects. In 1982, thrifts appear to have taken money out of the mortgage market. Their net holdings of mortgages fell by about $26 billion, although their holdings of securities backed by mortgages rose.

Governments The second largest source of funds consists of government agencies and mortgage pools based on their guarantees. This group accounts for about 27 percent of outstanding mortgages. In recent years, their market share has been larger. Note that in 1982, when the mortgage market was in a state of near collapse, they accounted for more than 80 percent of the funds advanced (including securities sold with government guarantees).

Commercial Banks Banks make up the third largest source of funds. Commercial banks are the largest construction lenders, furnishing nearly half of the money advanced in this submarket. They are also an important source for larger mortgages on income properties, and they provide short-term financing to other lenders. Banks differ widely in their approach to the home mortgage market. Some act almost like thrifts, putting most of their money into mortgages; other banks avoid this market completely.

Other Lenders Insurance companies, miscellaneous financial institutions, and direct loans from households are the other main sources of funds. In later chapters, when we study their operations in more detail, we will see tremendous variations in the types of loans each lender makes, in their reasons for being in the market, and in what they look for in deciding whether or not to lend.

Changing Sources

Variations in the amounts lent by different types of institutions reflect movements in the availability of credit and in interest rates. In 1981 and the first half of 1982, thrift institutions were in the midst of a financial crisis. Their deposit inflows were low and many institutions were in trouble. Rumors questioned the soundness and safety of the whole savings system. As a consequence, these institutions sold off mortgages, and their lending ground to a halt.

Life insurance companies were once major lenders on homes, but after 1980 they lent less than the amounts paid off. With drastic upheavals occurring in credit markets, insurance companies were unwilling to make fixed-rate loans on houses. They concentrated their mortgage lending in the commercial area, where their loans enabled them to share in any future increases in the income or value of properties.

A major group in the mortgage market is that of the large investment banking firms. They do not appear in Table 1-1 because they are primarily brokers and security underwriters. Salomon Brothers and First Boston, among others, are the main sources through which mortgage securities and the bonds and notes of the federal government agencies are sold. As a result, the interest rates borrowers now pay depend more on what Wall Street thinks will happen to rates than on the views of the management of local banks and thrift institutions.

THE MARKET FOR REAL ESTATE LOANS

The mortgage market is an **over-the-counter market** held together by telephones and computers. This does not make it unique, since the most active markets in the country—those for government bonds and short-term money funds—also depend completely on the interactions of borrowers, lenders, brokers, and dealers operating from offices throughout the country.

Well over 20,000 firms, with more than double that number of offices, participate in the real estate finance market. The firms range in size from Citibank, the country's largest financial institution with over $140 billion in assets, to single individuals making one or a few loans. Although competition is limited in some small towns, this has become far less true for the country as a whole. Anyone with a telephone or a computer can obtain the going price for a number of standard types of mortgages in a few minutes. Purchases and sales take place rapidly almost anywhere. As noted earlier, the number of mortgages bought and sold in the secondary market alone has run as high as 70 percent of all originations. Over 2.5 million mortgages are traded in a year.*

The Old Mortgage Market

A decade ago, books on real estate finance stressed the complexity and uniqueness of mortgage loans and the forces that separated the mortgage market from the general credit market. The reasons for this emphasis are clear:

- There was no organized market for obtaining mortgage money or price quotations.
- Thousands of submarkets, each somewhat separated from the others, existed in every city and town throughout the country. In each of these, a variety of mortgages and notes covering all types of loans on real property were traded.
- Each loan is tied uniquely to an individual property.

*Federal Home Loan Mortgage Corporation, *Secondary Mortgage Markets*.

- Although mortgage loans can range from a few hundred dollars to millions of dollars, they are usually small compared to most financial deals. Furthermore, a majority of borrowers are financially unsophisticated.
- Loan terms vary greatly depending on the specific factors affecting each loan, such as the location, type, age, and quality of the property, the creditworthiness of the borrower, and general money market conditions.
- Each state has different legal requirements, which cause considerable variation among specific mortgages.
- The residential market was dominated by specialized lenders regulated and subsidized by the federal government. Under the regulations, lenders were generally restricted to their own local areas.
- It was assumed that mortgages lacked liquidity; once made, they were difficult to resell.

Although the older books emphasized all of these factors, they did point out that a national mortgage market was developing. Even with all of their special features, local rates still remained near the national norm.

The New National Market

Although many of these same factors still exist today, emphasis must be placed on the unifying forces of the overall market. Local variations in prices and terms compared to the national average are far smaller. Differences in yields have tended to disappear. Consistency across local markets is far greater.

The growth of the secondary market has brought about major changes. The greatest force for change has been the important role in lending played by the government agencies—the Federal Housing Administration (FHA), the Veterans Administration (VA), the Federal National Mortgage Association (FNMA), called "Fannie Mae," and the Federal Home Loan Mortgage Corporation (FHLMC), called "Freddie Mac." One of the main objectives of the federal agencies has been to bring about a standardization of residential mortgages. They have been very successful in achieving this goal. Even those loans not planned for placement with Fannie Mae or Freddie Mac tend to be written so that they can be sold to them in an emergency.

Another major source of change has been the coming of age of the computer. Real estate brokers and other professionals can get an immediate printout of the rates and terms available in the market. With proper arrangements, loans can be applied for, the applications processed, and the final loan paperwork accomplished on the computer, far from the actual lender.

The terms and conditions for borrowing on income properties remain far more individual. But here, too, an information explosion has occurred. Knowledge of available terms and specific conditions is far more general and easier to obtain.

New Government Participation

The transformations in the mortgage market also reflect other government actions, such as the deregulation of deposit institutions and the frequent changes in the tax laws. The role of the FHA and VA in the market has varied depending on the tightness of the market and the federal administration's view of what the place of those agencies should be.

The government housing agencies experienced a tremendous growth based on their successful expansion of the secondary market and, more recently, their entry into the market for mortgage-backed securities. Government subsidies through federally assisted low-rent housing rose and then declined. Local issues of tax-exempt bonds fluctuated widely. The Reagan administration attacked the entire range of government housing programs on the basis that housing was being aided at the expense of other types of needed investments. How government housing programs evolve and change in the future will be the result of the ongoing political process.

A PREVIEW OF MAJOR CHANGES

Numerous and opposing forces have been at work in the mortgage market. The growth of the national market led to standardization of mortgages and the integration of mortgage and general market interest rates. In the early 1980s, higher rates, greater risks, and a shortage of long-term funds caused new methods and instruments of purchasing and borrowing to proliferate. (Each of these developments is discussed in more detail in later chapters.)

Greater Complexity

Another key force behind the transformation to more involved transactions has been inflation. It brought about much higher interest rates, which compensate lenders for the fact that the dollars they get back in payment may be worth less than those they lent. The higher rates mean that fewer families can generate sufficient cash flows to meet traditional mortgage terms.

Inflation does not necessarily raise borrowers' real costs, since property values and income also inflate. However, unless mortgage terms are adjusted to compensate for high rates, many borrowers have too little current income to enter the market. Furthermore, since rates fluctuate more, the risks to lenders of borrowers' defaults, of capital losses, and of untimely prepayments (which eliminate lenders' planned income from regular payments) are much greater. Lenders who fail to take these factors into account can be wiped out.

In the 1970s, inflation, interacting with fixed mortgage terms and tax subsidies, created a bonanza for borrowers. From 1975 to 1980, the rise in the costs of borrowing on mortgages lagged behind rises in the price level of real estate. Tax deductions and appreciated property values more than offset interest payments, so that the net costs of owning property were negative. This was a crucial factor in raising the demand for real estate and for mortgages, which led to the rapid rise in property values during the 1970s.

However, identical factors led to difficulties in the 1980s and to far more complex mortgage deals. The Federal Reserve Board raised the real cost of borrowing in order to fight inflation. Lenders drafted terms that they hoped would allow them to share expected gains. The anticipated increase in value became less certain as the rate of inflation declined. In fact, at times property values actually fell. Sound borrowing and lending called for far more knowledge and analysis.

Traditionally, real estate finance depended on loans at fixed rates for long periods—20 to 30 years. Such funds became much harder to find. Lenders who had made such fixed-rate loans lost large amounts and got out of the market. Thrift institutions saw their fixed-interest deposit base disappear. They had to match the amounts they charged for their loans to their new fluctuating deposit rates. Insurance companies found far fewer customers willing to make long-term saving commitments. Short-term interest rates more frequently rose above long-term rates, causing severe problems for fixed-rate lenders. All of these developments contributed to substantial changes in the terms and conditions of mortgage.

Residential Loans

The desire of lenders to avoid interest rate risks led to **adjustable-rate mortgages (ARMs).** In these loans, interest charges move in accordance with some money market rate, such as the interest paid on 3-month or 1-year U.S. Treasury securities, which are more closely related to lenders' cost of funds.

Because borrowers needed to solve the difficult problem of finding cash for high payments, **graduated payment mortgages (GPMs)** were developed, in which the scheduled payments rise over time. For the same reason, no- or **negative amortization mortgages** were introduced, in which the interest owed accumulates and is paid only when a property is sold or refinanced. Another new type—**shared appreciation mortgages (SAMs)**—sets interest below the market rates in return for an agreement between lender and borrower to split any profits arising from an increase in the value of the property.

When market interest rates rose, borrowers found that their low fixed-rate mortgages had considerable value. When such properties were sold, if the new owners could keep the old, low-interest mortgages rather than having to refinance, they could save interest costs and would be willing to pay more for housing. This led to legal and political battles over the right of lenders to demand payment upon resale (due-on-sale clauses) and the use by owners of more than one mortgage on a property.

The need for additional sources of funds created a major new market for bonds and certificates secured by a pool of mortgages, so-called **mortgage-backed securities.** (Mortgage-backed securities are discussed in Chapter 8.)

Loans on Income Properties

Since the mid-1970s, lenders in the commercial loan market have been anxious to reduce their risk and share in any profit. Those who have had money available to lend for income property could command the terms, since few income properties could be developed without outside funds.

Some commercial innovations have been similar to those in the residential market—adjustable rates, negative amortization, and shared appreciation. A critical development was a reduction in the length of loans. A great many mortgages now require that terms be renegotiated every three, five, or ten years.

Today, more and more loans for income properties force borrowers to give up a share of the profits. In some cases, all rents or incomes beyond minimum levels must be split with the lender. In other cases, if property values rise, the loans may be convertible into an ownership share. In many situations, the lender becomes a partner (joint venturer), receiving an ownership percentage in return for granting a loan with somewhat reduced interest rates.

Borrowers seeking to avoid relinquishing ownership rights have been willing to offer second, third, or even higher-order mortgages at much higher interest rates.

The acceptance by the market of these and similar innovations has increased the number of possible combinations and permutations of commercial mortgage terms and conditions. As later chapters demonstrate, the variety of loan arrangements available today greatly increases not only the potential ways of financing real property, but also the difficulty of analyzing those arrangements.

The Future

The changes in the mortgage market and the forces behind them raise important questions for the future. During the 1970s, many observers assumed that the rapid rise in real estate values during that period was based on immutable law. They concluded that features inherent in the real estate market made it certain that most future participants would profit. With further experience, others now believe that with the new, more complex mortgages, real estate markets are unlikely to revert to past conditions. Anticipated price increases can fail to materialize. Tax advantages will be smaller. Lenders are more likely to demand terms that protect against unexpected events. There have been strong pressures to get the government out of the provision of subsidies and to deregulate.

The chapters that follow explain the new developments in real estate finance. They show why the market has moved so rapidly away from the past and provide the background to understand the evolution of real estate finance. In these chapters are the tools to keep students and practitioners abreast of future innovations and to enable them to analyze the pros and cons of the wide variety of different lending and borrowing possibilities that are now available in real estate finance.

SUMMARY

In the process of financing real estate, developers and owners obtain financial capital from lenders and investors. They may obtain the funds directly or through individuals and firms established to help facilitate the process.

The mortgage market is the largest of all credit markets. It plays an important role in determining the number of housing starts as well as the sales and prices received for real property. When funds are available, demand for real estate rises, more construction takes place, prices increase, sales are brisk. In tight money periods, the opposite occurs.

The market is widely diversified, but it is tied together by mail, phones, and computers. Thousands of institutions and even more individuals make loans. These organizations range in size from very small to those with assets of $140 billion.

The mortgage market is intimately related to other credit markets and to monetary policies. Who is in the market, the terms they offer, and the loans they make vary widely depending on credit conditions.

The rate of innovation in mortgage types has been extremely high. Under the pressure of inflation and high, fluctuating interest rates, mortgage lenders were forced to change their product. Deregulation and the expansion of the secondary market under government leadership have led to massive shifts in the sources of funds and the types of loans.

KEY TERMS

adjustable-rate mortgage (ARM)
"creative financing"
debt
equity
graduated payment mortgage
    (GPM)
mortgage-backed securities

negative amortization
    mortgages
over-the-counter market
shared appreciation mortgage
    (SAM)
syndicators
thrift industry

QUESTIONS

1. In the light of recent developments, do you think that mortgages in the future will become more standardized or more diverse?
2. Fluctuations in housing starts are related to the movements of mortgage lending. Explain briefly how this comes about.
3. "When mortgage interest rates rise, more borrowers are able to obtain loans because lenders, anticipating higher profit, provide more credit." Evaluate this statement.
4. Discuss briefly some recent innovations in the mortgage market and what brought them about.

5. Who are the major lenders in the mortgage market.
6. What is the relationship between net mortgage lending and total mortgages outstanding?
7. Describe the trend of movements in the market shares of major mortgage lenders.
8. The mortgage market has many characteristics similar to other over-the-counter markets. Why, then, is there less mortgage information available in the financial press?

2 What Is a Mortgage?

OBJECTIVES

When you finish this chapter, you should be able to:

- describe the principal parts of a promissory note and a mortgage.

- explain what a standard fixed-rate mortgage is.

- understand how the share of the payment going to repay principal varies over time.

- explain affordability and its dependence on interest rates and on the term of a mortgage.

- recognize the similarities and differences between a mortgage and a deed of trust.

- discuss acceleration, due-on-sale, and rights of redemption.

- define defaults and foreclosure by judicial action or power of sale.

- offer reasons for recording mortgages and for borrowing on junior mortgages.

MORTGAGES AND DEEDS OF TRUST are central to real estate finance. In order to understand how they work, we must examine the concept of secured loans and their special features. Because the terminology of mortgage lending is important, much of this chapter is devoted to explaining the main terms as they appear in the standard fixed-rate mortgage. Mortgages are legal contracts covering individual loans involving large sums of money and long periods; therefore, they must be drafted carefully to cover many unique contingencies. Recently, however, the trend has been to use more and more standardized features in order to cut costs. Thus home mortgages tend increasingly to be similar to one another. Mortgages on income properties, however, remain more individualized.

MORTGAGES, NOTES, AND MORTGAGE BONDS

A favorite story among mortgage bankers tells of a builder who tried to buy a $300 suit on credit and was turned down. He then went next door to the bank, where he was quickly granted a $200,000 loan to build a house. The story illustrates the difference in the ability to borrow money on a secured as opposed to an unsecured debt. The bank assumed that it could collect because it held a mortgage secured by real property.

A **mortgage** is a contract that pledges a specific property as collateral to insure the repayment of a debt. The property serves as a **security,** or a promise that the borrower will meet the terms agreed upon. If the borrower fails to do so, the lender has the right to have the property sold to satisfy the debt. The ability to mortgage property means that borrowers obtain larger loans at lower interest and for longer periods. If they cannot pay, lenders expect that the mortgaged buildings will sell for enough to allow them to recover their money.

The amount of money borrowed and the terms of repayment for a real estate loan are described in a **promissory note** or in a *mortgage bond.* The notes and bonds are negotiable instruments. If not paid, the owner can sue to collect. A mortgage or deed of trust serves as an additional instrument to pledge a property as security for the repayment of the debt.

A typical promissory note, used when money is borrowed on real estate, contains the borrower's promise to pay and the terms of the loan. The note lists the interest rate, when and where the payments are due, prepayment rights or charges, and other pertinent information. In Figure 2-1, for example, prepayment is allowed without penalty; see clause 4. In the note, the borrower agrees to keep payments current and to accept the conditions that will cause the note to default.

Clause 8 makes clear that the note is a personal obligation and liability. In case of failure to repay, the borrower can be sued, as with any other debt. In

Figure 2-1
A Note to Accompany a Mortgage Contract

NOTE

...., 19......... ...., ...
                                                                     [City]   [State]

....
[Property Address]

1. BORROWER'S PROMISE TO PAY

In return for a loan that I have received, I promise to pay U.S. $... (this amount is called "principal"), plus interest, to the order of the Lender. The Lender is .... I understand that the Lender may transfer this Note. The Lender or anyone who takes this Note by transfer and who is entitled to receive payments under this Note is called the "Note Holder."

2. INTEREST

Interest will be charged on unpaid principal until the full amount of principal has been paid. I will pay interest at a yearly rate of ....%.

The interest rate required by this Section 2 is the rate I will pay both before and after any default described in Section 6(B) of this Note.

3. PAYMENTS

(A) Time and Place of Payments

I will pay principal and interest by making payments every month.

I will make my monthly payments on the .... day of each month beginning on ...., 19......... I will make these payments every month until I have paid all of the principal and interest and any other charges described below that I may owe under this Note. My monthly payments will be applied to interest before principal. If, on ...., ..., I still owe amounts under this Note, I will pay those amounts in full on that date, which is called the "maturity date."

I will make my monthly payments at .... or at a different place if required by the Note Holder.

(B) Amount of Monthly Payments

My monthly payment will be in the amount of U.S. $..

4. BORROWER'S RIGHT TO PREPAY

I have the right to make payments of principal at any time before they are due. A payment of principal only is known as a "prepayment." When I make a prepayment, I will tell the Note Holder in writing that I am doing so.

I may make a full prepayment or partial prepayments without paying any prepayment charge. The Note Holder will use all of my prepayments to reduce the amount of principal that I owe under this Note. If I make a partial prepayment, there will be no changes in the due date or in the amount of my monthly payment unless the Note Holder agrees in writing to those changes.

5. LOAN CHARGES

If a law, which applies to this loan and which sets maximum loan charges, is finally interpreted so that the interest or other loan charges collected or to be collected in connection with this loan exceed the permitted limits, then: (i) any such loan charge shall be reduced by the amount necessary to reduce the charge to the permitted limit; and (ii) any sums already collected from me which exceeded permitted limits will be refunded to me. The Note Holder may choose to make this refund by reducing the principal I owe under this Note or by making a direct payment to me. If a refund reduces principal, the reduction will be treated as a partial prepayment.

6. BORROWER'S FAILURE TO PAY AS REQUIRED

(A) Late Charge for Overdue Payments

If the Note Holder has not received the full amount of any monthly payment by the end of .... calendar days after the date it is due, I will pay a late charge to the Note Holder. The amount of the charge will be ....% of my overdue payment of principal and interest. I will pay this late charge promptly but only once on each late payment.

(B) Default

If I do not pay the full amount of each monthly payment on the date it is due, I will be in default.

(C) Notice of Default

If I am in default, the Note Holder may send me a written notice telling me that if I do not pay the overdue amount by a certain date, the Note Holder may require me to pay immediately the full amount of principal which has not been paid and all the interest that I owe on that amount. That date must be at least 30 days after the date on which the notice is delivered or mailed to me.

(D) No Waiver By Note Holder

Even if, at a time when I am in default, the Note Holder does not require me to pay immediately in full as described above, the Note Holder will still have the right to do so if I am in default at a later time.

Continued

Continued

(E) Payment of Note Holder's Costs and Expenses

If the Note Holder has required me to pay immediately in full as described above, the Note Holder will have the right to be paid back by me for all of its costs and expenses in enforcing this Note to the extent not prohibited by applicable law. Those expenses include, for example, reasonable attorneys' fees.

7. GIVING OF NOTICES

Unless applicable law requires a different method, any notice that must be given to me under this Note will be given by delivering it or by mailing it by first class mail to me at the Property Address above or at a different address if I give the Note Holder a notice of my different address.

Any notice that must be given to the Note Holder under this Note will be given by mailing it by first class mail to the Note Holder at the address stated in Section 3(A) above or at a different address if I am given a notice of that different address.

8. OBLIGATIONS OF PERSONS UNDER THIS NOTE

If more than one person signs this Note, each person is fully and personally obligated to keep all of the promises made in this Note, including the promise to pay the full amount owed. Any person who is a guarantor, surety or endorser of this Note is also obligated to do these things. Any person who takes over these obligations, including the obligations of a guarantor, surety or endorser of this Note, is also obligated to keep all of the promises made in this Note. The Note Holder may enforce its rights under this Note against each person individually or against all of us together. This means that any one of us may be required to pay all of the amounts owed under this Note.

9. WAIVERS

I and any other person who has obligations under this Note waive the rights of presentment and notice of dishonor. "Presentment" means the right to require the Note Holder to demand payment of amounts due. "Notice of dishonor" means the right to require the Note Holder to give notice to other persons that amounts due have not been paid.

10. UNIFORM SECURED NOTE

This Note is a uniform instrument with limited variations in some jurisdictions. In addition to the protections given to the Note Holder under this Note, a Mortgage, Deed of Trust or Security Deed (the "Security Instrument"), dated the same date as this Note, protects the Note Holder from possible losses which might result if I do not keep the promises which I make in this Note. That Security Instrument describes how and under what conditions I may be required to make immediate payment in full of all amounts I owe under this Note. Some of those conditions are described as follows:

Transfer of the Property or a Beneficial Interest in Borrower. If all or any part of the Property or any interest in it is sold or transferred (or if a beneficial interest in Borrower is sold or transferred and Borrower is not a natural person) without Lender's prior written consent, Lender may, at its option, require immediate payment in full of all sums secured by this Security Instrument. However, this option shall not be exercised by Lender if exercise is prohibited by federal law as of the date of this Security Instrument.

If Lender exercises this option, Lender shall give Borrower notice of acceleration. The notice shall provide a period of not less than 30 days from the date the notice is delivered or mailed within which Borrower must pay all sums secured by this Security Instrument. If Borrower fails to pay these sums prior to the expiration of this period, Lender may invoke any remedies permitted by this Security Instrument without further notice or demand on Borrower.

WITNESS THE HAND(S) AND SEAL(S) OF THE UNDERSIGNED.

....(Seal)
-Borrower

....(Seal)
-Borrower

....(Seal)
-Borrower

[Sign Original Only]

addition, however, as clause 10 points out, the debt is secured by an accompanying contract—a mortgage, deed of trust, or security deed—which can also be used to protect the lender from loss.

Personal **liability** means that if the property is sold but it does not yield enough to satisfy the lender's claim, the lender may seek a **deficiency judgment** or writ to collect the difference from the borrower. For example, if the lender receives $150,000 after costs from the sale of a foreclosed property on which the debt is $200,000, the lender may seek a judgment of $50,000, which the debtor would have to pay from other assets or from income.

States place many restrictions on deficiency judgments. In some states, they cannot be obtained if the mortgage was taken out in the course of a purchase (a **purchase-money mortgage**). In others, the value of the property must be determined separately, whatever the amount received in the foreclosure sale. Many states require that deficiency judgments will be granted only after costly court procedures and long delays. As a result, deficiency judgments have become rare, particularly for owner-occupied houses. However, the threat that they might be obtained must be taken into account in proper investment planning.

The last section of the note repeats a very important condition contained in the mortgage. It is a promise called a **due-on-sale clause.** If the borrower sells or transfers the property being used as a security, the lender has the option of requiring immediate payment of all sums still owed. When lenders make a loan, they consider the borrower's credit and reason for borrowing. The due-on-sale clause gives the lender a chance to refuse credit to a poor risk. What is more important is that it allows the lender to renegotiate the terms of the loan. If interest rates have risen, the lender can demand the new, higher market rate.

THE MORTGAGE AND THE DEED OF TRUST

The Mortgage Relationships

As has been noted, a mortgage is a contract that pledges rights in a specific property to insure repayment of a debt. A deed of trust serves the same purpose, but it introduces a trustee between the borrower and the lender. Both mortgages and deeds of trust require a note and a pledge of security for them to fulfill their purpose. Except in a legal context, the term *mortgage* is used generally to describe the many ways in which money can be borrowed with property as security. It also refers to the amount borrowed through a secured loan on real estate. Thus it encompasses deeds of trust as well.

The mortgage part of Figure 2-2 illustrates a typical mortgage situation. A borrower—also called a debtor or **mortgagor**—gives a note and a mortgage to the lender—also known as the creditor or **mortgagee**—as security for the money lent. Lenders usually *record* the mortgage instrument, for reasons to be discussed later. That is, they file it with the proper official to place it on the public record. When or if the debt is repaid, the mortgagee-lender returns a release for the mortgage.

Title and Lien Theories Two different theories of the nature of real estate mortgages are found among the states. They are called the title theory and the lien theory. Under the **title theory,** a mortgage transfers legal title to the mortgaged property from the mortgagor-borrower to the mortgagee-lender as a security for the loan. In theory, possession is also transferred, but most mortgages in title theory states carry provisions that allow borrowers to keep pos-

Figure 2-2
The Difference between a Mortgage and a Deed of Trust

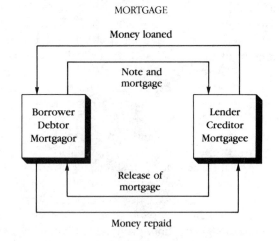

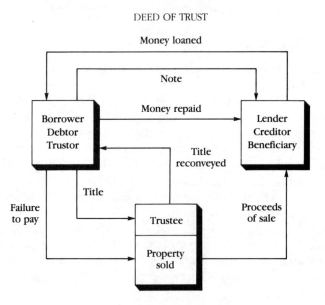

session as long as they do not default on their obligation. In case of default, the borrower's rights are terminated and the lender retains title and gains possession.

Most states use the **lien theory,** under which the mortgage creates a **lien**—a claim on the property as security—in favor of the lender. If the borrower fails to pay, the lender can go to court to enforce the lien in order to have the property sold for his benefit. In many states, the mortgage may include a *power of sale* clause, which allows the property to be sold in settlement of a debt without a judicial procedure.

The Deed of Trust

More complex relationships exist in a deed of trust than in a mortgage. Trust deeds introduce a third party at some additional expense, but they cut the cost of obtaining repayment when a security must be sold. The **deed of trust** involves three parties (refer again to Figure 2-2). The borrower signs a note to the lender—also known as the **beneficiary**—listing the conditions of the loan. The borrower also signs a trust deed that conveys the bare legal title of the property to a **trustee.** Such a deed contains a power of sale that the trustee can exercise if the borrower fails to meet the conditions of the loan. If the property is sold, the proceeds go to the lender-beneficiary. If no default arises, the trustee's title lies dormant. The grantor of the trust retains all normal ownership rights. When the debt is paid off, the trustee reconveys the title.

Although on the surface the deed of trust looks quite different from the mortgage, they serve the same function. Courts tend to treat them similarly. In practice, the variations among states in the ways in which they treat mortgages are greater than the differences between mortgages and trust deeds.

Deeds of trust are not allowed in all states. Where they exist, they are advantageous to lenders because they facilitate the foreclosure process. They tend to reduce slightly the interest rates compared to a standard mortgage.

THE STANDARD FIXED-RATE MORTGAGE

Many types of agreements can be entered into and secured by mortgages. These days, fewer contracts are of the kind traditionally considered standard. The number of payment patterns has been proliferating. However, an examination of the standard or **fixed-rate mortgage (FRM)** remains a good starting point. By first understanding the features of the standard mortgage, we gain a better grasp of why and how other types of agreement have evolved.

Mortgage Payments

How much a borrower must pay monthly, quarterly, or in total depends on the amount of the loan, on the interest and fees charged, and on the rate at which the debt is paid off or decreased.

1. The amount of money owed as debt is called the **principal.** In the usual case, lenders furnish cash. However, buyers often take over debts already in existence, and sellers often accept debt for part of their payment.
2. Lenders may charge a **loan fee**—typically from 1 percent to 3 percent of the amount lent. The fee may have to be paid at the time of the loan, or it may be included in the principal.

3. **Interest** is the charge for the use of money. It is usually expressed as a given percent per year of the principal. For example, a charge of $10 (the interest) for one year on a loan of $100 (the principal) yields a simple interest rate of 10 percent a year.
4. Loans must be repaid in a certain period. The length of this period is called the **term** of the loan—for example, 5, 15, or 30 years. The date of the final payment is the **maturity date** for the loan.
5. Most loans require repayment of part of the principal on an installment basis. In a standard mortgage, each monthly payment pays off some of the principal. The process of periodic repayment is called **amortization.**
6. The amount of each payment stated as a percent of the total loan is called the **mortgage constant,** or K. If the monthly payment on a $100,000 loan is $1,000, the monthly mortgage constant is 1 percent. In annual terms, if the annual payment is $12,000, the annual mortgage constant is 12 percent.

The amount of each payment is determined by the principal, interest rates, the term, and the form of amortization. Lenders set quite firm limits on the relationship between a borrower's or a property's income and payments. Amortization agreements must often be adjusted to arrive at periodic payments low enough to meet the lender's standards.

Equal Level Payments

The standard fixed-rate mortgage calls for equal monthly payments. Some of each payment goes to pay the required interest and some pays off part of the principal. Because the outstanding balance declines each month, the amount owed for interest on the outstanding principal also declines. This allows the sum applied to reducing the principal to increase each month.

EXAMPLE: Suppose that you borrow $50,000 on a mortgage at 12 percent interest and a term of 30 years. Table 2-1 contains an excerpt from a standard compound interest table summarizing the division of each payment between interest and principal. We note from column 2 that such a mortgage requires a monthly payment of $514.30, or $6,171.60 per year for each of the 30 years. Columns 3 and 4 demonstrate that in the first year most of your loan payments would be applied to cover the interest due, with the total reduction in principal being only $181.40, or less than .5 percent of the amount outstanding. However, the share going to interest declines every month because the interest rate applies against a smaller principal. Still, since so little has been paid off in the first year, most of your payments in the second year also go to interest, with the principal repayment rising only slightly. While the balance has shifted somewhat by the tenth year, 90 percent of the payment still covers interest.

In the final column, note that even after you have made payments for ten years, less than 7 percent of the debt is paid off. By year 20, principal payments

Table 2-1
Annual Summary of Monthly Payments
On a $50,000 30-Year Mortgage at 12 Percent Interest

Year	Annual Debt Service	Interest	Principal	Cumulative Principal Payments	End-of-year Principal Balance
1	$6,171.60	$5,990.20	$ 181.40	$ 181.40	$49,818.60
2	6,171.60	5,967.20	204.40	385.80	49,614.20
10	6,171.60	5,640.20	531.40	3,291.00	46,709.00
20	6,171.60	4,417.70	1,753.90	14,152.60	35,847.40
28	6,171.60	1,612.80	4,558.80	39,074.40	10,925.60
29	6,171.60	1,034.60	5,137.00	44,211.40	5,788.60
30	6,171.60	383.10	5,788.50	50,000.00	0.00

are more significant, but they still remain below one-third of the annual payment. Very few people stay in one house and make mortgage payments on it for 30 years, but it is only toward the end of the life of the loan that the amount going to principal increases sharply.

Figure 2-3 illustrates more completely how the standard FRM works. Part A shows the gradual drop in the share of the payment going to interest. The decline in interest on the amount owed becomes rapid only in the last one-third of the loan period. Part B shows that even though the interest requirements decrease steadily, only after half the life of the loan does the gradual increase in monthly amortization have much effect on the amount outstanding.

Prepayments

The standard FRM usually lets the borrower pay off the loan faster than agreed to in the mortgage. The ability of borrowers to prepay either part or all of the principal is a **prepayment privilege.** A **closed mortgage** does not allow prepayment; an **open mortgage** does. Most single-family home mortgages are open, but they usually specify a prepayment penalty if more than some share—perhaps 20 percent—is paid off in any of the first five years. Such penalties are set by agreement. A common penalty might be six months' interest, or the penalty might be between 1 percent and 5 percent of the amount paid off.

This penalty is assessed because lenders may lose money when a mortgage is prepaid. Loan fees do not cover the entire cost of making a mortgage. If interest rates have dropped, the lender will receive less income because the amount

Figure 2-3
Amortization of a Loan

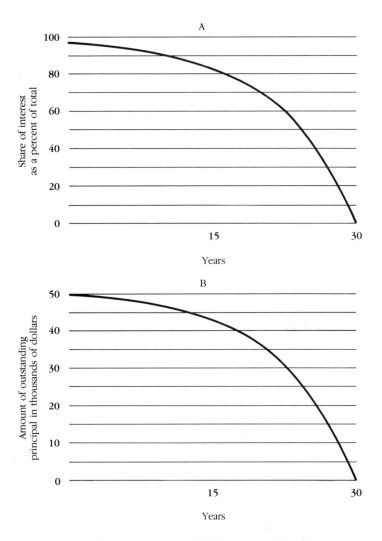

Amortization slowly decreases the share of a fixed mortgage payment going to interest and raises the share going to principal. In this example of a $50,000 12 percent loan for 30 years, the percent of each payment going to interest declines year by year (A), while the amount of principal still owed remains high until near the end of the loan period (B).

repaid must be reloaned at a lower interest rate. In recent years, many mortgages on income properties have been closed for 5 to 7 years, with penalties charged on prepayments that occur after the mortgage becomes open.

Loan Terms and Monthly Payments

Since payments depend on both the interest rate and the term, altering either will modify the amount required to be paid monthly. The lower the amount of payment required per dollar of loan, the larger the loan a borrower can afford, since less income is required to qualify for a loan of a given size.

Standard payment tables, such as Table 2-2, summarize the relationships between the required payments, interest rates, and the term of a loan. The table lists the monthly installments to amortize a $10,000 mortgage at different interest rates and a variety of maturities. The required payments rise with interest rates and fall as the period of amortization extends. For example, if the borrower agrees to pay 16 percent interest on a $10,000 loan and to amortize it over 5 years, the borrower would have to pay $243.13 per month. The same loan at 6 percent interest and a 40-year amortization would require only $55.02 per month. Of course, payments also increase with the size of the loan.

Standard payment tables enable us to find the monthly or annual payments on a loan of any size. For example, to find the annual payment of $6,171.60 in the second column of Table 2-1, take the $102.86 monthly payment on a 30-year 12 percent mortgage of $10,000 from Table 2-2 and multiply by 5 to find the amount of payment for a $50,000 loan. Multiply again by 12 to obtain the annual payment.

AFFORDABILITY

Lenders normally restrict the amount they will lend so that the monthly payment to cover principal, interest, and (frequently) property taxes and insurance (P.I.T.I.) does not exceed a certain percentage either of a family's income

Table 2-2
Monthly Payments to Amortize a $10,000 Loan in a Given Period

Terms in Years	Monthly Payments	Interest Rates					
		6%	8%	10%	12%	14%	16%
5	60	$193.33	$202.76	$212.47	$222.44	$232.68	$243.18
10	120	111.02	121.33	132.15	143.47	155.27	167.51
15	180	84.39	95.57	107.46	120.02	133.17	146.87
20	240	71.64	83.64	96.50	110.11	124.35	139.13
25	300	64.43	77.18	90.87	105.32	120.38	135.89
30	360	59.96	73.38	87.76	102.86	118.49	134.48
35	420	57.02	71.03	85.97	101.55	117.57	133.85
40	480	55.02	69.53	84.91	100.85	117.11	133.56

To amortize a $10,000 loan at 12 percent interest in 30 years, a borrower must pay $102.86 per month for 360 months.

or of the cash flow on an income property. Thus, both income and the size of the required payment determine how much can be borrowed. This concept, under which income and the required payment limit the ability to borrow enough to purchase a property, is called **affordability.** It plays a central role in all real estate financing.

Income Limits

EXAMPLE: Assume that a lender restricts the amount of a mortgage payment to 25 percent of a family's income. How much could a family with a monthly income of $1,755 afford to borrow for a house? Three separate factors are involved in setting the maximum mortgage the family could obtain:

1. the amount of the family's income
2. the limit on the share of the family income that lenders will permit to be allocated to the mortgage payment
3. the amount of the mortgage payment, which depends on the interest rate and term to maturity

If the family's income is $1,755 per month and lenders limit the mortgage payment to 25 percent of family income, the family could borrow as much as could be paid for with a payment of $438 per month. By dividing this sum by the required payments for a loan like that shown in Table 2-2, we can find the maximum loan amount allowed.

If interest rates were 10 percent, dividing the amount the family could afford by the payment per $10,000 ($438 ÷ $212), the family could borrow only about $20,000 if the loan had to be amortized over 5 years. In contrast, over $50,000 ($438 ÷ $85) could be borrowed if the amortization period was 40 years. Similarly, the table shows that the amounts that could be borrowed rise from under $20,000 ($438 ÷ $243) for a 5-year loan at 16 percent to almost $80,000 ($438 ÷ $55) for a 40-year loan at 6 percent interest—all for a family with $1,755 per month income. Note that the lower the interest, the more important the amortization period is in determining the size of the loan.

The Amount of Amortization

In order to increase the amount of a loan obtainable with a given income level, nonstandard mortgages have become more common. They have been especially prevalent in mortgages on income properties and in cases where sellers have financed a sale themselves. In many cases, for example, loans may be made without any amortization requirement. In an **interest-only loan,** the monthly payments cover the required interest. After a set period—say, five years— the entire principal must be repaid. In some cases **negative amortization,** in which payments are less than the interest owed, is permitted. The difference between the interest charge and the payment is added (or *accrues*) to the principal. When the mortgage becomes due, all the principal and accrued interest must be paid off.

Other agreements allow the amount of the payments to vary over time; either the interest charges or the rate of amortization may shift. A common method bases the amount of amortization on a period extending beyond the maturity date of the mortgage. For example, the level of monthly payments may be set at a rate that would amortize a loan over 30 years. In addition, the note requires that at the end of five years a payment must be made sufficient to repay all remaining principal. In these and similar examples, the final larger installment is called a **balloon payment.**

Loan-to-value Ratio

Affordability can also be affected by the required down payment. To protect the safety of deposit institutions and insurance companies, laws and regulations commonly restrict the amount most lenders can lend to a maximum percent of the appraised value of a property (or the selling price, if it is less). This maximum is usually expressed as a percentage of the value and is called the **loan-to-value ratio (LTV).** For example, a $50,000 mortgage on a house valued at $62,500 is said to have a loan-to-value ratio of 80 percent, or to be an 80 percent mortgage. This is typical, but the LTV may go up to 90 or 95 percent if mortgage insurance is obtained.

RIGHTS AND RESPONSIBILITIES OF BORROWERS AND LENDERS

Figure 2-4 is a uniform deed of trust. The Federal National Mortgage Association (Fannie Mae) and the Federal Home Loan Mortgage Corporation (Freddie Mac) require that this form be used for deeds of trust to be sold to them. There are only minor differences between this form and that which they require for mortgages. Both contain typical conditions outlining the rights and responsibilities of the lender and the borrower. The first page specifies the borrower, the lender, the trustee, and the property. It also refers to the underlying note and states that the borrower has the right to pledge the security.

The Covenants

The following sections outline agreements about the specific rights and duties of borrower and lender, called **covenants.** They enumerate special fees and charges as well as action to be taken if certain legal eventualities occur. They also require the borrower to keep adequate hazard insurance and to maintain the condition of the property. The lender can inspect the property to see that no waste is occurring. The covenants give the lender other rights, such as to

Figure 2-4
A Deed of Trust

──────────────── [Space Above This Line For Recording Data] ────────────────

DEED OF TRUST

THIS DEED OF TRUST ("Security Instrument") is made on ....,
19.......... The trustor is ....
.... ("Borrower"). The trustee is ....
.... ("Trustee"). The beneficiary is
...., which is organized and existing
under the laws of ...., and whose address is ....
.... ("Lender").
Borrower owes Lender the principal sum of ....
.... Dollars (U.S. $................................). This debt is evidenced by Borrower's note
dated the same date as this Security Instrument ("Note"), which provides for monthly payments, with the full debt, if not
paid earlier, due and payable on .... This Security Instrument
secures to Lender: (a) the repayment of the debt evidenced by the Note, with interest, and all renewals, extensions and
modifications; (b) the payment of all other sums, with interest, advanced under paragraph 7 to protect the security of this
Security Instrument; and (c) the performance of Borrower's covenants and agreements under this Security Instrument and
the Note. For this purpose, Borrower irrevocably grants and conveys to Trustee, in trust, with power of sale, the following
described property located in .... County, California:

which has the address of ...., ...,
                                        [Street]   [City]
California .... ("Property Address");
                    [Zip Code]

TOGETHER WITH all the improvements now or hereafter erected on the property, and all easements, rights,
appurtenances, rents, royalties, mineral, oil and gas rights and profits, water rights and stock and all fixtures now or
hereafter a part of the property. All replacements and additions shall also be covered by this Security Instrument. All of the
foregoing is referred to in this Security Instrument as the "Property."

BORROWER COVENANTS that Borrower is lawfully seised of the estate hereby conveyed and has the right to grant
and convey the Property and that the Property is unencumbered, except for encumbrances of record. Borrower warrants
and will defend generally the title to the Property against all claims and demands, subject to any encumbrances of record.

THIS SECURITY INSTRUMENT combines uniform covenants for national use and non-uniform covenants with
limited variations by jurisdiction to constitute a uniform security instrument covering real property.

CALIFORNIA—Single Family—FNMA/FHLMC UNIFORM INSTRUMENT   Form 3005 12/83

UNIFORM COVENANTS. Borrower and Lender covenant and agree as follows:

1. Payment of Principal and Interest; Prepayment and Late Charges. Borrower shall promptly pay when due the principal of and interest on the debt evidenced by the Note and any prepayment and late charges due under the Note.

2. Funds for Taxes and Insurance. Subject to applicable law or to a written waiver by Lender, Borrower shall pay to Lender on the day monthly payments are due under the Note, until the Note is paid in full, a sum ("Funds") equal to one-twelfth of: (a) yearly taxes and assessments which may attain priority over this Security Instrument; (b) yearly leasehold payments or ground rents on the Property, if any; (c) yearly hazard insurance premiums; and (d) yearly mortgage insurance premiums, if any. These items are called "escrow items." Lender may estimate the Funds due on the basis of current data and reasonable estimates of future escrow items.

The Funds shall be held in an institution the deposits or accounts of which are insured or guaranteed by a federal or state agency (including Lender if Lender is such an institution). Lender shall apply the Funds to pay the escrow items. Lender may not charge for holding and applying the Funds, analyzing the account or verifying the escrow items, unless Lender pays Borrower interest on the Funds and applicable law permits Lender to make such a charge. Borrower and Lender may agree in writing that interest shall be paid on the Funds. Unless an agreement is made or applicable law requires interest to be paid, Lender shall not be required to pay Borrower any interest or earnings on the Funds. Lender shall give to Borrower, without charge, an annual accounting of the Funds showing credits and debits to the Funds and the purpose for which each debit to the Funds was made. The Funds are pledged as additional security for the sums secured by this Security Instrument.

If the amount of the Funds held by Lender, together with the future monthly payments of Funds payable prior to the due dates of the escrow items, shall exceed the amount required to pay the escrow items when due, the excess shall be, at Borrower's option, either promptly repaid to Borrower or credited to Borrower on monthly payments of Funds. If the amount of the Funds held by Lender is not sufficient to pay the escrow items when due, Borrower shall pay to Lender any amount necessary to make up the deficiency in one or more payments as required by Lender.

Upon payment in full of all sums secured by this Security Instrument, Lender shall promptly refund to Borrower any Funds held by Lender. If under paragraph 19 the Property is sold or acquired by Lender, Lender shall apply, no later than immediately prior to the sale of the Property or its acquisition by Lender, any Funds held by Lender at the time of application as a credit against the sums secured by this Security Instrument.

3. Application of Payments. Unless applicable law provides otherwise, all payments received by Lender under paragraphs 1 and 2 shall be applied: first, to late charges due under the Note; second, to prepayment charges due under the Note; third, to amounts payable under paragraph 2; fourth, to interest due; and last, to principal due.

4. Charges; Liens. Borrower shall pay all taxes, assessments, charges, fines and impositions attributable to the Property which may attain priority over this Security Instrument, and leasehold payments or ground rents, if any. Borrower shall pay these obligations in the manner provided in paragraph 2, or if not paid in that manner, Borrower shall pay them on time directly to the person owed payment. Borrower shall promptly furnish to Lender all notices of amounts to be paid under this paragraph. If Borrower makes these payments directly, Borrower shall promptly furnish to Lender receipts evidencing the payments.

Borrower shall promptly discharge any lien which has priority over this Security Instrument unless Borrower: (a) agrees in writing to the payment of the obligation secured by the lien in a manner acceptable to Lender; (b) contests in good faith the lien by, or defends against enforcement of the lien in, legal proceedings which in the Lender's opinion operate to prevent the enforcement of the lien or forfeiture of any part of the Property; or (c) secures from the holder of the lien an agreement satisfactory to Lender subordinating the lien to this Security Instrument. If Lender determines that any part of the Property is subject to a lien which may attain priority over this Security Instrument, Lender may give Borrower a notice identifying the lien. Borrower shall satisfy the lien or take one or more of the actions set forth above within 10 days of the giving of notice.

5. Hazard Insurance. Borrower shall keep the improvements now existing or hereafter erected on the Property insured against loss by fire, hazards included within the term "extended coverage" and any other hazards for which Lender requires insurance. This insurance shall be maintained in the amounts and for the periods that Lender requires. The insurance carrier providing the insurance shall be chosen by Borrower subject to Lender's approval which shall not be unreasonably withheld.

All insurance policies and renewals shall be acceptable to Lender and shall include a standard mortgage clause. Lender shall have the right to hold the policies and renewals. If Lender requires, Borrower shall promptly give to Lender all receipts of paid premiums and renewal notices. In the event of loss, Borrower shall give prompt notice to the insurance carrier and Lender. Lender may make proof of loss if not made promptly by Borrower.

Unless Lender and Borrower otherwise agree in writing, insurance proceeds shall be applied to restoration or repair of the Property damaged, if the restoration or repair is economically feasible and Lender's security is not lessened. If the restoration or repair is not economically feasible or Lender's security would be lessened, the insurance proceeds shall be applied to the sums secured by this Security Instrument, whether or not then due, with any excess paid to Borrower. If Borrower abandons the Property, or does not answer within 30 days a notice from Lender that the insurance carrier has offered to settle a claim, then Lender may collect the insurance proceeds. Lender may use the proceeds to repair or restore the Property or to pay sums secured by this Security Instrument, whether or not then due. The 30-day period will begin when the notice is given.

Unless Lender and Borrower otherwise agree in writing, any application of proceeds to principal shall not extend or postpone the due date of the monthly payments referred to in paragraphs 1 and 2 or change the amount of the payments. If under paragraph 19 the Property is acquired by Lender, Borrower's right to any insurance policies and proceeds resulting from damage to the Property prior to the acquisition shall pass to Lender to the extent of the sums secured by this Security Instrument immediately prior to the acquisition.

6. Preservation and Maintenance of Property; Leaseholds. Borrower shall not destroy, damage or substantially change the Property, allow the Property to deteriorate or commit waste. If this Security Instrument is on a leasehold, Borrower shall comply with the provisions of the lease, and if Borrower acquires fee title to the Property, the leasehold and fee title shall not merge unless Lender agrees to the merger in writing.

7. Protection of Lender's Rights in the Property; Mortgage Insurance. If Borrower fails to perform the covenants and agreements contained in this Security Instrument, or there is a legal proceeding that may significantly affect Lender's rights in the Property (such as a proceeding in bankruptcy, probate, for condemnation or to enforce laws or

Continued

Continued

regulations), then Lender may do and pay for whatever is necessary to protect the value of the Property and Lender's rights in the Property. Lender's actions may include paying any sums secured by a lien which has priority over this Security Instrument, appearing in court, paying reasonable attorneys' fees and entering on the Property to make repairs. Although Lender may take action under this paragraph 7, Lender does not have to do so.

Any amounts disbursed by Lender under this paragraph 7 shall become additional debt of Borrower secured by this Security Instrument. Unless Borrower and Lender agree to other terms of payment, these amounts shall bear interest from the date of disbursement at the Note rate and shall be payable, with interest, upon notice from Lender to Borrower requesting payment.

If Lender required mortgage insurance as a condition of making the loan secured by this Security Instrument, Borrower shall pay the premiums required to maintain the insurance in effect until such time as the requirement for the insurance terminates in accordance with Borrower's and Lender's written agreement or applicable law.

8. Inspection.   Lender or its agent may make reasonable entries upon and inspections of the Property. Lender shall give Borrower notice at the time of or prior to an inspection specifying reasonable cause for the inspection.

9. Condemnation.   The proceeds of any award or claim for damages, direct or consequential, in connection with any condemnation or other taking of any part of the Property, or for conveyance in lieu of condemnation, are hereby assigned and shall be paid to Lender.

In the event of a total taking of the Property, the proceeds shall be applied to the sums secured by this Security Instrument, whether or not then due, with any excess paid to Borrower. In the event of a partial taking of the Property, unless Borrower and Lender otherwise agree in writing, the sums secured by this Security Instrument shall be reduced by the amount of the proceeds multiplied by the following fraction: (a) the total amount of the sums secured immediately before the taking, divided by (b) the fair market value of the Property immediately before the taking. Any balance shall be paid to Borrower.

If the Property is abandoned by Borrower, or if, after notice by Lender to Borrower that the condemnor offers to make an award or settle a claim for damages, Borrower fails to respond to Lender within 30 days after the date the notice is given, Lender is authorized to collect and apply the proceeds, at its option, either to restoration or repair of the Property or to the sums secured by this Security Instrument, whether or not then due.

Unless Lender and Borrower otherwise agree in writing, any application of proceeds to principal shall not extend or postpone the due date of the monthly payments referred to in paragraphs 1 and 2 or change the amount of such payments.

10. Borrower Not Released; Forbearance By Lender Not a Waiver.   Extension of the time for payment or modification of amortization of the sums secured by this Security Instrument granted by Lender to any successor in interest of Borrower shall not operate to release the liability of the original Borrower or Borrower's successors in interest. Lender shall not be required to commence proceedings against any successor in interest or refuse to extend time for payment or otherwise modify amortization of the sums secured by this Security Instrument by reason of any demand made by the original Borrower or Borrower's successors in interest. Any forbearance by Lender in exercising any right or remedy shall not be a waiver of or preclude the exercise of any right or remedy.

11. Successors and Assigns Bound; Joint and Several Liability; Co-signers.   The covenants and agreements of this Security Instrument shall bind and benefit the successors and assigns of Lender and Borrower, subject to the provisions of paragraph 17. Borrower's covenants and agreements shall be joint and several. Any Borrower who co-signs this Security Instrument but does not execute the Note: (a) is co-signing this Security Instrument only to mortgage, grant and convey that Borrower's interest in the Property under the terms of this Security Instrument; (b) is not personally obligated to pay the sums secured by this Security Instrument; and (c) agrees that Lender and any other Borrower may agree to extend, modify, forbear or make any accommodations with regard to the terms of this Security Instrument or the Note without that Borrower's consent.

12. Loan Charges.   If the loan secured by this Security Instrument is subject to a law which sets maximum loan charges, and that law is finally interpreted so that the interest or other loan charges collected or to be collected in connection with the loan exceed the permitted limits, then: (a) any such loan charge shall be reduced by the amount necessary to reduce the charge to the permitted limit; and (b) any sums already collected from Borrower which exceeded permitted limits will be refunded to Borrower. Lender may choose to make this refund by reducing the principal owed under the Note or by making a direct payment to Borrower. If a refund reduces principal, the reduction will be treated as a partial prepayment without any prepayment charge under the Note.

13. Legislation Affecting Lender's Rights.   If enactment or expiration of applicable laws has the effect of rendering any provision of the Note or this Security Instrument unenforceable according to its terms, Lender, at its option, may require immediate payment in full of all sums secured by this Security Instrument and may invoke any remedies permitted by paragraph 19. If Lender exercises this option, Lender shall take the steps specified in the second paragraph of paragraph 17.

14. Notices.   Any notice to Borrower provided for in this Security Instrument shall be given by delivering it or by mailing it by first class mail unless applicable law requires use of another method. The notice shall be directed to the Property Address or any other address Borrower designates by notice to Lender. Any notice to Lender shall be given by first class mail to Lender's address stated herein or any other address Lender designates by notice to Borrower. Any notice provided for in this Security Instrument shall be deemed to have been given to Borrower or Lender when given as provided in this paragraph.

15. Governing Law; Severability.   This Security Instrument shall be governed by federal law and the law of the jurisdiction in which the Property is located. In the event that any provision or clause of this Security Instrument or the Note conflicts with applicable law, such conflict shall not affect other provisions of this Security Instrument or the Note which can be given effect without the conflicting provision. To this end the provisions of this Security Instrument and the Note are declared to be severable.

16. Borrower's Copy.   Borrower shall be given one conformed copy of the Note and of this Security Instrument.

17. Transfer of the Property or a Beneficial Interest in Borrower.   If all or any part of the Property or any interest in it is sold or transferred (or if a beneficial interest in Borrower is sold or transferred and Borrower is not a natural person) without Lender's prior written consent, Lender may, at its option, require immediate payment in full of all sums secured by this Security Instrument. However, this option shall not be exercised by Lender if exercise is prohibited by federal law as of the date of this Security Instrument.

If Lender exercises this option, Lender shall give Borrower notice of acceleration. The notice shall provide a period of not less than 30 days from the date the notice is delivered or mailed within which Borrower must pay all sums secured by this Security Instrument. If Borrower fails to pay these sums prior to the expiration of this period, Lender may invoke any remedies permitted by this Security Instrument without further notice or demand on Borrower.

18. Borrower's Right to Reinstate. If Borrower meets certain conditions, Borrower shall have the right to have enforcement of this Security Instrument discontinued at any time prior to the earlier of: (a) 5 days (or such other period as applicable law may specify for reinstatement) before sale of the Property pursuant to any power of sale contained in this Security Instrument; or (b) entry of a judgment enforcing this Security Instrument. Those conditions are that Borrower: (a) pays Lender all sums which then would be due under this Security Instrument and the Note had no acceleration occurred; (b) cures any default of any other covenants or agreements; (c) pays all expenses incurred in enforcing this Security Instrument, including, but not limited to, reasonable attorneys' fees; and (d) takes such action as Lender may reasonably require to assure that the lien of this Security Instrument, Lender's rights in the Property and Borrower's obligation to pay the sums secured by this Security Instrument shall continue unchanged. Upon reinstatement by Borrower, this Security Instrument and the obligations secured hereby shall remain fully effective as if no acceleration had occurred. However, this right to reinstate shall not apply in the case of acceleration under paragraphs 13 or 17.

NON-UNIFORM COVENANTS. Borrower and Lender further covenant and agree as follows:

19. Acceleration; Remedies. Lender shall give notice to Borrower prior to acceleration following Borrower's breach of any covenant or agreement in this Security Instrument (but not prior to acceleration under paragraphs 13 and 17 unless applicable law provides otherwise). The notice shall specify: (a) the default; (b) the action required to cure the default; (c) a date, not less than 30 days from the date the notice is given to Borrower, by which the default must be cured; and (d) that failure to cure the default on or before the date specified in the notice may result in acceleration of the sums secured by this Security Instrument and sale of the Property. The notice shall further inform Borrower of the right to reinstate after acceleration and the right to bring a court action to assert the non-existence of a default or any other defense of Borrower to acceleration and sale. If the default is not cured on or before the date specified in the notice, Lender at its option may require immediate payment in full of all sums secured by this Security Instrument without further demand and may invoke the power of sale and any other remedies permitted by applicable law. Lender shall be entitled to collect all expenses incurred in pursuing the remedies provided in this paragraph 19, including, but not limited to, reasonable attorneys' fees and costs of title evidence.

If Lender invokes the power of sale, Lender shall execute or cause Trustee to execute a written notice of the occurrence of an event of default and of Lender's election to cause the Property to be sold. Trustee shall cause this notice to be recorded in each county in which any part of the Property is located. Lender or Trustee shall mail copies of the notice as prescribed by applicable law to Borrower and to the other persons prescribed by applicable law. Trustee shall give public notice of sale to the persons and in the manner prescribed by applicable law. After the time required by applicable law, Trustee, without demand on Borrower, shall sell the Property at public auction to the highest bidder at the time and place and under the terms designated in the notice of sale in one or more parcels and in any order Trustee determines. Trustee may postpone sale of all or any parcel of the Property by public announcement at the time and place of any previously scheduled sale. Lender or its designee may purchase the Property at any sale.

Trustee shall deliver to the purchaser Trustee's deed conveying the Property without any covenant or warranty, expressed or implied. The recitals in the Trustee's deed shall be prima facie evidence of the truth of the statements made therein. Trustee shall apply the proceeds of the sale in the following order: (a) to all expenses of the sale, including, but not limited to, reasonable Trustee's and attorneys' fees; (b) to all sums secured by this Security Instrument; and (c) any excess to the person or persons legally entitled to it.

20. Lender in Possession. Upon acceleration under paragraph 19 or abandonment of the Property, Lender (in person, by agent or by judicially appointed receiver) shall be entitled to enter upon, take possession of and manage the Property and to collect the rents of the Property including those past due. Any rents collected by Lender or the receiver shall be applied first to payment of the costs of management of the Property and collection of rents, including, but not limited to, receiver's fees, premiums on receiver's bonds and reasonable attorneys' fees, and then to the sums secured by this Security Instrument.

21. Reconveyance. Upon payment of all sums secured by this Security Instrument, Lender shall request Trustee to reconvey the Property and shall surrender this Security Instrument and all notes evidencing debt secured by this Security Instrument to Trustee. Trustee shall reconvey the Property without warranty and without charge to the person or persons legally entitled to it. Such person or persons shall pay any recordation costs.

22. Substitute Trustee. Lender, at its option, may from time to time appoint a successor trustee to any Trustee appointed hereunder by an instrument executed and acknowledged by Lender and recorded in the office of the Recorder of the county in which the Property is located. The instrument shall contain the name of the original Lender, Trustee and Borrower, the book and page where this Security Instrument is recorded and the name and address of the successor trustee. Without conveyance of the Property, the successor trustee shall succeed to all the title, powers and duties conferred upon the Trustee herein and by applicable law. This procedure for substitution of trustee shall govern to the exclusion of all other provisions for substitution.

23. Request for Notices. Borrower requests that copies of the notices of default and sale be sent to Borrower's address which is the Property Address.

24. Riders to this Security Instrument. If one or more riders are executed by Borrower and recorded together with this Security Instrument, the covenants and agreements of each such rider shall be incorporated into and shall amend and supplement the covenants and agreements of this Security Instrument as if the rider(s) were a part of this Security Instrument. [Check applicable box(es)]

☐ Adjustable Rate Rider   ☐ Condominium Rider   ☐ 2–4 Family Rider

☐ Graduated Payment Rider   ☐ Planned Unit Development Rider

☐ Other(s) [specify]

Continued

Continued
By Signing Below, Borrower accepts and agrees to the terms and covenants contained in this Security Instrument and in any rider(s) executed by Borrower and recorded with it.

....(Seal)
—Borrower

....(Seal)
—Borrower

——————————————————— [Space Below This Line For Acknowledgment] ———————————————————

take possession and manage the property under certain conditions and to substitute trustees. The lender agrees to request a reconveyance when all debts are paid.

Other clauses tend to be less uniform from one document to another, differing in accordance with agreements between the parties. Mortgages on income properties will have many more clauses which may require detailed individual bargaining.

Escrows   Clause 2 of the deed of trust provides that the borrower will pay with the monthly mortgage payment the amount needed to cover taxes and insurance. The lender will hold these sums in *escrow* (in trust) until they are needed to pay these items. Such arrangements reduce the risk to the lender that insurance will lapse or that unpaid taxes will become a lien prior to the debt. Many mortgages, however, do not require escrows.

Assumptions   Clauses 10 and 17 deal with the question of **assumptions,** which are agreements that shift the duty to repay the debt to the buyer, and the right to sell the property *subject to a mortgage.*

If not prohibited by a clause such as 17, owners of properties may sell them subject to an existing mortgage. If the mortgage has an interest rate below the current market, continuing the mortgage will be advantageous to the borrower. Also, fees or costs that might be demanded if a new mortgage loan were made can be avoided by selling subject to the existing mortgage.

If a property is sold in this manner, the new buyer usually agrees to assume and become responsible for the mortgage payments and to make them directly to the lender. In the example, because a due-on-sale clause (17) is included, the debt will become due in full if the transfer occurs without the permission of the lender. Lenders usually grant permission for a new buyer to assume the loan if they are paid a fee or if an agreement is reached for a higher interest rate.

Releases   Clause 10 provides that even if a lender agrees to an assumption by a new purchaser, the lender need not **release** the original borrower from any obligation. In case of default, the original borrower still remains responsible for the debt. However, if the buyer has a good credit rating, the lender may be willing to substitute a new note and release the original borrower.

Many borrowers do not worry about the lack of a release, particularly on individual houses. The lender's first claim is against the new buyer. Furthermore, in most states deficiency judgments against the original borrower would be difficult or impossible to obtain. In addition, sellers may feel that, having received some payment for the sale from the new buyer, they would not mind getting the property back, since it is worth more than the loan. However, if the amount they received was low or most of it went to cover selling costs, they might find that the debt owed exceeded the value of the property.

Acceleration   Clause 19 is a general acceleration clause in addition to the specific one that applies if a sale occurs. The lender has the right to claim the trust deed to be in default if the borrower fails to live up to any of the agreements or covenants. Upon **acceleration,** all amounts owed, including the entire debt, become due and payable immediately. Clause 19 also spells out the steps the borrower can take to halt acceleration and clear the default and the duties of the trustee if this clause is invoked.

The Right to Reinstate   Clause 18 outlines the conditions under which the borrower can reinstate the loan with its original terms. Even after the acceleration clause is invoked because of the failure to meet a covenant, the borrower has a limited period in which to correct any default.

DEFAULTS AND FORECLOSURES

Defaults

Probably more than two million deficiencies occur on mortgages every year. Borrowers are late in making payments (especially at Christmastime); tax or insurance bills get mislaid; properties are sold without notifying the lender. Each of these lapses creates a **default,** or failure by the borrower to perform according to agreement. A breach of any covenant is a default. It gives the lender the right to **foreclose**—that is, to force the sale of the property pledged as security in order to obtain funds to pay off the debt.

For most deficiencies and certain defaults, the lender takes no legal action; instead, a late payment penalty may be assessed. In more serious cases, where the ability to pay declines because of loss of a job, divorce, or death, the lender may extend the period of payment or recast the loan by altering the terms of payment. These are examples of **forbearance,** or the taking of more lenient action than allowed by law.

If the default cannot be cured, lenders may seek a **deed in lieu of fore-closure** in order to avoid costs and delays. If a borrower voluntarily grants a deed and possession, the lender will reconvey the mortgage. The borrower may simply want out of the agreement and may also want to avoid the stigma of foreclosure. Both sides save time and money by avoiding legal and court costs.

The Time to Gain Possession

The length of time required to foreclose a mortgage varies from one month to over two years. Three to four months is most typical. In recent years, many foreclosures have taken far longer, up to three or four years, because owners have declared themselves bankrupt to forestall foreclosure. Further, bankruptcy judges have wide powers and often delay foreclosure proceedings in an effort to make additional amounts available to other creditors.

In all states, there is some minimum period within which those who would lose by a foreclosure may reinstate their rights to the property by paying off the debt. This right existing prior to foreclosure is called an **equity of redemption.** In addition, about half the states grant a **statutory right of redemption** *after* foreclosure, which may result in further delays. This right gives borrowers a period after foreclosure in which to regain their property by paying off all debts owed. This period may be as long as a year, depending on the state. During this time the creditor and the property remain in a suspended state.

Foreclosure by Judicial Sale

If all else fails, the lender will foreclose. In most states this can be accomplished either by a judicial sale or by power of sale. Under the procedure of a **judicial sale,** the lender requests the court to sell the mortgaged property in order to obtain funds to repay the debt. A court hearing is required to determine that all rights have been respected and to make sure that all obligations, such as informing interested parties, have been carried out. Next, the court orders a public sale. The time and conditions of such sales differ depending on the law of each state.

Sales are conducted by a sheriff or a court officer. The results of the bidding are reported to the court, which confirms the sale if it appears reasonable. After a statutory period of redemption, the successful bidder receives a deed from the court. All junior liens named in the foreclosure proceedings are wiped out. (Junior liens are discussed in the next section.)

Usually the highest bid is made by the lender on the first mortgage in an amount equal to the debt. By bidding the amount owed, he obtains the property without having to put up more money and insures that no other bidder gets it for less than the outstanding loan. If any higher bids are received, funds from the sale go first to pay the cost of the sale and then to repay the foreclosing creditor. In the unusual case of a surplus, it is used to pay off junior liens in the order of their priority. If there are none or if they are more than covered, the debtor receives any amount left over.

Foreclosure by Power of Sale

Most deeds of trust and many mortgages contain a **power of sale** clause. In case of default, the lender can request the trustee to foreclose and to sell the property at a public auction without a judicial decree. The steps required for such a sale differ from state to state. Depending on the state, the sale may be conducted by a trustee or by a public officer or by the lender. California statutes, which are quite typical, outline the following procedures:

1. If a default occurs, the beneficiary requests the trustee to record a notice of default in the county recorder's office. The debtor and all others on record as requesting a notice must be informed.
2. The debtor or any other lienholder has 90 days in which to clear the default. He may reinstate the loan by meeting late payments plus penalties, by paying taxes, or by correcting any other fault.
3. After 90 days, if no reinstatement has occurred, the lender has the right to collect the entire debt plus costs. The trustee will record a notice of sale. In addition, public notice of the proposed sale is required for 20 days. The notice must be posted conspicuously on the property and in a public place, such as the courthouse. During this period, the notice must also appear at least weekly in a newspaper of general circulation.
4. After the notice period, the trustee conducts a public sale, usually on the steps of the courthouse. Typically, the amounts bid and the distribution of the proceeds are similar to those described under judicial sale.
5. The trustee gives a deed covering all the rights of the debtor to the high bidder. Junior liens are wiped out, but all higher-order rights remain in effect.

The power of sale saves court costs and is faster than foreclosure by judicial sale. Either the redemption period is reduced, or there is none at all. Some states forbid deficiency judgments if the power of sale is used; in others, they can be obtained only through a court proceeding. Still, when the contract allows a public sale without requiring a court action, this faster, cheaper technique will normally be used even though no deficiency judgment is possible. The saving of time and costs usually exceeds any possible claim.

THE ORDER OF JUNIOR MORTGAGES AND RECORDING

Although it is not a legal requirement, most mortgages are recorded, or filed with the proper official (usually at the county courthouse) to place it on the public record. **Recording** is necessary so that ownership of a property or claims against it become public information. Recording gives **constructive notice**—that is, notice available to all who search the public record—of the existing interest in the property. Lenders give such notice in order to protect the priority of their claims. In most cases, priority depends on being the first to have the record accepted by the public official. A *first mortgage* is one that is recorded first; others recorded later are *junior mortgages.* While priority is usually granted in the order of recording, other liens may have preference. For example, tax liens or assessments come before the first mortgage.

Junior Mortgages

Mortgages whose priority follows the first mortgage are called **junior mortgages.** It is not uncommon to find second, third, or fourth mortgages. Each is *junior to* those carrying a lower number. If a foreclosure sale occurs, the receipts are used first to pay off the first mortgage; then, if any funds are left over, they are used to pay off the second mortgage, and so on in order. When funds run out, the more junior mortgages receive nothing.

Because the order of recording is so crucial, in many states the process of closing the loan and examining the record to ascertain the order of priority is an extremely important ritual. In other states, the process of **escrow** is used. In this procedure, a neutral party is given the mortgage and the funds to be lent. Escrow agents are instructed to pay the money to the borrower only after they have assured themselves that the mortgage has been recorded with the agreed-upon priority.

Junior mortgages often carry special agreements or covenants. If the borrower defaults on a more senior mortgage, the total debt of the junior lien may be accelerated and become due. When foreclosing on a junior mortgage, in order to keep intact their claim to the property, lenders may have the right to clear defaults on higher-order mortgages by making the necessary payments. To ensure timely action, borrowers promise to give the junior lenders any notices received from prior lienholders.

Borrowers often demand a **subordination clause** that allows them to alter or substitute a new first mortgage. This clause keeps the junior mortgage from moving up to first if the borrower is able to get better terms by paying off the first mortgage and substituting a new one. Usually the clause will not permit the borrower to increase the amount owed on a prior lien.

Use of Junior Mortgages

Second mortgages are frequently used in at least three situations:

1. Sellers make a sale possible by accepting a junior mortgage. Some sales are feasible only if the seller does not demand all cash, but instead raises the price and accepts partial payment in the form of a junior mortgage. Such situations arise constantly. An existing mortgage that can be assumed may carry a below-market interest rate. In other cases, borrowers may not be able to meet the payments required by a larger first mortgage. The seller can agree that only the interest or some part of it due on the second mortgage need be paid, while the rest accrues as part of the principal to be paid off as a balloon in three or five years. For example, a house worth $80,000 may have an existing $65,000 loan with an interest rate 2 percent below the current market. The buyers might be willing to pay $85,000 if they could assume the existing loan and pay the additional $20,000 with $10,000 in cash and $10,000 from a second mortgage. They

might find this preferable to paying $80,000 made up of $65,000 from a new higher-rate first mortgage and $15,000 in cash.

2. Owners of land or buildings may allow their claims to be subordinated so that a builder can obtain the financing needed for developing or rehabilitating a property. Typically, someone may have been trying to sell a lot for a long time. A builder offers to buy it and perhaps pay somewhat above the market price. He explains, however, that he will pay for the land with some cash and a mortgage payable when the house to be built is finally sold. Furthermore, he will have to borrow construction money from a bank, which will lend only on a first mortgage. Looking at such an offer, the seller of the lot may agree to accept a mortgage that will be subordinated to and have second priority behind the bank's claim.

3. Many owners borrow against their equity, using a second mortgage, to obtain money for other needs. Risks and interest rates on second mortgages are usually lower than on personal or installment loans. For example, a group of doctors owns an office building whose value has gone up, and the doctors want to buy another property. Rather than selling the first building or refinancing it, they may be able to borrow against it on a second mortgage in order to obtain the down payment needed for their new purchase.

Wraparound Mortgages

The **wraparound mortgage** (or "wrap") is one of the most important types of junior mortgages, particularly in the sale of existing income properties. On a wrap, a second lender (frequently a seller) lends an amount over and above the existing first mortgage. The face amount of a wraparound mortgage equals the balance of the existing mortgage loan or loans plus the amount of the new loan. The borrower pays the wrap lender the interest and amortization on the face amount. The lender is responsible for making the necessary payments to the existing mortgage holders, retaining the difference between the amounts collected and paid out to cover the additional sums advanced.

Wraparounds are used for a variety of reasons, such as the following:

■ Many recent income property loans are closed for up to five or ten years. Original borrowers wanting to sell the property cannot pay off the loan. In other cases, heavy prepayment penalties make paying off the loan undesirable. Furthermore, the purchaser may want a larger loan than the outstanding closed loan. The seller advances additional financing through the wraparound procedure.

■ The interest rate on the existing mortgage may be below the current market rate. Both buyer and seller want to retain the existing loan to save having to pay the higher current rate.

■ The buyer wants a higher loan-to-value ratio or more extended terms than will be granted by a conventional lender. The seller is willing to furnish the desired terms, or finds another lender who will do so, because the wrap mortgage yields a higher return. It also provides more protection than a simple junior mortgage.

Table 2-3 shows how a wraparound mortgage works. A buyer offers $1.2 million for a property but has only $200,000 for the down payment. The property has an existing $800,000 mortgage at 12 percent interest. The seller agrees to accept a $1 million wraparound mortgage from the buyer at 14 percent and to continue to make the payments on the existing mortgage. The buyer receives an additional $200,000 in financing. The buyer has issued a mortgage for $1 million to the seller, but the existing mortgage for $800,000 has the first claim on the property and the seller's claim is junior to it.

The wrap lender collects $140,000 in interest and pays $96,000 in interest to the holder of the first mortgage. The remaining $44,000 is retained for a 22 percent return on the additional $200,000 advanced. The final two lines of Table 2-3 show that the high return results from the fact that the 14 percent interest applies to the entire wraparound mortgage. Thus, the wrap lender is able to retain 2 percent on the $800,000 of the original lender's loan. The yield will vary if the amortization—and therefore the remaining principal—on the two loans differs.

The wrap can run into problems similar to those of other junior mortgages. It may be harder for the borrower to be sure that payments are made promptly by the wrap lender and that a clear title can be obtained when the borrower has made all the payments. In some states, returns above the usury ceilings may be allowed; in others they are not. (The usury ceiling is the maximum rate of interest that may legally be charged.) Expected returns can differ from actual returns as a result of prepayments.

Table 2-3
The Return on a Wraparound Mortgage

	Amount	Interest	Lender's Interest Rate
Wraparound mortgage	$1,000,000	$140,000	14%
Existing first mortgage	800,000	96,000	12%
Wraparound lender lends	200,000	44,000	22%
Wraparound lender receives 14% on	200,000	28,000	14%
plus 2% (14 − 12) on	800,000	16,000	2%
for a total return of 22%			

SUMMARY

A mortgage is a contract pledging property as security for repayment of a debt. If the debtor fails to meet his or her obligations, foreclosure may occur. The lender can have the property sold so that the funds obtained can be used to repay the debt.

The conditions contained in mortgages are becoming more diverse and complex. The terms of the fixed-rate mortgage form a standard of comparison. The FRM calls for equal-level payments, each of which goes partly for interest and partly for some repayment of principal. The share going to principal increases steadily, initially at a slow rate but accelerating rapidly near the loan's maturity.

The amount of payment required rises with the rate of interest and with the amount borrowed, but it falls as the payment period lengthens. Because lenders limit the amount of income that can be committed to mortgage payments, the affordability of a loan and, therefore, of a property falls when interest rates rise and when the term is short.

The rights of borrowers and lenders vary depending on the law of each state and on the agreement or covenants they sign in the note and mortgage contract. Some states require a judicial procedure for foreclosure. Others allow a public auction under the terms of a deed of trust or of a mortgage with a power of sale. The length of time lenders have in which to declare a default or for borrowers to reinstate their loans also differs considerably, as does the ability to obtain a deficiency judgment.

Some mortgages allow a new owner to assume a debt. Others specify that the loan will accelerate so that the total outstanding amount will be due if a sale occurs. Similarly, some loans may be prepaid without penalty, while others may not. In closed mortgages, prepayments may not be made for a fixed period, if at all.

Junior mortgages have rights subordinate to other liens. They can be wiped out if the higher-order mortgagee forecloses. Usually the holders of junior mortgages can avoid such losses by foreclosing themselves and assuming the duties and covenants of the prior liens.

KEY TERMS

acceleration	deed of trust
affordability	default
amortization	deficiency judgment
assumptions	due-on-sale clause
balloon payment	equity of redemption
beneficiary	escrow
closed mortgage	fixed-rate mortgage (FRM)
constructive notice	forbearance
covenants	foreclose
deed in lieu of foreclosure	interest

interest-only loan
judicial sale
junior mortgages
liability
lien
lien theory
loan fee
loan-to-value ratio (LTV)
maturity date
mortgage
mortgage constant
mortgagee
mortgagor
negative amortization

open mortgage
power of sale
prepayment privilege
principal
promissory note
purchase-money mortgage
recording
release
security
statutory right of redemption
subordination clause
term
title theory
trustee
wraparound mortgage

QUESTIONS

1. Compare and contrast a mortgage and a deed of trust.
2. Define the following terms:

    promissory note   statutory right of redemption
    deficiency judgment   prepayment privilege
    due-on-sale clause   balloon payment
    power-of-sale clause   foreclosure
    equity of redemption   forbearance

3. Discuss the similarities and differences between foreclosure by judicial sale and foreclosure by power of sale.
4. Why is recording the mortgage important?
5. Mr. White has an annual income of $60,000 and is considering buying a $200,000 house with a mortgage. (a) Assume that he can obtain a mortgage for 90 percent of the cost of the house for 20 years at 10 percent interest and that the maximum mortgage payment to income is 25 percent. From Table 2-2, will he qualify for the loan? (b) If interest rates fall to 6 percent, how large a mortgage will he qualify for with a 20-year maturity loan? (c) At what term (time to maturity of the loan) will Mr. White just be able to borrow if interest rates are 12 percent?
6. "Since junior mortgages are subordinated to the first mortgage they are less desirable from a lender's point of view." Is this statement true? Why or why not?

7. Mrs. Brown borrows $30,000 from a thrift to finance her apartment. The interest rate is 12 percent and the term of the mortgage is 30 years. Using Table 2-2, what is the monthly mortgage payment and the mortgage constant? If the promissory note contains a provision that she can pay off the loan in a lump sum 10 years from now, (using Table 2-1) how much does she have to pay? (Assume that there is no penalty charge for prepayment.)

8. When the term of a mortgage increases or decreases, does the monthly payment change in the same direction? Does it change proportionally?

9. Briefly describe the important clauses in the covenants.

3 Interest Rates, Discount Rates, and Present Values

OBJECTIVES

When you finish this chapter, you should be able to:

- explain risks and returns.

- know the reason for default premiums.

- describe the market for loanable funds and interest rates.

- identify the component parts that make up mortgage rates.

- discuss the structure of interest rates and how it relates to mortgage interest.

- explain the debate over how closely mortgage rates track other rates.

- define real and nominal interest rates.

- recognize the importance of the time value of money in real estate finance.

- understand the principles of compound interest and discounting to find present values.

- use an interest factor table to find present values.

P EOPLE INVEST in real estate expecting ownership to yield material benefits and income. Whether they succeed or fail depends to a large extent on financial conditions, including interest rates and the availability of financing. The prices and yields of properties are interrelated—held together by prevailing interest rates. When interest rates shift, so do the values of property and the opportunities for profitable returns from ownership.

This chapter discusses some of the basic concepts of interest rates, returns, and risks. It examines the factors that determine general interest rates and those that cause interest on a particular loan to differ from the general or basic rate. The chapter also explains why borrowers on mortgages, like many other borrowers of funds, pay higher rates than those charged the best customers.

Although mortgage interest rates are primarily established by what happens in the overall credit market, mortgage borrowers pay an additional premium. The amount of this premium depends on the factors involved in each loan. Moreover, increases and decreases in the supply of and demand for credit cause both the general interest rates and these premiums to rise and fall. Both types of change affect mortgage rates.

Finally, the chapter examines in detail what is meant by the "time value of money." Property values and mortgage prices move up or down with interest rates because the rate affects the present value of future benefits. The last section focuses on how to measure and analyze changes in present value, using equations, formulas, and factor tables, as skills basic to real estate financing.

RETURNS FROM INVESTMENTS

The **return** on an investment consists of any cash received from the investment plus the change in its market value divided by its initial value. Returns reflect the change in an investor's wealth during a given period attributable to the investment. Returns are usually measured in terms of percentages over the course of a year. (Unless indicated otherwise, in this book rates of return, interest, and yields refer to the annual percentage rate.)

EXAMPLE: A bond bought for $100 paying cash interest of $9 was worth $103 at the end of the year. What was its return or yield? The answer is 12 percent, because ($9 + $3) ÷ $100 = 12 percent. If the price fell to $91, its return would be zero: ($9 − $9) ÷ $100 = 0 percent.

The Value of an Investment

Real estate investors and lenders give up current purchasing power for some promised future benefits, knowing that their actual return will be uncertain. In analyzing a loan or investment to determine its value, they must find the answers to five questions:

1. What is the amount of the promised benefits? Other things being equal, investors prefer properties that promise the greatest returns.
2. When will the benefits be received? Investors and lenders sacrifice present values for future ones. The sooner they receive the promised benefits, the better off they will be. We might agree to perform a job if we are paid $100 today, whereas we would refuse it if the promise were to pay $100 at the end of ten years.
3. What rate of interest could be earned on alternative investments? Because receipts are delayed in financing an investment, the investor must know how much is lost during the delay in order to choose among alternative investments. Therefore, the investor needs a measure of the cost of money over time so that he or she can know by how much to discount the future payments. This issue appears continually in real estate finance: to compare investments, we must adjust for time differences by using a correct discount rate.
4. What are the risks that the investor will receive less return than promised? Many real estate investments and loans promise high yields because of the considerable risk that the actual return will fall short of that promised. Investors must correct for the probability that the actual benefits will differ from those promised, subtracting a risk premium to project probable earnings.
5. How much income will be left once all costs are taken into account? Such costs include those for transactions, handling, and particularly taxes. Even safe junior mortgages on houses offer high rates because the costs of collecting and handling small monthly amounts are high. On the other hand, some real estate investments are especially attractive because their income is not subject to current taxes.

INTEREST RATES: A BRIEF REVIEW

In our economy, some families and businesses do not spend all of their purchasing power. They may be wealthy, have income higher than their spending desires, or want to accumulate for the future. Others want to spend more on consumption or investment than they have available. To acquire more purchasing power, those in the latter group create mortgages or other debt securities and sell them to those in the former group, who have surplus funds. The borrowers agree to return the funds at some future time and to pay interest in the interim. **Interest** is the rent or charge paid by borrowers for loans. It is the lender's "reward" for lending excess purchasing power instead of spending it himself.

Coupon Rates and Yields

We must now differentiate between two concepts in discussing interest rates: the coupon or face interest rate and the actual interest yield for holding an asset or making a loan.

The **coupon interest rate** or **face rate** is the promised interest payment included in the debt instrument. A mortgage note may promise to pay 10 percent interest a year for 4 years, at which time the entire principal will be repaid. If the loan is for $1,000, the borrower will pay 10 percent of the face value, or $100 annually. This is the coupon interest rate.

But the owner of the mortgage may have paid only $950 for it, either by lending less or by buying it from the original lender. Clearly, if he lends only $950 but still receives $100 a year, the rate of interest actually earned is higher than the coupon interest rate. (A question answered in the next chapter is "How much higher?") What is the expected return or yield to the lender?

The mortgage yield, as opposed to its coupon interest rate, takes into account the price paid and the expected amount to be received back over the entire life of the instrument. This is called the **yield to maturity.** It is the interest or discount rate that equates the present value of the investor's expected cash flows to the investment's current market price. As a corollary, the **present value** of an asset is the amount a buyer must pay to receive a future stream of payments each discounted at a specified market interest rate. Except for special cases, the terms *interest* and *discount rate* are used interchangeably. The concepts of interest and present value both derive from the fact that "time is money." The value of money differs depending on when it is received.

We discuss the ways of calculating the time value of money later in this chapter but delay until the next chapter the discussion of yields and rates of return, which differ from the coupon rate.

THE LEVEL OF INTEREST RATES

How much borrowers must pay in interest to borrow money depends on the time value of money in a period. The rent level for money—the basic interest rate—changes with the amount of money lenders are willing to make available by postponing their own purchases compared with the amount demanded by potential borrowers. Included in all interest quotations are additional charges to cover various risks involved in lending.

Mortgage and Other Interest Rates

We speak of "*the* interest rate," but a financial paper or magazine may list hundreds of different interest rates. On a typical day, there may be rates from 5 percent on short-term municipal notes to 21 percent on consumer finance loans. Rates differ because each contains unique features. Consumer loans are expensive to service (that is, to collect payments for), especially late ones, and run a considerable risk of default as a result, rates are usually high. Municipal bonds may carry a tax advantage; hence their rates may be lower. Other rates differ because of their term to maturity. For purposes of analysis, we can picture interest rates as forming a structure.

The Risk-free Rate

The **risk-free** (or representative) **rate** forms the base of the interest rate structure. Most analysts consider the interest rate on a 3-month U.S. Treasury bill (called a T-bill or treasury bill) as the best measure of this rate. These bills are virtually riskless, because the government can print money to pay them off if necessary. They are extremely liquid—billions of dollars in T-bills are traded daily—and they have a short term. All other loans have rates above the risk-free rate. Their rates form a hierarchy of separate rate classes that differ according to their particular features, such as degree of risk, time to maturity, marketability, and costs of making and collecting on loans. We call this hierarchy the **interest rate structure.**

Loanable Funds

The supply of and demand for loanable funds in the credit market determines the level of the basic interest rate. Some consumers, businesses, and governments demand credit in order to cover the shortfall of their revenues below their expenses. In the same market, other households, businesses, some government units, and the Federal Reserve have excess funds that they are willing to lend.

The amount of funds borrowed and lent depends on interest rates. As rates rise, many spending units save more and spend less. Therefore, they have more to lend. Simultaneously, when rates rise, some spending units demand fewer funds. They may postpone spending rather than pay the higher rates. Others will be excluded from the market by lenders doubtful of their ability to pay for new debts.

Figure 3-1 illustrates the operation of supply and demand in the funds market. The demand schedule for funds, d_1, slopes downward to the right, reflecting a greater willingness to borrow at lower interest rates. The supply schedule, s_1, rises to the right, because people have more to lend at higher rates. The intersection of the two schedules determines the amount of funds lent, F_1, and the prevailing interest rate, i_1.

Figure 3-1
Supply of and Demand for Loanable Funds

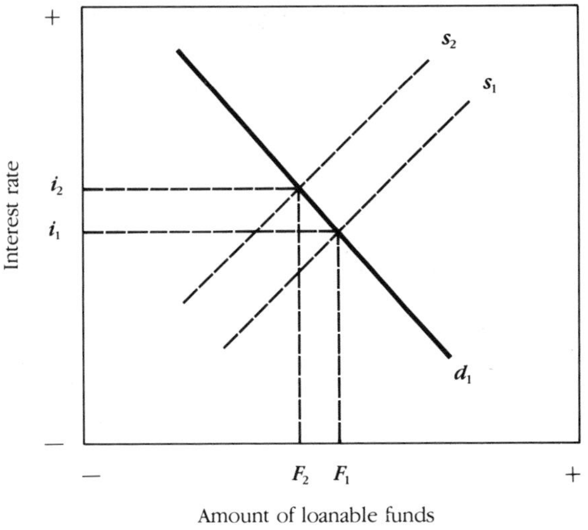

Amount of loanable funds

The shifted supply schedule, s_2, illustrates a critical force in the determination of interest rates, the Federal Reserve Board. As Chapter 5 discusses, the Federal Reserve can shift the supply schedule by creating more or less money. Schedule s_2 demonstrates a reduction in the money supply. This causes fewer funds (F_2) to change hands at a higher interest rate (i_2).

Figure 3-1 is a general model of the market that determines the risk-free interest rate. Far from being merely the market for treasury bills, it includes all supply and demand for borrowing and lending. Each influences the basic underlying rate. Moreover, the interest rate is not the rate quoted for treasury bills, for the actual market rate must be corrected for inflation. The basic rate is the risk-free *real interest rate,* which will be discussed shortly.

Not only is the risk-free real interest rate the basic component of rates charged on all loans, it also underlies the discount rate used by investors in valuing properties. The basic interest and discount rates are the same because people with excess purchasing power can choose to invest in either a physical or a financial asset. After corrections are made for differences such as risk and marketability, the return investors expect from each type of asset must be equivalent. If they were not, investors would bid up the price of one and bid less for the other until their expected rates of return converged.

THE COMPONENTS OF INTEREST AND DISCOUNT RATES

Interest and discount rates include certain major charges, illustrated in Figure 3-2. The figure is based on a mortgage interest rate of 13 percent, one

Figure 3-2
Components of Interest Rate

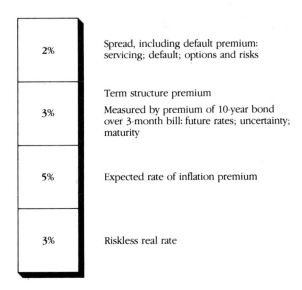

2%	Spread, including default premium: servicing; default; options and risks
3%	Term structure premium Measured by premium of 10-year bond over 3-month bill: future rates; uncertainty; maturity
5%	Expected rate of inflation premium
3%	Riskless real rate

The value of the components depends on the supply of and demand for loanable funds, on expected inflation, on risks, and on costs.

which prevailed in part of 1985. This was considerably higher than the 10 percent rate that prevailed earlier. The figure breaks down the total into four main components and shows the amount charged for each.

1. The riskless real short-term interest rate (3 percent).
2. A premium to cover an expected loss in purchasing power due to inflation (5 percent).
3. The **term structure premium,** a sum to pay for the risk and uncertainty of tying up money for long periods. One measure of this premium is the amount borrowers pay to obtain money for 10 years instead of 3 months. At the time period in the figure, 10-year government bonds yielded 11 percent, or a three-percentage-point premium over the T-bill.
4. The *spread,* or the charges to cover the cost of processing and servicing a mortgage and to cover the risk of default or uncertain returns. These needs account for 2 percent of the total.

The price of a 3-month treasury bill covers the first two costs. But mortgage rates include the last two charges as well. When the T-bill was yielding 8 percent, borrowers had to pay 13 percent on a fixed-rate mortgage.

When the interest rate rose above 13 percent, each of the four components underwent an increase. Comparing these rates to those when mortgage lenders demanded 16 percent, we would find that most of the additional premium went to cover a higher expected rate of inflation and greater uncertainty about future rates.

The discount factors used in valuing future incomes cover these same basic costs. However, the amounts needed for each component differ. For example, when mortgage interest rates were 13 percent, returns on many office buildings were being discounted at 16 percent. The spread was greater because management costs were higher and there was a greater risk that the buildings would not earn their projected income.

Real and Nominal Interest Rates

Borrowers and lenders on real estate have been plagued by major fluctuations in interest due to changing price anticipations. When the rate on mortgages moved to 13 percent, the burden seemed enormous for people accustomed to paying 7 or 8 percent. Yet most of the increase merely covered the cost of expected inflation (as gauged by the rise in the Consumer Price Index or other price indices).

This difference highlights the need to think in terms of both real and nominal interest rates. **Nominal interest rates** are the rates charged by lenders in current dollars. They are not corrected for the effect of inflation. **Real interest rates** are the nominal rates corrected for actual or anticipated changes in purchasing power. They are what people earn or pay on their loans after deducting the rate of inflation. Problems arise in measuring inflation, but for most purposes, changes in the Consumer Price Index (CPI) give an adequate indication of how purchasing power is changing.

Correcting for Inflation   Lending contracts are expressed in nominal terms. Experience shows that lenders and borrowers adjust their decisions to reflect the real return they expect. Take the case of a lender who would be willing to accept 4 percent interest in real dollars for a year's loan. What should she do if she expects prices to rise during the period of the loan? She lends $100 and wants to be paid back $104 in the same purchasing power. If prices rose 4 percent during the year, the $104 she got back at the end of the year would buy only the same amount of goods as the $100 originally lent. She would receive no real interest; the price increases would have wiped out the nominal interest earnings.

In order to earn a real 4 percent return, the lender would have had to ask approximately 8 percent in nominal interest. She would have to subtract the change in prices from the interest received to find the real interest rate. She would compare what she lent and what she got back in dollars with a constant purchasing power.

Experience also shows that although lenders try to obtain higher nominal interest rates in order to offset anticipated changes in purchasing power, they are not always successful because of uncertainties about future price movements. How interest rates and price changes compared between 1960 and 1985 is illustrated in Figure 3-3. One curve shows the percent changes in the CPI from the previous to the current December. Another curve shows the interest rate that would have been received from an investment the previous December in 1-year U.S. Treasury notes. The bottom curve shows the real interest rate yield minus the change in prices. It measures approximately the real interest rate earned in each year. Over most of this period, interest rates were considerably lower than people assume who think only in terms of nominal rates. In fact, from 1963 through 1980 real interest rates averaged under 1 percent. But a drastic change then occurred: from 1981 through 1985, real interest rates averaged over 5 percent.

The Term Structure of Interest Rates

The term structure premium, the second section of Figure 3-2, includes costs that arise if a mortgage ties up the lender's money for a long period. Interest rates on otherwise identical mortgages differ depending on their **time to maturity.** The explanation of why rates vary with time is called the theory of the **term structure** of interest rates. In most periods, longer-term riskless (treasury bond) rates are higher than shorter-term rates.

In 1985, borrowers had to pay 3 percent, or 300 basis points, more in order to borrow money for 10 years instead of 3 months. In financial markets, an interest rate of 1 percent is also spoken of as 100 basis points. A **basis point** equals .01 percent. A cost of 300 basis points for borrowing for a longer maturity has been typical. However, when money is tight, short-term money may rise above the long-term rate. In such periods, we say that the term structure is inverted.

Several factors explain why borrowers must pay a higher interest rate on longer-term loans:

1. Investors may think that future rates will be higher because of more inflation or a greater demand for borrowing. This means that they can increase their returns by buying a short-term note now and then rolling it over into a higher-yielding note later. If instead they tie up money in long-term mortgages, the rate they earn must compensate for the future lost opportunities.
2. Investors may fear to have their money tied up for long periods. When interest rates move, the capital values of long-term securities fluctuate widely, causing sharp movements in year-to-year total returns. Anyone unwilling to risk such fluctuations may demand a **liquidity premium** to compensate for such added risk. Borrowers may be willing to pay larger premiums in order to avoid the interest rate risk when they make a

Figure 3-3
Changes in Real Interest Rate

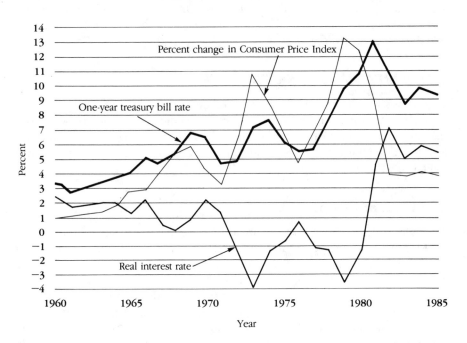

Real interest rates are the rates on 1-year treasury bills less the actual change in the year's Consumer Price Index.

Source: *Federal Reserve Bulletin.*

longer-term investment—for example, in a house. They may feel safer knowing that their future interest costs will be fixed. Because they may not be able to afford a sharp increase in future payments, they are willing to take out insurance through paying more for a fixed rate. They may also save by avoiding costs of refinancing.

3. Financial markets have a maturity mismatch. Many lenders want to avoid the risks of lending on a long-term security. On the other hand, borrowers feel safer with longer-term loans. This mismatch is solved by the borrowers paying a premium in order to entice enough lenders into accepting instruments with longer maturities.

4. Borrowers must pay an *option premium* that increases with the length of the loan. (Option premiums are explained in the next section.) This premium is required because borrowers have the right to prepay loans at times least favorable to lenders.

The **premium** for tying up money in a mortgage loan depends not only on its terms, but also on how high interest rates are and on the expected rate of prepayment. For example, the reason a 10-year bond was chosen to illustrate the term structure in Figure 3-2 is that, on the average, the cash flow from such a bond about equals that from a typical 30-year term mortgage. However, we will see that the repayment rates on mortgages vary far more than on bonds, and the risk is costly to lenders.

THE SPREAD AND RISK PREMIUMS

In addition to the risk-free rate and amounts needed to compensate for expected inflation and time to maturity, each specific interest rate in the interest rate structure contains a further amount, the **spread,** to cover risks and transaction and handling costs. The required spread is depicted as the top segment in Figure 3-2.

The Risks of Investing

When making an investment, including one in a mortgage or building, the investor projects an expected return. However, most investments contain a **risk** that returns will fall short of the amount expected. The risks vary from one segment of the rate structure to another. The rate of inflation may not be that expected, especially as the maturity is extended. Individual loans may not be repaid as a result of defaults. A rise in interest rates may cause values to fall. Future revenues from a building may be incorrectly projected. All of these and other risks must be compensated for through separate interest premiums in each discount rate.

Measures of Risk   Both the size and the probability of wrong estimates affect the amount of risk. The **expected return** of an investment is the weighted average (the mean) of all probable rates of return. The weights are based on the probability of a return occurring. The investor recognizes that the amounts received from a future investment may be more or less than that foreseen. The rate of return the investor expects is the mean of all these probable amounts.

One measure of risk is the weighted probable deviations from the mean (the standard deviation) of the expected amounts. Table 3-1 demonstrates how the standard deviation is calculated. Risks rise as the standard deviation increases— that is, as the dispersion of possible future returns broadens. Another measure considers both the probabilities that losses will occur and the possible size of each loss. The investor's need to consider the size of possible losses seems quite evident. Many people would feel that a 1 percent probability of a $1,000 loss is far riskier than a 50 percent probability of a $25 loss.

Table 3-1 further demonstrates how the expected return and a measure of risk are calculated. It also shows how two examples with the same expected return can have very different risks. An investment may earn from 2 percent to 20 percent, as shown in column 1 of Case 1. Column 2 shows the probability of each return. The expected return of 10 percent is the weighted average or mean

Table 3-1
Probabilities of Returns

Possible Rate of Return, %	Probability of Possible Rate of Return	Expected Rate of Return, %	Deviation of Possible from Expected, %	Deviation Squared	Deviation Squared Times Probability

Case 1

2	×	.1	=	.2	−8.0	64	=	6.4
6	×	.1	=	.6	−4.0	16	=	1.6
8	×	.2	=	1.6	−2.0	4	=	.8
10	×	.3	=	3.0	0	0	=	0
13	×	.2	=	2.6	3.0	9	=	1.8
20	×	.1	=	2.0	10.0	100	=	10.0
		1.0		10.0	Variance of return		=	20.6%

Standard deviation = $\sqrt{20.6\%}$ = 4.47%

Case 2

0	×	.5	=	0	−10.0	100		50.0
20	×	.5	=	10.0	10.0	100		50.0
		1.0		10.0	Variance of return		=	100.0%

Standard deviation = $\sqrt{100\%}$ = 10%

Source: Sherman J. Maisel and Stephen E. Roulac, *Real Estate Investment and Finance* (New York: McGraw-Hill, 1976), 276.

of the different return possibilities. The final three columns show that the variance of this case is 20.6 percent, or its standard deviation is 4.47 percent.

In Case 2, only two possible returns exist—either no return or 20 percent. The chances are even that either will occur. The expected return is the same, but the variance is now 100 percent and the standard deviation is 10 percent. Since most people try to avoid high risk when they can—that is, they are *risk-averse*—they would prefer to invest in Case 1.

Risk Premiums

In order to attract willing lenders and investors, an investment must carry a premium large enough to offset its potential losses. Interest rates contracted for on a group of mortgages must include a premium to make up for the probable defaults and foreclosures. The quoted rate of interest must be higher than the expected return. If the quoted rates did not include a risk premium, no one would buy mortgages.

A **default premium** is the different between the promised and the expected return due to the probability of a loss through default. It is the margin between what is paid for a risky mortgage compared to one that is default-free (riskless). The default premium (d) equals the difference between the promised yield (y) and the actual yield (r). In other words, $d = y - r$. For example, if a mortgage has an annual 1 percent chance of foreclosure and if the loss per foreclosure is 30 percent, the default premium is about .4 percent.* In order to actually return 12 percent, the interest rate charged on a mortgage will have to be 12.4 percent, including the default premium:

$$y = r + d \qquad y = 12\% + .4\% = 12.4\%$$

The promised return from any investment (except riskless ones) will contain some risk premium. The total risk premium rises as the degree of uncertainty grows and as the size of possible losses increases. The greater the risk, the higher is the expected return required from an investment. Moreover, the amount of risk premium rises faster than the actual underlying risk. This is because most investors are **risk-averse:** other things being equal, they prefer less risk to more.

Portfolio Risk   Because values of individual loans may not move together, the amount of risk in a portfolio may be less than the total risk we would calculate by summing the risk in individual loans. Since changes in values of individual investments may be offsetting, the **portfolio risk** depends on both the riskiness of the individual loans or investments it contains and on the relationships among them. **Diversification** is the policy of combining investments in a portfolio in such a way that its total risk is reduced.

EXAMPLE: Many studies have shown that investments in real property grow in value in an inflation, while inflation causes stock prices to fall. What if each 1 percent increase in the Consumer Price Index caused the expected price

---

*If the mortgage is foreclosed, the lender will lose 30 percent of its value. The probability that it will be foreclosed in any year is 1 percent. It has been shown that the default premium depends on the actual yield (r), the probability of default (P_d) and the expected loss (L):

$$y = \frac{r + L(P_d)}{1 - P_d}$$

$$d = y - r = \frac{r + L(P_d)}{1 - P_d} - r$$

$$d = \frac{.12 + .3(.01)}{1 - .01} - .12 = .0042$$

of a property to rise by 1 percent, while it caused the expected price of a stock to fall by .5 percent? By buying a $10,000 property and $20,000 worth of stock, the net expected effect of inflation on the portfolio would be zero; its effects on the two types of investment would be offsetting. The idea of diversification is to reduce the portfolio risk by holding investments with risks that react differently to possible future changes—in this example, the separate reactions of the investments to inflation.

The general rule is that the total risk in a portfolio depends not only on the expected individual variances, but also on the relationships of their movements to one another, their covariances. The **covariance** of the possible returns of two investments is measured by the extent to which they vary together rather than independently of each other. In calculating the portfolio risk, a correction is necessary for the *amount* of covariance; you do not simply add the individual risks. The optimum diversification occurs when the covariances between two investments is negative. They react in opposite ways, as in the reaction to inflation noted above.

Other Costs

In addition to the default risk premium, lenders have other costs. They may have to include an allowance for marketing the mortgage to others. A lender's return must cover (a) the cost of making and collecting the loan, (b) the charges needed to market mortgages, (c) risks due to lack of liquidity, delinquencies, defaults, and other forecast errors, and (d) profit.

Substantial costs are incurred in making, processing, and selling mortgage loans. Borrowers must be interviewed; credit must be checked; property has to be appraised. Some, but not all, of these costs are paid for by loan fees. The rest must be covered in the monthly interest payment. Charges must also be made to cover the servicing of the loan. Receipts must be accounted for; taxes and insurance checked and paid. Delinquent loans must be followed up. All of these different items—the processing, servicing, and operating costs as well as the risk premium—must be included in the spread.

Options

Most mortgages contain provisions allowing borrowers to pay off their loans before they are due. This prepayment privilege is equivalent to a *call option*. The borrower has the right, but not the obligation, to buy back—that is, to *call*—the loan. The due-on-sale clause is another form of option. It allows the lender to demand payment if a sale occurs.

Prepayment options are valuable. When market interest rates fall below the mortgage rate, borrowers usually prepay (call) their loans in order to refinance their debt at a lower rate. But when the loan is paid off, the lender must find a new investment, and its return will be lower than that of the prepaid mortgage. The borrower has won; the lender has lost. Since this privilege is valuable, the borrower must pay for it in an **option premium.**

The ability of the borrower to choose the time for prepayment has another advantage. When loans are made, lenders estimate the expected rate of prepayment. They set the term premium in the interest rate on the basis of when they expect the loan to be paid off rather than on the maximum possible period. For example, many 30-year fixed-rate mortgages are sold on the assumption that they will be entirely prepaid at the end of 12 years. However, if interest rates rise, borrowers are less likely to prepay and the lender is stuck with a below-market rate for a term well beyond that expected when the premium was set.

Consider a typical 13 percent fixed-rate mortgage. When interest rates fall to 10 percent, *if* the mortgage could not be prepaid it would be worth a good deal more than its initial value of 100. (Prices on mortgages are usually quoted in percent of the value of the principal. Thus a mortgage with $100,000 of principal which sells for $100,000 is said to be selling at 100, or at par. If it were selling at 80, it would sell for $80,000.) The mortgage could be sold at a premium, because the lender could collect 3 percent extra interest above current market rates. Unfortunately for the lender, however, when such premiums start to appear, the mortgage is likely to be paid off. The borrower calls it in by prepaying in order to save money by getting a new loan at 10 percent. Thus the call option reduces the selling price that would be expected when interest rates fall. On the other hand, if market rates rise above 13 percent, the mortgage will be worth far less than 100; it will sell at a discount. The lender receives less than the market rate. Because the borrower now has a bargain, he is less likely to prepay.

Although options in a mortgage are not priced separately, they are obviously valuable and must enter into the calculation of the interest rate charged. Chapter 4 explains in greater detail how options are valued. Option premiums depend upon the term of the mortgage, expected future rates, the volatility of interest, and any prepayment penalty. Studies show that, depending on circumstances, the annual premium required to cover the option features may range from 10 to 150 basis points (.1 percent to 1.5 percent). They also show that, until recently, most lenders badly underestimated the premiums needed to cover the options included in mortgages.*

Differential Risks and Spreads

Although the other charges apply to most mortgages, the premiums for options and risks differ greatly for every loan or investment. For example, many recent mortgages carry agreements that variable interest rates will not rise above an agreed-upon total. Each of these agreements has a different potential cost to the lender. As a result, the premiums for such terms depend on what is included and also on what is happening in credit markets when they are made.

---

*P. H. Hendershott and S. A. Buser, "Spotting Prepayment Premiums," *Secondary Mortgage Markets* 1, no. 3 (August 1984): 24.

A study of equity investments made in real properties shows still greater divergencies in interest and discount rates. The amount of risk included in each transaction varies tremendously, depending on how the purchase and loan are structured. Risk premiums for equities purchased under typical conditions are often from 4 percent to 6 percent above prevailing mortgage rates.

EXAMPLE: A major real estate consulting firm reports that for the year 1981 the expected yield on commercial real estate was 18.5 percent, while 10-year treasury bonds had an expected yield of 13.9 percent, or a spread of 460 basis points. For the first half of 1985, real estate yields had fallen to 13.6 percent and the 10-year treasury bonds to 11.1 percent. The yield had narrowed to 250 basis points.*

What factors might have caused the drop in each yield and the narrowing of the spread? Two obvious factors affecting the levels were a fall in expected inflation and an upward shift in the supply of loanable funds. (a) The Consumer Price Index rose at a rate of 8.9 percent in 1981 and a 3.7 percent rate in the first half of 1985. (Note, however, that expected inflation may not have fallen as fast as actual inflation.) (b) The supply of loanable funds went up as a result of an increase in the money supply. In 1981, the money stock (M1) grew at only half the rate of growth in spending (the GNP). In 1985, it grew at twice that rate. These different growth rates are indications that in 1985 the Federal Reserve Board acted to increase the supply of loanable funds and, thus, to reduce the real risk-free interest rate.

In addition to the fall in nominal interest rates, the real estate market also experienced a decrease in risk premiums. The fear of a financial panic and a shortage of funds disappeared, while the experience of high prior profits caused investors to look more favorably on real estate investments. The reduction in the interest used to discount future income caused a sharp increase in property values for the reasons analyzed in the next sections.

ARE MORTGAGE INTEREST RATES SEPARATE FROM OTHER RATES?

As we have just seen, every rate, including that for mortgages, contains basic charges for the risk-free interest rate, premiums for inflation, time to maturity, and defaults, plus a further spread to cover additional costs. A key debate among mortgage lenders and borrowers has concerned the degree to which the real estate financing industry's rate structure is so specialized that its spreads are or could be determined somewhat independently of other interest rates. Do mortgage rates depend so greatly on specialized lenders with separate sources of funds that they can vary considerably from rates in financial markets as a whole?

*Equitable Real Estate Group, *Emerging Trends in Real Estate: 1986* (New York: Equitable Group, 1986), 5.

A Local or a National Market?

It has been pointed out that, until recently, the market for mortgages seemed to be local and quite separate from the general credit market. Mortgage rates did not closely follow the movements of other interest rates.

Forty years ago, every mortgage loan was priced and sold on an individual basis. Values of each depended on the borrower's credit and on the selling price of the property pledged as security. Before loans could be sold, each mortgage had to be evaluated separately. Their poor marketability and the expensive process of checking their values raised their rates above others. Only when mortgage insurance and guarantees allowed sales of mortgages to be made on other than an individual basis did a competitive national market come into existence.

However, there is still disagreement as to the degree to which mortgage rates are unique. Do the rates charged for mortgages differ from other interest rates by more or less than one would expect, given their risks and need for servicing? To what extent do mortgage rates move away from the rest of the interest rate structure? These questions were the center of attention when the deregulation of deposit interest rates and of the savings and loan industry was under consideration. Did interest rate controls and special privileges for lending institutions keep mortgage rates lower than other market-determined rates?

Institutional Forces

A number of institutional factors could cause mortgage rates to differ from other rates:

1. When mortgages are subsidized directly through government programs, the subsidy could cause the rates charged to fall below the general market.
2. When savings and loans had surplus funds in a local area and were restricted to mortgage loans, an excess of supply over demand in a locality would mean equilibrium at a lower rate. (Equilibrium is a market situation with no impetus for change.)
3. If lenders are not too efficient or they do not seek maximum profits, they may charge rates below the market.

Many observers believe that such conditions formerly applied in the mortgage market and may still exist in particular situations. At times, local areas have had excess funds. Subsidies were important. Some institutions, depositors, and borrowers failed to obtain adequate information and therefore made bargains at rates below the general market. Deposit interest ceilings reduced the cost of funds to lenders, some of whom then lent at lower rates.

Others disagree with these points. They argue that mortgage rates must be fully competitive in the general credit market. Deposit institutions do not have enough funds to meet all the demands from those who want mortgages.

Large sums of money must be attracted from other lenders, such as commercial banks, insurance companies, and pension funds. They will not lend on mortgages unless they earn as much as they can obtain from other securities. To secure funds from these general lenders, mortgage borrowers must pay rates equal to those prevailing in the general market.

Money is said to be **fungible.** This means that it flows easily among markets. Any excess supply or demand spills over, causing all rates to equalize. Mortgage rates can differ from other rates only to the extent that (a) they contain unique premiums and features, such as those discussed with Figure 3-2, or (b) the market is inefficient (for example, some borrowers and lenders fail to obtain prevailing terms). But on the whole, as the national mortgage market has developed, rates have become more uniform. They move in close relationship to other, more representative interest rates.

The specific factors that enter into mortgage lending and rates are discussed in Part 2. Before discussing such relationships, we must examine more closely the time value of money, present values, and yields or rates of return.

THE TIME VALUE OF MONEY

How interest rates are determined is of critical importance to real estate finance because financing arrangements cover long periods. When someone buys a property, or lends or borrows on a mortgage, the revenues or cash flows are spread into the future as payments. How much they are worth today depends on the **time value of money.** Money has a time value because, if it can be lent or invested so as to earn a return, it grows to a larger sum in the future.

Compound interest means earning interest on interest. Compounding occurs when earnings are not paid out but instead are added to the principal and in the next period interest is earned on both the original principal and on the added or accrued interest. If money is lent at compound interest, how much the lender gets back in the future depends on the rate of interest, the frequency of compounding, and how long it is until he or she receives a payment.

Even small sums invested for medium periods at high interest rates, or for long periods at medium interest rates, grow to large amounts (see Table 3-2). A $100 investment at 25 percent compound interest would be worth $80,799 at the end of 30 years. A $100 investment compounded at 10 percent would be worth well over a million dollars after 100 years.

Compound Values

Investment advisers have dramatized the effectiveness of compound interest by urging new parents to plan for the cost of their children's college education by buying a **zero coupon bond** when a child is born. This type of bond pays no interest until it matures. Instead, the accumulated compound interest is paid with the principal at maturity. This is equivalent to buying a certificate of deposit with a guaranteed rate of interest for the entire period.

Table 3-2
Future Values of $100 at Selected Interest Rates and Maturities

Year	5%	10%	15%	20%	25%
1	105	110	115	120	125
2	110	121	132	144	156
3	116	133	152	173	195
4	122	146	175	207	244
5	128	161	201	249	305
6	134	177	231	299	381
7	141	195	266	358	477
8	148	214	306	430	596
9	155	236	352	516	745
10	163	259	405	619	931
15	208	418	814	1,541	2,842
20	265	673	1,637	3,834	8,674
25	339	1,083	3,292	9,540	26,470
30	432	1,745	6,621	23,738	80,779
35	552	2,810	13,318	59,067	246,519
40	704	4,526	26,786	146,977	752,316
45	899	7,289	53,877	365,726	2,295,887
50	1,147	11,739	108,366	910,044	7,006,492
75	3,883	127,190	3,567,287	86,814,737	1,854,603,075
100	13,150	1,378,061	117,431,345	8,281,797,452	490,909,346,530

Suppose you bought such a bond or deposit for $100. How much would it be worth ten years later? According to Table 3-2, the answer depends on the deposit's interest rate. In ten years, $100 compounded will grow to $163 at 5 percent interest, to $259 at 10 percent, and to $405 at 15 percent.

Finding a Future Value

EXAMPLE: To see how these figures are obtained, consider the mechanics of a savings account. If we put $100 into an account at 10 percent interest, what will it be worth at the end of the year?

1. The initial or present value, PV_0, equals 100.
2. The number of periods, n, equals 1.
3. The interest rate, i, equals .10.
4. The future value (FV_n) is to be solved for.

Since the **future value** is the present value of the principal plus the interest earned, at the end of the first year we will have $110. This is shown by a general equation and its solution:

$$FV_1 = PV_0(1 + i) \qquad FV_1 = \$100\,(1 + .10) = \$110$$

At the end of the second year, the future value will be the amount in the account at the end of the first year plus the interest earned in the second year. This comes to $121:

$$FV_2 = PV_1(1 + i) \qquad FV_2 = \$110\,(1 + .10) = \$121$$

Another way of thinking about this is that in the second year we again earn 10 percent, or $10, on the initial value and, in addition, 10 percent on the $10 of prior interest earnings, which equals $1. The total second-year interest earned is $11. Compounding allows us to earn interest on interest. For each year of compounding, we multiply by another $(1 + i)$; or, for year 2:

$$FV_2 = PV_0(1 + i)(1 + i) \qquad FV_2 = \$100(1.10)(1.10) = \$121$$

or:

$$FV_2 = PV_0(1 + i)^2 \qquad FV_2 = \$100(1.21) = \$121$$

In the third and in each succeeding year, we follow the same rule:

$$FV_3 = PV_2(1 + i) \qquad FV_3 = \$121(1.10) = \$133.10$$

or:

$$FV_3 = PV_0(1 + i)^3 \qquad FV_3 = \$100(1.331) = \$133.10$$

This gives us the general rule for compound interest. The final value equals the initial value times 1 plus the interest rate $(1 + i)$ raised to the power of the number of periods.

$$FV_n = PV_0(1 + i)^n \qquad\qquad (3.1)$$

Figure 3-4 helps demonstrate that the final value depends on both the number of years and the interest rate. Like Table 3-2, it also shows how fast the $100 would grow at different interest rates. Note that the interest earned in each year is not a simple arithmetic amount added to the previous principal; rather, each preceding sum of interest is compounded. As a result, the growth curve becomes steeper with each succeeding year. The speed with which it rises depends on the rate of interest.

Figure 3-4
Amount to Which $1 Will Grow at Different Interest Rates, Compounded Annually

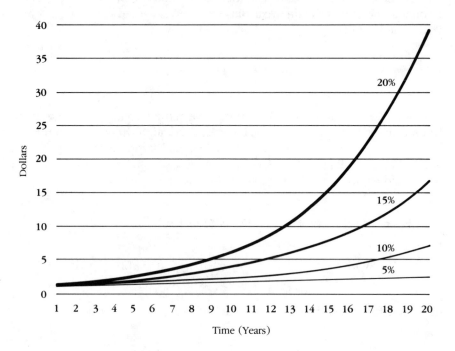

Finding the Present Value of a Future Payment

Just as money invested and held into the future grows in value, so a payment that need not be made until some future time has a smaller value at the present. The same concept of compounding can be applied in reverse to find the present value of payments to be made or received in the future.

The *present value* of an asset is the amount an investor must pay today to receive a future income at a specific interest rate. If a borrower promises to pay a lender $133.10 in three years and the lender wants to earn 10 percent on the loan, how much should she lend? According to Table 3-2, the lender would have to invest $100 today at 10 percent to receive $133, or $133.10 (not rounded), three years from now. Finding the present value, or **discounting,** is simply the reverse of finding a future value:

1. $FV_3 = \$133.10$
2. $i = .10$
3. $n = 3$ and you want to find
4. PV_0, the present value.

Using Equation 3.1,

$$FV_n = PV_0(1 + i)^n \qquad \$133.10 = \$100(1 + .10)^3$$

Dividing through by the compound interest factor $(1 + i)^n$ gives:

$$PV_0 = \frac{FV_n}{(1 + i)^n} \qquad \$100 = \frac{\$133.10}{(1 + .10)^3} \tag{3.2}$$

Instead of dividing by the compound interest factor, we can multiply by its reciprocal. The amount by which we multiply the future value to obtain its present value is called the **discount factor.** Thus the 3-year discount factor at 10 percent interest is $1 \div 1.10^3 = 1 \div \$133.10 = .751315$.

Interest Factor Tables

Most problems of compounding and discounting are now solved using financial calculators or computers. However, it is sometimes more convenient to solve them with annual interest factor tables (see Table 3-3). Such tables contain compound **interest factors.** Each column in the table gives the factors for a separate interest operation.

For example, column 2 of Table 3-3 shows the interest factor (IF) for future values (FV), or IFFV, the amount a dollar grows to each year when compounded at 10 percent interest. In writing, the interest rate and years are usually specified in a parenthesis after or under the interest factor. Thus IFFV(10%,3) is a factor at 10 percent interest for three years into the future. Multiply this factor by the initial amount (PV_0) to get the future value (FV_3).

How much will the lender in the previous problem receive if she invests $100 at 10 percent interest for three years? On Table 3-3, find the amount $1 would grow to in three years at 10 percent interest IFFV(10%,3). This is shown in column 2 as $1.331. Next, multiply this factor by the size of the principal—in this case $100. The answer is $1.331 \times \$100 = \$133.10$.

In the same way, we can solve problems like Equation 3.2 to find present value. For example, what is the present value of a payment of $133.10 in three years when the proper discount rate is 10 percent. Column 5 of Table 3-3 lists the interest factors for present values IFPV. To find the present value of a sum due in three years, note that IFPV(10%,3) is .751315. Multiply this by $133.10 to find the answer: $100.

THE PRESENT VALUE OF A STREAM OF RECEIPTS

One of the most common problems in real estate finance occurs when an investor is offered a property or a mortgage with a stream of estimated cash

Table 3-3
Annual Interest Factor Table
Effective Rate 10 Percent

Year	IFFV Amount of $1 at Compound Interest	IFΣFV Accumulation of $1 per Period	$\frac{1}{\text{IF}\Sigma\text{FV}}$ Sinking-fund Factor	IFPV Present Value Reversion of $1	IFPVA Present Value of an Annuity of $1 per Period	$\frac{1}{\text{IFPVA}}$ Installment to Amortize $1
1	1.100000	1.000000	1.000000	0.909091	0.909091	1.100000
2	1.210000	2.100000	0.476190	0.826446	1.735537	0.576190
3	1.331000	3.310000	0.302115	0.751315	2.486852	0.402115
4	1.464100	4.641000	0.215471	0.683013	3.169865	0.315471
5	1.610510	6.105100	0.163797	0.620921	3.790787	0.263797
6	1.771561	7.715610	0.129607	0.564474	4.355261	0.229607
7	1.948717	9.487171	0.105405	0.513158	4.868419	0.205405
8	2.143589	11.435888	0.087444	0.466507	5.334926	0.187444
9	2.357948	13.579477	0.073641	0.424098	5.759024	0.173641
10	2.593742	15.937425	0.062745	0.385543	6.144567	0.162745
11	2.853117	18.531167	0.053963	0.350494	6.495061	0.153963
12	3.138428	21.384284	0.046763	0.318631	6.813692	0.146763
13	3.452271	24.522712	0.040779	0.289664	7.103356	0.140779
14	3.797498	27.974983	0.035746	0.263331	7.366687	0.135746
15	4.177248	31.772482	0.031474	0.239392	7.606080	0.131474

Table 3-3 71

16	4.594973	35.949730	0.027817	0.217629	7.823709	0.127817
17	5.054470	40.544703	0.024664	0.197845	8.021553	0.124664
18	5.559917	45.599173	0.021930	0.179859	8.201412	0.121930
19	6.115909	51.159090	0.019547	0.163508	8.364920	0.119547
20	6.727500	57.274999	0.017460	0.148644	8.513564	0.117460
21	7.400250	64.002499	0.015624	0.135131	8.648694	0.115624
22	8.140275	71.402749	0.014005	0.122846	8.771540	0.114005
23	8.954302	79.543024	0.012572	0.111678	8.883218	0.112572
24	9.849733	88.497327	0.011300	0.101526	8.984744	0.111300
25	10.834706	98.347059	0.010168	0.092296	9.077040	0.110168
26	11.918177	109.181765	0.009159	0.083905	9.160945	0.109159
27	13.109994	121.099942	0.008258	0.076278	9.237223	0.108258
28	14.420994	134.209936	0.007451	0.069343	9.306567	0.107451
29	15.863093	148.630930	0.006728	0.063039	9.369606	0.106728
30	17.449402	164.494023	0.006079	0.057309	9.426914	0.106079
40	45.259256	442.592556	0.002259	0.022095	9.779051	0.102259
50	117.390853	1,163.908529	0.000859	0.008519	9.914814	0.100859
100	13,780.612340	137,796.123398	0.000007	0.000073	9.999274	0.100007

flows and must determine what the investment is worth. The task is to find the present value of the cash flows.

First, the investor must decide what interest rate she needs to earn to make the investment worthwhile. She must estimate the four interest components, shown in Figure 3-2, that she believes are necessary for this particular investment. If the payments come from a well-secured mortgage, the risk—and therefore the required interest—will be less than if they come from a building whose future rents are uncertain.

Having picked a proper interest rate, the investor finds the investment's present value by multiplying the expected income stream by the discount factors for that interest rate.

EXAMPLE: Someone is offered an apartment house whose net cash flow will be $10,000 at the end of the first year, $20,000 at the end of the second year, and $20,000 every additional year. The investor will also receive $120,000 cash upon its sale at the end of the fourth year. If he wants to earn 15 percent a year, how much is the house worth to him? To solve this problem, the investor must find the present value of each of the projected receipts (CF_j) and add them together. Here is the general equation for finding the present value of a future stream of cash flows:

$$PV = \frac{CF_1}{1 + i} + \frac{CF_2}{(1 + i)^2} + \frac{CF_3}{(1 + i)^3} + \cdots + \frac{CF_n}{(1 + i)^n} \tag{3.3}$$

One way of visualizing how the equation is solved is to put it in the form of a table, such as Table 3-4. The cash flow for each year is multiplied by the discount factor IFPV($15\%, j$) for the specified interest rate. Such factors are found in tables such as Table 3-3 (column 5) for each interest rate.

The top row of Table 3-4 shows the first year's $10,000 cash flow multiplied by .8696, the 1-year 15 percent discount factor IFPV($15\%, 1$). The product ($8,696) shown in column 4 is the present value of the first year's net revenue. (The table assumes that all payments are received at the end of a period.) When the present values for each of the four years are added together, the total is $117,014. This is the property's present value to the investor and is the upper limit he should be willing to pay under the assumptions that (a) he believes the estimated cash flows are correct and (b) he is willing to accept 15 percent a year return for the effort involved.

If the discount rate changes, the estimated value of the building is altered. If the discount rate fell from 15 percent to 10 percent, the amount of discount for each cash flow would be smaller. The total present value of the building would rise to $136,268.

The investor may instead find the **net present value (NPV),** which is the present value of all positive cash flows less the negative ones. In the example of Table 3-4, if the apartment house cost $100,000 its net present value would be $17,014, since the initial payment would be negative with an IFPV of 1.

Table 3-4
The Present Value of an Income Stream
At 15 Percent Interest

Year	Income and Reversion	Present Value Discount Factor	Present Value Amount
1	$ 10,000	0.8696	$ 8,696
2	20,000	0.7561	15,123
3	20,000	0.6575	13,150
4	20,000	0.5718	11,435
4	120,000	0.5718	68,610
Total			$117,014

THE PRESENT VALUE OF AN ANNUITY

The difficulty of finding present values grows as the number of years increases. Present values can be found readily by use of a financial calculator or computer. However, if an investor does not want to use either and is willing to simplify the problem by assuming that the average income over the period is received in each year, he or she can find the present value from interest factor tables, such as Table 3-3.

The right to receive a fixed income per period is called an **annuity,** defined as a series of payments for a specified period. If the cash flows are equal—that is, if they are annuities—the interest factors needed to solve them can be found in column 6 of Table 3-3, called the "Present Value of an Annuity of $1 per period." PVA is the present value of an annuity which runs for n years; I is the periodic receipt. We have seen that the present value of income received at the end of the first year is $I \div (1 + i)$. The second year's receipt is worth $I \div (1 + i)^2$, and so on. The value of the annuity is the sum of the present values of these receipts, or:

$$
\begin{aligned}
\text{PVA} &= I\left(\frac{1}{(1 + i)}\right) + I\left(\frac{1}{(1 + i)^2}\right) + I\left(\frac{1}{(1 + i)^3}\right) + \cdots + I\left(\frac{1}{(1 + i)^n}\right) \\
&= I\left[\frac{1}{(1 + i)} + \frac{1}{(1 + i)^2} + \frac{1}{(1 + i)^3} + \cdots + \frac{1}{(1 + i)^n}\right] \\
&= I\left[\frac{1 - \dfrac{1}{(1 + i)^n}}{i}\right] \qquad\qquad (3.4) \\
&= I(\text{IFPVA})
\end{aligned}
$$

In this equation, IFPVA is the abbreviation for the interest factor for an annuity.

Use of an Annuity Interest Factor

To find the value of an apartment house, we must separate the problem into that of valuing (a) the annual income stream and (b) the selling price I_n (the **reversion** or final return to the owner). The present value of the property equals the present value of the annuity plus the present value of the reversion:

$$PV = I(\text{IFPVA}) + I_n(\text{IFPV}) \qquad\qquad (3.5)$$

The apartment has an annual net income of $15,000 and a net sales price at the end of 10 years of $120,000.
When:

Annual income stream $= I = \$15,000$
Present value of annuity factor $=$ IFPVA $= 6.145$
$\qquad\qquad\qquad$ (10%,10)
Selling price (reversion) $= I_n = \$120,000$
Present value of reversion $=$ IFPV $= .386$
$\qquad\qquad\qquad$ (10%,10)

Then:

$$\$15,000(6.145) + \$120,000(0.386) = \$138,495$$

Column 6 of Table 3-3 shows that a payment of $1 per year for 10 years has a present value of 6.145. Column 5 of that table shows that the present value of a reversion in year 10 is .386. To find the value of the apartment, multiply the projected income by the annuity factor and the selling price by the factor for a reversion, then add them together. The answer is $138,495.

This example illustrates a basic point that recurs frequently in the book. At medium to high discount rates, present values of amounts that will not be received until well into the future become rather small. In column 5 of Table 3-3, for example, at 10 percent a $1 reversion occurring at the end of 10 years is worth $.39. However, if it occurs after 30 years, it is worth only $.06, and the present value of $1 that will not be received for 50 years is less than $.01.

COMPOUNDING MORE FREQUENTLY THAN ANNUALLY

The discussion of compounding thus far has used examples based on annual compounding and discounting. Yet we know that most mortgage payments are made monthly. Bonds compound interest twice a year. Some banks advertise that they compound interest continuously. How much difference does this make? The sooner we receive interest, the longer it will be invested and compounded.

To find the amount of interest due if it is compounded more frequently than annually, we simply correct the formula for compound interest for the additional subperiods. If m is the number of subperiods in a year, the interest rate received in each subperiod is $i \div m$, and the total number of periods in n years is $m \times n$. Equation 3.1 in a more general form becomes:

$$FV_{mn} = PV_0\left(1 + \frac{i}{m}\right)^{mn} \tag{3.6}$$

For example, a 30-year term mortgage has 360 monthly payments. If the annual interest rate is 10 percent, the interest rate in each period is .00833. We want to see the difference made by the additional compounding.

Increased Income To demonstrate how more frequent compounding increases the amount received, we can compare the interest earned in 1 year at 10 percent by a $100 savings account compounded monthly and yearly. For monthly compounding, the value of m—the number of periods in a year—is 12; i is 10 percent, and n is 1 year. The formula $i \div m$ gives us the interest that would be earned in 1 month: $.83. By the end of the year, the interest if compounded monthly, will have multiplied 12 times, and the amount in the account will be $110.47 By contrast, the interest in the account if compounded annually would be $110. The amount of interest earned when payments are compounded monthly instead of annually increases by $.47. This is the difference in annual interest payments due to the more rapid compounding.

The more often a sum is compounded, the larger the amount received will be, as the results from other periods of compounding in the course of a year will show. For example, at 10 percent interest, the amount of the annual payments on $100 for different subperiods and the total differences over 10 years are as follows:

Subperiods	Future Values	
	1 year	10 years
Annual	$110.00	$259.37
Semiannual	$110.25	$265.33
Monthly	$110.47	$270.70
Continuous*	$110.52	$271.83

If loans or accounts run for over a year, this additional interest continues to be compounded. If no money is withdrawn for 10 years, with monthly compounding the original savings account will have grown to $270.70. For the 10

*Note that the formula for continuous compounding is $FV_n = PV_0 e^{rn}$.

years, total interest is $11.33 more when interest is compounded monthly than when it is compounded annually. The total amount received will depend on the frequency of compounding.

SUMMARY

Property values, costs of borrowing, and rates of return depend on the interest rates established in the market plus the premiums required because of the additional costs and risks of each particular investment. When these rates change, the impact on the present value of an investment is compounded because of the time value of money.

Mortgage interest rates are heavily influenced by the general level of interest rates. The representative or base interest rate—that on the 3-month U.S. Treasury bill—is determined by the demand for and supply of credit.

The base interest rate includes an inflation premium. Nominal or market interest rates must be corrected for changes in prices before the real interest rate can be estimated. In recent years, rises and falls in inflation have accounted for much of the fluctuations of interest rates.

Other interest rates, as measured by the interest rate structure, reflect the market's pricing of the unique features of each type of security. Mortgage rates are higher than those on T-bills because they have a longer maturity, because they are more costly to service and to market, and because they contain additional risks.

The premiums, which vary with the time to maturity, are determined by the term structure. They may reflect higher expected rates in the future. Premiums may also be necessary to pay lenders for assuming the risks of illiquidity, which most spending units prefer to avoid.

Disagreement exists as to how much the structure of mortgage rates can differ from that of other rates. How much, if at all, can rates be influenced by limits on deposit interest or by the regulated activities of thrift institutions? To the degree that mortgage markets are still local, that information about other rates is poor, and that lenders do not try to obtain optimum profits, mortgage rates can differ from those of other rates. However, since mortgages must usually attract funds from the general funds market, their rates must be competitive. Mortgage rates may move at a somewhat different pace from general interest rates because of inefficient markets and lags in adjustments, but the divergences have narrowed greatly.

Money has a time value: the longer the use of purchasing power is postponed, the more can be earned on it. Conversely, purchasing power to be received in the future is not worth much if it is long delayed or if the interest rate used to discount the future cash flow is large.

To calculate the value of a stream of future payments, determine an interest rate related to the basic market rate and the costs and risks of the investment. Next, multiply each flow by a discount factor that depends on when the payment will be received and the interest rate. If the payments are evenly spaced and equal, they form an annuity, and annuity interest factors can be used in calculating their present values.

KEY TERMS

annuity	nominal interest rate
basis point	option premium
compound interest	portfolio risk
coupon interest rate	premium
covariance	present value
default premium	real interest rate
discount factor	return
discounting	reversion
diversification	risk
expected return	risk-averse
face (interest) rate	risk-free rate
fungible	spread
future value	term structure
interest	term structure premium
interest factors	time to maturity
interest rate structure	time value of money
liquidity premium	yield to maturity
net present value (NPV)	zero coupon bond

QUESTIONS

1. Why should investors look at the actual return instead of the book return when evaluating an investment?
2. Which of the following 1-year investment opportunities is worth more?
   a. Promised return = 12 percent
      Loss per foreclosure = 20 percent
      Foreclosure rate per year = 5 percent
   b. Promised return = 15 percent
      Loss per foreclosure = 40 percent
      Foreclosure rate per year = 9 percent
3. What are the components of a typical mortgage interest rate?
4. List and explain the factors causing mortgage interest rates to be higher than some other rates, yet lower than still others.
5. Why are long-term interest rates usually higher than short-term rates?
6. Notice on Figure 3-3 that for some years the real interest rate was negative. What does this mean?
7. An apartment house has a projected net income of $12,000 per year and its net sales price after five years is $100,000. Given its risks, you would

not buy it unless you felt sure it would return 16 percent a year. How much would you be willing to pay for the property?

8. You are offered a choice of two certificates of deposit, each due in three years. One promises to pay 11 percent a year simple interest. The other promises 10 percent a year with interest compounded monthly. Which would give the highest return? Show the calculations.

9. You buy a mortgage with a principal value of $1,000 that pays 8 percent interest at the end of each of the next five years. It repays the principal also at the end of five years. You want to earn at least 10 percent on the price you pay for the mortgage. What is the maximum amount you should be willing to pay?

10. You are offered a mortgage which accrues interest. It will either pay you $10,000 at the end of four years or $16,000 at the end of eight years. If the interest rate is the same for the entire period, what is the interest rate? At that interest rate, how much should you pay for the mortgage?

4 Debt Service, Rates of Return, and Leverage

OBJECTIVES

When you finish this chapter, you should be able to:

- understand the relationships among interest rates, terms to maturity, and mortgage payments.

- explain how the concept of annuities and reversions can be used to calculate mortgage payments and unpaid balances.

- understand the complexities of finding internal rates of return and yields.

- know why changes in market interest rates determine the value and price of fixed-rate mortgages.

- define effective yields and costs, and show how they are affected by points, discounts, and prepayments.

- calculate different types of yields on equities.

- describe leverage and explain how it works.

- show why leverage increases both profit opportunities and risks.

- know what is meant by a prepayment option and how it affects mortgage interest rates.

A KNOWLEDGE of interest and discount rates and of present values forms the basis for analyzing many problems that constantly recur in finance: What is the actual interest rate when mortgages are made or sold with discounts? How are payment schedules calculated and used? An investor who is told that a property will yield a return of 20 percent should be certain which yield is meant—the face or coupon rate or the effective interest rate.

This chapter builds on the preceding one in order to analyze some fundamental elements common to all real estate investment analyses. First it explains the factors that enter into mortgage payments. More and more real estate transactions hinge on the financing arrangements. Borrowers and investors as well as lenders must know what is involved in payments, how to calculate their effective yields, and how to evaluate their costs and benefits.

In recent years the number of mortgages bought and sold has equaled 70 percent or more of the mortgages created in a year. Even though the payments on them may be constant, the prices at which they trade change daily. Essential to pricing and trading mortgages are projections of when they will be paid off. Among the largest and most active financial markets are those for mortgage securities. How these markets operate can be understood only by knowing the relationships among the present values of future mortgage payments.

Properties are bought and sold daily that are priced according to their expected yields. Part of this chapter outlines the simple algebra of yields and of the factors that influence them. Although the actual calculations and their degree of sophistication vary tremendously from market to market, more and more offerings contain detailed data and analysis for use by investors in making their purchase decisions.

As examples of mortgage payments and rates of return on both properties and mortgages, the chapter examines two types of problems. First it focuses on the effects of leverage on ownership returns and risks. Many real estate experts consider this the most important topic in real estate finance. Second, the chapter considers the effect of prepayments on mortgage returns—a critical issue in all mortgage purchases and sales.

THE USE OF FINANCIAL CALCULATORS AND COMPUTERS

Chapter 3 showed how interest factor tables could be used to solve certain interest problems, and this chapter will discuss others. However, among professionals the use of these tables has declined because modern technology has outmoded them in many cases. Although some financing problems with a good deal of data require a personal computer, most solutions for which tables were formerly used can be found more quickly and accurately with a financial calculator. The tables now serve primarily as an introduction and a way of explaining the intricacies of the problems so that the right questions can be asked and the proper numbers inserted into the computer or calculator, and as a check to see that the answers make sense. They are also useful for very specific questions, such as what the mortgage payments will be for a certain typical mortgage.

Financial Calculators

In solving interest and discount problems, financial calculators use five keys to insert the values for each of five main variables:

1. the interest or discount rate (i)
2. the number of periods (n)
3. the initial principal or present value (PV_0)
4. the future or terminal value (FV_n)
5. one or a number of periodic payments (I_j)

Financial problems are mainly of two types: (a) single-sum problems, such as finding a single present or future value, which require four keys, and (b) problems concerned with a stream of payments, which use the fifth key in addition to the first four.

EXAMPLE: What is the future amount (FV_3) an investor will receive if he deposits $100 in principal ($PV_0$) at 10 percent interest (i) for 3 years (n)? Enter these three items using the specified keys, hit the COMPUTE and FUTURE VALUE keys, and see the answer displayed: $133.10. If the number of years (n) and the principal (PV_0) were the same as above but we wanted to know what interest rate the investor would need in order to attain a final sum (FV_3) of $133.10, the calculator could solve for the interest rate. The answer is 10 percent.

Computers

Although calculators solve many problems rapidly, computers are best for entering a long series of unequal payments. Financial spreadsheets to solve such problems have become the most popular programs for personal computers. Many spreadsheets come equipped with real estate overlays. These are specially formatted programs that solve quite complex problems rapidly. Furthermore, they can answer "What if ... ?" questions. When one or two variables are changed, the program immediately shows how yield and values are altered.

MORTGAGE PAYMENTS

In addition to solving other types of problems, many financial calculators are programmed to answer a series of questions about mortgage payments. The key to finding answers to many mortgage questions is that if the mortgage constant continues to be paid over time, the mortgage payment is an *annuity*, which is the right to receive a fixed income per period for a specified time. Understanding this simplifies many problems, such as the following:

- You are offered a $100,000 mortgage at 10 percent interest with a 30-year term. How much will you have to pay each month?
- You are buying a house, and the current owners tell you that five years previously they took out a mortgage and have made the monthly payments. You can now assume the remaining principal as part of the sale. What is the remaining principal that you will owe?
- Owners of real estate can take a tax deduction for their yearly mortgage interest payments. You know what your total mortgage payments were for the year. How much of the total year's payments went for principal, and how much for interest?

All of these questions can be answered by using specially prepared tables or by using a financial calculator. If a calculator is not available, the answers can also be solved using annuity formulas along with a set of interest factor tables.

The Monthly Payment

It is easy to find the monthly payment on a $100,000, 10 percent, 30-year mortgage without a calculator by looking up the answer in a book with interest amortization tables. A typical book may contain tables ranging from 5 percent to 25 percent interest, in increments of .25 percent. A separate table for each interest rate shows years along the top and mortgage amounts down the side. To find a monthly payment on a $100,000 30-year loan, locate the 10 percent table (see Table 4-1 on page 84) and look under the heading "30 Years" and opposite the $100,000 amount. The payment is $877.57.

This amount can also be found using the general formula for the present value of an annuity and a calculator or logarithmic tables to solve the equation. In making a loan, a lender buys an annuity with a monthly interest rate of $i \div m$. For $100,000—the present value of the annuity (PVA)—the borrower agrees to make 360 monthly payments (I). Using Equation 4.1, we find again that the required monthly payment is $877.57.

$$\text{PVA}_{mn} = I \left[\frac{1 - \dfrac{1}{\left(1 + \dfrac{i}{m}\right)^{mn}}}{\dfrac{i}{m}} \right] \tag{4.1}$$

$$I = \text{PVA}_{mn} \left[\dfrac{\dfrac{i}{m}}{1 - \dfrac{1}{\left(1 + \dfrac{i}{m}\right)^{mn}}} \right]$$

$$I = \$100,000 \left[\dfrac{.0083}{1 - \dfrac{1}{(1.0083)^{360}}} \right] = \$877.57$$

Financial calculators have keys to solve this problem directly; insert the interest rate, the number of payments, and the amount of the loan, then solve for the payment. The calculator gives slightly more exact figures. In addition, it can be used for odd numbers, whereas tables usually contain only round sums.

Monthly Interest Factor Tables

Table 4-2 contains a standard series of interest factors similar to the annual data in Table 3-3. However, here all interest payments are compounded monthly instead of annually. When using interest factor tables, make sure that they cover the correct periods. Many books contain tables for monthly, quarterly, semiannual, and annual interest factors.

Mortgage payments are an annuity running for the period of the loan. Therefore, the required payment in the previous problem can be found using the interest factors in column 6 of Table 4-2 on pages 86 and 87. To find a mortgage payment (I) using Equation 4.2, divide the proper interest factor, IFPVA, from column 6 at 30 years (360 payments), into the loan to obtain the monthly payment of $877.57.

$$\begin{aligned} \text{PVA} &= I(\text{IFPVA}) \\ &\quad (10\%, 360) \\ \$100,000 &= I(113.951) \\ I &= \$877.57 \end{aligned} \tag{4.2}$$

Interest factor tables make calculating the monthly payment even simpler. Column 7 in Table 4-2 lists the installment payment needed to amortize $1 of loan. Find the appropriate factor opposite the 30-year term of the loan: .008776. Multiply the factor by $100,000 to find a required monthly payment of $877.60. (Small differences are due to rounding.)

Table 4-1
Interest and Amortization Table
Monthly Payments, 10 Percent

Principal	Years						
	1	5	10	15	20	25	30
1,000.00	87.92	21.25	13.22	10.75	9.65	9.09	8.78
5,000.00	439.58	106.24	66.08	53.73	48.25	45.44	43.88
10,000.00	879.16	212.47	132.15	107.46	96.50	90.87	87.76
15,000.00	1,318.74	318.71	198.23	161.19	144.75	136.31	131.64
20,000.00	1,758.32	424.94	264.30	214.92	193.00	181.74	175.51
25,000.00	2,197.90	531.08	330.38	268.65	241.26	227.18	219.39
30,000.00	2,637.48	637.41	396.45	322.38	289.51	272.61	263.27
40,000.00	3,516.64	849.88	528.60	429.84	386.01	363.48	351.03
50,000.00	4,395.79	1,062.35	660.75	537.30	482.51	454.35	438.79
75,000.00	6,593.69	1,593.53	991.13	805.95	723.77	681.53	658.18
100,000.00	8,791.59	2,124.70	1,321.51	1,074.61	965.02	908.70	877.57
125,000.00	10,989.49	2,655.88	1,651.88	1,343.26	1,206.28	1,135.88	1,096.96
150,000.00	13,187.38	3,187.06	1,982.26	1,611.91	1,447.53	1,363.05	1,316.36
200,000.00	17,583.18	4,249.41	2,643.01	2,149.21	1,930.04	1,817.40	1,755.14

Outstanding Mortgage Amounts

What about the problem of calculating the principal outstanding on a loan after some payments have been made? Many lenders make tracking a loan easy by furnishing a computer printout, such as the excerpt in Table 4-3 on page 88, that shows how much of each year's payments goes to principal and how much to interest, and also the amount still outstanding on the principal.

EXAMPLE: Table 4-3 presents the basic information for a $100,000, 10 percent, 30-year loan. In the fifth year of such a loan, how much of the payments goes to interest and how much to principal? The table gives the answer at once. The balance outstanding at the end of year 4 is $97,402. Payments for year 5 are $10,531, of which $828 goes to principal and $9,703 to interest. At the end of the year, the balance still owed on the loan is $96,574.

The amount outstanding can also be calculated directly using a financial calculator, or it can be obtained from the interest factors in tables such as Table 4-2. Recall that the outstanding principal of a loan must be equal to the present value of the remaining payments. Thus, to find the outstanding balance at the end of year 5, locate in column 6 of Table 4-2 the factor for the present value of an annuity with 25 years of payments remaining. After 5 years of payments, 300 monthly payments remain. This factor is 110.047, which is then multiplied by the amount of the monthly payments. The balance after 5 years of payments is $96,574.

$$PVA = I(IFPVA) \qquad PVA = \$877.57(110.047) = \$96,574$$
$$(10\%,300)$$

Amount of Interest Paid

This same method of calculating provides the answer needed for tax purposes to the question of how much interest is paid in any year. From the interest factor tables (Table 4-2), we can calculate that at the beginning of year 5 the outstanding principal was $97,402.

$$PVA = I(IFPVA) \qquad PVA = \$877.57(110.99) = \$97,402$$
$$(10\%,312)$$

By subtracting the amount outstanding at the end of the year from that at the beginning, we find that the total payment on principal was $828. During the previous year the payments totaled $10,531. The amount of interest paid, therefore, was $9,703. This is the amount to show on a tax return.

INTERNAL RATES OF RETURN

Chapter 3 pointed out that there is a difference between the face or coupon rate on a mortgage and its actual or effective yield or interest rate. When we borrow or lend on a mortgage we usually want to know not only its coupon rate, but what it costs us. Similarly, in choosing among investments, it is common to compare their rates of return while making necessary adjustments for risks and transaction costs. An investor offered a choice of securities or of buildings will attempt to estimate expected yields in order to pick the highest risk-return payoff.

To find the yields, we must calculate the internal rate of return (IRR), also called the expected yield or the **effective interest rate.** The concept is closely related to the discussion of discount rates and present values in Chapter 3.

The technique for finding the internal rate of return is the reverse of the present value process. It asks: "If one knows the cost of an asset, what rate of discount (internal rate of return) is needed to make the present value of the future income flow equal to the cost?" More formally, the **internal rate of return** is that rate of return at which the present value of all future inflows is

Table 4-2
Monthly Interest Factor Table
Effective Rate 10 Percent

Months	IFFV Amount of $1 at Compound Interest	IFΣFV Accumulation of $1 per Period	$\frac{1}{IFΣFV}$ Sinking-fund Factor	IFPV Present Value Reversion of $1	IFPVA Present Value of an Annuity of $1 per Period	$\frac{1}{IFPVA}$ Installment to Amortize $1
1	1.008333	1.000000	1.000000	0.991736	0.991736	1.008333
2	1.016736	2.008333	0.497925	0.983539	1.975275	0.506259
3	1.025209	3.025069	0.330571	0.975411	2.950686	0.338904
4	1.033752	4.050278	0.246897	0.967350	3.918036	0.255230
5	1.042367	5.084031	0.196694	0.959355	4.877391	0.205028
6	1.051053	6.126398	0.163228	0.951427	5.828817	0.171561
7	1.059812	7.177451	0.139325	0.943563	6.772381	0.147659
8	1.068644	8.237263	0.121400	0.935765	7.708146	0.129733
9	1.077549	9.305907	0.107459	0.928032	8.636178	0.115792
10	1.086529	10.383456	0.096307	0.920362	9.556540	0.104640
11	1.095583	11.469985	0.087184	0.912756	10.469296	0.095517
12	1.104713	12.565568	0.079583	0.905212	11.374508	0.087916

Years							Months
1	1.104713	12.565568	0.079583	0.905212	11.374508	0.087916	12
2	1.220391	26.446915	0.037812	0.819410	21.670855	0.046145	24
3	1.348182	41.781821	0.023934	0.741740	30.991236	0.032267	36
4	1.489354	58.722492	0.017029	0.671432	39.428160	0.025563	48

Table 4-2   **87**

5	1.645309	77.437072	0.012914	0.607789	47.065369	0.021247	60
6	1.817594	98.111314	0.010193	0.550178	53.978665	0.018526	72
7	2.007920	120.950418	0.008268	0.498028	60.236667	0.016601	84
8	2.218176	146.181076	0.006841	0.450821	65.901488	0.015174	96
9	2.450448	174.053713	0.005745	0.408089	71.029355	0.014079	108
10	2.707041	204.844979	0.004882	0.369407	75.671163	0.013215	120
11	2.990504	238.860493	0.004187	0.334392	79.872986	0.012520	132
12	3.303649	276.437876	0.003617	0.302696	83.676528	0.011951	144
13	3.649584	317.950102	0.003145	0.274004	87.119542	0.011478	156
14	4.031743	363.809201	0.002749	0.248032	90.236201	0.011082	168
15	4.453920	414.470346	0.002413	0.224521	93.057439	0.010746	180
16	4.920303	470.436376	0.002126	0.203240	95.611259	0.010459	192
17	5.435523	532.262780	0.001879	0.183975	97.923008	0.010212	204
18	6.004693	600.563216	0.001665	0.166536	100.015633	0.009998	216
19	6.633463	676.015601	0.001479	0.150751	101.909902	0.009813	228
20	7.328074	759.368836	0.001317	0.136462	103.624619	0.009650	240
21	8.095419	851.450244	0.001174	0.123527	105.176801	0.009508	252
22	8.943115	953.173779	0.001049	0.111818	106.581856	0.009382	264
23	9.879576	1,065.549097	0.000938	0.101219	107.853730	0.009272	276
24	10.914097	1,189.691580	0.000841	0.091625	109.005045	0.009174	288
25	12.056945	1,326.833403	0.000754	0.082940	110.047230	0.009087	300
26	13.319465	1,478.335767	0.000676	0.075078	110.990629	0.009010	312
27	14.714187	1,645.702407	0.000608	0.067962	111.844605	0.008941	324
28	16.254954	1,830.594523	0.000546	0.061520	112.617635	0.008880	336
29	17.957060	2,034.847258	0.000491	0.055688	113.317392	0.008825	348
30	19.837399	2,260.487925	0.000442	0.050410	113.950820	0.008776	360
40	53.700663	6,324.079581	0.000158	0.018622	117.765391	0.008491	480
50	145.369923	17,324.390796	0.000058	0.006879	119.174520	0.008391	600
100	21,132.414600	2,535,769.752020	.000000	0.000047	119.994322	0.008334	1200

Table 4-3
Payments to Interest, Principal, and Outstanding Balance
On a $100,000 30-Year Mortgage at 10 Percent Interest

Year	Annual Debt Service	Interest	Principal	Cumulative Principal Payments	End-of-year Principal Balance
1	$10,530.86	$9,974.98	$555.88	$555.88	$99,444.12
2	10.530.86	9,916.77	614.09	1,169.96	98,830.04
3	10,530.86	9,852.47	678.39	1,848.35	98,151.65
4	10,530.86	9,781.43	749.43	2,597.78	97,402.22
5	10,530.86	9,702.96	827.90	3,425.68	96,574.32
10	10,530.86	9,168.71	1,362.15	9,061.98	90,938.02
15	10,530.86	8,289.70	2,241.16	18,335.44	81,664.56
20	10,530.86	6,843.46	3,687.40	33,593.14	66,406.86
25	10,530.86	4,463.95	6,066.91	58,696.77	41,303.23
30	10,530.86	548.91	9,981.95	100,000.00	0.00

equal to the present value of all negative outflows. This is usually simplified to assume that the only outflow is the initial purchase. In practice, however, many real estate transactions are structured so that payments on the original purchase continue even as benefits are being received from the building. This means that negative flows can continue for several periods.

The formula for finding present values knowing the interest or discount rate and the future revenues—Equation 3.3—can easily be turned into an equation for finding internal rates of return, Equation 4.3. Let us call the capital cost or known present value of a property COS. Then we substitute the unknown internal rate of return (IRR) for the interest rate (i) and solve the equation. As a specific illustration, let us use the example of the apartment house from Table 3-4. It is bought for $117,014 and sold at the end of four years, with the cash flows shown in the table and repeated below in the internal rate of return equation:

$$\text{COS} = \frac{I_1}{(1 + \text{IRR})} + \frac{I_2}{(1 + \text{IRR})^2} + \frac{I_3}{(1 + \text{IRR})^3} + \ldots + \frac{I_n}{(1 + \text{IRR})^n} \qquad (4.3)$$

$$\$117,014 = \frac{\$10,000}{(1 + \text{IRR})} + \frac{\$20,000}{(1 + \text{IRR})^2} + \frac{\$20,000}{(1 + \text{IRR})^3} + \frac{\$20,000 + \$120,000}{(1 + \text{IRR})^4}$$

As in the calculations for the problem using Equation 3.3, the IRR will be 15 percent.

Effective Yields

Effective yields are another example of internal rates of return, which arise when the principal or par value stated in a mortgage or bond differs from its actual or market price. For example, a borrower agrees to pay 10 percent interest on a $100,000 mortgage; however, he receives only $95,000 in cash because the lender charges fees of 5 percent. What actual interest rate is the borrower paying? We will see shortly that the answer is found by substituting in Equation 4.3.

The **effective yield** or cost of the mortgage is the discount rate that equates the present value of expected cash flows with the current market price. For a mortgage, it is the actual interest cost to the borrower. Yields change as the result of either a move in the market price or an alteration in the investment's expected cash flow.

Market interest rates change daily; the coupon or contract interest rates on fixed-rate mortgages do not. Consequently, the market value or price of the mortgage must change so that the effective yield will match rates being offered in the market. If new mortgages are being made at 11 percent, no one will pay $100 for a mortgage yielding only 10 percent. The price of the existing mortgage must drop so that its return will equal that on a new one.

The amount the price drops will also be affected by changes in the expected cash flow. Most mortgages are prepaid at some time. Yields differ depending on when prepayments are expected. Furthermore, because the borrower has the option of determining when to prepay, the yield must reflect both current market interest rates and the value of any prepayment option.

Points and Discounts   In executing a mortgage, the borrower agrees to a stated principal and interest rate. The amortization schedule of payments is based upon these par amounts. However, the actual amount of cash disbursed by the lender will often be less than the contract principal. Lenders charge loan fees to cover origination costs and to increase their effective yields. These fees or discounts are measured in points. A **point** is 1 percent of the loan balance. Thus, if the borrower agrees to pay three points on a $100,000 loan, the lender pays out only $97,000. The fee or discount is $3,000, or three points.

Market Yields   If the lender sells the loan in the market, the price received will depend on market interest rates and effective yields. For example, a lender who made a $100,000, 10 percent, 30-year loan found that market interest rates had risen to 11 percent when the loan was offered in the market. At what price would such a loan sell? Table 4-4, an excerpt from a book of such tables, shows that if this loan is expected to be prepaid at the end of 12 years, it would have to sell at a price of $93,590 in order to earn the market yield of 11 percent.

The table shows the present value of an annuity and a reversion or principal payment on 10 percent mortgages with either 300 or 360 monthly payments, given current market interest rates. The present value or price will differ

Table 4-4
Prepayment Mortgage Values

PREPAYMENT MORTGAGE VALUES   **10.00 %**
                                                              MONTHLY PAYMENT MORTGAGE

Description: This table shows the price to pay for a mortgage at the yield rate. The yield is to prepayment.

Example: The price of a 10.00%, 30 year mortgage, prepaid in 5 years, to yield 8.00% is $108.10.

25 YEAR MORTGAGE PREPAID IN

YIELD	3 yr	4 yr	5 yr	8 yr	10 yr	12 yr	15 yr
0.0	129.56	139.19	148.69	176.22	193.61	210.02	232.33
1.00	126.20	134.57	142.73	165.95	180.25	193.48	211.02
2.00	122.94	130.12	137.05	156.39	168.00	178.54	192.16
3.00	119.77	125.83	131.63	147.49	156.77	165.03	175.45
4.00	116.69	121.71	126.46	139.20	146.47	152.81	160.62
4.25	115.94	120.70	125.21	137.22	144.03	149.95	157.18
4.50	115.19	119.71	123.97	135.27	141.64	147.15	153.84
4.75	114.44	118.72	122.74	133.35	139.31	144.42	150.59
5.00	113.71	117.74	121.53	131.47	137.02	141.75	147.44
5.25	112.97	116.77	120.33	129.63	134.77	139.15	144.38
5.50	112.24	115.81	119.14	127.81	132.58	136.61	141.40
5.75	111.52	114.86	117.97	126.03	130.43	134.14	138.51
6.00	110.80	113.92	116.81	124.27	128.33	131.72	135.70
6.25	110.09	112.99	115.67	122.55	126.27	129.36	132.97
6.50	109.38	112.06	114.54	120.86	124.25	127.06	130.32
6.75	108.68	111.15	113.42	119.20	122.27	124.82	127.74
7.00	107.98	110.24	112.31	117.56	120.34	122.62	125.23
7.25	107.29	109.34	111.22	115.95	118.45	120.48	122.80
7.50	106.60	108.45	110.14	114.38	116.59	118.39	120.43
7.75	105.92	107.57	109.07	112.82	114.77	116.35	118.12
8.00	105.24	106.70	108.02	111.30	112.99	114.36	115.88
8.25	104.57	105.83	106.98	109.80	111.25	112.41	113.70
8.50	103.90	104.98	105.94	108.33	109.54	110.51	111.58
8.75	103.24	104.13	104.93	106.88	107.87	108.65	109.52
9.00	102.58	103.29	103.92	105.46	106.23	106.84	107.51
9.25	101.93	102.45	102.92	104.06	104.62	105.07	105.55
9.50	101.28	101.63	101.94	102.68	103.05	103.34	103.65
9.75	100.64	100.81	100.96	101.33	101.51	101.65	101.80
10.00	100.00	100.00	100.00	100.00	100.00	100.00	100.00
10.25	99.37	99.20	99.05	98.69	98.52	98.39	98.25
10.50	98.74	98.40	98.11	97.41	97.07	96.81	96.54
10.75	98.11	97.62	97.18	96.15	95.65	95.27	94.87
11.00	97.49	96.84	96.26	94.90	94.26	93.77	93.25
11.25	96.87	96.06	95.35	93.68	92.89	92.29	91.68
11.50	96.26	95.30	94.45	92.48	91.55	90.86	90.14
11.75	95.65	94.54	93.56	91.30	90.24	89.45	88.64
12.00	95.05	93.79	92.68	90.14	88.96	88.08	87.18
12.25	94.45	93.04	91.81	89.00	87.70	86.73	85.76
12.50	93.86	92.31	90.96	87.88	86.46	85.42	84.37
12.75	93.27	91.58	90.11	86.78	85.25	84.14	83.02
13.00	92.69	90.85	89.27	85.69	84.07	82.88	81.71
13.25	92.10	90.13	88.44	84.63	82.90	81.65	80.42
13.50	91.52	89.42	87.62	83.58	81.76	80.45	79.17
13.75	90.95	88.72	86.81	82.55	80.64	79.28	77.95
14.00	90.38	88.02	86.00	81.53	79.55	78.13	76.76
14.25	89.81	87.33	85.21	80.53	78.47	77.01	75.60
14.50	89.25	86.65	84.43	79.55	77.42	75.91	74.46
14.75	88.69	85.97	83.65	78.59	76.38	74.83	73.36
15.00	88.14	85.30	82.88	77.64	75.37	73.78	72.28
15.25	87.59	84.63	82.13	76.70	74.37	72.75	71.22
15.50	87.05	83.97	81.38	75.79	73.40	71.74	70.19
15.75	86.50	83.32	80.64	74.88	72.44	70.75	69.19
16.00	85.97	82.67	79.90	73.99	71.50	69.79	68.21
16.25	85.43	82.03	79.18	73.12	70.58	68.84	67.25
16.50	84.90	81.40	78.46	72.26	69.68	67.92	66.32
16.75	84.38	80.77	77.75	71.41	68.79	67.01	65.40
17.00	83.85	80.14	77.05	70.58	67.92	66.13	64.51
17.25	83.34	79.53	76.36	69.76	67.06	65.26	63.64
17.50	82.82	78.91	75.67	68.95	66.23	64.41	62.79
17.75	82.31	78.31	75.00	68.16	65.40	63.57	61.95
18.00	81.80	77.70	74.33	67.38	64.60	62.76	61.14
18.25	81.30	77.11	73.66	66.61	63.81	61.96	60.35
18.50	80.80	76.52	73.01	65.86	63.03	61.18	59.57
18.75	80.30	75.93	72.36	65.12	62.27	60.41	58.81
19.00	79.81	75.35	71.72	64.38	61.52	59.66	58.06
20.00	77.87	73.09	69.23	61.57	58.65	56.80	55.25
25.00	68.96	62.93	58.29	49.88	47.07	45.44	44.23
30.00	61.22	54.45	49.49	41.27	38.84	37.57	36.73

30 YEAR MORTGAGE PREPAID IN

YIELD	3 yr	4 yr	5 yr	8 yr	10 yr	12 yr	15 yr
0.0	129.74	139.53	149.23	177.78	196.25	214.14	239.63
1.00	126.36	134.86	143.20	167.28	182.46	196.89	216.92
2.00	123.08	130.37	137.46	157.51	169.84	181.32	196.89
3.00	119.89	126.05	131.98	148.41	158.28	167.28	179.18
4.00	116.79	121.89	126.75	139.95	147.68	154.59	163.50
4.25	116.03	120.87	125.48	137.93	145.17	151.61	159.87
4.50	115.28	119.87	124.22	135.94	142.71	148.71	156.35
4.75	114.53	118.87	122.98	133.99	140.31	145.88	152.93
5.00	113.79	117.89	121.75	132.07	137.95	143.11	149.61
5.25	113.05	116.91	120.54	130.18	135.65	140.42	146.39
5.50	112.32	115.94	119.34	128.33	133.40	137.79	143.26
5.75	111.59	114.98	118.16	126.51	131.19	135.23	140.22
6.00	110.87	114.03	116.99	124.73	129.03	132.73	137.27
6.25	110.15	113.09	115.83	122.97	126.91	129.29	134.41
6.50	109.44	112.16	114.69	121.24	124.84	127.91	131.63
6.75	108.73	111.24	113.56	119.55	122.82	125.59	128.92
7.00	108.03	110.32	112.44	117.88	120.83	123.32	126.30
7.25	107.33	109.42	111.34	116.24	118.89	121.11	123.75
7.50	106.64	108.52	110.25	114.64	116.99	118.95	121.27
7.75	105.96	107.63	109.17	113.06	115.12	116.84	118.86
8.00	105.28	106.75	108.10	111.50	113.30	114.79	116.52
8.25	104.60	105.88	107.05	109.98	111.51	112.78	114.25
8.50	103.93	105.01	106.01	108.48	109.76	110.82	112.04
8.75	103.26	104.16	104.98	107.00	108.05	108.91	109.89
9.00	102.60	103.31	103.96	105.55	106.37	107.04	107.80
9.25	101.94	102.47	102.95	104.13	104.72	105.22	105.77
9.50	101.29	101.64	101.96	102.73	103.12	103.44	103.79
9.75	100.64	100.82	100.97	101.35	101.54	101.70	101.87
10.00	100.00	100.00	100.00	100.00	100.00	100.00	100.00
10.25	99.36	99.19	99.04	98.67	98.49	98.34	98.18
10.50	98.73	98.39	98.09	97.36	97.00	96.72	96.41
10.75	98.10	97.60	97.15	96.08	95.55	95.14	94.69
11.00	97.48	96.81	96.22	94.82	94.13	93.59	93.01
11.25	96.86	96.03	95.30	93.58	92.74	92.08	91.38
11.50	96.24	95.26	94.39	92.36	91.37	90.61	89.79
11.75	95.63	94.50	93.50	91.16	90.03	89.17	88.25
12.00	95.02	93.74	92.61	89.98	88.72	87.76	86.74
12.25	94.42	92.99	91.73	88.82	87.44	86.38	85.27
12.50	93.82	92.25	90.87	87.68	86.18	85.04	83.85
12.75	93.23	91.51	90.01	86.56	84.94	83.72	82.46
13.00	92.64	90.78	89.16	85.46	83.73	82.44	81.10
13.25	92.05	90.06	88.32	84.38	82.55	81.18	79.78
13.50	91.47	89.34	87.50	83.31	81.38	79.96	78.49
13.75	90.90	88.63	86.68	82.26	80.24	78.76	77.24
14.00	90.32	87.93	85.87	81.23	79.13	77.58	76.02
14.25	89.76	87.24	85.07	80.22	78.03	76.43	74.83
14.50	89.19	86.55	84.28	79.23	76.96	75.31	73.67
14.75	88.63	85.86	83.49	78.25	75.91	74.22	72.53
15.00	88.07	85.19	82.72	77.28	74.87	73.14	71.43
15.25	87.52	84.52	81.95	76.34	73.86	72.09	70.35
15.50	86.97	83.85	81.20	75.41	72.87	71.06	69.30
15.75	86.43	83.19	80.45	74.49	71.90	70.06	68.28
16.00	85.89	82.54	79.71	73.59	70.94	69.08	67.28
16.25	85.35	81.90	78.98	72.70	70.01	68.12	66.30
16.50	84.82	81.26	78.26	71.83	69.09	67.17	65.35
16.75	84.29	80.62	77.54	70.97	68.19	66.25	64.42
17.00	83.77	79.99	76.84	70.13	67.31	65.35	63.51
17.25	83.24	79.37	76.14	69.30	66.44	64.47	62.63
17.50	82.73	78.76	75.45	68.49	65.59	63.61	61.76
17.75	82.21	78.14	74.76	67.68	64.76	62.76	60.92
18.00	81.70	77.54	74.09	66.89	63.94	61.93	60.09
18.25	81.20	76.94	73.42	66.12	63.14	61.12	59.29
18.50	80.69	76.35	72.76	65.35	62.35	60.33	58.50
18.75	80.19	75.76	72.10	64.60	61.58	59.55	57.73
19.00	79.70	75.17	71.46	63.86	60.82	58.79	56.98
20.00	77.75	72.89	68.95	61.02	57.92	55.90	54.13
25.00	68.79	62.67	57.93	49.23	46.23	44.47	43.09
30.00	61.02	54.15	49.07	40.56	37.99	36.61	35.65

depending on how long the annuity is to be received and on market interest rates.

The logic behind the lower selling price should be clear. Because of prevailing market rates, investors demand an 11 percent return. We know from an earlier discussion that the monthly payments on the 10 percent loan will be $877.56. If the mortgage was bought for $93,590 instead of $100,000, each monthly payment would yield a slightly higher current interest rate because the amount invested was less than that used to calculate the monthly payment. In addition, the amount of principal repaid will exceed that paid by the new purchaser. The higher current interest rate plus the additional principal together raise the yield from 10 to 11 percent.

Estimating the Effective Yield

On Table 4-4 note that in the case of mortgages that sell at yields higher than their contract or coupon rate, the earlier they are paid off, the higher the price. For yields below par, a more rapid expected prepayment lowers prices. At an 11 percent market yield, a 10 percent mortgage is worth $93,590 if it is expected to be repaid in 12 years, and $96,810 if in 4 years. Conversely, at 8 percent the price would fall from $114,790 at 12 years to $106,750 at 4 years.

To see why prices, yields, and prepayments interact in this way, we must go "behind the table" to look at the factors that determine relationships between coupon rates and effective yields.

Prices   If the coupon rate, the term, and the market yield are known, finding the market price is straightforward. The price should be the present value of the expected cash flows discounted at market interest rates. Equation 4.4 shows the general solution to finding the present value of an annuity plus a final payment. It is identical to Equation 3.5 except, in that case, the present value was obtained for a building; here we are using it to solve for the present value of a stream of mortgage payments.

EXAMPLE: What price should be paid for a $100,000, 10 percent, 30-year mortgage that is expected to be prepaid in 12 years if the market interest rate is 11 percent?

The annuity or monthly payments run until the mortgage is prepaid. The reversion (I_n) is the principal (BAL) prepaid at that time. We find from mortgage payment tables such as Tables 4-1 and 4-3 that the monthly payments are $877.57 and the outstanding principal at the end of 12 years is $87,771. Solving Equation 4.4 shows that if the mortgage is expected to be prepaid at the end of 12 years, its present value is $93,590.

$$PV = I(\text{IFPVA}) + \text{BAL}(\text{IFPV}) \qquad\qquad (4.4)$$

$$I(\text{IFPVA}) = \$877.57(79.773) = \$70,006$$
$$(11\%,144)$$

$$\text{BAL}(\text{IFPV}) = \$87,771(.2687) \ = \underline{\$23,584}$$
$$(11\%,144)$$

$$\text{Price} \qquad\qquad\qquad = \$93,590$$

Use of the interest factors gives us the same results as we find by looking in Table 4-4.

Yields   The problem of finding the effective yield, given the price, payment, and prepayment period, is identical to finding an internal rate of return. Without a financial calculator, it is difficult because it can only be solved by trial and error. However, we can try to find it by using tables of interest factors.

EXAMPLE: What is the yield that will be earned if we buy a $100,000, 10 percent, 30-year mortgage for $96,000 and expect it to be paid off at the end of 12 years? In this case, we know the price and cash flow and must solve for the yield. That is, we must find the interest factors that will give the single correct yield when they are entered into the equation.

$$PV = I(\text{IFPVA}) \quad + \quad \text{BAL}(\text{IFPV})$$
$$(?,144) \qquad\qquad\qquad (?,144)$$

$$\$96,000 = \$877.57(\text{IFPVA}) \ + \ \$87,771(\text{IFPV})$$

The values of the interest factors are unknown, as is the yield. However, an arbitrary starting point is 11 percent. On a table of interest factors we find that at 11 percent and with 144 payments, the factor for "the present value of an annuity of one" IFPVA is 79.773, and for "the value of a reversion of one" IFPV is .2687. From this we can find the value of the mortgage if market yields were 11 percent. The previous solution of Equation 4.4 shows that the value would be $93,590. We recognize that if market interest rates were 11 percent, a price of $96,000 would be too much to pay for this mortgage, so the market yield must be lower.

Since this is a 10 percent mortgage, if it were bought at a yield of 10 percent, its present value would be par, or $100,000. Therefore, the true effective yield must fall somewhere between these two arbitrary choices. We can find exactly where it falls by interpolation. Given the known present values and yields at 11 percent, we want to find the approximate yield (call it X) to go with the mortgage bought for $96,000:

Yield	Present Value
10%	$100,000
X%	$ 96,000
11%	$ 93,590

The difference between the present values at 10 percent and X is $4,000, and between those at 10 and 11 percent is $6,410. We assume that the yield will be the same fraction of the distance between 10 and 11 percent: Thus $4,000 ÷ $6,410 = .62 percent. Adding .62 percent to 10 percent gives an estimated yield of 10.62 percent (check by interpolating in Table 4-4).

RETURNS ON EQUITY

The calculation of the rates of return on equities follows the same rules as those for mortgages or other debts, but it is complicated by several features of equity:

1. Since the return to the equity is the residual return after payment of other expenses, including the amounts due on the mortgage, no fixed cash flow is promised. This means that yields must be estimated from projected income.
2. Because the equity yield comes after mortgage payments, if the returns on debt and equity differ (as they usually do), the yield on the equity will depend on what percentage of the total is paid for through debt borrowing and what part through equity.
3. Investors are interested in their yield after they have paid their taxes or received any tax benefits. Yet each potential buyer's tax rate may differ. This means that a piece of property will have a different potential yield for each investor.

If the real estate market were efficient and had excellent information, these differences would not matter. All investors would be able to calculate their expected yields, and the price would be set just high enough for the investor with the highest yield to outbid the others. In fact, information is poor enough and projections differ sufficiently so that investors using different yield estimates compete in the market. In some markets, it is said that the successful buyer is the one who mistakenly estimates the highest yield, but it is also true that the successful buyer may be the one who best sees prospects for raising the future cash flow.

Rate of Return on the Asset

Properties produce revenues and generate expenses. **Net operating income (NOI)** is the difference between revenues and expenses. It is the cash flow available to the owner of the entire property (the capital assets or the investment). In its most general form, the **rate of return on assets (ROR)** is simply the net operating income divided by the total value of the assets (the purchase price).

$$\text{Rate of return on assets (ROR)} = \frac{\text{net operating income}}{\text{total capital investment}}$$

$$\text{ROR} = \frac{\text{NOI}}{\text{price}}$$

Thus, if NOI is $100,000 and the property is bought for $1 million, its ROR is 10 percent.

$$\text{ROR} = \frac{\text{NOI}}{\text{price}} = \frac{\$100,000}{\$1,000,000} = 10\% \tag{4.5}$$

Although more accurate estimates require consideration of all cash flows over the entire ownership (holding) period, many investors calculate this return for a single period, using an adjusted or normalized net operating income based on current information. This return is also called the **free-and-clear return** and the **overall rate.**

Debt Service   When the financing of a property consists of both debt and equity, the net operating income must be split, with the equity owner getting what is left after the mortgage lender has received the payments due to him or her. **Debt service (DS)** consists of the contracted-for payments to the lender. Its amount depends on the amounts borrowed and on the mortgage constant. If a person borrows $800,000 and the mortgage constant is 11 percent, the debt service is $88,000. When this is paid and subtracted from the net operating income, the residual return to the equity owners is called the **before-tax cash flow (BTCF).**

Return on Equity

Another and one of the most popular methods of calculating yields is called the rate of **return on equity (ROE),** also known as **cash-on-cash return** and broker's equity return. Along with the free-and-clear return, it is the one found most often in brokers' offering sheets. The return on equity divides the annual cash flow (NOI) after debt service (DS) by the investor's equity (E). The difference of NOI minus DS is the before-tax cash flow (BTCF):

$$\text{Return on equity (ROE)} = \frac{\text{net operating income less debt service}}{\text{equity investment}} \qquad \textbf{(4.6)}$$

$$\text{ROE} = \frac{\text{NOI} - \text{DS}}{\text{E}} = \frac{\text{BTCF}}{\text{E}}$$

EXAMPLE: Investors purchase the same $1 million building as in the previous example, but they make a down payment (they put up equity) of $200,000 and borrow $800,000, for which the debt service (DS) payment is 11 percent a year, or $88,000. The NOI remains at $100,000. Then, from Equation 4.6:

$$\text{ROE} = \frac{\$100,00 - \$88,000}{\$200,000} = \frac{\$12,000}{\$200,000} = 6\%$$

The effect of borrowing in this case is to reduce the return on equity. This is called *negative leverage,* and in the next section we see why it occurs.

The After-Tax Internal Rate of Return

The problem with using either the free-and-clear or the cash-on-cash rate of return is that they do not take account of appreciation; yet for many properties this is the largest component in the benefits received. These rates of return also do not account for taxes, which have a significant impact on most investors. As a result, most professionals use the after-tax internal rate of return (IRR) in estimating yields. For this purpose, the cash flows for which present values are equated with the equity investment include the annual **after-tax cash flows (ATCF)** and the final cash flow—that is, the reversion (REV) or the amount received back after taxes upon the sale or refinancing of the property.

Equation 4.3, the general equation for yields, can be rewritten with the amount of equity (E) investment and with the final cash flow (ATCF_n) consisting of the last year's operating income plus the reversion:

$$E = \frac{\text{ATCF}_1}{1 + \text{IRR}} + \frac{\text{ATCF}_2}{(1 + \text{IRR})^2} + \frac{\text{ATCF}_3}{(1 + \text{IRR})^3} + \cdots + \frac{\text{ATCF}_n}{(1 + \text{IRR})^n} \qquad \textbf{(4.7)}$$

EXAMPLE: Investors buy an apartment house for $300,000, paying $117,014 in cash and borrowing the rest on a mortgage. Their after-tax return at the end of year 1 is $10,000, and it is $20,000 at the end of each of the following three years. They sell the property at the end of the fourth year, and after paying off their mortgage, selling expenses, and taxes, they net $120,000. What is their yield or rate of return? Solving Equation 4.7 (as we have done with the identical equation twice before), we find that their IRR is 15 percent.

$E = \$117{,}014$; $ATCF_1 = \$10{,}000$; $ATCF_{2,3,4} = \$20{,}000$; $REV = \$120{,}000$:

$$\$117{,}014 = \frac{\$10{,}000}{1 + IRR} + \frac{\$20{,}000}{(1 + IRR)^2} + \frac{\$20{,}000}{(1 + IRR)^3} + \frac{\$140{,}000}{(1 + IRR)^4}$$

LEVERAGE, EQUITY, AND DEBT

One of the unique features of real estate is the large percentage of the cost of a property that can be covered by borrowing. Because loans are secured by property, the amount investors can borrow tends to be much larger than in any other type of investment. Many people believe that the best feature of real estate investments is the ability to control large assets through small payments. They are using other people's money to gain potential benefits.

How much buyers pay from their own resources compared with the amount borrowed is a critical determinant of potential risks and returns. With part of the property paid for through debt, a rise in a property's net selling price, or in its net operating income, relative to interest rates will magnify the rate of return on the equity. One of the reasons for the great popularity of real estate as an investment is that, although it is risky, the leverage obtained by using debt financing can lead to high rates of profitability.

The Potential Impact of Leverage

The impact of borrowing on yields can be analyzed by measuring the amount of leverage and estimating its effects on the required equity and all future cash flows. **Leverage** is the share of the purchase price or the value of an asset covered by debt. It is sometimes defined simply as the use of other people's money. The higher the loan-to-value ratio, which is the percentage of a property financed with debt, the greater the **financial leverage.** If leverage increases the yield, it is said to be positive. **Negative leverage** reduces the yield.

To analyze the effect of leverage on the yield of a property, we must estimate the degree to which a change in the relationship between debt and equity shifts the cash flows from a property and, therefore, its rate of return. Leverage changes the cash flow in four ways:

1. It alters the initial negative cash flow to pay for the equity.
2. It alters the operating income or annual cash flows.
3. It can change the amount of taxes paid.
4. It can shift the cash flow when the property is sold or refinanced.

How much it alters a yield depends on how much is required to be paid on the debt relative to what the property earns.

The next section examines the effect of leverage through its influence on the amount of equity and (a) the cash flows received during the operating period and (b) the cash flows upon sale. To see the full impact, the two effects must be added together. Both flows are taken after taxes. The tax effects of leverage are complex; they are discussed in detail in Chapter 16.

HOW LEVERAGE WORKS

To understand how leverage works, consider a property purchased for $1 million that has an annual net operating income of $100,000 a year. (More complex cases are analyzed in Part 4.) Lenders will lend up to 80 percent of the property's value at an annual interest rate of 9 percent with no required amortization of principal. After considering various leverage possibilities, the new investors decide to take out an $800,000 mortgage with a debt service of $72,000 a year. How will the leverage affect their yield?

Leverage in the Operating Period

First, consider the operating period between purchase and sale by itself. The property costing $1 million with an annual net operating income of $100,000 has a free and clear return of 10 percent, as found by using Equation 4.5.

$$\text{ROR} = \frac{\text{NOI}}{\text{capital investment}} = \frac{\$100,000}{\$1,000,000} = 10\%$$

If no leverage is used, this is also the cash-on-cash or return on equity (ROE).

As a result of borrowing, the return on assets (ROR) is unchanged but, because the equity and cash flow after debt are altered, the return on equity (ROE) rises to 14 percent, as found by using Equation 4.6:

$$\text{ROE} = \frac{\text{NOI} - \text{DS}}{\text{E}}$$

$$\text{ROE} = \frac{\$100,00 - \$72,000}{\$200,000} = 14\%$$

The use of other people's money has increased the yield of the property.

Leverage has raised the yield because the debt service constant (K) is less than the rate of return on total assets. In this case, ROR is 10 percent and K is 9 percent, so each dollar of assets makes a positive contribution to the owners' yield. In fact, we can separate the earnings into the part coming from the owners' own capital and that from the debt. Each $1 of assets earns $.10. The owners get that amount on each of their $200,000 in equity, or $20,000 ($200,000 × $.10 = $20,000). In addition, they receive the difference between the earnings and the debt service for every dollar of assets bought with debt. They earn $.01 on each of the debt-financed assets, since that is the amount by which the ROR exceeds the debt service. Thus they earn $8,000, or $800,000 × ($.10 − $.09) = $8,000, on these assets.

The two income sources added together and divided by the equity yield the return on equity of 14 percent ($20,000 + $8,000 ÷ $200,000). This is also the difference between the net operating income and the debt service divided by the equity.

The above example can be generalized to state that positive leverage will exist from operating cash flow, and the return on equity will grow as the percentage of debt increases if the free-and-clear return is greater than the debt service constant (ROE ↑ if ROR > K). Conversely, negative leverage exists if the debt service constant exceeds the rate of return on capital assets (ROE ↓ if ROR < K). If the leverage alters the return, the greater the amount of leverage, the larger will be the change in the return.

EXAMPLE: How leverage from operations works is demonstrated in Table 4-5. A property bought for $1 million has a net operating income of $100,000. The first two columns show the percent of leverage—the loan-to-value ratio—and the amount of equity. Column 3 shows that the free-and-clear return (ROR) is 10 percent. Columns 4 and 6 show the debt service constant to be 9 percent in the first case and 11 percent in the second.

When K is less than ROR, positive leverage exists. The cash-on-cash (ROE) return rises from 10 percent at zero leverage to 14 percent at 80 percent. As the amount of leverage grows (the equity diminishes), the effect of leverage multiplies. The final column shows the opposite effect, negative leverage, in which K exceeds the free-and-clear return. The greater the leverage, the more the return on equity falls.

The effect of leverage increases as the gap between debt service and operating income narrows, making it either more profitable or more dangerous. Furthermore, since with more leverage less is being earned by the equity-financed assets, the danger of being unable to meet the debt service also grows. With a 40 percent leverage and an 11 percent K, use row 2 of the table to calculate that earnings could still meet the debt service if ROR fell to 4.4 percent. On the other hand, at 80 percent leverage, if ROR dips below 8.8 percent, income will be insufficient to carry the mortgage. Clearly, the greater the leverage, the greater the risk.

Leverage and Appreciation

Using other people's money can be even more profitable and risky when the potential for gain or loss at time of sale is also considered. Since the amount

Table 4-5
The Effect of Leverage on the Return on Equity (ROE)
$1 Million Purchase; $100,000 Annual NOI

Percent Leverage	Equity ($000)	Return on Capital Assets (ROR)	Positive Leverage (ROR > K)		Negative Leverage (ROR < K)	
			Debt Service Constant (K)	Return on Equity (ROE)	Debt Service Constant (K)	Return on Equity (ROE)
0%	$1,000	10%	9%	10.0%	11%	10.0%
40	600	10	9	10.7	11	9.3
60	400	10	9	11.5	11	9.0
80	200	10	9	14.0	11	6.0

borrowed must be paid back at sale, all of the increase or decrease in the property's net selling price goes to the equity holder. The greater the leverage, the greater the impact on the equity holder.

EXAMPLE: The same $1 million property is sold at the end of four years for $1.1 million. The total profit is $100,000 after payment of buying and selling costs. Table 4-6 shows the impact of leverage on the equity holders' profit. Again, four leverage ratios are illustrated. As shown in column 4, the percentage increase in the equity grows from 10 percent with no leverage to 50 percent with 80 percent leverage. The percent appreciation per year goes from 2.4 to 10.7 percent, according to column 5.

The potential for negative leverage and the enhanced risk should be evident again, even though it is not illustrated. What if the net selling price was only $800,000? At 40 percent leverage, the equity holders would lose one-third of their original investment. At 80 percent, they would be wiped out. If the property sold for only $700,000, the mortgage lender would still be repaid at 70 percent leverage but would suffer loss at any higher percentage.

The Total Effect of Leverage

The total impact of leverage is the result of the gains or losses realized both through operations and through sales, together with any enhancement or reduction due to tax effects. The joint effects are measured by solving for the internal rate of return on the equity. When Equation 4.7 is used to estimate the yield, the cost or price to the owner which must be equated to the cash flows

Table 4-6

The Effect of Leverage on the Return from Appreciation

$1 Million Purchase Price Sold for $1.1 Million

	Equity		Percent Appreciation		Internal Rate of
Percent Leverage	Down Payment ($000)	Cash on Sale ($000)	Total	Compounded per Year	Return from Operations and Appreciation
0%	$1,000	$1,100	10.0%	2.4%	12.1%
40	600	700	16.7	3.9	14.1
60	400	500	25.0	5.7	16.4
80	200	300	50.0	10.7	27.4

shifts with leverage, as does each of the cash flows. Thus, in the case of 80 percent leverage with the debt service constant at 9 percent, Equation 4.7 becomes:

$$\$200,000 = \frac{\$100,000 - \$72,000}{1 + IRR} + \frac{\$100,000 - \$72,000}{(1 + IRR)^2} +$$
$$\frac{\$100,000 - \$72,000}{(1 + IRR)^3} + \frac{\$328,000}{(1 + IRR)^4}$$

Solving this equation with a financial calculator, we find the answer of 27.4 percent, as shown in column 6 of Table 4-6.

The table also brings out how quickly the IRR changes with leverage. When only small sums are invested, both the potential rate of return and the risks accelerate rapidly.

Changing Leverage

Because of the impact of leverage on risk and returns, the amount to be borrowed and the mortgage constant both play key roles in the bargaining between buyers and sellers and between borrowers and lenders. The lower the required payment per dollar of loan (the mortgage constant), the more dollars of borrowing can be carried by any cash flow. Thus, leverage and the amount borrowed can be increased if either the interest rate or the amount of principal repayment can be reduced.

Since lenders do not like to lower interest charges, borrowers use many different techniques to reduce the amount of principal repayment and the mortgage constant. Some loans are **straight** or interest-only nonamortizing loans. The amount of principal remains constant. In others, the mortgage constant is below the interest rate. As a result, unpaid interest accrues; it is added to and becomes part of the outstanding principal. In most of these cases, the term of the loan is limited to 3, 5, or 10 years. The loan must be paid off or refinanced at that time.

PREPAYMENTS

The importance of estimating potential yields has grown as more mortgages are traded in the secondary market. Fluctuations in interest rates are frequent and large, causing wide ranges in mortgage prices. Their movements and actual yields depend on both the market interest rates and when they are likely to be prepaid. As Chapter 8 will explain, many mortgages are grouped together into **mortgage pools** and securities based on them are traded. Such pools of government-guaranteed mortgages with 9 percent coupons sold in 1982 at less than $65 per $100 par value. Within six months their prices rose more than 30 percent, to over $85. Investors received an actual return of over 45 percent for the year. During the same period, pools of mortgages with 16 percent coupons rose in price from $98 to $110. Their total return was under 30 percent. These differences in return were caused by how interest rate movements affect prepayments.

Pricing Conventions

Quoted yields on mortgages depend on an artificial pricing convention. Yields are calculated from a cash flow which assumes that no prepayments will occur until the end of year 12. At that point, all mortgages are prepaid completely. Figure 4-1 shows the cash flow pattern assumed under this convention. (This pattern was used to estimate the yields in the previous section.) For the first 12 years, each payment includes some amortization, but it primarily covers interest. At the end of the 144th month, the remaining principal is paid off.

Such prepayment patterns, however, are not the way things work in practice. Instead, actual cash flows from a pool of identical mortgages look more like those in Figure 4-2. Some mortgages are paid off every year. The amount of interest received drops steadily because the outstanding principal is declining.

Moreover, how much is prepaid in any year varies greatly. In some years, the prepayment rate has been as high as 12 percent a year on all mortgages selling at or below par. In other years, it has fallen as low as 1 percent. It has usually averaged between 6 and 8 percent. For mortgages selling above par, the rate is much higher. Most government-guaranteed mortgages issued at 17 percent in 1982 were paid off within two or three years.

Figure 4-1
Total Payment on a 30-Year Mortgage under the Standard 12-Year Prepayment Assumption

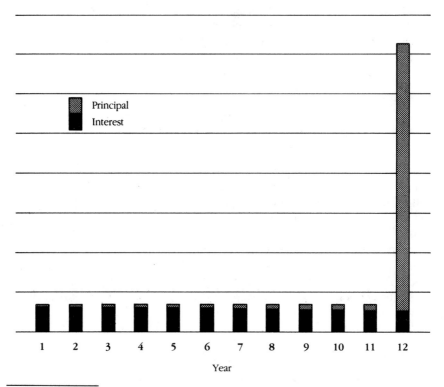

Source: Salomon Brothers.

The lesson from history is that anyone buying or selling mortgage loans must analyze the discounts and premiums carefully. Acting as though the conventional assumption of a 12-year prepayment were correct will almost always lead to paying the wrong price for a mortgage. Changes in the probable rate of prepayment cause large variations in yield that must be estimated.

Influences on Prepayment

Because prepayment rates are so important, an increasing amount of effort has been expended in trying to explain why they rise and fall. The knowledge that has been developed shows that borrowers appear to make logical decisions. Such knowledge helps in estimating what will happen in the future. Projected cash flows from tables such as Table 4-2 are inserted in Equation 4.3 to estimate the effective yield from a mortgage. This yield, together with the length of time over which payments are expected, determines the market price of the mortgage.

Figure 4-2
Typical Payment Pattern on a Pool of 30-Year Standard Mortgages

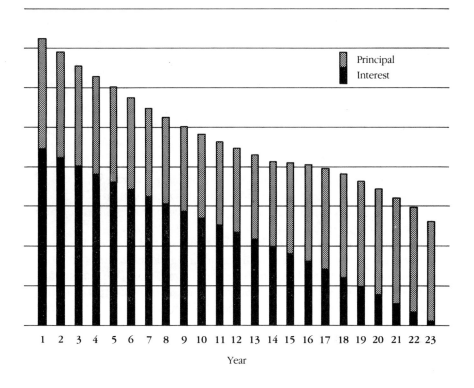

Year

Source: Salomon Brothers.

Here are some of the forces causing prepayment rates to rise:

1. When property values rise and loan-to-value ratios fall, mortgages are paid off more rapidly. Buyers of the properties find that it is not worth their while to assume the existing mortgages. Furthermore, original owners step up their rate of refinancing mortgages; they want to use their greater equity for other purposes.
2. The higher the level of current market rates compared to outstanding coupon rates, the smaller the number of prepayments there are. With low market rates, people refinance their existing high-rate mortgages. Borrowers are aware of opportunities to save money.
3. However, the turnover of mortgages slows when discount points rise above normal. Added points raise the cost of both the current and future refinancing.
4. Older mortgages have a higher probability of prepayment. This factor is in

addition to the fact that they may have lower coupons and loan-to-value ratios.

5. Affluent borrowers tend to pay off faster. Older borrowers who have less extra income prepay more slowly.

6. When the economy is booming, housing turnover and mortgage payoffs increase.

7. The volume of prepayments varies widely among states and regions. If bought at the same discount, identical-seeming mortgages from different states will have different payment rates. For example, in 1983 the rate of prepayment in Texas was twice as high as it was in the state of Washington.*

Prepayment Options

It has been noted that most mortgages contain prepayment options. The right to buy back a mortgage—that is, to prepay—is a **call option.** On the other hand, lenders can demand repayment only if a due-on-sale clause is included and if the property is actually sold.

The value of prepayment clauses can be measured by option theory. Two researchers estimate that under typical conditions a mortgage that contains the right to prepay without penalty costs the lender from 50 to 80 basis points a year more than one that does not permit prepayment.[†] This means that a mortgage with a no-penalty prepayment option should carry an extra risk premium of close to .75 percent. However, if a mortgage requires a prepayment penalty of six months' interest, the value of the option would be cut in about half.

Evidence indicates that when prepayment options were included in mortgages, lenders were unaware of the risks they were taking. The options were granted with insufficient charges for the risks they contain. This was one reason thrift institutions got into trouble: they were selling their product below their real costs. Their spreads were too narrow.

Option Values   Why should prepayment risks and costs be so great? Figure 4-3 gives an insight into why. The solid line shows the present value—measured on the vertical axis—of a portfolio equivalent to one of 30-year 13 percent mortgages that have no prepayment options. The horizontal axis records market interest rates. When market rates rise, the value of such a portfolio will fall. At each higher interest rate, the discount to be applied to future cash flows increases, and their present value falls. If interest rates decline, each future payment is discounted by a smaller interest factor, and present values rise.

*M. Waldman, H. Petty, and N. Lowen, "Mortgage Prepayments: The Regional Difference," *The Mortgage Banker* (January 1985): 25–27.

†P. H. Hendershott and S. A. Buser, "Spotting Prepayment Premiums," *Secondary Mortgage Markets* 1, no. 3 (August 1984):21–25. See also J. Green and J. B. Shoven, "The Effect of Interest Rates on Mortgage Payments," Federal Home Loan Bank of San Francisco, *Special Report* (June 1984).

The dashed line in the figure shows the present values at each interest rate of a portfolio of similar 13 percent mortgages that can be prepaid at the borrower's option. The prepayable mortgages have a higher yield in the mid-range of the table reflecting the premiums they include which are required to cover the potential losses from inopportune prepayments. As interest rates rise above 13 percent, the value of this portfolio declines. Higher discount rates depress present values. Moreover, its fall in value is somewhat more rapid than that of the noncallable mortgage.

The left side of the figure shows market interest rates below 13 percent. Initially the value of the callable portfolio rises, just as does that of the noncallable

Figure 4-3
Present Value of Cash Flows from Two Securities When the Initial Level of Interest Rates Is 13 Percent

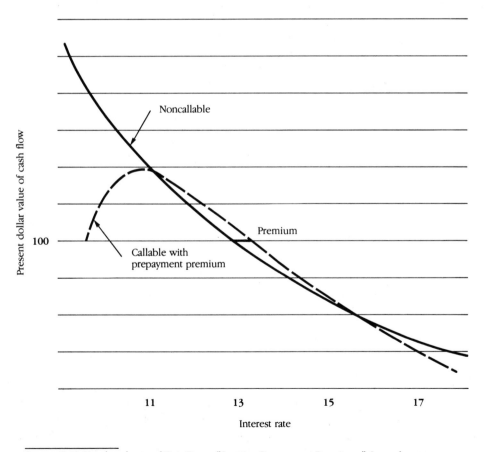

Source: P. H. Henderschott and S. A. Buser, "Spotting Prepayment Premiums," *Secondary Mortgage Markets* 1, no. 3 (August 1984): 23.

one. But if interest rates continue to drop instead of rising, the value of the prepayable portfolio falls. What is happening? Because borrowers can refinance at lower rates, they will prepay their mortgages. Lenders will have to reinvest the principal they receive at the lower market rates. The mixed return from those mortgages still paying the 13 percent rate plus the new lower-rate reinvestments yield a cash flow below that of the initial portfolio. Moreover, its present value falls below that of the similar closed mortgage portfolio, which forbids prepayments.

Option theory enables experts to measure the differences in value of the two portfolios. The call option premium should be just large enough to equalize the present values of the two portfolios, including a necessary premium for differential risks.

SUMMARY

An annuity is the right to receive a series of equal payments for a term of years. The fixed-rate mortgage is a typical annuity. By recognizing that the principal of a mortgage is the present value of the future annuity payments, we can calculate the size of payments needed to amortize a loan, given its interest rate and term. We can also find the outstanding balance at the end of any period, and the proportion of the payments that should be applied to interest and to principal.

The value and price of existing fixed-rate mortgages move with changes in interest rates. Buyers will pay only the amount which makes their effective yield equal to current market interest rates. Loans may sell at discounts or premiums, which are measured in points. A point equals 1 percent, or 100 basis points, of the loan.

If loans are sold at a discount or premium, their expected yield or cost is affected by the possibility that they may be paid off prior to their maximum term. The earlier money is received, the greater its present value. Mortgage payments are based on the concept of an annuity amortizing the principal over the full term. If market interest rates differ from the face or coupon rate, any prepayment will change the value and yield of the mortgage.

The yield or internal rate of return on an asset is the discount rate that makes the present value of all future cash flows exactly equal to its cost. In most situations, projections show a series of cash flows plus a final flow or reversion equal to an assumed selling price or repayment of the balance of a loan. The discount rate that equates these flows to the asking price for the asset is its yield or IRR.

The rate of return on an investment can be defined in a variety of ways. This chapter introduced three definitions which differed with respect to the cash flows covered. These three, as well as others, are used in specific real estate transactions. Part 4 examines the results arising from the use of these different definitions.

Leverage is one of the most important concepts in real estate. If the rate of return on the capital assets during the operating period differs from the debt service, leverage will cause the yield of a property to be multiplied. The greater the leverage, the larger the multiplication. If the return on assets exceeds the debt service, the effect of leverage is positive; if it is less, negative leverage raises losses. The impact of leverage during the operating period can be augmented or offset by the effect of leverage on the cash flow from a sale or refinancing.

Many mortgages contain a valuable prepayment option. If interest rates rise, loans need not be paid off. If rates fall, properties can be refinanced at a lower rate. In the early 1980s the value of the option was much higher than lenders had allowed for. Since then, it has played a significant role in the setting of mortgage rates and terms.

KEY TERMS

after-tax cash flow (ATCF)
before-tax cash flow (BTCF)
call option
cash-on-cash return
debt service (DS)
effective interest rate
effective yield
financial leverage
free-and-clear return
internal rate of return (IRR)

leverage
mortgage pools
negative leverage
net operating income (NOI)
overall rate
point
rate of return on assets (ROR)
return on equity (ROE)
straight

QUESTIONS

1. You are thinking of buying a house and there are two financing options open to you: a $20,000 10 percent loan for 30 years, or two loans, one for $10,000 at 6 percent for 10 years and one for $10,000 at 10 percent for 15 years. Which is the better deal if the market interest rate is 9 percent?

2. Mrs. Jones takes a mortgage on an office building for 10 years under the following terms, which pay off the loan completely: years 1 to 3, 36-month by payments at $1,000 per month; years 4 to 7, 48 payments at $2,000 per month; years 8 to 10, 36 payments at $3,000 per month. The market interest rate is 10 percent. How much does she borrow?

3. Given the answer to Question 2, Mrs. Jones asks to make constant monthly payments. How much should this payment be? If there were a balloon with half of the principal to be paid at the end of year 10, how much should the monthly payment be?

4. You invest $700,000 in a property that returns $30,000 per year for the following 10 years. You intend to sell it at the end of year 10, and the expected receipt upon sale is $800,000. If your discount rate is 10 percent, what is your *NPV?*

5. Using the information in Question 4, if you believe you should not accept a yield of less than 15 percent, at what price would you consider this investment worthwhile?

6. You have an option to buy a $100,000, 10 percent, 30-year, 360-payment mortgage for $90,000 and expect it to be paid off at the end of year 12. What is your expected yield?

7. Many buildings are purchased with leverage so great that cash flows for the first four years are negative. Yet investors are pleased to engage in such transactions. Using the concept of leverage, explain why such arrangements may make sense.

8. An investor buys a $500,000 building. She is offered loans with a mortgage constant of 11 percent and can borrow any amount up to 80 percent of the price. She projects a rate of return (ROR) of 12 percent, but believes that a 10 percent probability exists that it could fall as low as 8 percent. If she wants less than a 10 percent probability of having to supply additional funds, what is the maximum loan she should take?

9. Explain why, when market interest rates on mortgages are 10 percent, the price of mortgages with 12 percent coupons is such that their yields may be more than those with 14 percent coupons, even though both have the same term to maturity.

10. What is the monthly payment required to fully amortize a $20,000 10 percent mortgage over 180 payments? What will the outstanding balance be after 60 payments have been made?

PART

2

The Availability and Sources of Mortgage Funds

5 Fluctuations in Mortgage Credit and Interest Rates

OBJECTIVES

When you finish this chapter, you should be able to:

- explain why interest rates and credit fluctuate as they do.

- explain the advantages of financial intermediaries.

- describe the main sources and uses of financial funds.

- know what the Federal Reserve does and what it tries to achieve.

- explain how monetary policy works.

- discuss the relationships among financial assets, liabilities, and the money supply.

- illustrate a typical credit cycle and discuss its causes.

- offer reasons for the amplified impact of credit cycles on mortgage lending.

- show how knowledge of cycles enters into planning for financing real estate.

REAL ESTATE FINANCE depends heavily on the levels of interest rates and the availability of credit. They in turn depend on the supply of and demand for loanable funds. Knowledge of the sources of mortgage funds and how they react in credit cycles is essential for participants in the real estate industry. Instability in the credit and real estate markets has increased. Most funds flow through financial institutions, whose ability to lend depends on the supply of and demand for credit and on changes in the supply of money.

Credit cycles have existed for most of United States history. The Federal Reserve System and the government deposit insurance agencies were established in an effort to moderate some of their unfortunate consequences. Knowing how and why the Federal Reserve operates is central to understanding the fluctuations of interest rates and credit. In addition to explaining how monetary policy and the credit cycle work, this chapter examines their impact on real estate finance. When the flow of funds through financial markets is increased or decreased, reactions in the mortgage market are magnified as a result of institutional forces. Proper planning for both borrowers and lenders begins with an understanding of how and why the flows of mortgage funds, and their costs, act as they do.

INSTABILITY IN THE MORTGAGE MARKETS

One of the most frustrating experiences encountered by real estate sales people, builders, and developers is to have a sale or project all set to go, only to see it fall through because of inability to obtain the necessary credit. Unfortunately, during the 1970s and 1980s, such failures became increasingly common as financial markets and credit supplies became less stable.

Figure 5-1 measures changes in the **federal funds rate**—the interest rate at which financial institutions lend credit to each other overnight. This is one of the most active markets and is another good measure of the risk-free rate. The figure reflects how unstable interest rates have been over the past 25 years. It also measures the degree to which credit markets were tight or easy during this time. Periods of **tight money** are those in which interest rates are high because the demand for funds exceeds the supply. Note that in a single year, such as mid-1972 to mid-1973, interest rates rose more than 125 percent, while in other years they fell 40 percent or more. Interest rates reached heights never dreamed of even a few years earlier. The period-to-period movements also grew far more volatile. Changes in the amount of lending have been even greater than the movements shown in the figure.

111

Figure 5-1
Monthly Federal Funds Rate, 1960 to 1985

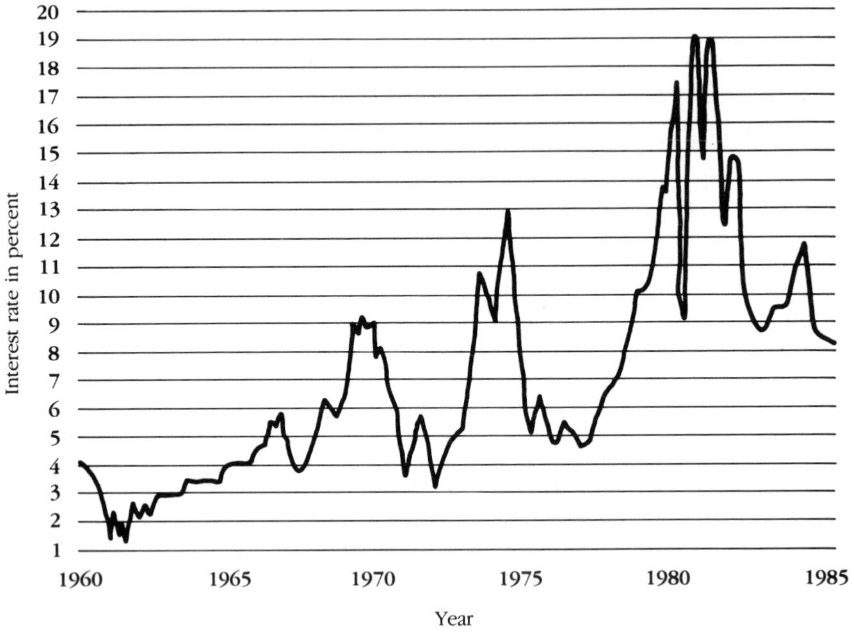

Credit Crunches

These fluctuating rates greatly increase the dangers of losses to both borrowers and lenders. In every period of high rates, the number of foreclosures has risen and there have been widespread failures of builders and developers. In the mid-1980s major financial institutions, such as Continental Illinois Bank (one of the ten largest banks) and Financial Corporation of America (the largest savings and loan company) had to be rescued by government deposit insurance agencies. More banks, savings and loans, and individual lenders and investors have failed in recent years than in any period since the Great Depression of 1929–1933.

The number and size of the failures did not surprise those familiar with financial history. The interactions of lenders, borrowers, and the Federal Reserve lead to cycles in credit availability and costs. Periods of tight and easy money have alternated for the past 200 years. There is no reason to believe they will end. What forces cause financial markets to react as they do? What gives rise to frequent credit crunches?

A **credit crunch** occurs when the supply of credit falls short of demand. Interest rates shoot up and credit availability almost disappears. As costs of borrowing increase, firms and individuals find that they entered into overoptimistic plans. Incomes are insufficient to meet the high interest rates and debt burdens they assumed. Losses and failures proliferate, and the values of both financial and real assets fall.

Credit Crunches and Real Estate Activity

Experience tells real estate salespeople, developers, and builders that, on average, mortgage funds will be hard to obtain and will become very expensive about every four years, although the range around the average is wide. When the general credit market plunges, the reactions of the mortgage market are even more pronounced because fluctuations in credit and interest have an especially strong impact on real estate markets. Credit crunches and the period of tightening that precedes them cause sharp drops in mortgage availability. Because it is more sensitive to interest rate and credit movements, real estate demand falls farther than does activity in the rest of the economy.

A larger proportion of real estate than of other investments is financed through borrowing. When the percentage that can be borrowed falls, so does demand. Because debt service takes a larger share of income than for most other goods, rising interest rates cut affordability faster. Furthermore, many real estate investments can be postponed. Existing vacancies can absorb new demand for a period.

The Cycle of Housing Starts

The net effect of all these factors is to make housing production one of the most unstable elements in the entire economy. Table 5-1 shows the results of credit and interest rate movements on housing starts. Declines of 35 to 65 percent in the number of starts are common.

While other parts of the real estate market do not react as violently, mortgage lending and the sales and prices of existing properties do follow similar patterns. Cycles in interest rates and in the availability of financing cause equivalent shifts in demand throughout real estate markets. However, prices do not fall as far as output does because owners of existing properties delay sales in the hope of avoiding major losses.

Reasons for the Increasing Instability of Credit Cycles

In the past 15 years, wider movements in interest rates and huge credit crunches forced lenders, anxious to avoid disaster, to rethink and reshape their lending policies. They reduced the length of loans and increased the number of variable-rate loans. Borrowers had to take unwanted interest rate risks that previously they had been able to avoid. What caused this increased volatility? The following six forces appear to be significant:

1. Inflation. Soaring prices meant that nominal interest rates rose much

Table 5-1
Peaks and Troughs in the Cycles of New Private Housing Starts
At Seasonally Adjusted Annual Rates

	Months between High and Low	Amount in One Month in Thousands			Percent Decline	Three-Month Averages in Thousands			Percent Decline
		High	Low	Difference		High	Low	Difference	
Oct. 1947–Feb. 1949	16	1,036	821	215	(20.8)	1,014	846	168	(16.6)
Aug. 1950–July 1951	11	1,889	1,154	735	(38.9)	1,881	1,182	699	(37.2)
Dec. 1954–Mar. 1957	27	1,703	1,068	635	(37.3)	1,664	1,080	584	(35.1)
Dec. 1958–Dec. 1960	24	1,604	1,063	541	(33.7)	1,589	1,157	432	(27.2)
Dec. 1965–Oct. 1966	10	1,656	843	813	(49.1)	1,522	931	591	(38.9)
Jan. 1969–Jan. 1970	12	1,768	1,085	683	(38.6)	1,679	1,236	442	(26.4)
Feb. 1972–Feb. 1975	36	2,540	904	1,636	(64.4)	2,458	967	1,491	(60.7)
Apr. 1978–May 1980	25	2,197	815	1,382	(62.9)	2,114	907	1,207	(57.1)
Jan. 1981–Nov. 1981	10	1,547	837	710	(45.9)	1,410	874	536	(38.0)
Feb. 1984–		2,208							

faster than in the past. Furthermore, lenders, who had suffered large losses through reacting too slowly in the past, reacted more rapidly.

2. Supply shocks, especially those due to the record-breaking rise in oil prices. In the 1970s, two large and rapid increases in oil prices, engineered by the Organization of Petroleum Exporting Countries (OPEC), raised the demand for money and credit far faster than their supply. The result was higher interest rates.

3. More dependence on interest movements to control demand in the economy. The desire for more freedom in markets led to a greater reliance on the use of prices rather than other means to curtail demand. In the credit markets, this led the Federal Reserve to shift its emphasis from influencing interest rates to controlling the money supply. Interest rate ceilings were removed. Rates had to rise faster and higher, and fall more rapidly, in order to achieve impacts equal to those of smaller movements in the past.

4. Deregulation of financial institutions. The same pressures for greater reliance on market forces caused the dismantling of many controls over financial institutions. The results were wider fluctuations in rates and more drastic crunches.

5. Fiscal policy out of control. Huge government deficits and borrowing put more pressure on the credit market. When public opinion demanded a stronger battle against inflation, the entire burden fell on monetary policy and tighter credit.

6. Major changes in financial markets. Credit market debt rose from $1 trillion in 1965 to over $7.3 trillion in 1985. Funds from abroad became

more significant as financial markets became increasingly international. Mortgage loans and many other types became the basis for issuing securities. As a result, their demand and prices were influenced more strongly by day-to-day financial market movements.

THE MARKET FOR SAVING AND LENDING

To understand why and how mortgages become more or less available and mortgage interest rates rise and fall, we must examine the underlying sources and movements of credit. New credit arises from savings, from repayments or sales of existing assets, and from the creation of money by the Federal Reserve. Most mortgage funds are accumulated and lent through financial institutions that act as intermediaries between those with excess purchasing power and those who want to borrow. However, some are lent directly by individuals or nonfinancial firms, as when sellers accept notes as partial payment.

Financial Markets

The mortgage market is a specialized segment of the general lending market. Funds for lending are accumulated by individuals, firms, or governments that do not consume all the income they earn in a period. They have excess purchasing power, which they save and thus make available for transfers to firms and individuals eager to spend more than their current income. Borrowers want credit in order to increase consumption or to invest in houses, buildings, equipment, or other goods.

However, most financial activity is not based on such new saving but rather on the transfer of past savings in the form of existing assets; that is, money made available by the repayment of debts is re-lent. Many loans, such as those between banks, have a maturity of only a day or two. People who believe they have found a better investment sell real or financial assets accumulated in the past. Others sell assets to pay for a new car or a trip. They use past savings to raise current consumption above their current income. Every day billions of dollars of securities are bought and sold; checks and wire orders transfer over a trillion dollars among individuals, firms, and government.

Although we can distinguish between new and old savings, practically speaking no one can tell whether the funds from an individual mortgage loan came from new savings or old. A home buyer may be using current income, past savings, or someone else's new savings.

The Market for Loanable Funds

In financial markets, funds are transferred between savers (lenders) and borrowers (spenders) in a variety of ways. While some loans and securities are bought and sold in organized markets, most loans are made over the counter at financial institutions. Figure 5-2 offers a simplified view of loan channels. At

Figure 5-2
The Flow of Saving and Lending

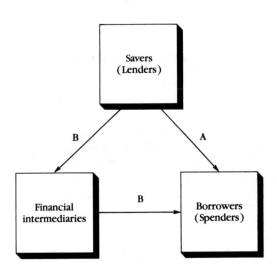

the apex are the savers (lenders). They have funds available for use by others. As the diagram shows, they can channel the funds either directly to borrowers (A) or indirectly through financial intermediaries (B).

In A, savers deal directly in the money or capital markets. They buy securities—notes, bonds, common stock, or other financial instruments issued by corporations or governments. The issuers use these funds for investments or for current operating expenses.

Financial Intermediaries   Most funds do not follow this direct route. Instead, savers deposit money with banks, savings and loans, or other financial institutions. These firms act as **intermediaries,** as in B. They gather the funds from savers and buy securities from or make loans to the ultimate investors.

The number and size of intermediaries or middlemen have expanded enormously because they make financial investing far more efficient. They solve many of the problems that plague individuals who try to invest or lend directly. We can identify some of the reasons individuals use financial intermediaries.

1. Intermediaries offer liquidity and a range of denominations. A mortgage is both expensive and time-consuming to sell for cash; in other words, it is illiquid. If, instead, a saver deposits the money in a savings bank and the bank buys the mortgage, the saver can obtain cash or transfer the funds elsewhere at any time. The funds are not "locked in"; they are liquid. The saver has flexibility because the deposit can be in any amount from one dollar to millions of dollars.

2. Financial intermediaries diversify their assets, thereby reducing their risks. Most savers are lucky if they save enough to buy a single mortgage. If it then defaulted, their loss would be catastrophic. Not so for the intermediaries, however. Intermediaries lower their risk by owning thousands of different assets of many types. Without diversification, more loans would be restricted to risk-free ones.

3. Institutions can afford greater expertise. They have staffs who trade constantly in the money market, who can properly underwrite loans, who can take action to collect if payments are delayed. Most individuals do not have the time or skills to perform these and similar tasks well.

4. Economies of scale exist in the handling of funds as in any other business. Large computers keep track of accounts. Funds are transferred through clearing houses and the Federal Reserve to thousands of destinations almost simultaneously. A loan officer can spend full time finding the best loans. All of these economies reduce transactions costs.

5. Deposit insurance increases the safety of savings deposits. Savers who choose a federally insured institution and do not exceed the $100,000 insured limit in each account need not worry about not being able to collect if the institution defaults; their accounts are safe. They need not waste time in examining institutions' balance sheets and operating statements before choosing where to place their funds.

Of course, these services are not free. The bank or savings and loan must make a spread between the amount paid the depositor and the fees charged to the borrower. The interest rates they pay are enough lower than those they receive to cover their expenses, their risk and losses, and their profit.

Nevertheless, the advantages of intermediaries are so great that they now dominate the field of lending and investing. Over 80 percent of funds flow through financial institutions rather than directly from lender to borrower. For better services, they can charge the borrower less and pay the saver more than would be possible without them. Their reduced costs and more skilled lending have been extremely beneficial. As a result, the financial system in most cases works more efficiently than when it depended on individual lending. Before World War I only a few consumers could obtain loans. Now the family without a credit card or installment loan is rare. If buyers had to accumulate the entire price in cash before they could make a purchase, we might have as few automobiles as China or the Soviet Union, and individual homeownership would be exceptional. The proliferation of financial institutions acting as intermediaries has been a key element in the nation's rapid growth and prosperity.

THE FLOW OF FUNDS

Credit crunches and the availability or lack of mortgage funds come about as a result of decisions made by millions of consumers or investors, lenders or savers, and financial institutions, including the Federal Reserve. Households, businesses, and governments decide whether or not to *save*—that is, to spend or not to spend current income on consumption. They also decide whether or not to *invest*—that is, to purchase new goods that will last for more than one year. They are also constantly making decisions as to whether to buy or sell their existing financial assets, including common stock. In the Gross National Product (GNP) Accounts, such purchases or sales are classified as financial transactions, not investments.

Along with deciding whether to invest and to save, individuals and businesses must finance their activities. They can spend more than their income by borrowing, or they may spend less and lend excess funds to others, either directly or by placing them with financial institutions which will do the lending. In addition, the Federal Reserve and banks together create new money for lending.

Changes in decisions to save and invest, to borrow and lend, and to create money cause fluctuations in credit and interest rates. A sudden increase in the demand for funds or a decrease in the supply may make interest rates shoot up. To understand these driving forces in real estate markets, we must be able to trace these changes back to their origins. The Flow of Funds Accounts help us to do this.

Sources and Uses of Funds

The **Flow of Funds Accounts** are a special set of accounts similar to the more familiar *National Income and Product Accounts.* They show who borrows and who lends, who saves and who invests, as well as the channels through which credit moves, for the entire economy of the United States. They make it possible for analysts to estimate potential changes in the supply of and demand for credit and the resulting pressures on interest rates.

Tables 5-2 and 5-3 are simplified summaries of the kind of information contained in these accounts. The first row of Table 5-2 contains estimates of the amount of net savings for the year 1984 by each of five decision-making sectors of the economy: households, businesses (divided into nonfinancial and financial), governments, and foreign. It also shows the total amount of saving for the economy. Note that a group's net saving equals its change in net worth.

The columns in Table 5-2 divide the financial activities of each decision group to indicate where they obtain the funds they use (sources) and what they do with their available funds (uses). Total sources and uses must be equal for each individual group and for the economy as a whole. Similarly for the entire economy, savings equals investment, borrowing equals lending, and the amount of money created is held by its users. However, within each group this is not true since a group can borrow to finance its investment or can lend excess savings.

Households   Families and individuals account for most of the net savings of the economy. People accumulate funds for retirement, for emergencies, and to

Table 5-2
Sources and Uses of Funds by Major Sectors, 1984
(in billions of dollars)

Sources of Funds	Households	Business Nonfinancial	Business Financial	Government	Foreign	Total
Net saving (change in net worth)	306	126	15	(172)	94	369
Borrowing (change in liabilities)	247	181	621	304	11	1364
Money creation	—	—	27	9	—	36
Total sources	553	307	663	141	105	1769

Uses of Funds	Households	Nonfinancial	Financial	Government	Foreign	Total
Net investment (change in physical assets)	164	190	15	—	—	369
Lending (change in financial assets)	360	111	648	141	104	1364
Money holdings	29	6	—	—	1	36
Total uses	553	307	663	141	105	1769
Gross capital expenditures	465	479	21	—	—	965

Source: Federal Reserve Board, "Flow of Funds Accounts," Z.1.
Note: discrepancies, a separate item in the accounts, have been distributed to investment and lending.

upgrade their standard of living. Households are also important investors. They buy houses and consumer durable goods. Their gross capital expenditures (shown as a separate item at the bottom of the table) on these items exceeded $465 billion in 1984. However, about 65 percent of this gross investment was offset by depreciation of the existing stock. Households issued mortgages and contracted for consumer debts. Except for financial institutions and governments, they were the largest borrowers. But households lent even more than they borrowed. Their net investment, lending, and accumulation of money equaled $553 billion.

Businesses   Businesses are divided into two dissimilar groups. Nonfinancial businesses are the largest investors in both gross and net amounts. They invest

Table 5-3
Net Borrowing and Investment Flow of Funds
(in billions of dollars)

Use	1979	1980	1981	1982	1983	1984	1985
Mortgages	$166	$129	$108	$ 86	$176	$214	$ 233
Governments	125	153	156	274	312	340	497
Other private borrowing	200	143	224	130	155	334	341
Total	$491	$425	$488	$490	$643	$888	$1,071
Gross investment	$455	$437	$516	$447	$502	$674	$ 670

Source: Federal Reserve Board, "Flow of Funds Accounts," *Federal Reserve Bulletin,* Table 1.57, and *Economic Report of the President,* Table B-1.

more than they save, funding their investments by borrowing considerably more than they lend.

In contrast, financial businesses account for only a minor share of capital expenditures. However, they do the largest amount of the borrowing and lending. In fact, since most borrowing and lending goes through them as intermediaries, the total flow of funds is much greater than the actual amount of final lending to users. Most of the lending of the other groups is actually deposits which show up as the borrowing of the financial sector. As we shall see shortly, banks are also the primary source for the creation of new money.

Governments   The key point that stands out in the table about governments is their large amount of dissaving. This reflects the huge deficits of the federal government. Most of the funds needed to cover the dissaving had to be borrowed in the market. A small percentage, however, was paid for by the Federal Reserve's creation of money.

No capital expenditures or investments are shown for governments. By definition in the GNP and Flow of Funds Accounts, governments are assumed not to invest. Expenditures for roads, schools, aircraft carriers, and the like are shown as being consumed in the period they are paid for. If the government maintained capital accounts, a good part of their expenditures would show up as investment, and the net *dissaving,* or deficit, would be less. Government purchases of mortgages and other loans are also shown as expenditures.

Governments are major borrowers to fund their deficits. In addition, since this table includes government-sponsored agencies such as Fannie Mae and Freddie Mac as part of the government sector, other borrowing and lending is also large—particularly, as will be seen throughout this book, in the mortgage market.

The Foreign Account   In normal periods, the Foreign (or Rest of the World) Account is not large because it includes only capital items. Most exports and imports and similar transactions are paid for currently. The net saving by foreigners primarily reflects the net surplus of the current account for trade and services.

The mid-1980s was an unusual period for foreign borrowing and lending. The United States had been a net overseas investor for over 60 years. The rest of the world had steadily increased its debt to the United States. In the period covered by the table, however, large trade deficits and the desire of foreigners to invest in United States markets caused the rest of the world to lend this country more than it borrowed. The claims of the United States against the rest of the world decreased while theirs against the United States rose. The shifts were so great that the United States became a net debtor.

Shifts in Lending and Investing

Analysts estimate what is happening to the demand and supply of credit by studying each of these accounts in detail. If households want to buy more cars or houses, they will have to increase their borrowing. Interest rate forecasters try to find where the additional funds they need might come from.

Shifts in spending and lending are primary causes of instability and inflation. Most of the swings in demand that bring on unemployment or price increases occur in durable goods and especially real estate construction. These goods need financing to be sold. However, no one knows to what extent the swings in output are due to shifts in credit, or whether they reflect changes in real demand. These two movements are so closely related that it is nearly impossible to separate them into cause and effect.

Table 5-3, also taken from the Flow of Funds Accounts, pictures what happened to borrowing between 1979 and 1985. Several points are significant for real estate finance. Clearly, mortgages play a critical role in the market. However, the relative share of mortgages declined in the first half of the 1980s. Their share of the total fell from 34 to 22 percent. Initially, a sharp drop occurred in the actual amount of mortgage borrowing. By 1982, it was only 52 percent of its previous peak. Borrowing by other private borrowers also declined from 1979 to 1982. Its fall from 1979 to 1980 was sharper than that of mortgages. By 1985, other private borrowing had expanded at a much faster clip—it was about 70 percent above its 1979 level—while mortgages had grown by 40 percent.

Perhaps the most startling increase was in borrowing by governments. By 1985, issues of government debt were almost four times as large as in 1979. This change, of course, merely mirrors the relaxation of fiscal policy which occurred in 1982. The table makes it easy to understand why the government deficit became such a critical economic issue.

The last row shows the related movements in private investment. It mirrors the changes in private borrowing, but is less volatile because much of investment occurs with a lag or through contracts awarded in prior periods. When the economy experiences a credit crunch, investment falls, as do other demands and output.

THE FEDERAL RESERVE SYSTEM

The **Federal Reserve System** consists of the Board of Governors in Washington, D.C., and 12 Federal Reserve district banks, which together act as the central bank of the United States. Bitter attacks on the Federal Reserve are often heard at conventions of real estate brokers, builders, and mortgage lenders. Several years ago, builders from all over the country mailed two-by-fours to Paul Volcker, chairman of the Board of Governors of the Federal Reserve System, to let him know they were in trouble and losing money. They need not have bothered; Volcker knew only too well.

The credit crunches of 1979 to 1980 and 1981 to 1982 were engineered by the Federal Reserve, with the support of both Presidents Carter and Reagan, for the purpose of ridding the country of double-digit inflation. Both Democratic and Republican administrations opted for tight money, even though they were aware of the drastic effects it would have on housing and the real estate market. To most Americans, Volcker and the Federal Reserve System became heroes of the hour for conquering inflation. But to those who lost their jobs or businesses, they were villains.

What the Federal Reserve Tries to Do

The Federal Reserve (or the "Fed," as it is also called), in conjunction with the financial system, determines the amount of money and credit in the United States. The aim of monetary policy is to help the nation reach its economic goals of stability in output, full employment, no inflation, and optimum growth. **Monetary policies** are government actions, or instruments, taken to influence the stock of money and the assets and liabilities of financial institutions. Changes in money and financial assets alter the amount of spending and, therefore, of the demand for output. The objective of monetary policy is to tailor the amount of money and credit so that the demand for production will equal the country's productive resources. Changes in monetary policy affect demand and spending by the public. How much is spent in each period determines the level of output and its growth, as well as employment and prices. These are the ultimate goals of monetary policy.

If the amount of money and credit rises too rapidly, demands for goods, services, and labor exceed their supplies, resulting in inflation. As the growth of money and credit slows, so does demand. The result is lower output and unemployment of labor and resources, leading to more stable prices. Because of the way the economy operates and because of external shocks, rarely are all economic goals achieved. More commonly, some goals are reached at the expense of others. At one time, the economy may experience rapid growth and full employment with inflation. At other times, fairly stable prices with slower growth and slack output prevail.

Assets and Prices

Controlling money is difficult because no one really knows what it is or how much exists at any time. Money can be anything that people use to obtain monetary services. Historically, all sorts of things have served as money—for example, stones, beads, cattle, precious metals.

Money can be defined in many ways. The most common definition of **money** (known as M1) is currency in circulation (primarily Federal Reserve notes, such as $10 bills) plus the checkable deposits of the banking system. Measured in this way, the money supply grew by $66 billion in 1985. A basic definition of **credit** is the amount of net borrowing in the economy. This is the "total" line in Table 5-3. Total credit grew by about $1.07 trillion in 1985.

From the public's point of view, money is an asset, not a liability. It consists of the claims of individuals and firms against the government and financial institutions. As our monetary assets expand, we feel more liquid and richer. Our willingness to spend grows. The monetary assets of the public are simultaneously the liabilities of the financial system. To follow the process by which money is created, we have to grasp what happens on both sides of financial balance sheets. Banks are able to expand their assets by paying for mortgages or loans through the creation of new deposit liabilities and, therefore, the amount of money. (This fundamental concept in economics—that *banks create money by going into debt in the form of deposits*—is one of the hardest to grasp.)

The Federal Reserve's Monetary Instruments

High-powered money—also called the **monetary base**—consists of currency in circulation and the mandatory deposits, or legal reserves, of the banking system in Federal Reserve banks. The fulcrum of our monetary control system is the requirement that banks maintain a certain percentage of legal reserves against their deposits. By lowering or raising the amount of reserves, the Fed can inhibit or promote the growth of bank deposits and assets. Three main factors determine how much money is available for spending:

1. The Federal Reserve controls the amount of high-powered money.
2. Depository institutions, principally commercial banks, issue deposits to the public in accordance with the amount of high-powered money made available to them, their legal requirements, and their profit opportunities.
3. The public in turn decides whether to hold currency, demand deposits, or other types of assets that can function as money.

The Federal Reserve controls the amount of high-powered money and influences the amount of bank and savings and loan deposits through the use of the four types of instruments of monetary policy:

- open market purchase and sale of securities
- the discount rate
- legal reserve requirements
- selective credit controls

Instruments are the regulations and operations that the Fed controls directly, in contrast to the money supply and interest rates, which are called *targets* and which can be influenced only indirectly.

The primary instrument, discussed in the next section, is called an **open market operation,** through which the Federal Reserve directly controls the amount of high-powered money by buying and selling government securities. The next three instruments are less important and are used infrequently.

One of the best known is changing the **discount rate.** This is the rate of interest that banks borrowing from the Fed must pay. The rate imposed on banks affects both the amount they borrow from the Federal Reserve and the minimum interest rates banks offer and take in the money market. Although discount rate changes make the headlines, they are most often used to ratify movements in market interest rates that have already occurred as the result of the prior use of open market operations.

The Federal Reserve also has the right to change the **legal reserve requirements.** These legal requirements establish the ratio of reserves to deposits that banks must hold. Though powerful, this instrument has some undesirable side effects, and it has not been used in the last 20 years.

At various times in the past, Congress has granted the Fed the right to control some of the lending terms set by financial institutions. These instruments are called **selective credit controls.** During the Korean War, for example, limits were set on the loan-to-value ratios and the maximum lengths of time over which mortgages could be amortized.

DETERMINING THE AMOUNT OF MONEY AND CREDIT

To understand how the Federal Reserve actually controls money and credit, we must understand the way open market operations work and how they cause banks to alter their lending, creation of deposits, and interest charges. How the Federal Reserve and the banks together determine the money supply can be illustrated using **T-accounts,** which are a means of showing the interrelationships of the balance sheets of the Fed, the banks, and the public.

The Federal Reserve's Balance Sheet

The first of the T-accounts we study is the Federal Reserve's own balance sheet of assets and liabilities (see Tables 5-4 and 5-5). On the asset side in Table

Table 5-4
Factors Influencing the Monetary Base, January 1986
(in billions of dollars)

Sources (Assets)		Uses (Liabilities)		
Federal Reserve credit		Reserve of banks		50
U.S. government securities	191	Deposits at Fed	29	
Loans (discounts)	3	Vault cash	21	
Float plus other Fed assets	15			
Subtotal	209	Currency held by public		161
		Treasury deposits at the Fed		9
Gold stock, treasury currency, other	27	Other liabilities		16
Monetary base	236			236

The Federal Reserve controls the total size of the monetary base by open market purchases or sales of securities. They add to or offset movements in all other categories to insure that bank reserves follow an agreed-upon path.

5-4, the Fed's largest holdings consist of $191 billion of government securities, all of them purchased in the open market. Loans or discounts also appear on the Fed's balance sheet. These amounts are borrowed from the Fed by banks at the discount rate. Other assets consist of gold, buildings, and miscellaneous items.

The Federal Reserve's largest liability is $161 billion of currency in circulation. By law, every dollar issued by the Fed must be secured by a dollar of government securities. However, the liability that has the greatest effect on the money supply and credit is the reserves of commercial and savings banks. Under the law, banks must hold as legal reserves a specified ratio of their deposits at the Fed plus vault cash to their own deposits. The Federal Reserve also has a group of miscellaneous liabilities, including deposits of foreign banks and the Treasury.

An Open Market Purchase by the Federal Reserve

What happens when the Federal Reserve engages in an open market operation? To simplify the explanation, we assume that (a) all assets and liabilities except government securities and the reserves (deposits) of banks at the Fed remain constant, and (b) the required reserve ratio is 20 percent. In other words, for every dollar of their deposits, banks must keep 20 cents in reserves at the Fed. Therefore, they may issue deposit liabilities equal to five times their reserves, but no more.

Assume that the Federal Reserve decides to engage in an open market operation by buying $100 million of treasury bills. To do so, it calls for bids from

Table 5-5
Expansion of Deposits as a Result of Federal Reserve Open Market Operations
(in millions of dollars)

Federal Reserve				Commercial Banks			
Assets		Liabilities		Assets		Liabilities	
U.S. government securities	100	Commercial bank deposits (reserves)	100	Deposits at Fed	100	Deposits	100
				Required reserves	**20**		
				Excess reserves	**80**		
				Total assets	100	Total liabilities	100

The Federal Reserve alters the monetary base and the deposits banks hold with it by purchasing securities in the open market. The economy must hold the expanded monetary base (the Fed's liabilities) in the form of either bank reserves or currency.

government bond traders. It buys those offered by the market at the lowest price. In this example the low bidder is Salomon Brothers, one of the largest dealers in government bonds. The Fed pays for its purchase by writing a check to Salomon Brothers, which deposits the check in its bank. Salomon's bank in turn deposits the check with its central banker—the Federal Reserve.

This chain of events is illustrated in Table 5-5. The Fed owns an additional $100 million of securities. It owes $100 million more to one of its member banks. As a result of the transaction, high-powered money in the form of bank reserves has also increased by $100 million. The banking system has an additional asset—a deposit at the Fed—and an additional liability, a deposit owed to Salomon Brothers. That firm, the seller of the bonds, would have made a profit on the sale. They have been paid in the form of a bank deposit, which they can use to buy bonds from someone else.

The Expansion of Deposits

Another important change has occurred as a result of this transaction. The new bank deposit created when Salomon Brothers sent the Fed's check to its bank forces that bank to hold more in its account at the Fed to meet the legal reserve requirement. As illustrated by the boldface items under the commercial banks' account in Table 5-5, the banking system now has $80 million in excess reserves. This remainder of the $100 million in added reserves is in excess of the bank's required legal requirements of $20 million.

How banks with excess reserves can increase their assets and their profits is shown in Table 5-6. In the stage following the open market operation, the second stage of the expansion of deposits, banks buy an additional $80 million of mortgages. They issue checks to their new borrowers, who are home sellers, builders, and the like. They in turn redeposit the checks in the banking system.

Table 5-6
Expansion of Commercial Bank Deposits
(in millions of dollars)

		Assets		Liabilities	
	Mortgages		80	Deposits	180
	Deposits at Fed		100		
	Required reserves	**36**			
	Excess reserves	**64**			
Second stage*	Total assets		180	Total liabilities	180
	Mortgages		80	Deposits	244
	Bonds		64		
	Deposits at Fed		100		
	Required reserves	**48.8**			
	Excess reserves	**51.2**			
Third stage	Total assets		244	Total liabilities	244
	Mortgages		100	Deposits	292.8
	Bonds lending		92.8		
	Deposits at Fed		100		
	Required reserves	**58.56**			
	Excess reserves	**41.44**			
Fourth stage	Total assets		292.8	Total liabilities	292.8
	Loans and securities		400	Deposits	500
	Deposits at Fed		100		
	Required reserves	**100**			
Final stage	Total assets		500	Total liabilities	500

Banks that receive new reserves expand their assets and liabilities (deposits) by making loans and purchasing securities. The maximum expansion of deposits equals the increase in reserves (less any leakage into currency) times one over the required reserve ratio.

*First stage is exhibited in Table 5-5.

As a result of making new mortgage loans, the assets and deposits of the banks have risen to $180 million.

In stage three, banks may buy bonds in order to use up the excesses or they may expand consumer loans. Every action of the banks to increase their assets raises their deposit liabilities by the same amount. By the final stage, banks have used up all the excess reserves created by the Fed's open market operation. With a 20 percent reserve requirement, a $100 million purchase by the Federal Reserve leads to a $500 million expansion of deposits.

Banking Is a Closed System   At this point some skeptics might ask, "What if those who are selling bonds, houses, and other things do not want to hold their deposits?" Individuals usually deplete their deposits by issuing checks against their accounts to make purchases. However, to collect, sellers must deposit the checks in their *own* accounts. Bank deposits would not be reduced except for leakages of funds into the currency supply caused by drawing cash from the banks.

In a closed banking system, the banks determine the total amount of deposits in accordance with the amount of reserves created and the legal requirements set by the Federal Reserve. If people do not want to hold deposits, they can spend them faster. But the total amount remains the same. It is true that currency may be held instead of deposited, and money can be transferred abroad, making the analysis somewhat more complicated. However, it remains true that the Federal Reserve and the banking system control the amount of deposits and of money created.

The T-accounts reflect how the creation of deposits is controlled. However, money is defined as the amount of currency (issued by the Fed) plus deposits. Therefore, the Fed, by controlling deposits, also controls the money supply. Although the government is somewhat better off if people hold currency instead of bank deposits, the Fed does not try to control the composition of the money supply. Banks can obtain either currency or reserves, depending on their customers' desires.

On bank balance sheets, when deposits expand, the offsetting growth on the asset side consists of bank loans and security holdings. As a result, open market operations also have a major influence on how much banks lend and on interest rates.

Monetary Policy

Open market operations are the main instrument used by the Federal Reserve to control the money supply and, less directly, interest rates. Although its control over deposits and money is not complete, the Fed can hit its targets within 2 or 3 percent at most times. Deciding *how much* to move the money supply is the heart of monetary policy. The Federal Reserve Board meets weekly to consider this problem. A broader group, the Open Market Committee, meets monthly to analyze potential changes in spending, inflation, output, and unemployment. The Fed decides how much growth in money and credit appears optimal in order to influence spending so that it grows at a rate likely to achieve the nation's economic goals.

At the same meetings in which it chooses the desired levels for the monetary targets, the Fed sets its instruments at the levels it believes will enable the targets to be hit. If the Fed tightens money and raises interest rates, spending, output, and prices will all grow more slowly. If it expands credit and lowers interest rates by making money easier, spending, output, and prices will grow more rapidly.

Figure 5-3
The Phases of a Credit Cycle

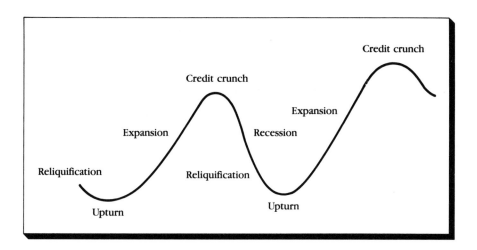

CYCLES IN THE FLOW OF FUNDS AND CREDIT

Our economy frequently experiences cycles in credit and in the flow of funds.* Fluctuations in the demand for and supply of credit and in the value and liquidity of balance sheets cause the demand for houses, building, and other goods to follow similar cycles. The **credit cycles** consist of periods called expansions, crunches, recessions, and upturns. Crunches and downturns in cycles of this type occurred in 1966, 1970, 1974, 1980, and 1982.

Figure 5-3 charts a prototype of a credit cycle. It starts with a reliquification period and an **upturn,** leading to an expansion with rising interest rates. The expansion ends in a credit crunch, followed by a **recession,** also called a contraction. Again, this ends in a reliquification period and an upturn. The following description of a credit cycle reveals the forces behind the cyclical patterns.

The Expansion

As recessions come to an end, money is usually easy; funds are readily available; interest rates are comparatively low. Expectations of greater profits rise. People want to borrow, and lenders to lend. Credit is easy to obtain, and demand for goods—especially durable goods—picks up. The economy enters into an **expansion** of jobs and output.

---

*For an excellent description of credit cycles, see O. Eckstein and A. Sinai, "The Mechanisms of the Business Cycle in the Postwar Era," in *The American Business Cycle Today: Continuity and Change,* ed. R. J. Gordon (Chicago: National Bureau of Economic Research, University of Chicago Press, 1986).

Causes of Tighter Credit   As the expansion gathers momentum, the economy begins to boom. Eventually demand exceeds the limit of both available resources and available funds. Spending in many sectors outruns normal growth and the ability to produce. Accelerating inflation may make borrowing seem extremely profitable. Desires to borrow and to invest grow faster than the willingness to save and to lend.

In order to end a recession and bring about an expansion, the Federal Reserve will have speeded up the growth rate of money. If credit is expanding at an unsustainable pace, the Fed may be forced to cut back on the reserves it furnishes. If inflation has increased, the Fed may decide credit should be curtailed and interest rates raised for the purpose of slowing the growth in demand.

Some or all of these pressures cause interest rates to shoot up. Credit becomes harder to obtain. A period of tight money begins.

The Credit Crunch

Extended expansions and booms are often topped off by tight money, bringing on a credit crunch accompanied by deteriorating balance sheets. Excesses in the expansion lead to a period of correction. Borrowers find that they overestimated their ability to make profits and to earn the cash flow needed to meet payments promised on loans. Higher interest requirements arising from variable interest rates may exacerbate debt servicing problems.

Interest rates soar to even greater heights because liquidity evaporates. Losses from asset sales become more frequent. Some borrowers dump assets even at low prices in an effort to meet loan payments. Spending—previously at a high level because of borrowing—declines. Earnings fall; the inability to pay worsens; jobs are lost; and the drop in spending accelerates. Debt burdens become even heavier. Bankruptcies and failures of financial institutions become more common. The credit crunch has led to a recession.

Cycles in credit and real demand are reinforced by cycles in expectations. When the economic horizon looks bright, investors and lenders become more and more optimistic. They lower the standards by which they judge prospective loans. When the market weakens, investors and lenders become pessimistic. Loans they would have sought eagerly a few weeks before they now reject. They raise their estimates of default risk, increasing interest charges still more.

Reliquification and Upturn

How long a recession lasts depends on the amount of correction necessary for past excesses, on the underlying growth rate of the economy, on the speed with which the Federal Reserve reverses policies, and on how fast expectations react.

If the rate of bankruptcies continues high, people will hesitate to increase spending even though their own financial situation is healthy. A spurt of growth may develop from foreign orders or from a new technology, shortening the recession. The Fed can increase the growth rate of the money supply, in an attempt to bring interest rates down in order to reinforce an upturn. Eventually expectations begin to rise as pessimism about the availability and terms of money turns to optimism.

During a recession, consumers and businesses gradually reliquify their balance sheets. With lower purchases and no new borrowing, their cash flow can be used to pay off old debts. The share of debt to equity and of debt service to income falls. If they so desire, firms and consumers can now begin to spend more.

Eventually, some or all of these positive pressures bring a halt to the spending decline. The recession ends, and the economy once again enters an expansion period. Although economists, businesses, and government have striven for over 60 years to control such cycles in the flow of funds and while victory has often been proclaimed, few observers believe that we have seen the last of credit cycles and crunches.

THE IMPACT OF CYCLES ON MORTGAGE LENDING

When credit cycles hit the mortgage and real estate markets, they react more violently than most other sectors of the economy. The amplitude of the fluctuations is far greater; the expansions go higher and contractions fall lower before a turning point occurs. Three related factors cause stronger reactions in mortgage and real estate markets:

1. Buildings are more dependent on credit than other parts of the economy because of their durability.
2. The flow of funds to and through the leading mortgage lenders fluctuates more than that to the credit market as a whole.
3. A mortgage becomes a less desirable asset when interest rates are high and rising rapidly. Lenders shift to other assets that appear safer and more desirable.

Higher interest rates and less availability of funds decrease both the supply of and demand for real estate finance. Given the large amount of leverage, higher interest rates and lower loan-to-value ratios make it harder for buyers to put together successful deals. Potential income appears too low to carry the sharply increased debt services. In addition, the squeeze on balance sheets hits those who are already highly leveraged. As we shall see, lending for construction and development is among the riskiest of all. Failures rise rapidly, especially in new developments. Finally, many purchases are postponed in the hope that future debt service will be less. Many of the transactions that do take place depend on the use of creative financing rather than on new loans.

Disintermediation

When money becomes tighter and interest rates rise, funds flow out of depository financial institutions into direct market investments, such as treasury bills or money market funds. These shifts in the channels of funds are called **disintermediation.** In the past, thrift institutions lost funds because regulations prevented them from raising their deposit interest rates as high as market rates. Knowledgeable savers withdrew their deposits in order to earn higher interest rates through direct purchases of market instruments. Disintermediation was one of the forces causing the abolition of interest rate ceilings.

However, even with deregulation the rates offered by institutions still lag behind those of the market. The intermediaries already have high volumes of deposits. It does not pay for them to try to match the market. They are better off paying lower rates on their outstanding deposits, even though it means losing some marginal funds to the market.

But this loss of funds does affect their mortgage lending. Frequently institutional lenders have outstanding commitments based on prior high growth rates. When their deposit growth slows, and they begin to lose funds to the market, they lack money even to take care of prior commitments. Lenders abruptly slam the mortgage window shut and stop making new loans or commitments.

A Smaller Share to Mortgages

In addition to having fewer funds available for lending, institutions cut the share of loans on mortgages. With high and rising market rates, mortgages become less profitable. Lenders realize that if interest rates drop, fixed-rate mortgages are likely to be prepaid rapidly. If rates rise, the loans will engender capital losses. When cycles move rates up, mortgages become riskier. The chances of default increase, and borrowers cannot afford higher risk premiums.

Many lenders halt mortgage lending because funds are sufficient only to take care of priority customers. Institutions find it more profitable to lend to old, steady customers who have banked with them over time. Bankers say you buy the right to credit in tight periods by being a good customer in other times. Many mortgage borrowers are onetime "over-the-counter" customers. Since home buyers borrow only every eight years or so, they do not build up a regular relationship with lenders. They have not earned the right to be considered priority borrowers.

Many lenders look on the mortgage market as a marginal one. When they have excess funds, they start making mortgage loans or increase the share of mortgages in their portfolios. When money is tight, they reduce their mortgage lending or move completely out of the mortgage market. This has been less true of funds for income properties. Insurance companies and pension funds traditionally have had a more even flow of funds. They have been willing to commit their funds further in advance and at a steady pace. This is one reason why their role in the market for large properties has been much greater. However, as credit cycles have become more volatile, their sources of funds have also fluctuated more. This has influenced their lending, and especially their willingness to make commitments at fixed interest rates.

Usury laws are another factor that has cut the share of mortgage lending when money is tight. **Usury** is collecting interest above the legal limit. As part of the movement toward deregulation, many states have repealed or loosened their usury laws. However, in certain cases, these laws still inhibit lending. If the legal limit on mortgage interest charges is below the rate that other markets or forms of investment are paying, lenders will not make mortgage loans, preferring to invest elsewhere at the higher rate.

The Credit and Mortgage Cycles and Real Estate Demand

The changes in interest rates and in the availability of mortgage credit cause similar cycles in the demand to purchase and construct real property. As noted earlier, the impact on demand is especially great because financing plays such a major role in determining the price of properties. Low interest rates mean low discount factors and high present values for future income flows. In contrast, high discount factors reduce the present value and the prices paid for expected cash flows.

Changes in demand are exacerbated by the fact that when credit is easy to obtain, output, employment, and demand for space rise. Rising values raise expectations, and investors take a more optimistic view of future demand and profits. They pay more for each dollar of future income, even as estimates of the amount of income go up also. When the crunch comes, the situation reverses. Lack of credit decreases demand. Investors turn pessimistic and lower their projections of future income and prices. GNP and the demand for space fall at the same time as the new space induced by the prior boom reaches the market. As the projections of future cash flows fall, larger discount rates (caused by higher interest) lead to lower present values.

PLANNING FOR THE CREDIT CYCLE

The history of real estate finance shows that periods of tight money, credit crunches, and high interest rates recur frequently. However, the timing and amplitudes of these movements have been highly irregular. Experience fails to tell us when the next turning point will occur, or how high rates will go. Many banks and savings and loans have failed because, when rates were high compared to the past, managers thought they were near a peak. To lock in high rates, they increased their lending, only to find they had guessed wrong when market interest rates continued to climb. Firms that had gambled on hitting the peak in rates experienced large losses, and many failed.

The credit cycle causes a related cycle in building. It is one of the reasons why lending on new projects is so risky. As long as builders can obtain funds, they will continue to build; they can make money from the construction and development process even if the final project is unsuccessful.* As a result, when credit is easy to obtain, too many projects are started. When the excess building space comes on the market, investors and lenders are surprised to find that rents fail to rise as fast as projected and vacancies are far more numerous. Again, the consequences are defaults and foreclosures.

Forecasting

To protect against these dangers, some analysts emphasize the need to forecast the current state of the credit cycle. The Flow of Funds Accounts were developed and are used to forecast future changes in the supply of and demand for credit and, therefore, of potential interest rates. Daily papers carry statements of "Fed watchers," who spend full time trying to explain what the Federal Reserve is doing and to guess what it is likely to do.

These kinds of forecasts and analysis are easy to obtain. Many large banks, other lenders, and brokerage houses provide periodic reports and analyses to their customers and others who request them. One can buy financial newsletters of all kinds that publish both individual analyses and summaries of 40 or more analysts. However, the interest rate predictions of even the best of these analysts have been poor. Moreover, the typical investor or lending manager cannot hope to beat the money and capital markets on a regular basis. Financial theory shows why this is so. At any time, market rates are based on the best forecasts of thousands of experts who spend full time on this task. The chances appear slim that any individual spending less time and with poorer sources of information would be able to beat the experts at their own game.

Experience and theory demonstrate that the information provided by the market itself as to what it thinks is going to happen to rates equals or beats the average forecast. To find what the market thinks is going to happen to interest rates, we need only look at the rates set daily in the financial future markets and reflected in the term structure of interest rates. Unfortunately, the market forecasts, though cheap, are not very good either. Lenders and borrowers tend to be overly optimistic or pessimistic, and the future holds too many unexpected events. Consequently, neither source—the market nor the experts—tends to be accurate about the future of interest rates.

Diversification and Hedging

Even though borrowers and investors cannot beat those in the market in forecasting its movements, they can still profit from the knowledge that cycles will occur. They can plan their portfolios of assets and liabilities to minimize its risks, thereby reducing their chances of failure to a size they are willing to accept.

---

*For a detailed discussion of one expert's view of this issue, see A. Downs, *The Revolution in Real Estate Finance* (Washington, D.C.: Brookings Institution, 1985), Ch. 6.

Proper choices of leverage, cash flows, and debt service will keep investors from being ruined by unforeseen events.

Some people are risk-takers. They welcome large risks in the hope of large gains. Many of our major financial failures in recent years have occurred in firms that knowingly adopted high-risk policies and lost. Other people prefer to seek lower returns with lower risks. Knowledge of how credit markets work and cycles occur is essential for properly planning risks. The key point in planning is to recognize that the unexpected is likely to happen.

Chapter 9 discusses how savings and loan associations are learning to use portfolio diversification and hedging in the futures markets to protect themselves against interest fluctuations. They use gap and duration analysis to estimate their risks under several interest rate scenarios. Individual investors plan in similar ways. Personal computers and financial spreadsheets permit them to find mortgage terms that can be met under different assumptions of interest rates, inflation, and net operating income. These allow investors to choose debt service and portfolios that will meet specific objectives under a variety of future possible conditions. Investors and lenders can select the risk-to-return ratios they desire. But to make the necessary decisions, planning for the credit cycle is vital. Unless they take into account probable future cycles, some investors and lenders will find themselves in situations they could have avoided.

SUMMARY

Instability in interest rates, credit, and real estate markets has increased. This instability has been augmented by inflation, deregulation, more emphasis on the use of prices rather than ceilings to halt the excess growth of credit, plus fiscal policy out of control.

The fluctuations in credit and rates result from the structure of our financial system. Financial markets bring together people who have excess purchasing power to lend and those who want to borrow. While some funds pass directly from households and corporations to borrowers, most lending takes place through financial institutions acting as intermediaries. The advantages of the financial intermediaries are great enough to make it worthwhile paying them the spread they charge to cover their costs and profits.

The Flow of Funds Accounts assist analysts in tracing the causes and effects of fluctuations in the demand for and supply of credit. The accounts divide economic units into major sectors. They reveal how each spends or saves, borrows, and lends. The types of loans and securities flowing between the sectors and their constituent parts are shown in detail.

The Federal Reserve affects all financial markets. It influences the amount of money, lending, and interest rates. It sets monetary and credit targets in order to sway spending and, therefore, inflation and output. The Fed uses its monetary instruments—particularly open market operations—to help it achieve its targets and the nation's goals. It helps determine the amount of credit by controlling high-powered money and the deposits bank can create.

Our financial history has been replete with financial cycles and credit crunches. In expansions, interest rates rise because the demand for funds outruns the supply. The Federal Reserve may slow the monetary growth rate to reduce inflationary pressures. Higher interest rates and tighter money cause a credit crunch. People cannot meet their debt obligations. Balance sheets deteriorate. Demand, output, and income fall. A recession finally brings about a drop in interest rates, eventual reliquidation, and the beginning of a new expansion.

In credit crunches, mortgage and real estate markets are hit harder than most others. Traditional mortgage lenders lose funds through disintermediation. At higher interest rates, the risks of losses on mortgages rise faster than on other financial assets. Required debt services exceed the carrying capacity of many properties.

Knowledge that credit crunches will recur need not mean that more effort should be spent trying to forecast interest rates. The record holds out too little hope for success. Rather, it means that loans and portfolios must be planned so that they remain viable even under conditions of high inflation and record short-term rates.

KEY TERMS

credit
credit crunch
credit cycles
discount rate
disintermediation
expansion
federal funds rate
Federal Reserve System
Flow of Funds Accounts
high-powered money
instruments
intermediaries

legal reserve requirements
monetary base
monetary policies
money
open market operation
recession
selective credit controls
T-accounts
tight money
upturn
usury

QUESTIONS

1. Why does the mortgage market react so strongly to credit crunches?
2. Explain why the volatility of credit markets has increased.
3. What are the main reasons for financial intermediaries?
4. What do the Flow of Funds Accounts try to measure?
5. How can businesses invest more than they save?
6. Explain how monetary policies work.
7. Do the monetary instruments allow the Fed to achieve its monetary goals effectively?
8. How is money created when the Fed performs an open market operation?

9. Can you trace the relationship between the credit cycle, money, and mortgages?
10. Explain what disintermediation is and how it affects the mortgage market.
11. What can an investor do to avoid the risks of credit cycles?
12. Test your grasp of how deposits expand by checking to see that a 10 percent reserve requirement on a $100 million purchase by the Federal Reserve would allow deposits to grow by $1 billion.

6 The Sources of Mortgage Funds

OBJECTIVES

When you finish this chapter, you should be able to:

- recognize the main participants in the separate parts of the mortgage market.

- explain why some institutions make or buy certain types of mortgage loans and not others.

- describe the forces that have shaped the savings industry.

- discuss the types of regulations that govern thrift institutions in deciding whether or not to make a loan.

- describe the role of commercial banks in the field of real estate finance.

- understand why life insurance companies moved most of their lending operations from the individual home market to the commercial property market.

- explain why pension funds may become a major source of real estate funds, and why this may or may not affect mortgage rates.

- discuss the potential sources of money to be found among private lenders willing to take high risks or to structure loans in unusual ways.

SINCE CREDIT is the lifeblood of the real estate industry, where to find funds for borrowing is a crucial question. Just as important in many situations are the terms that will be granted. This chapter explores the main sources of mortgage money. It explains how and why lenders differ in their willingness to make certain types of loans. Most mortgages are originated by deposit institutions, which have received state or federal charters and assistance in the form of deposit insurance and tax subsidies. The kinds of loans they can make are subject to regulation. Since 1980 these regulations have been relaxed.

Most lenders have concentrated on particular types of loans. Which kinds they accept depends on their organization, location, size, sources of funds, and the regulations under which they operate. However, the differences between lending institutions are rapidly disappearing. The mortgage market is gradually becoming homogenized.

WHO LENDS AND ON WHAT?

Where borrowers go to seek mortgage credit depends on for how long a period they want the money, the type of property, the size of the loan, and on the amount they want to borrow compared to the value of the property. Different lending markets exist to handle any combination of these variables. What loans lenders make and the conditions they attach often depend on where they obtain their money and on what other loans they can make.

Types of Lenders

One method of classifying lenders is by type of institution (see Table 6-1). Most mortgage loans originate with the *deposit institutions.* The largest group, in terms of both assets and individual offices, consists of commercial banks. About 21 percent of their assets are in mortgages. But from the point of view of real estate finance, savings institutions are more influential. Although they hold fewer assets and have fewer offices, their total mortgage lending is greater. The dominance of savings institutions is especially strong in the field of residential mortgages, where they hold about 40 percent of all loans.

Insurance companies and *pension funds* are the most diverse group. Their importance is much greater in the area of income properties and farms than in residential mortgages. Their lending policies follow from the fact that their funds are long-term. They have fewer neighborhood lending offices than the former group.

Life insurance companies are traditional mortgage lenders. They still hold about 21 percent of their assets in mortgages, primarily nonresidential. On the

Table 6-1
Sources of Mortgage Loans
Rounded Data, 1986

	Deposit Instititions		Life Insurance and Pension Funds	Other Private and Mortgage Companies	Federal and State Agencies
	Savings Institutions	Commercial Banks			
Total assets*	$1,420	$2,250	$1,700	n/a	n/a
Mortgage loans*	760	420	190	200	600
(percent of total)	54%	21%	12%	n/a	n/a
Organization	All sizes, local and regional; mutual and stock	Regional; stock	National; mutual and stock	Local; stock	National and local
Market	Mainly local	Local	National	Local	Local
Source of funds	Deposits	Deposits	Insurance reserves and pension funds	Equity and short-term borrowing	Borrowings
Preferred types of loans	Long-term and construction; residential	Construction and long-term; commercial, income, and single-family	Long-term; income properties	All types; as agents or for sale to final lenders	Residential
Typical restrictions	Loan-to-value, terms; type	Loan-to-value, terms	Few	None	Loan-to-value, terms

*In billions of dollars.

Source: Based on *Statistical Abstract of the United States*, 1985.

other hand, pension funds engage in very little real estate finance. They are a key target of those interested in making more credit available for housing.

Mortgage companies, in the third group, are major originators but minor long-term lenders. A great many of their mortgages are sold to the federal agencies or through mortgage pools. All sorts of other private lenders can be found, but except for mortgage companies, their lending is not on a large scale. Their significance is due to their ability to make riskier and offbeat loans.

The final group consists of federal and state *government agencies.* The amount of their lending, especially in tight money periods, makes them important. Their lending is restricted, however, by their public purpose. As we saw in Chapter 1, government funds became an increasingly substantial part of the mortgage market in the 1960s. They now account for almost 30 percent of all outstanding residential loans. Because funds made available through this source contain some subsidy, the size of loans that can be purchased by government agencies or included in government-guaranteed pools is limited.

This chapter and the next describe lenders primarily in accordance with this four-way division by type of institution. However, other classifications are also significant. Lenders may operate in either the primary or the secondary market for loans. They may be either construction or long-term lenders. They may make conventional or government-insured loans. Lenders also differ with respect to the size of loans and types of property they cover. Many mortgage lenders have been organized as **mutual associations,** in which theoretically each borrower and depositor shared in any earnings and, in most cases, could vote for directors. Others were organized as **capital stock companies,** similar to other corporations. Recently, more and more mutuals have been converted to capital stock companies.

Deposit Institutions A basic difference among institutions stems from how they raise their funds. Deposit institutions—commercial banks, savings and loan associations, savings banks, and credit unions—play a special role in our economy and financial system. They create most of our money supply and hold most of our savings. For this reason, they have always been subject to special chartering and regulation. However, these regulations did not succeed in maintaining the desired level of safety. Their record from 1780 to 1940 was one of frequent failures, with the number of bankruptcies becoming critical in every depression.

As a result, the government established deposit insurance funds to reimburse depositors in case of failure. In return for these and other privileges, enterprises have been restricted as to the risks they can take and the types of assets they can buy. In the past, there were also strict controls over interest rates paid on deposits and limits to the localities in which institutions could operate.

In the United States, state and federal authorities have maintained a dual system of chartering and supervision. Each state has its own regulations, which may differ considerably from federal ones and from those of other states. By deciding whether to obtain a federal or a state charter, institutions could choose their prime regulator. However, because most state deposit insurance funds turned out to be untrustworthy (Ohio and Maryland had major failures in 1985), almost all deposit institutions must now carry federal insurance. This means that even state-chartered corporations are subject to many federal requirements.

While federal supervision has become more nearly universal, deregulation at the federal level has broadened the scope of much lending. Many controls have disappeared, and a bank or savings institution can now operate in several states. Many savings and loan associations and savings banks transformed themselves from mutual associations into normal stock corporations.

Even though many critical lending restrictions have been removed, skills, traditions, and some remaining regulations cause major differences to prevail in how institutions operate. All generalizations as to what firms do and what rules apply are apt to be misleading. Some commercial banks operate much more like typical savings institutions than like their neighboring banks. Although the reverse is less true, some savings institutions are moving rapidly into the field of nonmortgage lending.

Primary and Secondary Markets

Individuals or firms seeking funds usually operate in the **primary mortgage market.** This is where loans are originated. The borrower finds an institution willing to process and actually make a loan. But these initial lenders may not want to hold loans on a long-term basis for a number of reasons: (a) they may have insufficient funds; (b) they may prefer other types of loans; or (c) they may make their profits through servicing—that is, administering loans for others—rather than lending.

For these and similar reasons, many—and, at times, most—loans are sold in the **secondary mortgage market.** In this market, existing loans are bought and sold. Many lenders, such as life insurance companies, pension funds, and the government agencies, do not establish a wide network of local offices. It is more efficient for them to buy loans in the secondary market from local originators.

Most money in the primary market comes from deposit institutions. In a typical year, savings institutions originate 40 to 45 percent of the value of all new mortgages. Commercial banks account for 35 to 40 percent. Most other primary originations are made by mortgage companies.

The Length of the Loan

Where money comes from also depends on the length of a loan and on the type of property. Construction and development lenders differ from long-term lenders. Among long-term loans, about two-thirds are made on one- to four-family houses and primarily to owner-occupiers (those who own and live in their residences). Other markets exist for loans on income properties and farms. Each of these markets appeals to a different group of lenders. Similarly, separate markets may exist for loans of varying sizes. Some lenders are interested only in making loans of a million dollars or more, while others will not lend over $100,000 on a single property.

Construction Lenders   Commercial banks dominate the construction loan market; savings institutions and mortgage companies account for most of the remainder (see Figure 6-1). The operations of banks and savings institutions in the residential construction loan market are similar. However, lending for more complex commercial and industrial buildings has been almost the exclusive preserve of commercial banks.

As Chapter 18 will show, construction lending is complex. It is also the riskiest of all real estate lending. In fact, construction loans are among the two or three types causing the heaviest losses to commercial banks. Because construction lending on larger properties is more complex than on individual houses, it requires a high level of skill and tends to be concentrated in a limited number of institutions in each area.

Long-Term Lenders   Figure 6-2 illustrates the amount of mortgages originated by institutions, as well as their final lending after sales and purchases of mortgages in the secondary market. The sharpest differences are found in the

Figure 6-1
Construction Lending by Type of Institution and Property for 1985

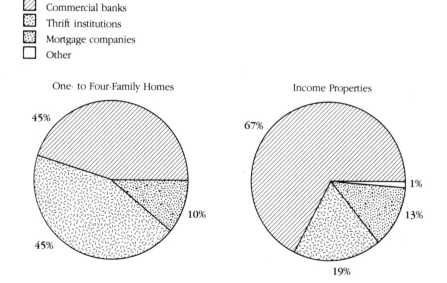

Source: Department of Housing and Urban Development.

Figure 6-2
Long-Term Mortgage Lending for 1985

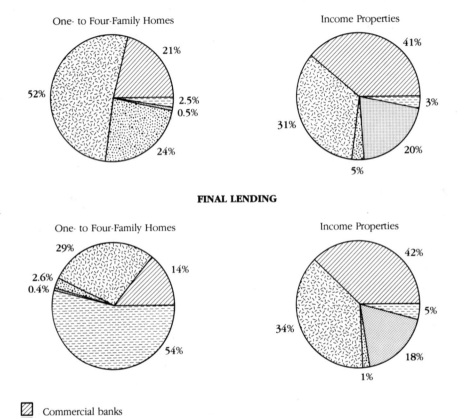

ORIGINATIONS

One- to Four-Family Homes

21%

52%

2.5%
0.5%

24%

Income Properties

41%

3%

31%

20%

5%

FINAL LENDING

One- to Four-Family Homes

29%

14%

2.6%
0.4%

54%

Income Properties

42%

5%

34%

18%

1%

▨ Commercial banks
▨ Thrift institutions
▨ Mortgage companies
□ Insurance companies
▤ Government and mortgage pools

Source: Department of Housing and Urban Development.

case of mortgage companies and the government agencies. Mortgage companies are major originators for single-family houses, but they hold only a small share of loans in their permanent portfolios because they sell the loans individually or as pools in the secondary market. In contrast, government agencies and related mortgage pools originate relatively few mortgages, but, not untypically, in 1985 they ended up with over 50 percent of the total. Another noteworthy fact is the significant part played by insurance companies and pension funds in lending on income properties, in contrast to their minor role in one- to four-family units.

The figure does not reflect the sums lent by individuals or the net amount of lending in a year. In some years, but not in 1985, individuals made up a significant part of the market, as Table 1-1 indicates. Earlier discussions also point out the importance of payments in reducing the total outstanding on older loans. Repayments (excluding construction loans) in a year amounted to over 40 percent of mortgage originations. Consequently, the net increase in portfolios is less than 55 percent of the amount of lending shown in Figure 6-2. Repayments vary a great deal among lending sectors, depending on the size, age, and type of loans they hold.

Conventional Loans versus Government-backed Loans

One of the traditional divisions of the mortgage market has been between loans backed by government agencies, particularly the Federal Housing Administration (FHA) and the Veterans Administration (VA), and all others, called **conventional loans.** The FHA and VA loans have had the advantage of greater acceptance in the secondary market, lower down payments, lower interest rates, assumable loans, and no prepayment penalties, as well as the assurance of an independent appraisal concerned with the borrower's interest. Their disadvantages have included limited loan-to-value ratios, maximum interest ceilings leading to large discounts, detailed and complex regulations, and longer processing time.

The differences between conventional and government-insured loans have been disappearing. Many conventional loans are acceptable to the secondary market because they carry private mortgage insurance. On the other hand, they may carry a maximum loan amount and be written on government-specified forms so that they can be eligible for purchase in the secondary market by the government-sponsored agencies, particularly the Federal National Mortgage Association (FNMA or Fannie Mae) and the Federal Home Loan Mortgage Corporation (FHLMC or Freddie Mac). At the same time, the FHA maximum interest ceilings have been removed and processing has speeded up. Choice between the two types depends on market conditions and other special features.

SAVINGS INSTITUTIONS

When seeking a mortgage loan—particularly one on a residential property—the obvious place to start has been at a savings institution. (The terms *savings* and *thrift* for these institutions are used interchangeably. We also no longer differentiate between savings and loan associations and mutual savings banks. They have become intermingled, and many have switched charters and adopted the title of savings bank.) In typical years, thrift institutions account for more than half of the loans made on single-family homes and for over 60 percent of those on apartment houses. However, their share falls sharply in periods of tight money. While not as numerous as commercial banks, the offices of these institutions blanket the country; most borrowers do not have to travel far to find several potential sources. Both regulation and practice have made their loan-to-value ratios and time to maturity among the most liberal. However, their interest rates, points charged, and prepayment penalties have tended to be somewhat higher than those of banks or insurance companies.

Organization

The savings industry consists of savings and loan associations, federal savings banks, mutual savings banks, and credit unions. In some states, institutions performing these same functions carry local names such as cooperative banks, homestead associations, and building and loans. Credit unions do only a minor mortgage business; therefore, we do not include them in the following discussion.

Both federal and state governments charter and regulate the firms in this industry. Savings and loans accept deposits and lend money in a variety of categories. However, they generally emphasize mortgages. For historical reasons, savings and loans and mutual savings banks were separate, somewhat antagonistic industries, but the changes of the 1980s have moved them so close together that their similarities now outweigh their differences. Therefore, they can be treated as a single group. Both have had the dual function of promoting savings and homeownership.

These institutions began as local, small-scale, self-help mutual organizations. However, drastic changes have taken place. Most loans are now made by large capital stock organizations that have a number of branches covering one or several states. In 1986, the largest association had over $28 billion in assets. The top 100 accounted for 45 percent of the industry's deposits. There were close to 4,000 savings institutions in 1986, approximately 25 percent of which were capital stock associations and 75 percent mutuals. The capital stock associations held over 40 percent of all deposits.

Nearly 500 institutions transferred from the mutual to the stock category in the early 1980s. Moreover, from 1980 to 1985, over a thousand institutions disappeared. Some closed down, burdened with large losses and negative net worth; others were forced to merge by regulatory action, while still others merged voluntarily. In 1984 the largest association—Financial Corporation of America—required assistance from the Federal Savings and Loan Insurance Corporation (FSLIC) to prevent failure. This government agency required it to remove its senior officers and directors, and to change completely its mode of operations.

The damage to the thrift industry occurred because it had not been prepared for high market interest rates. Associations had borrowed short and lent long; when rates shot up, they had to pay more to obtain deposits than they were earning on the mortgages in their portfolios. (Chapter 9 discusses in more detail the implications for the future of these industry changes.)

Regulation and Deregulation

The federal government fostered the thrift industry to give small savers a safe place to accumulate funds and to increase the number of homeowners. The government provided assistance through three major aids:

1. The most important has been the **Federal Savings and Loan Insurance Corporation (FSLIC).** With federal deposit insurance, associations can attract vast amounts of money. It is assumed, but is not a matter of law, that they are backed by the good faith and credit of the United States. Depositors look to the insurance corporation rather than to the institutions for the safety of their funds.
2. The thrift institutions obtain federally subsidized credit from the Federal Home Loan Bank System (FHLBS) and its subsidiary, the Federal Home Loan Mortgage Corporation (Freddie Mac). These institutions furnish liquidity; they make advances at low rates, and they also conduct a substantial secondary mortgage market operation.
3. The thrift institutions were also given a tax subsidy through a special bad-debt reserve. If they placed over 60 percent of their assets in residential mortgages and other qualifying assets, their taxes were reduced. These benefits reached a maximum when they maintained 82 percent of their assets in the qualifying categories.

Specialization   The concepts behind the aid to the industry seemed logical. With funds costing less, the savings and loans would reduce the rates on their mortgages. In addition, the public would benefit from the existence of specialized thrift institutions which would know their customers and the local real estate market. Local expertise would enable them to do a better job of valuing properties. Their better market knowledge would allow them to lend to borrowers whom other lenders could not reach. They could tailor loans to individual needs.

However, several flaws marred the concept in practice. When they were small, the associations were able to lend to families who would not have qualified at other institutions. But when the bulk of loans were made by billion-dollar national organizations, their specialized local knowledge was no better than that of other institutions. Many critics claim that subsidies and special aids led to inefficiencies or higher profit rates, not to lower mortgage rates, and certainly not to higher interest for depositors. A still more serious flaw was that the thrifts' needs for diversified portfolios in order to reduce risks conflicted with the advantages of specialization.*

Nondiversification   When interest rates shot up, the cost of nondiversification became clear. It is a major investing error to put all one's eggs in one

---

*See American Assembly, *Financial Services,* ed. G. J. Benston (Englewood Cliffs, N.J.: Prentice Hall, 1983).

basket. When a firm concentrates most of its loans in fixed-rate mortgages, it is betting on stable or falling interest rates. Also, even with the backing of the Federal Home Loan Bank System, it lacks liquidity.

Indeed, most savings and loans were locked into fixed-rate mortgages and suffered heavy losses as rates increased. *Disintermediation*, the withdrawal of deposits to obtain higher rates elsewhere, became critical as treasury bills and money market funds offered rates well above the interest rate ceilings of the thrifts. As depositors recognized that savers were subsidizing borrowers, they became a lobby against the ceilings.

Changing the Rules   The lack of diversification brought about failures on a large scale. These, together with lobbying by depositors, led to new laws that attempted to ameliorate the situation. At the federal level, the Depository Institutions Deregulation and Monetary Control Act of 1980 and the Garn–St. Germain Depository Institutions Act of 1982 authorized major changes. Under the new federal laws, both savings and loan associations and mutual savings banks could obtain charters as federal savings banks. They could also shift from mutual to capital stock ownership. Interest rate ceilings were gradually removed, and the types of loans they could make were expanded. Meanwhile, to convince associations to maintain state rather than federal charters, states competed by expanding the types of loans and businesses in which the thrifts could engage.

Sources of Funds   As a result of deregulation, the ways in which thrifts obtain their funds have altered dramatically in recent years. Traditionally, most savings were in passbook accounts with comparatively low interest rate ceilings. By the time the ceiling on passbook interest rates was finally removed in 1986, these accounts had become only a minor source of funds, making up less than 15 percent of all liabilities.

Beginning in the 1970s, thrifts were allowed to compete with commercial banks for demand deposits. They issue **NOW accounts,** negotiable orders of withdrawal, which pay interest but are otherwise virtually indistinguishable from other checking accounts on which interest is illegal. **Money market certificates** and other market rate accounts pay market interest rates and also have checking privileges. The thrifts' largest source of funds has become **certificates of deposit** and other time accounts, which, because they are for a fixed number of days, lose interest if cashed before their due date.

Advances from the Federal Home Loan Banks have been another major source of funds. These are discussed in more detail under government programs in Chapter 7. They can be extremely important when institutions face a liquidity crisis.

The Thrifts' New Powers

The effect of deregulation has been to relax almost all the special lending restrictions on thrift institutions. Their authorized operations come much closer to those of commercial banks. In fact, in several states, the level of restraint has fallen below that for banks and below that considered minimal by most students of financial history.

Regulations differ considerably from one state to another. In many cases they tend to be more lenient than federal regulations. The latter, however, give the best picture of what thrift institutions can do. Although they continue to emphasize the importance of residential mortgage lending, federal regulations now allow many other functions. They specify limits for these other functions, but these limits are so broad that only a few institutions approach them. Because of the rapidity of regulatory change, any list of activities allowed savings and loans is bound to be incomplete. However, the following list does illustrate the general trend in regulations for thrifts:

1. Mortgages on improved residential properties continue to be the most important lending category. Standard residential mortgages can be made for up to 90 percent of value. If the amount of the loan above 90 percent is insured by private mortgage insurance, the loan-to-value ratio can be as high as 95 percent.
2. Firms can make loans backed by government insurance or guarantees on any terms authorized by the government agencies. They can also buy any of the securities issued by these agencies.
3. If secured by a mortgage on the property, construction loans can be made for up to 75 percent of value. Combination loans can also be made. **Combination loans** are construction loans which can be assumed by the buyer of the new home. At the time of sale, the loan is increased to 90 or 95 percent of the selling price. Such loans are efficient because they avoid the cost of dual underwriting and other fees.
4. Junior mortgages are authorized provided the total mortgage debt does not exceed 90 percent of value. Thus loans for modernization and expansion, education, travel, or other purposes can be made based on second mortgages.
5. Many associations act as mortgage bankers. They originate loans and then sell them in the secondary market.
6. Mortgages can be made on commercial and industrial properties, but the total in these categories is limited to 40 percent of total assets.
7. As more and more people have moved into mobile homes in order to reduce their housing costs, mortgages on these homes have become more important. They constitute a sizable outlet for thrift funds.
8. Many other types of more specialized loans, such as loans on leases and unimproved land, can now be made. Other nonconforming loans are also permitted, but their terms and amounts are limited by the regulations.
9. In recent years, savings and loans attempted to expand their profits by entering into joint ventures for land development and construction. They have also purchased income properties for their own accounts. Such

investments and loans are usually handled through **service corpora-tions**—special subsidiaries authorized to conduct nontraditional activi-ties. Federally chartered and regulated associations remain under tight limits for investments of this type, but some states allow their state-chartered associations almost unlimited powers. For example, in Califor-nia and Texas from 1982 to 1986, this led to much speculation, overbuild-ing, and many failures.

10. Under the new laws, the thrifts have been permitted to make many kinds of nonmortgage loans and investments although the percentage of their assets allowed for such loans is limited. They can issue credit cards, make installment and other consumer loans, buy bonds and commercial paper, and make commercial loans.

11. Through their service corporations, associations have entered into many other kinds of real estate activities. Some own brokerage and title com-panies; others act as trustees and escrow agents.

The list of activities allowed thrifts under current regulations is so long and restrictions so loose that competitors and other interested parties have raised questions as to whether the concept of specialized mortgage-thrift insti-tutions still makes sense. How should such institutions be defined, and what special functions should they perform? One suggested solution is to require that they hold some minimum percentage of assets in mortgages, mortgage-related securities, or government securities. Associations must now hold 60 percent of their assets in these categories in order to qualify for some privileges. Powerful lobbies have battled over whether eligibility for federal deposit insurance should depend on the thrifts meeting this 60 percent requirement.

THE USE OF NEW POWERS

A wide gap exists between the right to enter specific markets and make new loans and the actual use of these powers. It takes a good deal of time for organizations to alter their operations after regulations change.

Before Deregulation

Savings and loan associations have traditionally been conservative mort-gage lenders. Most of them concentrated on 30-year fixed-rate mortgages on existing homes. Loan-to-value ratios clustered around 80 percent, although some went as high as 95 percent on loans carrying private mortgage insurance. Their interest rates and fees tended to be somewhat higher than those of other lenders. In the 1980s, many firms shifted to adjustable as opposed to fixed-rate mortgages.

Larger savings and loan associations always did a good deal of construction lending, especially on combination loans on single-family developments or apartments for which they would also be the final lenders. Some associations also lent on commercial properties. However, apartment houses and commercial buildings each accounted for less than 10 percent of their mortgages.

Mutual savings banks had more varied portfolios. They were more likely to buy government-insured or -guaranteed mortgages. They held sizable amounts of corporate bonds and limited holdings of common stock. More of their mortgage portfolios were in income properties. However, since all mortgages formed a less important share of their assets, the actual percentage of their loans on income properties did not differ greatly from that of the savings and loans. In a few states, mutual savings banks were active in making consumer and installment loans.

After Deregulation

In the deregulated world, the thrifts have the right to much greater diversity. Most firms have experimented with the new powers, but on a small scale. They make auto loans, issue credit cards, and make some commercial loans. However, the bulk of their activities remains with home mortgages, and they still concentrate on "economical home financing." They fear the dangers of expanding too rapidly into unknown types of markets. They recognize that it takes time to build organizational skills in new areas of business.

In contrast, the most rapidly growing associations between 1982 and 1986 have been state-chartered thrifts that use all the flexibility they are legally allowed. They have rushed into direct investments, large-scale construction loans, and joint building ventures. The capital-to-asset ratio of many of these institutions was low when they initiated these investments. As a result, these high risks have tended to be at the expense of the FSLIC and the rest of the industry—because they had insufficient capital to cover losses from these new high-risk activities, many of these thrifts failed.

Their failures brought about demands for more complete regulation. The FSLIC and many savings and loan executives feared that such firms were using the availability of federal deposit insurance to attract funds for speculative purposes. Federal controls were tightened in an effort to reduce losses to the insurance funds and to keep pressure on for the aid of homeownership.

COMMERCIAL BANKS

Commercial banks are the largest and most widespread category of all intermediaries. They are the principal sources of short-term credit and of most business lending. They create the largest share of the money supply through their demand deposits. In 1986 the United States had approximately 15,000 commercial banks holding over $2.25 trillion in assets.

Real Estate Lending

Commercial banks perform three distinct functions in real estate finance: (a) They are the primary sources for construction and interim (short-term) financing. (b) While ranking below savings institutions and government agencies and pools, they are a major source of long-term lending. (c) Directly and through nationwide subsidiaries, they conduct an extensive business in originating, trading, and servicing mortgages.

While historically real estate lending was a minor part of commercial banking, this is no longer true. Banks have expanded into all phases of real estate finance, as Table 6-1 makes clear. Over 20 percent of their assets consists of mortgages. Considering their dominance in other mortgage-related activities, their total impact on real estate lending comes close to that of the thrifts, despite the fact that their share of the single-family residential market is considerably smaller.

Organization

Commercial banking organizations vary in size from Citicorp, the largest with over $140 billion in assets, to small community banks with less than $1 million. Most banks are state chartered, but national banks, which are chartered and regulated by the Comptroller of the Currency, hold the largest share of assets. State regulation of real estate lending by banks varies greatly, as it does with thrifts. However, because most banks are insured by the Federal Deposit Insurance Corporation they must comply with its criteria.

Although most banks are local, most lending is performed by large regional, national, and international organizations. The share occupied by real estate on the balance sheets of large and small banks varies tremendously. Large money center banks do little long-term real estate lending compared to other activities. However, this situation has been changing. Some of the largest banks now own thrift institutions. Many have mortgage subsidiaries with offices spread across the country. Some of the large regional banks always did and still do a sizable amount of real estate financing. Many smaller banks hold the largest share of their assets in real estate loans.

The funds of commercial banks come from demand and savings deposits, short-term certificates of deposit, and overnight borrowing in the federal funds market. They avoided long-term real estate lending because of their dependence on short-term funds. By law prior to deregulation, their permanent mortgage loans were limited to a certain percentage of their time deposits or capital. However, since deregulation legal restrictions play only a minor role in most banks' decisions as to mortgage lending.

Short-Term Lending

The most significant real estate activities of commercial banks consist of short-term lending. They dominate the market for construction loans on commercial and industrial properties, and they share the residential market in construction equally with savings institutions.

A great deal of bank lending is limited to two years, sometimes extending to five. This is **interim lending.** Banks lend if a long-term lender gives a **take-out** (or permanent) **loan** commitment. An insurance company or one of the government agencies agrees that if the property is completed and sold to a creditworthy buyer, a permanent long-term loan will be granted. On the basis of commitments of this type, banks provide interim credit. They run the risk that the property will not be completed or that it will not be sold on terms that meet the commitment. If such failures occur, they will have to foreclose. However, take-out commitments mean that the banks avoid the risk of interest rate increases or of the nonavailability of funds when the sale is completed.

Warehousing

Banks also lend to mortgage companies and large builders on notes collateralized by a group of mortgages or construction loans. This process is called **warehousing.** The warehousing of loans is similar to the financing of inventories or accounts receivable in other industries. Mortgage lenders build up an inventory of unsold mortgages in the process of construction lending or in order to accumulate a large enough pool of mortgages to sell in the secondary market. The amounts they lend exceed their own capital, so they must borrow.

EXAMPLE: In a typical warehousing transaction, the ABC Mortgage Company opens a line of credit with the Second State Bank, allowing it to borrow up to $5 million. ABC signs a note secured by its net worth and by an agreement to assign individual mortgages as they are made.

In the course of each month, ABC makes 30 loans at an average of $120,000 each. As each loan is made, ABC writes a check against its account at Second State and transfers the new mortgage to the bank's custody. The bank advances the funds against ABC's note. At the end of the month, the bank holds 30 mortgages and ABC owes $3.6 million. ABC then sells the mortgages to a pension fund. The bank receives the fund's check and releases the mortgages.

What percentage of value a bank advances to a mortgage company in the warehousing process and how much leeway in paperwork it allows depends on each company's credit rating and the bank's prior experience with the company and in similar lending.

Long-Term Lending

Many of the long-term loans originated by banks and their mortgage subsidiaries are for sale to others. However, banks also retain loans for their own accounts. Banks are a particularly good source of funds for income properties and also for customers who do other business with them and who want to borrow to buy a home. Banks also advertise and compete actively for so-called **equity loans.** These junior mortgages allow homeowners to borrow against any increased equities in their homes. Because they carry above-normal interest rates, junior mortgages are an important source of profit.

While banks can now compete with most other lenders, and while some of them do make all kinds of loans, most banks remain conservative in their appraisals. Banks tend to avoid maximum terms, except for loans that can be sold in the secondary market. Although their loan-to-value ratios and time to maturity lag behind those of other lenders, their interest rates and fees tend to be lower. They often skim the best loans in the market by offering to lend at somewhat lower rates and fees.

LIFE INSURANCE COMPANIES AND RETIREMENT FUNDS

Lenders in the insurance and retirement fund category are the most diverse. They consist of four main groups: (1) life insurance companies, (2) private uninsured pension funds, (3) state and local retirement funds, and (4) a miscellaneous group comprised primarily of private trusts and endowments. The total assets of these groups in 1986 were over $1.7 trillion.

Statements about the size of the pension industry must be interpreted carefully. The Social Security Trust Fund and other United States government retirement funds are sometimes included. However, these invest only in U.S. government securities. Furthermore, some of the assets of insured pension funds are counted twice. Some pension assets also appear as liabilities of life insurance companies. This double-counting overstates the total assets of this group.

Sizes and Mortgage Portfolios

Over 2,000 life insurance companies range in size from the largest, Prudential, with over $70 billion in assets, to those with less than $1 million in assets. More than 500,000 pension funds vary in size from over $23 billion to those with only a few dollars. About 5,500 of them have assets of over $5 million each. If individual retirement accounts (IRAs) are each counted as a pension fund in itself, the number of funds runs into the millions.

At the end of World War II, life insurance companies formed the second-largest group of financial institutions and one of the most important sources of mortgage funds. Their relative size and the share they place in mortgage loans has fallen since then; in 1986 their total assets were about $780 billion. One-third of this amount came from insured pension funds. They held mortgages totaling about $170 billion, or 22 percent of the total; mortgage-backed securities of about $50 billion; and direct real estate investments of about $27 billion.

Private uninsured pensions and state and local retirement funds had about $1.2 trillion of assets in 1986. Less than 3 percent of these were mortgage loans. Private pension funds had only about 1 percent of their total assets in mortgages. State and local retirement funds placed about 5 percent of their money in mortgages, a majority of which were residential. In addition, the two together placed between 4 percent and 5 percent of their assets in securities backed by mortgages. They also held some direct equity investments in real estate.

The Future

Most discussions of real estate finance point to pension and retirement funds as the great untapped future source. These funds have been the fastest growing, but their real estate loans and investments remain small. Many of those engaged in real estate believe that if more pension money flowed into real estate finance, interest rates would drop and credit would be easier to obtain.

Although pension funds are furnishing more funds to the real estate market and their importance is likely to grow, this change should not make much difference in relative mortgage rates. As earlier chapters note, belief to the contrary assumes that financial markets have imperfections that block money from flowing freely among them. If more loans were made by pension funds, mortgage rates would indeed drop initially. But if markets are efficient, real estate lenders would go elsewhere to fill the gaps left by the partial departure of pension money to real estate lending. Rates would return to their previous level. The moral of the story is that increasing potential flows from any source to one segment of the total market will not reduce rates unless current charges are higher than they should be. Higher than normal rates should prevail only if inefficiencies exist in the movements of funds among markets.

Life Insurance Companies

Life insurance companies are chartered in all states. Although most of them are headquartered in Texas, Louisiana, and Arizona, the largest firms—those holding the bulk of assets—are in the northeast and in California. Most companies conduct their mortgage operations at their headquarters. They use mortgage brokers throughout the country for originating and servicing loans. Some of the largest, however, maintain regional offices for direct lending or to improve communications with local mortgage companies.

Most of the firms are capital stock corporations, but many of the largest are mutuals. Insurance companies are regulated primarily by the states. The state in which a company obtains its charter and maintains its headquarters is normally its leading regulator. However, other states usually do not allow insurance companies to enter unless they operate under equivalent regulations. These host states may set additional standards for loans made within their borders.

States tend to impose stricter requirements for loan-to-value ratios and maturity terms on insurance companies than they do on thrift institutions and banks. They also establish maximum percentages of assets that can be placed in individual loans and in real estate as a whole. However, such limits are rarely binding, except for smaller companies.

Sources of Funds Life insurance companies obtain most of their funds from four sources:

1. The largest and most traditional source is in the reserves of policyholders. Such savings are accumulated early in the life of insurance policies so that

level premiums can be maintained later on. If savings did not accumulate, premiums would rise sharply with the age of the insured, since the cost of insuring a life goes up with age.

2. Between a quarter and a third of the money comes from insured pension funds. Many companies that operate a pension system turn over the funds under a contract with an insurance company.

3. Other money comes from annuities—amounts held by the insurance company to be paid out over a person's lifetime. When those who have pension benefits or are insured retire or die, the form of settlement is often that of a lifetime annuity.

4. Insurance companies also have capital and reserves of their own. These, too, require investment.

Pension Funds

Private pension funds are regulated and assisted by the federal government. They have grown rapidly because a firm's contributions to its pension fund are not taxed, nor are the fund's earnings. Pension funds were once virtually free of regulations and restrictions. In 1974, as a result of mismanagement, conflicts of interest, and in certain cases an inability to pay promised benefits, Congress passed the **Employees Retirement Income Security Act (ERISA).** This act established minimum investment standards and attempted to make certain that funds were used to pay pensions and not to aid the businesses that had contributed to the pension funds.

Pension trustees use a variety of investment techniques. Some invest by contract with life insurance firms. Others use commercial banks to serve as trustees and to handle all investments. Many are managed internally but employ outside consultants and investment managers. Most funds lack the necessary infrastructure to make and supervise real estate loans, however. That is one reason why real estate assets are insignificant in most portfolios. Furthermore, management fees tend to be too low to cover the higher investment costs required for the proper handling of real estate loans.

A few funds do recognize that diversification into real estate can be beneficial and are therefore willing to incur the higher costs involved in managing real estate. They believe that their net returns will be as good as or better than they could achieve by putting funds elsewhere. Others have bought increasing amounts of mortgage-backed securities, and this market is increasing rapidly.

State and Local Retirement Funds

State and local governments were early participants in the retirement-pension movement. Between 6,000 and 7,000 organizations have a total of over $300 billion in assets. Most of these funds manage their investments themselves. Traditionally their investment policies have been more conservative than those of the private uninsured funds. They have maintained a larger share of their money in fixed-rate assets, such as bonds and mortgages, rather than in common stocks. Because they are more subject to local political pressure, many have put more money into housing loans. They have tried to support local builders and home buyers having trouble because of mortgage shortages. Even so, with a few prominent exceptions, real estate remains a small item in their portfolios.

Operations and Real Estate Lending

On the whole, lenders in the insurance-pension category make mortgage loans only when they promise a return as high as or higher than the returns available in markets that they can engage in with less effort. With the exception of the larger companies, they generally act through mortgage brokers. Their main emphasis has been on large loans, where handling costs are less per dollar invested. They furnish most of the credit for the big commercial and industrial buildings.

Low Liquidity   These institutions need far less liquidity than most other financial groups. Their liabilities tend to be stable and they are not payable until well into the future. In addition, cash requirements can be predicted quite accurately on a statistical basis. Therefore, long-term real estate loans would seem to be ideal for their portfolios. In theory, they borrow—and therefore can lend—on long terms. They are not caught in the "borrow short–lend long" bind suffered by deposit institutions.

In fact, however, they have less freedom than it would appear. Investment managers and insurance companies are judged in the market by their short-term results. If their total returns lag behind those of other companies, funds entrusted to them will be withdrawn and new accounts will dry up. Consequently, as interest rates became more volatile, they too have feared to make long-term fixed-rate loans.

Types of Loans   In the 1960s and 1970s, the holdings of insurance companies and pension funds of many fixed-rate mortgages and bonds caused their returns to suffer. As a result, when money became tight, they would lend only if they were granted the right to share in the potential profits of the buildings on which they lent. Chapter 19, which discusses loans on income property, describes in detail some of the methods insurance companies and pension funds have developed for this sharing process.

Both insurance companies and pension funds have also been willing to purchase large buildings for their own account. At times, the companies buy buildings directly. In other cases, they purchase shares in trusts established for the purpose of investing the funds of a number of pension and insurance companies. This enables those that otherwise could not afford a diversified portfolio of large buildings to remain diversified.

If you read the signboards listing the financing sources on new large-scale developments, you are likely to find that banks are furnishing the interim financing against permanent loan commitments from a life insurance company or pension fund. Because their flow of funds is more stable, these firms are willing to give commitments to lend several years in the future, providing the terms they obtain are to their liking. Many people believe that this has caused cycles of overbuilding in commercial properties. Construction continues under the older commitments even when vacancies have risen to such a high level that the new buildings are bound to be unprofitable.

Because of the difficulty of managing small individual loans, in the past insurance companies bought government-insured or -guaranteed mortgages on residential properties in the secondary market. In this way they avoided the need to check individual credit ratings and appraise properties. They made their purchases on the strength of the government insurance guarantees. Currently, they usually buy mortgage-backed securities rather than individual loans, still seeking those that are guaranteed or insured by government agencies. As Chapter 8 points out, such purchases require far fewer skills than does mortgage lending. Mortgage-backed securities are more like bonds, which these firms have traditionally held in their portfolios. Their purchases have widened the market. They have also made investment bankers who underwrite and trade the securities an important part of the real estate finance industry.

In 1985 several large insurance companies announced that they were returning to the single-home mortgage market. They had been absent from this type of lending for over 20 years. Apparently, they now saw new profit opportunities and were willing to make the overhead investments needed to build an individual home mortgage business.

OTHER PRIVATE MORTGAGE LENDERS

The final group of private lenders shown in Table 6-1 includes some mortgage companies and a variety of miscellaneous other lenders. We discuss mortgage companies separately in Chapter 8, because their significance is closely related to that of the secondary market.

The remaining miscellaneous sources account for between 7 percent and 10 percent of outstanding loans. Chapter 5 pointed out why their share of the total rises sharply in periods of tight money. In 1981 and 1982, over one-quarter of new mortgage money came from this diverse category. Individuals and non-financial corporations account for the largest segment of this group. Since they are not regulated except for usury laws, they are the prime source of "creative financing." Foreign individuals and partnerships have been especially willing to make high-risk loans. Other lenders include mortgage investment trusts, finance companies, credit unions, and insurance companies that do not provide life coverage.

Mortgage Investment Trusts

Real estate investment trusts (REITs) are similar to closed-end mutual funds, but they invest in real estate loans and equity rather than buying stocks or bonds. REITs give small investors an opportunity to buy a small piece of a package of mortgages or of large buildings. They raise their money by selling common stock or bonds, or by borrowing from banks and the money market. They use the funds to purchase properties, make mortgage loans, or a combination of the two. They pay no corporate profits taxes if they meet certain criteria and if they also distribute annually 95 percent of their net income. This means that the recipients of their dividends avoid double taxation. The shareholder pays income taxes on the basis of the source of the REIT's dividend—income, capital gains, or the nontaxable return of the shareholder's capital investment.

REITs specializing in mortgage lending are called *mortgage investment trusts.* In theory, REITs have substantial advantages. They can afford centralized, skilled management. They can borrow money in addition to selling stock shares. Since a market exists for their shares, individuals obtain greater liquidity by investing through a REIT rather than directly. Owners can liquidate without having to sell a property or mortgages. The REITs can offer tax savings to individuals. They are not taxed themselves; yet through careful timing of capital gains and return of capital dividends, they can lower taxes for their shareholders.

The History of REITs   Some REITs have a long history, but most of them originated after advantageous tax law changes were passed in the 1960s. A tremendous speculative binge followed in the early 1970s, ending with a large number of bankruptcies and a collapse in the share value of most REITs.

Their difficulties were multifold. Since they borrowed short and lent long, they suffered badly when the term structure of interest rates shifted. They were stuck with fixed-rate assets yielding less than their current costs of money. Creative accounting allowed them to record as current income interest that might or might not be earned in the future, and thus to overstate their real profits and to create a dangerous amount of leverage. They claimed profits as money was lent, even though the loans were poor and had only a slight chance of being repaid. As a result of this accounting, they literally threw money at weak developers and developments. Many of these had to be foreclosed, leading to enormous losses.

The industry shakeout eliminated many of the weakest REITs. Others lost large amounts but were able to avoid bankruptcy. Although a few that had been cautious continued to function well, even their owners suffered because their share prices dropped drastically as a result of the industry's bad reputation.

Operations   In the mid-1980s, the renewed success of the survivors of the early period underscored the basic advantage of this type of organization: REITs were particularly useful for IRA investments. New REITs once again entered the market. They promised not to repeat the earlier errors, and they were believed. In 1985, over $2.5 billion was raised by new REITs and the total assets of the trusts increased by over $4 billion.

Mortgage investment trusts have emphasized specialized lending for construction and development. They take high risks in return for sizable participations in any profit. In such cases, they make medium-term loans while obtaining an equity position granted for making the loan funds available.

Other Financial Institutions

Finance companies, credit unions, and other insurance companies with no-life coverage all do a limited amount of mortgage lending. Credit unions have grown rapidly, and mortgages have been a useful outlet for their funds. Mortgages have helped them maintain good relations with their members. Other insurance companies have fairly large investment programs. To the extent that mortgages yield competitive returns, these companies will buy them. On the other hand, because mortgage investments require special skills, few such companies are very active.

Finance companies, which are located throughout the country, specialize in high-risk consumer loans. They find that equity (second mortgage) loans to homeowners fit in with their normal operating patterns. As a result, they have increased their mortgage portfolios by $1 billion to $2 billion a year.

Other Lenders

The remaining group of lenders is too diverse to describe in detail. The largest source of miscellaneous loans continues to be households. They participate primarily through second mortgages, discussed in Chapter 2. Most make junior mortgages, which they grant because the new owners have insufficient funds to cover the difference between the largest available first mortgage and the selling price.

For similar reasons, nonfinancial corporations and syndicates make second, third, and even fourth mortgages primarily for income properties. Each group holds and sells large amounts of property. If offered a high enough price, interest rates, or participation, they will accept very junior mortgages with all their inherent risks. Foreign investors are another prime source of junior loans. They invest in the United States primarily to diversify their portfolios away from their home countries. They do not need liquidity, and many are accustomed to assuming high risks in return for large potential gains.

These miscellaneous lenders have been among the most dynamic participants in financing income properties. Their ability to realize the large profits they expect depends on what happens to real estate prices and profits and on the real estate cycle. They expanded their lending in an effort to share in the high profits of the period from 1975 to 1982. The fact that they made funds easily available helped to create the fast rise in prices that characterized the period.

Under more normal circumstances, these lenders tend to find the market highly competitive and more difficult.

SUMMARY

Mortgage lenders may operate in the primary or secondary market and make construction or long-term loans. Lenders may specialize in residential lending or income properties, making either conventional or FHA-VA loans. Few lenders operate in all markets.

Most real estate loans are made or bought by deposit institutions. To protect their depositors and the insurance funds, the type, size, and amount of loans they may make are subject to regulation.

Savings institutions receive government aid on the assumption that their operations will help increase saving and homeownership. Pressures toward deregulation and use of market forces to determine the most efficient loans have given thrifts the ability to make more different kinds of loans. The need for savings institutions to diversify and to pay depositors competitive rates also pushed the regulators into doing away with many regulations. Pressures toward reregulation built up because of the poor experience of some lenders.

Commercial banks, with their greater need for liquidity, have put more effort into short-term construction and interim lending. However, some operate in the housing market in a manner similar to thrifts. Many large banks conduct substantial mortgage banking business, through either their real estate departments or their mortgage subsidiaries.

Life insurance companies were major mortgage lenders in the past, but they have recently become far less important in the residential market. Their size and ownership of long-term funds enable them to give firm commitments and to make loans on large commercial and industrial projects. When money is tight, they have been able to insist on the right to participate in income increases and profits.

Pension funds would seem to be logical real estate investors and sources of funds because their need for liquidity is slight. However, because most are not organized to handle diverse individual loans, their participation in the real estate market has been minimal. A shift in attitudes and the development of mortgage-backed securities has increased the funds they devote to mortgages. Their total, however, remains fairly limited.

While other private lenders (outside of mortgage companies) are not major suppliers of mortgages, they may at times play a critical role. They are especially important in periods of tight money and in making loans which institutions cannot or would not make.

KEY TERMS

capital stock companies

certificates of deposit

combination loans

conventional loans

Employees Retirement Income
   Security Act (ERISA)
equity loans
Federal Savings and Loan
   Insurance Corporation (FSLIC)
interim lending
money market certificates
mutual associations

NOW accounts
primary mortgage market
real estate investment trusts
   (REITs)
secondary mortgage market
service corporations
take-out loan
warehousing

QUESTIONS

1. Describe the differences between primary and secondary mortgage markets.
2. "Government-backed loans are much safer than conventional loans." Do you agree with this statement? Give your reasons.
3. What are the characteristics of savings institutions?
4. Describe recent changes in the savings industry.
5. Can you think of some reasons justifying government assistance to savings and loan institutions?
6. What effect has the deregulation of savings and loans had on their sources of funds?
7. In view of the current regulations governing thrift institutions listed in this chapter, do you agree with the claim that thrifts are no longer specialized mortgage institutions?
8. The increased diversification of thrifts helps the healthy growth of the housing industry. Evaluate this statement.
9. What are the differences between savings and loans and commercial banks in mortgage lending?
10. What are the principal types of mortgage loans that insurance companies make? Why?
11. What is a REIT?
12. Why did many REITs fail in the 1970s?

7 The Government and Housing Finance

OBJECTIVES

When you finish this chapter, you should be able to:

- explain what is meant by a national housing policy.

- analyze some of the pros and cons of abolishing housing aids.

- define a federally sponsored agency and list the main ones in the housing sphere.

- discuss the organization and functioning of the principal housing agencies.

- describe the ways in which tax preference programs work.

- know what state housing finance agencies are and what they do.

G OVERNMENT ASSISTANCE to real estate has been popular but controversial. For most of their history, the direct assistance programs to renters have been bitterly debated. In contrast, aid through financial institutions, the secondary market, and tax preferences has been generally accepted. However, criticism by neoclassical economists and the Reagan administration, together with a desire for tax reform, have led to frequent attacks against many of the programs.

What should the role of the government be in the financing of real estate? Its importance has increased steadily, but that involvement is now being questioned. Those who think that the private market should be paramount in all or most situations have urged a cutback in all of these programs. They base their views on the belief that attempts to promote the economy and family welfare through aid in the financing of real estate have instead brought about inefficiency and an unfair distribution of income.

To be able to analyze the pros and cons of this debate, and to use the programs if necessary, students of real estate finance must understand how and why the programs developed and how they work. When builders and real estate professionals argue for the continuation or expansion of government programs, are they primarily reflecting their own self-interest, or are they concerned about the welfare of families and the economy as a whole?

This chapter provides an overview of government assistance to real estate finance, the size and variety of the programs and the premises on which the policies have been based, along with their counterarguments. It then introduces the different agencies and regulations. Chapters 8 and 9 explain how the programs operate and their significance in the purchase, sale, and ownership of property.

THE VARIETY OF GOVERNMENT HOUSING PROGRAMS

Since 1933 and the New Deal, the government's housing programs have profoundly influenced the ability of families to obtain mortgage funds at affordable rates. In years of tight money, up to 80 percent of all residential mortgage loans were aided by some form of government program. Even at their minimum, these programs accounted for at least 20 percent of mortgage lending. While not quite as significant, a great deal of the decision making in the development and purchase of income properties (particularly apartment houses) is also highly influenced by government policies.

Government support of real estate finance has taken a variety of forms. The following list divides these forms of support into four types, with further subtypes:

1. *Tax expenditures,* the most expensive category, are administered through
    the Internal Revenue Service (IRS).
    a. Housing expenditures (but not other consumer expenditures) that
        may be deducted from income subject to federal income tax.
    b. Benefits to owners of apartments and other real estate from special
        privileges that reduce their income taxes.
    c. Mortgages from state and local housing agencies at below-market rates
        (these agencies raise their funds through tax-exempt bonds).
2. *Direct subsidy* programs reduce a family's rent or mortgage payments.
    These were among the earliest and most controversial programs.
    a. Public low-rent programs.
    b. Community development and slum clearance.
    c. Special assistance through the Federal Housing Administration (FHA),
        established in 1934, or the Government National Mortgage Association
        (GNMA), called "Ginnie Mae."
    d. Programs for rural areas and farmers through the Farmers Home
        Administration (FmHA).
3. Programs involving *intermediaries* provide smaller and more indirect
    subsidies.
    a. Special aid to financial intermediaries, such as deposit institutions, in
        the form of federal deposit insurance and tax breaks to reduce the
        cost of funds.
    b. Establishment of federally sponsored agencies to increase the flow and
        lower the cost of mortgage credit. These agencies include the Federal
        National Mortgage Association (FNMA), called "Fannie Mae," the
        Federal Home Loan Banks, the Federal Home Loan Mortgage
        Corporation (FHLMC, or Freddie Mac), and the Federal Land Banks.
4. Programs developing the *secondary mortgage market* are the most
    important of all.
    a. The FHA.
    b. Veterans' loan guarantee programs, enacted following World War II in
        a major expansion.
    c. The GNMA, the FmHA, the FNMA, the FHLMC, and the Federal Land
        Banks, now grown in importance.

The Size and Scope of the Government Programs

In 1985, the total expenditures for government aid in real estate were about
$63.2 billion, or roughly 5 percent of total federal expenditures (see Table 7-1).
By far the largest amounts went out in the form of **tax expenditures,** which
are amounts not collected in taxes because of special credits or exemptions in
the tax code included to foster particular actions by taxpayers.

Tax Expenditures   Because homeowners could deduct mortgage interest
and property taxes from their taxable income and because they could defer

Table 7-1
Federal Budget and Tax Expenditures
for Housing and Community Development
(in billions of dollars)

Type of Expenditure	Year 1985	Year 1986	Year 1987
Tax Expenditures:			
Deductibility of interest and property taxes	34.4	37.3	40.8
Capital gains exclusion	3.6	3.8	4.4
State and local finance agencies	2.4	2.9	3.0
Depreciation and miscellaneous	2.5	2.7	2.9
Subtotal	42.9	46.7	51.1
Low-rent Housing and Community Development:			
Low-rent housing	11.7	11.9	10.8
Rural low-rent housing	4.0	3.3	1.7
Community development	4.6	4.6	3.9
Subtotal	20.3	19.8	16.4
Total	63.2	66.5	67.5

Note: Figures for 1985 are actual; figures for 1986 and 1987 are estimates from the Office of Management and Budget.

Source: *Budget of the United States, Fiscal Year 1987* (Washington, D.C.: U.S. Government Printing Office, 1986), pp. 5-59, 5-66, 5-79, 6d 132–40.

capital gains, tax collections of the federal government were reduced by about $38 billion a year. The exemption from income taxes for bonds issued by state and local housing agencies costs $2.4 billion. The remaining $2.5 billion resulted from accelerated depreciation on buildings, tax subsidies to thrift institutions, and similar programs. All of these will be cut considerably by the enactment of tax reforms.

Although these are by far the most expensive of all government housing programs, the estimates of tax expenditures vary a great deal depending on the assumptions used. Some observers object to the concept of tax expenditures on the theory that potential taxes are not subsidies since they have not been enacted into law. They believe that exemptions should not be examined one by one and that failure to tax should not be thought of as a subsidy even when the tax law is reshaped to promote a particular function.

Low-Rent Housing and Community Development   The costs of the programs usually thought of as government housing aids, namely low-rent housing and community development, include those of public housing projects, housing for the elderly and disabled, low-income (Section 8) housing, housing vouchers, the rural housing program of the FmHA, and community development subsidies (see Table 7-1). Section 8 housing was the principal method of subsidizing housing between 1974 and 1985. Housing vouchers have been debated for 50 years. They became the centerpiece of the Reagan administration's housing agenda but were voted for only grudgingly by Congress. Community development subsidies have been used for all kinds of local needs. About one-third of these funds went directly for housing.

All of these programs together cost about $20.3 billion per year. Under the pressure to cut taxes and reduce the budget deficit, they have undergone a steady contraction in real (inflation corrected) terms. (For more on direct federal housing assistance, see the appendix to this chapter.)

The Federal Credit Programs   The government programs to increase housing credit are of three categories (see Table 7-2). First, and largest, are insurance and guarantees for private mortgages. In recent years, the FHA and the VA have insured or guaranteed about $60 billion a year; the total outstanding exposure is over $350 billion. The FHA programs are self-supporting; the losses on VA guarantees are not large and are considered a veterans' benefit, offered in lieu of the bonuses paid in earlier years.

Second are portfolio loans made by the government-sponsored housing agencies. In the mid-1980s, these agencies did up to $50 billion a year in transactions, resulting in average portfolio increases of about $20 billion a year. Their outstanding portfolios totaled over $240 billion. Third, these agencies together with Ginnie Mae issued or guaranteed about $100 billion a year in bonds or certificates backed by private mortgages. Only part of the mortgage-backed securities add to the government exposure. All of the guarantees by Ginnie Mae, plus some of the other agency certificates, largely duplicate guarantees already given by the FHA and the VA. Thus they are already counted. If all of the over $400 billion in the third category is added to the over $600 billion in the first two, double-counting occurs. (Federal Land Bank loans have not been included.)

The credit programs on the whole are self-supporting. Their costs to the government are low. They incur some risk; also, they do not pay the taxes that might be collected if their functions were performed by private firms. Congress has used some of the agencies in the credit sphere to administer direct subsidies. Such costs, however, should appear in Table 7-1 as part of the low-rent programs.

Table 7-2
Government Programs to Increase Housing Credit
(in billions of dollars)

Program	Transactions			Outstandings		
	1985	1986	1987	1985	1986	1987
Mortgage Insurance and Guarantees						
Federal Housing Administration	47	49	37	195	221	240
Veterans' mortgage loan guarantees	12	12	15	131	136	144
Total	59	61	52	326	357	384
Portfolio Loans						
Federal National Mortgage Association	20	17	17	97	102	109
Federal Home Loan Mortgage Corporation	5	4	5	13	14	17
Federal Home Loan Banks	12	10	9	87	97	106
Farmers Home Administration	3	2	1	28	29	29
Total	40	33	32	225	242	261
Mortgage Pools and Securities						
Federal National Mortgage Association	19	22	24	49	67	87
Federal Home Loan Mortgage Corporation	35	39	40	92	123	149
Government National Mortgage Association	36	43	40	201	235	265
Total	90	104	104	342	425	501

Note: Figures for 1985 are actual; figures for 1986 and 1987 are estimates from the Office of Management and Budget.

Source: *Special Analysis Budget of the United States, Fiscal Year 1987* (Washington, D.C.: U.S. Government Printing Office, 1986), Part 2, F.

THE PROS AND CONS OF A NATIONAL HOUSING POLICY

Over the past 50 years, virtually every country in the world has developed a range of government housing policies. The United States would be unique only if it abolished them. The stated goal of the United States's **national housing policy** is to insure every household the opportunity to live in a decent house, in a suitable environment, at a cost that leaves sufficient income available for other needs. Before describing how programs to achieve these goals operate, we must consider their traditional justifications. We also look into the attacks on them articulated by neoclassical economists and the Reagan administration. To the degree that these latter arguments are accepted, government support of real estate finance will be phased out.*

In the past, several programs operated only intermittently. Their activity depended on the state of the economy. In depressions or recessions, low housing starts caused administrations and Congress to open wide the spigot of housing funds; in prosperity they turned down the flow. In contrast to these periodic fluctuations, the *neoclassical* view attacks the basic concepts of housing policy. It holds that special aids to real estate create inefficiencies and are wasteful, and that the programs should therefore be permanently dismantled.

The Arguments for a National Housing Policy

Why is more and better housing in the national interest? Three arguments are frequently advanced.

1. Housing is a national concern rather than an individual one, because houses carry important **externalities**—the benefits and damages to others that make the sum greater than its parts. Slums and bad neighborhoods diminish everyone's welfare. Deterioration of neighborhoods imposes heavy costs on individuals. Such changes cannot be reversed by private action alone. By maintaining property values, we all gain. A related argument holds that when people obtain a stake in the economy through homeownership, political stability and national welfare are enhanced.
2. Cycles in housing production cause undesirable fluctuations in the gross national product and in output. If the cycles can be stopped, national economic efficiency will rise and the cost of housing will fall.
3. The credit cycle imposes further costs. The greater the fluctuations are in the availability of credit, the higher the risks are of purchasing and building houses. Also during periods of tight money affordability suffers. If the

---

*For a more detailed discussion of these issues, see S. J. Maisel, "The Agenda for Metropolitan Housing Policies," in J. M. Quigley and D. L. Rubinfeld, *American Domestic Priorities* (Berkeley: University of California Press, 1985). The Reagan administration proposals and arguments are contained in U.S. President's Commission on Housing, *The Report of the President's Commission on Housing* (Washington, D.C.: U.S. Government Printing Office, 1982). Also see A. Downs, *The Revolution in Real Estate Finance* (Washington, D.C.: Brookings Institution, 1985).

government can bring about smoother flows of mortgage money by intervening to provide funds regularly, it will reduce waste.

The arguments for aid to other kinds of property are usually based on the desirability of expanding our stock of capital. Since buildings are a significant part of the capital stock, programs to accelerate investment often include increasing construction among their goals.

Market Failures　The proponents of a national housing policy claim that market forces alone cannot bring about the desired goals.

1. By definition, the market, which depends on individual desires for profit, will not achieve the externalities. This means that slum clearance, redevelopment, and wider homeownership are all proper spheres for government action.
2. The fluctuations in mortgage credit are caused by natural market forces. They are reactions to movements in private demand and monetary policies. Credit and production cycles can be offset by government policies that change market institutions so as to even out the flow of mortgage funds to borrowers. Greater stability in housing finance and construction will reduce risks and costs, as well as increase the efficiency, growth, and output of the economy.
3. Most important are the problems raised by the large amount of capital tied up in houses. (a) Few homeowners or landlords can accumulate the equity required to buy a house; they need mortgages with large loan-to-value ratios. (b) Over 12 million families, or 15 percent of the total—mainly those not in the labor market—are poor. Their incomes are too low to afford decent housing without government aid. (c) The large capital requirements also mean that the affordability of decent housing may be a problem for many other families, especially those who have not previously owned a house. Action to assist groups who have adequate income but cannot accumulate enough capital to buy their first house may help both them and the nation.
4. If there are widespread benefits, the government can afford to experiment with innovative but risky policies that would be beyond the scope of any individual firm.

The Arguments against a National Housing Policy

The arguments against assistance to real estate follow from the neoclassical view that any interference with the market is likely to do more harm than good. They can be summarized in six arguments.

1. Because the market knows best, any interference—even for theoretically

worthy purposes—will decrease the market's efficiency. Externalities are not significant.

2. Housing programs have made mortgage credit too good a bargain. Too many houses have been built, permitting families to occupy too much space. Households—especially singles—should double up rather than occupy individual dwellings.

3. Housing production has expanded at the expense of other investments. A decrease in housing expenditures would allow more productive investment elsewhere. The national savings rate fell because rising home values made homeowners wealthy and they consumed more.

4. Cheaper and more available housing does not mean better neighborhoods. Slums and poor environments are the result of poverty or failure to maintain property. Urban or housing policies cannot solve these problems.

5. Housing is a natural place for cyclical instability to be concentrated. A decrease in housing production can be absorbed by a drop in vacancies rather than in occupied space. When demand in the economy increases too rapidly, it is good to have housing as a safety valve to let the economy blow off steam. Therefore, efforts to make housing less cyclical do more harm than good.

6. In their current form, tax expenditures are especially bad. They subsidize the rich at the expense of the poor. Under present housing policies, the higher your income, the more you save in taxes.

Each of these arguments can also be applied to programs that aid real estate outside the housing sphere.

Lack of Consensus

No agreement has emerged on which of the two positions is correct. Espousing the neoclassical arguments, the Reagan administration attempted to end many of the programs, but it did not try to alter the most expensive policies. They concluded that the tax expenditure deductions for mortgage interest payments had become such a sacred cow that they could not drum up enough political support to terminate them.

Rejecting the neoclassical arguments, proponents of housing programs attacked the position of the Reagan administration. They contended that no proof had been advanced to show that housing investment was actually too large or that it had occurred at the expense of other, more vital types. Homeowners saved more, not less, because repayments on mortgages are a form of forced saving. Statements that externalities were small did not prove that they actually *were* small. While admitting that housing cycles have not been eliminated, they believed that the possibility of doing so still exists. Because success is so rewarding, it is worthwhile continuing to try. As long as poverty exists, subsidies are needed. Current subsidies might be inefficient, but the best way of improving them would be to alter tax expenditures.

The lack of consensus probably means that housing policies will continue. If so, their efficiency can be improved. The anticyclical programs have not been successful, and tax expenditures clearly contain a good deal of waste.

The agencies that exert the most influence on real estate finance are those that increase the flow of mortgage credit. The most expensive programs, however, are those involving tax expenditures, and this is likely to remain true even with tax reform. Partially because of the Reagan administration's efforts to abolish them, but also for other reasons, the direct subsidy programs have had even less significance recently than in the past. These programs are extremely complex and require a great deal of expertise. The appendix to this chapter contains a brief analysis of the main programs and key issues.

THE GOVERNMENT AGENCIES IN THE MORTGAGE MARKET

There are four major types of action the government has taken to bolster the private housing market (see also Table 7-3):

1. The government charters deposit institutions, increases their available funds through deposit insurance, and regulates the types of loans they make. Most observers believe that the savings and loan industry would be much smaller were it not for active government intervention. (Some believe the economy would be more efficient if savings and loans were much smaller.) In recent years deposit insurance has been essential to the growth and survival of the savings and loans.
2. The government insures and guarantees lenders against losses from mortgage defaults. It also guarantees the purchasers of mortgage-backed securities based on these mortgages against losses from a failure to pay interest and principal. As a result, from 20 percent to 25 percent of residential loans are backed by the full faith and credit of the federal government.
3. Supplementing the insurance and guarantees, the government has established a set of agencies to foster the secondary market. These agencies borrow money on their own credit. They then use this money to buy mortgages, or they lend it to other lenders. Recently, a good deal of the borrowing has been through mortgage-backed securities.
4. Through the internal revenue code, the government helps owners of real estate by providing preferential tax treatment through tax expenditures.

The Types of Agencies by Their Funding

Independent Agencies Each of these policies is planned and administered by a somewhat different type of agency in relation to the federal government's

Table 7-3
Federal Government Real Estate Finance Policies

Agencies	Actions
1. Insurance and Regulatory Policies	
Federal Savings & Loan Insurance Corporation (FSLIC) Federal Deposit Insurance Corporation (FDIC) Federal Home Loan Bank Board (FHLBB) Comptroller of the Currency Federal Reserve Board	Provide deposit insurance and liquidity reserves. Regulate types of lending on real estate, development, and construction.
2. Mortgage Insurance and Guarantees	
Government National Mortgage Association (GNMA) Farmers Home Administration (FmHA) Federal Housing Administration (FHA) Veterans Administration (VA)	Insure and guarantee lenders against losses from defaults on mortgages. Guarantee purchasers of mortgage-backed securities against defaults. Make some direct loans.
3. Secondary Market Operations	
Government National Mortgage Association (GNMA) Farmers Home Administration (FmHA) Federal National Mortgage Association (FNMA) Federal Home Loan Mortgage Corporation (FHLMC) Federal Home Loan Banks (FHL Banks) Federal Land Banks	Purchase mortgages for holding in portfolio. Issue securities backed by pools of privately written mortgages. Furnish funds for lending.
4. Tax Expenditures	
Internal Revenue Service (IRS)	Subsidize homeowners; property developers and owners; state and local housing finance agencies and industrial development bonds; and deposit institutions.

funding responsibility. The agencies fostering and regulating the deposit institutions (except for the Comptroller of the Currency), the first group in Table 7-3, are **independent agencies** that are part of the government but have a nontax source of funds. They are headed by boards that are granted a good deal of leeway in their operations.

Direct Government Agencies   The second group of agencies, operating the mortgage insurance and guarantee programs as well as direct subsidies, are traditional government agencies dependent on budgetary appropriations. The FHA and GNMA are operating arms of the Department of Housing and Urban Development (HUD), subject to direction from the secretary of that agency. The FmHA is a branch of the Department of Agriculture. The VA is also a long-established agency. The IRS, which operates the tax system, is part of the Department of the Treasury.

Sponsored Agencies   Except for the GNMA, the agencies that are active in the secondary market are of an entirely different type. The four major ones—the FNMA, the FHLMC, the Federal Home Loan Banks, and the Federal Land Banks—are **sponsored agencies.** The government has no direct responsibility for their debt. They are not included in the federal budget and do not count as part of the federal deficit.

Over the years, a substantial effort has been mounted to make money available for mortgage lending without requiring government appropriations or the direct lending of the government's own funds. By removing the mortgage agencies from the government budget, the amount of their lending and their flexibility were enhanced. Agencies included in the budget are subject to constraints when the government deficit is of concern. Such periods often coincide with the greatest shortage of mortgage funds. As a result, this has often caused agencies in the budget to operate in a way that makes the housing cycle worse. They have lent less when they should have been lending more.

To counteract this tendency, the sponsored agencies were removed from the budget and were made semi-independent. They raise their capital from private investors and lenders. Furthermore, the government disclaims ultimate responsibility for their debt. In theory, they are on their own and are not part of the government.

The Sponsored Agencies and the Government's Implied Commitment   Despite the semi-independence of the sponsored agencies, the market clearly believes that the government has a very strong implied commitment to step in and pay off the debt if necessary. In most crisis situations, the sponsored agencies have the right to borrow limited sums directly from the U.S. Treasury. The market assumes that the government supervises the agencies closely enough to make sure that they will be able to meet their required payments. It assumes that in time of need, the limits of their government borrowing will be increased.

Although the sponsored agencies are not legally a part of the government, their close relationship allows them to raise their funds at a lower rate than if they did not have government backing. In fact, they usually pay interest rates only slightly above those paid by the Treasury. People assume that the government will back them. However, there have been periods when agencies' losses became excessive and the spread between their bonds and those of the government widened from 10 or 15 to over 150 basis points. The sponsored agencies also have certain tax advantages. For example, some interest payments are not taxed by states. Furthermore, they can operate with less capital and assume greater risks than if they were purely private organizations.

In the debate over President Reagan's suggestions either to increase the fees or to privatize the sponsored agencies, builders and real estate lobbies have argued that such moves would lower the efficiency of very valuable agencies. They claim that the financial risks in the secondary market are too large and uncertain to have them assumed by private industry. They point to the failures of private insurance of savings and loans, to limits on the amount of private mortgage insurance, and to runs on deposit institutions. The government can avoid runs and panics because it cannot go bankrupt. As a result, many financial operations can be profitable for the government even though they are beyond the scope of private firms. The other arguments on both sides are similar to those over national housing policy in general.

THE TRADITIONAL GOVERNMENT AGENCIES

The Department of Housing and Urban Development was established in 1965 to recognize the importance of programs in the urban sphere, which had developed at a rapid pace after 1932. The department administers the numerous programs described in the appendix to this chapter, and it also includes the GNMA and the FHA.

The Government National Mortgage Association

The **Government National Mortgage Association (GNMA),** called **"Ginnie Mae,"** was created in 1968 when the FNMA moved out of the government to become a sponsored agency. The GNMA is part of HUD; its operations are included in the HUD budget and its personnel are regular government employees.

The GNMA performs three major functions:

1. It guarantees mortgage-backed securities, its principal activity. These operations are covered in Chapter 8.
2. It manages a portfolio of federally owned mortgages. At times, the government has made direct mortgage loans or has acquired mortgages from other lenders. These have been turned over to the GNMA. It has sold

some of them and receives payments against the outstanding balance on the others. This is a minor operation and has been declining steadily.

3.   Its special assistance function provides support for housing for which financing is not readily available, particularly housing for low-income families. At times, the GNMA's activities in this sphere have been extremely important. However, they declined sharply in the face of the Reagan administration's opposition to subsidized housing programs and the large federal budget deficit.

Lenders have often been unwilling to buy high-risk mortgages—especially on multifamily projects—even if they are insured by the FHA. Many of these projects have amortization periods of up to 40 years, with great interest rate risks. These programs would fail unless the government supplied a market. Through its special assistance function, Ginnie Mae purchases loans that appear uneconomic to the private market. In the 1980s, most of these have been projects built with Section 8 guaranteed contracts.

In earlier periods, the GNMA **tandem plan** directly subsidized borrowers by buying at par mortgages which carried below-market interest rates. For low-income families, Congress authorized special mortgage programs with interest rates well below the market. No private lenders would provide funds at these rates, since they could earn more elsehwere. The GNMA agreed to buy the loans at 100 cents on the dollar. If the GNMA then sold them in the market, it would absorb a loss equal to the difference between market interest rates and the bargains given the low-income families. On mortgages it held, its losses each year equaled the difference between the rate collected and the interest the government paid on the amount borrowed for Ginnie Mae to purchase the mortgages. Both types of losses are paid for by funds appropriated in the budget.

Farmers Home Administration

Much of the lending on rural houses is done through the **Farmers Home Administration (FmHA),** part of the Department of Agriculture. To qualify for a loan or a subsidy from FmHA, a homeowner must buy a farm or choose a house in a rural political subdivision of less than 10,000 population. Additionally, he or she must have been rejected for regular financing by a bank or other mortgage lending institution. This is one of the least known government programs. However, in the mid-1980s its yearly expenditures exceeded $2 billion and made up between 15 percent and 20 percent of total government direct housing assistance.

The FmHA makes loans for housing, farms, and many other rural programs. Some loans used appropriated funds; others depend on government guarantees or assistance contracts. Loans have been made and serviced by local offices operating in most rural counties. However, these programs have also been prime targets for those who desire to cut government deficits. As a result, their functioning has varied greatly over time.

The terms of these loans and the amounts of subsidies available change with congressional action. Loans have been as high as 100 percent of appraised value. The amount of subsidy has depended on the level of market interest rates, a family's estimated needs, and the availability of government funds. As in the urban programs, the agencies' costs come either from paying higher interest rates than are collected from the subsidized borrowers or from making direct payments to reduce the interest charges of lenders. The expenditures are funded by government appropriations.

THE FEDERAL HOME LOAN BANK SYSTEM

The **Federal Home Loan Bank System (FHLB System)** was founded under President Herbert Hoover. It is a mixture of an independent federal agency—the Federal Home Loan Bank Board (FHLBB)—and a group of still more independent sponsored agencies. In case of need, Congress and the administration would have to pass new legislation giving the other parts of the system special aid through direct appropriations or guarantees.

The other members of the Federal Home Loan Bank System include the 12 regional Federal Home Loan Banks (FHL Banks), the Federal Savings and Loan Insurance Corporatoin (FSLIC), and the Federal Home Loan Mortgage Corporation (FHLMC, or "Freddie Mac"). In addition, the system encompasses private savings and loan associations and savings banks that take out membership.

The three members of the FHLBB are appointed by the president of the United States with the advice and consent of the Senate. They also serve as directors of the FSLIC and the FHLMC. The 12 regional FHL Banks are quasi-governmental agencies. Their stock is owned by their member savings and loans, which elect a majority of their directors. Their presidents are elected by the individual bank directors with the consent of the FHLBB. Each of these presidents has certain responsibilities to his or her members and directors. However, each is expected always to keep the public interest paramount.

Advances

The FHLB System's regulatory and deposit insurance functions are the lifeblood of the thrift institutions. In addition, however, the FHLB System is also a major source of funds for its member associations. The FHL Banks borrow in the money and bond markets on consolidated notes and bonds. They lend these funds to associations to meet unexpected withdrawal demands, to provide seasonal liquidity, and to cushion the shock of a slowdown in deposits in periods of disintermediation. These loans from the banks to the associations are called **Federal Home Loan Bank advances.**

Availability of short-term loans is important when a local crisis creates a sudden need for funds by a member institution. Since most assets are in hard-to-liquidate mortgages, availability of another source of money gives institutions time to accumulate cash through their normal flow of funds and through sales of mortgages. The ability to obtain the advances allows them to tie up fewer assets in cash or short-term bills.

The loans also serve as a long-term base of funds. They increase the money available to the home mortgage market. This is particularly true for localities where the need for credit outruns local savings. In a typical year, half or more of the member associations borrow from the FHL Banks. The outstanding advances totaled over $90 billion in 1986.

The funds to lend come from three sources: (1) Member associations are required to buy capital stock in the banks. (2) The FHL Banks accept deposits from their members. (3) Most important, the banks issue consolidated obligations of bonds, notes, or certificates in the general money market. These instruments are secured by the capital of the banks, the notes of their members, and mortgages. This technique allows the FHLB System to attract money into mortgages from sources that could not or would not buy mortgages directly. A bank or insurance company buys these notes in competition with other bonds, even if its own mortgage portfolio is filled. The total money in the mortgage market expands.

Attracting additional funds has been a significant accomplishment of the system. It also serves to widen the geographic distribution of mortgage money. Most of the FHL Banks' borrowing takes place in areas with ample money supplies, while advances go mainly to shortage areas. The improved liquidity for emergencies is also a major advantage. This means that member associations can hold more mortgages than would otherwise be possible.

THE FEDERAL LAND BANKS

The **Federal Land Banks** were established by the Federal Farm Loan Act of 1916. They are part of the overall Farm Credit System. Their structure and operations are similar to those of the Federal Home Loan Banks, but they are more complex because their lending membership is more varied. These banks account for a majority of all farm mortgage lending.

The mortgage loans of the Farm Credit System can be made on farms, ranches, rural houses, and farm-related businesses through a widespread network of local Federal Land Bank associations. Borrowers must become members of their local land bank association through the purchase of stock equal to 5 percent of their loan. When a loan is repaid, the stock can be sold back to the association.

Funds for the mortgages are raised in the market by sale of consolidated issues of the 12 Federal Land Banks. As with other federally sponsored agencies, the securities sell at a favorable rate. The actual interest rate charged to borrowers on mortgages varies with the total cost of money to the Federal Land Banks. They have greatly increased the availability of credit in rural areas. Their rates are lower and their terms more liberal than those of other lenders. When borrowers fall behind, payments are often rescheduled rather than the loan being foreclosed.

The farm depression of 1985 and the sharp drop in farmland values led to the insolvency of some parts of the system because so many loans went bad. The system as a whole came under sharp criticism for poor management and for having helped fuel speculation and overoptimism that carried land prices up too fast and too far.

Although some critics suggested that the Farm Credit System should not be granted special federal aid, Congress and the Reagan administration decided that the cost to the economy of such a policy would be too great. They concluded that a better approach would be to restructure the system in order to improve its management, to force it to pool its reserves, and then to underwrite future potential losses with a guarantee of appropriated funds. The government would make good on its implied promises to those who had lent to this and to the other sponsored agencies. When faced with the need to decide whether to let a sponsored agency falter, the decision was made to grant it full government backing.

THE FEDERAL NATIONAL MORTGAGE ASSOCIATION

The largest, and in some ways the most interesting, of the federally sponsored credit agencies is the **Federal National Mortgage Association (FNMA),** commonly known as **"Fannie Mae."** It was established by Congress in 1938 to set an example for private lenders as to how to operate in the secondary mortgage market. It has been reorganized several times. Since 1968, when it was moved out of the government budget and became a sponsored agency, it has become one of the country's largest financial intermediaries, with assets of over $100 billion.

The FNMA has performed five major services:

1. It has established procedures to demonstrate that mortgages can be successfully bought and sold in the secondary market.
2. It has acted to provide needed liquidity to the market at critical times.
3. It has established a successful market for future commitments when other lenders have been out of the market.
4. It has increased the total flow of money to the mortgage market by issuing its own notes and bonds to attract new funds.
5. It issues mortgage-backed bonds.

The Organization of the FNMA

The FNMA is a federally sponsored agency. Its common stock and other securities are owned by private individuals and organizations. It has a fifteen-member board of directors, five of whom are appointed by the federal government and ten elected by the stockholders. Its common stock, which is bought and sold on the New York Stock Exchange, has been subject to sharp speculative rises and falls.

While Fannie Mae's management is similar to that of other private corporations, the election of its president is subject to approval by the president of the United States, who may also remove him or her. In its operations, the management must walk a fine line between its responsibilities to the American public—because of its special charter, special borrowing, and tax advantages—and its responsibility to its private owners. This dual responsibility has led to several disagreements with the secretary of the Department of Housing and Urban Development, who retains nominal regulatory powers and must see that Fannie Mae fulfills its public responsibilities.

Fannie Mae got into trouble in the early 1980s because it had not properly balanced its portfolio. Its mortgage loans had a longer average maturity than the securities on which it borrowed. When interest rates rose, it had to pay more for its current borrowing than it was receiving on its loans (as did savings and loans). As a result, it began to lose money. When short-term interest rates receded from their peak, it was saved from deeper troubles. The association was also helped when it issued mortgage-backed securities based on swaps of its debt for mortgages of equal maturity, as well as by other fee operations.

THE FEDERAL HOME LOAN MORTGAGE CORPORATION

The Emergency Home Finance Act of 1970 authorized the establishment of the **Federal Home Loan Mortgage Corporation (FHLMC), or "Freddie Mac."** The savings and loan industry wanted an agency competitive with Fannie Mae, which they felt was dominated by builders and mortgage bankers. Furthermore, they wanted a secondary market established for conventional mortgages equivalent to that maintained for FHA and VA mortgages by Fannie Mae. At that time, the FNMA acted as a secondary market only for government-issued or government-guaranteed loans. The act establishing the FHLMC authorized the FNMA to deal in conventional loans also.

As noted previously, the three members of the FHL Bank Board are the directors of the FHLMC. Capital comes from the Federal Home Loan Banks. The corporation engages in a wide variety of secondary market operations. It buys and sells mortgages and, in addition, will *participate* (buy part of a mortgage) with member savings and loans.

The basic operations of Freddie Mac are similar to those of Fannie Mae. However, it has put greater emphasis on the issuing of mortgage-backed securities, keeping only an insignificant number of mortgages in its own portfolio. Its outstanding holdings of mortgages in 1986 were over $100 billion.

FANNIE MAE AND FREDDIE MAC IN THE SECONDARY MARKET

The FNMA and the FHLMC operate in a niche between private lenders and borrowers. They package individual mortgages into a form the market wants. Their size, skills, and government sponsorship bring many investors into the mortgage market who would not think of buying individual mortgages. Together they have been the largest source of mortgage funds. In the extremely tight money year of 1982, when their operations made a peak impact, they accounted for more than 60 percent of total loans on one- to four-family houses. Ginnie Mae mortgage pools accounted for another 20 percent in that year.

Operations

Fannie Mae and Freddie Mac buy loans from mortgage companies, banks, savings and loans, and other approved lenders. Freddie Mac also accepts participations from savings and loans. Most of Fannie Mae's business is with mortgage companies, while Freddie Mac deals mainly with thrifts. The lenders continue to service the loans, remitting the payments they receive in bulk to the agencies.

Through their regulations, the two together have exerted an overwhelming influence on the types of loans made. They have standardized mortgage instruments, appraisals, and most documentation. Their criteria for qualifying borrowers and properties establish market norms. Their requirement that mortgages submitted to them with down payments of less than 20 percent be insured led to a major expansion of private mortgage insurance. The current listings of mortgage interest charges in any locality reveal a major jump for loans exceeding the maximum amount the agencies are authorized to buy or guarantee ($133,250 in 1986).

These sponsored agencies hold mortgages in their own portfolios, but they also issue mortgage-backed securities that they guarantee. The servicers collect monthly mortgage payments and remit to the agencies, who in turn pay the investors.

Commitments

One of the key functions and sources of income of these agencies is the issuance of commitments to buy mortgages for fixed periods. A **commitment** is a pledge to purchase or make a loan if qualified loans are presented. They will make commitments with firm prices for from 30 days to 6 months or more in the future. The commitments may either be priced at current market interest rates or they may be open, the rate determined by prevailing market rates at the time of delivery. In some cases, the purchaser of the commitment agrees to a mandatory delivery of a qualified loan within the specified period; in other cases delivery may be voluntary. The fees charged depend on the length of a commitment and whether or not it is mandatory. Left to themselves, lenders would always deliver if interest rates rise (and prices fall), and they would sell elsewhere at a price better than that of the commitment if interest rates fall (and prices rise).

The availability of commitments removes many risks from lenders and from their builder-customers. Firm take-outs are usually necessary to obtain interim financing. With fixed rates, lenders can work out their own hedging strategies. The size and skills of the agencies enable them to obtain or create the options needed to protect against losses on the commitments. The amount they are charged tends to be lower than that available to most lenders from other sources.

Sources of Funds

The FNMA and the FHLMC have many available sources of funds. Fannie Mae has kept a large volume ($100 billion) of mortgages in its own portfolio and earns income on them. It has raised money by selling short-term notes of from 30 to 360 days and by issuing long-term bonds. It also requires lenders who sell to it to buy some of its stock. In recent years, it has also sold mortgage-backed securities as well as guaranteed some sold by lenders. Freddie Mac's capital comes from the Home Loan Banks; otherwise, it uses the same sources of funds. However, its portfolio (over $13 billion) is small compared to the mortgage-backed securities it has issued or to Fannie Mae's portfolio.

Swaps

Between 1982 and 1985, lenders swapped over $100 billion of mortgages with the FNMA and the FHLMC. In a **swap**, lenders transfer mortgages to the agency, which pays for them with mortgage-backed securities. The rate on these securities approximates those on the underlying mortgages, since both are transferred at par. At one time a lender might swap a pool of 8 percent mortgages and receive a 7.5 percent Fannie Mae *pass-through* security, while simultaneously swapping another pool of 12.5 percent mortgages for 12 percent pass-throughs. Both securities would show up as having the same principal value on the lender's books even though the 12 percent pass-throughs would be worth far more in the market. *Pass-throughs*, discussed in Chapter 8, are securities backed by mortgages whose monthly payments depend on the interest and repayments made on the mortgages in the pool that collateralizes them. The actual payments and the maturities of the pass-throughs vary depending upon the action of the mortgage borrowers, in contrast to bonds, which usually have a fixed schedule of payments.

Why should lenders swap in this way? The answer is that they gain liquidity: their balance sheets show government agency securities rather than mortgages. In addition, if they need cash, they can obtain it immediately, since securities can be sold more quickly and cheaply than can mortgages.

Such transactions have been abetted by creative accounting. Many swapped mortgages carried interest rates far below the market. If the mortgages had been sold, the lender would have had to report large losses. Instead, the lenders were allowed to show the agency securities at the same price as the mortgages for which they traded. Even though the Fannie Mae securities might be worth only 70 cents on the dollar, for example, they could be carried on the books at a full dollar. No loss had to be shown unless they were sold. Lenders gained liquidity and improved their balance sheets without having to show a loss. Both the accounting profession and the regulators accepted the fiction that their capital was not impaired.

THE FUTURE OF THE SPONSORED AGENCIES

In the mid-1980s, the sponsored agencies came under attack from several directions. The poor experience of Fannie Mae and large losses suffered by parts of the Farm Credit Administration raised questions as to the extent of the federal commmitment to the safety of the sponsored agencies' borrowings. Simultaneously it was asked whether it made sense, if the implied federal guarantee was unlimited, to allow the agencies to operate without firm government controls.

Furthermore, the Reagan administration wanted to curtail the agencies' operations for other reasons. It believed that they were competing with the U.S. Treasury for funds. This raised the total cost of government borrowing. The situation was exacerbated by huge deficits and the need for the Treasury to be constantly in the money market. Also, for philosophical reasons the administration desired to avoid all competition with the private market. It felt that the sponsored agencies were a form of unfair competition. Therefore, it urged Congress to require the agencies to pay fees to the Treasury as a way of offsetting their advantages.

This effort to change policy seemed nonsensical to those concerned with housing finance. The agencies had been established because the private market had failed to maintain an even flow of housing credit at reasonable rates. Did it make sense to penalize the agencies for performing well the functions for which they had been established? Because both sides felt strongly, this debate over the functions of the sponsored agencies will continue.

TAX EXPENDITURES

In the debate over tax reform, tax expenditures for housing became a central issue. Total expenditures in this sphere were over $48 billion in 1985. There are several justifications for extending benefits:

■ They help families to own and live in better homes.
■ They increase the amount of good rental housing available for moderate- and low-income families.
■ They increase the amount of building in the economy.
■ Some of the special housing benefits are aimed specifically at first-time buyers who otherwise could not afford to buy.

The arguments against the benefits originate primarily with those who believe that they are inefficient and that the least needy benefit the most. The amount of lost revenue is high compared to housing benefits that could be purchased for similar amounts through other programs. However, the right to deduct interest for mortgage payments has enjoyed such tremendous political support that almost all tax-reform proposals avoid tackling it.

There has been less reluctance, however, to attack the other tax expenditures. For example, President Reagans's tax-reform proposals in 1985 called for ending the deduction of state and local property taxes, which accounted for over $10 billion of tax expenditures; for abolishing most tax subsidies to lending institutions; for ending the use of tax-exempt bonds for housing finance; and for phasing out accelerated depreciation of rental properties. Congress was unwilling to approve many of the suggestions, preferring other types of actions.

Deductions from Taxable Income

The right of homeowners to deduct mortgage interest payments and property taxes from their gross taxable income is called a tax expenditure or subsidy because homeowners reduce the taxes they pay by the amount of the deduction times their marginal tax bracket.

EXAMPLE: Consider a family that rented a house for $8,000 a year in 1985 and had $30,000 in taxable income after all deductions. Their federal income tax would have been $4,706. What if, instead, the family had bought the house for $80,000, with interest and property tax payments of $8,000? Because this amount could be deducted from their net taxable income, that income would have been reported to the IRS as $22,000 rather than $30,000, and they would have had to pay only $2,814 in taxes. Through this tax expenditure, the government would have helped lower their housing costs by $1,892 to assist them in becoming homeowners rather than renters.

Some observers have claimed—incorrectly—that the deductibility of mortgage interest and property taxes on owner-occupied houses is not a special tax expenditure because these items are deductible in any business. This argument fails to recognize that the income from ownership of business-related property must be reported and the deductions are legitimate expenses of creating the income. Thus, a landlord receiving $8,000 in rent would report it as income, and the deduction of interest and taxes would merely reduce his reported taxable income. (A tax expenditure would arise only if the deductions were excessive.) In contrast, homeowners do not have to report the value of the housing services or rental equivalences they receive as income, and thus they are able to subtract the housing expenses from an income already reduced below its real value. (In some countries, imputed rent from ownership must be included in taxable income.)

This type of subsidy has been criticized because the more expensive the house and the higher one's income, the greater is the amount of the government's tax expenditure. As a second example, assume that another family bought a $200,000 house with deductions of $20,000 for interest and taxes, and that their marginal tax bracket was 30 percent. Their tax saving would be $6,000 a year, in contrast to the $1,892 saved by the family with the more modest house and income.

The effect of lowering tax rates and of cutting the differences among brackets is both to decrease the amount of taxes each family saves and to narrow the differences in the tax subsidy. Increasing the standard deduction has also reduced the amount of tax preferences, since fewer families find it worthwhile to itemize deductions.

Other Tax Expenditures

Another major tax expenditure delays the time at which taxes must be paid and may reduce them to zero. Homeowners can defer taxes upon gains made when selling a house if they reinvest the amount they receive from selling their principal residence within two years before or after purchasing another principal residence for as large a sum. Owners over 55 years of age can exclude up to $125,000 of capital gains upon the sale of their house. These two privileges cost over $3 billion a year in tax expenditure.

Owners of income properties can reduce their personal income taxes because they are allowed to deduct depreciation allowances from income at a rate that exceeds real economic depreciation. Chapter 16 explains how this privilege reduces taxes. The time value of money means that a tax not paid today—even if paid in the future—lowers the cost of the tax.

New multifamily apartment houses have received further tax preference subsidies by accelerating the rate of depreciation. At times special tax benefits as well as subsidies have been made available for apartments that contain units for low-income families or for units made available through the rehabilitation of existing structures. Units under these special programs have made up a sizable proportion of all additions to the nation's stock of rental units. When President Reagan in 1985 proposed doing away with this preference, builders claimed that rents for new low-rent units would rise by 38 percent to 45 percent.*

STATE AND LOCAL AGENCIES FOR HOUSING FINANCE

Another important tax expenditure is the ability to use tax-exempt bonds for housing finance. This program has led to one of the least known but the fifth largest source of mortgage funds. State and local agencies held over $70 billion in mortgages in 1986. Although this is a large amount of money, these agencies have remained out of sight of almost all except those employed in the industries or who have obtained a mortgage from them. Despite their low profile, they have been crucial sources of money to those engaged in developing moderate- or low-cost properties. They are also important to first-time home

---

*For a complete explanation of this benefit and conflicting claims, see A. R. Cerf, "Low Income Housing and Tax Reform: A Potential Crisis," Center for Real Estate and Urban Economics, University of California, Berkeley, Working Paper 85–103 (November 1985).

buyers and to those concerned with obtaining more housing for lower-income groups. Their appeal to these parties has been demonstrated by the battles faced by the Reagan administration in its efforts to abolish this type of financing.

Organization

The key concept behind **state and local housing finance agencies** has been their ability to issue bonds exempt from federal income taxation. They use tax-exempt bonds to raise funds at a reduced rate. The lower cost of these funds can then be passed through to the mortgage borrower. Normally, tax-exempt bonds (called **municipal bonds**) have interest rates that are only 70 to 80 percent of the interest on equivalent taxable bonds. If mortgage interest rates are 12 percent, these agencies can cover their cost and issue mortgages at a rate about 2 percent (200 basis points) below that of the private market.

These savings to the borrower are indirectly subsidized by the federal government. Because they gain in after-tax income, buyers of tax-exempt bonds accept lower interest rates. They do not have to pay federal income tax on the interest received from the state and local agencies. In 1983 and 1984, tax-exempt bonds issued for housing subsidy purposes made up between 35 and 40 percent of all tax-exempt issues. Because of this loss in revenue, federal administrations have attacked these subsidies as unwarranted.

The structure of the state and local agencies is complex. Because Congress has placed limits on the amount of bonds that can be issued in each state, all but one state have established housing agencies in order to ration the state's total funds going to its localities. Many state housing agencies operate directly in the loan market because they enjoy economies of scale and marketing.

In addition, many localities issue their own bonds, often backed by banks' letters of credit. These bonds may be sold by local governments, local housing agencies, or private firms under special arrangements that confer the tax-exempt features on them. In most cases, the bonds are backed by mortgages, but some may be general obligations of a state or locality.

Operations

The variety of agencies has produced many different programs. Most can be classified into four groups:

1. funding of single-family ownership through mortgage revenue bonds
2. subsidies for construction or rehabilitation of multifamily units, frequently using industrial development bonds
3. bonds for veterans' programs
4. bonds for low-rent public housing

After 1980, federal laws restricted the use of loans funded by tax-exempt mortgage revenue bonds. On the whole, loans were limited to first-time buyers of modestly priced houses (those priced below 110 percent of the average cost of new units in the area). In addition, most agencies placed restrictions on the maximum income borrowers may have; such as the restriction that loans may be made only to those with incomes in the lowest 40 percent of the families in the local area.

Programs

The Council of State Housing Associations and home builders' associations claim that these programs have been of special importance to first-time home buyers. They estimated that in 1984, first-time buyers purchased between 35 and 40 percent of all houses sold. Of the 1.5 million or so first-time buyers, about 1 million had incomes moderate enough for them to qualify for these programs. Of those who could qualify, about one-fourth, or 250,000, actually obtained mortgages at reduced rates from these agencies.

Rental Units In the multifamily sphere, funds have been raised through tax-exempt state and local industrial development bonds. The developments meet all market criteria. However, the mortgage on the entire building carries a subsidized rate. In these cases, the subsidized financing also often results in a saving of 200 basis points on the whole mortgage. Typical regulations require that 20 percent of the units be rented at below-market rates to families meeting moderate income limitations. However, the borrower may charge market rents for the remaining 80 percent of the units. In theory, the entire subsidy then goes to the 20 percent of the units to be occupied by moderate- and low-income families, whose rents should be well below the market.

Veterans' Programs State programs for veterans have existed for many years. They are a type of bonus awarded for service during periods of war. In the mortgage sphere, they work much like the single-family tax-subsidized program. However, eligibility is based on status as a war veteran rather than on income. When the funds are raised through general obligation bonds of a state, the bonds sell at lower rates than mortgage revenue bonds. Eligible veterans thus realize savings from two sources: the basic one through tax-exempt financing, and the use of the credit of the state, which is often rated AA or AAA.

Objections to Tax-exempt Bond Programs

Attacks on state programs of these types have been of two main kinds. Those who believe that all special subsidies are bad feel that these programs should never have been started. Others hold that the use of tax-exempt bonds creates added inefficiencies—the amount of tax saving to the buyers of the bonds is greater than the benefits received by the borrowers. In other words, the government does not get what it is paying for.

Those who support the programs argue that low-income and first-time home buyers need subsidies to improve their housing. While these programs may not be entirely efficient, they are in place and working. Until a better solution to the low-income housing problem is found, they should be retained.

The laws and regulations for use of mortgage revenue and industrial development bonds have been tightened several times. Controls over the use of the funds from the bonds were made more specific. Most of the authority to issue tax-exempt bonds expired in December 1983. However, it was then reenacted for another four years. Because they have remained under strong criticism, the bonds may again be phased out or changed drastically in 1987.

SUMMARY

The United States and most other nations have adopted a wide range of housing policies. Their aim is to insure every household a decent dwelling at a cost they can afford. These policies are justified by the argument that the free market cannot solve housing problems by itself. The poor cannot pay market rents. Slums are recognized to be harmful, but no private firm can afford to undertake clearing them up. Credit cycles cause production to fluctuate and reduce construction efficiency. Most families have trouble accumulating all the capital buying a house requires.

Housing policies try to deal with these problems by assisting families to rent or buy adequate shelter, by allowing easier access to affordable credit, and by lowering interest rates through greater market efficiency. Some critics argue that the failures of the free market are not as severe as pictured and its advantages are far greater. They claim that most housing policies lower efficiency because they interfere with normal market operations.

In 1985, housing policies cost about $63.2 billion, or about 5 percent of total federal expenditures. Most money went for tax expenditures (which, some argue, are not real costs). Other amounts went primarily to subsidize the rents of lower-income families. Depending on how duplications are eliminated, the government insured, guaranteed, or lent on mortgages between $125 and $225 billion a year and had outstanding commitments of between $450 and $800 billion.

The different types of real estate finance programs are spread among a wide variety of governmental agencies. Chartering, regulation, and insurance of deposit institutions are handled primarily by so-called independent agencies. Housing assistance to low- and moderate-income families and the issuance of insurance and guarantees of both mortgages and mortgage-backed securities are housed in traditional departments and agencies. Secondary market operations are mainly the responsibility of government-sponsored agencies.

Four major housing agencies are sponsored by the government. Their size and government backing permit them to borrow more cheaply and take greater risks than private firms. Each of them would be in the top size group of all

American financial institutions. Key reasons for their existence are the belief that they can increase the flow of credit into mortgages in tight money periods; that they can lower mortgage interest rates, and that they can experiment with more liberal lending than can private firms.

Tax expenditures are reductions in taxes that would be paid if the programs were not made part of the tax law. Homeowners have benefited from reduced housing costs by being able to deduct mortgage interest and property tax payments from the income on which their taxes are computed. State and local housing finance agencies borrow money on tax-exempt bonds so that they can lend it on mortgages at interest rates below the market.

KEY TERMS

commitment
externalities
Farmers Home Administration
   (FmHA)
Federal Home Loan Bank
   System (FHLB System)
Federal Home Loan Bank
   advances
Federal Home Loan Mortgage
   Corporation (FHLMC, Freddie
   Mac)
Federal Land Banks
Federal National Mortgage
   Association (FNMA, Fannie
   Mae)

Government National
   Mortgage Association
   (GNMA, Ginnie Mae)
independent agencies
municipal bonds
national housing policy
sponsored agencies
state and local housing
   finance agencies
swap
tandem plan
tax expenditures

QUESTIONS

1. Do you agree that tax expenditures are housing subsidies? Why or why not?
2. What are the basic arguments of those who object to a national housing policy?
3. Among the arguments for a national housing policy, which one do you think is the strongest? And which is the weakest?
4. What are the major roles played by the FmHA?
5. Since owning a home brings tax advantages, why do many people still rent?
6. What are the advantages and disadvantages of state and local agencies in the mortgage market?
7. What are the uses of advances from Federal Home Loan Banks?

8. What are the differences between the operations of Federal Home Loan Banks and those of the Federal Land Banks?
9. Should the federal government continue with its moral commitments to the sponsored agencies? Why or why not?

APPENDIX TO CHAPTER 7
DIRECT FEDERAL HOUSING ASSISTANCE

Government subsidies to assist in funding the housing of low-income families started in the Great Depression. Ever since, they have been the subject of constant debate and almost annual legislative changes. By 1986, these programs included over 4.2 million housing units. Most direct subsidies have been aimed at renters. Only a few programs have directly subsidized homeowners. Rather, aids to homeownership have usually been indirect, through huge tax expenditure and credit programs.

A large number of programs exist for channeling federal aid to needy families. Before examining their specifics, we look at some general issues which form the background against which these programs have developed.

Eligibility

Most direct assistance programs provide that subsidies should be available only to families whose incomes are too low to cover the rents or costs of standard housing without unduly sacrificing other consumption. When rents are too high in relation to income, the programs will subsidize a portion.

These criteria require determining what incomes should be eligible for subsidy and what the rental costs are of a standard dwelling. Many programs set a limit on the cost or rent of units that are eligible for a subsidy. Given the diversity of rental costs in this country, a fair price in one region could be completely inadequate in others. The limits contained in many programs provide that the Department of Housing and Urban Development (HUD) can raise the maximum subsidy for high-cost areas.

Consequently, many programs limit subsidies to costs or rents that do not exceed some percentage—such as 80 percent—of the median rent or housing cost in the area. In the same way, limits on maximum incomes for those eligible have shifted from a flat amount to a certain percentage of the median income in the locality. Under a percentage criterion, lower-income families may be defined as those whose incomes do not exceed 50 percent of the median income in the area.

Other problems arise in selecting which of the poor are to receive subsidies. Programs are curtailed by limited government appropriations, so that only a small percentage of those eligible are accepted for subsidizing. Those who receive assistance can be thought of as having won a lottery. A major criticism has been that only one of two similar families might receive a large subsidy—

perhaps half of the rent—while the other would receive nothing, simply as a result of luck or knowing how to manipulate the system.

The Amount and Form of the Subsidy

The government subsidizes either the dwelling's cost or a family's rent. For units to be included in a direct assistance program, their rent must fall below the maximum established for the program. The maximums are based on market rents adequate for decent, safe, sanitary units. Eligible families normally receive help to cover the difference between the market rent of a unit and the amount they can afford to pay.

How much of its own income should a family pay for housing, and how much should be subsidized? Most programs assume that a family should pay some share of its income as rent. This share may be from 20 percent to 30 percent of gross income, depending on the program. The percentage may be adjusted according to the size of the family, and similar criteria. The subsidy covers the difference between the maximum the family can afford and the estimated fair market rate.

How does this work? Suppose the median rent for a family unit in an area is $500 per month. The maximum rent for a unit to be subsidized is set at 80 percent of the median, or $400. A family must pay 30 percent of its income for rent. In this case, a family with an income of $1,000 per month could occupy a $400 apartment and still receive a subsidy. It would pay $300 a month from its own resources, while the subsidy would pay the remaining $100.

New or Existing Buildings?

Should government aid concentrate on new construction, or on major rehabilitation, or should it mainly use existing structures? Initially, most programs required new construction. The idea was that housing would improve only if the supply was enlarged. Otherwise, subsidies would merely raise rents, leaving many worse off. Furthermore, construction increases jobs and incomes.

Present-day emphasis has shifted to subsidizing existing units, on the assumption that they are cheaper. For a given total subsidy, more families can be helped in existing units. Even if these units require substantial rehabilitation, they will be cheaper than new construction. It is assumed (perhaps incorrectly) that additions to the supply of units are not needed to keep rents down.

Management and the Type of Financing

How the programs should be managed has also been a controversial issue. At first, most management responsibilities were assumed by HUD together with state and local authorities. Then emphasis shifted to nonprofit associations and the private market.

The earliest projects were financed entirely with government funds. This put too great a strain on the federal budget. All of the capital had to be appropriated and expended at the time of construction. In order to make the budget look better, programs shifted to long-term assistance contracts, under which subsidies were to be paid each year for the following 10 to 40 years.

With such contracts, local authorities could issue tax-exempt bonds and builders could get FHA-insured mortgages. In some cases, the government bought mortgages at a loss through the GNMA. Other programs did not depend on contracts, but the entire subsidy came through federal purchases of mortgages at below-market interest rates. In the latest programs, the families receive vouchers that allow the landlord to collect the rent assistance month by month.

THE MAJOR SUBSIDY PROGRAMS

The many subsidy programs can be classified into low-rent public housing, Section 8 housing, housing vouchers, and other programs. They differ primarily in their approach to the kinds of questions just discussed. For example, what form should the subsidy take? Should it be in new or existing units? Who should manage the program?

Low-Rent Public Housing

One of the earliest direct subsidy programs was the **low-rent public housing program** authorized by the United States Housing Act of 1937. Large projects built under this act are still found in most cities. Under this scheme, HUD provides technical and financial assistance to local housing authorities that plan, build, and operate public housing projects that charge below-market rent. Housing authorities can build new projects, rehabilitate existing structures, purchase units from builders, or lease units from private owners.

The dwellings are rented to low-income families at rents below the market or economic cost. The difference between the actual cost of operating the unit and the rents collected from the tenants is covered by a subsidy from the federal government, the state, or a local agency. Most of the federal subsidy consists of annual contributions made to cover the debt service on the bonds of the local authority. These bonds, which are tax-exempt, cover the necessary capital costs for the acquisition of the public housing project. Because they are based on federal contracts guaranteeing funds to repay them, the bonds carry AAA ratings. This fact, together with tax exemption, means that their interest rates are among the lowest of all.

Section 8 Housing

The **Section 8 program** is by far the largest direct assistance program, accounting for about half of all low-rent payments. It gets its name because it was authorized by Section 8, a 1974 amendment to the U.S. Housing Act of 1937.

HUD contracts with private owners, developers, or state and local housing agencies to subsidize the units of eligible families. Rents are limited to the fair market rent for an adequate unit. Tenants must pay 30 percent of their gross income in rent. The subsidy covers the difference between the rents private owners are authorized to charge and the amounts the low-income families must pay.

At first Section 8 emphasized new construction. Many projects were developed by state and local agencies. However, private developers were also active. They obtained FHA-insured mortgages based on their Section 8 contracts with HUD. In recent years, most of the contracts have covered existing units, some of which are completely rehabilitated. The program was designed to avoid a concentration of low-income families in large projects, as had happened with public housing, and it has succeeded to some extent.

Housing Vouchers

The Reagan administration sought to cut back the low-rent programs and to make sure that any additional assistance programs took the form of allowances through **housing vouchers**. This concept, developed in the 1930s, had been used experimentally during the 1970s. Under this program, housing allowances are made available directly to low-income families to use to cover part of the rent in any decent, safe, and sanitary unit. A family who qualifies for housing assistance is granted a voucher through its local housing authority. The government agrees to make up the difference between a fixed percentage (such as 30 percent) of the family's income and the general rental level of standard houses in the locality.

Other Programs

Many other programs exist or have been tried. Their administration is the major function of HUD. Among the largest and politically most popular have been direct loans for the elderly or handicapped under Section 202 of the Housing Act of 1959. Nonprofit sponsors may get large loans at the federal government's borrowing rate for long terms (from 30 to 50 years). Eligible households must be at least 62 years old or handicapped. Through Section 8 there can be contracts with the sponsor for up to 100 percent of the units.

The federal government has granted subsidies for community development and redevelopment that can be used as the recipient local government sees fit. However, about a third of the subsidies have been spent for major rehabilitation of rental units, increasing the local supply of decent, low-rent housing.

Many programs have used special FHA insurance to obtain lower interest rates than those available in the market because the FHA assumes most of the lender's risks. Some programs secure financing with below-market rates because the GNMA buys the mortgages at a loss. The number and types of eligible families vary with each of these programs. In some with mortgages insured by FHA but at market rates, no income restrictions apply. Their purpose is to increase the stock of rental housing.

As Chapter 16 explains, the Tax Reform Act of 1986 includes special tax credits for the construction and rehabilitation of low-income housing.

SUMMARY

The appendix to Chapter 7 describes the operations and some of the issues concerning programs that give direct assistance to households with incomes too low to meet the minimum rents on a standard housing unit. Households are required to pay some percentage of their income (such as 30 percent) as rent. The government pays the difference to bring their total payments up to the minimum rent level. Many methods have been used for these payments. Currently, the main ones are Section 8 contracts, with private landlords guaranteed assistance payments, and housing vouchers which recipients can use for any standard unit they find.

KEY TERMS

low-rent public housing program
Section 8 program
housing vouchers

QUESTIONS

1. What are the problems associated with determining the eligibility of families receiving housing subsidy? Can you suggest some solutions?
2. Suppose the government provides subsidies that are either inversely proportional to each family's income or directly proportional to the building's price. What do you think the impacts will be in each case?

8 The Secondary Market and the Securitization of Mortgages

OBJECTIVES

When you finish this chapter, you should be able to:

- explain what the secondary mortage market is, why it has grown, and how it operates.

- discuss the principal characteristics of mortgage banking.

- describe the main features of FHA mortgage insurance.

- know how the major programs of the FHA work and differ.

- recognize the differences between the FHA and VA programs.

- contrast private mortgage insurance with the government programs.

- list the main features of mortgage-backed securities.

- discuss the significance of the growth of mortgage-backed securities for the interrelationship between the mortgage and capital markets.

TWO OF THE MOST DYNAMIC innovations in mortgage lending have been the growth of the secondary mortgage market and the related transformation of mortgages into instruments similar to traditional corporate bonds. Changes are continuing at a rapid pace. The growth of mortgage-backed securities has hastened the integration of mortgages into the overall capital markets. It has increased the liquidity and marketability of mortgages and has opened up large additional sources of capital. The integration of mortgage lending into the major national financial markets has reduced local variations in rates and availability. The mortgage market reacts more rapidly to general credit conditions now than when it consisted of small isolated submarkets.

Much of the expansion has been based on government programs. Modern mortage insurance was developed by the Federal Housing Administration (FHA), which, along with the Veterans Administration (VA), dominated the field until the 1970s. In recent years, however, the volume of insurance written by private morgage insurers (PMIs) has exceeded that of the government agencies.

The mortgage-backed security market developed out of the guarantees issued by the Government National Mortgage Association (GNMA) or "Ginnie Mae," the Federal National Mortgage Association (FNMA), or "Fannie Mae," and the Federal Home Loan Mortgage Corporation (FHLMC), or "Freddie Mac." These government agencies have continued to hold sway over the field. Among the more controversial issues raised by President Ronald Reagan's administration was whether the insurance and guarantee programs were proper governmental functions or whether they ought to be performed by entirely private firms.

This chapter shows how the secondary market functions and the services it performs. It describes mortgage banking activities and outlines the way in which mortgage insurance and mortgage-backed securities operate. Since on average the number of mortgages sold in the secondary market or used as collateral for securities equals two-thirds or more of those originated in a year, the importance of these activities in real estate finance is obvious.

FUNCTIONS OF THE SECONDARY MARKET

In the primary mortgage market, lenders receive applications and process loans through closing. Then they either hold the mortgages for their own account or sell them. The secondary market is where these existing mortgages are bought and sold. Even before making loans, originators may receive secondary-market commitments to purchase the loans at agreed-upon rates.

There are two common types of operations in the secondary market:

1. Loans may be sold on an individual basis by a mortgage originator to other investors, who then hold the debts in their own portfolios. The sales

may be of single mortgages, as is true for most income property, or more often in batches, as with home mortgages. In some cases only part of each loan is sold. This is done through the sale of **participations.** The original owners sell a portion of each instrument, retaining the rest for themselves. They collect and forward the other participants' shares of interest and principal payments. If defaults occur, all losses are split according to ownership shares. The concept of participation is that sharing makes the originators more careful in underwriting loans.

2. In the second type of operation, the form of the debt is transformed through securitization and the securities are sold. In the process of **securitization** or **collateralization,** the mortgage originator or a packager buys mortgages that are then placed in the custody of a trustee. A specified group or pool of mortgages held by the trustee is used as collateral for the issuance of *mortgage-backed securities* (MBSs) or **participation certificates.** Each of these securities conveys the ownership of an undivided interest in the mortgage pool. Investors are forwarded their share of the interest and principal payments collected from the mortgages in the pool. Investors are usually guaranteed full and timely payment of interest and principal by a government agency or a private insurer.

The key advantage of these securities is that they are rated and traded in the same way as bonds. Investors look to the guarantor for the security; they do not have to examine or be concerned with the creditworthiness of each borrower and the value of each mortgage.

Most of the mortgages in the secondary market carry some type of **mortgage insurance.** Mortgage insurance covers some or all of the risk to the investor arising from borrower's defaults. It reduces the need to evaluate individual loans. If the borrower defaults on the loan, the insurer pays the lender.

In most cases, when originators sell mortgages they retain the servicing function, for which they are paid a percent of the monthly payment. **Servicing** is the administration of loans. Servicers collect the payments, keep records, handle defaults, and send the secondary market participants the amounts they are owed.

Although it has a long history, the secondary market for residential loans today reflects primarily the result of government policies. It blossomed after World War II, under the aegis of the FHA insurance and the VA loan guarantee programs. It grew still faster after 1968 with the expansion of the FNMA and the GNMA. These two agencies increased their portfolio investments and initiated the development of mortgage-backed securities. While originally limited to FHA and VA loans, the government agency programs have also included privately insured conventional loans since the early 1970s.

The development of a completely private market for residential loans has proceeded at a much slower rate. There is disagreement about the cause of the slow growth between those who attribute it to unfair government competition and those who believe that the risks of losses and the instability of funds are so great that government participation is needed. The market for nonresidential mortgages has remained private. Participants in this market have been able to issue some MBSs, and they hope the market will expand.

How the Market Works

Figure 8-1 contains a simplified presentation of the functioning of the secondary mortgage market. Borrowers apply for loans to a primary or origi-nating lender, who usually services the loans as well. When a loan is approved, a borrower signs a mortgage in return for funds. Before making such loans, lenders who intend to sell them in the secondary market usually get a firm insurance commitment from the FHA, the VA, or a private mortgage insurer. Thus most of the home mortgages shown as passing through the secondary channels to the investors carry some form of insurance. In addition, originators may also get a commitment from one of the agencies or other investors to buy the mortgage when closed, either at a fixed rate or at the market.

Direct Sales   When lenders have accumulated enough loans, they enter the secondary market. In the first channel, some mortgages are sold directly to final investors. This was the basic technique used until other instruments were devel-oped in the 1970s.

Brokers or Dealers   Rather than seek a final buyer directly, many lenders use a mortgage broker or a dealer to find investors for whole loans. This is the second channel. The difference between dealers and brokers is that dealers buy and sell mortgages for their own account, and brokers merely match up pro-spective buyers and sellers, often also carrying out the paperwork.

Mortgage-backed Securities   A third channel is that of mortgage-backed securities. Lenders may originate securities based on a pool of mortgages. The key advantage of mortgage-backed securities is that buyers can make investments of any size they want and need not examine each mortgage in detail. A purchaser of individual mortgages must check to make sure that the property exists, that the note and lien are legal, that the amount of the loan is well secured, and that the borrower's credit is good. Furthermore, even if the individual mortgages are serviced elsewhere, an account must be maintained for each mortgage.

Mortgage-backed securities avoid these problems because the issuer and, usually, another agency guarantee that these tasks have been carried out prop-erly. The issuers do all the necessary accounting and remit as a whole the funds due for a pool; each security holder is forwarded his proper share. This sim-plification and the fact that the securities carry credit ratings from the national credit-rating agencies, such as Standard & Poor's, mean that the mortgages can be traded in an active market in the same way as bonds. Thus they gain desirable liquidity and sell at lower yields.

Figure 8-1
Operations in the Secondary Mortgage Market

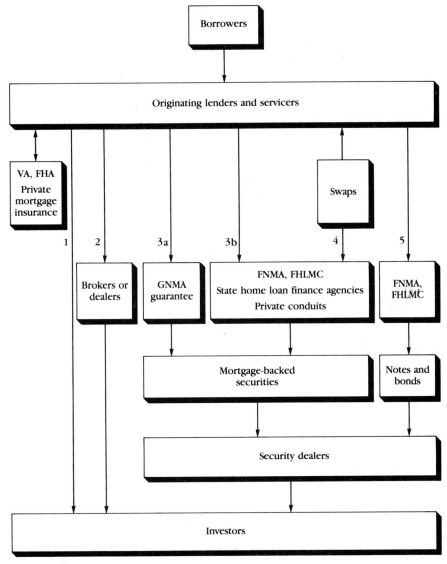

Figure 8-1 also illustrates the two main methods of issuing mortgage-backed securities. In the first (3a), the selling lender originates the securities and obtains the necessary insurance or guarantees that the payments will be met. Most of these securities carry guarantees issued by the GNMA, although state and local housing finance agencies often use bank letters of credit for their backing. Some private insurers have also been used. However, several large losses through private insurers in 1985 made the market wary of such guarantees.

The second method (3b) consists of government and private conduits. Mortgages are bought by the FNMA, the FHLMC, or private packagers. They pool their purchases and issue the mortgage-backed securities against them. The securities are backed by the general assets of the issuer in addition to the specific mortgage collateral.

In both cases, the securities are sold to dealers—usually major Wall Street investment banking firms—who sell them to a wide variety of final investors. In the first case, the issuer does the servicing and is responsible for collecting the monthly mortgage payments and passing them through to the investors. In the second case, the servicer sends the funds to the agency or conduit, which handles the paperwork for the security owners.

Although these conduits sell most of the securities to dealers and through them to final investors, an exception is *swaps,* the fourth channel. In making swaps, lenders trade their mortgages with the FNMA or the FHLMC for the agency's securities. Then the lenders can either hold the securities they receive or sell them in the market.

Purchases for Portfolio   The fifth channel is the portfolio operations of the government agencies. They buy mortgages from the lenders and hold these assets to maturity or for sale when the market improves. They finance their portfolios by selling agency notes and bonds in the traditional manner.

Figure 8-1 details the transformation of the secondary market from one in which distant investors had a few selected correspondents who sold carefully scrutinized individual loans to them, to one in which hundreds of firms issue mortgage-backed securities sold to thousands of investors on the strength of the insurance or guarantees they carry. The logic for this is simple. Many investors do not have the experience or staff to handle individual loans. They are accustomed to buying corporate and government bonds. To the degree that mortgages can be transformed into securities equivalent to bonds, these investors will buy and hold them. Mortgage-backed securities accomplish this transformation. So do the bonds and notes used to finance the portfolios of the federally sponsored agencies.

The Advantages of the Secondary Market

The secondary mortgage market grew because of a mismatch of funds in primary markets, because risks are reduced, because of instability in the flow of funds, and in order to lower mortgage interest rates.

1.   In many local markets, the demand for mortgage money far exceeds the supply. Fast-growing areas need funds; older, more established ones have surpluses. The secondary market draws funds from excess to deficit locations.

2. Portfolios made up of loans from a variety of primary lenders reduce risks. A portfolio of loans diversified in terms of localities and underwriters suffers less danger of large-scale defaults due to a local depression or lapse in credit standards. The desire for diversification means that a sizable number of loans move from one savings and loan or bank to others, as well as to other types of institutions.

3. Some major lenders, such as insurance companies, pension funds, and the government agencies, do not have local offices. They prefer to buy loans originated and serviced by local institutions.

4. The government promoted the secondary market as a method of combatting the credit cycle and housing depressions. The FHA was established to help get the country out of the Great Depression. By tapping funds not directly available for real estate and by borrowing in the capital market, the FHA and housing agencies help to keep mortgage funds flowing when other lenders cut back.

5. The programs also aimed at reducing and standardizing mortgage interest rates. Some higher rates were caused by geographic imbalances. For example, borrowers in the growing West paid considerably higher rates than New Englanders, where an excess of funds existed. The secondary market narrowed the gap between the rates. In addition, the margins between the interest rates for mortgages and those for corporate bonds narrowed. The program reduced risks, improved lending standards, and raised efficiency. The government agencies were large and diversified, could spend funds on research, and could provide lenders with a safer investment. They were able to standardize mortgage flows, instruments, and lending techniques.

6. The secondary market also reduces costs of handling and holding mortgages because marketability and liquidity are enhanced. Prior to the FHA, every mortgage sold on the secondary market had to be handled individually. The lender had to check both the property and the individual buyer. Insured loans and mortgage-backed securities eliminate this need. Standardized loans and securities have led to an active market: (a) Lenders can obtain cash almost instantaneously. (b) Loans are handled in large batches with considerable efficiency. (c) Lending institutions can obtain any amount of loans they desire. Although they would not buy mortgages if they had to set up a major program to handle individual loans, they are willing to hold mortgage-backed securities.

New Sources of Capital

In addition to lowering mortgage costs and improving the efficiency of the market, the growth of the secondary market brought in large new sources of capital. Initially, in the 1940s and 1950s, the FHA and VA programs allowed eastern savings banks and insurance companies that had excess funds to invest them in the growing West and South, where funds were short. Their return was higher than they could obtain elsewhere, and borrowers paid less.

The growth of mortgage-backed securities has brought other new sources of capital into the market. Pension and mutual funds as well as individuals buy mortgage-backed securities in competition with stock and bonds. Because investors have a free choice about where to put their money, the rate on mortgages must be completely competitive with other market rates; otherwise, they will invest elsewhere. This inherent need to be competitive has been a major factor in the integration of the mortgage with other credit markets.

MORTGAGE BANKING COMPANIES

Mortgage banks are vital players in the secondary market. Also known as mortgage companies, these firms are not banks, since they do not accept deposits. Their mortgage portfolios are not large, since they hold few mortgages as permanent investments. Rather, their assets consist primarily of mortgages held temporarily until enough can be accumulated to sell in the secondary market. Mortgage companies operate under general corporation laws. They need no special charters or state supervision. However, in many states they must have licenses as real estate brokers. Most are registered as approved lenders by HUD and the other government agencies. This means that they meet minimum capital standards, are familiar with and operate under the procedures established by HUD, and are subject to audit.

Although only about 750 companies belong to the National Association of Mortgage Bankers, HUD has approved over 7,000 lenders to perform mortgage banking functions. These include various types of institutional lenders and many firms that are primarily real estate brokers or builders. Most of the largest mortgage companies are owned by commercial banks, which bought into this field in order to acquire lending offices outside their home states. Other major corporations, such as General Motors; Sears, Roebuck; and Weyerhaeuser, also own large mortgage banking firms. The major investment banking firms, such as Salomon Brothers, Morgan-Stanley, Goldman-Sachs, and Merrill-Lynch, do a sizable mortgage banking and securities business. Most of the small firms and a few of the largest are independents; the level of entrepreneurial skills required is high.

The major function of mortgage companies is to act as *correspondents*— that is, to find, process, and service mortgage loans for institutions that are located in other parts of the country and that do not want to open the offices needed to attract customers or to handle the collection process. After they sell the loans, the mortgage companies usually continue to service them for a fee.

Mortgage companies developed because real estate lending usually occurs at the local level. Loans must be solicited, applications handled, appraisals made, land and credit records checked, and construction inspected at the place where the property is located. Without local correspondents, financial institutions interested in lending outside their own regions would require many local offices. It is more efficient to have these functions performed for a number of companies or security holders by a correspondent that knows the local area. In addition, large lenders and the government agencies may have five to ten regional offices to improve communication and the supervision of local mortgage companies.

How Mortgage Companies Function

The operations of mortgage bankers can be divided into four parts:

1. They obtain and prepare loans for sale to others, or act as brokers and negotiators.
2. They sell mortgages, either as whole loans or in packages through mortgage-backed securities.
3. They service most of the loans they sell.
4. They conduct mortgage-related activities, such as selling insurance.

Mortgage bankers originate about 75 percent of the FHA and VA home loans. Most of these are packaged and sold as GNMA pass-through securities (described later in this chapter). They also originate conventional loans, most of which are sold to the FNMA, but also to savings institutions, insurance companies, and pension funds. In 1985, these companies originated over $66 billion in residential mortgages, or nearly one-fourth of the market. They estimate that they service a slightly larger share of all outstanding mortgages.

They also handle a substantial share of the negotiations and act as brokers on nonresidential properties. They may serve as agents for the mortgages paid for by the bonds issued by state housing finance agencies. One lucrative activity in recent years has been handling the sale and lease-back of corporate headquarters, shopping centers, and warehouses to limited partnerships (syndications). Many of these individual deals—such as the selling of Rockefeller Center in New York City—amount to from $500 million to over $1 billion.

Obtaining Loans

In their basic function—making loans on single-family homes—mortgage companies handle both new construction loans (especially for large builders) and individual loans on existing houses, called **spot loans.** Usually they operate against commitments that they buy from long-term lenders such as Fannie Mae, savings institutions, life insurance companies, or pension funds. They may also hedge by buying contracts in the financial futures markets.

Mortgage companies bridge the financing gap caused by the lag between the start of construction, the contract for a sale to individual borrowers, and the final insurance, guarantee, or sale to an investor. A good deal of uncertainty characterizes this period. The builder may not finish construction; eligible borrowers may not appear; interest rates may shift; the borrower's credit may be rejected. Putting together a final package for sale requires on-the-spot negotiations.

During the origination period, mortgage companies accumulate pools of mortgages. Most lenders want sizable packages rather than single mortgages. The minimum pool for issuing securities is $1 million, but larger amounts are more efficient. In contrast, loans on nonresidential properties, since they are large, usually are sold individually.

Selling Loans

In effect, most loans are presold during the period in which they are being closed. The government agencies post prices daily at which they will buy mortgages. These prices vary by type of mortgage. The agencies also quote their charges for committing to buy at these prices for 30, 60, 90, or 180 days into the future. They also sell commitments at a reduced rate to buy at future market prices. In the same way, mortgage companies can obtain commitments from investment bankers to buy future GNMA securities or loan packages.

Mortgage companies leverage their capital heavily through bank loans (warehousing), but they also use the commercial paper market if they are large enough. To obtain these loans, they need either a great deal of capital or fixed-rate take-out commitments. Without final commitments, banks will not lend them the money they need to close loans and gather mortgages while making up a sale package or issuing a security.

Servicing and Other Activities

Although the primary job of mortgage bankers is to originate the loans, their main income is derived from servicing them. In origination, they find the borrower, underwrite the loans, complete the mortgage documents, and make and close the loans with their own funds. After the mortgages are sold, they collect and account for the monthly payments, maintain escrow accounts, examine properties periodically, and handle delinquencies and foreclosures.

They may also perform a wide variety of functions based on or related to their origination and servicing operations. Since they liquidate foreclosed properties, they usually have property management duties and may act as real estate brokers. Since properties must be insured, they often sell insurance. Mortgage companies may also do consumer lending on second mortgages.

Income

Mortgage bankers charge fees for originating and closing loans. However, origination fees for residential mortgages do not usually cover the full cost of putting the mortgages on their books. In contrast, the fees for brokering or originating the much larger loans on nonresidential properties are profitable.

The companies may make or lose money on their warehousing operation. The mortgages they hold accrue interest at the current mortgage rate. The money they pay the banks is at short-term rates—perhaps the banks' prime lending rate plus 1 to 3 percent. A mortgage rate higher than that charged by the bank yields a positive source of income called **positive carry.** If the bank rate is above the mortgage rate, mortgage companies lose on the carry. Since long-term rates usually exceed short-term ones, on average warehousing is a positive source of income.

Mortgage companies may also lose or gain from their exposure to market interest movements. Rarely will the commitments they have bought exactly match the interest rates on loans they make. Their interest rate risk may be raised by decisions to buy more or fewer commitments than they need. If such market speculations are successful, their earnings rise. If they bet wrong on interest rate changes, they may lose heavily.

Servicing Fees

Normally, however, other sources of income are minor compared to the fees for servicing. The contract to sell mortgages or mortgage-backed securities usually contains an agreement about a servicing fee. Depending on the services they perform, mortgage companies charge fees ranging from 15 to 44 basis points per year. A typical contract might allow them to retain three-eighths of a percent of the outstanding principal from the interest they collect, with the remainder forwarded to the investor. If their actual servicing cost is one-eighth of a percent and their fee is 37.5 basis points, they earn one-fourth of a percent on their entire servicing portfolio.

They also earn income from their **float.** The float arises because they deposit in their banks the monthly mortgage payments they receive, together with taxes and insurance escrows. On average, these sums may stay in their accounts for 30 days or more until they are finally paid out. The bank may either credit them with interest on these amounts or simply lower the interest it charges on their loans.

Because they are substantial sources of potential income, servicing contracts are traded in the market. The prices paid for them vary depending on the age of the portfolio, the average size of loans, interest rates, and the location of the property. Servicing contracts often sell at prices equal to 2 to 3 percent of the outstanding principal on the mortgages in a portfolio.

The miscellaneous activities of mortgage companies form a final source of income, which can vary from extremely significant to almost nothing. On the whole, the industry has been profitable, but incomes fluctuate widely with the availability of mortgage funds.

Deposit Institutions as Mortgage Bankers

Many savings and loan associations, savings banks, and commercial banks do a large mortgage banking business. They originate mortgages and then either sell them directly to other institutions or to Fannie Mae or Freddie Mac; or they obtain GHMA private guarantees and issue mortgage-backed securities.

It is not hard to see the advantages institutions gain by being in the mortgage banking business. They can help pay for their staffs and overhead by increasing their origination and servicing activities. At the same time, since the mortgages are not on their books, they do not have to increase their capital or the risk of owning additional assets. They can offer types of loans that they do not want to hold in their own portfolios. Thus many savings and loans, trying to reduce their interest rate risk and not wanting fixed-rate loans, have continued to make such loans provided that they can sell them in the secondary market.

Over the past four years, savings and loans have also increased their liquidity by swapping mortgages for securities. If securities must be sold, an immediate market exists, whereas it takes a considerable period of time to sell mortgages. They may need added liquidity to guard against a run on deposits out of their accounts. At the same time, they can keep the profitable servicing business.

FEDERAL INSURANCE AND GUARANTEE PROGRAMS

The establishment of the Federal Housing Administration in 1934 was a critical factor in the development of secondary mortgage markets. Ten years later, the loan guarantee program of the Veterans Administration was added. The two are usually considered together for analytical purposes. Annually, the programs together have insured or guaranteed between 10 percent and 40 percent of the value of all new loans on one- to four-family houses in the United States.

Currently, most of the money for these mortgages comes through the sale of Ginnie Mae–guaranteed mortgage-backed securities. In 1986, outstanding FHA and VA mortgages made up nearly 25 percent of the value of all mortgages held by lenders. The Reagan administration's suggestion that the FHA either be sold to private investors or that all fees be raised, down payments increased, and an income limit—a maximum of $40,000—be placed on borrowers may drastically change the way the FHA operates.

The FHA System

The FHA makes no loans. Approved private lenders write and then sell or hold the individual mortgages. The FHA insures that borrowers will make the agreed-upon payments of interest and principal to the lender. If a default occurs, the FHA becomes responsible for repaying the lender.

The FHA was established to help foster a national mortgage market and to "encourage improvement in housing standards and conditions." Standard forms and the existence of the government insurance helped to bring about the national market.

To improve housing conditions and affordability, the FHA acted to lower down payments, to lengthen amortization periods, and to lower interest rates. At times, the government has subsidized some FHA mortgages, either by assuming without extra fees the risks from overly generous terms or by paying part of the interest cost. The FHA also inaugurated detailed *minimum property standards* covering design, materials, plumbing, heating, and so on for a structure; but in 1985 they were phased out as part of the push for deregulation.

Advantages and Disadvantages of the FHA System

The FHA program sparked major improvements in all mortgage lending. It laid the foundation for the use of long-term fully amortized loans with low down payments. It improved property standards and brought about more uniform valuation procedures. It developed new techniques for determining who could qualify for loans. Its experience made possible private mortgage insurance and led to the development of mortgage-backed securities.

The reasons for the widespread adoption of FHA programs are not hard to find.

1. Down payments are usually lower than on other loans.
2. Amortization periods are as long or longer. However, other lenders have adopted maturities with amortization periods equal to those of many FHA programs.
3. The borrower receives an independent appraisal and an assurance of minimum property standards and conditions.
4. No prepayment penalties are charged.
5. Mortgages are assumable. Both assumability and the avoidance of prepayment penalties can cut costs greatly if the owner must move in the first several years after taking out the loan.
6. The FHA often led the way in designing new payment formulas to increase affordability.
7. More funds are available in the secondary market at slightly lower rates if loans carry FHA insurance.
8. In some cases, the mortgage interest payments may be subsidized.

Disadvantages

In view of all these advantages, some may wonder how other types of loans compete. The answer is that the program also contains built-in drawbacks. Although some of these became less significant than in the past, others came to the fore as the Reagan administration attempted to add hurdles to FHA operations in order to shift more activity to private insurers.

1. The main constraint is a strict limit on the amount of an insured loan. In 1986 the maximum mortgage in many parts of the country was limited to $67,500, but it went to $90,000 in high-cost localities. In the past, Congress has lifted the limit when it threatened to strangle the program. The limit establishes the maximum loan. Buyers can make larger down payments if they want a FHA-insured loan on a more expensive house.

2. Some sellers see as a disadvantage the need for a FHA appraisal and the requirement that the appraiser check to see that the house is in good condition and complies with the building codes. Without these checks, sellers might be able to sell for a higher price with loans from other sources. However, if they have sought FHA insurance, buyers may be disinclined to exceed the FHA appraisal. They are also likely to demand that required repairs be made as noted in the FHA report. Builders of new developments have felt that FHA minimum property standards were too restrictive.

3. The time required to obtain a FHA appraisal and commitment for a specific mortgage has often been excessive. FHA appraisals must be made before conditional commitments are issued for a property. Then, at one time, the FHA had to approve the individual borrower. Often these delays tied up a property for considerable periods. Furthermore, the deal would fall through eventually if the borrower was rejected. Now the FHA will arrange to delegate underwriting decisions to approved lenders. This can cut delays effectively.

4. In the past, the FHA set maximum interest rates on its loans. Mortgages at below-market interest rates could only be sold at a discount. Now rates are negotiated between borrower and originating lender, doing away with discounts and points.

5. For borrowers with good credit or who did not want maximum terms, private mortgage insurance might be cheaper. With standard rates for all FHA insurance, borrowers with good credit were subsidizing marginal ones. Rates now vary somewhat with the terms of the loan, thus eliminating some of the previous disadvantages.

6. The FHA sets higher standards for some loans than private insurers. Loans to nonowner-occupiers are 85 percent of the maximum available for owner-occupiers. (Upon resale, however, a loan with a low down payment may be assumed by a nonoccupant.) The difference in maximum terms reflects the FHA objective of promoting homeownership. It serves to cut out borrowers for other purposes. Somewhat similar regulations forbidding initial second mortgages and increasing down payments on houses not inspected by the FHA during construction also curtail demand for FHA loans.

Programs

The FHA has administered over 40 different programs since its inception. Periodically, Congress has changed the insurance and added or modified the types of property covered, the percentages insured, the maximum loan amounts, and interest rates and fees. Since each set of regulations alters the risks to the FHA, separate insurance funds are set up for each type of program. For example, in addition to the primary programs (203b), others exist to insure loans on cooperatives and condominiums, loans to nonprofit sponsors, projects in redevelopment areas, rehabilitated housing, housing for the elderly, low-market subsidized rents, and many others.

FHA programs are identified by the title or section of the National Housing Act of 1934 that authorized them. Most of the sections have been added since the original act was passed. For example, Section 242, covering hospital mortgages, was added in 1968; Section 245, for graduated payment mortgages, was passed in 1974. Because the specifics of each program change frequently, anyone interested in obtaining maximum loans with minimum down payments should check with the nearest HUD office to find the current rules and regulations.

Title I of the original act authorized an early consumer loan program. This program insures loans for the modernization and repair of houses. It now covers mobile homes (manufactured housing) as well. Limits on the amounts and terms for Title I loans are quite low. In 1985, they were $17,500 and 15 years for consumer loans, and $22,500 and 20 years for mobile homes. Under this title, the lender does the complete underwriting and acts as a coinsurer with the FHA. The lender gets back only 90 percent of any losses.

Title II covers most of the programs. The great majority of FHA insurance has been written for new and existing single-family, owner-occupied homes under Section 203b. In earlier years, another important single-family program was Section 235 for subsidized housing. More recently, Section 245, authorizing graduated payment mortgages, has also become important.

In the multifamily sphere, Section 207 was the initial and standard program. Currently, however, most multifamily insurance falls under Section 221d. This covers the financing for the purchase, construction, and rehabilitation of projects for low- and moderate-income families. It has included subsidized below-market interest rate programs and some projects by state and local housing finance agencies. At present, however, HUD subsidies for mortgage interest rates are not being granted. As a result, the main use of Section 221d recently has been in conjunction with Section 8 contracts with nonprofit associations and private developers.

Section 203b authorizes approved lenders to obtain FHA insurance on mortgages for one- to four-family houses. Under the statutes, HUD establishes the maximum limits of an insured loan for each area. The maximum loan of $67,500 to $90,000 for single-family houses rises with the number of units in a building. Thus, a four-plex has a loan ceiling 60 percent higher than that for a one-family house.

FHA insurance has always featured low down payments. Most buyers try to obtain a loan covering as much of the purchase price as possible. In 1985, the maximum insured mortgage could equal 97 percent of the first $25,000 plus 95 percent of the remainder of the acquisition cost of a house up to the loan limit. In addition to this amount, the borrower can include in the insured loan 95 percent of the prepaid mortgage insurance premium. If the buyer is a veteran, the maximum percentage insured can be increased somewhat.

Section 245 authorized graduated payment mortages (see Chapter 11). These allow homeowners to make smaller monthly payments at first. Payments then gradually increase in size for up to ten years. Under the most popular schedule of payments, the initial monthly payments rise by 7.5 percent a year for five years. Since this schedule means that negative amortization exists during the first five years, under Section 245 the minimum down payment must be increased somewhat in order to avoid exceeding the maximum loan-to-value ratio at a later time. However, these extra down payment requirements can be waived for first-time homeowners (those who have not owned a home for the preceding three years).

Section 221d(3) and *Section 221d(4)* programs help finance the construction or substantial rehabilitation of multifamily projects (five or more units) for low- and moderate-income families. Units under this program may qualify for assistance under the HUD Section 8 program. Under Section 221d(3), nonprofit and cooperative sponsors can qualify for insured loans equaling 100 percent of the project's costs. Section 221d(4) covers other types of owners and allows up to 90 percent of approved costs. The terms of loans under Section 221d can be as long as 40 years. Maximum limits per loan depend on the number of units in a project and on a maximum cost per unit, which differs with the locality.

HUD has expanded its coinsurance to cover these programs. **Coinsurance** has been discussed by HUD for many years. The idea is that lenders will be more careful if they share in the risk. The FHA insurance programs have been plagued by the long time and extremely onerous conditions required to obtain insurance, particularly in multifamily projects. Under the coinsurance program, approved lenders can qualify to make loans without the necessity of detailed individual authorizations from HUD. As with other coinsurance programs, the lender assumes part of any losses. In this case, the FHA covers only 90 percent of losses on a project.

Obtaining an FHA-insured Loan

Because of the role played by FHA-insured loans in real estate finance, would-be borrowers and real estate salespeople should understand how they work. A borrower applies, usually through a broker, to an approved FHA lender. The lender calls the local HUD-FHA office to obtain a case number and to order an appraisal by an FHA fee appraiser. The appraiser estimates the value of the property and also checks that it meets FHA standards. The property must comply with local building codes, must present no hazards to health or property values, must be in a neighborhood free of environmental or noninsured flood dangers, and must have no other deleterious effects.

The FHA notifies the lender and prospective borrower of the estimated value and of any property deficiencies requiring correction through a HUD **conditional commitment.** This commitment says that HUD will insure a loan if the borrower qualifies as creditworthy and if all other requirements are met. It shows the maximum mortgage amount and maturity as well as estimates of closing costs and of the monthly expenses over and above the mortgage payment.

The conditional commitment will be made final if the borrower's credit qualifies and the property has been brought up to standard. Most FHA loans are now made by lenders who have been approved by HUD to process and directly close single-family loans. However, it is primarily the largest lenders who use this system; many small- or medium-sized lenders have not qualified.

Approval of individual borrowers requires a good deal of documentation. The borrower's ability to carry the loan amount must be confirmed. The borrower must have enough savings for the down payment (second mortgages are not permitted) and an income sufficient to meet FHA credit standards. Both must be confirmed through a credit check. If the borrower qualifies, a direct endorsing lender can close the loan and send the necessary documentation to HUD, which then issues the mortgage insurance certificate. Other lenders must submit all documentation to the FHA. Upon approval of the borrower, the FHA issues a final commitment, and the loan can be closed. After receipt and checking of the closing documents, the FHA issues the mortgage insurance certificate.

The Monthly Payments

The interest rate on the loan may be negotiated between the borrower and lender. The amount of the monthly payment will depend on the amount of the loan, the interest rate, and the amortization period. Payments must also include escrow amounts to cover taxes and fire and hazard insurance. The monthly mortgage payments plus utilities and maintenance make up the FHA's definition of the estimated monthly housing expense. This is the amount that the FHA uses to specify the minimum income a borrower must have to qualify for insurance.

Ending the FHA Coverage

FHA insurance can be terminated by repayment of the loan, by a mutual agreement between the borrower and lender, or by default. When the insurance is ended without default, two types of refunds are possible:

1. The FHA will return the amount of its unearned insurance premium to the borrower. Because mortgage insurance premiums are paid in advance covering the full term, an earlier termination of the policy means that the FHA has not earned all the amounts it was paid for the full-period risks.
2. FHA insurance is mutual. Loans made in a period and under a given program are pooled. If the loss experience on the pool is better than expected, some premium may be returned to the borrowers. It usually takes ten years for a pool's loss experience to stabilize.

Defaults and Forbearance   If the borrower is delinquent for three months, the lender must inform both the borrower and the FHA of the existence of the default. The borrower is also told of the possibility of **forbearance.** This allows a delay in foreclosure and a possible reshaping of the loan. If the default is due to circumstances beyond the borrower's control and a reasonable prospect of repayment exists, HUD may accept assignment of the mortgage. HUD pays for and services the loans it accepts. The borrower will be given time to make up the delinquency, and other terms may be altered.

If no assignment occurs, the lender must acquire title from the borrower by some voluntary means or must institute foreclosure proceedings. The lender can either retain the title or transfer it to HUD; most are transferred. On transfer of title, the lender applies to the FHA for reimbursement of the principal, delinquent interest, and other costs of the foreclosure. The FHA pays the claim from its reserves and then must sell the house. The insurance fund is reduced by the costs of carrying the house and by any deficit between what it paid out and what it receives from the sale.

VETERANS ADMINISTRATION LOAN GUARANTEES

The Veterans Readjustment Benefit Act of 1944 established a system of **mortgage guarantees** as a veterans' benefit. The system roughly parallels that of FHA insurance. While instituted as a benefit for war veterans, it now covers all those who have served minimum periods in the military and naval service and have not been dishonorably discharged.

To enable veterans to purchase better homes on easier terms than would otherwise be available, Congress has agreed to guarantee lenders against some or all losses on these veterans' mortgages. As a result, VA-guaranteed mortgages usually have lower down payments and lower interest rates than conventional loans.

The VA guarantee covers 60 percent of the loan, or $27,500, whichever is less. Although for most of its history the VA set no maximum limit on the amount of the loan, in 1986 it attempted to set a $90,000 ceiling on mortgages to which its guarantee could be applied, but under congressional pressure the proposal was withdrawn. Barring limits, individual lenders set their own maximums, usually four times the amount guaranteed by the VA, or $110,000, except in unusual cases.

Generating a Loan

Veterans apply to the VA for a **certificate of eligibility,** which permits a veteran to apply to lenders to have a loan guaranteed on a specific proposed property. The lender asks the VA for a **certificate of reasonable value (CRV).** This is an approved appraiser's estimate of how much the property is worth.

Provided that the loan does not exceed the CRV and the lender finds that the borrower qualifies for a loan based on his income and credit record, most lenders can close loans without further VA approval. Upon notification, the VA issues the guarantee. The VA charges a 1 percent funding fee, which may be included in the loan. Otherwise the guarantee is free, paid for by the government as a benefit to the veteran.

Advantages and Disadvantages

VA-guaranteed loans have all the advantages of the FHA-insured loans, plus some added ones:

1. Since the VA charges a below-market fee and no insurance premium, it is cheaper than other forms of loan insurance.
2. For most of its history, down payments were not required. This opens the market to a group who have not accumulated any savings.
3. It may be easier to qualify for a VA loan than for any other loan.
4. The VA sets a maximum interest rate that may be slightly below the market.
5. Because the loan cannot exceed the valuation of the certificate of reasonable value, sellers eager to close may reduce their price to the VA appraiser's estimate. The sellers may also pay some mortgage discount points, since veterans cannot.

The disadvantages of VA-guaranteed loans are also similar to those of FHA insurance:

1. Obtaining the CRV may take longer than a conventional approval.
2. The maximum allowed interest rate may be below the market. In such cases, lenders will demand points; that is, the loan will be discounted. Since the amount of charges veterans are permitted to pay is limited, a seller who wants to make the sale may have to pay the points. Many sellers refuse to pay, preferring to hold out for conventional loans.
3. The guaranteed loan cannot exceed the CRV. If a veteran agrees to pay more than the VA's appraisal, the total difference must be paid by the veteran in cash. This need for a larger down payment will torpedo most deals.
4. The size of a loan is limited by any ceiling imposed by the VA and by the fact that the amount of loss the VA will cover is limited to $27,500 (in 1986).

On balance, the advantages of the VA guarantee are so great that these loans have been very popular. More than 12.5 million loans have been guaranteed. They have been used especially often in the sales of new houses in developments. Builders arrange for the loan terms and all the paperwork. They can decide what points they are willing to absorb so as to be able to advertise and make sales with no down payment. They may absorb a substantial amount because the VA loan acts as a key selling point and speeds up their sales.

PRIVATE MORTGAGE INSURANCE COMPANIES

Encouraged by the successful underwriting insurance experience of the VA and the FHA, a group of *private mortgage insurance companies* (MICs) reentered the field in 1957. Such companies had existed earlier, but the Great Depression drove them into bankruptcy. Because of poor underwriting practices and inadequate reserves, the earlier insurance became useless.

Modern companies were started under a Wisconsin law of 1956, which called for much stricter state regulation. In 1985, 14 **private mortgage insurers (PMIs)** belonged to the field's trade association, the Mortgage Insurance Companies of America. Some other companies also sold insurance. Although primarily insurers of lenders against losses on individual mortgages, the firms perform other related functions. They may have mortgage subsidiaries that buy and sell mortgages and issue mortgage-backed securities. They act as brokers between lenders and investors. They also insure pools of mortgages, thus enabling private firms called *conduits,* which pool mortgages from several lenders, to issue mortgage-backed securities.

Growth of the Industry

While the private mortgage insurance industry started with only a limited volume, by the early 1980s private insurers had become a dominant part of the mortgage insurance business. They began to write more insurance than the FHA and the VA combined. For the years from 1973 to 1982, private industry had insured 15 percent of the value of all new mortgages, which was slightly less than the FHA and VA total. Each of those two agencies had insured 9 percent in this period. The number of units insured by the FHA and the VA together was about one-third greater than that of the private industry.

In 1984, the amount of new private mortgage insurance written exceeded $63 billion. This total amounted to over 30 percent of the volume of all mortgages on one- to four-family houses originated in that year. (Private mortgage insurers do only a small volume on income properties; their underwriting experience on commercial properties has been poor.)

Simultaneous with its achievement of a new peak in volume in 1984, the profitability of the mortgage insurance industry reached a new low. For its first 25 years, the mortgage insurance business had been a virtual gold mine. Inflation and rising house prices kept losses low. But the recessions and slowed inflation of the early 1980s turned the situation around, and by 1984 the cost and losses of the companies ran well above their receipts. They had to raise their premiums and their underwriting standards. In 1985, losses caused one of the major companies to withdraw from the market. A shortage of capital caused others to tighten their standards in order to reduce their volume of insurance.

Causes of Growth   After 1970, as a result of the creation of a secondary market for conventional loans by Freddie Mac and Fannie Mae, the volume written by mortgage insurance companies rose sharply. The agencies had received the authority to buy conventional mortgages with loan-to-value ratios of up to 95 percent, provided that all of their exposure above 80 percent was insured. This was the opening the MICs needed for greater expansion. They wrote $63.4 billion of new insurance in 1984, compared to only $1.2 billion in 1970. The total insurance in force rose from $7 billion to $192 billion.

The forces behind this growth were primarily those factors which made FHA and VA insurance and guarantees disadvantageous. The private insurers were burdened with less red tape; lenders could obtain a firm commitment in a day or two rather than in the one to six weeks or more taken by the government agencies. When the FHA and VA had interest-rate ceilings, the private insurers did not. As a result, if the buyer obtained a privately insured loan, sellers did not have to pay points to absorb the discount between the FHA and VA ceilings and the market rates.

There is no limit on the size of an insured loan. Thus lenders must use private insurance if the size of the loan exceeds the FHA maximum or the amount at which the risk based on the VA guarantee becomes too high. Until recently, private insurance was also considerably cheaper than FHA because the private firms skimmed the market. They took only the best loans, leaving those with the greatest risks to the government. They also allowed the insurance to be canceled whenever the lender decided adequate equity had been built up. Until recently, FHA policies had to be paid for the life of the mortgage.

The government forbids due-on-sale clauses and prepayment penalties in the mortgages it insures and guarantees. This is not true of the PMIs. As a result, lenders may prefer private insurance, while borrowers may not realize that they have a choice.

Operations

In a typical insurer-lender relationship, the mortgage insurance company rates lenders based on their net worth, the quality of their assets, their underwriting capabilities, and their procedures for handling delinquent loans. The insurer also screens out lenders with deteriorating loss records. When it finds a lender that is qualified, it issues a master policy. This policy sets forth the terms and conditions under which the MIC will insure individual mortgages. All insurers determine their own standards for property and borrowers' credit. Typically these follow industry norms, although those of each MIC differ to some extent. The insurer imposes no minimum number or type of loan to be submitted by lenders for insurance.

Lenders usually deal with several mortgage insurance companies. A lender who wishes to insure a mortgage submits a separate application for it to the insurer. The application must be accompanied by all loan documents, such as an appraisal report, the borrower's loan application, and verifications of credit and down payment ability. The lender usually receives a rapid reply as to whether or not a policy will be issued. Speed has been a big selling point of the PMIs.

Insurers offer a variety of policies. They typically insure loans up to 95 percent loan-to-value ratio on single-family houses and duplexes. They offer a number of combinations of down payment and percentage of the loan insured. When down payments are between 5 percent and 10 percent, the insurance usually covers the top 25 percent of the loan. In the case of a $120,000 house with a mortgage of $110,000, insurance coverage would be 25 percent of the $110,000 mortgage, or $27,500.

With a 15 percent to 20 percent down payment, the mortgage insurance might cover only 20 percent of the loan. For example, if the $120,000 house had a $100,000 mortgage, the insurance coverage would be 20 percent of $100,000, or $20,000. Because the insurer's exposure is reduced in the second example, mortgage premiums would be lower.

Defaults

If an insured borrower defaults, the lender can claim any unpaid principal plus accrued interest and other expenses, such as taxes and legal fees, that result from the borrower's failure to pay. The insurance company responsible for the claim has two choices in each case.

1. The insurer can pay the lender the percentage of the claim agreed to in the insurance policy. The lender retains the mortgage lien and can foreclose or take any action deemed most desirable. For example, if the claim is for $50,000 and the coverage is 20 percent, the insurer could send the lender $10,000, and have no other obligation.
2. The insurer can pay all of the amount due the lender and take title to the property. The insurer must then arrange for its sale, but collects the entire proceeds.

The insurer chooses whichever path is more profitable in the light of what is happening to property values and of the cost and difficulties of handling the foreclosed property. Such costs are usually high where the insurer is based far from the property.

MORTGAGE-BACKED SECURITIES

As their name implies, **mortgage-backed securities (MBSs)** are securities—a bond, a note, or a certificate—issued against and collateralized by a pool of mortgages usually held by an independent custodian or trustee. Each security represents a share—an undivided interest—in the pool. We can differentiate among six major types of mortgage-backed securities, keeping in mind that many other possibilities exist.

1. Ginnie Mae **pass-through certificates.** The original and largest amount of securities take the form of Ginnie Mae pass-through certificates. As

detailed in the next section, these certificates are issued and sold by private mortgage firms based on a guarantee by Ginnie Mae that the scheduled interest and principal payments will be met in a timely manner. Because the GNMA is part of HUD, this guarantee carries the full faith and credit of the United States government. One major problem with pass-throughs is that the monthly payments and the actual maturity of the securities are uncertain. They may be paid off in anywhere from 2 to 30 years. How much an investor receives each month and the maturity of a certificate depend on how fast prepayments occur. Receipts include interest, scheduled principal payments, and all prepayments. They will differ in every period.

2. Pass-through certificates issued by the federal agencies or private conduits. Similar pass-throughs have been issued by the FNMA and the FHLMC, as described in an earlier section on swaps. These carry the guarantee of the sponsored agency. Others have been issued by private mortgage companies or conduits. For these, a private insurer or a bank letter of credit usually guarantees the timely payment. Some of these insurers have failed, causing sizable losses.

3. **Collateralized mortgage obligations (CMOs).** These are a special variant of the pass-through certificate. The objective of the CMOs is to find a market among investors who want semiannual instead of monthly payments and who want short- or intermediate-term bonds rather than the possible 30-year life of a straight mortgage pass-through (even though their average life is much shorter). They do this by putting together a pool of mortgages and issuing bonds in a number of classes, A–1, A–2, A–3, and A–4—there are usually four—against them. Each bond has a fixed semiannual interest payment, although the last series may include a zero-coupon bond. The terms of the bonds specify that all principal payments (including prepayments) will go to the first class (A–1) of bonds until they are paid off. With no prepayments, they might have a maximum term of 4 years. With prepayments, they might be paid off in a year or two. When the first class has been retired, all principal payments go to pay off the second (A–2) class, and so on.

4. **Mortgage-backed bonds.** These are ordinary bonds backed by a company's assets, but also secured by a mortgage or a pool of mortgages. An investor makes a standard bond investment. The issuer of the bonds assumes the risk of losses or gains if interest rates change and if prepayment rates vary. On the pass-through types, the investor assumes the interest rate risk caused by the fact that the rate of prepayment can be delayed or accelerated.

5. **Builders' bonds.** These are bonds issued by builders and covered by mortgages on homes they build and sell. These bonds have usually taken the form of Ginnie Mae pass-throughs. Builders have sold these bonds as a way of reducing their reported profits and income tax. The houses for which the bonds are issued qualified for installment sales treatment under the tax laws. (Installment sales are discussed in Chapter 16.)

6. Bonds backed by a single mortgage. Some bonds may be backed by a single mortgage on a large commercial building. Their security is only the building, since the issuers have no other assets. Wall Street firms sell bonds varying in length from 1 to 15 years based on a mortgage deposited with a trustee for the benefit of the bondholder. Such bonds are rated by Standard & Poor's and are sold and traded in the same way as other corporate bonds.*

How Mortage-backed Securities Work

Although each of the types of securities discussed above functions differently to some extent, they are similar enough that one description of how the GNMA program works can apply them to all (see Figure 8-2). The central figure is the lender, who must be approved and must meet certain capital standards set by Ginnie Mae. The lender lends money to borrowers, receiving individual mortgages in return. The lender gathers these mortgages together in a pool as collateral for the securities. Then it applies to Ginnie Mae for a commitment that Ginnie Mae will guarantee the pool by issuing a guarantee certificate.

Each pool must meet minimum qualifications. It must hold at least $1 million of mortgages, and all the mortgages in a pool must be insured or guaranteed by a government agency and must be similar in interest rate and type of maturity. Ginnie Mae charges a nominal 6 basis points per year for its guarantee, but it still makes a profit.

Issuing the Securities   When Ginnie Mae agrees to issue the guarantee, the lender places the mortgages in a pool and ships the mortgage documents to a custodian, who holds them for the benefit of the GNMA and the investors. Upon receiving an assignment of the mortgages, Ginnie Mae issues a guarantee certificate. On the basis of this certificate, the lender can then sell the securities to a dealer who makes a market in Ginnie Maes. The dealer, in turn, sells them to final investors.

Depending on what has happened to interest rates and whether the mortgages were hedged when issued, either in the futures market or by buying a fixed-price commitment, the lender may gain or lose on the sale. The lender services the mortgages and sends to the investors all interest and principal payments less a 44-basis-point servicing fee and the 6 basis points for the GNMA. The amount of the monthly check to the investors will vary depending on the number and amount of prepayments in the pool during that month.

Under the most popular plan, called the **modified pass-through,** the lender is responsible for the scheduled monthly payments to the investor whether or not they are received from the borrower. Ginnie Mae guarantees that the lender will meet the contract terms. It steps in only if the lender fails to perform.

---

*See *Ratings on Commercial Mortages: A New Approach* (New York: Salomon Brothers Real Estate Services, 1986).

Figure 8-2
The GNMA Pass-through Security

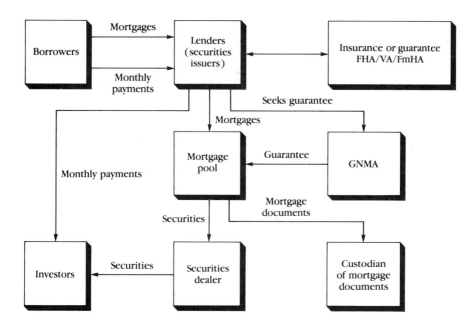

Since the individual mortgages are insured or guaranteed, the risk that lenders will not be able to meet their obligations is slight unless fraud occurs. That is why the GNMA's premium is low.

Ginnie Mae guaranteed securities are very popular. An active futures market exists for them. They are held by many mutual bond funds, particularly those aimed at individual retirement accounts (IRAs) or other pension accounts. Although no default risk exists, the interest rate risk may be considerable. Securities that carry high interest rates relative to the current market are likely to be prepaid at a rapid rate. Any premiums paid for such securities may be lost.

As the secondary market continues to grow, the types of securities continue to increase. The FNMA and the FHLMC have continued to expand the scope and scale of their own offerings. Securities are able to attract funds for the mortgage market that would not or could not be invested in individual mortgages. They are one of the fundamental forces behind the tremendous expansion in the secondary market.

SECURITIES ON COMMERCIAL BUILDINGS

Because of the lack of government guarantees, the securitization of commercial mortgages has lagged far behind developments in the residential market. Since individual commercial mortgages tend to be large, it is hard for private mortgage insurers to obtain a sufficiently diversified portfolio. In addition, as we shall see in Part 4, the valuation of income properties is more difficult than is that of individual homes. The risks in a portfolio of commercial mortgages are large, and they have a considerable variance.

In an effort to broaden the market, Standard & Poor's in 1984 agreed to rate commercial mortgages, either in pools or individually for large buildings.* The ratings depend on the debt service coverage, the loan-to-value ratio, the *seasoning* (how long the loan has been in existence), the minimum property size, the loan terms, and the payment history.

The Standard & Poor's model projects possible income shortfalls in accordance with past declines in property income. If deficits appear possible, they can be offset by letters of credit or insurance guaranteeing some additional source of credit support. The use of third-party guarantees or pledges of other assets to assure debt or lease payments is known as **credit enhancement**. It has become increasingly common and important in the financing of real estate.

In 1985, a few large mortgage-backed securities were issued based on such credit ratings. The interest rates paid by the borrowers were lower than they could have obtained on standard mortgages. Investment bankers were enthusiastic and projected a rapid growth in this form of securitization. At the same time, securities based on other types of collateral, such as second mortgages, also entered the market.

The idea of finding a wider market and new sources of capital for real estate finance based on mortgages as collateral for all types of securities has an obvious appeal for those in the industry. Only time will tell the degree to which the success of securities backed by residential mortgages can be copied for other types of mortgages.

SUMMARY

The secondary market for mortgages, which integrates the mortgage and capital markets, has expanded rapidly. It has caused the gap between mortgage interest rates and those in more general markets to narrow. Geographic differences tend to disappear, and the marketability and liquidity of mortgages are enhanced. The growth of the market stemmed from mortgage insurance and mortgage-backed securities. Investors no longer must investigate the borrower and the underlying property for individual mortgages.

Mortgage banking companies form an integral part of the secondary market. They originate loans and sell them to investors, while continuing to service them. They also act as brokers on large loans for commercial properties. An increasing share of their business has been to generate securities sold by dealers to final investors. This contrasts with their original function of acting as local correspondents for out-of-state lenders, such as life insurance companies.

*See Standard & Poor's *Credit Week,* Supplement, November 19, 1984.

The Federal Housing Administration (FHA) regenerated the mortgage insurance business and provided a major impetus to the secondary market. The FHA primarily insures loans with low down payments on moderately priced houses. The basic principles of appraising and underwriting loans, which it established, are now used by most lenders. The amount of a loan it insures is limited and no second loans are permitted. The FHA also has high-risk and subsidized programs, primarily to assist multifamily projects for low- or moderate-income families.

The Veterans Administration (VA) loan guarantee program operates as a benefit or bonus for veterans. It guarantees loans with no down payments. However, it does not guarantee the full loan but only the top part. Loans cannot exceed the VA's certificate of reasonable value; nor can the interest rate exceed the VA ceiling. While in theory the amount of a loan could be unlimited, most lenders restrict their loan amounts to four times the VA guarantee.

Private mortgage insurance firms have taken over a major share of the market. They give faster service, are not limited in the size of the loan, have no interest rate ceilings, and allow the lender to include due-on-sale clauses and prepayment penalties. They also insure loans more readily on other than owner-occupied houses. MICs do not guarantee the entire loan, but pay all of a loan up to 20 percent or 25 percent of the principal plus foreclosure expenses.

Mortgage-backed securities have become an extremely important factor in the secondary market. They are sold to investors who lack the skill or interest to buy whole loans. The securities are issued by mortgage firms, private lenders, private conduits (which pool mortgages from several lenders) and the government agencies. The securities consist of a share in a pool of mortgages backed by the insurance or guarantee of the GNMA, a government agency, or a private insurer.

Although pass-through certificates have been the most common instrument in the market, they have a significant disadvantage in that the monthly payments to investors change periodically depending on the number and the amount of prepayments made against the mortgages in the pool. Some pools have been paid off in 2 or 3 years; others threaten to have small amounts dribbling in for the full 30 years. Mortgage bonds and consolidated mortgage obligations are some of the ways the market has used to make the mortgage-backed securities more like regular bonds and, therefore, more saleable in the market.

KEY TERMS

builders' bonds	**coinsurance**
certificate of eligibility	**conditional commitment**
certificate of reasonable value	**credit enhancement**
(CRV)	**float**
collateralization	**forbearance**
collateralized mortgage	**modified pass-through**
obligations (CMOs)	**mortgage-backed bonds**

mortgage-backed securities
  (MBSs)
mortgage guarantees
mortgage insurance
participations
participation certificate
pass-through certificate

positive carry
private mortgage insurers
  (PMIs)
securitization
servicing
spot loans

QUESTIONS

1. What role did the government play in the development of the secondary mortgage market?
2. What are the main channels for selling mortgages in the secondary market?
3. Discuss the different ways in which a mortgage company obtains its revenue.
4. Since the FHA programs provide many advantages, how can private insurers compete?
5. Describe the major differences between FHA and VA programs.
6. What led to the growth of private mortgage insurance?
7. Distinguish among the different types of mortgage-backed securities.
8. What is the major risk involved in investing in pass-through certificates?
9. Why do you think the government has not pooled its efforts in one single agency to provide a source of funds?
10. Explain the reasons why many deposit institutions do a large mortgage banking business.
11. What have been the effects of the growth of the secondary mortgage market?

9 Change and the Mortgage Market of the Future

OBJECTIVES

When you finish this chapter, you should be able to:

- describe the forces causing change among financial institutions.
- define and explain a shortage of mortgage money.
- discuss how thrift institutions have changed and why.
- list the six causes of losses in firms lending on mortgages.
- explain how systems of asset-to-liability management work.
- define duration and gap analysis.
- discuss key factors determining the future size of deposit institutions.

T HE FINANCIAL SERVICES industry has undergone major transformations in the 1980s. The size of firms has mushroomed; companies have broadened their product lines and are fighting to enter new spheres; lenders on mortgages are becoming more diverse. The movements which have occurred make it appear likely that the mortgage market of the future will differ considerably from that of the past. To prepare for change, those in real estate finance must understand what has been happening and where events are likely to lead.

A new economic environment, advanced technology, deregulation, and increased competition are all putting financial service firms under stress. Changes in the thrift industry have been both dynamic and traumatic, and observers fear that these changes will create a shortage of mortgage money. We want to know what this means and portends.

Because thrift institutions have been so significant in real estate finance, an understanding of what has occurred in the thrift industry is necessary for knowledge of the future. Savings institutions have been given broad new powers. Some current problems have arisen because many deposit institutions have failed to control their risks. They could be lax in this respect because depositors, lulled by the existence of government insurance, felt no need to investigate the safety of individual firms.

Many observers feel that the changes and innovations are occurring so rapidly that the mortgage market of the future will be vastly different from that of the past. The major adjustments to deregulation taking place now are likely to accelerate in the future, but whether or not they will be revolutionary is less certain. For example, we often hear that a shortage of mortgage money is almost inevitable. And many fear that the future will see the industry dominated by large-scale, homogenized financial institutions. This chapter examines the forces at work behind these predictions, as well as future prospects.

THE FORCES FOR CHANGE

Some of the major forces that produce change in the mortgage market can be examined in terms of three general areas: the economic environment, technology, and competition and regulation.

The Economic Environment

The past two decades witnessed several economic disruptions. Related forces also buffeted the mortgage market, among the most critical of which were the huge fluctuations in interest rates. Higher inflation, changes in the operation of monetary policies, growth in international financial markets, a larger federal deficit, and more extreme cycles in output and unemployment all led to much sharper and wider swings in interest rates than had been previously experienced. Rates rose to levels unprecedented in the history of the United States. The mortgage and related savings markets experienced severe reactions from these high rates. In 1986, when rates fell toward earlier levels, many financing techniques that seemed to have disappeared as a result of high rates reappeared. The amount of refinancing soared.

During this period the country was moving from a manufacturing to a service economy. The share of services in the economy, and particularly financing services, became far more significant than in the past. But although service industries are traditionally more stable than other sectors of the economy, this now appears less true.

Our capital markets have become increasingly international. For years, Americans barely thought about the value of the dollar or of foreign trade. Then the interaction between exchange rates, trade and capital flows, and foreign interest rates began to influence activity, interest rates, and the availability of capital even in primarily domestic industries such as real estate finance.

Technological Change

New technology has simplified many mortgage tasks. The computer has reduced the cost of servicing and originating loans. It has increased the amount of information available to decision makers. Transactions that previously would have taken weeks can now be proposed and completed in minutes.

With the proliferation of computers came growth of telecommunications. Markets are no longer isolated; trading takes place simultaneously in all parts of the country and in several parts of the world. Loans in San Francisco can be made on-line from institutions in Virginia or Texas.

The automation of the deposit function through **automatic teller machines** (ATMs) has eliminated the need for many branches of banks and savings institutions. Since ATMs can be located anywhere—in the nearest drugstore or supermarket—most deposit and cash functions can be performed outside of the deposit institution itself.

Competition and Deregulation

During the 1970s, large and small deposit institutions fought over regulations. The large ones were under growing competitive pressure. The small ones, believing themselves sufficiently isolated by distance so that their customers would not be wooed by higher rates, argued against deregulation.

Then came the growth of money market funds, the explosion of mortgage loan volume by the federal agencies, and new entries into what had been restricted markets. American Express and Sears, Roebuck competed for funds and business. Merrill Lynch and Salomon Brothers became major participants in real estate finance. General Electric, General Motors, Ford Motor Company, and other industrial firms demanded a share of the financial services industries. The deposit institutions could not continue to operate in the old ways.

Forced by changes in the market and responding to a more market-oriented philosophy, in 1980 the government began to deregulate at a rapid pace. Many regulations no longer worked; they were holdovers from an earlier, simpler economy with different problems. The need to change regulations forced the removal of interest rate ceilings, which had held down rates to artificially low and noncompetitive levels. Because their rates *were* noncompetitive, traditional savings accounts became a minor share of total deposits. Adjustable-rate mortgage were authorized. New types of loans and investments were approved. Banks and savings and loans were allowed to expand outside their home states. Savings and loans and savings banks converted from mutuals to stock companies.

The Removal of Interest Rate Ceilings   For the mortgage market, the most significant event was the removal from 1980 to 1986 of interest rate ceilings on deposit accounts at banks and thrift institutions, commonly called **Regulation Q.** The institutions lost a cheap source of funds. The one-quarter of a point advantage the thrifts had had with a higher ceiling than that of commercial banks was phased out. Deposit institutions had to decide for themselves what rates to offer in a competitive market.

In addition to increasing competition, the demise of deposit rate ceilings also promoted stability by eliminating a major cause of disintermediation. As rates offered to savers in the treasury bill market and by money market funds moved far above the interest rate ceilings of thrifts, disintermediation became far more serious. Repeal of rate ceilings allowed the institutions to react more rapidly by moving their rates closer to those of the market. Banks and savings and loans could now stem the sharp outflows of their funds by offering competitive rates. On the other hand, they now had to compete with every service and product at their disposal.

The watchword that described this new situation was the need to change regulations so as to assure all players in the financial arena "a level playing field." That is, everyone would be allowed to compete in the financial market unimpeded. How this was to come about was less clear. Did deregulation mean no more deposit insurance, identical tax laws, identical supervision (or none at all)? Some feared that a "level playing field" would lead to less stability, with players rushing back and forth from one end of the field to the other in pursuit of an elusive ball.

While developments from these new changes remained unclear, the *fact* of change was most manifest in a new aggressiveness. Maurice Mann, former president of the San Francisco Home Loan Bank, underscored this change by his capsule description of the savings and loan industry in the first 15 years after World War II. He claimed that savings and loans had a "3-6-3 rule"—they borrowed money at 3 percent, lent it out at 6 percent, and were on the golf course by 3 P.M. Those new to the field of real estate finance find it hard to imagine the easy life of that period.

The new economic environment, expanded technology, and more competition shook the thrift industry and the mortgage market to their roots. The protection from competition enjoyed by the deposit institutions disappeared. Whether this will mean a diminished market share with fewer assets for each institution is not certain. The new shape of the markets is still in the process of development.

The Financial Services Industry

Many types of firms have entered various parts of the financial services market. Their aim is to fuse what had been separate, protected markets. Sears, Roebuck and Merrill Lynch own large real estate brokerage firms and mortgage banking operations in addition to their traditional functions. Investment bankers and money management firms have become extremely important borrowers and lenders in real estate finance; they have founded consumer banks and are anxious to expand. Prudential Insurance Company has entered the business of stock brokerage and has turned again to residential real estate finance, as it did in the 1950s, for expansion.

A key issue is the degree to which firms whose deposits are insured by the government should be allowed to affiliate with firms in other industries. Because of bad loans made through affiliates prior to the Great Depression in the 1930s and because of fear of financial domination by a few conglomerates, federal laws have forbidden mergers between deposit institutions and other forms of investment and commerce. That barrier is now under attack. Insurance of deposits offers a less expensive source of funds, which can provide a competitive advantage over noninsured firms. Opponents of reducing the barrier do not want other than traditional deposit institutions to share these benefits.

The New Environment

The turmoil in the financial services industry has raised numerous questions about the future of real estate finance. As the following section discusses, many observers worry that a shortage of mortgage money could develop as a result of deregulation. Thrift institutions have been the largest suppliers of mortgages. But observers argue that the lending practices authorized by the new rules may threaten the future of home financing. For if thrifts were to shift from mortgages to other investments, as now allowed, this would decrease the availability of mortgage funds and raise mortgage interest rates.

Real estate lending and investment has always been dangerous because of its long development cycle. Speculation takes over periodically, and supply far outruns demand. Vacancies shoot up, followed by defaults. From 1970 to 1982 these dangers were hidden behind the cloak of inflation. People built into their plans the assumption that prices would continue to rise. Stable prices increased the probability of losses and defaults.

Deregulation was forcing changes. Many savings institutions were failing even as others rushed to get new charters. The ability to make all types of commercial loans, to engage in joint ventures, to own property, and to lend on nonresidential property has been greatly expanded. It was unclear what types of policies would be required to handle the new functions. Firms were uncertain how to react to the changed environment—an environment that raised questions about the future look of the savings industry and about how thrifts would operate in the mortgage market.

A SHORTAGE OF MORTGAGE MONEY

Rapid change in the thrift industry and the experience of 1980–1982, when thrifts greatly reduced funds flowing to residential loans, led to frequent "scare" articles proclaiming the existence of or imminent danger of a shortage of money, particularly for housing finance. The logic was simple. Thrifts have been the major suppliers of housing mortgages (over 50 percent of the private market). They now have freedom to put their money elsewhere. If they partially withdraw from the mortgage market, as allowed by deregulation, it will create a shortage of lendable funds for mortgages. But is this scenario accurate? What is meant by a shortage? How could one develop, and how can one be curbed once it begins?

What Is Meant by a Shortage

Individuals know when they are short of funds. The bank bounces their checks; they are forced to cut back on expenditures or go into debt. But what is a *market* **shortage of funds?** Look again at Figure 3-1, which shows a simplified market for funds. When supply falls, the supply curve for funds shifts to the left. A new equilibrium occurs at a higher interest rate. All borrowers willing to pay the higher interest rate receive funds. The only unsatisfied customers are those unwilling or unable to pay the market rate.

The concept of supply and demand illustrate what most observers mean by a shortage of funds. Prospective borrowers deemed worthy to receive a loan by generally accepted criteria find that they cannot afford market interest rates, or are unwilling to pay them. If more funds came into the market, the supply curve would shift to the right and these borrowers would be included among those taking out loans at the lower interest rate. Thus one definition of a shortage is interest rates that are too high for worthy borrowers.

However, some borrowers willing to pay the going rate may still find no loans available. For such a situation to occur, the market must be segmented and information about prevailing terms and rates among the submarkets must be poor. For some reason the borrower's demand is ineffective. Either she cannot find a lender willing to accept her bid for funds, perhaps at slightly higher than the market rate, or the lender cannot obtain enough information about the profitability of the loan and therefore accepts another loan that is less profitable but about which more is known.

Segmented Markets

When mortgages were purely local, the market for them was segmented into submarkets. Thrift institutions sometimes passed their government subsidies on to borrowers and accepted less than market interest rates, as a result of segmentation. Loans were made to selected borrowers even though others would have paid more. Such situations probably persist in isolated cases. Information about prevailing rates is far from perfectly disseminated. Some borrowers may obtain bargains even as others pay more, but this occurs in all markets.

In truth, a single interest rate for everyone, at equilibrium, is an abstraction. On any list of prices at which lenders are offering mortgage money, there will be differences in interest rates of up to 1 percent or more. These may reflect differences in real values from the consumer's point of view, such as convenience, greater ease of qualification, or more rapid decisions by lenders. However, some higher rates prevail because potential borrowers are ill informed about alternatives on the market.

Despite variations, however, when half or more of all mortgages are sold in the secondary market, segmentation cannot be great enough to create a shortage of funds. These mortgages are traded anonymously; they carry only a number, not a case history. Their prices depend on what is happening in the national or international capital markets.

Most local markets have sufficient competition so that lenders cannot make an excessive markup over the secondary market rate. However, competition is not perfect because the markets are oligopolistic. That is, they are dominated by a few sellers, who are aware of the impact of their own decisions on their margins. Nevertheless, entry into the market by new lenders is relatively easy. When rates stay too far out of line, as they have at times, new entrants gain market shares and bring the price down.

High Interest Rates

If a shortage appears to exist because some worthy borrowers cannot pay market interest rates, it is not a result of the functioning of the mortage market or of where thrifts or other deposit institutions invest their funds as a result of deregulation. Market interest rates depend on the *overall* flow of borrowing and lending, saving and investing, and on monetary policy. Because mortages are a large factor in the market, their demand does influence overall rates. But so do all other demands and supplies.

High mortgage interest rates reflect a general shortage of funds. If we believe lower rates are necessary, we must either (a) try to alter the overall supply of and demand for funds or (b) offer some or all mortgage borrowers subsidies that will reduce their real interest costs.

The Overall Market   When talk of shortages arises, attention properly turns to methods of influencing the overall market. Monetary policy can be altered.

Although more difficult, the rate of saving can be raised. Government deficits, which compete for funds, can be lowered. The government can influence other borrowing demands through taxes and subsidies. These are all long-term solutions. The growth of the secondary market has largely overcome the short-term problem of mortgages being crowded out in credit crunches more so than other borrowing. The problems that existed in the past have diminished to the degree that the Federal National Mortgage Association (FNMA), the Government National Mortgage Association (GNMA), the Federal Home Loan Mortgage Corporation (FHLMC), and the other agencies have successfully integrated the capital and mortgage markets.

Subsidies   Major debates continue over whether mortgage interest rates should be subsidized at all times, only when they seem high, or not at all. One issue arises over the value judgment that housing is so important that some or all mortgage borrowers ought to pay less than market interest rates. A second question is whether subsidies can work. Have the subsidy techniques used in the past been successful or not?

Chapter 7 outlined the advantages and disadvantages of government expenditures to reduce borrowing costs both to individual homeowners and to the thrift institutions. Each case requires an analysis of costs and benefits. Could targeting be improved so that the neediest receive more, with less being wasted on subsidies to those deemed less worthy? How do tax expenditures for homeowners, for thrifts, and for income property owners compare with each other and with other forms of aid? Direct subsidies to borrowers lower their costs, but it is argued that a lucky few are gaining at the expense of others. Subsidies to thrift institutions, it is claimed, end up mainly as higher profits or waste and inefficiency. The subsidies are not passed through to either borrowers or savers. Wealthier homeowners gain at the expense of the less well off. Given these negative facts, supporters of subsidies should be forced to show more specifically the gains they yield.

THE THRIFT INDUSTRY IN TRANSITION

The new economic environment has caused rapid changes among savings and loan associations and mutual savings banks. More than one-quarter of all firms have closed or merged. Others have been propped up with assistance from the Federal Savings and Loan Insurance Corporation (FSLIC) and the Federal Deposit Insurance Corporation (FDIC) deposit insurance agencies. The failures include some of the largest firms in the industry. During the first half of the 1980s, most firms operated with a negative market net worth. When interest rates rose far above the mortgage coupon rate, many mortgages were worth only 60 or 70 cents on the dollar. However, deposit insurers did not close down the thrifts at that time because the thrifts did not have to show mortgages at their real values in calculating net worth for regulatory purposes.

As the decade progressed, many associations continued to be in poor shape even after interest rates fell; their losses had been so great that they had difficulty recovering. However, the deposit insurers allowed many of these firms to continue operating because they were swamped with even worse cases. The insurers couldn't handle all of the failures expeditiously and wanted to spread their losses over a longer period.

In contrast, firms that were more skillful in portfolio management or that entered the market after the period of low interest rates began were very profitable. Many firms were eager to enter and take on the risks of the new deregulated environment.

The New Game

Deregulation offered the industry new opportunities. Deposit interest rate ceilings were gone. New types of accounts could be offered. Checking acocunts were no longer the sole prerogative of commercial banks. Money could be borrowed in all parts of the capital market, including **Eurodollars** (dollar funds raised outside the United States).

The lending side of the balance sheet also opened up. Consumer and commercial loans were authorized, although with restrictions. Joint ventures, which could engage in all types of projects, were permitted. Institutions, no longer limited to passive lending, could share in the profit and risks of their customers as full-fledged investors. Some states permitted almost complete freedom for institutions to lend or invest as they saw fit.

Savings institutions were no longer restricted to lending within their local areas or states. In fact, several—primarily through mergers—began to operate in a number of the largest states. It seemed clear that at least the largest firms would become national lenders. Major companies from outside the industry, such as Citicorp and Chase Manhattan Bank, among the largest commercial banks, and Sears, Roebuck, and Ford Motor Company, bought and operated savings and loan subsidiaries.

An industry that had been composed mainly of mutual firms began to shift rapidly to stock corporations. This transfer of ownership form was fostered by the regulators, who were eager to attract new capital into the industry. The capital growth of mutual firms is restricted primarily to reinvestment of earnings. Because they had trouble acquiring additional capital, the regulators tried to phase them out. Stock companies, in contrast, can raise additional funds by issuing new stock.

BACKGROUND OF THE SAVINGS INDUSTRY

Until 1980, the savings and loan industry was one of the great post–World War II success stories. The industry raised its share of household saving deposits from 14 percent in 1947 to 41 percent by 1980. Assets of the largest firms grew from only a few million to well into the billions of dollars.

The key to this growth was the existence for most of the period of an upward-sloping yield curve. Firms borrowed short, paying low ceiling rates on their deposits, and lent on mortgages at the long-term rates. The spread was great enough to guarantee profitability for all but the most badly mismanaged firms.

Other factors also contributed to the prosperity of the savings industry. The government's deposit insurance meant that depositors did not have to be concerned with the safety of the individual association. They could move their savings to a more convenient office or one offering better toasters or slightly higher rates without having to investigate that firm first. Although interest rate ceilings restricted competition on deposit rates, the thrifts were allowed an advantage of .25 percent over commercial banks. Competition among thrifts was reduced by restricting the number of new entrants, even as existing firms were allowed to branch into new territories.

The government helped in other ways as well. Firms received a tax subsidy if they continued to specialize in residential mortgage lending. They could maintain reduced liquidity by their ability to borrow from the Home Loan Banks. They could obtain long-term advances at rates only slightly above the low federal agency borrowing rate.

Regulation and Supervision

The gifts from the federal government, however, did not come without strings attached. In return, associations had to specialize in housing finance. They were to provide one of the channels for improving housing conditions. They could offer only limited types of deposits, all of which carried interest rate ceilings. They had to concentrate their loans in residential mortgages which had to meet specific criteria.

The associations were subject to examination and supervisory pressure when they moved too far from the norm. Since the regulating agencies were dominated by the industry's trade associations, however, supervision and regulation were not onerous. Only occasionally were regulations adopted that were opposed by the industry. The working relationship between the industry and the regulators was so close that many outside observers felt it was at the expense of the public.

The Impacts of Change

The new economic environment destroyed part of the base of the thrift industry's growth. The most vital changes were due to the record high interest rates, and to a reversal of the yield curve: for considerable periods, short-term rates exceeded long-term ones. More calamitous was that the short-term rates paid on deposits far exceeded the long-term rates being collected from the mortgage loans made previously at even lower rates. Liabilities cost more than assets paid.

Competition for funds heated up. Savers would no longer accept low-ceiling interest rates when treasury bills and money market funds offered rates that were much higher. Disintermediation forced the thrifts to replace low-rate deposits with much more expensive market funding. They could not pay off the deposits by selling old loans without showing the large losses incurred by the mortgages when interest rates rose. If they held on and did not sell, regulators neglected the drop in values and allowed the mortgages to be carried at book.

Deregulation brought further difficulties to older savings and loans. New entrants were not encumbered by old low-coupon mortgages. They could offer higher deposit rates because they were making new loans at the market. Even though they were small and had limited capital, because savers looked no father than the deposit insurance in evaluating where to put their money, these small firms could attract large volumes of deposits by bidding higher rates. In fact, savers were not even careful to check the security of the promised insurance. Crises arose in Ohio, California, Maryland, and other states among nonfederally insured institutions; state insurance funds had insufficient assets to meet runs on deposits.

New Assets

The new lending powers also caused problems for thrifts, because institutions took far greater risks under deregulation than before, in efforts to make larger profits. In the past, lenders could get by with only minimal skills. Home mortgages are all quite similar, and they have a low default rate. Except in cases of fraud or extreme underwriting irresponsibility, it is difficult to accumulate large default losses in portfolios of single-family owner-occupied homes.

The same freedom from losses, however, does not apply on other types of mortgages or on loans to developers. Losses shot up when firms began to lead on condominium projects, on commercial construction, and on similar riskier ventures. Even larger losses were sustained because many loans were made at a distance with unknown, unskilled developers. Firms lent anywhere if the promised profits were high enough, and many found to their sorrow that restricting thrifts to local lending made some sense. Joint ventures also turned out to be a mine field for many. The skills needed to underwrite individual home loans differ widely from those necessary for new, large projects. Furthermore, many of the new entrepreneurs were far too sanguine. The inflationary spiral made all sorts of deals appear sound, particularly to new lenders who had not experienced past periods of adversity.

By 1986, problems in the thrift industries seemed to have multiplied. Many firms still had not recovered from their losses on low-coupon fixed-rate mortgages. Some of these firms, and many newcomers, attempted to recoup by taking large risks. Lending losses, which previously had been nominal, soared. In contrast, other firms, following more traditional and cautious policies, saw their profits rise. The spread of profits and losses across the industry was unusually wide.

RISK AND INSOLVENCY

One result of dynamic change has been that losses and failures among banks and savings institutions rose to new highs. In 1981 and 1982 the thrift industry as a whole suffered losses. As late as 1984, over 40 percent of the firms in the industry were still operating unprofitably. The number of firms with negative net worth was at a record.

The deposit insurance agencies—the FSLIC and the FDIC—were faced with the task of deciding whether to declare hundreds of firms insolvent in order to liquidate or merge them, or to allow them to continue operating. The choices were difficult. Insolvent firms permitted to stay in business may take undue risks in an effort to recoup. Any added losses would be at the expense of the insurer, since no private equity would have remained, while profits would go to stockholders. Still, the insurers delayed action in hope that the situation would not deteriorate further and they would not have to act.

Lending Risks

What had happened to transform extremely profitable firms into ones with such losses? Individual lenders failed to measure properly and plan for the risks they were assuming. As Chapter 3 pointed out, risk is the probability that the returns on a loan or a portfolio of loans will fall below the amount expected. All loans carry some risks, but normally the interest rate charged the borrower is sufficient to cover them. Problems arise mainly from improper management of a firm's portfolio. If firms fail to diversify, income and capital enough to handle a flow of average losses are inadequate to cover a concentration of losses.

At least six factors can contribute to produce heavy losses in a given portfolio:

1. *Poor underwriting.* Either because of poor management or because they take large risks in the hope of large profits, firms make an unusual number of poor loans. Historically, single-family mortgages have had an excellent loss record. The number of deficiencies and defaults has been low and losses through foreclosures small. Although the number of defaults on individual loans has multiplied, except for special circumstances it has not been large enough to cause institutions to fail.

   Serious losses usually arise from a concentration of loans in large projects or from those outside the single-family sphere. (a) Many families simply walk away from badly designed and constructed developments rather than continue to pay on their mortgages. Resales can be made only at greatly reduced prices. (b) Big condominium projects turn out to be overpriced. (c) Large-scale purchases of land fail to reach the completion stage. (d) Construction loans are made on commercial projects with large cost overruns, or they may be too expensive and fail to rent up.

   Most heavy losses occur because lenders become greedy. For promised high gains, they enter into deals about which they know too little.

They cooperate with a distant association that knows even less than they do. They finance inexperienced developers because the good ones have an ongoing relationship with prior lenders.

2. *Fraud.* A surprising number of major losses are due to fraud, both within the firm and among customers. It has been particularly common among savings and loans because the conflict-of-interest laws have been rather lax. Individuals have profited from loans to related firms, planning to gain personally through loans made by the savings and loans that they own or manage.

3. *Interest rate risks.* The difficulties of the thrift industry as a whole, rather than those of specific firms, arose mainly from their assuming too much interest rate risk. When market rates rose to record highs, the value of fixed-rate mortgages dropped steeply. The ability to continue carrying mortgages on their books at face value concealed the losses for a time. However, delay did not make the problem go away. Rates paid on deposits rose above the yields of the mortgages. The losses that would have resulted if sales of old mortgages had been forced did not occur. However, the steady drain, month after month, of negative margins was enough to wipe out equities. Interest rate risk remains among among the thorniest problems for individual institutions. The next section discusses ways of decreasing it.

4. *Depressions and recessions.* After interest rates, the greatest risks to thrifts have developed when incomes declined, either nationally or locally. When this happens, borrowers do not earn enough to pay back their loans. Because too few have sufficient income to make purchases, the resale market dries up, causing larger losses from foreclosures.

   The Great Depression of 1929 to 1932 wiped out a huge number of deposit institutions. Although the recession of 1980 to 1982 was far less severe, it added to the other pressures that institutions were experiencing. Loans that would have paid off in a normal economy went bad. As the last such period shows, the risk posed by recessions and depressions is a continuing one.

   A related danger arises from cycles concentrated in one sector of the real estate market. For example, because development profits are high, a major expansion in office buildings or apartments occurs, financed by lenders seeking loans. Construction runs far ahead of the rate at which occupants can begin to use the space. Consequently, as a result of default, lenders must take back completed but unrented buildings.

   Crises can also develop in local markets. A city's main industry may decline; an air base or the largest factory in town closes down. If most of a lender's loans are concentrated locally, any such development will be a shock. On the other hand, portfolios with proper geographic diversification will hardly be affected by local cycles.

5. *Inflation and deflation.* When prices alter sharply, the projections underlying loans fail to materialize. Lenders tend to become careless in periods

of rapid inflation. Rising prices bail out even poor loans. Difficulties in meeting payments do less damage because rising prices increase owners' equity. Even if they are in trouble, borrowers will make solid efforts to meet their payments. If they fail, they can still sell out at a profit.

When inflation slows, many income assumptions go wrong. Because the owner's equity has not risen, it may not even cover selling costs. Owners default rather than add to their losses. The lender must take back the property—and the losses.

6. *Liquidity.* A traditional requirement of deposit institutions is that they maintain sufficient liquidity to cover withdrawals. **Liquidity risks** are of two types. First, money may simply not be available. In 1985, the state insurance funds of Ohio and Maryland had insufficient liquidity to pay out to state-insured institutions. The savings and loans dependent upon them faced runs on their deposits. They had to close down, reopening later to allow only limited withdrawals. Many of these thrifts failed or were taken over by banks or other associations with sufficient capital and liquidity.

A second liquidity risk is that extra costs may be generated if mortgages must be sold to obtain cash. The Home Loan Banks and the Federal Reserve will lend funds for a period to maintain an institution's liquidity, but they want to be paid back before long. Institutions that must liquidate mortgages, particularly mortgages not designed for sale in the secondary market, will incur losses.

The secret of successfully managing a loan portfolio is to avoid losses from these six factors. Basic to success are policies of diversification and careful underwriting. Some mistakes always occur. However, if the concentration of any single type of loan is low, losses will not be disastrous. Escaping the perils of interest rate risk and liquidity risk requires careful planning. The following section explains how this is accomplished.

ASSET-TO-LIABILITY MANAGEMENT

Interest rate risk remains a persistent problem for all deposit institutions, especially for mortgage lenders. Unless they plan carefully, their assets and liabilities will be mismatched; they will borrow short and lend long. When interest rates rise, they will lose; if rates fall, they will gain.

Asset-to-liability management is a system of measuring the degree to which a portfolio is mismatched and its exposure to risk. It shows the degree of risk in a portfolio, offering methods by which a firm can reduce or increase its risks. As in most invesment situations, there is a trade-off between risk and profits. A firm can reduce its risk, but only at the expense of lower profits. With a proper system based on duration or gap analysis (covered next), a firm can determine the amount of risk it is willing to accept and how to hold to that level with the least cost in lost profits.

A firm whose risk is too high can decrease the average maturity, or duration, of its loans by lending on adjustable-rate mortgages or on short-term consumer and commercial loans. Similar results can be achieved by increasing the average length of its liabilities—issuing bonds, borrowing on longer-term advances, conducting interest rate swaps, or concentrating on longer-term deposits.

Measuring Interest Rate Risk

The **duration** of a portfolio is a measure of its weighted average life or maturity. Weights are based on the present value of future payments. (The appendix to this chapter analyzes duration in more exact terms.) Duration provides a direct measure of potential interest rate risk. The value of a portfolio changes as a function of how much interest rates move and of the portfolio's duration. Values will fall when interest rates rise. The percentage fall in the value of a portfolio is equal to its duration times the percentage change in interest rates. The two examples that follow show how duration influences losses and gains.

EXAMPLE: The portfolio of a typical savings and loan has a duration of three years. What happens to the value of such a portfolio if interest rates rise from 8 percent to 13 percent (less than actually occurred)? To find the decline in the portfolio's value, multiply the 4.6 percent (.05 ÷ 1.08) increase in interest rates by its duration of 3, or:

$$3\left(\frac{.05}{1.08}\right) = 3(.046) = 13.8\%$$

The value of a portfolio would fall by 13.8 percent; a $100 million portfolio would decline to $86.2 million. If the duration was only 1, a similar calculation shows that the decline in value would be only 4.6 percent. The difference between the declines when the duration is 3 and when it is 1 shows the degree to which changing a portfolio's duration alters its risk.

EXAMPLE: A 13 percent mortgage which has an average prepayment rate of 5 percent a year has a duration of about 5.5. If prepayments do not change, the value of such a mortgage will fall by about 31 percent if interest rates rise to 18 percent (.05 ÷ 1.13 × 5.5 = 31%). However, we know that prepayments in a pool or portfolio of mortgages will change, causing problems in duration analysis. To find the duration of a portfolio, the cash flow of each mortgage must be projected; yet they depend on future interest rates. If interest rates rise to 18 percent, prepayment will be less than previously assumed, and the duration of a mortgage might climb from 5.5 to 7. As a result, duration estimates based on lower interest rates would be understated, as would the projected decline in the portfolio's value.

Gap Analysis

Another method of measuring interest rate risks is **gap analysis.** This shows to what extent the interest income of an institution responds to interest rate changes in each period. It is measured by the gap between the expected cash flows of assets and liabilities in a series of future periods. Some institutions prefer this method because it comes closer to book-value accounting. Duration analysis, on the other hand, resembles changing the stated value of a portfolio to agree with its market value.

EXAMPLE: Table 9-1 helps demonstrate how gap analysis works. The first column of figures lists all assets and liabilities that mature in the next 6 months. The second column shows those maturing in 6 months to a year, and so on. The gap is the difference between the assets and liabilities in a period. Each column would carry its current interest rate until renewal, when it would take new market rates. For ease of demonstration, look at part 1 of the table. Let us assume that all assets are earning 10 percent interest and all liabilities cost 9 percent. This firm shows net interest receipts of $33 million (3300 × .10 − 3300 × .09 = 33).

What happens if interest rates rise 1 percent (100 basis points) on both assets and liabilities? The income of the portfolio changes only to the degree that assets and liabilities mature and are reinvested. This occurs every day for some of the assets and liabilities. Renewals carry the new rates. At the end of 6 months, $900 million of assets carry the 1 percent higher rate, as does the $2 billion of liabilities. The income of the firm has fallen by $11 million at an annual rate. It has lost one-third of its expected income. This occurs because the

Table 9-1
Measuring the Gaps
(millions of dollars)

	1–180 Days	180–365 Days	1–5 Years	Over 5 Years	Total
1.					
Assets maturing	$ 900	$500	$800	$1,100	$3,300
Liabilities maturing	2,000	300	600	400	3,300
Gaps	($1,100)	$200	$200	$700	$0
2.					
Assets maturing	$1,800	$500	$200	$800	$3,300
Liabilities maturing	2,000	300	600	400	3,300
Gaps	($200)	$200	($400)	$400	$0

1 percent interest rate increase is multiplied by the negative gap of $1.1 billion. At the end of the year, the drop in annual income has decreased to $9 million (1100 − 200 × .01) because in the second 6 months $500 million of assets and only $300 million of liabilities mature.

In part 2 of the table, if the shortest-term assets had been $1.8 billion and the assets over 1 year had been reduced by that amount, any interest rate changes would not have altered income at all during the first year. The small negative gap in the first 6 months would have been offset by an equivalent positive gap in the second half of the year.

Duration analysis would not have yielded the same result as in this example. At the end of the year, all assets and liabilities with maturity of less than a year would be at par. On the other hand, the 1 percent increase in market interest rates would have lowered the value of all longer-term assets and liabilities. Since the longest-term assets show a gap of assets over liabilities, the value of the portfolio would have declined.

Which gives the truer picture, duration or gap analysis? Gap analysis shows how reported (book income) would change. Duration analysis shows what would happen if some or all of the long-term portfolio had to be liquidated. Furthermore, it predicts future losses that will have to be taken into income at a later date. Some assets would still be earning 10 percent long after the market had moved to 11 percent, whereas most liabilities would have moved up to the 11 percent rate. The firm's interest rate margin would fall.

OFFSETTING STRATEGIES

The object of an asset-to-liability analysis is to find some level of portfolio risk the lending firm is willing to accept. It should not necessarily be zero. Institutions are paid for accepting interest rate risks; it is a burden they can assume more readily than most of their customers as part of their financial intermediation. Institutions can intermediate interest rate risks because they have larger portfolios and can diversify better than can most borrowers. Many customers seek fixed-rate loans or ones with limited variability because they fear the gamble of rapid changes in their borrowing cost.

How much interest rate risk a lending firm can accept is a function of its capital and of its own risk desires. Management must decide the amount of risk it wants to take. Dangerous situations arise primarily when portfolios are built without a recognition of the pitfalls they may hold.

Balancing Portfolios

When it selects a desirable risk-to-return trade-off, how does the thrift achieve it? The answer: with difficulty. The normal mismatch prevalent in institutions has become so great that a completely balanced position is hard to attain.

However, firms can achieve a sizable improvement over past practices by choosing among the following alternatives:

1. The most dramatic choice would be to hold only adjustable-rate mortgages. Depending on their specifications, the duration of these mortgages probably falls between 1 and 2. In choosing such a tactic, however, the firm must sacrifice revenues. Returns on variable-rate mortgages are lower than those on fixed-rate ones.

2. Another set of possibilities exists on the liability side. Liabilities can be lengthened. The firm can issue long-term bonds, especially if they are backed by mortgages. Thrifts can obtain long-term advances from the Home Loan Bank System. Or marketing of intermediate-term deposits can be emphasized. In all of these cases, higher rates must be paid for the longer-term debt.

3. It is also possible to shorten the average asset maturity by making non-mortgage loans. Consumer, student, and commercial loans have a relatively short maturity.

4. Ways can be found to hedge part of the portfolio. Mortgages can be sold for delivery at future dates. Mortgage contracts can be sold in the organized *futures market*. The price variations in the future contracts when interest rates move will be in the opposite direction and will roughly offset the price movements in the firm's mortgage portfolio. Similarly, *put options* can be purchased, allowing lenders at their option to deliver mortgages in the future at a fixed interest rate.

5. Swaps of interest rates of different maturities are also possible. An **interest rate swap** is a contract between two institutions to exchange payment streams on an amount of debt for a fixed period, usually for from 2 to 12 years. Through a swap, a savings and loan can change the interest rate received on mortgages from fixed to variable, or vice versa. It does not switch the asset, but its cash flow of payments for the swap period becomes variable instead of fixed.

    For example, thrifts have many short-term variable-rate deposits that they use to fund long-term mortgages. The Student Loan Marketing Association (SLMA) has many short-term loans that it funds with longer-term bonds. Its long-term liabilities exceed its long-term assets. The thrift agreees to pay a fixed rate—perhaps 10 percent interest on $10 million for the next 5 years—to SLMA. The association agrees to pay the thrift the auction rate on 3-month T-bills every three months. The thrift has swapped a fixed-rate 5-year asset for a variable-rate one, thereby decreasing the duration of its portfolio.

None of these management techniques is costless. Most require accepting a lower interest rate. In addition, the feasible amounts involved in many of them are limited. An institution cannot suddenly decide to lower the duration of its portfolio or remove negative gaps and expect to accomplish this rapidly. Such reshuffling takes time. Only with a conscious management policy consistently applied can a firm reach its desired risk-to-return trade-off.

The increased attention to portfolio policy is only one aspect of the changing mortgage scene. Progress away from the mediocre markets of the early 1980s is proceeding rapidly. The industry has become so dynamic that predicting where it will be only a few years into the future is almost impossible. In the meantime, it is important to understand why change is occurring and to recognize the forces shaping the future.

PROBABLE DEVELOPMENTS

The thrift industry will find it difficult to settle down, for as of 1986 the forces promoting rapid change have not diminished. Failures must be weeded out without placing too great a burden on the industry or the public. More capital is required if lending is to expand.

The whole future structure of the financial services industry remains in doubt. A basic question is whether the country should maintain a group of deposit institutions that primarily specialize in housing finance. Should thrift institutions be granted special privileges and tax breaks if they agree to maintain home mortgages as their principal business? As we have seen, the answer depends on (a) whether markets can be segmented and (b) who gains and by how much from government funds spent for this purpose.

Capital

Because savings institutions had low risks and were under the supervision of the FSLIC, they have operated with little or no real capital. Commercial banks did little better. However, if deposit institutions are to have less supervision and take more risks, they need more capital. Managements should be betting their own or their stockholders' funds and not those of the deposit insurers. Without adequate capital, the investment strategy of deposit institutions becomes a game of "heads I win, tails you lose." Risks that are large and not well thought through can be taken because the firm has the chance of winning big, while if it loses, costs to the firm's owners are small. It is like a lottery in which the owners have bet a small amount of capital, but the odds are greatly in their favor because the public has put a large sum in the pot but gets no tickets.

Economies of Scale and Scope

The key factor behind government aid has been the concept of specialization. Thrifts were assisted for the purpose of encouraging easier family saving and cheaper mortgages. But such aid may not be justified if lenders are no longer restricted to housing finance. The idea of a "level playing field" means no advantages for any firm. Henceforth competition, not government policy, is to bring about the most efficient market.

The growth of large statewide or national institutions removes the supposed advantages of management by locally involved neighbors. Most savings associations now control their lending by criteria that differ only slightly, if at all, from those of national lenders. In fact, many adopt the standards promulgated by Fannie Mae (the FNMA) and Freddie Mac (the FHLMC).

Furthermore, specialization in mortgages was in large part the cause of the crises of the thrifts. With portfolios concentrated in fixed-rate mortgages, they were extremely vulnerable to interest rate movements. Although portfolios consisting entirely of fixed-rate mortgages can be hedged against interest rate risks, it requires a good deal of skill—perhaps more than small or medium-sized firms can afford.

Small local firms are less viable because economies of scale have become more substantial. Marketing and advertising costs decline considerably as the size of an institution grows. Loan officers can become more specialized. A single person can devote full time to handling commercial lending rather than dealing with such loans only on rare occasions, and with less expertise.

Technology may also have brought about significant new economies of scale. The computer and ATMs may again make specialization in collecting savings and making mortgages worthwhile. If so, they too probably contribute to the development of larger firms.

In addition, technology may well have increased the economies of handling more product lines by a single firm. It may be cheaper to market a number of products to the same customers. **Economies of scope** arise when it costs less to market and produce a package of products than to specialize in individual products.

Thrifts can broaden their product lines to include more types of financial products, such as new savings accounts, insurance, real estate brokerage, development and construction loans, and some commercial loans. They may gain efficiency through their ability to sell several different services to the same customers. Anyone with a deposit account knows that you now receive a variety of offers from your friendly financial service institution. Selling by mail is expensive; therefore, it is more cost effective when done using a mailing list of customers who are satisfied with other services. Products may reinforce one another in other ways as well. The skills acquired in lending may lead to better development decisions. People who borrow also buy real estate and insurance, and vice versa.

Economies of scope are likely to foster larger firms. The larger the customer base, the cheaper it is to develop and make use of additional skills. Learning costs may also be reduced. As change occurs, large firms find it easier and cheaper to learn and adopt new skills. On the other hand, small firms find it harder to spend the time or manpower needed to learn new tasks. For lack of economies, and for other reasons, they tend to be followers and copiers, not innovators.

Geographic Change

Technology also makes it easier to manage institutions from a distance—further minimizing the supposed advantage of local lending. Computers and telecommunications allow decisions to be made and audited rapidly from a central location. Exceptions can be noted and acted on immediately rather than after a delay.

Branches developed primarily as a way of collecting funds. They may be done away with as a result of ATMs. For years, banks tried to move their managers and loan officers out onto the streets to insure active marketing rather than a passive acceptance of loan requests. If computers can handle the cash function semiautomatically, more employees can be put to use performing previously neglected tasks. Most big banks have cut back on their branches in a given geographic area. Expansion continues through more ATMs or by moving into new territory.

Competition

What is less clear is whether faster and better communications have actually increased effective competition. The banking and savings industries have been oligopolistic. Price competition has been unwelcome. With money rates posted publicly, any cuts by one institution are likely to be matched by another. Price competition can be expensive. As a result, most competition has occurred in nonprice areas—more appliances for opening accounts, more free coffee for customers, more branches. Even deregulation has not changed this.

THE FORM OF THE FUTURE

Over the past hundred years or more, the thrift and banking industries have debated the advantages of scale and of locally owned institutions. For most of this period the results were a standoff. Small firms had political clout and no severe economic disadvantages. They were able to maintain state laws limiting branches and keeping competition out of their local markets. The United States has had over 20,000 deposit institutions. If it had followed the path of other industrialized countries, there would have been only about 200 or 300 separate firms.

Smaller institutions fought hard against the entry of larger ones into their markets. They argued that absentee owners took more from a community than they contributed. They pointed out the danger of concentrating economic and political power in a few hands rather than in many. Their fears were illustrated by an early cartoon, which showed a large cow eating in the Midwest breadbasket while being milked in Wall Street. Insurance agents have been able to restrict institutional insurance sales by citing potential conflicts of interest. Can a prospective borrower really shop for the best insurance if a lender suggests that the loan will best be protected if the borrower buys the fire insurance from the lender's own company? On the other hand, consumers have argued that forbidding banks to sell insurance precludes the convenience of being able to obtain a loan and insurance simultaneously.

Under the impact of change and deregulation, many of the laws preventing the entry of larger firms into local markets seem to be crumbling. Many states that had the strictest no-branching laws have now allowed statewide operations. Others permit entry by firms throughout the region. Congress authorized mergers of savings and loans across state borders to reduce the rescue costs of the FSLIC. Nationwide banking seems on its way.

Fewer and Larger Firms

What do all these factors add up to? Most observers foresee a sharp reduction in the number of deposit institutions and an increase in the size of the largest. Yet we are unlikely to see the high concentration of firms that exists in other countries. Experts have estimated that by the turn of the century we could see the number of firms decline from 20,000 toward 3,000.*

Current experience shows that small firms can continue to operate profitably if they find a proper niche. Some lending tasks call for specialized skills. Some customers want and can pay for unusual service. Entrepreneurial lenders who have the capital and skills necessary to expand their operations often prefer to stay small. At the other extreme, the number of nationwide firms handling all types of financial services is likely to be fairly small; betwen 50 and 100 seems reasonable.

No one knows how fast such change is likely to occur. In the first place, it depends on the political process. When change has strong opponents it lags well behind its economic justification. Secondly, technological change is dynamic; it might make the need for larger firms obsolete—allowing the current situation of many smaller firms to continue. For example, relatively inexpensive personal computers and microcomputers have obviated the need for massive and costly mainframe computers in many uses. Similar developments could affect the financial services industry.

California, which has roughly 10 percent of the nation's population, is often seen as a model for the future. It may present a picture of what to expect from unlimited nationwide banking. California has between 600 and 700 commercial banks and savings institutions, about 20 to 25 of which operate on a statewide basis. Perhaps double that number are important in local areas. The rest operate with a limited number of branches, or with none. Applying the California experience to the whole country, one might expect 6,000 to 7,000 institutions—about one-fourth of the present number. On the other hand, economies of scale and scope seem to be growing. This would mean fewer nationwide deposit institu-

---

*For a discussion of some of these issues, see F. E. Balderston, *Thrifts in Crisis* (Cambridge, MA: Ballinger, 1985) and the references therein.

tions than would be estimated from multiplying the number in California firms—a number still far larger than would be expected from the experience of other countries.

Integration of Financial Service Firms

Because of technology, economic forces, and the changing political climate, more integration will take place, reducing the amount of specialization and the differences between financial service firms. Deregulation has meant that the powers of commercial banks and thrifts are becoming more alike.

Both types of institutions own national mortgage companies. They still differ, however, with respect to their ability to merge with other kinds of financial institutions, and particularly with commercial or manufacturing firms.

By law, bank holding companies are limited in the types of activities in which they can engage. A strict prohibition exists forbidding nonbanking firms from owning and operating commercial banks. Because thrifts have had inadequate capital in the past few years, this same prohibition does not apply to them; regulators have been happy to welcome additional capital from any source.

Some relaxation of what banks can do appears probable. In the future, banks will be able to enter more areas of financial services. Conversely, other purely financial service firms will be able to move into commercial banking. However, removing the curtain between banking and commerce seems less likely; the separation has a long tradition. This also means that commercial and manufacturing firms buying savings institutions will have trouble expanding the range of financial services they offer. Their additional capital is welcome to bail thrifts out of trouble—but not to take them out of the home finance market.

SUMMARY

The financial services industry has changed rapidly in the past decade. Inflation and high interest rates necessitated a rethinking of portfolio strategies. Technological change—particularly computers, telecommunications, and their offspring, automatic teller machines—caused major changes in how the industry operated. Deregulation heightened competition.

The ability of thrifts to lend elsewhere than for home finance has caused some observers to fear a shortage of mortgage money. They mean either that interest rates are so high that some borrowers are unwilling to pay them, or that some who might have obtained mortgages at below-market rates in the past no longer can do so. To the degree that mortgage and capital markets are integrated, mortgage rates depend on the overall supply of and demand for funds. If mortgages are to be subsidized, difficult choices must be made as to the most efficient methods.

One major cause of change results from the reorganization of the thrift industry. Savings and loans grew rapidly in a protected market that has now eroded. To offset the effects of the new competitive environment, they have been granted new powers to alter the types of assets and liabilities they hold.

Losses and failures among financial institutions shot up in the 1980s for various reasons. Initially, the largest losses were among firms that had assumed excessive interest rate risks. However, many firms also experienced a sharp deterioration in the quality of their assets. They moved too rapidly into new lending spheres and failed to diversify properly.

Asset-to-liability management enables firms to measure and control their interest rate risk. The amount of risk can be measured through estimates of the duration of a portfolio or by gap analysis of the mismatch of assets and liabilities. The amount of duration or gap can be reduced by actions to shorten assets or lengthen liabilities.

The number of financial institutions has been declining slowly. With new powers to branch within states and regions and with national banking on the horizon, a drastic reduction in numbers appears possible. How fast change occurs will depend on both technological and regulatory change. The scope of financial firms will widen. Less certain is the degree to which commercial and manufacturing firms will be allowed to expand to the ownership of deposit institutions.

KEY TERMS

asset-to-liability management
automatic teller machines
duration
economies of scope
Eurodollars

gap analysis
interest rate swap
liquidity risk
Regulation Q
shortage of funds

QUESTIONS

1. What is meant by a shortage of mortage money?
2. In a segmented mortgage market, would you expect wide variations in mortgage rates? Why or why not?
3. What factors contributed to the growth of the savings industry prior to 1980?
4. Discuss the main forces for change that have created problems for the thrift industry.
5. Why did losses at savings and loans increase dramatically in the first half of the 1980s?
6. Compare and contrast gap and duration analysis.
7. Suggest some guidelines for better asset-to-liability management for a thrift.
8. What do you think will be the main forces determining future development in the savings industry?

9. Using Table 3-3 or a calculator, find the duration of a $100,000, 10 per-
cent mortgage amortized over 10 years. If it is expected to be paid off at
the end of year 5, what is its duration?
10. Discuss the main factors that have caused changes in the financial service
industry.
11. What changes do you expect to see in the financial service industry over
the next five years? Explain why.

APPENDIX TO CHAPTER 9
DURATION

Duration is a measure of the weighted average time before payments are
received from interest and principal on a mortgage or loan. The weights used
in the calculation are the relative present values of the payments. Thus, duration
(D) can be expressed as:

$$D = \sum_{t=1}^{n} w_t(t) = W_1 + w_2(2) + \ldots + w_n(n)$$

where: t is the time period when a payment is received, usually expressed in
years;
w is a weight;
n is the number of periods.
The weight (w) represents the present value (PV) of each payment as a
proportion of the present value of the mortgage (which is also its price). It will
change as interest rates and prepayments alter. When P is the amount of payment
in a period, i is the market interest rate, and PV(P_t) is the present value of P_t,
the weight of the payment received in period t is as follows:

$$w_t = \frac{\dfrac{P_t}{(1+i)^t}}{\displaystyle\sum_{t=1}^{n}\dfrac{P_t}{(1+i)^t}} \quad \text{and} \quad \sum_{t=1}^{n}\frac{P_t}{(1+i)^t} = \text{price}$$

The duration then is

$$D = \frac{\displaystyle\sum_{t=1}^{n}\dfrac{tP_t}{(1+i)^t}}{\displaystyle\sum_{t=1}^{n}\dfrac{P_t}{(1+i)^t}} = (1)\left(\frac{\dfrac{P_1}{1+i}}{\text{price}}\right) + (2)\left(\frac{\dfrac{P_2}{(1+i)^2}}{\text{price}}\right) + \ldots + (n)\left(\frac{\dfrac{P_n}{(1+i)^n}}{\text{price}}\right)$$

Or assume that a $1,000 mortgage is written at 10 percent with interest to be paid at the end of each year, and the principal is to be received at the end of year 4. Its duration is:

$$D = (1)\left(\frac{\frac{100}{1.10}}{1000}\right) + (2)\left(\frac{\frac{100}{(1.10)^2}}{1000}\right) + (3)\left(\frac{\frac{100}{(1.10)^3}}{1000}\right) + (4)\left(\frac{\frac{(1100)}{(1.10)^4}}{1000}\right) = 3.487$$

$$D = \quad .0909 \quad + \quad .1653 \quad + \quad .2254 \quad + \quad 3.0053 \quad = 3.487 \text{ years}$$

If interest rates were lower, the duration would be longer, since the present value of the later payments would be greater. For example, at 4 percent interest, the duration of this mortgage would be 3.75 years. On the other hand, if pre-payments were expected, the duration would be less, since the early payments would be larger. If it were all prepaid at the end of year 2, the mortgage would have a duration of 1.91 years.

While duration increases with the term to maturity, the rate of increase slows as the period of the mortgage extends. The duration of a mortgage does not increase by much when maturity is extended from 20 years to 30 years, because the present value of payments to be received 20 years or more out is low.

The risk to a mortgage or a portfolio depends on its average duration. For small changes in interest, the relationship between duration and price volatility (the interest-elasticity of the mortgage or portfolio) is approximately

$$\frac{\Delta PM}{PM} = -D\frac{\Delta i}{1 + i}$$

That is, the percentage change in the price of a mortgage (PM) equals the percentage change in market interest rates times the negative of its duration. The interest rate risk depends on the duration and on the probabilities of interest rate movements.

Households: Affordability and Decisions to Borrow and Buy

10 Mortgages and Affordability

OBJECTIVES

When you finish this chapter, you should be able to:

- explain what it costs to own a house and how such costs have varied over time.

- discuss the mortgage tilt problem and the relationship of inflation to housing costs.

- understand how to measure the costs of owning and renting.

- define at least two types of affordability.

- construct indexes of affordability and recognize the problems in using them.

- identify the kind of factors entering into the decision as to how expensive a house to buy.

PEOPLE WHO DO NOT own a home are often told they are making a great mistake. Owning a home is said to be one of the best investments one can make. But many would-be buyers say they cannot afford to buy a house because their income is not high enough to pay for the one they want. This conflict arises because of the difference between the actual economic costs of owning a house and the cash flow payments needed.

This chapter analyzes the differences between these two measures of ownership costs. How much a family can or should pay for a house depends not only on whether it can meet the monthly payments, but also on the amount of actual sacrifice of other consumption and savings it is willing to make. The two differ because of tax deductions, because of the opportunity costs of lost income from equity, because a building may depreciate or appreciate, because mortgages amortize, and because transactions cost money.

In many periods, homes have been excellent investments, with the actual costs of homeownership at times approaching zero. This chapter shows how actual costs are calculated and why they vary, and describes ways to measure the ability of households to afford a house. It also enumerates some of the factors that enter into the decision of whether to rent or buy and how expensive a house it is reasonable to consider.

BUYING VERSUS RENTING

Among the most basic decisions every family must make are whether to rent or to buy and how much to spend for housing. Once the decision to buy has been made, the key decisions are what house to buy and how to finance it. These choices determine how we live, how much we spend for shelter, how much will be available for other types of consumption and saving, and how profitable an asset we own. Knowledge of how to make the best decisions possible is valuable to everyone involved in real estate finance. Since most sales of property depend on financing, those brokers and salespeople who have intimate knowledge of all available possibilities will sell more property. Lenders who know enough to avoid making poorly underwritten loans that do not fit a family's financial needs will avoid losses due to borrower defaults.

The Costs of Ownership and Renting

Renters know what their occupancy costs will be for the period of the rental agreement. The amount a renter agrees to pay in rent is the measure of his or her current sacrifice. In comparing renting to owning, occupants must also project future rents over some logical horizon. Many families incorrectly choose to rent because their rent payments at a single point in time are less than the cash payments needed for ownership. They fail to consider two factors: how much rents may rise, and the actual economic costs of ownership.

Buying a house involves different kinds of costs. The purchase price, closing costs, and the amount borrowed determine the initial expenditures and the annual or monthly costs. The **initial expenditures** consist of the down payment and necessary closing costs. The initial amount needed depends on the loan-to-value ratio of the mortgage, on points, and on whatever other costs are involved in obtaining title.

At least four different concepts can be used to analyze and measure **annual or monthly payments:**

1. The **mortgage payment,** covering interest and any amortization of principal.
2. **Housing expenses,** or the amount of the mortgage payment plus property taxes and mortgage and hazard insurance. These items are often abbreviated as **P.I.T.I.** (*Principal, Interest, Taxes, Insurance*).
3. **Annual cash costs,** equivalent to annual rent payments, include P.I.T.I. plus necessary maintenance and repairs, reduced by any savings in annual income tax payments that result from the shift to ownership. (Income tax withholding can be reduced to provide the cash needed for mortgage payments.)
4. **Actual economic costs of ownership** measure the amount of income sacrificed to own and occupy a house. In deciding whether to rent or buy and how much to spend, prospective owners must look beyond the annual payments to the actual economic costs, which reflect the fact that the buyer of a house acquires an investment as well as a source of housing services. The investment results must be added to the annual cash costs to arrive at the actual economic costs. This means that (a) the **opportunity costs,** or the income not received on the equity tied up in the property, must be added to the annual cash costs, and (b) when a house is sold, the amount of cash received back will differ from the initial cash payments. How much is received back depends on the selling price, selling costs, and the amount of mortgage amortization that has taken place. This difference, divided by the number of years of ownership, must be added to or subtracted from the other costs to obtain the actual economic costs of ownership.

EXAMPLE: The difference between mortgage payments, housing expenses, cash costs, and actual economic costs can be found in the first column of Table 10-1.

Section 2 contains both the P.I.T.I. and the cash costs. For 1960 to 1970, the payments on the mortgage, real estate taxes, and insurance average $1,747 a year over the 10-year period. Adding maintenance costs and subtracting the tax savings reduce the annual cash costs to $1,606.

Table 10-1
A Comparison of Cash-Flow and Actual Costs of Homeownership

	1960–1970	1970–1980	1980–1985
1. Acquisition, or capital, cost			
Purchase price	$19,100	$23,000	$62,200
Closing costs	669	805	2,177
Total	$19,769	$23,805	$64,377
Initial expenditures			
Down payment	$1,910	$2,300	$6,220
Closing costs	669	805	2,177
Total	$2,579	$3,105	$8,397
Receipts on sale			
Selling price	$23,000	$62,200	$74,800
Less selling costs (10%)	(2,300)	(6,220)	(7,480)
Less mortgage outstanding	(14,631)	(18,291)	(54,895)
Total	$6,069	$37,689	$12,425
Receipts less initial			
expenditures	$3,490	$34,584	$4,028
2. Annual cash costs			
Mortgage payment (P.I.)	$1,326	$1,885	$7,405
(Interest rate)	(6.67%)	(8.36%)	(12.95%)
Real estate tax (1.6%)	337	681	1,096
Insurance (0.4%)	84	170	274
P.I.T.I.	$1,747	$2,736	$8,775
Plus maintenance (1.0%)	211	426	685
Less tax deduction (25% rate)	(352)	(582)	(2,099)
Total	$1,606	$2,580	$7,361
3. Annual economic costs			
Mortgage payments	$1,326	$1,885	$7,405
Real estate tax	337	681	1,096
Insurance	84	170	274
Maintenance	211	426	685
Less tax deduction	(352)	(582)	(2,099)
Plus interest on equity (after tax)	193	270	868
Subtotal	$1,799	$2,850	$8,229
Annualized receipts less initial expenditure	(349)	(3,458)	(1,771)*
Total	$1,450	($608)	$6,458

*Closing and selling costs amortized over 10-year span for comparison with other periods.

Sources: Existing house prices for 1970 to 1985 are from the National Association of Realtors; interest rates are from the Federal Home Loan Bank Board; taxes, maintenance, and insurance, and 1960 house price are estimates based on FHA and census data.

Section 3 of the table shows that the actual economic costs are further reduced to $1,450. This results from the addition of $193 a year in opportunity costs and a savings of $349 a year, reflecting appreciation, transaction costs, and the average annual mortgage amortization. (We will return to this table in the next section.)

The Owner's Choices

In seeking a sound decision to rent or buy, in theory families should first ask, "With our current and expected income, how much do we want to spend for shelter over a period of three, five, or ten years?" Next they must find out what they can get for that amount in both the rental and ownership markets.

Owners Spend More   In fact, however, the choice is seldom made in that way. Most owners spend more on actual housing costs than do renters.* One reason for this is that buyers have a better selection of housing that is available to them. The rental market offers less choice, especially in desirable locations. Pride of ownership is also a factor; people are willing to spend money to fix up their own homes but would consider it a waste to put money into a rental unit. Ownership also appears to yield a "psychic income," and one's standard of living and expenditures rise with ownership.

Buying has another advantage: a family can control a much larger investment than is usually available to them. Extremely high leverage, possible in buying a house, increases a typical family's assets several hundredfold. Thus the decision to buy is and should be treated as a combination consumption and investment decision. What a family spends for a house determines what housing services the family consumes, while the *actual* cost of these services rises or falls depending on their investment results. These results, in turn, depend on the amount of the family's leverage, on what happens to the market in general, and on the family's skills in purchasing and making financing arrangements.

Lenders' Limits on Borrowing

Even though potential buyers make logical decisions as to how much to spend for housing based on their desired standard of living and projected economic costs, they often find that lenders do not agree. Consequently, families may not be able to raise the amount needed to complete a purchase.

Lenders may be reluctant to grant a loan because they base their decisions on the family's current income and expenditures, not on projected economic costs. Their experience causes them to beware of expectations. Lenders formulate general lending criteria and minimize their risks by making only rare exceptions.

---

*See I. S. Lowry, C. E. Hillestad, and S. Sama, *California Housing* (Santa Monica: The Rand Corporation, 1983), 93.

Lenders usually limit their loans in accordance with a family's ability to raise cash for the down payment and with the ratio of expected housing and other debt payments to income. These ratios are **expense-to-income ratios,** and each lender determines maximum ratios a family can assume in qualifying for a loan. Lenders generally use two separate ratios. One is the ratio of housing expenses to income. As noted previously, housing expenses consist of payments on the mortgage, property taxes, and insurance (P.I.T.I.). Although some lenders take into account expenses for maintenance and utilities as well as income tax savings, this is usually not the case. Maximum ratios of housing expenses to gross monthly income allowed by lenders tend to range from 25 percent to 28 percent.

A second ratio considers P.I.T.I. plus other installment debt payments that have more than 10 months to run. The maximum range for the ratios of these **total monthly payments** to gross monthly income, is usually 33 percent to 36 percent.

When either ratio goes slightly over the maximum, lenders may de-emphasize the criteria on the basis of other factors: the buyer's assets and liabilities, past credit history, past spending habits as measured by savings, and potential for increased earnings. These have been shown to reflect borrowers' willingness and ability to pay the mortgage on time.

Even more important is the percent of down payment. Ratios at the top of a lender's range would be acceptable if the down payment was 20 percent; an applicant might be rejected if the down payment was only 5 percent. Higher down payments mean that borrowers have a greater incentive to meet the payments, since they have more to lose if they default. Furthermore, even if they default, receipts from a foreclosure are less likely to fall below the amount of the loan.

EXAMPLE: Table 10-2 summarizes how a lender would calculate the two expense-to-income ratios. In a loan application, Peter reports that his base monthly income is $2,310, supplemented by an annual bonus that averages $230 a month. Bonuses and other secondary income, such as overtime, commissions, or pay for second jobs, are usually counted if they are typical of the job, can be substantiated by past records, and are likely to continue. The application showed that Cindy earned $620 a month in regular part-time work; this is counted also.

Housing expenses or P.I.T.I. estimated at $815 a month and long-term debt payments at $230 add up to total monthly expenses of $1,045. The ratio of expenses to gross income is 25.8 percent and the total expense ratio is 33.1 percent. If these ratios were above the lender's maximum, a special consideration of other assets, saving habits, and the amount of down payment would be required to determine the amount of risk.

WHAT IT COSTS TO OWN A HOUSE

Although lenders put most emphasis on monthly cash outlays, families must recognize that they are making a combined consumption and investment

Table 10-2
Ratio of Monthly Housing Expenses to Income

Category of Expense or Income	Amount
Income	
Base employment income (Peter)	$2,310
Base employment income (Cindy)	620
Annual bonus (monthly average)	230
Total	$3,160
Housing expenses (P.I.T.I.)	
Monthly mortgage payment	$720
Taxes and hazard insurance	95
Total P.I.T.I.	$815
Long-term debt payment	
Automobile	$180
Furniture	50
Total	$230
Total monthly expenses	$1,045

$$\frac{\text{Housing expenses}}{\text{Gross income}} = \frac{\$815}{\$3,160} = 25.8\%$$

$$\frac{\text{Total monthly expenses}}{\text{Gross income}} = \frac{\$1,045}{\$3,160} = 33.1\%$$

decision. In deciding how much to spend and borrow, they should take into account the potential difference between P.I.T.I., annual cash costs, and actual economic costs.

How can families calculate their potential actual costs and compare them with their cash outlays? Table 10-1 summarizes such differences and highlights the significant cost variables through the experience of families who bought houses, lived in them for a period, and then sold them. The three columns of costs on the table reflect those of typical homeowners who bought in 1960, in 1970, and in 1980. In each case, the information covers the median-priced house bought in the initial year. It assumes that the house was financed at terms typically available at the time of purchase and that it was lived in for 10 years if bought in 1960 or 1970 and for five years in the case of the 1980 purchase. It was then sold at the median price for existing houses prevailing in the last year of the period. (This overstates the expected sales price slightly, because the total universe of houses probably grew somewhat in price and quality over the period.)*

Acquisition Costs and Initial Expenditures

In calculating cash flow and economic costs, the initial expenditures follow the same rule. Buyers decide how much they need or want to spend for a house and what leverage to use. Choices depend on market prices in their localities, on how much they can borrow, and on lenders' terms. These factors determine the amount of both initial and annual (monthly) costs. In 1960, the typical (median) American family bought a house that cost $19,100 (see section 1 of Table 10-1). It had to pay $669 in closing costs, and its cash payments were based on a 90 percent mortgage. A 10 percent down payment plus closing costs required an initial cash expenditure of $2,579, or 13.5 percent of the purchase price. By 1970 the median house had risen in price to $23,000, and by 1980 to $62,200.

Annual Cash Costs

The typical homeowner's annual cash costs for each period include the mortgage payments based on average interest rates in the year of purchase, plus sums for real estate taxes and insurance (P.I.T.I.). (See section 2 of Table 10-1.) Although taxes and insurance differ from one locality to another, the percentages shown in Table 10-1 for each (1.6 percent and .4 percent) are typical for the country as a whole. They have been applied to the *average value* (the purchase price plus the sales price divided by two) of the house over the entire period.

To cover expenditures for maintenance and repairs, 1 percent of a house's value is added to P.I.T.I. Since such costs vary widely depending on the age and condition of each house, these expenditures should be projected specifically for every potential purchase.

Tax Savings   A deduction for tax savings should also be projected individually. A major factor lowering annual cash costs has been the ability to reduce income taxes through the deductibility of mortgage interest payments and property taxes. These costs can be deducted from one's taxable income in calculating federal (and many state) income taxes. Previous discussions of tax expenditures explained the logic of these deductions as well as how they work. They also pointed out that how much one gains depends on marginal tax brackets. Table 10-1 uses a 25 percent marginal tax rate applied to interest and property tax payments in its calculations. These result in a sizable reduction in the required

---

*For more detailed data and a related analysis, see K. T. Rosen, *California Housing Markets in the 1980s: Demand, Affordability, and Policies* (Cambridge, Mass.: Oelgeschlager, Gann, & Hain, 1984), Ch. 2.

cash flow payments. In the period 1980 to 1985, for example, these deductions reduced annual payments by over $2,000 per year. Although President Reagan urged the removal of some of these deductions, the Tax Reform Act of 1986 retained both the mortgage interest and the property tax deductions. However, the act considerably reduced the gain for families whose other itemized deductions fall below the amount allowed under the standard deduction. Some of the assumed deductions from homeownership are offset by the amounts needed to raise the total of itemized deductions up to the standard deduction.

The table reflects the sharp increase in the price of housing and of interest rates that occurred over this period. Cash flow payments after tax benefits rose from $1,606 in the period from 1960 to 1970 to $7,361 in the period from 1980 to 1985—well over a 350 percent increase. Payments went up because houses cost more, interest rates were higher, and property taxes rose.

Actual Annual Costs

Section 3 of Table 10-1 contains an estimate of the actual annual ownership costs for a typical house in each of these periods, showing how and why they varied from the cash payments in section 2 even though these make up the bulk of the total. The annual costs of ownership must be adjusted for two other costs or gains: opportunity cost and the results of investing in the property upon its sale.

Opportunity Costs   The first is the opportunity cost of the earnings lost from not being able in invest the initial payments and mortgage amortization elsewhere. In 1980, for example, the buyer had to pay out nearly $8,400 upon closing. If this money had not been put into the house, it would earn a return elsewhere. How much it would earn depends on each individual. Money in savings accounts would not return much; money used to avoid installment or credit card payments would earn a good deal.

As with maintenance costs and tax savings, opportunity costs vary so much among families that each one must estimate its own in projecting its actual economic costs. For Table 10-1 we have used the initial mortgage interest rate in each period as an estimate of what a typical family might pick. This rate should be calculated net of taxes, since if the equity funds were invested elsewhere their return would be taxed. Alternatively, the net opportunity cost can be estimated by using the return on tax-exempt bonds rather than the mortgage rate less marginal taxes. For example, in 1970 the assumed interest rate is 8.36 percent. A tax saving of 25 percent reduces it to 6.27 percent. This rate is multiplied by the initial equity plus the average equity buildup from repayments of principal over the 10-year holding period. The estimated opportunity cost after taxes is $270 per year, which is an estimate of the after-tax amount that would have been earned if the equity tied up in the house had been invested elsewhere.

Appreciation   In estimating the gap between the cash costs and the economic costs, it is still more important to include a correction for investment results. **Appreciation** or depreciation can be measured roughly by the difference between an owner's initial cash payment and any amount received back when a property is sold. The size of the correction depends on (a) the difference between the purchase and selling prices, (b) **transaction costs,** or the amount of closing costs at purchase plus selling costs, and (c) the equity built up, or amortization of the mortgage. In most cases, no subtraction is necessary for a possible capital gains tax, since several methods exist to postpone or avoid the tax on one's principal home.

Receipts on Sale   Section 1 of Table 10-1 also contains estimates of the amount received when a house is sold. The change in the value of a house may dominate all other factors in determining the actual costs of ownership. Changes in selling prices depend on how good a buy was made originally, on what happens to the neighborhood, on the maintenance of improvements and site, and on the rate of inflation. In most post–World War II periods, housing prices have risen so that, even after paying transaction costs, sellers have gotten back more than they paid.

However, not all sellers have been equally fortunate. Results have depended on the period, the locality, and the individual house. In the mid-1980s many owners experienced no increase in values. Some who bought in 1982 at the height of the buying boom and had to sell during the following three or four years were fortunate if they got back enough to cover their down payment.

Among the factors that may cause receipts to fall below expenditures are *selling costs,* which vary between 8 percent and 12 percent of the sales price. Included in these costs are agent's fees, attorney charges, prepayment penalty, mortgage points, escrow and stamp fees, plus the risks of having to redecorate or hold a unit vacant while a sale is being made. Transaction costs per year are estimated as the closing costs plus selling costs divided by the number of years. Given these large charges, it rarely pays, except in periods of rapid inflation, to buy a house if one expects to have to move within the next three years.

Even before selling costs are subtracted, the existing mortgage must be paid off or transferred to the new owner. The mortgage will be less than it was at the time of purchase because of amortization. Using Table 4-3, it is easy to see that the cumulative monthly repayments of principal on a 30-year 10 percent mortgage will be 3.4 percent at the end of 5 years and 9.1 percent at the end of 10 years. Unless a house is owned for more than 10 years, therefore, amortization will be less than selling costs. As a result, even over 10 years, unless the sales price exceeds the purchase price, final cash receipts at sale will be less than initial cash payments.

The gap between the initial expenditures and receipts upon sale, together with the opportunity costs, reflect the investment results of owning a home. The actual gain over the period is shown on the bottom line of section 1 of

Table 10-1. In section 3, the second-to-last line shows the average of these gains on an annual basis. In the last line, these gains are subtracted from the other costs, resulting in a final estimate of actual costs on an annualized basis.

As we shall see in Part 4, investment results are normally calculated in present-value terms to reflect any variances between the timing of income and expenditures. In calculating economic costs of homeownership, however, the neglect of present value makes only a minor difference because one's income from the house, both in rents saved and in psychic returns, rises, as do costs, at the same rate as the house appreciates. This assumption, that costs and income will move at the appreciation rate, is only roughly true if mortgage terms are fixed.

The Final Economic Cost Estimate

The final line of Table 10-1 shows estimates of the annual economic costs to own the median home in each of the periods since 1960. Although the estimates are not exact, differences in the movements of the averages are great enough for us to be certain that individual homeowners whose results cover a wide range around the averages experienced tremendous variations in actual costs. In the first period, with inflation and interest rates low, the annual cost of ownership averaged about 7.6 percent of the purchase price of a house. This was somewhat below the annual cash costs, but not by much. Because house values appreciated and equity built up through mortgage amortization, a gain upon sale exceeded the equity's opportunity costs by $156 annually, and this was the amount by which actual costs fell below cash costs.

The results in the second period were far different. Inflation of the general price level and a still more rapid appreciation of housing prices caused the cost of ownership to be negative. The annual rate of appreciation actually exceeded owners' annual after-tax costs. As people realized what a good deal ownership was, they bid up housing prices, speeding up appreciation still further and cutting the real costs of those who owned homes.

In the last period, however, the market caught up with inflation. Nominal interest rates rose to 12.95 percent. The rapid appreciation in house prices slowed drastically. As a result, the annual economic costs from 1980 to 1985 for the median house bought in 1980 rose to $6,458. The true cost of homeownership, even after tax benefits, rose to over 10 percent a year. Ownership expenses were certainly much higher than many buyers had expected, given the opposite results of the prior decade. If they had realized how much their actual costs would run, they might have bought cheaper houses or even remained renters.

INFLATION AND OWNERSHIP COSTS

The dichotomy between cash costs and economic costs can cause major difficulties for potential buyers. As inflation waxes and wanes, the two measures move apart. In periods of inflation, renters want to become buyers and to buy more expensive houses, anticipating major benefits and low costs. In contrast, lenders, basing their decisions on housing expenses that seem high because of the inclusion of inflationary expectations in mortgage rates, are less willing to lend. Potential buyers are rejected on the grounds that they cannot afford the cash payments on the houses they want.

In the following sections we examine the impact of projected and actual price movements on nominal housing payments and the actual economic costs of housing. We also look at two separate measures of affordability—one based on mortgage payments and the other on actual costs—and see how widely they have differed. The differences between them is one major reason for the development of so many new mortgage instruments.

Inflation and Appreciation of Houses

In deciding whether to buy or rent, prospective buyers must project their expected economic costs against rents. As the experiences of the 1970s and early 1980s showed, results of this comparison will depend heavily on how much housing prices rise during the ownership period. Housing prices tend to move with the general rate of inflation. The relationship was close in the 1950s and 1960s. In the 1970s, however, houses appreciated more rapidly than inflation; in the 1980s the two movements were again generally similar.* On the whole, housing prices should be expected to track the general price level, but individual houses and localities experience widely dispersed results around the average.

Nominal and Real Costs

Ownership costs can be divided into two categories (see Table 10-3):

1. Some costs change over time in line with the movements of a price index such as the Consumer Price Index (CPI). Maintenance costs, property taxes, insurance, and transaction costs move at roughly the rate of inflation (see section 1 of the table). After tax deductions, these costs total about 4 percent of the amount paid for a house. They vary somewhat depending on one's marginal tax bracket and on the actual time between buying and selling. If no inflation occurs, these costs should not change much. If inflation does develop, they will rise at about the inflation rate. In other words, these costs are likely to stay constant in real terms after adjustment for inflation.

2. However, mortgage interest and opportunity costs march to a different drum. In Chapter 3 we saw that mortgage interest rates include a premium equal to expected inflation. When prices are expected to rise, interest rates go up, and vice versa. An inflation adjustment is already built in

---

*Data on housing prices and costs are available in various editions of the *Economic Report of the President* and construction and census publications of the U.S. Department of Commerce.

Table 10-3
Nominal and Economic Costs of Ownership

1. Semiconstant Expenditures (Costs Rise with Prices)

	Percent of House Value
Property tax (less tax deductions)	1.2%
Maintenance and insurance	1.4
Annual cost of transactions over 10 years	1.4
	4.0%

2. Interest Rates and Appreciation as a Percent of House Value

	1. Expected	2. Actual	3. Expected	4. Actual	5. Marginal Tax 15%	6. Marginal Tax 33%
Mortgage interest rate	8.00	8.00	15.00	15.00	10.00	10.00
Interest after tax (25%)	6.00	6.00	11.25	11.25	8.50	6.70
Housing appreciation or depreciation	3.00	10.00	10.00	4.00	3.50	3.50
Real interest cost	3.00	(4.00)	1.25	7.25	5.00	3.20
Economic cost	7.00	0.00	5.25	11.25	9.00	7.20

to fixed-rate mortgages. If inflation rises faster than expected, the real rate of interest falls; a rise in inflation below expectations means higher real interest costs.

Table 10-3 demonstrates the significance, in estimating actual economic ownership costs, of the *expected appreciation rate*—that is, the expected change in the price at the time of sale. If this projection is wrong, the actual cost of ownership will differ greatly from that anticipated when the decision to purchase was made. The cost of ownership of a house as a percent of the cost of a house can be expressed in the following equation:

$$OC = K + (r + \dot{P}^e)(1 - t) - \dot{P}^b \tag{10.1}$$

where   OC   = expected annual cost of ownership as a percent of the acquisition cost of a house

K = fixed-rate expenditures: net property taxes, maintenance, insurance, and so on, as a percent of house costs

r = real interest rate

$\dot{P}^e$ = expected rate of inflation.*

t = marginal income tax rate

$\dot{P}^h$ = expected percentage change in housing prices

EXAMPLE: Real after-tax interest costs and economic costs can be calculated from the data in Table 10-3. It shows that the real economic cost of ownership (OC) in column 1 is 7 percent of the purchase price, since:

Nominal mortgage interest rates ($r + \dot{P}^e$) are: 8%
Expected inflation ($\dot{P}^e$) and house appreciation ($\dot{P}^h$) are: 3%
Real mortgage interest rates (r)(8 − 3) are: 5%
Tax rates (t) are: 25%
Fixed-rate expenditures (K) are: 4%

Therefore:

$$OC = 4 + (5 + 3)(1 - .25) - 3 = 7$$

Projected and Actual Ownership Costs

Table 10-3 helps illustrate two important relationships between ownership costs and inflation. It shows how dependent actual costs are on inflation and how far off projections can be. The table also demonstrates that the amount of tax preference arising from the deductibility of mortgage interest increases with the rate of inflation and with a person's marginal tax bracket.

How this works is demonstrated in section 2 of the table. The first and third columns show projections of real costs of ownership based on knowledge of mortgage interest rates and recent inflation and housing price changes. The first row shows the mortgage interest rate—8 percent in column 1 and 15 percent in column 3. The second row shows the after-tax interest rate under the assumption that the purchaser would receive tax savings of 25 percent of all interest payments.

Row 3 shows the expected rate of appreciation in houses, based on the projected rate of inflation. The expected real after-tax interest cost is found in row 4 by subtracting the appreciation rate from the after-tax interest rate. The final row contains the projected economic costs of ownership obtained by adding the real interest cost (which applies to both the equity and the mortgage) to the

---

*The dot indicates a percentage rate of change of the variable that is the change (ΔP) in a price index over the index (P): $\left(\dfrac{\Delta P}{P}\right)$

semiconstant expenditures from section 1 of the table. Expected costs are estimated as 7 percent in column 1 and as 5.25 percent in column 3.

Table 10-3 illustrates well the two points noted earlier:

1. It emphasizes the relationship of economic costs to appreciation and depreciation and inflation, while showing how far estimates can err if the appreciation projections are wrong.
2. It demonstrates that the amounts of tax preferences arising from the deductibility of mortgage interest increase with the rate of inflation and with a person's marginal tax rate.

Projected and Actual Economic Costs

Columns 1 and 2 of Table 10-3 illustrate what happens when actual inflation and housing appreciation exceed expectations, as happened in the 1970s. At the beginning of the decade, a person obtaining an 8 percent mortgage and expecting a continuation of a 3 percent appreciation rate would have projected an annual cost of ownership of 7 percent.

Column 2 reflects more closely what actually happened. It shows the results when housing prices rise an average of 10 percent a year, rather than the projected 3 percent. The semiconstant costs for taxes and so on, which do rise with inflation, stay at 4 percent in real terms. The after-tax mortgage interest rate of 6 percent, however, is reduced by the 10 percent inflation in house prices to result in a negative 4 percent real rate. As a result, the actual economic costs of ownership would be zero. (Table 10-1, with somewhat more exact data, shows that they were actually negative in the 1970s.) It is no wonder that people rushed to buy—often not just one, but several houses—in the early 1980s.

Lower than Expected Inflation   People who eagerly bought houses failed to realize that the market interest rates and prices were also adjusting to the previous experience. Although delays and lags may occur, the average price expectation in the market becomes "built into" the interest rates and prices quoted. You make money only if your guess as to where the market is going is better than the average.

Columns 3 and 4 of Table 10-3 reflect more closely the situation in 1982. The previous inflation rate had become embedded in both interest rates and prices. Expected inflation of 10 percent translated to interest rates of 15 percent. Because tax deductions are larger at high interest rates, the expected costs of ownership were below the previous initial example. The expected real cost of the interest and appreciation factor was 1.25 percent. The expected total cost from both parts together was 5.25 percent of the acquisition cost.

But we know that house prices did not continue to climb at prior rates. In fact, some came down. Column 4 shows what happens to costs if housing prices rise only at an average 4 percent a year for the 10 years after 1982. Interest less appreciation rises to 7.25 percent, or to nearly six times the initial expected rate.

Total economic costs, at 11.25 percent, are more than twice as high as anticipated. However, this would be reduced somewhat if the mortgage could be refinanced at a lower rate.

The Tax Break

The final two columns, 5 and 6, demonstrate how differences in costs result from variations in marginal income tax rates (explained in Chapter 16). They also show why, in 1986, some real estate brokers opposed a cut in federal income tax rates. A cut in the marginal tax rate, since it reduces the amount of tax preference (subsidy), may raise a family's housing costs. These brokers feared that higher relative housing costs would reduce housing demand and sales. However, other brokers reasoned that increases in after-tax income resulting from lower tax rates would offset the direct effects of higher housing costs.

The final two columns indicate that as long as mortgage interest rates remain deductible, people in higher tax brackets will continue to enjoy lower costs of ownership. With a 10 percent mortgage and an expected inflation of 3.5 percent, an owner in the lower bracket with a 15 percent marginal tax would be looking forward to a 5 percent real rate. The owner in a 33 percent marginal tax bracket could figure on a real interest cost of only 3.2 percent. Their respective projected economic costs would be 9 and 7.2 percent. As explained more fully in Chapter 16, the higher-income family has an even greater tax advantage. To deduct housing expenses, a family must forgo the $5,000 (1988) standard deduction. Its benefit from deducting mortgage interest and property taxes is reduced by any shortfall of other deductions below $5,000. Usually higher-income families will have a smaller shortfall, if any.

In summary, the actual real costs of homeownership depend on relatively fixed maintenance, tax, and transaction costs, on the rate of inflation and interest rates, on how fast house prices rise, and on the buyer's income tax bracket. If the house is bought as an investment, how good or bad an investment it turns out to be also depends on leverage, as explained in Chapter 3. Further discussion of investment returns and unexpected changes in inflation will be covered in Part 4.

Readers aware that efficient economic markets tend to adjust to average expectations of the future are not surprised by the difference in results between simple projections and realization. At any time, the market's expectatons of inflation should be included in both the price of a house and interest rates in calculations of the real cost of ownership. Expected inflation should not lower housing costs, except for those in above-average tax brackets. Purchasers gain or lose only to the extent that their projections are better than those of the market or when actual housing price movements differ from the expected.

MORTGAGE TILT AND AFFORDABILITY

Although, on average, expected inflation will have only a minor impact on actual housing costs after interest rates and house prices have adjusted to market expectations, it will strongly influence a family's ability to buy because of the limit that lenders place on the amount of cash housing expenses that a family can assume. As we shall see shortly, mortgage lenders' estimates of affordability and their willingness to lend have varied greatly and have differed considerably from projected economic costs. In these discussions, **affordability** is defined as the ability of a family earning median income to meet the cash flow payments required to own a median home.

Potential owners who could afford to buy a house if their actual costs were 6 percent to 10 percent of its price often find that they cannot get financing. Because the cash flow needed to carry the mortgage is too high, lenders will not make a mortgage loan. Even though a potential borrower has more than enough income to meet the actual cost of homeownership, lenders fail to qualify the borrower because the projected expense-to-income ratio exceeds the lender's maximum.

What Families Can Afford to Buy

The inability of prospective buyers to obtain financing for houses whose actual economic costs they could afford is due to what has been called **mortgage tilt.*** Nominal mortgage interest rates include an inflation premium that raises them far above the real rate and above actual costs. If the expected inflation actually occurs, family incomes and house prices will rise at approximately the same pace. As a result, mortgages will be manageable even though income-to-expense ratios appear very high. Mortgage tilt results because inflation expectations are included in the interest rate and expense estimate but not in the income estimates. It is the initial upward tilt of the mortgage rate above current incomes that causes an affordability problem based on traditional standards of lenders.

However, since most incomes will rise at about the rate of inflation, families—although squeezed at first—will soon be able to pay the high interest rates. Payments are high only in nominal, not in real terms. Because rising productivity usually causes wages to go up faster than other prices, a family can expect its own income to rise even faster than the rate of inflation.

Let us assume that nominal interest rates are 15 percent, made up of a 5 percent real rate and a 10 percent expected inflation. A family deciding to make a large current sacrifice—and able to find a lender—pays 50 percent of its current income to cover the mortgage payment. With an inflation rate of 10 percent, this mortgage payment rapidly becomes a much smaller share of income. In fact, if the family's income rises at an expected inflation rate of 10 percent annually, its mortgage payment after 30 years would be less than 3 percent of its income.

*See J. R. Kearl, "Inflation, Mortgages, and Housing," *Journal of Political Economy* 87 (October 1979): 1115–1138.

We can look at the same point from another angle. In 1970 the median household had a monthly income of $822. What if they agreed to pay a constant 25 percent of their income for a house and their income grew at the rate of the actual inflation in the decade of 7.8 percent a year? In the first year they would pay $206 a month. At the end of 10 years they would be paying $437 a month. At the end of 30 years they would find that the $206 payment had risen to $1,961 per month. Their ability to pay would have grown because of inflation by more than 800 percent. Compounding raises income and lowers dollar values rapidly.

Furthermore, if inflation actually develops, the lender does not have to worry about an individual family's income keeping up with inflation. Even if a family suffers hard times and its wages lag the average, property values are likely to rise at the inflation rate. This means that the mortgage is well secured. If the family cannot pay, the property can still be sold at a profit. This ability to transfer houses by sale was what kept the foreclosure rate and losses so low in the 1970s.

The idea that property prices will rise lies behind the willingness to lend with negative amortization or with interest accruals. Lenders expect to be repaid from the sale of a property. They need not believe that incomes will be high enough to retire a loan.

The Experience of the 1970s

The 1970s seemed to demonstrate that the theory actually worked. During the ten years from 1970 to 1980, the Consumer Price Index went up at a rate of 7.8 percent a year. The median household income rose 7.9 percent annually. For a family working at the start of the decade, the actual increase in wages would have been several percent a year higher, since wages rise with experience and training. New entrants into the market and a growing percentage of retirees pulled down the overall average. At the same time, the selling price of the median house increased at an annual rate of 10.5 percent a year.

The variance of changes during this period, however, could have caused problems. Annual movements in the inflation rate ranged between 3.3 percent and 11.3 percent. Although movements in incomes and house prices were highly correlated with inflation, differences did occur. Consequently, real incomes actually fell in three years during the 1970s, and real housing prices fell in one.

INDEXES OF AFFORDABILITY

To show how affordability changes from period to period, **affordability indexes** have been constructed. Both mortgage payment and economic cost affordability are measured. The indexes bring out the vast difference between the two concepts of affordability. From 1970 to 1981, the percentage of home buyers who had sufficient income to qualify for a loan to purchase a house dropped 60 percent. Yet during most of that period actual economic costs were falling, not rising. Clearly, how one measures housing affordability can be critical for the average American family as well as for builders and others trying to sell houses.

Mortgage Payments and Income

The relationship to income of money that must be paid to meet mortgage and other housing expenses determines whether one can get a loan. Without a mortgage, most people cannot buy. One simple measure of affordability is to compare median mortgage expenses with median incomes. Such measures for the United States as a whole are shown in Table 10-4. These data are published monthly by the National Association of Realtors and receive wide newspaper publicity. Although P.I.T.I. would make a better index than mortgage payments alone, the published indexes use only mortgage payments.

The second column of the table gives the median sales price of existing homes in the United States. Note that the typical price nearly tripled in 15 years, rising from $23,000 to $74,800 in 1985. If prices for new houses were used, the prices would be somewhat higher and the percentage who could qualify would be lower, but the trends would be similar.

The third column shows median household incomes in the same years. A comparison of columns 2 and 3 reveals the first cause of the affordability squeeze: the prices of houses rose faster than incomes. Between 1970 and 1981, the

Table 10-4
Affordability Measured by Cash Flows
80 Percent 30-Year Mortgage; 25 Percent Maximum Mortgage Payment-to-Income Ratio

Year	Median Sales Price of Single-family Housing	Median Family Income	Effective Mortgage Interest Rate	Annual Mortgage Payment	Payments Percent of Income (Median)	Index (Income/ Income to Qualify)	Percent of Families Affording Median House
1970	$23,000	$ 9,867	8.36%	$1,676	17.0%	147.2	70.7%
1975	35,300	13,719	9.21%	2,778	20.2%	123.5	61.7%
1980	62,200	21,023	12.95%	6,582	31.3%	79.9	36.6%
1981	66,400	22,388	15.12%	8,121	36.3%	68.9	28.8%
1985	74,800*	27,940*	12.01%*	7,392*	26.5%	94.5	47.2%

*Preliminary estimates

Sources: National Association of Realtors, "Monthly Report on Existing Housing"; *Federal Home Loan Bank Board Journal,* various issues; U.S. Bureau of the Census, *Consumer Income,* Series P-60, various issues.

median house price rose 188 percent, while average incomes went up only 117 percent. From 1981 to 1985 the two rose together at about the same rate. In 1970, the median selling price was roughly 2.3 times the median income, while the ratio by 1985 had risen to 2.7.

However, the main reason why the percentage of families who could buy houses fell after 1970 is reflected in column 4. Effective interest rates were 8.36 percent in 1970. They actually fell to 7.6 percent in 1972, but then rose steadily to 15.12 percent in 1981 and to 15.33 in 1982 before receding again to 12.01 percent in 1985 and to 10 percent in 1986.

The joint effect of rising housing prices and rising interest rates is seen in the sharp increase in annual mortgage payments found in column 5. On mortgages with an 80 percent loan-to-value ratio amortized over 30 years, the annual payment rose from $1,676 in 1970 to $8,121 in 1981. By 1985, as a result of the drop in interest rates, annual mortgage payments actually declined. The percentage increase in expenses from 1970 to 1985 was 341 percent.

The Index of Affordability

Column 7 presents an index of affordability. It shows the ratio of the median income to the amount of income needed to qualify for the median loan, on the assumption that the latter is four times the mortgage payment. That is, lenders pick 25 percent as the maximum ratio of mortgage payment to gross income. One way of thinking about this affordability index is to say that, for 1980, a family earning the median family income of $21,023 had 79.9 percent of the income needed to qualify for the purchase of the median-priced resale home of $62,200.*

In 1970, the index was 147.2. The family with the median income could easily afford the median house—and, in fact, those much lower down the income scale could qualify. In 1981, the median family had only 68.9 percent of the required income, or affordability had been cut more than in half. By 1985, the index had recovered to 94.5, and it was actually over 100 by the end of that year.

Affordability indexes of this type must be used carefully. They tell us that housing expenses have risen faster than income, and thus fewer people can afford to buy. They summarize the previous information about increases in mortgage payments and incomes. But such indexes do not really reflect how many families have been priced out of the market, although they are often used for this purpose.

Percent Eligible

The final column provides a somewhat better picture of affordability, answering a slightly different question. Assume that lenders will grant mortgages only to households whose mortgage payment-to-income ratio is no higher than

*National Association of Realtors, "Report on Existing Home Sales."

25 percent; that is, those whose annual income is at least four times their payments. If lenders follow this rule, what percentage of households could afford to buy the median-priced house?

To answer this question, we must go beyond the measure of median income to look at the total income distribution—that is, at the number of households at each income level. The question then becomes, What percentage of households have an annual income at least four times as large as the median payment of a given year? In 1970, 70.7 percent of families could have qualified to buy the median house. By 1981, the number eligible had fallen to 28.8 percent. It stood at 47.2 percent in 1985.

Analysis similar to that of the final column can lead to statements such as that in 1985, only 47.2 percent of households could afford to buy a house; or its converse, that 52.8 percent of households could not buy a house in 1985. These statements are not strictly accurate, however; they do not take into account the distribution of housing prices. By definition, half of the houses produced cost less than the median. Some households shown as frozen out of the market can afford these lower-priced units.

The Effect of Local Markets on Affordability   Furthermore, the index makes no provision for the fact that housing markets are local. In California, for example, housing prices rose far more than the national average; therefore, the affordability problem was much worse. On the other hand, in many states price increases were far below the average. The index also does not take into account the fact that during part of this period, lenders raised and then lowered the allowable expense-to-income ratio. Data show that many families pay more than 25 percent of their income on their mortgages.

It is also true that many families do not need as large a mortgage, and therefore have lower monthly or annual expenses. They can afford to put more money down because they have available assets—particularly from the sale of houses bought in the past. Even though many households can buy only if they obtain a loan-to-value ratio of 95 percent or higher, the average loan-to-price ratio is about 78 percent.*

Still, while these and similar caveats show that the indexes cannot be used literally as an exact measure of what happens to affordability, the general picture they paint is true. When housing expenses rose rapidly, many families found it far more difficult to buy a house than was true 15, 25, or 40 years ago. The gap between income and the required cash flow payments became especially great for first-time home buyers. Many who wanted to buy a house found that they could not obtain a mortgage which would enable them to do so.

ACTUAL COSTS AND AFFORDABILITY

The difficulty is deciding how much to spend for a house and whether a prospective owner is better off buying or renting depends, as we have seen, on

---

*1985 Statistical Abstract of the United States, table 1329.

the accurate projection of a future selling price. Estimates of the actual cost of homeownership will vary greatly given the year-to-year range in price movements. How many people can afford to buy or should decide to buy will vary with these price change projections. In turn, the percentages of those who can afford to buy will differ considerably from the cash flow limitations set by mortgage lenders.

A Second Affordability Index

Table 10-5 helps measure affordability on the basis of projected economic costs. It highlights the difference between decisions based on comparisons of income and mortgage payments and those that use economic costs. The data for incomes, mortgage rates, and housing prices are the same as those in Table 10-4. Based on these data, columns 2 through 5 estimate the actual costs for owning the median-priced house, using the technique from Table 10-3. The estimated economic costs is found by projecting the real after-tax interest rate and adding to it 4 percent to cover payments for insurance, property taxes, maintenance, and transaction costs.

Table 10-5
Affordability Based on Economic Costs

	Projected Economic Costs*					Percent of Families Affording Median House Based On:	
Year	Mortgage Interest Rate	Appreciation†	Real After-tax Costs (in percent)	Estimated Economic Costs (in dollars)	Annual Mortgage Payment	Economic Costs	Mortgage Payment
1970	8.36%	5.23%	5.04%	$1,159	$1,676	82.7%	70.7%
1975	9.21%	8.17%	2.74%	966	2,778	91.8%	61.7%
1980	12.95%	13.80%	−0.09%	(54)	6,582	100.0%	36.6%
1981	15.12%	13.20%	2.14%	1,421	8,121	92.1%	28.8%
1985	12.01%‡	3.00%‡	10.01%‡	7,486‡	7,392‡	46.4%‡	47.2%‡

*Estimated economic costs = costs (in percent) × median house price
$1,159 = 0.0504 × $23,000, where:
costs (in percent) = mortgage interest rate × (1 − marginal tax rate) − appreciation rate + semiconstant costs (in percent)

For 1970: 5.04 = 8.36 × (1 − 0.25) − 5.23 + 4.0

†Estimated appreciation rate equals average of three prior years.   ‡Preliminary estimates.

Source: Table 10-4; National Association of Realtors, "Monthly Report on Existing Housing"; *Federal Home Loan Bank Board Journal,* various issues; U.S. Bureau of the Census, *Consumer Income,* Series P-60, various issues.

EXAMPLE: In 1970, the nominal mortgage interest rate is 8.36 percent before taxes and 6.27 percent after taxes (assuming a 25 percent marginal tax saving). From this, a projected appreciation rate of 5.23 percent is subtracted to obtain the real after-tax interest rate of 1.04 percent. Next, 4 percent is added to the real interest rate to arrive at the economic costs of ownership as a percent of the purchase price of a house. Thus, the $1,159 estimated economic cost in column 5 is found by multiplying the median house price of $23,000 by the economic cost of 5.04 percent.

To project the expected rate of inflation, the table uses a simple rule. It assumes that the rate of appreciation in housing prices that prevailed in the three years prior to a purchase will continue for the entire holding period. As column 3 shows, the expected inflation rates range from 13.8 percent in 1980 to 3 percent in 1985.

Although logical and handy, this projection procedure has several drawbacks. Buyers may use more or less complex rules than simply averaging the previous three years' appreciation rate. In a rapid inflation, more weight may be put on the most recent period. If inflation has been slow, they may weigh other factors more heavily. In addition, of course, projections—no matter how logical—will probably be wrong. Inflation and appreciation vary a good deal. Few forecasters can boast of a good prediction record.

Comparing Affordability

A comparison of columns 5 and 6 of Table 10-5, even if rough, emphasizes the wide divergence between economic costs and cash costs, even when measured, as here, by mortgage payments alone. Estimated economic costs in dollars are considerably lower in every year in the table except 1985. (They are higher only when expected inflation and appreciation are 3 percent or less.) In 1980, when mortgage payments were near their peak, projected economic costs were slightly negative.

The last two columns compare the percentage of families who could meet the economic costs with those eligible on the basis of mortgage payments. They help show why the use of an expense-to-income ratio based on cash costs causes an affordability problem for families convinced that they can afford the economic costs of a house. In each column it is assumed that families can allocate a maximum 25 percent of their income to housing. In 1980, using economic costs as the criterion, every family who could make a 10 percent down payment could have afforded the median-priced house. In contrast, in that year only 36.6 percent of the families could qualify for an 80 percent mortgage loan to buy the house if restricted to a 25 percent mortgage payment-to-income ratio. In most years, the great majority of families could have met the economic costs of ownership. Only in 1985 was the percentage able to afford the median house below 50 percent.

If we look at the percentage of people who actually own homes, real affordability appears to fall somewhere between the two concepts. If owners had to finance their present homes at prevailing interest rates with an 80 percent mortgage, many—if not most—families could not afford to meet the cash payments. They can live where they do because they have built up equity in the past, have used other assets, or have an older, low-rate mortgage. A great deal of the problem of cash flow and affordability is concentrated on new families and those who have not owned homes in the past.

A Drop in the Inflation Rate

The next chapter will show that many solutions offered for the mortgage tilt problem depend for their logic on the past relationships between inflation and real housing costs. They propose new types of contracts to correct for the gap between them. Similarly, the decision to buy rather than rent often depends on a projection of what prices will prevail in the future.

Bearing in mind the sharp changes in actual costs, both up and down, we can see why problems persist. Actual house prices will differ from projections. If houses must be sold in the first few years of ownership, the fact that closing and selling costs need to be amortized over a relatively short period will also cause annual costs to be higher than anticipated.

The most serious problems will arise if the rate of inflation and housing appreciation have been overestimated. If housing prices go up more slowly than expected, actual ownership costs will be higher. Incomes rising more slowly than anticipated will mean that families will not be able to meet future payments. Furthermore, since the expected increase in property values will not be realized, foreclosures and losses are more probable. Basing the ability to qualify for loans on projected inflation greatly magnifies risk. It adds another significant factor to those entering into the traditional underwriting process.

MAKING THE BUY-OR-RENT DECISION

The preceding sections describe the factors that determine how much it costs to own a house and how these costs have varied from year to year. But what about the actual decision of whether to buy or rent? How can prospective homeowners decide whether this is the time to buy and how much to spend? What are the advantages, if any, of renting? The answers depend on making the best possible estimates of future economic costs and then deciding how much real economic sacrifice and risk a family is willing to assume in order to live in the owned home of their choice.

More than the Cost of Shelter

Decisions to buy houses are based on far more than relative costs of shelter. In fact, if markets are operating well, the actual costs of buying and renting are not far apart. Ownership is somewhat cheaper because buyers get a tax break and the maintenance costs of owner-occupiers are probably lower than those of landlords, since owners do more for themselves. However, for moderate income families, the difference in actual cost between owning and renting is probably slight.

Even so, most people who can qualify as borrowers opt to buy. Almost 65 percent of households own a home. The percentage of ownership rises steadily with income and with age up to retirement. At retirement about 90 percent of couples are homeowners. Furthermore, people do not buy in order to pay less rent. In actual costs, people who own spend about one-third more for shelter than do renters. The decision to buy usually means allocating much more of a family's nominal and real income to housing than is spent for rent.*

Quality of Life   People who buy do so because they have a wider choice and can better satisfy their space needs. The quality of a family's living environment has a direct effect on its quality of life. Where and how families live influences their friendships, their children's education, and often their jobs and the time spent in automobiles. People choose to buy so that they can tie down their preferred lifestyle. They may also obtain a significant psychic income from homeownership.

People often begin to search for new space because they are dissatisfied with what they have. House sites include a mixture of status, access, convenience, municipal services, and job opportunities. Altered circumstances modify space needs. The composition of families changes; more children require more space. When they leave home, space needs may shrink again. Rising incomes allow families to upgrade their housing.

A *Major Investment*   For most families, a house constitutes their largest investment outside of education, training, and human capital. How good an investment it turns out to be depends on when a purchase is made and how carefully the purchase agreement and financing are worked out.

Housing investments can be highly leveraged. Ownership greatly increases the assets the family controls, and it adds diversification to its portfolio. Senior citizens tie down their shelter costs; they have a fixed income and want a fixed rent. But as the previous discussions have shown, the actual results from a housing investment depend on real interest rates, on real—as opposed to anticipated—inflation, and on the owner's marginal tax bracket. For many families, the purchase of a home turns out to be by far their best investment. For others, because prices fail to rise as expected, ownership leads to foreclosure and perhaps personal bankruptcy.

*Data on tenure are found in U.S. Bureau of the Census, *Annual Housing Surveys,* Series H-150, and in the *Statistical Abstract of the United States,* various years.

Calculating the Costs of Ownership

The types of estimates needed for calculating both cash flow and actual costs can now be summarized.

1. The acquisition or capital cost is most important because it determines the size of necessary outlays. How much one pays depends on what choices are made and on bargaining. Also included are closing, financing, and other charges that must be paid before title passes. The amount required in cash is the difference between the acquisition cost and the mortgage loan.
2. Cash payments depend on the size of the mortgage, on interest rates, on the type of mortgage, and on property taxes and hazard insurance. They are reduced by any income tax savings. The condition of the house determines how much must be spent on maintenance and repairs.
3. The cash payments must be adjusted to estimated actual cost by including opportunity costs, plus allocations for each year for the difference between the initial expenditures and the receipts at the time of sale. These, in turn, depend on the sales price, closing and selling costs, and the amount of mortgage amortization.

Tables 10-1, 10-3, 10-4, and 10-5 have demonstrated how widely actual costs vary, depending on the difference between actual and anticipated inflation in housing prices. Some people who bought in the early 1970s found that their actual costs per year were virtually zero. In contrast, a family buying in 1982 and forced to sell in 1984 probably paid between 16 percent and 18 percent a year in actual costs. The costs were unusually high because of high interest rates, low actual price increases, and the need to amortize closing and selling costs over only a two-year period.

Using the Expense-to-Income Ratios   There is no precise answer to the question of the proper amount to allocate to housing. A family with minimum assets needing a maximum loan-to-value mortgage will probably find the amount it can spend—both the cash cost and the actual cost—limited by the qualification rules of mortgage lenders. Families with large existing home equities or other assets must decide how much of other consumption and saving they are willing to forgo to buy a specific house.

In making this decision, however, prospective buyers should recognize what actual costs are likely to be and the risks that these estimates will be wrong. If market expectations are realistic and are properly incorporated into both interest rates and housing, actual economic costs for an average family should be between 7 percent and 9 percent of acquisition costs. Someone who buys a $100,000 house can expect his or her actual costs to vary between $7,000 and $9,000 a year. The buyer's cash payments will depend, of course, on the size of the down payment and the mortgage terms.

on past profits in owning a home, on how long a house has been occupied, and on how well the cash flow affordability problem can be solved.

KEY TERMS

actual economic costs of
   ownership
affordability
affordability indexes
annual cash costs
annual or monthly payments
appreciation
expense-to-income ratio

housing expenses
initial expenditures
mortgage payment
mortgage tilt
opportunity costs
P.I.T.I.
total montly payments
transaction costs

QUESTIONS

1. Compare and contrast P.I.T.I. costs and cash payments.
2. A family with a monthly income of $2,000 is thinking of taking a $50,000, 30-year, 10 percent mortgage. The property tax and insurance per month are 8 percent and 6 percent of the monthly mortgage payment. The household has a monthly installment payment on their automobile of $500. Maximum housing expense ratio is 28 percent, while maximum total monthly payment ratio is 36 percent. Can this family qualify for the loan?
3. From Table 10-1, discuss the major factors determining the deviation of actual economic costs from the annual cash flow.
4. Distinguish nominal interest rates from real interest rates. Show examples in each case relating to mortgage interest rates.
5. What are the factors determining the actual economic cost of owning a house?
6. Calculation of expected cost of ownership as a percentage of the cost of a house:

    nominal interest rate = 10 percent
    marginal income tax rate = 30 percent
    expenditures other than interest = 5 percent

    The inflation rate for the next ten years is expected to be 6 percent, and the house price is expected to rise at the same rate. Calculate the expected cost.
7. What is the mortgage tilt problem?
8. Define affordability in detail.
9. What are the problems of using the two affordability indexes mentioned in the text?
10. Explain the differences between the two affordability indexes.

11 Creative Financing and Alternative Mortgage Instruments

OBJECTIVES

When you finish this chapter, you should be able to:

- discuss the reasons for alternative mortgage plans and creative financing.

- describe how adjustable-rate mortgages work.

- show how seller carry-backs, contracts of sale, lease-options, and builder buy-downs attempt to solve the problems of inadequate cash for down payments and income for monthly payments.

- give reasons why payments and interest rates in some mortgages do not move together.

- outline the reasons for agreeing to more rapid amortization or for rejecting it.

- list and explain various techniques for using the equity in a house as a source of additional cash.

DECISIONS ON THE amount to spend for a property frequently depend on how much can be borrowed and in what form. The types of loans available and the methods of creative financing have mushroomed. **Creative financing** consists of the use of nontraditional loans and combinations of loans to better meet the needs of borrowers and lenders. Usually it allows buyers to reduce initial or monthly payments below those required by a standard mortgage. Creative financing is especially prevalent in periods of tight money. D. M. Jaffee, who defines creative financing somewhat more narrowly as those funds advanced by noninstitutional lenders, estimates that in 1981 creative financing by his definition accounted for half of all existing home sales.* In markets such as California, as high as 70 percent of sales used some form of creative financing. Although the examples in this chapter are taken mainly from residential financing, almost all of the techniques discussed here are important in the financing of income properties as well. Chapter 19 demonstrates that income property uses even more complex methods in addition to those discussed here.

To comprehend what has been happening in the mortgage market and to learn where to seek and how to choose the best mortgages, those in real estate finance must analyze the various new types of financing. We want adequate options so as to be able to select those that can solve specific financing problems as they arise. This chapter analyzes the reasons for the development of the creative and alternative types of financing and shows how the new instruments attempt to meet borrowers', lenders', and builders' felt needs. It describes these methods of borrowing and lending and compares their advantages with their disadvantages.

THE BACKGROUND

There are many explanations for the development of new lending practices in the 1970s and 1980s. Rising and fluctuating interest rates and inflation put tremendous pressure on borrowers and lenders. A concentration on fixed-rate mortgages meant that lender portfolios had a long duration, with large interest rate risk. Furthermore, fixed-rate mortgages were underpriced, both because of their interest rate risk and because of their standard prepayment and assumption options. As a result, lenders developed new offerings so that they could either share their risks with borrowers or charge enough to cover them.

Borrowers unable to qualify at the new high rates needed some way to cut their monthly payments. They were reluctant to give up the fixed-rate mort-

---

*D. M. Jaffee, "Creative Finance: Measures, Sources, and Tests," *Housing Finance Review* 3, no. 1 (January 1984): 1–18.

gage. However, if they were offered advantageous terms or if they could not borrow on standard mortgages, buyers were willing to share part of the risk. They also saw advantages in having mortgages with payments that started low but rose as their income increased.

Owners who held low-interest mortgages had a good deal. The present values were high because of the below-market interest on payments that would be made in the future. But if they sold their house and the loan was repaid, this profit would disappear. It was worthwhile, therefore, for sellers to offer junior mortgages to potential buyers so that the old mortgage with low rates could be retained. Both buyers and sellers could gain at the expense of the lender. But more than simply retaining profitable loans was at stake; creative financing might also be the only way potential borrowers could obtain financing.

Other concerns led to different kinds of new loans. Some families were worried about the heavy interest burden they were assuming; they saw it stretching far into the future. Others desired ways of increasing their saving. They wanted to build up their equity more rapidly by amortizing their loans faster than on the standard mortgage. Because more rapid payments were advantageous to lenders, the lenders eagerly created mortgages of this type.

The inflationary increase in house values meant that older owners had large potential capital gains. The equity in their houses had expanded tremendously. To make funds available for other purposes, new mortgages were needed to allow them to borrow against the equity.

For 40 years, the fixed-rate mortgage amortized over a long period had been the predominant investment in the market; there were few variations from it. Until these new developments, most mortgage lenders saw little advantage in changing, and consumers and many regulators opposed it.

But the need for new types of mortgages became so evident that opposition to them began to evaporate. By 1983 the dam had burst. Regulations controlling the kinds of mortgages lenders were allowed to issue almost disappeared. Within the few remaining regulatory constraints, lenders could issue any kind of a mortgage that a borrower would agree to. In the first three years of this new, freer market, the Federal National Mortgage Association (FNMA) bought over 100 different kinds of new, nonstandard mortgages.

Alternative Mortgage Plans

The market responded to these needs by creating a vast array of new financing techniques. These added to or built upon the standard fixed-rate mortgage. For our purposes, we can divide them into four categories. The individual mortgages will be defined and explained in the sections that follow.

1. The most important is the adjustable-rate mortgage. In 1985, more than half of the loans made on single-family homes were of this type, although with easier money their share fell sharply by 1986.
2. The second category includes many of the methods used by sellers to

reduce the down payment or monthly payments of buyers compared to those required for traditional mortgage loans.

3. The third group aims to reduce monthly payments also, but these instruments, in contrast to those from sellers, are provided by the major financial institutions, and several can be insured by the Federal Housing Administration (FHA) or guaranteed by the Veterans Administration (VA).

4. The last group includes a potpourri of other types of new financing arrangements, each developed to take care of special needs.

The New Developments

As we examine the list of new variations, it will become clear that coiners of acronyms have had a field day: some nickname has been attached to most of the new forms. But the fun of innovation and coining names has carried proliferation beyond reasonable limits. It is necessary to sell mortgages in the secondary market. There are considerable advantages to being able to pool mortgages and offer securities backed by them. For this reason, too much differentiation makes little sense. In order to be saleable in pools, mortgages must be easy to understand and have a track record that the market can evaluate properly.*

While all sorts of mortgages can be engineered and many can be used in the future for special purposes, most activity will probably be concentrated in developing a limited number of types. It is not worthwhile—indeed, it is nearly impossible—to list and discuss all of the many possible forms that a mortgage can take. What is needed is an understanding of the forces that have led to alternative instruments, and a knowledge of their major advantages and drawbacks. Beyond that, those interested in a certain type of mortgage should examine it carefully and in detail. No one should accept a mortgage without carefully studying its covenants and simulating its conditions to see how they would work if either favorable or unfavorable events occurred in the future.

ADJUSTABLE-RATE OR VARIABLE-RATE MORTGAGES

The most common nontraditional mortgage today is the **adjustable-rate mortgage (ARM),** in which the contract interest rate adjusts periodically. Usually it changes with a predetermined market index, or it may be subject to renegotiation at intervals.† These mortgages, also known as *variable-rate* mortgages, are complex. Knowing what terms are included in an ARM, a borrower can logically compare it with the fixed-rate mortgages available at the same time. ARMs start with lower payments that make it easier for borrowers to qualify for

*J. M. Guttentag, "Solving the Mortgage Menu Problem," *Housing Finance Review* 2, No. 3 (July 1983): 227–252.

†The Federal Reserve and the Federal Home Loan Bank Board have prepared a simple but detailed explanation of ARMs called *Consumer Handbook on Adjustable-Rate Mortgages.* It is available from most lenders free of charge.

a larger loan. Interest costs should be less over the period of the loan than with fixed rates.

A borrower on an ARM usually accepts the risk that future payments may be higher in exchange for a lower initial rate and a belief that interest payments will be less over the entire mortgage period. Whether the trade-off is worthwhile depends on how much risk is acceptable and on comparisons of possible future costs. (Such comparisons are illustrated in the first figure in Chapter 12.)

Purpose and Types

The objective of adjustable-rate mortgages is to bring about a fairer sharing of interest rate risk. If possible, this should be accomplished without subjecting the borrower to undue shock or greater likelihood of default. It is also vital that lenders make a full, clear disclosure of the terms so that borrowers understand the real meaning of the contract.

There are three distinct types of adjustable-rate mortgages. Frequently aspects of all three are mixed in a single contract.

1. The first type of ARM provides for variable loan payments. Monthly payments are adjusted by the amounts required to cover added or reduced interest costs.
2. The second type of ARM provides for variations in the maturity of the loan. Monthly payments remain the same; but when interest charges change, amortization of principal changes by the same amount but in the opposite direction. Negative or accelerated amortization modifies the outstanding principal and the term to maturity of the mortgage. Frequently, after a minimum period (such as five years), payments will adjust also to take account of the principal at that date.
3. In the renegotiable or **roll-over mortage,** interest rates and amortization amounts are renegotiated at the end of a fixed number of years. If no new terms can be agreed upon, the loan may be called.

EXAMPLE: To illustrate how these mortgages work, consider a $100,000 ARM with a 30-year maturity and an initial interest rate of 10 percent. The monthly payment on the mortgage will be $877.57 (see Table 4-1). At the end of the second year, when the principal balance outstanding is $98,830 (see Table 4-3), an agreed-upon index rises to 11 percent.

1. Under the adjustable payment contract, the monthly payments will rise to $949.76. This is the amount a borrower must pay to amortize the outstanding balance at 11 percent interest for the remaining 28 years.
2. Under the adjustable maturity contract, mortgage payments will remain at $877.57. Since the actual interest charges on the outstanding balance in the 25th month will be $905.94, negative amortization will occur. The outstanding balance will increase month by month. Most mortgages require

that at some point the amount of payments be increased in order to stop the loan from continuing to grow. If interest rates are falling, the balance will decrease faster than was agreed to initially and the maturity will be less.

Clearly, the adjustable maturity mortgage gives more protection to borrowers. They will not need higher income to meet higher payments. If the value of the property is increasing at least at the rate of negative amortization, lenders will also be better off even though their cash flow will not increase. They will be earning interest at the market rate and will be repaid in full when the property sells. They are less likely to be forced to foreclose as a result of payments growing too fast for the borrower's income.

How an Adjustable-Rate Mortgage Works

While many types of adjustable-rate mortgages exist, most contain certain basic features. These include the preliminary or initial rate; the index; dates for changes and notices thereof; any limits on rate and payment alterations; any maximum amount of lifetime changes permitted; and assumption and prepayment covenants. Many of these features are contained in an adjustable-rate note rider to a basic mortgage, shown in Figure 11-1.

The Index From the borrower's viewpoint, the most significant features of the contract are the intial rate, the specification of the index, the original index value (not contained in the note), and the limits on authorized adjustments. The most common indexes are those using rates on U.S. Treasury securities (6 months, 1-, 3-, or 5-year rates) or the average cost of funds for savings and loan associations insured by the Federal Savings and Loan Insurance Corporation (FSLIC).

On most ARMs, the interest rate charged the borrower rises or falls in accordance with movements in the rate (value) of a specified index. The **index** measures the amount of change that can occur in the effective interest rate. Each adjustable-rate mortgage specifies which index will be used. In the example in Figure 11-1, clause 3.2 specifies that the index value is the rate as made available by the Federal Reserve Board for 1-year constant-maturity treasury notes and bonds.

The Initial and the Effective Interest Rate It is important to recognize the difference between the initial and the effective interest rates. The **initial interest rate** is that paid until the first change date. It is chosen arbitrarily by the lender and may bear no relationship to the rates the mortgage will carry later.

The **effective interest rate** consists of the initial rate and the rate that replaces it at the first change date. The replacement rate is determined by the value of the index on a given date or average of dates, plus a margin added to the index as specified in the contract. Clause 3.3 shows a margin of 2 percent.

Figure 11-1
A Note Rider to an Adjustable-Rate Mortgage

NOTE TYPE

PROMISSORY NOTE
ADJUSTABLE RATE

BORROWER:

DATE: March 1, 1986	LOAN NUMBER:
LOAN AMOUNT: $100,000.00	MONTHLY PAYMENT: $769
INITIAL INTEREST RATE: 8.5 percent	FIRST PAYMENT DUE: April 1, 1986
	TERM-FULL PAYMENT DUE: March 31, 2016

FOR VALUE RECEIVED, Borrower (jointly and severally if more than one) promises and agrees to the following:

1.   PAYMENT. To pay to the order of ___ . FEDERAL SAVINGS AND LOAN ASSOCIATION or its successors ("Lender"), at its principal office or at such other place as Lender may designate, in lawful money of the United States, the Loan Amount with interest on the unpaid balance at the Effective Interest Rate, principal and interest payable in consecutive monthly installments as stated above, commencing on the due date shown above and continuing on the same day of each succeeding month until fully paid, subject to adjustment as provided hereafter. Payments received shall be credited first on interest and other charges then due and the remainder on principal. Interest due and not included in a monthly installment shall be calculated on the basis of the actual number of days elapsed over a 365-day year.

2.   PRINCIPAL BALANCE ADJUSTMENT. If, at any time, the monthly payment is insufficient to pay the interest due, the amount of unpaid interest shall be added to the principal and bear interest at the Effective Interest Rate.

3.   INTEREST RATE ADJUSTMENT.

   3.1   Effective Interest Rate. The Effective Interest Rate of this Note is the Initial Interest Rate until adjusted, and thereafter shall be the adjusted interest rate in effect from time to time.

   3.2   Index. Any adjustments of the interest rate shall be based upon changes in the following index ("Index"):

The weekly average yield on United States Treasury securities adjusted to a constant maturity of 1 year, as made available by the Federal Reserve Board.

   Index Value. The particular Index Value which is to be used in the calculation of an interest change shall be the last such value received prior to the date of calculation by Lender from the U.S. Government through the U.S. mail.

   If the Index is no longer available, Lender shall choose a new index which is based upon comparable information.

   3.3   Establishing New Rate. The Effective Interest Rate of this Note is subject to change on the first day of   April
19 87   , and on that day of every   12   month(s) thereafter (each, successively, the "Change Date"). The Effective Interest Rate shall not be changed if the value of the change is less than   0.125%   . The method used to determine the Effective Interest Rate is: (Check one box for method used.)

      (a) [x] Subject to the limitations on interest rate changes appearing elsewhere in this Note, and subject to the right of Lender in its sole discretion to expressly waive an indicated increase in the Effective Interest Rate, as to each Change Date, Lender will calculate and change the Effective Interest Rate by adding   2.00%   to the Index Value last received prior to the Change Date, except in the case of a concurrent payment adjustment pursuant to 4.4 below, in which instance Lender will calculate and change the Effective Interest Rate by adding   2.00%   to the Index Value last received by Lender 45 days before the Change Date. The sum will be the Effective Interest Rate.

      (b) [ ] Subject to the limitations on interest rate changes appearing elsewhere in this Note, and subject to the right of Lender in its sole discretion to expressly waive an indicated increase in the Effective Interest Rate, a change between the Initial Interest Rate and any Effective Interest Rate under this Note shall be made in an amount equal to the amount of the change between the Initial Index Value and the Index Value last received prior to the Change Date, except in the case of a concurrent payment adjustment pursuant to 4.4 below, in which instance the change between the Initial Interest Rate and the Effective Interest Rate of this Note shall be made in an amount equal to the amount of the change between the Initial Index Value and the Index Value last received by Lender 45 days before the Change Date.

   3.4   Maximum Rate Adjustments. Notwithstanding the provisions of 3.3 above, the maximum adjustments in the Effective Interest Rate shall not exceed the following:

Maximum Increase	Maximum Decrease
2 % each Change Date	2 % each Change Date
2 % annually	2 % annually
5 % for term of loan	5 % for term of loan

4.   PAYMENT ADJUSTMENT.

   4.1   Periodic Adjustment. If the interest rate is adjusted, the monthly payment of principal and interest shall be adjusted, commencing on the first day of   April   , 19 87   , and on the first day every   12   month(s) thereafter (the "Adjustment Date"), to permit amortization of the unpaid balance with interest in equal monthly installments over the remaining term ("Full Amortization").

   4.2   Maximum Payment Adjustments. Subject to equalizing adjustments as provided in paragraph 4.3, adjustment of the monthly payment of principal and interest shall not exceed the percentage of the amount of the monthly payment immediately preceding such adjustment as follows:

Maximum Increase	Maximum Decrease
7.5 % each Adjustment Date	7.5 % each Adjustment Date
7.5 % annually	7.5 % annually
30.0 % for term of loan	30.0 % for term of loan

   4.3   Equalizing Adjustment. If the interest rate is adjusted, and the monthly payment has not been adjusted to fully amortize the unpaid balance, the monthly payment of principal and interest shall be adjusted, commencing   months from the due date of the first payment, and on every fifth anniversary of that date thereafter, to permit Full Amortization. However, if the monthly payment has been adjusted so as to fully amortize the unpaid balance, this paragraph 4.3 shall not be applicable.

   4.4   Notice of Payment Adjustment. In the event of an adjustment of the monthly payment, Lender shall send a written notice of at least 30 days before the Change Date (see 3.3 (a) and (b)) to Borrower containing the following information:
      (a) The effective date of the payment change;
      (b) The new Effective Interest Rate; and
      (c) The amount of the new monthly payment.

   4.5   Sufficiency of Notice. Any notice to Borrower will be given by mailing it first-class mail addressed to Borrower at the property described in the Security Instrument or such other address for the Borrower as shown on Lender's records.

Continued

Continued

5.   The following paragraph will be operative only if the box below is checked with an "X".
☐   OPTION TO EXTEND OR REDUCE TERM: If, at the end of _____ months from the due date of the first payment, or between subsequent Adjustment Dates, there is a net increase in the Effective Interest Rate, Borrower shall have the option on each Adjustment Date to extend the term of this Note, provided that such extension will permit Full Amortization over such extended term. In all circumstances under this Note, the total term of this Note shall not exceed 480 months from the date hereof. If the Borrower exercises said option to extend, the monthly payment shall be adjusted by Lender to permit Full Amortization. Borrower shall provide Lender with written notice of Borrower's intention to elect said option, to be received by Lender no later than the Adjustment Date. Such written notice shall be in a form provided by Lender.
     If at any Adjustment Date subsequent to Borrower's exercising the foregoing option, there has been a net decrease in the Effective Interest Rate since the prior Adjustment Date, Lender shall either concurrently maintain or adjust the monthly payment to permit Full Amortization over the term that existed prior to such extension.
6.   LATE CHARGE. To pay to Lender a late charge of 5% of any installment due if such installment is not received by Lender within 15 days after its due date. It would be impracticable or extremely difficult to fix Lender's actual damages if any installment is not paid when due, and said late charge shall be deemed to be Lender's damage for any such late payment, but shall not limit Lender's right to compel prompt performance of any obligation or exercise other remedies under this Note or the Security Instrument. No late charge assessed shall exceed the maximum permitted by law.
7.   DEFAULT. Upon default in the payment of any installment when due, or in the performance of any obligations of the Security Instruments executed with this Note, the entire unpaid balance and accrued interest shall become due and payable immediately at Lender's option.
8.   PREPAYMENT. Borrower shall have the right to pay all or part of the principal without penalty at any time, unless the box below is checked with an "X".
☐   In which event the following paragraph shall be operative:
     Privilege is reserved to make prepayments of principal on any installment date on condition that if the aggregate amount prepaid in the prior 12 month period plus the amount of the present prepayment exceeds 20% of the original principal amount of this Note, Borrower shall pay Lender an amount equal to 6 months interest upon such excess amount. Such additional amount shall be due and payable whether said prepayment is voluntary or involuntary, or effected by the exercise of any acceleration provision contained in this Note, or the Security Instrument, except for an acceleration pursuant to the exercise of any due-on-sale provisions.
9.   TRANSFER OF THE SECURITY OR A BENEFICIAL INTEREST IN BORROWER.
     9.1 If all or any part of the security or an interest therein is sold or transferred by Borrower or if Borrower is not natural persons but contains a corporation, partnership, trust or other legal entity and a beneficial interest in Borrower is sold or transferred without Lender's prior written consent, excluding
     (a) a transfer by devise, descent or by operation of law upon the death of a joint tenant, tenant by the entirety, or partner,
     (b) the grant of any leasehold interest in all or any part of the security of 3 years of less not containing an option to purchase,
     (c) sales or transfers of beneficial interests in Borrower provided such sales or transfers, together with any prior sales or transfers of beneficial interests in Borrower, but eliminating sales or transfers under subparagraph (a) above, do not result in more than 25% of the beneficial interests in Borrower having been sold or transferred since commencement of amortization of the Note,
     (d) the creation of a lien or other encumbrance subordinate to the Security Instrument, or
     (e) the creation of a purchase money security interest for household appliances,
Lender may, at Lender's option, declare this Note immediately due and payable and Lender may invoke any remedies permitted by the terms of this Note, the Security Instrument, or provided by law.
     9.2 Lender shall not exercise its option if:
     (a) Borrower causes to be submitted to Lender all information required by Lender to evaluate the transferee as if a new loan were being made to the transferee;
     (b) Lender determines that Lender's security will not be impaired and that the risk of a breach of any covenant or agreement in the Security Instrument is acceptable;
     (c) thereupon and thereafter interest is payable on this Note upon terms acceptable to Lender; and
     (d) changes in the terms of this Note and the Security Instrument as required by Lender are made.
10.   WAIVERS.
     10.1 Lender may waive all or part of any right, option, payment or charge in its favor, and a waiver or a failure of Lender to exercise its rights shall not affect enforcement respecting subsequent events. Lender's subsequent acceptance of any payment hereunder shall not be deemed a waiver of any default by Borrower, or of any sale or transfer of the security, regardless of Lender's knowledge thereof upon acceptance of such payment.
     10.2 Presentment, protest, and notice of dishonor are hereby waived by Borrower, and all sureties, guarantors and endorsers hereof. The right to plead any and all statutes of limitations as a defense to any demand or claim on this Note, or on any guaranty thereof, or to any agreement to pay the same, or to any demand or claim secured by the Security Instrument, or other security, securing this Note, against Borrower, sureties, guarantors or endorsers is expressly waived, to the extent permitted by law, by each and all said parties.
11.   AMENDMENTS. This Note may not be amended or modified orally, and no provision of this Note may be waived or amended except in writing signed by the parties hereto which expressly refers to this Note.
12.   ATTORNEY'S FEES. To pay reasonable attorney's fees and costs if Lender seeks legal advice following a default or refers this Note to an attorney for collection or to reclaim, protect, preserve or enforce its interest in this Note or any security, including proceedings under Eminent Domain or Federal Bankruptcy Law.
13.   SECURITY. This Note is secured by property subject to a pledge, hypothecation or other encumbrance under written instruments dated the same date as this Note ("Security Instrument(s)").

_____   _____

_____   _____

CF4582E (3/85)

EXAMPLE: Table 11-1 illustrates how the effective rate is calculated. Mortgage A has an initial rate of 8 percent, which is also the effective rate until the first change. The current value of the index is 8.5 percent (not shown in the contract), and the margin is 3 percent in this example. Adding the value of the index to the margin gives the effective rate at the first change, found in the last two rows. If, 45 days before the first change, the index is 8.5 percent, the effective rate will be 11.5 percent. If the index is 7 percent, the effective rate will be 10 percent. The interest rate is adjusted in the same way on each future change date.

Teasers   The fact that the initial rate and the current value of the index need not be related has led to the use of teasers. A **teaser** is a mortgage with an initial

Table 11-1
Interest Rate on Adjustable-Rate Mortgage

	Mortgage A	Mortgage B
Interest rate	8.0%	10.0%
Current index value	8.5%	8.5%
Margin	3.0%	2.0%
Effective rate on first change date:		
Index remains constant at 8.5%	11.5%	10.5%
Index moves down to 7.0%	10.0%	9.0%

rate well below the current value of the index plus the margin. Since the current rate of the index is not contained in the note, in order to know whether a teaser is being used, a borrower must obtain the current value of the index, either from the lender or from its source, then calculate what the current effective rate would be using the index. Teasers are offered by lenders wanting to attract borrowers, or by sellers who pay part of the first period's interest in order to make their deal look more attractive and to enable more potential buyers to qualify.

On the first change date, borrowers choosing a loan because of a teaser may be subject to payment shock, since their interest costs may shoot up even though the index stays stable or even drops. To find what risks they run, borrowers must consider the relationships among the initial rate, the current value of the index, and the margins offered by each lender.

An example of these relationships is the two mortgages in Table 11-1. At first glance, mortgage A looks like a better deal because its initial rate is 8 percent, not 10 percent as for mortgage B. But what happens at the first change date tells the real story. Because the margins differ (assuming they both use the same index), the rate of interest on A will always be 1 percent higher than the rate on B as soon as the effective rate becomes the index plus margin. If interest rates stay constant, the rate on A will jump from 8 percent to 11.5 percent, while B will rise only to 10.5 percent. If the index moves up, the shock for the borrower on A will be still greater, since the total increase would be the 3.5 percent teaser plus any movement in the index unless the amount of adjustment is limited by a clause in the contract.

In some ARMs, as in Figure 11-1, changes occur every year on the anniversary of the loan. Other loans have change dates varying from 6 months to 5 years apart. In some contracts, monthly changes are required. The predominant choices are for changes to occur either every 6 months or once a year.

Clause 4.4 specifies that the lender will calculate the required change and notify the borrower. The notification must be sent 30 days in advance of the date the altered payments are due. This gives the borrower more time to adjust or to negotiate a new loan.

Maximum Changes (Caps)   Clause 3.4 of the agreement specifies the maximum amount by which the interest rate can change, or the **cap.** In this case, the increase is limited to 2 percent on any change date. Note, however, that if the index jumped 4.5 percent before the first change date and then held constant, the interest rate would automatically rise 2 percent on the first date, 2 percent on the second, and yet again .5 percent on the third. The note also provides that in this case the maximum increase or decrease from the initial rate for the term of the loan shall be 5 percent.

While the interest cap limits the increase in costs, many borrowers also fear that payments may rise more rapidly than income, thus putting a squeeze on other expenditures. This is a reason for decoupling the amount of interest charged from the amount of payment. In addition to the limits on interest rate changes imposed in clause 3.4, a separate limit is placed by clause 4.2 on the amount of increase in any monthly payment (in this case 7.5 percent). Provisions may specify that payments change less often or to a smaller degree than do interest rates.

Variable-maturity mortgages allow interest changes to rise or fall but hold payments constant. In all cases, if payments adjust more slowly than interest rates, there will be negative amortization and the principal will increase. If interest falls more rapidly than payments, the principal will be paid off faster.

Lifetime Maximums   In addition to limits on the periodic changes in interest rates and payments, caps may be placed on the maximum total change in interest rates, in payments, and in negative amortization. Clause 3.4 in the figure specifies that the effective interest rate may not rise by more than 5 percent. Similarly, cause 4.2 holds additional payments to 7.5 percent per year, with a maximum of 30 percent above the initial rate. In Table 11-1, in contrast, the maximum increase over the initial payment for mortgage A would be over 40 percent because of the 3 percent difference between the initial rate and the index plus margin on that date.

Negative amortization also is frequently limited in ARMs. A contract may specify that the outstanding principal may not exceed 125 percent of the original. Sometimes the limit is expressed as a maximum percent either of the original appraised value or of a current appraisal. Other specifications, such as clause 4.3, call for a change in payments at least every 5 years. As a rule, in cases of this kind the payments are increased in such a way that the total loan balance will be paid off over the original maturity. In any case, if the principal rises, payments will be adjusted to ensure that the maturity does not exceed 40 years.

Prepayments and Assumptions   Other covenants are not shown in Figure 11-1 because they appear in the basic mortgage. Some regulators require that prepayments without penalty and assumptions be allowed for all adjustable-rate mortgages. The market is usually willing to go along, since such concessions appeal to borrowers and have only a slight cost to lenders.

Renegotiable-Rate or Roll-over Mortgages

Renegotiable-rate mortgages are special forms of adjustable-rate ones. They have been the most common form used in Canada for years. One type is basically a short-term (1- to 5-year) mortgage with a balloon. When the mortgage comes due, the borrower and lender renegotiate the terms of any renewal. Another form has a long-term (25- or 30-year) mortgage but the rate and payments are subject to renegotiation at agreed-upon intervals. A borrower who does not accept the new terms can refinance elsewhere. If the rate is acceptable, the loan is renewed automatically.

Advantages and Disadvantages of ARMs

Adjustable-rate mortgages aim to reduce risks to lenders and thereby to reduce their costs. To realize these gains, lenders may offer lower rates, at least initially, than those on fixed-rate mortgages. They can do so because they incur less risk. At the same time, if market rates rise, they are not locked into previous low rates. The advantages of ARMs follow from those factors.

- More buyers can qualify as a result of lower rates and payments.
- Mortgage lenders can continue to attract funds, since they earn and can pay market rates. Disintermediation and shortages are less likely.
- Borrowers taking out loans in periods of high interest can profit from a drop in rates without the need to refinance.
- Lenders may reduce origination charges to attract borrowers.
- No prepayment penalties and the right to assume are usually included.

The disadvantages arise parimarily from the lack of a fixed rate and from the much greater complexity of the ARMs.

- Borrowers greatly increase their interest rate risk.
- If adjustments are large, defaults may go up and losses due to payment shock will rise.
- Borrowers do not profit from rising rates. A low starting interest rate may disappear as rates go up.
- Negative amortization may cause equity to fall below zero, with the result that borrowers will be more willing to walk away from the debt.
- Borrowers have trouble understanding what they are agreeing to. Teasers are especially nefarious.
- Although computers make it easy to recalculate payments, borrowers do not like fluctuating payments.
- The caps on payments will shift some of the interest rate risk back to the lender. How the risk is split is determined by the specific caps agreed upon.

- Under the fixed-payment, variable-maturity mortgage, payments do not change. Lenders may be caught in a cash flow bind even though they are free of interest risk. The cash outflow from borrowers will exceed their costs when rates fall, since amortization speeds up and maturity falls rather than payments being reduced.

CREATIVE FINANCING BY SELLERS

The second category of new techniques consists of those primarily offered by sellers, either in order to help buyers qualify for a larger loan or to improve the seller's return by using existing lower-rate mortgages and the tax law to their advantage. These become particularly prevalent when money is tight, rising, as noted earlier, to over 50 percent of the market in 1981.

Sellers may offer one of the following types of creative financing:

- Seller carry-backs
- Contracts of sale
- Lease options
- Buy-downs

The Objectives of Sellers

Sellers who find it difficult to sell a house because too many would-be buyers lack adequate financing often turn to methods of creative financing. Lowering the buyer's required down payment and monthly payments increases the number of potential buyers.

Buyers like creative financing because of lower initial payments. They can buy a more expensive house than a traditional lender would allow. Buyers may also share in the savings obtained using existing mortgages with lower interest rates. However, their problems may become serious when the time to refinance arrives. Under certain arrangements in this category, they may have trouble obtaining a clear title. They may also find that additional liens have been created that raise their costs.

Sellers agree to furnish part of the financing in order to increase demand. They may allow borrowers to profit from the lower rates on existing mortgages on the property, or they may charge the borrower less than market rates on what is owed to the seller. To compensate for their assistance, sellers usually obtain a higher price for the property than they could if only standard financing were available. Less often, their profit comes through obtaining interest rates higher than they could get elsewhere on the funds they provide.

But sellers must also be aware of possible problems. Particularly for 100 percent or over 100 percent financing, they may end up repossessing their property with less equity than before the sale. Lack of sophistication may cause them to allow buyers to take out other financing that becomes a lien on the property. Buyers may continue to occupy the house without making payments during a lengthy and expensive foreclosure period.

Seller Carry-backs

The most common seller-assisted financing is the **seller carry-back;** the purchaser assumes or buys subject to the existing mortgage or mortgages and the seller accepts part of the price in the form of a junior mortgage. Common also, especially for income properties, are *wraparound mortgages* (see Chapter 2). In some cases, the seller may grant a first mortgage to cover all the buyer's needs, especially if the existing mortgage is low or absent.

In addition to saving on interest costs, buyers frequently need smaller down payments and lower monthly payments in order to qualify for the purchase. Any terms may be included that are agreeable to the buyer and seller, provided they are not usurious. Amortization may be zero or negative. The selling price can be adjusted to cover added risks and costs.

Whether or not sellers agree to assist buyers depends on the terms being offered in the market compared with those on the existing loan. Assumptions are most advantageous when market rates are well above the original ones. Savings are also possible, depending on the size of prepayment penalties and on the points and fees a new loan will engender.

Due-on-sale Clauses

Whether an existing mortgage can remain in effect upon the sale of the property depends on its particular covenants. Many contain due-on-sale clauses. Others specifically permit assumptions but frequently require payment of a fee. The amount of the fee compared to costs of refinancing may be important in deciding which technique is best. Even with due-on-sale clauses, however, the lender may be willing to continue the loan if some of the terms are altered. Continuing an altered mortgage may be preferable to obtaining a new loan.

Equity and the Amount of the Second Mortgage

If the gap between the existing loan and the selling price is too great, assumptions are not feasible. The difference between the two is the seller's equity. The amount of the equity depends on the amount of the initial down payment, on how much amortization has taken place, and on any appreciation in the property's value. Equity can be measured by subtracting the mortgage balance from the net selling price. The gap widens, and the equity rises, with the length of time a house has been owned and with the rate of appreciation.

EXAMPLE: Table 11-2 illustrates a seller carry-back used because it increases the selling price. A house is bought for $50,000 with a $45,000 mortgage at

Table 11-2
An Example of a Seller Carry-back

Owner's Equity		Sale Financing		
			A	B
Original purchase	$50,000	Sales price	$60,000	$63,000
Original mortgage	45,000	Down payment	6,000	6,300
Down payment	$5,000	Required financing	$54,000	$56,700
Amortization	1,500	Original mortgage	43,500	43,500
Appreciation	10,000	Second mortgage	$10,500	$13,200
Owner's equity	$16,500			
		Monthly payment	$105	$110
		Balloon payment at 5 years	$12,275	$13,200
Present value at 12%	$16,500	Present value at 12%	$17,477	$18,510

12 percent interest. After 6 years the owner decides to sell. The market values and sale price are $60,000. The owner's equity is $16,500—the sum of the down payment, amortization, and appreciation.

In the sales financing scenario A, a buyer agrees to the $60,000 sale price, but she has only $6,000 for a down payment after meeting other closing costs. The required financing of $54,000 is covered by assumption of the $43,500 first mortgage plus a $10,500 second mortgage from the owner. The terms of the second mortgage are 16 percent interest, payable at the rate of 1 percent a month with the remainder accruing. The mortgage is payable at the end of 5 years. The amount owed will be the initial principal plus accrued interest.

An equally probable scenario, as in B, would be for the owner to list the $60,000 house for $65,000, specifying a willingness to carry a second mortgage. The final sales price might be $63,000 with a $6,300 down payment and a $13,200 second mortgage. This could be payable with 10 percent interest, or at a rate of $110 a month. The balloon payment at the end of 5 years would be $13,200. In such cases, sellers receive their reward through a higher sales price rather than by charging a higher interest rate. As long as they do not charge less than the minimum interest rate in the Internal Revenue Service code, they will save on taxes. If they do not charge the minimum, they will be taxed at an imputed rate. Since the higher price is made up mainly through a larger balloon payment, the buyer may also be willing to accept the trade-off.

Before deciding which approach to a sale is best, the owner can calculate the present value of the separate possibilities. The last line of Table 11-2 shows the present value of the cash flows from the three separate scenarios (neglecting any differences in taxes and transaction costs) discounted at 12 percent. Scenario B has a present value of about $1,000 more than scenario A, and about $2,000 more than an outright sale. The seller would have to weigh these potential returns against the risks, costs, and bother of a second mortgage. Even more important to the decision, however, is the seller's estimate of how long it would take to sell the house under different arrangements. Most sellers accept carry-backs in order to avoid the long delays that can arise in trying to find a buyer who both has the necessary down payment and can meet an institutional lender's qualification criteria.

Contracts of Sale

Contracts of sale are also known as land contracts, installment sales contracts, or contracts for deeds. They serve as financing devices. A **contract of sale** provides for a down payment and monthly payments. However, the buyer (*vendee*) does not receive legal title from the seller (*vendor*) until an agreed-upon number of payments have been made.

Land contracts are a traditional method of selling property, particularly vacant land for which institutions will make only limited loans, when buyers have only a small down payment or their credit is too poor to qualify for a normal mortgage. As Chapter 16 explains, land contracts may also be used for tax purposes to gain the advantages of installment sales. In recent years they have been used to avoid the acceleration of, and the need to repay, a low-interest mortgage that may occur under due-on-sale clauses. Whether they can actually be used for this purpose is a complex legal question that differs from state to state. Land contracts can be a legal quagmire. They should not be entered into without competent legal advice.

Legal Rights Under a contract of sale, although sellers agree to grant a legal title in the future, they retain it in the interim. They can sell these rights or borrow against their interest. Judgments can be entered as liens against the property. Purchasers receive what is known as **equitable ownership.** They are considered to be the unofficial owners subject to the unpaid purchase price. They too can sell or borrow on their interests. The contract may or may not give them the right of possession and may specify what improvements they can and cannot make. They too can borrow on and create liens against their interest as well. Neither the vendor's nor the vendee's rights are ended by death.

The buyer has the right to a clear title when the conditions of the contract are met. However, this may be hard to achieve because the owner's title may not have been clear at the time of the original contract, or liens may intervene. If the legal owner dies, action through the courts may be needed to obtain title.

Recording the Contract Sellers often do not want to record the contract because they do not want existing mortgages to accelerate. They wish to avoid the cost of clearing title if the sale falls through. Sellers may prefer to collect and make the mortgage payments themselves in order to be sure no default occurs.

The buyer's interests are often the opposite. Upon completing their payments, they have the right to clear title free of any encumbrances except those agreed to in the contract. Without a recording, other liens may have come into existence. Buyers also must be sure that payments to the seller actually go to pay off the mortgage. Making payments to financial institutions, trusts, or escrow accounts often serves to accomplish this.

Sale and Foreclosure   If buyers fail to meet their payments, sellers have a choice of action, depending on the contract and the state. They may evict the buyer or sue, as under other contracts. They may use a trustee and power of sale or foreclose. Usually the buyer loses all prior payments. Normally the costs to the seller of regaining possession are less than under a mortgage. However, the courts and legislatures continually revise the rights under contracts of sale to make them fair to both parties. As a result, in some states there are only slight differences between a land contract and a mortgage. Legal changes create additional reasons why it is advisable to use a good real estate attorney before signing any such contracts. The contract of sale is useful mainly where the buyer must take risks because of insufficient funds for an adequate down payment or an inability to qualify for a mortgage.

Lease Options

A **lease-option** agreement gives the tenant the right to use the property and also to purchase it within a specified period of time. The agreement sets out the price of the property and the other terms that will apply at the time of sale. The lessee decides sometime during the option period whether or not to exercise the option. The price of the option may simply be part of the rent or it may require an additional initial fee. If the option is exercised, some or all of the lease payments may apply against the purchase price. Both the lease and the option may be assigned to third parties.

Instead of merely including an option, some leases provide for purchase agreements. The lease and contract of sale are drawn at the same time, and the agreement specifies the future closing date. The contract will also indicate how much, if any, of the lease payments will be included as a payment on or are to be used to reduce the amount due. The difference between the **lease-purchase** and the lease-option is that, under the former, closing the sale is required and the seller can sue for specific performance (that is, collect damages if the purchase is not made).

Buy-downs

In periods of high interest rates or slow sales, buy-downs become increasingly important. A **buy-down** is a payment to the mortgage lender by the seller in order to reduce the interest rate and the monthly payments of the borrower. Buy-downs are lump-sum payments, usually by builders, that reduce the borrower's interest rate. Typically, such reductions last only three to five years. One common form of a buy-down, called 3-2-1, reduces interest payments in the first year by 3 percent, in the second year by 2 percent, and in the third by 1 percent.

At least three factors have made buy-downs popular:

1. Everyone likes a bargain. A builder offers the buy-down as a concession similar to the discount offered by a car salesman. It makes the deal more attractive.
2. Lower initial mortgage payments make houses more affordable. If the lender agrees to apply an unchanged percentage-of-income rule to the bought-down payment, people who could not afford a house at the original rate may now qualify. However, in doing so lenders increase their risks. As a result, most lenders will not use the same expense-to-income ratio on a buy-down as they would on a standard mortgage. They will, however, be somewhat more lenient in qualifying buyers. If a borrower's income has not risen by the time payments rise, the borrower may be forced to default.
3. Builders profit either by selling the property at a higher net price (taking their payment for the buy-down into account) or by selling more rapidly, thereby reducing holding costs.

How a Buy-down Works

Greater affordability makes the buy-down particularly attractive to builders. How it works is summarized in Table 11-3 and in the example below.

EXAMPLE: A builder finds that the houses he thought would sell for $100,000 are failing to sell. He believes that this is happening because, with

Table 11-3
Builder Buy-down with 12 Percent 30-Year Fixed-Rate Mortgage,
$10,000 Dealer Contribution

	Selling Price	Type	Mortgage	Payment		Interest Rate	
				Initial	Final	Initial	Final
1.	$100,000	No concession	$95,000	$977	$977	12%	
2.	90,000	Price reduced	85,000	874	874	12%	12%
3.	100,000	5-year buy-down*	95,000	755	977	9.2%	12%
4.	100,000	3-year buy-down†	95,000	645	977	7.8%	12%
5.	100,000	3-2-1 buy-down‡	95,000	734 (year 1)	977	8.9%	12%
				814 (year 2)			
				896 (year 3)			

*$10,000 buys a $222 annuity at 12% for 60 months; payment becomes $755.
†$10,000 buys a $332 annuity at 12% for 36 months; payment becomes $645.
‡$5,093 buys a 1-, 2-, and 3-year annuity; two of $81 and one of $82. In the first year, when all three are effective, payments are reduced by $243; in the second by $163; in the third by $81.

interest rates at 12 percent, too many would-be buyers cannot qualify. After surveying the market and his rapidly escalating costs, he decides it is worthwhile to sacrifice income of $10,000 per house rather than to continue with an unsold inventory. How can he recover the most for his expenditure?

1. As we see in the first row of the table, the builder has been trying to sell each house at its listed price of $100,000, with a down payment of $5,000 and a mortgage loan of $95,000. If interest rates are 12 percent with a 30-year term, each monthly payment will be $977. This is the payment rate from which the buy-down occurs. After the buy-down period, payments on the loan will rise to this level.
2. In the second row, the builder reduces the price by $10,000 to $90,000. With a mortgage of $85,000, monthly payments are $874. The reduction in payments is $103 per month, compared to those on the $95,000 mortgage, and a family could qualify with an income $5,000 lower. The borrower gains not only from lower monthly payments, but also because any time the loan is prepaid the outstanding principal will be considerably less than on the larger mortgage.
3. In the third row, the builder pays the lender $10,000 for the purpose of buying down interest payments for 60 months. The lender reduces the monthly payments so that the present value of the payments not received exactly equals the builder's payment. At a 12 percent discount rate, this reduction is $222. The builder's $10,000 payment equals the present value of 60 payments of $222 each, discounted at 12 percent. The builder can advertise a current interest rate of 9.2 percent when the market is 12 per-cent. After 5 years payments rise to $977, the regular payments on a 12 percent loan, for the remaining 25 years.

   If the lender allows the buyer to qualify on the basis of the $755 monthly payment, the reduction in the annual income required to qualify is more than $10,000, assuming a maximum 25 percent mortgage pay-ment-to-income ratio. Compared to the previous case, in which the concession was applied to the price of the house, the buy-down lowers required income by more than twice as much. This greatly increases the number of potential buyers and makes such buy-downs very popular with builders.
4. In the next row, the $10,000 builder's concession is used to cover pay-ments for only 3 years. Payments are reduced to $645 a month. The pres-ent value of a reduction of $332 for each of 36 months equals his $10,000 payment to the lender. The initial interest rate is 7.8 percent. If the lender does not change eligibility rules, families will need $16,000 less in annual income then they would in a non-buy-down situation.
5. In the 3-2-1 buy-down, the builder cuts his concession roughly in half, but the first year's interest is only 8.9 percent. The builder must put up only a little over $5,000 to match reductions of $243, $163, and $81 for the first three years. Moreover, the initial qualifying income is slightly less than for

a $10,000 buy-down spread over 5 years. The builder's costs fall because the borrower's payments go up at an earlier time. They reach the $977 level by the end of the third year.

The advantages to the builder of using a buy-down rather than a straight concession are clear: more potential buyers can qualify at less cost to the builder. Greater demand means more rapid sales at a better price. On the other hand, it is riskier for both the buyer and the lender. In the 5-year buy-down, unless the buyer's income has increased by a third by the end of year 5, the buyer may default. For the lender, such buy-downs mean that foreclosures and losses due to mortgage shock will rise. For the shorter-period buy-downs, income must increase even more rapidly, and the time horizon for risks is shorter. Furthermore, if the buyer prepays the loan—which is probable—he will always have to pay off a larger outstanding principal than is true in the second case, in which the price of the house and the amount of the mortgage were reduced directly.

Which of the four types of creative financing discussed under this category is actually used depends on the kind of property and the particular market. Carry-backs are most common on sales of existing houses and when the seller does not need the cash for another purchase. Contracts of sale are used mainly for selling land and for inexpensive houses. In such cases, foreclosure costs would exceed feasible down payments. Lease options are more unusual and are used primarily in very weak markets. Buy-downs are found most often in sales of new units when the builder can arrange a number of contracts and when low initial interest forms a major marketing tool.

Advantages and Disadvantages of Sellers' Creative Financing Techniques

Each of these financing methods has its advantages. Although they vary from one method to another, some or all of the following apply:

- The down payment can be as little as the seller will agree to accept. A buyer qualifies on the strength of the seller's—not a lender's—judgment.
- The continuation of the existing mortgage may mean a lower interest rate.
- Prepayment penalties and other transaction costs may be avoided or postponed.
- Monthly payments may be reduced, allowing more potential buyers to qualify and thus raising demand. A sale may be possible only if creative financing is used.
- Builders and sellers may not have to reduce their prices as much as with other techniques.
- The seller's security is better under the contract of sale and lease-option than with a mortgage for the same amount. One reason more favorable

terms can be granted is that the property can be regained faster and with fewer risks.

However, the advantages may be more than offset by these added difficulties:

- Buyers may have to pay for the better terms possible under creative methods with a higher sales price. They might buy for less if they could obtain traditional financing.
- Buyers may pay more for the property under a buy-down than with traditional financing. Moreover, they face the difficult prospect of increasing payments.
- The buyer is confronted with a balloon payment or need to fulfill a contract that may come at an inopportune time.
- On contracts and options, the buyer cannot be sure of receiving a clear title, even though the property has been paid for.
- Mortgage payments through the seller may be diverted and not credited to the buyer.
- The seller gets less cash from the sale and has more equity tied up than in traditional mortgages.
- The seller's risks are greater in creative financing than by traditional means. Buyers are more likely to default since their equity is less. The sale may fall through without the seller receiving adequate compensation for the time the property is tied up, and its condition may have deteriorated.
- The tenant does not receive full tax benefits when a lease is used in conjunction with the sale.
- The seller must administer the contract, lease, or mortgage, or sell it at a heavy discount.

The disadvantages so outweigh the advantages that under normal circumstances these techniques are not common. Their share of the market rises when credit is tight and interest rates are high. Such mortgages are made at all times, however, to handle the special circumstances of buyers with adequate income but few savings, of sellers who are happy to gain the higher rates on second mortgages or who want to sell on an installment basis, and to facilitate the sale of special or unique kinds of property.

REDUCING MONTHLY PAYMENTS

A third group of techniques also serves to cut borrowers' monthly payments, but they are used primarily in mortgages issued by institutions. They are forms of creative financing and are aimed mainly at solving the problem of mortgage tilt. In a period of inflation, housing is an excellent investment. Yet in such periods many families cannot invest because of the mortgage tilt problem. Current interest rates include a premium for future inflation, whereas incomes used to qualify borrowers depend on current, not future, income. If a family's income or the value of a property also rises with inflation, initial monthly payments can be set lower than those required later. They can move with the price level, or with time, or with the value of the property. Reduced payments in earlier years permit more families to qualify for a loan and to buy a house sooner or one with greater value.

Although many types of mortgages have been suggested and tried in this category, we describe only three:

1. Graduated payment mortgages and others that reduce payments or allow negative amortization.
2. Price-level adjusted mortgages and others in which payments change with the rate of inflation.
3. Shared appreciation mortgages, in which the interest yields depend on how much the value of the house has appreciated.

The first and last types have been used fairly regularly, but their share of the market has not been significant. The second type, although it appears to have major theoretical advantages, has hardly been used at all.

Reduced Amortization Mortgages

Payments can be reduced by minimizing amortization or allowing it to become negative. Some loans permit payments of interest only or of partial interest, or they allow all of it to accrue. Any unpaid interest adds to the outstanding principal. **Graduated payment mortgages (GPMs)** call for a gradual increase in monthly payments over the initial years of a mortgage. Interest rates may be fixed or adjustable. If the payment schedule is graduated but fixed and the interest rate is adjustable, the loans are called **dual interest-rate mortgages (DIMs).**

The GPM is used by many types of lenders and has been authorized for FHA-insured loans (Section 245) and VA guarantees. Contracts call for fixed interest rates and payments that rise according to an agreed-upon schedule. The most common forms specify that monthly payments will increase by 7.5 percent at the end of each of the first 5 years. They then remain constant at this higher level. Table 11-4 illustrates how payments rise each year by 7.5 percent until they reach a final level in year 6. Meanwhile, the outstanding balance also rises with the first amortization payment occurring in the sixth year. Other possibilities include an increase of 3 percent a year for each of 10 years, and there are many variations between these two.

GPMs assume that the borrower's income will rise. Buyers gain by not being constrained by their first year's income. They can pick a house that will meet their needs over a longer future period. Note from the table that if lenders maintain a maximum 25 percent mortgage payment-to-income ratio and a house has an $80,000 mortgage at 13 percent with a 30-year maturity, a GPM allows a

Table 11-4
Examples of Graduated Payment and
Price-level Adjustable Mortgages
$80,000, 30-Year Term to Maturity

	GPM		PLAM	
Year	Payment	Beginning of Year Balance	Payment	Beginning of Year Balance
1	$685	$80,000	$429	$80,000*
2	736	82,315	464	85,167*
3	792	84,216	501	90,571*
4	851	85,846	517	91,763†
5	915	86,854	532	92,849†
6	984	87,187	549	93,838†

Note: GPM interest rate is 13%. PLAM real interest rate is 5%, plus inflation rates below.
*8% inflation
†3% inflation

family to qualify with an income of $2,740 per month. Under a standard mortgage, the family's required income would be $3,540.

The example also reveals that even though lenders' interest charges do not change, they increase their risk of defaults with GPMs. If a safe payment ratio should not exceed 25 percent at any time, safety requires that the family's income rise steadily and reach $3,936 per month by the end of year 5. If inflation declines or if the borrower's income increase drops below the average, the borrower will have trouble meeting the payments. Furthermore, negative amortization raises the principal balance to $87,347. If the value of the house rises less, the lender's safety margin falls as well. Defaults, foreclosures, and lender losses have been higher on these mortgages.

In the standard GPM, interest rates are fixed. However, the contract could just as well contain an agreement that interest rates will adjust in accordance with an index. These are called **graduated payment adjustable mortgages (GPAMs).** Moreover, payments need not move with interest rates. Instead, the difference in interest charges can be added to or subtracted from the principal balance as in DIMs. They are dual rate because the scheduled payments and the actual rate of interest charged move at different speeds. How far they depart from each other depends on the movements in the index that determines the actual effective interest rate.

In many cases, varying the amounts of the payments causes the term to maturity to change. Increasing balances can rapidly extend the term to maturity. As a result, most such mortgages contain an agreement that payments will be adjusted when the outstanding balance exceeds a certain percent (125%) of the original, or when the maturity based on the scheduled payments is longer than 40 years.

Price-level Adjustable Mortgages

A **price-level adjustable mortgage (PLAM)** increases the outstanding principal in accordance with a price index. Payments remain constant in real terms but rise in nominal dollars. The initial payment is low because the interest payment does not include the premium for expected inflation. The PLAM has decided theoretical advantages, but it has had few actual applications. It appears too complex. Under this scheme, the payment for each year is based on (a) a constant real interest rate, (b) the principal, which rises at the end of each year by the amount of inflation, and (c) the amount of amortization required to pay off the mortgage in its remaining life.

Table 11-4 presents the example of an $80,000 30-year PLAM with a real interest rate of 5 percent. The first payment is $429 a month; this amount will amortize a mortgage at 5 percent interest over 30 years. At the beginning of year 2, the principal balance is shown as $85,167. This is found by applying an inflation factor (here, 8 percent) to the $78,858 balance at the end of year 1. The monthly payment in year 2 is recalculated as $464, which is the amount needed to amortize that year's beginning balance at 5 percent real interest over the remaining 29 years. Payments continue to change year by year, following the same rules. Each year, the outstanding balance is adjusted by the previous year's inflation rate. The payment for the year is set as the amount required to amortize the inflation-adjusted balance over the rest of the original term, based on the constant fixed interest rate (5 percent in this example).

Every year, because the principal is being amortized over a shorter period, the payment constant rises. The actual payment depends on what has happened to inflation and on the outstanding balance. Note in the table that in year 4 the monthly payment goes up by only $16, compared to $37 in the previous year. With declining inflation, the principal owed did not rise as fast as before. At some point, the amount of amortization exceeds the rate of inflation, causing the principal to decline and to reach zero by the end of year 30.

The low initial payment based on real interest rates greatly increases affordability. Payments rise with actual inflation, not by an arbitrary amount. Even though the value of a house and the income of the borrower varies somewhat around the inflation level, both are more likely to move with inflation than with the indexes used or the graduated payments agreed to for the other types of alternative mortgages.

However, in a period of strong inflation the outstanding principal will rise rapidly. Borrowers' payments will go up even faster than the outstanding balance because the time for amortization is shorter. Furthermore, the more rapid the inflation, the greater will be the dispersion of individual income and house prices. This means that more families will not have the necessary income to meet the higher payments.

Shared Appreciation Mortgages

In a **shared appreciation mortgage (SAM),** the lender accepts a lower than market rate of interest in return for a specified share of any appreciation in the value of a property. The appreciation may be calculated when the house is sold or it may be based on an appraisal at the end of a fixed number of years. If the house is not sold, the lender must be paid off through refinancing. In a typical arrangement, the lender might agree to lend $80,000 on a $100,000 house. The interest rate is lowered to 8 percent instead of a market rate of 12 percent. The mortgage is amortized over 30 years.

For accepting the lower interest, the lender is promised one-third of any increase in value above the $100,000 purchase price. After 5 years, if the house sells for $121,000, the lender receives $7,000 in recompense for having reduced interest charges by $3,200 a year. Obviously, such arrangements, if they are to work, need a high rate of inflation. The trade-off between how much interest is reduced and the share of appreciation is subject to bargaining.

While the SAM lowers monthly payments and thus increases affordability, it has a major flaw. House appreciation depends on maintenance and improvements as well as on time and inflation. How can the borrower and lender know whether they will be rewarded or penalized for the owner's extra or substandard performance in maintaining and improving the property?

Advantages and Disadvantages of Mortgages to Reduce Payments

Since the key reason for loans in this category is to reduce the borrower's initial payments, their advantages are similar to those of other forms of creative financing.

- Low initial payments increase affordability. First-time home buyers can get more house at their current income level.
- The rate of increase in payments for GPMs can be determined in advance.
- ARMs should carry lower interest rates than fixed-rate mortgages, since they reduce the lender's interest risk.
- Except in periods of rapid inflation, PLAMs should have less risk because the amount of debt and payments track actual, not assumed, inflation.
- The SAM allows borrowers to qualify with less income. It also shares the risk of inflation-related interest changes between borrowers and lenders.

The main disadvantages of loans in this category arise from their dependence on asumptions of future increases in income and house values, which may not be realized:

- Negative amortization and increasing loan balances raise the risk of default.

- The borrower's income and the prices of houses may not track either assumed increases or actual inflation.
- All mortgages with required balloons or payment changes can cause payment and refinancing shocks.
- Lenders may not want their mortgage loan balances to increase automatically, especially if the interest rate is fixed or if housing prices do not move with interest rates.
- SAMs are complex. It is difficult to share appreciation when it is unclear how much of any change in value is due to actions of the owner rather than to the economy.

OTHER BORROWING ARRANGEMENTS

The final category of creative and alternative financing techniques contains a variety of methods of borrowing on real property, each of which has developed to meet a special need. We discuss three main types of methods:

1. Faster-amortization mortgages reduce maturities and may lower costs.
2. The increased equity in homes is a potential source of financing for non-housing expenditures. A number of techniques are available for this purpose.
3. Some changes in ownership and borrowing maximize the use of any available tax preferences.

Faster Amortization

Loans in this category take the opposite tack from most of the creative financing approaches. Rather than lowering monthly payments, these require higher payments to fund a faster amortization compared with a standard fixed-rate, 30-year mortgage.

The most common kind increases payments by using a 15-year term to maturity. In early 1986, 15 percent of all mortgages were claimed to be of this type. A second type is a **growing equity mortgage (GEM),** in which the initial payments start as though the mortgage were for a standard 30-year term. The amount of the payments then increases, based either on an agreed-upon rate, such as 3.5 percent per year, or on an adjustable index. The total amount of the increases is applied to amortization, causing the mortgage to be paid off in 12 to 15 years. The actual maturity depends on the rate at which payments increase and on market interest rates. To avoid the borrower being tied down to a required rate of increase in payments, the lender can use indexes, such as those for interest rates or the gross national product, to determine the rate of the step-up in amortization. Another form of GEM increases amortization by requiring that payments be made twice a month.

Why Pay off Faster?   There are several reasons why people agree to more rapid amortization.

- More rapid payoffs lead to somewhat lower interest rates. On average, 15-year mortgages have rates about one-third of a percent less than 30-year mortgages. When a 30-year mortgage carries a 10 percent rate, the rate on one of 15 years might be 9.6 percent. Because rates are slightly lower, it is claimed, the increase in monthly payments is minor, but this is a matter of judgment. On an $80,000 mortgage, the monthly payments on one for 15 years would be $840, compared with $702 on a 30-year mortgage at 10 percent. Shortening the term raises the amount of each payment by 19.7 percent.

- Some prospective borrowers add all the interest payments together for loans of different maturities and then compare them. On an $80,000 30-year mortgage at 10 percent paid until maturity, the interest charges will total $172,741. On a mortgage of the same amount and rate but amortized over 15 years, the interest payments will total $74,743. This difference looks tremendous and both convinces and frightens many people. However, such a comparison makes no economic sense because it ignores the time value of money. It also neglects the reductions in costs that stem from the ability to deduct interest payments from taxable income.

  EXAMPLE: if a person's real borrowing costs were determined by the 18 percent she paid on a bank credit card or installment loan, additional mortgage payments would be a bargain. At 18 percent, the present value of her future payments on the 30-year loan above would be $46,584; on a 15-year loan it would be $52,160. By taking the longer loan, she would be immediately $5,575 better off. Furthermore, she would not have to struggle to meet the larger payments. If money were worth 10 percent to her, the total amount of the payments for both loans would have the same present value. If her money were worth only 8 percent, she would save between $5,000 and $6,000 by taking the shorter loan because she would be borrowing excess money worth only 8 percent to her. Both the gains and the losses would depend also on taxes and on any differences in the treatment of interest earned or paid. Clearly, if interest on home mortgages is deductible for tax purposes and interest on personal loans is not, the use of a longer-term mortgage will reduce costs even if the interest rates are equal.

- Some people must force themselves to save. By paying off a mortgage in 15 rather than 30 years, for example, they increase their savings more rapidly because their debt has fallen faster. If they wish to save more and cannot accomplish it any other way, rapid payoffs may make sense, since the lower principal owed means that they have a higher equity and reduced leverage.

Why Take a Large, Long Loan? The disadvantages of faster amortization are also evident.

- By agreeing to larger payments and faster amortization, a borrower has less money available for other uses.
- Rapid payment may increase a borrower's default risk. Meeting a higher monthly payment may be more difficult than finding the cash for a smaller one.
- It is more difficult to qualify for a 15-year mortgage than for a 30-year one. This need not be true for the GEM, since its initial payment would be the same as for a 30-year loan.
- If the borrower must default, he or she loses more money by having increased the equity using the 15-year mortgage. The borrower would have been better off saving the extra money elsewhere. It would then have been available as a source of mortgage payments over the period of hard times that led to the default.
- Most consumers cannot borrow as cheaply anywhere else as they can on a mortgage. If they can pay off other debts as a result of making smaller mortgage payments, the longer mortgage costs less than the shorter one. Equity builds up faster on a shorter mortgage. Before choosing the term, prospective borrowers must add the opportunity cost of the higher equity to the interest payments in order to find the actual cost of the respective mortgages. Comparing total interest payments alone makes no sense.
- Many people of moderate income have no other way of obtaining leveraged investments except through their house mortgage. A larger mortgage allows an investor to obtain more leverage. (As Chapter 4 explained, the effects of leverage may be good or bad depending on how well the investment is made and on future inflation and housing prices.) More debt and more leverage protect the homeowner against inflation, since the value of the property rises while the debt does not.

Using the Owner's Equity

Lenders have developed a number of methods that enable owners to take advantage of the rapid buildup in equity that occurs when houses appreciate. Although equity buildup from mortgage amortization always leads to an ability to increase borrowing, the importance of techniques to use this possibility rises with inflation and with the number of families who have occupied the same home for a long period of time.

One of the most important ways to obtain cash without selling a property is through refinancing. A new mortgage can include sufficient funds to repay the outstanding mortgage and still leave a remainder of cash available for other uses. As Chapter 12 explains, whether or not refinancing is worthwhile depends on how the new and old interest rates differ, on the amount of the prepayment penalties, on origination costs, and on how badly additional cash is needed.

Reverse Annuity Mortgages   Many retired couples find themselves with a different set of problems: they have a large equity in their home, but a reduced income. They would like to keep living in the house and use the existing equity to help maintain their standard of living. This is the purpose of the **reverse annuity mortgage (RAM),** a mortgage under which the lender agrees to advance the principal over time rather than immediately.

Although many forms of RAMs are possible, the simplest entails a mortgage for an agreed-upon sum that would be advanced to the borrower in fixed payments as an annuity over several years. Each payment made increases the outstanding balance on the loan and is split, part going to the borrower and part to pay the interest on the outstanding principal. If payments stay constant, the amount received by the borrower falls as the balance and interest due on it rise.

The loan is usually repaid in one of three ways:

1. The borrower dies and the loan is settled by the estate.
2. The property is sold.
3. After the fixed number of payments has been made, if an appraisal shows that the value of the house has risen, a new set of payments could be renegotiated. If not, the house will be sold.

EXAMPLE: A couple owns a $100,000 house with no outstanding liens. They sign a RAM to borrow up to $90,000 at 12 percent interest. The first year they are paid $5,000; this amount becomes the outstanding balance. The second year the amount advanced against the mortgage is $5,600, but they receive only $5,000; the remainder is paid to the lender as interest. The outstanding loan is now $10,600. Payments to them continue until the outstanding balance reaches $90,000. At that point the house could be reappraised. If the value has increased, the loan could continue to grow in order to meet further payments. If not, the house would be sold to pay off the loan.

Insurance Annuities   The uncertainty of how long the payments will be needed creates problems for borrowers with RAMs. This uncertainty can be transferred to an insurance company by using the proceeds of a mortgage to purchase a lifetime annuity. The payments from the insurance company go partly to meet the interest on the mortgage and partly to the owner-borrower. When the property is sold, the mortgage is repaid. If the sale occurs because the owner no longer wants to remain in the house, any proceeds above the amount needed to pay off the mortgage go to the seller. In addition, the full monthly annuity payments are now no longer split. If the sale is at death, the annuity ends. The advantage of the annuity over the RAM is that the owner-borrower can stay in the house regardless of how long he or she lives.

Using Potential Tax Savings

The final two techniques for creative and alternative financing use the tax preferences through depreciation allowances, interest deductions, and other costs that can be charged off against taxable income. Their purpose is to transfer the tax savings from owners in low tax brackets to owners for whom the tax preferences are worth more.

In a **sale-leaseback** an owner sells the property but retains occupancy. A rental lease is signed simultaneously with the sale. At the same time, a trust or other method of guaranteeing the rent payments is established. Such agreements work best among members of a family. Elderly parents might sell their existing equity to one of their children. Conversely, a high-income couple might buy a second house and lease it to a son or daughter who is in college or is just starting out on a career.

EXAMPLE: In a sale-leaseback equivalent to an RAM, a couple with a $100,000 house but with little income sells the house to their daughter. She finances it with a $90,000 mortgage. The parents use the $100,000 to buy a lifetime annuity. The daughter signs a lifetime lease agreement with her parents, and they pledge part of the annuity payments to meet their rents to her. She assigns the rents as additional security on the mortgage. This also assures the parents that the mortgage will not be foreclosed, since part of the annuity guarantees the mortgage payment. They are certain that they can continue to live in the house as long as they wish.

The rent they are charged can be reduced by the amount of tax savings the daughter engenders through deduction for depreciation, interest payments, and property taxes. On a $100,000 house, these deductions can run as high as $16,000 a year. If she is in a 30 percent tax bracket, the savings that could be used to reduce the parents' rent would be $4,800 a year.

There are many other types of participation financing. (Several that are used with commercial property are discussed in Part 4, Chapter 19.) One fairly common form for individual homes is called equity sharing or equity participation. In an **equity sharing** arrangement, two parties purchase the house jointly. The one who occupies it pays his share of the costs while paying rent to the other to cover her (or an institution's) share. When the house is sold, each participates in the sales price in accordance with his or her share.

The same additional benefits arise from tax savings as under the sale-leaseback. Other advantages and disadvantages are similar to those for the SAM. The shared equity arrangement has been specifically authorized under a special section of the Internal Revenue Code.

Since shared appreciation and equity sharing mortgages are difficult to arrange and to police on individual homes, they are more likely to be used among relatives or close friends, where trust and willingness to compromise are greater. Both types of loans furnish equity to those who cannot raise a down payment, and both allow for tax savings.

Advantages and Disadvantages

Most of the techniques in the last category depend on the existence of sizable equity in a property, or on the existing tax laws and rulings. For those whose homes have large equity, there are four main advantages:

- They enable the homeowner to obtain cash, which can be used to spend or invest elsewhere.
- Borrowing against equity in a home may be the only way a family has of raising money.
- The RAM permits homeowners to continue to live in their own home, a right that may be guaranteed them for the rest of their lives.
- Some of these techniques have sizable tax advantages.

There are also major disadvantages to these types of mortgages:

- Even though they cost less than other forms of borrowing, the funds obtained using these techniques may be expensive in terms of both interest and other transaction charges.
- The risks of default rise when equity is reduced.
- When interest rates are high, RAMs may not offer much current income. They are also too complex for many potential users.
- Without insured annuities, how long payments on RAMs will continue is uncertain. Insurance may be expensive, depending on the amount of risk transferred to the insurance company and on sales and other transaction costs.
- Arrangements to reduce taxes depend on the tax laws and on relative marginal tax rates, which may change in ways that make these techniques more trouble than they are worth.

SUMMARY

New mortgage plans and creative financing developed during the 1970s and 1980s to fill special needs. Inflation made it more difficult for borrowers to qualify, and lenders wanted to transfer interest risk to borrowers. Some borrowers hoped to reduce their high interest costs through faster amortization. Owners desired to use some of the increased equity they had achieved through luck or successful investing.

Borrowers should pay lower interest rates on adjustable-rate mortgages because they assume more risks, among them the risk of payment shock. They can limit the risks to those they are willing to accept by understanding the details of the contract and by choosing mortgages with acceptable caps for changes in interest charges and payments. Borrowers must watch for the margin above the index, for differences between the initial rate and the effective rate indicated by the index in the current market, and for the maximum changes allowed by the caps.

Creative financing includes several methods through which sellers assist buyers by helping them finance a purchase. Since the buyers' equity is lower, risks of default are greater. Sellers grant financing in order to make a sale or get a higher price. Both buyers and sellers can reduce their risks by carefully structuring rights. They need to make sure that all payments are properly met and that property can be transferred without liens additional to those specifically provided for.

Monthly payments can be reduced by separating the amount of interest charged from the payments. This means that amortization can be either negative or positive. The changes can either be prescheduled or made dependent on an external index.

Lenders' risks are reduced when borrowers amortize the principal more rapidly, providing they can meet their payments. Borrowers can save costs through faster amortization when lenders charge a lower interest or when their opportunity costs for the higher equity are below market interest rates. On the other hand, borrowers may lose to the extent that faster amortization and higher payments cause them to borrow elsewhere for goods and services at higher rates. If borrowers discount future payments at the mortgage interest rate, the term of a loan does not affect its actual costs, since the much higher interest amounts paid on a larger loan have the same present value as paying off a loan with larger payments over a shorter period.

In shared appreciation and shared equity loans, the lenders and borrowers divide potential risks and profits. Problems can arise in deciding the size of gains and losses and in assigning responsibility among the sharing parties. Reverse annuity mortgages have been unpopular because their results have been uncertain. Insured lifetime annuities can reduce some risks of how long the payments to the borrower will be made. Shared equities and leasebacks may achieve reduced costs through tax advantages.

KEY TERMS

adjustable-rate mortgage (ARM)
buy-down
cap
contract of sale
creative financing
dual interest-rate mortgage (DIM)
effective interest rate
equitable ownership
equity sharing

graduated payment adjustable
    mortgage (GPAM)
graduated payment mortgage
    (GPM)
Growing equity mortgage
    (GEM)
index
initial interest rate
lease-option

lease-purchase
price-level adjustable
   mortgage (PLAM)
reverse annuity mortgage
   (RAM)
roll-over mortgage

sale-leaseback
shared appreciation mortgage
   (SAM)
seller carry-back
teaser

QUESTIONS

1. Describe how a contract of sale works and its drawbacks.
2. Recalculate Table 11-3 using 10 percent as the initial mortgage rate from which to be bought down.
3. Discuss the advantages and disadvantages of the seller carry-back, contract of sale, and lease-option.
4. What are the three basic types of ARMs?
5. Compare and contrast the advantages and disadvantages of ARMs with those of seller carry-backs.
6. Distinguish graduated payment adjustable mortgages from adjustable-rate mortgages.
7. Explain how the PLAM works. Why do you think it has not been implemented?
8. What criteria would you use to choose between a longer loan with a smaller monthly payment and a shorter loan with a larger payment? (Assume they have the same present value.)
9. How do RAMs differ from other mortgages?
10. In general, would you prefer the types of mortgages discussed in this chapter to standard mortgages? Which do you think would be most useful to (1) a lender and (2) a borrower? Explain your reasoning.
11. Look in the most recent *Federal Reserve Bulletin* for the latest rate on 1-year, constant maturity treasury notes and bonds. Assuming that this was the index for mortgages A and B in Table 11-1, what would each one's effective interest be if this were the index value on the next change date?

12 The Borrower's Mortgage Loan Decision

OBJECTIVES

When you finish this chapter, you should be able to:

- describe the process of finding a mortgage that fits a borrower's needs.

- understand how computers help in the selection process.

- know the factors to look for in deciding which loan is best.

- explain how to evaluate a fixed-rate mortgage compared with an adjustable-rate mortgage.

- compare an existing and a proposed loan to determine whether refinancing is cost-effective.

T HE TWO PREVIOUS chapters have described the complexities of deciding how much to spend and borrow, as well as the types of mortgages available. This chapter and the next analyze some of the reasons for choosing a particular mortgage. They also discuss the residential lending process and the effects of mortgage availability on the demand for housing.

Borrowers deciding what type and how large a mortgage to seek must confront a number of issues. The most important is finding a mortgage for which they can qualify. **Qualification** is the process by which a lender determines that a borrower can be expected to meet promptly the payments required by the mortgage contract.

In addition, because borrowers can often trade off costs, amounts, and risks, they must choose among a variety of risks and effective interest rates. They may decide to go for lower current payments based on an adjustable rate, knowing that rates will rise if high interest rates come back. They can agree to a step-up in payments over the next five years based on a graduated-payment contract. If they decide on an adjustable-rate mortgage, they must choose an index and decide how much extra interest to pay to include caps that will protect against still higher future payments.

In determining how large a mortgage to take and the amount of the down payment, borrowers also select differing risks of default. Many borrowers faced with a balloon payment due in only a few years have nightmares worrying about how to meet it. Others, unwilling to accept such risks, opt for more conventional financing.

Prospective borrowers cannot avoid making projections of cost when choosing a mortgage. Whether a fixed-rate or adjustable-rate mortgage will work best depends on future interest rates. Actual costs—and therefore how expensive a house to buy—are determined by projected future appreciation or depreciation. Affordability hinges on the outlook for increases in income. The costs of ownership can change drastically, depending on how long a mortgage is outstanding.

Potential borrowers need to find the loans actually available in their locality when they want the money. This requires searching for the mortgage that can meet their needs at the least cost. Computers have speeded up this process in many cities. In choosing the best mortgage, borrowers must analyze the factors that cause certain loans to be preferable to others.

FINDING THE RIGHT LOAN

The process of obtaining a loan involves a good deal of strategy on the part of the borrower, the real estate salesperson, and the lender. The borrower wants to obtain money in the shortest possible time, with the least bother, and on the best available terms. Since most offers to buy make a sale contingent on the availability of a mortgage loan on specified terms, the salesperson's commission depends on financing availability. A smoothly operating loan procedure assures the lender that the risks and benefits of a loan are properly balanced and that it conforms to policy.

Shopping for a Mortgage

Finding the right mortgage loan is becoming easier. More and more offices have computers that can be used on-line to obtain specific information on loans being offered by a variety of lenders. Newspapers carry compilations of the best terms available locally. Real estate brokers maintain up-to-date files on loan terms.

Anyone making an offer to buy needs current mortgage information. Because financing is crucial for most purchases, the sales contract usually contains a **contingent financing clause** which makes the sale depend on the buyer's securing specified terms. Typically the offer enumerates the required amount, a maximum interest rate, limits on points, a minimum maturity, and whether Federal Housing Administration (FHA) insurance or a Veterans Administration (VA) guarantee is required. The contingency clause should make clear that if a loan is not available on the terms listed, the buyer can cancel the offer and get back all deposits. A contingent-upon-financing clause that specifies below-market terms or leads to long delays means that other sales opportunities are lost. Sellers should therefore limit the time borrowers can take to obtain a loan, to avoid holding the property off the market for an excessive period.

Assuming a Loan

Depending on whether rates are rising or falling, the best place to begin looking for a loan may be the existing one on the property. If rates have been rising and the seller is willing to accept a junior mortgage for part of the price, assuming an existing loan will usually cost less. In addition, a freely assumable mortgage may have better terms than those currently available. Even if a due-on-sale clause exists and the lender demands fees or a change in terms, obtaining permission for an assumption may still be worthwhile; prepayment penalties may be avoided and closing costs reduced.

USING COMPUTERS TO FIND A MORTGAGE

The mid-1980s witnessed a growing use of computer networks to help potential borrowers search for loans for which they could qualify. Over a dozen companies offer on-line services. A prospective borrower can go to a real estate broker or mortgage banker who uses one of the services and obtain the desired information through a personal computer. The specific services offered differ widely from one company to another:

1. The simplest offerings consist of a printout, supplemented by details on the terms currently being granted on mortgages by a variety of lenders.
2. Some firms further act as mortgage loan counselors. They discuss the types of loans for which a borrower can qualify. They also indicate what additional factors might qualify a borrower for others.
3. When income and property information are supplied, some firms will make preliminary commitments on actual loans. The final loan will depend on meeting the necessary underwriting criteria.
4. The computer can be used to prepare the standardized documents needed by the underwriters. The loan application can be filled out and signed, the credit check carried out, and an appraisal ordered.

How far the loan process is carried depends on the individual company. Some merely furnish information. Some prepare the documents needed for qualification and turn them over to a lender. Others actually make the loan.

In most cases, firms charge lenders for carrying information in the data base on the lenders' loans; the borrower pays nothing until documents are ordered, at which time the borrower pays the usual charges for a credit report and drawing up of documents or perhaps a commitment fee applicable against costs if the loan is granted. A service may contain data on as many as 2,000 types of mortgages from hundreds of lenders. The data supply information on individual mortgages in considerable detail. For each mortgage, specifications may include minimum down payments, maximum size of loan, interest rates, amortization schedules, points and fees, specific indexes, spreads, and caps for adjustable-rate mortgages. Information on interest rates and points is used to calculate the effective costs or yield. Most important, the data bases include the minimum underwriting criteria of the different lenders.

Qualifying for a Loan

What should a borrower expect from a broker or banker using a computer? The borrower is asked what type and size of loan he or she wants, what kind of property the loan is for, what down payment the borrower can make, and what maturity is under consideration. In addition, a potential borrower furnishes information on income, debts, assets, and funds available for the down payment, as well as maximum acceptable mortgage payments.

The computer searches its files on the basis of this information. It can supply a great deal of detail on each prospective loan, including its interest rate, that meet the borrower's criteria. It can translate the borrower's financial data into the maximum loan available in each loan category, and can show how expensive a house could be bought, the minimum down payment, closing costs, and monthly expenses. If the borrower can almost but not quite qualify, a loan counselor might come on-line and suggest how some of the included factors might be altered in order to obtain the most desirable loan.

If a loan is found, the borrower fills out the loan application. The service company either commits for a loan or refers the borrower to the lender, who processes the loan far faster than through traditional channels.

Mortgage bankers and thrift institutions worry about competition from these services. If they do not supply information on their offerings to the data bank, they will lose customers; if they do, they will have to compete in price terms or be ignored. They fear that national firms will undercut their market. To compete, they will be forced to offer better service or better terms. On the other hand, most consumer advocates welcome the added competition. It increases the flow of information and reduces the ability of isolated sectors of the market to continue to make loans on noncompetitive terms.

WHICH MORTGAGE IS BEST?

What is best in a loan depends on a borrower's needs. To some, the interest rate may be the most important; others may need to find a loan with the smallest down payment. One firm may be more willing to qualify a marginal borrower than others. Lenders differ in their willingness to count supplementary income or to overlook past credit deficiencies. Other borrowers may feel that assumability and no prepayment penalties are crucial because they plan to move in two or three years. In adjustable-rate mortgages the index and terms of adjustment as well as the margin above the index may differ. Other variations may be found in the points charged and in the insurance fee.

Another of the borrower's main objectives should be to clearly understand the terms. Borrowers must know what they sign. The lender's explanations should be clear and should spell out what might happen under diverse conditions. No borrower should suddenly be confronted with an unexpected jump in payments without warning, or be forced to refinance at much higher rates or to default.

Because most borrowers enter the market only infrequently, they require advice and guidance in equating and trading off the separate loan factors. Brokers should know the best sources of loans; they and the chosen lender should explain the differences between available mortgages. Points, fees, and penalties can be translated into interest rates if the prospective borrower can predict how soon the loan will be paid off. The differences between fixed-rate and adjustable-rate mortgages should be taken into account and clarified by examples. In many cases, however, the need to qualify for the loan may override considerations of cost or other features.

The Decision Criteria

At least four different kinds of factors must be considered in deciding what mortgage to take.

1. Will the mortgage make the desired purchase possible? For some, initial cash costs may be critical; they want the lowest down payment and closing costs and a maximum loan-to-value mortgage. Others may want to start with the smallest possible monthly payments in order to meet the lender's maximum expense-to-income ratio for a loan.

2. How do actual costs compare among mortgages? Costs vary with interest charges, fees, points, and prepayment penalties. Because charges may occur now or at some time in the future, borrowers should compare costs on the basis of their present values.

3. What are the risks of default and of higher charges in the future? Such risks depend on the size of future payments, especially if one of them is a balloon, and on whether future interest rates are adjustable, in which case the caps may be critical. They also vary with the amount invested.

4. A variety of other aspects of lending influence borrowing decisions. Who lends makes a difference; institutions differ with respect to speed and the certainty of obtaining the loan. Forbearance, if needed, may be more probable on a VA- or FHA-approved loan. Contracts of sale, lease options, and wraparound mortgages can all cause the borrower the problems of making sure that the first mortgagee receives the payments rendered and also of obtaining clear title when the loan is paid off. Dealing with individuals can be either far easier or far more difficult than confronting an institution. Borrowers should also remember that interest payments will be tax deductible, while payments through the house's price will not be. Opportunities to pay or obtain additional funds vary according to the terms of the mortgage and the source of the funds.

The Mortgage Menu

A prospective borrower has found a house she would like to buy. It costs much more than she planned, but she is convinced that it meets her needs and its economic costs seem reasonable. She can make the purchase with the proper type of financing. She makes the offer to buy, including contingent financing terms that establish minimum conditions without which the sale cannot proceed. If the offer is accepted, she then must find the best terms under which to borrow.

Either the prospective borrower or her broker may come up with a wide variety of mortgage choices. The owner may be willing to carry back a loan or to sell on a contract of sale. The market has available many kinds of fixed-rate mortgages, each differing somewhat in rates, fees, and clauses. An even wider range exists among adjustable-rate mortgages.

Table 12-1 is an example of a typical table of available mortgages that is similar to many carried weekly by local newspapers. It includes the prices quoted at the end of the previous week for a selected group of banks, savings and loans, and mortgage companies. The table gives the quoted rate and points for four different types of mortgages.

In the table, note the wide differences in rates and points quoted. The interest rates vary from 11.375 percent for bank B on a 30-year, fixed-rate mort-

Table 12-1
Example of Available Mortgage Terms
Mortgage That Will Qualify for Sale to FNMA or FHLMC

| | 30-Year Fixed | | 15-Year Fixed | | FHA | |
| | | | | | Rate | Points + Origination Fee |
Institution	Rate	Points	Rate	Points	Rate	Fee
Bank A	10.125	1.75	9.75	1.25	9.875	1.50 + 1%
Bank B	11.375	2.50	10.75	2.50	10.000	2.00 + 1%
Bank C	10.000	4.00	9.75	3.50	10.000	2.00 + 1%
Savings and Loan A	10.375	1.25	10.00	1.25	10.125	1.00 + 1%
Savings and Loan B	10.125	2.00	9.75	2.00	10.000	1.00 + 1%
Savings and Loan C	10.500	3.50	10.00	3.25	9.750	3.00 + 1%
Savings and Loan D	11.000	2.00	10.75	1.50	10.250	0.00 + 1%
Savings and Loan E	11.250	2.50	10.75	2.50	10.250	2.00 + 1%
Mortgage Company A	9.750	4.75	9.50	4.75	9.500	4.00 + 1%
Mortgage Company B	10.125	5.25	9.75	5.00	10.250	4.00 + 1%

One-Year Adjustable (ARM)

Institution	Initial Rate	Points	Cap Annual	Cap Maximum	Index	+ Margin
Bank A	8.500	4	2	14.500	T-bill*	+ 2.625
Bank B	8.000	2	2	14.000	1-yr T†	+ 2.000
Bank C	8.125	3	2	15.000	1-yr T†	+ 2.250
Savings and Loan A	8.250	4	2	14.500	T-bill*	+ 2.750
Savings and Loan B	8.750	3	2	14.670	T-bill*	+ 2.500
Savings and Loan C	8.500	2	2	14.500	1-yr T†	+ 2.000
Savings and Loan D	9.500	4	2	14.750	T-bill*	+ 2.750
Savings and Loan E	9.250	3	2	15.000	T-bill*	+ 3.000
Mortgage Company A	8.750	3	2	13.875	T-bill*	+ 2.750
Mortgage Company B	8.500	3	2	14.875	1-yr T†	+ 2.250

* 6-month treasury bill
† 1-year treasury note

gage to 8 percent for the same bank's rate on an adjustable-rate mortgage. Similarly, the discount (points) varies from 5.25 at mortgage company B to no points but a 1 percent origination fee on an FHA loan at savings and loan D. There are large differences in rates and points among individual institutions for each type. Wide variations also appear among offerings across the four loan categories at each institution.

It is difficult to single out any specific institution as the low-priced or high-priced provider. Naturally, none wants to be labeled the high-priced lender. Each seems to have developed a flexible marketing strategy that permits it to vary its quoted interest rate and points to differentiate it somewhat from its competitors. Each marks down the particular type of loan it wants, placing higher charges on the ones it finds less desirable at a particular time.

Affordability

As we have seen, one of the most important loan criteria is finding enough money needed to buy the house. This may point to owner financing. When interest rates were at their peak in 1982, most houses were sold by assuming existing lower-rate mortgages, accompanied by an owner's second mortgage. Buyers could not qualify for high-percentage-rate loans when interest rates ran from 15 percent to 18 percent. Keeping the old loan assured them of both lower interest cost and reduced payments.

Owners who take back a second loan or use a contract of sale can set the payments as low as necessary to clinch a sale. Interest-only loans with balloons are common in owner financing. If desirable, interest may be partially accrued, resulting in a steady increase in the outstanding balance. The adjustable-rate mortgage (ARM) is another way of lowering initial payments.

Under such circumstances, buyers must be convinced that interest rates are going to fall or that inflation will raise future incomes and house prices. The prospective borrower can agree to higher future payments if she feels certain that the forces causing high interest rates will also raise income. The inclusion in the interest rate of a premium that covers inflationary expectations makes such an assumption logical. Graduated payment or buy-down mortgages can also make sense under these circumstances.

Owner financing can also keep down payments low enough to solve the problem of buyers with inadequate cash. However, if owners will not cooperate, choosing FHA and VA loans can also lead borrowers to lower down payments. These programs are specifically aimed at keeping cash requirements low, particularly for first-time buyers.

Borrowing Costs

The costs of owner financing and buy-downs are likely to be high and hard to pin down. Rather than appearing in interest rates and mortgage discounts, they show up in a sales price higher than that which would be charged for a cash purchase. When creative financing is common in an area, appraised values tend to be high. Houses with creative financing often sell at 5 percent to 10 percent above true market values. Buyers must be aware of how much of the house price actually covers financing costs. They can then equate their mortgage needs and desires with both direct and indirect charges.

The previous chapter discussed the differences between fixed-rate and adjustable-rate mortgages and illustrated how the latter work. Here we consider how to incorporate some of these factors into the borrower's decision about which mortgage to choose. The same types of criteria apply to loans on both residential and income properties. Important factors in the decision are the differences among the indexes offered, the size of the margin above the current level of the index, the points, and the expected future levels of the index.

Indexes Each index used to adjust the rate in adjustable-rate mortgages has unique features. For example, 1- or 2-year treasury note rates are more stable than 3- or 6-month treasury bills, but they also have a higher average cost over a period of years. Which of these rates is best may depend on the current shape of the yield curve in relation to an average that runs over a long time, and on the quoted margin. A flat curve and similar margins make indexes based on shorter-term U.S. Treasury rates preferable.

The **Savings and Loan Cost of Funds Index**—another frequently used index—is complex because it is derived from both current and past saving contracts. In addition to market interest rates, it reflects the redeposit of older funds plus shifts among types of savings. Before agreeing to its use, the borrower should try to find estimates of where it is headed and why, since all but the least informed lenders use studies of this kind before deciding on what prices to quote.

Margins A key criterion for choosing the best index is to consider the *margins* (the amount added to the index) offered and the difference between the initial rate and the current index rate plus the margin. The value of the original index as listed in the mortgage contract may be well below the market. Too many borrowers have been caught with such teasers (low initial rates that rise sharply later). The crucial factors in an ARM's rate are the current and expected rate of the index and the margin paid above the index. Indexes based on U.S. Treasury rates should be lower on average than those using the cost of funds for federally insured savings and loans; thus, they are likely to carry a wider spread. If an index has a narrow spread, it may be a bargain.

Since most borrowers are risk-adverse, they should receive a lower initial interest rate for accepting the uncertainty of an ARM. Borrowers are sacrificing options with ARMs and should be paid for giving up a fixed interest rate. Therefore, the rate of interest on an ARM should be 1 percent to 2 percent lower than that on a fixed-rate mortgage.

Points and Discounts The origination charges on an ARM should be lower than on a fixed-rate mortgage also, since this is one way the lender is paying the borrower for the lost options. Moreover, the points charged by lenders differ, as Table 12-1 made clear. Bargaining over points may be possible. It is easier for lenders to adjust points in individual cases than to alter interest rates.

Because of the danger that later payments may jump well above initial ones, adjustable-rate mortgage instruments should normally allow for prepayment without penalty. If interest rates adjust to market rates, they should also allow assumptions by new buyers with minimal fees; it pays lenders to keep outstanding loans that are earning market rates. Weekly tables of available mortgages rarely show prepayment penalties, but they may be significant if the chances of the borrower moving are high or if the penalties continue for the life of the mortgage.

Borrowing Risks

Borrowing risks arise from the possibility that (a) the borrower will not be able to meet future payments, (b) interest payments will be higher than expected, or (c) actual shelter costs will run above budget.

If the price of the house or the borrower's income does not grow with inflation, the borrower may be squeezed in his ability to make payments. The specific problems differ depending on the borrowing contract. Adjustable rates should fall if inflation declines, and payments should be easier to meet. On the other hand, real interest rates have risen even as nominal ones fell. Housing prices rising less than expected can mean that shelter takes a larger share of income than had been planned.

Owner financing may cause similar risks. Contracts of sale usually call for a balloon payment or the need to purchase after a few years. They assume that rates will fall and values rise so that refinancing will be easy. If both do not occur, borrowers may be forced to default. GPMs and adjustable rates with rising indexes can mean that payments go up faster than the ability to pay. ARMs with adjustable maturities lead to negative amortization and the possibility that the balance owed will exceed the value of the house.

Adjustments and Caps To avoid some of these dangers, the borrower may decide to pay extra for caps that adjust only at longer intervals—such as every three or five years instead of semiannually or annually. Also important are the amount of change allowed in each period and the maximum overall change. The smaller each of these separate caps is, the lower the borrower's risks are of both higher payments and defaults.

Other Mortgage Choice Factors

Because methods of borrowing and the desires of borrowers differ so greatly, the list of other factors that may be considered when choosing a mortgage is extremely broad in scope. To some, borrowing from an institution may be most important; others put too much faith in the lending capabilities of individuals, who may fail to perform as expected. Contracts of sale, lease options, and wraparound mortgages—all complex contracts—can lead to undesired legal entanglements. If properly drawn, these alternatives are desirable because they can solve problems; if left to chance, they can cause expensive difficulties.

Similar statements can be made about tax savings. Purchases of real estate can lead to tax benefits even under tax reform, as we shall see in greater detail in Chapters 16 and 19. Sale-leasebacks and shared equities are examples of financing aimed at taking advantage of such possibilities. Again, however, the borrower should seek expert advice in tax matters.

Other potential mortgage features, such as those which use existing or future equities, are also complex. They can be advantageous to borrowers, but each must be carefully crafted to meet the borrower's specific situation. This is one reason that most of the more complex contracts are seldom found in the usual offerings of financial institutions, which are set up to deal with volume, not individuals. In most cases, institutions lack both the desire and the skill to handle individual variations on single-family house mortgages.

Choosing a Lender

The key criterion in choosing a lender is that it makes the type of loan the borrower is seeking. Some lenders do not make FHA and VA loans; others may not lend above the Federal National Mortgage Association (FNMA) or the Federal Home Loan Mortgage Company (FHLMC) maximum. Others limit their loans to a 15-year maturity.

If a number of lenders are available that can grant a loan at similar terms, costs and the quality of service become crucial criteria. Many lenders suffer from a rapid employee turnover; their personnel are often inexperienced. Others are understaffed and cannot give fast service. Some lenders cannot be depended upon; if the market shifts against them, they may enforce rules that they would normally overlook. Others are to be avoided because they raise fees or demand new restrictions just as the loan is about to close. Imagine how frustrating it is to a borrower when last-minute adjustments must be made under the threat of having to start the entire process over again with another lender.

CALCULATING EFFECTIVE INTEREST RATES

Every day, some potential borrowers must decide whether to pick a fixed-rate or an adjustable-rate mortgage. In order to make sound choices, they need to know the expected costs of each as well as the additional risks they run if they select the ARM. Calculations to find the expected *effective interest rate* are quite straightforward for a fixed-rate mortgage (FRM). As we saw in Chapter 4, the yield, or *internal rate of return* (IRR) to the lender, is the effective rate. It depends on the interest rate agreed upon, any initial points (discounts), and any prepayment penalties. The expected time until the loan is paid off determines the period over which each of these is amortized and, therefore, the effective rate. Projections are more complex for an adjustable-rate mortgage (ARM), since their effective costs depend on the initial rate, the index, the margin, any points, and possible future rates of the index, subject to any caps.*

How can a borrower find the effective interest rates (costs) on possible mortgages? Taking specific offers in hand, the borrower must find the implied rates, which will differ depending on the actual length of the loans. Figure 12-1 demonstrates the results of comparing the effective rates of a specific ARM and fixed-rate mortgage. The lines reflect possible future mortgage rates, and the data at the bottom show the effective interest rates for each separate interest path and for several prepayment periods.

The Fixed-Rate Mortgage   In Figure 12-1, the projected rate for the FRM is 12.18 percent if it is paid off at the end of 3 years, and it then falls steadily to an expected rate of 10.67 percent if it is paid off at the end of 10 years. How are these numbers derived?

The agreed-upon interest for the FRM is 10 percent, and the initial charge is four points. (The other minor fees are not considered, since they will be the same for each mortgage.) A prepayment penalty of 2 percent is assessed if the mortgage is prepaid at the end of 3 years, and a penalty of .5 percent if it is prepaid at 5 years.

The borrower can find the IRR easily by working with an even figure for the mortgage, such as $10,000, while solving Equation 12.1, which is the same as Equation 4.4. To find the 12.18 percent at 3 years, we must find the IRR. This requires inserting in the equation the amount borrowed (PV), the monthly payment (I), and the amount to be paid off (BAL). The IRR can be found by inserting these numbers directly into a financial calculator, or it can be approximated by using the interest factor tables.

$$\text{PV} = I(\text{IFPVA}) + \text{BAL}(\text{IFPV}) \qquad\qquad\qquad \textbf{(12.1)}$$
$$(?, 36 \text{ mo.}) \qquad (?, 36 \text{ mo.})$$

The question mark represents the IRR. Then if

PV = $10,000 less 4 points = $9,600
I = monthly payment for a $10,000, 10 percent, 360-month mortgage
      = $87.76
BAL = principal after 36 payments plus 2 percent prepayment penalty =
      1.02(9815) = $10,012

$$\$9{,}600 = 87.76(30.03) + \$10{,}012(.6955)$$
$$\phantom{\$9{,}600 = }(12.18\%, 36) \quad (12.18\%, 36)$$
$$\phantom{\$9{,}600 = }\text{IRR} = 12.18\%$$

---

*Because the borrower can receive a tax deduction for interest, comparisons of effective rates are more accurate if they are made on an after-tax basis. However, the differences in the relative rates of return on a before-tax and after-tax calculation are minor enough for them to be neglected.

Figure 12-1
Projected Rates on Adjustable-Rate Mortgages

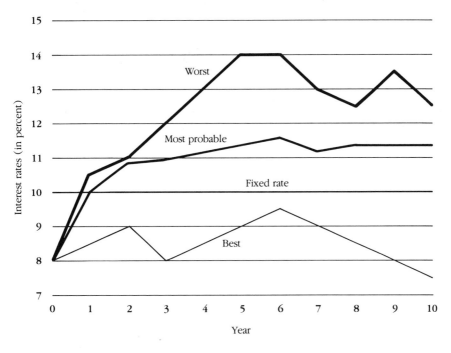

Effective Interest Rates by Period until Mortgage Is Paid Off

Period:		Adjustable-Rate Mortgage		
End Of	Fixed-Rate Mortgage*	Market Expectation	Best Scenario	Worst Scenario
Year 3	12.18%	10.30%	9.24%	10.51%
Year 5	11.14	10.54	8.88	11.16
Year 7	10.83	10.73	8.95	11.79
Year 10	10.67	10.82	8.85	12.00

*Including four points at origination and a 2 percent prepayment penalty at 3 years and .5 percent at 5 years.

In the same way, the estimated effective rates are found if the mortgage is prepaid at the end of years 5, 7, or 10. The specific years chosen depend on how long a time the borrower expects will elapse before he sells or refinances. The average mortgage is prepaid in 8 years and younger families are likely to move sooner than this. Because the initial points are amortized over a longer period and the prepayment penalty disappears, the effective interest rate declines with time.

The Adjustable-Rate Mortgage   The technique used to estimate the cost of the ARM is identical, but it is complicated by the fact that only the initial rate is known. One method of proceeding is to calculate the IRRs for a "most likely" case plus those for best- and worst-case scenarios, as in Figure 12-1. Lenders should be willing to assist with these calculations.

Financial markets predict rates in the future every day by the prices at which they buy and sell bonds of different maturities—the term structure yield curve. These predictions by the market can be considered to be the market's best estimate of where the index will be on each of the future change dates. The market's prices can therefore be used to derive its estimate of the "most probable" interest rates that are likely to be paid on an ARM.* To estimate the best and worst cases, the borrower can find the maximum by which interest rates have gone up or down in any past seven-year period. This experience, limited by the caps in a mortgage, provides the base for estimating the "worst" and "best" lines in Figure 12-1.

The table in Figure 12-1 reflects the effective interest rates under each of these scenarios. For a mortgage prepaid at the end of the seventh year, the rates range from 8.95 percent to 11.79 percent, with 10.73 percent being the amount based on the market's estimates, which supposedly incorporate the knowledge of the best experts in the field.

On the basis of projections of possible future rates, the borrower must assign some weights in order to compare a single weighted estimate to the FRM. Individual borrowers should assign these weights on the basis of their own estimates of the risks.

If no special risks in meeting higher payments are foreseen, then the *most likely* rate for the ARM can be compared directly with the FRM. However, borrowers who are risk-averse may want to assign a higher probability to the worst case. As an example, a borrower might choose 7 years as the most likely holding period. Weights such as .30, .60, and .10 must then be assigned to each of the possible interest rates. How much weight to assign to each case will depend on the borrower's belief in the likelihood of each outcome and on his own risk aversion. Table 12-2 shows the results of assigning weights and using them to project an average based on these probability weights. The results in this case give an expected rate for the ARM of 10.87 percent. If the distribution around the market's estimate was expected to be normal, its return of 10.73 could be used. Very risk-averse borrowers might assign a 100 percent probability to the worst case and thus use 11.79 percent as their estimate.

From Table 12-2 we could conclude that if borrowers expected to keep the mortgage at least seven years, they would select the fixed-rate mortgage. Any of the ARM scenarios except the best case save so little that it is not worth taking the extra risk. On the other hand, if they were sure they would pay off the loan

*For those unfamiliar with how market quotations can be used to find expected future rates, see J. C. Van Horne, *Financial Market Rates and Flows,* 2d ed. (Englewood Cliffs, N.J.: Prentice-Hall, 1984), 106–108.

Table 12-2
Calculating a Weighted Expected Effective Interest Rate for a
Mortgage Prepaid at End of Year 7

Scenario	Probability	Possible Interest Rate in Percent	Expected Rate in Percent
Worst case	.30	11.79	3.53
Market expectation	.60	10.73	6.44
Best case	.10	8.95	0.90
Expected rate, ARM			10.87
Expected rate, FRM			10.98

within five years, borrowers would take the ARM. Figure 12-1 shows that the ARM will cost less than, or about the same as, the FRM in all three cases for five years or less.

REFINANCING

Before proceeding to the actual loan process in the next chapter, we should discuss choosing whether to seek a new mortgage in order to **refinance.** Over 20 percent of new mortgages—and, in some years, such as 1986, a much higher percentage—are taken out by borrowers to pay off old ones. We think of loans as being made at the same time as a sale, but that need not be true. Borrowers refinance for at least three basic reasons:

1. They may be able to reborrow at a lower interest rate.
2. They may be able to increase the size of their loan.
3. They may be able to improve their loan conditions—for example, by obtaining a fixed-rate mortgage in place of one with variable rates.

Because the process can be expensive, it may be difficult to decide when to refinance. Borrowers may have to pay a prepayment penalty and meet the costs of new credit reports, title searches, and other fees. The new loan may require a discount of several points, and less favorable conditions may be imposed. If the existing lender agrees to do the refinancing, some of these costs may be reduced. That is why it is often best to start searching for funds from the old lender.

If the purpose of refinancing is to obtain a larger loan, borrowers may be willing to accept higher costs. On the other hand, instead of refinancing, a better solution might be a second mortgage. Even though a second mortgage carries a higher interest rate, it avoids the penalties and discounts involved in refinancing.

What if the borrower's purpose in refinancing is to reduce interest costs? A common rule of thumb says that refinancing is a good idea if a new loan has rates at least 2 percent lower than the old one, and if it will not be paid off for at least three years. As with many rules of thumb, this one is probably wrong as often as it is right; better decisions can be made by using knowledge of present values.

The Decision to Refinance

EXAMPLE: In a typical refinancing situation, a house was bought a year earlier with a $100,000 30-year fixed rate mortgage at 12 percent (see Table 12-3). The existing mortgage has monthly payments of $1,028.60. Its outstanding balance is $99,637, which is the present value at 12 percent of the existing mortgage. A somewhat larger loan can be obtained at 10 percent for 30 years. Is refinancing worthwhile?

1. To refinance, the borrower must obtain funds sufficient to pay off the existing balance plus $6,172 to meet the prepayment penalty of six months' interest.
2. To obtain a new mortgage, the borrower must pay a 3-point discount, or $3,174. (The table ignores possible closing charges and similar fees because they differ so from state to state, but they should be included in individual cases.)
3. The new mortgage principal must be $108,983 merely to refinance the old mortgage. Monthly payments on this amount would be $956.43. If the $72.17 a month reduction in payments is important, some additional costs of refinancing might be justified. Because the interest payments can be deducted from taxable income, the saving in after-tax payments will be only about $51.96 for a borrower in the 28 percent marginal tax bracket.*

Before making any decision, however, the borrower would like to know the full cost of refinancing—that is, how much he will have to pay or save. The answer depends on how long the new loan will be outstanding. To take account of the time value of money, the borrower should compare the present value of the saving in monthly payments with the present value of the additional balances that will have to be paid when the mortgage is retired. How this can be done is demonstrated in Table 12-3, which first calculates the differences neglecting tax effects and then considers taxes under the assumption that the borrower is in a 28 percent tax bracket.

---

*The amount of tax saving decreases year by year as less of each payment goes to interest and more to principal. Therefore, the calculations in Table 12-3 for the "tax savings" figures are only partially correct.

Table 12-3
Does It Pay to Refinance?

---

1. Calculation of required new loan to refinance a $100,000, 30-year mortgage at 12 percent after 1 year to be refinanced with a 10 percent 30-year mortgage:

Outstanding balance, old loan	$ 99,637
Prepayment penalty	6,172
Discount on new loan (2 points)	3,174
Total	**$108,983**

---

2. Change in cash flow:

	Principal × Mortgage Constant =		Monthly Payments Pretax	Tax Savings
Current	$100,000 × 0.010286 =	$1,028.60		$740.59
Refinanced	$108,983 × 0.008776 =	956.43		688.63
Reduction in mortgage payments = $		72.17		**$ 51.96**

---

3. Calculation of present value of change in costs.

a. Present value of savings in monthly mortgage payments:

IFPVA × savings in monthly payments

For 3-year pretax example:

PV = (IFPVA = 30.991236) × (savings in monthly payment = $72.17)
(10%, 36 mo.)
PV = 30.991236 × 72.17 = **$2,237**

Savings by year of prepayment:

			End of Year			
	3	5	7	10	...	29
Pretax	$2,237	$3,397	$4,347	$5,461	...	$8,178
Tax savings	$1,610	$2,446	$3,130	$3,932	...	$5,888

b. Present value of additional payment at payoff of new loan:

	Outstanding Balance			
End of Year	Old Loan	New Loan	Difference	Present Value of Difference
3	$98,248	$106,969	$ 8,721	$6,469
5	97,004	105,250	8,246	5,012
7	95,424	103,152	7,728	3,849
10	92,220	99,107	6,887	2,544
29	0	10,879	10,879	606

Continued

Table 12-3, (*continued*)

4. Adding the savings in payments to the cost of the additional balance (same as Equation 3.5). For 3-year pretax example:

$$PV = (IFPVA \times 72.17) \quad - (IFPV \times \$8,721)$$
$$(10\%, 36 \text{ mo.}) \qquad (10\%, 36 \text{ mo.}) \qquad\qquad (12.2)$$

Pretax PV = $(30.991236 \times 72.17) - (0.741740 \times 8,721) = -\mathbf{\$4,232}$

Tax savings PV = $(30.991236 \times 51.96) - (0.741740 \times 8,721) = -\mathbf{\$4,859}$

Savings or (cost) by year of prepayment:

End of Year

	3	5	7	10	...	29
Pretax	($4,232)	($1,615)	$ 449	$2,917	...	$7,572
Tax savings	($4,859)	($2,566)	719	$1,388	...	$5,282

Section 1 of the table shows that the amount needed to pay off the old loan consists of the $99,637 outstanding balance plus $6,172 as a prepayment penalty. To borrow this $105,809, three points, or $3,174, must be paid. Thus, a new loan of $108,983 is needed simply to refinance the old loan.

Section 2 calculates the reduction in mortgage payments that results from borrowing more at a lower interest rate. The first column neglects tax savings (as do many borrowers); the second column takes into account savings from taxes.

Section 3 calculates the present value of the change in costs. Part a shows the savings that result from the reduction in monthly mortgage payments. First, an example is calculated for a new loan prepaid at the end of year 3. The monthly savings are multiplied by the interest factor for a 36-month annuity (IFPVA, 10%, 36 mo.), resulting in a pretax savings of $2,237. These savings, as shown, grow from this amount to a saving of $8,178 if no prepayments occur and the loan lasts 29 years. The savings based on the slightly smaller reductions on an after-tax basis run from $1,610 to $5,888, assuming a constant saving of $51.96 per month and neglecting the decrease in tax savings over time.

Part b of section 3 shows the present value of the additional balance that must be paid off as a result of the larger loan. The costs drop with time because the additional balance declines (except at the end of year 29) and because present values of later payments are discounted more heavily. Thus, these extra costs run from $6,469 at 3 years to $606 at 29 years.

Section 4 puts the savings and the costs together. If the loan is paid off in 3 years, refinancing is not worthwhile. The cost of the additional loan needed because of the points and prepayment penalty ($6,469) more than offsets the monthly savings ($2,237), resulting in a total added cost of $4,232. The data in section 4 show that, in this example, it does not pay to refinance unless the new mortgage will be outstanding for at least 7 years. Each case will differ, of course, depending on the cost to refinance and the difference in interest rates. The ability to deduct interest from taxable income makes refinancing less worthwhile since it takes longer for the savings in monthly payments to offset the increased balance which must be repaid on the larger loan.

This example illustrates that the rule of thumb is wrong because it does not use enough information. A reduction in interest rates is significant, but so are the costs of refinancing. Prepayment penalties and the loan fees are high enough here so that no gain is realized unless the new loan is outstanding for 7 years. In addition, refinancing precludes the possibility of using the prepayment option later at a still lower rate. Consequently, in such situations, many would prefer to delay. Their actual choice would depend on projected future interest rates, on the importance of a lower monthly payment, and on when the new loan might be paid off.

In any case, whether a prospective borrower is interested in a loan on a newly purchased property or on one to be built, or wants to refinance, after deciding on what type of loan to seek he or she must go through processing by the lender. This process is the subject of the next chapter.

SUMMARY

Lenders vary in the terms they offer, in their service, and in how they qualify borrowers. The best loan for a family will depend on which of these features it finds most important. Companies using computers to supply loan information and, in some cases, to qualify borrowers are increasing the competition in most markets.

Finding a mortgage that makes a purchase possible is essential. If several mortgages pass this test, a choice based on costs, risks of default, and lender can be made. Computers are being used increasingly to provide potential borrowers with lists of available mortgages and lenders.

In deciding what mortgage to take, the most difficult choices may lie between fixed-rate and adjustable-rate mortgages. Comparing their costs requires a forecast of future interest rates. In choosing among ARMs, the prospective borrower must know the margin above the index and the expected level of the index compared to those of other available indexes.

A sizable number of refinancings occur, particularly after a drop in interest rates. Deciding whether to prepay and refinance requires a consideration of all penalties and fees involved as well as how long the new mortgage is expected to be outstanding. The present value of both payment streams must be compared.

KEY TERMS

contingent financing clause
qualification
refinance
Saving and Loan Cost of Funds Index

QUESTIONS

1. What are the main factors that should be compared when deciding which mortgage is best?
2. Explain how you would use knowledge of the current value of an index in deciding among adjustable-rate mortgages that differ as to initial rates and type of index.
3. Why should the initial and expected rates on ARMs be lower than those on FRMs?
4. Under what circumstances would a borrower be better off using a second mortgage rather than refinancing?
5. What are the main factors that determine whether refinancing is or is not worthwhile?
6. A homeowner has a 13 percent mortgage with an outstanding principal of $99,112.21. Monthly payments are $1,103,40. The prepayment penalty is 6 months' interest. The homeowner can get a 10 percent mortgage with a maturity of 360 months by paying 2 points. If the borrower decides to refinance and to include the prepayment penalty and points in the amount borrowed, what will the new monthly payment be?
7. Explain why the fact that mortgage interest rates may be deductible from taxable income affects the advisability of refinancing.
8. Explain the importance of contingent financing terms in an offer to purchase.

13 The Lender's Mortgage Loan Process

OBJECTIVES

When you finish this chapter, you should be able to:

■ know the process through which lenders value a house offered as security.

■ list the main features that determine the value of a house.

■ explain the sales-comparison approach to valuing a house and its relationship to the cost and income approaches.

■ discuss the process of closing and the main features of the items involved in the settlement.

■ cite significant federal legislation that regulates mortgage lending, and explain how various acts operate.

■ discuss the process of applying for a loan and underwriting.

■ list the principal factors that cause loans to go bad.

■ explain how lenders qualify prospective borrowers in terms of their projected income, expenses, payment habits, and net worth.

T HE PREVIOUS CHAPTER discussed the factors borrowers take into account in deciding what type of financing to seek. This chapter examines the factors that lenders consider when determining whether a prospective borrower qualifies for a loan. We follow the lending process from the application through the commitment process to loan closing. The processes for obtaining a mortgage loan on either a home or an income property follow the same general path; but, as we shall see in Part 4, the negotiations, decisions, and factors that must be included for income property mortgages are far more detailed and complex.

Once a borrower decides which mortgage offering looks best, the actual process of obtaining the money begins. For lender and borrower alike it consists of five steps:

1. The loan application and interview.
2. Underwriting by the lender to determine whether the borrower and property qualify for a mortgage.
3. The decision to issue or deny a loan commitment.
4. The acceptance of the offer, or possible negotiations and appeal.
5. The closing or settlement of the loan.

The rest of this chapter discusses how each step in the process works from the lender's point of view.

THE LOAN APPLICATION AND INTERVIEW

In order to avoid poor loans, lenders need a standardized underwriting procedure. Loans that are to be sold in the secondary market require specific documentation to prove that proper care was taken in the origination process. Because of the dominant role in the secondary market of the Federal Home Loan Mortgage Corporation (FHLMC) and the Federal National Mortgage Association (FNMA), most lenders use the standardized form they prepared jointly.

The loan application is usually supplemented by an interview with the borrower. Together they serve (a) to welcome prospective borrowers, (b) to aid them in making their financial decisions, (c) to obtain preliminary offers to borrow, subject to further negotiations, (d) to secure part of the information necessary for evaluating loans and servicing them if granted, (e) to inform prospective borrowers of lending and servicing procedures, and (f) to screen out unlikely applicants and thus save unnecessary effort.

The Loan Application

Figure 13-1 is a standard loan application form. The top line shows the amount of loan requested and the proposed terms of repayment. It ends with the signatures of the applicants requesting the loan. The application is a preliminary offer of a contract. It may be accepted, rejected, or met by a counteroffer. While final terms may require substantial negotiation, the borrower's submission of a completed loan application form mandates a reply from the lender.

The **loan application** describes the property, the borrowers, their income, employment, credit history, assets and liabilities, and whether or not they intend to occupy the house personally.

1. The first section, in addition to listing the terms requested, specifies the property.
2. The second section asks the prospective borrowers for marital information, current and recent addresses, and information concerning employers.
3. A third part asks for income information and for estimates of monthly housing expenses. It shows the costs involved in the purchase and the cash required for closing. The amount of income and estimated expenses allow for decisions as to whether the family can meet maximum expense-to-income ratios. The form shows how much cash will be required at closing, which permits a comparison with available sources of funds.
4. Other sections of the form ask for a credit history and credit references so that the information contained on the application can be checked. In addition to furnishing necessary data as to the source of the required cash, the balance sheet section is also an indication of whether assets are high enough to make up for a high expense-to-income ratio.

The Loan Interview

Interviews may occur before or after receipt of the loan application. Many people shop for loans from several sources; even so, they must be treated courteously. Frequently, however, no formal application follows. In other cases, the preliminary interview makes it clear that the applicant will not qualify for a loan. Such clients should be discouraged as soon as possible from making a formal application.

The interview is extremely important in the lending process. Its nature depends on the size of the firm and its type of operations. Usually loan officers with the responsibility of analyzing the loan and recommending its approval or rejection also handle the interviews. They may specialize by type of loan, or they may deal with many sorts of loans. The larger the loan or the more complex it is, the higher in the organization's structure will the interview and final negotiations take place. As the complexity of the loan application and its attachments

Figure 13-1
Residential Loan Application

RESIDENTIAL LOAN APPLICATION

MORTGAGE APPLIED FOR	Conventional ☐ FHA ☐ VA ☐	Amount $	Interest Rate %	No. of Months	Monthly Payment Principal & Interest $	Escrow/Impounds (to be collected monthly) ☐Taxes ☐Hazard Ins. ☐Mtg. Ins. ☐
Prepayment Option						

SUBJECT PROPERTY

Property Street Address		City		County	State	Zip	No. Units
Legal Description (Attach description if necessary)						Year Built	

Purpose of Loan: ☐ Purchase   ☐ Construction-Permanent   ☐ Construction   ☐ Refinance   ☐ Other (Explain)

Complete this line if Construction-Permanent or Construction Loan	Lot Value Data	Original Cost	Present Value (a)	Cost of Imps. (b)	Total (a + b)	ENTER TOTAL AS PURCHASE PRICE IN DETAILS OF PURCHASE.
Year Acquired $		$		$	$	

Complete this line if a Refinance Loan		Purpose of Refinance	Describe Improvements [ ] made [ ] to be made
Year Acquired	Original Cost	Amt. Existing Liens	Cost: $
	$	$	

Title Will Be Held In What Name(s)	Manner In Which Title Will Be Held

Source of Down Payment and Settlement Charges

This application is designed to be completed by the borrower(s) with the lender's assistance. The Co-Borrower Section and all other Co-Borrower questions must be completed and the appropriate box(es) checked if ☐ another person will be jointly obligated with the Borrower on the loan, or ☐ the Borrower is relying on income from alimony, child support or separate maintenance or on the income or assets of another person as a basis for repayment of the loan, or ☐ the Borrower is married and resides, or the property is located, in a community property state.

BORROWER				CO-BORROWER			
Name		Age	School Yrs	Name		Age	School Yrs
Present Address No. Years ☐Own ☐Rent				Present Address No. Years ☐Own ☐Rent			
Street				Street			
City/State/Zip				City/State/Zip			
Former address if less than 2 years at present address				Former address if less than 2 years at present address			
Street				Street			
City/State/Zip				City/State/Zip			
Years at former address ☐Own ☐Rent				Years at former address ☐Own ☐Rent			
Marital Status: ☐Married ☐Separated ☐Unmarried (incl. single, divorced, widowed)	DEPENDENTS OTHER THAN LISTED BY CO-BORROWER NO AGES			Marital Status: ☐Married ☐Separated ☐Unmarried (incl. single, divorced, widowed)	DEPENDENTS OTHER THAN LISTED BY BORROWER NO AGES		
Name and Address of Employer	Years employed in this line of work or profession? ____ years Years on this job ____ ☐Self Employed*			Name and Address of Employer	Years employed in this line of work or profession? ____ years Years on this job ____ ☐Self Employed*		
Position/Title	Type of Business			Position/Title	Type of Business		
Social Security Number***	Home Phone	Business Phone		Social Security Number***	Home Phone	Business Phone	

GROSS MONTHLY INCOME				MONTHLY HOUSING EXPENSE**			DETAILS OF PURCHASE	
Item	Borrower	Co-Borrower	Total		PRESENT	PROPOSED	Do Not Complete If Refinance	
Base Empl. Income	$	$	$	Rent	$		a. Purchase Price	$
Overtime				First Mortgage (P&I)		$	b. Total Closing Costs (Est.)	
Bonuses				Other Financing (P&I)			c. Prepaid Escrows (Est.)	
Commissions				Hazard Insurance			d. Total (a + b + c)	$
Dividends/Interest				Real Estate Taxes			e. Amount This Mortgage	( )
Net Rental Income				Mortgage Insurance			f. Other Financing	( )
Other† (Before completing, see notice under Describe Other Income below.)				Homeowner Assn. Dues			g. Other Equity	( )
				Other:			h. Amount of Cash Deposit	( )
				Total Monthly Pmt.	$	$	i. Closing Costs Paid by Seller	( )
				Utilities			j. Cash Reqd. For Closing (Est.)	$
Total	$	$	$	Total	$	$		

DESCRIBE OTHER INCOME

⟡ B–Borrower   C–Co-Borrower

NOTICE:† Alimony, child support, or separate maintenance income need not be revealed if the Borrower or Co-Borrower does not choose to have it considered as a basis for repaying this loan.	Monthly Amount
	$

IF EMPLOYED IN CURRENT POSITION FOR LESS THAN TWO YEARS COMPLETE THE FOLLOWING

B/C	Previous Employer/School	City/State	Type of Business	Position/Title	Dates From/To	Monthly Income
						$

THESE QUESTIONS APPLY TO BOTH BORROWER AND CO-BORROWER

If a "yes" answer is given to a question in this column, explain on an attached sheet.	Borrower Yes or No	Co-Borrower Yes or No	If applicable, explain Other Financing or Other Equity (provide addendum if more space is needed).
Have you any outstanding judgments? In the last 7 years, have you been declared bankrupt?			
Have you had property foreclosed upon or given title or deed in lieu thereof?			
Are you a co-maker or endorser on a note?			
Are you a party in a law suit?			
Are you obligated to pay alimony, child support, or separate maintenance?			
Is any part of the down payment borrowed?			

This Statement and any applicable supporting schedules may be completed jointly by both married and unmarried co-borrowers if their assets and liabilities are sufficiently joined so that the Statement can be meaningfully and fairly presented on a combined basis; otherwise separate Statements and Schedules are required (FHLMC 65A/FNMA 1003A). If the co-borrower section was completed about a spouse, this statement and supporting schedules must be completed about that spouse also. ☐ Completed Jointly ☐ Not Completed Jointly

ASSETS		LIABILITIES AND PLEDGED ASSETS			
Indicate by (*) those liabilities or pledged assets which will be satisfied upon sale of real estate owned or upon refinancing of subject property					
Description	Cash or Market Value	Creditors' Name, Address and Account Number	Acct. Name if Not Borrower's	Mo. Pmt. and Mos. left to pay	Unpaid Balance
Cash Deposit Toward Purchase Held By	$	Installment Debts (include "revolving" charge accts)		$ Pmt./Mos.	$
Checking and Savings Accounts (Show Names of Institutions/Acct. Nos.)				/	
				/	
				/	
				/	
Stocks and Bonds (No./Description)				/	
				/	
				/	
Life Insurance Net Cash Value				/	
Face Amount ($)		Other Debts Including Stock Pledges			
SUBTOTAL LIQUID ASSETS	$				
Real Estate Owned (Enter Market Value from Schedule of Real Estate Owned)		Real Estate Loans		/	
Vested Interest in Retirement Fund					
Net Worth of Business Owned (ATTACH FINANCIAL STATEMENT)					
Automobiles (Make and Year)		Automobile Loans			
				/	
Furniture and Personal Property		Alimony, Child Support and Separate Maintenance Payments Owed To			
Other Assets (Itemize)					
				/	
		TOTAL MONTHLY PAYMENTS		$	
TOTAL ASSETS	A $	NET WORTH (A minus B) $		TOTAL LIABILITIES	B $

SCHEDULE OF REAL ESTATE OWNED (If Additional Properties Owned Attach Separate Schedule)								
Address of Property (Indicate S if Sold, PS if Pending Sale or R if Rental being held for income)		Type of Property	Present Market Value	Amount of Mortgages & Liens	Gross Rental Income	Mortgage Payments	Taxes, Ins. Maintenance and Misc.	Net Rental Income
			$	$	$	$	$	$
		TOTALS →	$	$	$	$	$	$

LIST PREVIOUS CREDIT REFERENCES

B–Borrower C–Co-Borrower	Creditor's Name and Address	Account Number	Purpose	Highest Balance	Date Paid
				$	

List any additional names under which credit has previously been received

AGREEMENT: The undersigned applies for the loan indicated in this application to be secured by a first mortgage or deed of trust on the property described herein, and represents that the property will not be used for any illegal or restricted purpose, and that all statements made in this application are true and are made for the purpose of obtaining the loan. Verification may be obtained from any source named in this application. The original or a copy of this application will be retained by the lender, even if the loan is not granted. The undersigned ☐ intend or ☐ do not intend to occupy the property as their primary residence.

I/we fully understand that it is a federal crime punishable by fine or imprisonment, or both, to knowingly make any false statements concerning any of the above facts as applicable under the provisions of Title 18, United States Code, Section 1014.

_____ Date _____ _____ Date _____
Borrower's Signature   Co-Borrower's Signature

INFORMATION FOR GOVERNMENT MONITORING PURPOSES

Instructions: Lenders must insert in this space, or on an attached addendum, a provision for furnishing the monitoring information required or requested under present Federal and/or present state law or regulation. For most lenders, the inserts provided in FHLMC Form 65-B/FNMA Form 1003-B can be used.

FOR LENDER'S USE ONLY

(FNMA REQUIREMENT ONLY) This application was taken by ☐ face to face interview ☐ by mail ☐ by telephone

_____   _____
(Interviewer)   Name of Employer of Interviewer

FHLMC 65 Rev. 8/78   **REVERSE**   FNMA 1003 Rev. 8/78

Source: Federal Home Loan Mortgage Corporation, "Residential Loan Application," Form 65, and Federal National Mortgage Association, "Residential Loan Application," Form 1003, revised August 1978.

increases (for example, when a loan on a new shopping center is being proposed, rather than for a single-house loan on an existing structure), more skill and training are required of the interviewer.

The interviewer is a salesperson, a public relations expert, and a lending analyst. The interview serves as a screening device to prevent unnecessary paperwork. Acceptance of applications for loans that are sure to be refused causes wasted effort and ill will. On the other hand, unsatisfactory prospective borrowers must be turned away without losing their respect or friendship.

Interviewers can be valuable sources of education for borrowers. In explaining the logic behind the information called for on the application, they can aid prospective borrowers in making a proper decision as to what financial obligations to incur. Families are often attracted to a certain house and try to borrow far more than they can repay. The interviewer must explain why everyone will be better off if this is not done.

Interviewers can also improve future servicing of loans. They can explain the firm's procedures. They can stress the need for promptness, pointing out that borrowers should take the initiative and seek out the lender if any problems develop. If borrowers know what they are expected to do and why, future relations will be more cordial.

All of these other duties, however, merely supplement the interviewer's main function of getting as much information as possible in order to judge the prospective borrower's creditworthiness. The loan officer must gather from the applicant all the specific details necessary for a proper evaluation. Part of this information is furnished on the application form, but the information which the interviewer gathers from informal discussion and the give-and-take of questions and answers may be still more significant.

Loan repayments depend partly on the borrower's desires, partly on the likelihood that his or her income will continue, and partly on family relations. Since judgment of these factors tends to be subjective, evaluation of the same data by different interviewers may vary greatly. The skilled loan officer has the best judgment in these areas.

Interviewers must also be negotiators. They must realize during the discussion what prospective terms are likely to be unsatisfactory and where changes might be made to minimize future risk. During the interview process, they can probe to discover whether the borrower is willing and able to make changes in critical items. It is often much easier to negotiate differences before they are put down in black and white.

When the conference is finished, the loan application and the interviewer's notes should contain the information necessary for further processing of the loan. Unsatisfactory requests should have been withdrawn. At the end of the interview, the loan officers should be able to indicate whether a loan will probably be granted, but they must also be careful to point out that they do not have the final responsibility. Additional information will be obtained from the credit and appraisal reports.

AVOIDING POOR LOANS

Borrowers want loans on the best possible terms, while lenders want to be sure that a loan is profitable. To satisfy both aims, the risks and rewards must be balanced. **Underwriting** consists of evaluating the risks of a loan to determine whether benefits balance risks. Loan underwriters examine loan applications and the documentation accompanying each case. They weigh many aspects of a mortgage. They compare its interest rates and fees with the probability of repayment and with the estimated present and future value of the property to be used as security. The sharp increase in defaults that occurred in 1984 was taken by many lenders as a sign that they had placed too much reliance on expected inflation and had been poor underwriters.

The Quality of a Loan

To be acceptable, a mortgage must meet certain minimum standards developed from past underwriting and default experience.

1. The underwriter examines the borrower's records to judge the likelihood that the borrower will continue to make timely payments until the loan is paid off. To qualify a borrower, the underwriter relates income and expected income to the terms of the mortgage. The underwriter must also judge, on the basis of the borrower's credit history, the probability that the borrower will make sacrifices to continue payments rather than walking away from the property if problems arise.
2. The underwriter also examines the qualifications of the property to answer an important question: If the borrower defaults, will the property provide enough value for the lender to recover its investment?

What Causes Losses

Successful underwriting calls for a sound processing procedure to analyze each loan in order to ascertain that its reward outweighs its risks. It also requires a set of standards to estimate its dangers. Studies of defaults and foreclosures reveal 10 to 15 factors that cause the risks of a loan to deviate from the average.* Knowledge of these factors and how they interact is vital to the lender's making the types of adjustments that can lower excessive risks. Neither borrowers nor lenders want loans that are doomed to failure.

1. The largest losses are due to unsatisfactory loan characteristics.
    a. The single most important loss factor arises from low down payments; that is, from high loan-to-value mortgages. Every reduction in the

---

*For an example, see H. F. Peters, S. M. Pinkus, and D. J. Askin, "Default: The Last Resort," *Secondary Mortgage Markets,* 1 no. 3 (August 1984): 16–20.

down payment ratio increases the probability of loss for the lender; 95 percent mortgages have five to ten times the probability of failure of those with larger down payments.

  b. Junior liens also increase losses. The addition of secondary liens is simply another way of reducing down payments.

2. The relationship of an owner's income to monthly housing expenses is significant. Housing expenses depend on the height of interest rates, the time to maturity, and other amortization features. The larger the monthly payments compared with income, the more dangerous is the loan.

3. Other owner characteristics can also lead to defaults.

  a. Some people will stop making payments when their income drops. Loss of a job is a major cause of delinquencies. A buyer with an irregular employment history or who is in a fairly new job is a greater risk.

  b. Unmarried owners have a higher than average loss record.

  c. Family events like divorce, serious illness, or death can also increase defaults. However, on an actuarial basis, such events are expected and are figured into the average loss ratio. These events are random and will not be discovered during the underwriting process.

  d. Forces that cause people to have a poor credit rating are not likely to change. Those with unsatisfactory past records are therefore more likely to become delinquent.

  e. Houses bought on speculation or for rent to others have a higher loss ratio. For this reason, most lenders demand more down payment when a house is not owner-occupied.

4. Characteristics of the property and its location can add risks. Older houses and those with unusual designs are somewhat riskier than newer houses and those of conventional design.

5. Other important factors are the growth of demand and rising housing prices. Areas of slow growth have larger losses, as do periods of declining inflation.

QUALIFYING BORROWERS

A **qualified borrower** is one who can reasonably be expected to meet regular monthly payments without servicing difficulties. A qualified borrower has the capacity to pay both the down payment and the monthly payments. Thus, to qualify a borrower, housing expenses must be calculated, the borrower's available cash ascertained, and his or her future income estimated.

The borrower's present income and its future stability should be sufficient to cover payments. Otherwise, enough assets must be available to meet payments if income declines temporarily. To make a correct estimate, the underwriter must consider the borrower's occupation, employment history, educational background, and training for the position.

Along with ability to pay, the borrower must have the desire to pay. This is projected from the credit history. Those who have met debt payments promptly in the past or have shown a desire and willingness to save are more likely to meet payments in the future. Larger down payments also increase the desire not to default.

Chapter 10 pointed out that lenders use shortcuts, such as a rule of thumb that a maximum expense-to-income ratio must not be exceeded, but such ratios need not be the final determinant of whether credit is granted. Other factors, such as the credit record, assets, and down payments, are all taken into account.

Stable Income

Do the prospective buyers earn enough, and is their income sufficiently stable to meet the monthly payments? That is the key question for the lender. Although every lender may use a somewhat different income formula, definitions such as that of the FHLMC are common: **stable monthly income** "is the borrower's gross monthly income from primary employment-based earnings plus recognizable secondary income."

Secondary income includes such items as bonuses, commissions, overtime, or part-time employment. These are included if they are typical for the occupation and can be substantiated by earnings during the previous two years. In the same way, self-employment income must be proved by use of the previous two years' profit-and-loss statements and balance sheets, or by signed federal income tax returns.

Job experience is used to evaluate probable stability and durability of income. Too-frequent job changes are suspicious, but they are favorable if they indicate upward progress. Education and training are plus factors; they can lead to more rapid advancement.

Underwriters must be careful not to allow the borrower's race, color, religion, national origin, sex, or marital status to influence their credit evaluations. The income and assets of all co-borrowers—all who sign the note—are given equal weight. For example, a wife's regular part-time job is taken fully into account.

Property Income

The loan application in Figure 13-1 has a schedule for owned real estate as part of the balance sheet. This item receives special consideration. Because of leverage, only properties owned for a considerable period and whose rents have risen are likely to produce much positive income. On the other hand, if worse comes to worst, their equity can be called on to help meet mortgage payments.

Special rules apply if the property is not to be owner-occupied. The borrower's income must be sufficient to meet all personal expenses plus all the monthly expenses of the property, including maintenance and repair. Income can include 75 percent of gross monthly rents on rental property, except that proposed rentals of second homes cannot be included.

Expense-to-Income Ratios

Chapter 10 (Table 10-2) demonstrated how expense-to-income ratios are arrived at from the information on the loan application. The underwriter estimates the amount of reported income which can be considered stable for lending purposes. She also checks the estimated housing expenses and calculates the ratios of housing and debt payments to income.

Most lenders and the secondary market use maximum expense-to-income ratios in determining whether or not a borrower qualifies. In 1986, these ranged between 25 and 28 percent for *P.I.T.I.* (mortgage principal, interest, taxes, and insurance) and between 33 and 36 percent for total debt payments. These ratios could be exceeded, however, if logical reasons existed for doing so.

Adjustable Payments

Many mortgages have monthly payments that increase either automatically, as in the case of buy-downs and graduated payment mortgages, or that may alter as a result of movement in an interest rate index. The possibilities that such increases will raise the expense-to-income ratio on the mortgage to an unacceptable level must be planned for when the loan is made. What appears initially as an adequate ratio may be too high if monthly payments rise.

To avoid having an expense ratio that is too high, lenders can demand a lower starting ratio, while borrowers can insist on a *cap* (maximum increase) on the upward adjustment of payments. Lenders often lower the maximum expense-to-income ratio they will accept—from 28 to 25 percent, for example—on adjustable-payment mortgages.

In certain mortgages, payments do not increase; instead, the amount of principal grows as a result of negative amortization. Such arrangements are acceptable on the assumption that the value of the house will rise faster than the mortgage principal. If the house price rises fast enough, a loan-to-value ratio of under 100 percent can be maintained. But such assumptions may be wrong. Any mortgage with potential negative amortization increases the lender's risk. It requires more careful underwriting to guard against the borrower's equity becoming negative.

One way of curtailing the risks of negative amortization is to demand a higher down payment—such as 10 percent rather than 5 percent—even on insured loans. Another way may be to include a requirement that negative amortization never raise the principal on a loan above 100 percent of the property's initial value. Still another way, as noted, may limit the outstanding principal to 125 percent of the initial amount. This last restriction may also require that if the 125 percent level is reached, the loan will have to be recast. Monthly payments will be increased enough so that the larger principal will be amortized over the term of the original mortgage.

Assets and Liabilities

The loan application includes a statement of the borrower's assets and liabilities. This is used to make certain that cash is available for closing the loan. It also serves as an indication of the borrower's net worth and a measure of past financial success.

If the statement does not show enough cash to close the sale, additional funds will probably have to be borrowed. More debts mean a higher ratio of debt payment to income. Some lenders do not agree to the existence of junior mortgages, since they reduce the owner's equity. Others do not object, but they may require a smaller expense-to-income ratio. The Federal Housing Administration (FHA) does not insure a first mortgage when a second is required.

The borrower's ability to accumulate net worth is very important. Ingrained saving habits are likely to continue. Also, assets form a source from which payments can be funded if necessary. Families with a good record in meeting past payments will probably continue to do so. The borrower's proven ability to live without borrowing may be even more favorable; it shows that the family has been able to live within its means.

The many factors that enter into a decision as to whether or not a buyer is qualified make the need for skilled underwriting evident. They also explain the advantage to borrowers and real estate brokers of knowing how different underwriters operate. Since judgments too often are made in a simplistic manner based only on ratios, it is important in marginal cases to be able to find lenders who use their considered judgment. Many loans and sales can be saved by a well-thought-through approach by the borrower to a receptive lender.

QUALIFYING THE PROPERTY

Although the borrower's credit is important, many lenders consider the real property underlying a mortgage to be the basic source of its security. Lenders want their mortgages to be on properties that if foreclosed will return sufficient cash to pay off accrued interest, the remaining principal, and other related expenses. If a property is valuable enough, no foreclosure will be necessary; borrowers who cannot continue payments can sell the property or transfer ownership in order to cash out their equity. If foreclosure is necessary, sufficient value in the property will minimize any loss.

Underwriters make their decisions as to whether a property will support a proposed mortgage on the basis of an appraisal report. Figure 13-2 shows an appraisal report on an FHLMC-FNMA form. In large institutions, appraisals are usually done by staff appraisers; other firms use independent fee appraisers.

The **appraisal** estimates the current market value and indicates the probable future trend of that value. The **market value** is the price at which a willing

Figure 13-2
Residential Appraisal Report

RESIDENTIAL APPRAISAL REPORT   File No. _____

Borrower John J. Jones	Census Tract 1005.00 Map Reference 33-B4

Property Address **482 Liberty Street**

City **Cincinnati**   County **Hamilton**   State **Ohio**   Zip Code **46260**

Legal Description **Lot 78, 1st Section Happy Acres Farm 2nd Addition to City of Cincinnati**

Sale Price $ **75,700**   Date of Sale **03-01-84** Loan Term **30** yrs Property Rights Appraised [X] Fee [ ] Leasehold [ ] DeMinimis PUD

Actual Real Estate Taxes $ **797.11** (yr) Loan charges to be paid by seller $**None**   Other sales concessions **None**

Lender/Client **XYZ Federal Savings and Loan Assoc.** Address **1702 Penn Avenue, Cincinnati, Ohio**

Occupant **Owner**   Appraiser **William B. Faust** Instructions to Appraiser **I-75 to Colerain Exit to Beech-wood Avenue, Beechwood to Liberty, Second House on Left.**

NEIGHBORHOOD

					Good	Avg.	Fair	Poor
Location	[ ] Urban	[X] Suburban	[ ] Rural	Employment Stability	[ ]	[X]	[ ]	[ ]
Built Up	[X] Over 75%	[ ] 25% to 75%	[ ] Under 25%	Convenience to Employment	[ ]	[X]	[ ]	[ ]
Growth Rate [ ] Fully Dev.	[ ] Rapid	[X] Steady	[ ] Slow	Convenience to Shopping	[ ]	[ ]	[X]	[ ]
Property Values	[ ] Increasing	[X] Stable	[ ] Declining	Convenience to Schools	[X]	[ ]	[ ]	[ ]
Demand/Supply	[ ] Shortage	[X] In Balance	[ ] Over Supply	Adequacy of Public Transportation	[ ]	[X]	[ ]	[ ]
Marketing Time	[ ] Under 3 Mos.	[X] 4–6 Mos.	[ ] Over 6 Mos.	Recreational Facilities	[ ]	[ ]	[X]	[ ]
Present Land Use 80% 1 Family 10% 2–4 Family 10 % Apts. ___% Condo ___% Commercial				Adequacy of Utilities	[ ]	[X]	[ ]	[ ]
___% Industrial ___% Vacant ___%				Property Compatibility	[ ]	[X]	[ ]	[ ]
Change in Present Land Use [X] Not Likely	[ ] Likely (*)		[ ] Taking Place (*)	Protection from Detrimental Conditions	[ ]	[X]	[ ]	[ ]
(*) From _____ To _____				Police and Fire Protection	[ ]	[ ]	[X]	[ ]
Predominant Occupancy [X] Owner	[ ] Tenant		___% Vacant	General Appearance of Properties	[ ]	[X]	[ ]	[ ]
Single Family Price Range $ 55,000 to $ 80,000 Predominant Value $65,000				Appeal to Market	[ ]	[X]	[ ]	[ ]
Single Family Age 10 yrs to 20 yrs Predominant Age 15 yrs								

Note: FHLMC/FNMA do not consider race or the racial composition of the neighborhood to be reliable appraisal factors.

Comments including those factors, favorable or unfavorable, affecting marketability (e.g. public parks, schools, view, noise) **shopping is approximately two miles away at I-75 and Colerain, City Park One mile North. Other recreational facilities of a private nature, fire protection is voluntary unit. Other aspects average or better.**

SITE

Dimensions **60 X 125 X 72 X 140**   = **8,745** Sq. Ft. or Acres   [X] Corner Lot

Zoning classification **R-2 (Min. Size 7500 Sq. Ft.)**   Present improvements [X] do [ ] do not conform to zoning regulations

Highest and best use: [ ] Present use [ ] Other (specify) _____

	Public	Other (Describe)	OFF SITE IMPROVEMENTS		
Elec.	[X]		Street Access: [X] Public [ ] Private	Topo **Level**	
Gas	[X]		Surface **Macadem**	Size **Typical in Neighborhood**	
Water	[X]		Maintenance: [X] Public [ ] Private	Shape **Typical in Neighborhood**	
San.Sewer	[X]		[X] Storm Sewer [X] Curb/Gutter	View **Average**	
				Drainage **Good**	
[ ] Underground Elect. & Tel. [X] Sidewalk [ ] Street Lights				Is the property located in a HUD Identified Special Flood Hazard Area? [X] No [ ] Yes	

Comments (favorable or unfavorable including any apparent adverse easements, encroachments or other adverse conditions) **NONE**

IMPROVEMENTS

[X] Existing [ ] Proposed [ ] Under Constr. No. Units **1** Type (det, duplex, semi/det, etc.) **Detached** Design (rambler, split level, etc.) **Rambler** Exterior Walls **Brick**

Yrs. Age: Actual **10** Effective **10** to **12** No. Stories **1**

Roof Material **Cedar Shake Shingle**	Gutters & Downspouts [ ] None **Galvanized Iron**	Window (Type): **Double Hung – Wood** Insulation [ ] None [X] Floor
	[X] Storm Sash [X] Screens [X] Combination	[X] Ceiling [X] Roof [X] Walls

BSMT

[ ] Manufactured Housing	80 % Basement	[ ] Floor Drain	Finished Ceiling No
Foundation Walls	[X] Outside Entrance	[ ] Sump Pump	Finished Walls No
Concrete	[X] Concrete Floor	0 % Finished	Finished Floor No
[ ] Slab on Grade [ ] Crawl Space	Evidence of: [ ] Dampness [ ] Termites [ ] Settlement		

Comments **A very attractive house – above average maintenance**

ROOM LIST

Room List	Foyer	Living	Dining	Kitchen	Den	Family Rm.	Rec. Rm.	Bedrooms	No. Baths	Laundry	Other
Basement											
1st Level	X	X	X	X		X		3	2		
2nd Level											

Finished area above grade contains a total of **7** rooms **3** bedrooms **2** baths. Gross Living Area **1645** sq. ft. Bsmt Area **1316** sq. ft.

INTERIOR FINISH & EQUIPMENT

Kitchen Equipment: [X] Refrigerator [X] Range/Oven [X] Disposal [X] Dishwasher [X] Fan/Hood [ ] Compactor [ ] Washer [ ] Dryer [ ]

HEAT: Type **FWA** Fuel **GAS** Cond. **Good** AIR COND: [X] Central [ ] Other _____ [X] Adequate [ ] Inadequate

					Good	Avg.	Fair	Poor
Floors	[X] Hardwood	[ ] Carpet Over						
Walls	[ ] Drywall	[X] Plaster [ ]		Quality of Construction (Materials & Finish)	[X]	[ ]	[ ]	[ ]
Trim/Finish	[X] Good	[ ] Average [ ] Fair [ ] Poor		Condition of Improvements	[X]	[ ]	[ ]	[ ]
Bath Floor	[X] Ceramic			Room sizes and layout	[ ]	[X]	[ ]	[ ]
Bath Wainscot	[X] Ceramic	[ ]		Closets and Storage	[ ]	[X]	[ ]	[ ]
Special Features (including energy efficient items) **Soft water system**				Insulation—adequacy	[X]	[ ]	[ ]	[ ]
R-38 insulation ceiling; CR-19 walls; R-11 floors				Plumbing—adequacy and condition	[ ]	[X]	[ ]	[ ]
--hot water heater insulated; automatic setback				Electrical—adequacy and condition	[ ]	[X]	[ ]	[ ]
ATTIC: [X] Yes [ ] No [ ] Stairway [X] Drop-stair [ ] Scuttle [ ] Floored **thermostat**				Kitchen Cabinets—adequacy and condition	[ ]	[X]	[ ]	[ ]
Finished (Describe) _____ [ ] Heated				Compatibility to Neighborhood	[ ]	[ ]	[X]	[ ]
CAR STORAGE: [ ] Garage [ ] Built-in [ ] Attached [ ] Detached [X] Car Port				Overall Livability	[ ]	[X]	[ ]	[ ]
No. Cars 1 [X] Adequate [ ] Inadequate Condition **Good**				Appeal and Marketability	[ ]	[X]	[ ]	[ ]

PROPERTY RATING

Yrs Est Remaining Economic Life **40** to **50** .Explain if less than Loan Term

FIREPLACES, PATIOS, POOL, FENCES, etc. (describe) **Fireplace in living room; rear concrete covered patio (22X12); 4 ft. high chain link fence around rear yard.**

COMMENTS (including functional or physical inadequacies, repairs needed, modernization, etc.) **Additional insulation and automatic thermostat were added in 1979. (floor & ceiling)**

FHLMC Form 70 Rev. 7/79   ATTACH DESCRIPTIVE PHOTOGRAPHS OF SUBJECT PROPERTY AND STREET SCENE   FNMA Form 1004 Rev. 7/79

VALUATION SECTION

Purpose of Appraisal is to estimate Market Value as defined in Certification & Statement of Limiting Conditions (FHLMC Form 439/FNMA Form 1004B). If submitted for FNMA, the appraiser must attach (1) sketch or map showing location of subject, street names, distance from nearest intersection, and any detrimental conditions and (2) exterior building sketch of improvements showing dimensions.

COST APPROACH

Measurements			No. Stories		Sq. Ft.
42	x 37	x	1	=	1554
24	x 3.8	x	1	=	91
	x	x		=	
	x	x		=	
	x	x		=	

ESTIMATED REPRODUCTION COST – NEW – OF IMPROVEMENTS:

Dwelling 1,645 Sq. Ft. @ $38.09	=	$ 62,658
1,316 Sq. Ft. @ $ 7.89	=	10,383
Extras Soft wtr. sys.; d/w, disp.;		
range/oven; f/h; fireplace	=	3,240
Special Energy Efficient Items R-30 insulation	=	500
Porches, Patios, etc. & fence	=	1,800
Garage/Car Port 200 Sq. Ft. @ $ 6.50	=	1,300
Site Improvements (driveway, landscaping, etc.)	=	3,050
Total Estimated Cost New	=	$ 82,931

Total Gross Living Area (List in Market Data Analysis below) 1,645

Comment on functional and economic obsolescence: Largest house on street with other houses ranging from 1,300 to 1,400 sq. ft. In Happy Acres Farm subdivision, there are 11 other houses with floor plan similar to subject.

	Physical	Functional	Economic		
Less Depreciation $ 13,500		$ 7,500		= $ (21,000)
Depreciated value of improvements				= $ 61,931
ESTIMATED LAND VALUE (If leasehold, show only leasehold value)				= $ 15,500
INDICATED VALUE BY COST APPROACH				$ 77,400

The undersigned has recited three recent sales of properties most similar and proximate to subject and has considered these in the market analysis. The description includes a dollar adjustment, reflecting market reaction to those items of significant variation between the subject and comparable properties. If a significant item in the comparable property is superior to, or more favorable than, the subject property, a minus (-) adjustment is made, thus reducing the indicated value of subject; if a significant item in the comparable is inferior to, or less favorable than, the subject property, a plus (+) adjustment is made, thus increasing the indicated value of the subject.

MARKET DATA ANALYSIS

ITEM	Subject Property	COMPARABLE NO. 1	Adjustment	COMPARABLE NO. 2	Adjustment	COMPARABLE NO. 3	Adjustment
Address	482 Liberty St.	478 Liberty Street		225 West 17th Street		110 East 16th Street	
Proximity to Subj.		Adjacent		2 blocks West		3 blocks SE	
Sales Price	$ 76,700	$ 65,000		$ 73,500		$ 67,500	
Price/Living area	$ 46.62	$ 46.43		$ 44.54		$ 42.19	
Data Source	Sales Contract	Present Owner		Appraiser's files		Selling Broker	
Date of Sale and Time Adjustment	3-1-84	1-29-84	–	2-14-84	–	12-17-83	–
Location	Average Suburb	Similar	–	Similar	–	Similar	–
Site/View	Corner Lot	Inside Lot	1,950	Inside Lot	1,950	Corner Lot	–
Design and Appeal	Rambler - Avg.	Similar	–	Similar	–	Similar	–
Quality of Const.	Good	Good	–	Good	–	Good	–
Age	20 years	19 years	–	20 years	–	13 years	(3,250)
Condition	Good	Good	–	Good	–	Int. Paint/Fair	950
Living Area Room Count and Total	Total 7 / B-rms 3 / Baths 2	Total 6 / B-rms 3 / Baths 1.5	7,500	Total 7 / B-rms 3 / Baths 2	–	Total 7 / B-rms 3 / Baths 1	2,800
Gross Living Area	1,645 Sq.Ft.	1,400 Sq.Ft.		1,650 Sq.Ft.		1,600 Sq.Ft.	
Basement & Bsmt. Finished Rooms	80% Bsmt Area Unfinished	Full Bsmt Rec. Room	(1,950)	Full Bsmt, Rec. Rm. ½ Bath	(2,800)	50% bsmt Unfinished	3,200
Functional Utility	Good	Good	–	Good	–	Fair	2,800
Air Conditioning	Central	Central	–	None	2,500	Central	–
Garage/Car Port	1 Car Att.C/P	Similar	–	2 Car Att.Gar.	(4,000)	2 Car Att. Gar.	(4,000)
Porches, Patio, Pools, etc.	Fence, Rear Patio	Fence, Rear Screen Porch	(1,200)	Fence, Rear Patio	–	No Fence, Rear Screened Porch	(500)
Special Energy Efficient Items	R-38 Insulation in ceiling. Solar HW Heater	No solar HW Heater	3,900	No Solar HW Heater	3,900	Inf. insulation No Solar HW Heater	4,600
Other (e.g. fireplaces, kitchen equip., remodeling)	Fireplace Range/Oven, Disp., D/Washer	Similar	–	No Fireplace	1,800	No Fireplace No Solar HW Heater	2,300
Sales or Financing Concessions	84% Conv., No Concessions	80% Conv. No Concessions	–	80% Conv. No Concessions	–	80% Conv., No Concessions	–
Net Adj. (Total)		X Plus; ☐ Minus $ 10,200		X Plus; ☐ Minus $ 3,350		X Plus; ☐ Minus $ 8,900	
Indicated Value of Subject		$ 75,200		$ 76,850		$ 76,400	

Comments on Market Data: Sale No. 1 is recent sale of smaller house next door to subject and indicated value reflects considerable net adjustments as does sale No. 3. Sale No. 2 is most comparable to subject and required only a few moderate size adjustments, consequently most weight is assigned to its indicated value.

INDICATED VALUE BY MARKET DATA APPROACH .... $ 77,000

INDICATED VALUE BY INCOME APPROACH (If applicable) Economic Market Rent $ 650 /Mo. x Gross Rent Multiplier 116 = $ 75,400

This appraisal is made X "as is" ☐ subject to the repairs, alterations, or conditions listed below ☐ completion per plans and specifications.

Comments and Conditions of Appraisal: Property is at the top of the neighborhood value, but at estimated value it is readily saleable.

Final Reconciliation: Most weight is given to market approach as the comps are recent sales and are fairly similar and in close proximity to subject. Less weight is assigned to cost approach due to the difficulty in reliably establishing depreciation. Least weight given to income approach.

Construction Warranty ☐ Yes X No Name of Warranty Program _____ Warranty Coverage Expires _____

This appraisal is based upon the above requirements, the certification, contingent and limiting conditions, and Market Value definition that are stated in

☐ FHLMC Form 439 (Rev. 10/78)/FNMA Form 1004B (Rev. 10/78) filed with client, December 1, 19 83 ☐ attached.

I ESTIMATE THE MARKET VALUE, AS DEFINED, OF SUBJECT PROPERTY AS OF March 7, 19 84 to be $ 77,000

Appraiser(s) *William B. Faust*

Review Appraiser (If applicable) *John R. Kelly* X did ☐ Did Not Physically Inspect Property

FHLMC Form 70 Rev. 7/79   REVERSE   FNMA Form 1004 Rev. 7/79

Source: Federal Home Loan Mortgage Corporation, "Residential Appraisal Report," Form 70, and Federal National Mortgage Association, "Residential Appraisal Report," Form 1004, revised July 1979.

seller would sell and a willing buyer would buy at the time of the appraisal. It is the price that would be set in an efficient, knowledgeable, well-operating market under normal supply and demand conditions.

The fair market value of a property can be more or less than its actual selling price. The sales price can be affected by how much knowledge the buyer has about the property's worth, the need of the seller for a quick sale, financing terms, and similar factors. One of the key purposes of qualifying the property is to make certain that the mortgage is based on a realistic and not an inflated selling price. The value of a house depends on its neighborhood, site, and improvements, as detailed on the appraisal report and discussed in the following paragraphs.

Neighborhood

The top third of page 1 of Figure 13-2 lists the kind of neighborhood features that influence value. Location plays a significant role in determining whether a specific house meets a buyer's requirements. **Location** refers both to the political and geographic area and to the particular site in a neighborhood.

Most people want to live in an attractive, well-maintained neighborhood, free of such adverse features in their surroundings as a manufacturing plant, a crowded freeway, or a noisy nightclub. Houses in such undesirable locations are sold, but at a diminished value. Amenities that may raise values include good views, streets with flowers and trees, and easy access to jobs, stores, schools, and recreational facilities.

Governmental factors can also have a substantial bearing on value. How good are the schools? Are public transportation and other municipal services adequate? What are the zoning and building codes, and are they enforced? How do taxes compare with those in surrounding communities? The answers to these questions help determine the worth of the neighborhood from the standpoint of home ownership.

Surrounding Properties   A good deal of emphasis is placed in the appraisal on the other properties in the neighborhood. Well-developed neighborhoods with harmonious land uses are preferred. Appraisers assume that owner-occupiers maintain their properties better and enhance an area's general appearance. Houses priced well above those of the surrounding neighborhood may be more difficult to sell. Age is not significant provided properties are well maintained.

The purpose of analyzing the neighborhood before the borrower is approved is to try to guard against a lack of market appeal when the time comes for the property to be resold. Lower values may be caused by either missing or detrimental factors. In addition, appraisers are expected to warn against trends that may cause prices to fall in the future or not to rise at the same rate as those in other sectors. The appraiser must consider both the plus and minus factors in evaluating the neighborhood influences on a particular property.

The Site

Lots that do not meet the prevailing neighborhood pattern or that lack utilities or the usual street improvements are worth less. The appraisal form lists a number of specific site items that may affect value. Some houses may be built in slide areas or on fill; special care must be taken to check the construction in such cases. The appraiser must also check whether a property is in a flood zone. On the other hand, if the site has special amenities, it is worth more. A fine view, good landscaping, beautiful trees are all items that can make a house more desirable. Streets vary in their size and maintenance. How these factors influence future prices requires the appraiser's good judgment. A great deal depends on what is normal for the area. It is the appraiser's job to comment on any unusual features and to point out how they affect the value of the property.

Physical Improvements

The bottom sections of the first page of the sample appraisal report describe the house's improvements, number and type of rooms, and quality of construction and equipment. These features are also important to the degree that they raise or lower values relative to other houses in the area. In evaluating the improvements, the appraiser must estimate the remaining economic life of the building and ascertain the care that has been given to its maintenance. If it is below standard, the appraiser must estimate the cost of bringing the property back to a normal condition.

Because of the shock caused by rising energy costs in the 1970s, appraisers now place a good deal of emphasis on the amount of insulation in a house and the efficiency of its heating and cooling systems. High utility payments mean that less money is available for other uses, such as maintenance or improvements. They lower the value of the house and could endanger monthly payments.

Special attention must also be given to unusual configurations of rooms and to floor plans. Some people have extreme needs or tastes. For example, a large house with only a single bedroom will be worth far less per square foot than will one of similar size with three bedrooms. Older houses may have too few bathrooms; additions may cause peculiar entry and interior traffic patterns.

When obtaining the necessary information on the improvements, the appraiser must measure not only the square feet in the house, but also in the garage, carport, or other areas that cost less than the main building. These data are necessary for calculating estimated reproduction costs (discussed in the next section).

The "bottom line" in the property rating is appeal and marketability. The appraiser must judge the property's overall attractiveness to the average buyer. Future values depend on there being enough prospective purchasers to make an adequate market for the house when it is resold. The appraiser must comment on any unusual features. Those rated only fair or poor must be given special attention by the underwriter. They often require a special examination to make sure that they will not cause a default on the mortgage.

VALUATION ANALYSIS

The main point of the appraisal is to arrive at an estimate of market value. The details on location, site, and improvements are primarily background to the valuation process. Appraisers speak of using and correlating three approaches to *valuation:* the sales (market) comparison, cost, and income capitalization approaches. In fact, they are not really correlated; appraisers consider all three, but they place most reliance on the method that provides the best available data for the property being valued.

The discussion of income property in Part 4 emphasizes that the joint approach through all three techniques is necessary. With single-family homes, however, almost all weight is placed on the sales comparison method for existing houses. It is supplemented by the cost approach on new or substantially rehabilitated units. Only minor weight is given to the income approach.

A property's value depends on the possibilities of substitution and the degree to which an improvement to the property is useful. **Substitution** is the ability to obtain equal benefits from another property. It is significant because a knowledgeable buyer will not pay more for a property than an equally desirable one will cost. Few people would pay $120,000 for a house if they saw an almost identical one for sale at $110,000.

Spending money on improvements does not increase a property's value unless the improvements are in demand. An owner might ask $130,000 for a house similar to one selling for $110,000 because he had spent an extra $20,000 on very expensive paint, carpets, and bathroom fixtures. If the average buyers feel that these improvements contribute only $5,000 to the amenities of the house, that is all that these features will add to its price. The house would sell for $115,000 and the other $15,000 would not be recovered by the investor.

Sales (Market) Comparison Approach

Most buyers use a simple **sales (market) comparison approach** in deciding what they will pay for a property. Using this method, they do not have to look at many houses before they have a fairly accurate picture of how much houses of the type they are seeking are worth. Appraisers use not only their own knowledge, but also specific data on recent sales. The appraisal form allows a comparison of the house being valued with three similar ones. The comparable properties are usually ones in the same neighborhood in order to minimize the need to adjust for locational differences.

The sales comparison approach consists of four steps:

1. Find recent sales of similar or **comparable properties** and obtain accurate data on their improvements and selling prices.

2. Analyze and compare the subject property with each of the others in order to reveal any differences between them with respect to improvements, financing, time of sale, and other features.
3. Calculate necessary adjustments in the selling price to make it equivalent to that of the subject property.
4. Determine a best estimate of the value of the subject property.

A key part of the appraiser's job is finding the prices of good comparable properties that have been recently sold. They use public records, multiple listing sales, information from other appraisers and brokers, plus any other data they can find.

Comparisons The middle part of page 2 of Figure 13-2 is an example of how the comparison technique works. Necessary positive (+) adjustments arise when a comparable property is inferior to the one being appraised. They are necessary to bring the value of the comparable property up to that of the subject one. Thus comparable number 1 in the example has 245 fewer square feet and a half bath less. The appraiser estimates that it would sell for $7,500 less because of these differences. Since for this comparison the comparable is inferior, this amount must be added to its selling price in order to estimate the value of the subject property.

In the same way, if the comparable has superior features, a minus (−) adjustment is necessary. Comparable number 1 has a full basement and finished recreation room, while the basement of the property being appraised is unfinished. The appraiser must subtract $1,950 from the comparable's price to equalize the two.

When all the separate items are listed, valued, and summed, we note that $10,200 must be added to the price of the comparable property to make its value equivalent to that of the subject. The comparable sold for $65,000. Adding $10,200 in order to raise its selling price to what the subject property would sell for, the appraiser finds $75,200 ($65,000 + $10,200) to be the estimated value of the subject property. In the same way, $3,350 is to be added to the selling price of comparable number 2 and $8,900 is to be added to the price of comparable number 3 to indicate the value of the property being appraised.

Other, more general adjustments may also be required. Although not necessary in this case, special attention must be paid to financing concessions, which can affect the price by from 5 percent to 10 percent. Somewhat unusual properties—older or larger ones—may not sell as frequently, so that sales over a longer period must be compared. Adjustments may be based on estimates of the average increase or decrease in the price level for all houses in the area during the period since the last sale. Such estimates require constructing a neighborhood housing price index.

Finally the appraiser uses judgment to arrive at an indicated value. The estimate is not simply an average of the adjusted comparables. The weight placed on each of the comparables will differ depending on how large its adjustments have been and on the appraiser's feeling for which provides the best information.

The Cost Approach

In the **cost approach**— also called the *replacement cost* or *reproduction cost approach*—the appraiser estimates the cost of reproducing the improvements on the subject property in terms of today's costs of labor, building materials, and supplies. In estimating **reproduction costs,** the identical building is replicated. For **replacement costs,** estimates cover construction of a building with the same functions and services, but with contemporary design because exact reproduction is illogical or impossible. An example is shown on the top of the second page of Figure 13-2. Since land cannot be reproduced, the appraiser uses market comparisons to derive the value of the land. In this case the costs of the basic structure are estimated by multiplying the cost per square foot by the number of square feet. Such costs are available from appraisal manuals or from local banks or builders. Costs of other items are calculated on a unit basis— for example, for each bathroom or fireplace.

Having obtained an estimate of what the building would cost to produce today, the appraiser next subtracts estimated **depreciation,** or the loss in value, from this new cost. If costs rise more than depreciation, the estimated value of the building will exceed its original cost. Buildings may depreciate because they are older and have used up part of their economic life, because they have been poorly maintained (**physical depreciation**), or because they contain features that are no longer adequate to perform their function (**functional obsolescence**).

The final value obtained from this approach is equal to the estimated cost if the building were new, minus the depreciation and plus the land value. The need to estimate depreciation sharply reduces the usefulness of this approach. The older the building, the greater is the inaccuracy. Measuring the actual value lost as a result of time can be accomplished in reality only by using the sales approach. Some buildings built 200 years ago retain all their basic values because they were well designed and maintained; others built 10 years ago may be out of date. Depreciation is far from a simple function of age.

For new buildings, the cost approach makes sense on the assumption that people will not pay much more for a building than it costs to build. But this neglects the development process, which increases the total value of the building above its costs. On the other hand, new buildings may be worth less than they cost to build; they may be overimproved or poorly designed. Nevertheless, because of substitution, costs are a good indicator of the value of a properly planned and built new house.

Recognizing the weakness of the cost approach in the case of older buildings, the FHLMC requirements state that it can be skipped if adequate market comparisons are available. In contrast, if the cost approach must be used because of lack of market data, lenders ask for a more *conservative,* or lower, appraisal because market acceptance has not been demonstrated.

The Income Approach

The **income capitalization approach** for single-family houses depends on the often difficult task of finding enough sales of rented units to provide a data base. Under this technique, the appraiser estimates what the subject unit would rent for. This estimate is then multiplied by a gross rent multiplier, found from other sales in the neighborhood, to obtain the estimate of value.

The **gross rent multiplier (GRM)** is simply the selling price of a house divided by the amount it rents for. Thus, in the example of the property appraised in Figure 13-2, from sales of other houses that have been rented the appraiser might find that an average house that rents for $700 has been selling for $81,200. These data furnish the information necessary to derive the gross rent multiplier:

GRM = selling price ÷ rent = $81,200 ÷ $700 = 116

The GRM in this case is 116. The estimated rent for the subject property is $650. Multiplying this by the GRM, the appraiser would estimate the value by the income approach as $75,400.

Value = rent × GRM = $650 × 116 = $75,400

Since information on sales of comparable rental units is not easy to obtain, and since rather small errors either in the gross rent multiplier or in estimates of what a house will rent for result in large errors in the valuation, this technique is rarely useful for owner-occupied houses. The income approach carries more weight in the case of units bought for investment or for duplexes and quadriplexes. In these cases, the rental income is expected to cover part of the monthly mortgage payments.

Reconciliation of Estimates

The appraiser derives the final estimated market value by reconciling the valuations derived by the different approaches. However, the final estimated value is not an average; the appraiser usually depends primarily on the value found through sales comparisons. The other data serve as a check to make sure that the estimated value is reasonable.

The appraisal should provide a comprehensive and logical analysis of the location and property. It should explain reasons for any deviations of the final estimates from the indicated value found by the sales data approach. It must also be compared with the listed selling price.

THE LOAN COMMITMENT

On the basis of the qualifications of the borrower, the examination of the property, and its value, underwriters complete their task by recommending to the lender's loan committee whether or not a commitment should be issued. Underwriters reach their recommendations by weighing all the factors needed to make a loan successful. Great strengths in some areas may offset weaknesses in others.

Most lenders use **loan committees** to make the final decision. The composition of the loan committee may range from only a senior officer to the whole board of directors. How many members are included and from what level usually depends on the size and type of loan under consideration. A $100,000 loan might be approved at a branch; a $5 million loan might require a vote of the board of directors.

If the loan is approved, the lender issues a **loan commitment.** This is a binding contract that offers to make a loan if the buyer accepts and meets specified conditions. The commitment form sets forth the terms of the loan and certain legal requirements and conditions. For example, it might require that necessary repairs noted in the appraisal report be completed, that a termite certificate be furnished, and that hazard and flood insurance be at a certain level. It will also usually specify a time period within which the borrower must accept the offer and another within which the loan must be closed. After the borrower accepts the commitment, arrangements are made for the final closing.

Negotiations

In some cases, the lender may reject the application or may set conditions—such as a higher down payment—that the would-be borrower cannot meet. Rejected applicants can return to the lender to find out what caused the denial. They can also negotiate to see if either the objections can be removed or different terms can be arranged.

The lender's decision is based on the judgment of the underwriter and the loan committee. The lender can be asked what caused the loan to be turned down and what changes could make it acceptable. Altering some terms, such as the down payment, discount, or maturity, might make an agreement possible. Moreover, errors may have crept into the information used. If the applicant is able to discover and rectify them, the loan may turn out to be a good one for both parties.

Equal Credit Opportunity

The amended **Equal Credit Opportunity Act** of 1974 aims to make certain that no potential borrower is discriminated against by lenders. The act places special emphasis on the equitable treatment of women when they apply for loans. It prohibits certain kinds of actions and mandates others:

- It prohibits discrimination on the basis of race, color, religion, national origin, age, sex, marital status, and the receipt of public assistance.
- It forbids asking certain questions—for example, about divorce or pregnancy—that could be used to make decisions on prohibited grounds.
- It provides that secondary income cannot be arbitrarily rejected; rather, it must be judged on logical grounds. Emphasis is placed on the protection of the rights of working women to credit. Previously many lenders arbitrarily approved less credit for women with incomes on the assumption that they were more likely to leave the work force.
- The lender must notify the applicant within three days of the action taken on a loan request. If a request is denied, reasons for the disapproval must be listed. The rejected borrower must be given an opportunity to rebut the reasoning by furnishing additional credit information.

The Equal Credit Opportunity Act is one of a series of consumer protection steps taken by the federal government. Closely related is the **Fair Credit Reporting Act.** It requires that the information in credit reports be relevant, accurate, and treated as confidential by the recipients. Applicants have a right to know what credit bureau supplied the report. They have the right to examine their credit file and correct any errors, and to file an explanatory statement to offset any derogatory information.

The act prevents the use of outdated credit information, on the assumption that borrowers can reform. Outdated information includes credit problems that occurred more than 7 years earlier and, in the case of bankruptcies, those that took place over 14 years previously. The act also forbids asking neighbors certain questions, such as about the applicant's lifestyle.

CLOSING OR SETTLEMENT

The act of actually making and settling the loan is called **closing** or **settlement.** How this is done differs greatly from one state to another. Procedures also vary depending on whether the loan is made at the time a property is sold or whether it is a refinancing or secondary loan. In some states, closing is an elaborate ceremony, with buyers, sellers, lenders, and various attorneys present. In the case of some large, complex properties, from 50 to 100 persons might be present, with an even greater number of documents. Several dress rehearsals may be required before the actual closing. At the other extreme, the closing process may take place over a period of time, conducted entirely by an escrow agent. The buyer, the seller, and the lender each deliver documents, money, and instructions to the agent. When all instructions have been met, the agent closes the escrow, records the necessary documents, and disburses the money.

The Settlement Statement

The amounts that a buyer must pay and a seller will receive are shown in a **settlement statement.** In the sample settlement statement in Figure 13-3, the first page summarizes the information and the second page presents it in more detail.

Buyer–Seller Payments   The left side of page 1 in the figure, "Summary of Borrower's Transaction," lists the amounts for which the buyers are responsible. They have agreed to pay $90,000 for the house. They must also pay $3,878.13 in settlement charges, as page 2 shows. The gross amount the buyers must pay is $93,878.13.

The lender will advance $72,000 on a mortgage, and the buyers are owed $323.57 for the proration of taxes. The buyers have deposited $9,000 on their purchase contract. The net is that they are credited with $81,323.57 and must put up an additional $12,554.56 in cash at the closing.

The right side of page 1, "Summary of Seller's Transaction," shows that the sellers get credit for the sale price. They must meet their share of the settlement costs, unpaid taxes, and the broker's commission. They must also pay off their outstanding mortgage, including any prepayment fees. The sellers are due $90,000 and owe $47,873.57. Thus, they will receive $42,126.43 from the escrow account. The holder of their previous mortgage will be paid $42,100. The remainder will be split among the claims shown on the second page of the settlement statement.

Commissions and Fees   Page 2 of the figure, "Settlement Charges," gives an indication of the transaction costs involved in the purchase and sale of a house. The largest amount goes to the broker's commission. Next largest are the discounts paid to the lender. Then come the fees for the title company, to make sure that the title is good and to insure this fact. The remainder is paid out in bits and pieces for several other services.

How these various costs are split between the buyer and the seller differs from one part of the country to another. Most locations divide them in a customary manner. Who *actually* pays, however, may be subject to negotiation. The specific items required are also different in each state. In California, attorneys' fees are unusual because of the use of escrow and title companies, but in some states they may constitute a major cost.

Impounds and Prepaid Interest   The deposits required by lenders to avoid delayed payments, primarily for hazard insurance and taxes, are called **impounds, escrow accounts,** or **reserves.** They need not exist, but are usually specified in mortgages with low down payments. In typical cases, the borrowers may be required to pay the first year's insurance in advance. In addition, monthly payments include amounts needed to establish reserves for insurance and taxes so that sufficient money will be available in the account to make the payments when due. Sums already accumulated in the account are returned to the seller upon closing.

Prepaid interest occurs if the day of the month on which interest is due differs from the date of closing. Assume that interest is paid at the end of the month and that the first payment will be due on May 31. If the loan is closed on April 15, the buyers will owe 15 days' interest.

Prorations   Most agreements provide that buyers and sellers **prorate,** or divide, certain charges according to the time each owns a house. Assume that taxes are paid at the end of each six-month period. On April 15, the sellers will have owned the house for three and a half months of the first tax period. They will have to pay 58.3 percent (3.5 ÷ 6) of the projected tax bill to the buyers. The buyers receive credit for this amount, but if an escrow account is required, they will have to deposit that amount immediately. The sellers get back the sums they may have already deposited in insurance or other escrow accounts.

The Real Estate Settlement Procedures Act

The purpose of the **Real Estate Settlement Procedures Act (RESPA),** enacted in 1974, is to protect consumers by reducing the costs of settlement. It also attempts to improve their decisions as to which lender offers the best deal with respect to both interest rates and closing costs. It does this by requiring lenders to furnish applicants with information about settlement charges in a uniform manner. Certain types of charges are prohibited. The act applies to all federally related mortgage loans on one- to four-family houses. A **federally related mortgage loan** is one made by any lender insured or regulated by a federal agency, or guaranteed or insured by the FHA or VA, or planned to be sold to a federally sponsored agency. Thus it includes almost all loans made by institutions.

Information   Within three days of accepting a loan application, a lender must supply to each mortgage applicant a booklet prepared by the Department of Housing and Urban Development (HUD). This booklet contains information about real estate transactions and settlement costs. It informs borrowers of problems they can get into when borrowing on a mortgage. It also explains how relevant consumer protection laws can assist them.

At the same time, the lender must give the borrower a good-faith estimate of what settlement costs will be. This allows borrowers to plan for the cash they will need, as well as to make comparisons among lenders. The information is similar to that shown in the settlement statement in Figure 13-3, but it may be summarized more succinctly.

Figure 13-3
Settlement Statement Form

Form Approved
OMB NO. 63-R-1501

HUD-1 Rev. 5/76

A.

U.S. DEPARTMENT OF HOUSING AND URBAN DEVELOPMENT

SETTLEMENT STATEMENT

B. TYPE OF LOAN
1. ☐ FHA   2. ☐ FmHA   3. ☒ CONV. UNINS.
4. ☐ VA   5. ☐ CONV. INS.
6. FILE NUMBER: 15-000,000   7. LOAN NUMBER: 002150200
8. MORTGAGE INSURANCE CASE NUMBER:

C. *NOTE: This form is furnished to give you a statement of actual settlement costs. Amounts paid to and by the settlement agent are shown. Items marked "(p.o.c.)" were paid outside the closing; they are shown here for informational purposes and are not included in the totals.*

D. NAME OF BORROWER:	E. NAME OF SELLER:	F. NAME OF LENDER:
Peter S. May	Paul T. Jones	**Federal Savings and Loan Association**
Cindy P. May	Sally Q. Jones	

G. PROPERTY LOCATION:	H. SETTLEMENT AGENT:	I. SETTLEMENT DATE:
3042 Alameda Palo Alto, CA 94304	AC Title Company	April 15, 1986
	PLACE OF SETTLEMENT: 205 University Palo Alto, CA 94302	

J. SUMMARY OF BORROWER'S TRANSACTION		K. SUMMARY OF SELLER'S TRANSACTION	
100. GROSS AMOUNT DUE FROM BORROWER:		**400. GROSS AMOUNT DUE TO SELLER:**	
101. Contract sales price	$90,000.00	401. Contract sales price	$90,000.00
102. Personal property		402. Personal property	
103. Settlement charges to borrower *(line 1400)*	3,878.13	403.	
104.		404.	
105.		405.	
Adjustments for items paid by seller in advance		*Adjustments for items paid by seller in advance*	
106. City/town taxes to		406. City/town taxes to	
107. County taxes to		407. County taxes to	
108. Assessments to		408. Assessments to	
109.		409.	
110.		410.	
111.		411.	
112.		412.	
120. *GROSS AMOUNT DUE FROM BORROWER*	$93,878.13	420. *GROSS AMOUNT DUE TO SELLER*	$90,000.00
200. AMOUNTS PAID BY OR IN BEHALF OF BORROWER:		**500. REDUCTIONS IN AMOUNT DUE TO SELLER:**	
201. Deposit or earnest money	9,000.00	501. Excess deposit *(see instructions)*	
202. Principal amount of new loan(s)	72,000.00	502. Settlement charges to seller *(line 1400)*	5,450.00
203. Existing loan(s) taken subject to		503. Existing loan(s) taken subject to	
204.		504. Payoff of first mortgage loan	42,100.00
205.		505. Payoff of second mortgage loan	
206.		506.	
207.		507.	
208.		508.	
209.		509.	
Adjustments for items unpaid by seller		*Adjustments for items unpaid by seller*	
210. City/town taxes to		510. City/town taxes to	
211. County taxes 1/01 to 4/15	323.57	511. County taxes 1/01 to 4/15	323.57
212. Assessments to		512. Assessments to	
213.		513.	
214.		514.	
215.		515.	
216.		516.	
217.		517.	
218.		518.	
219.		519.	
220. *TOTAL PAID BY/FOR BORROWER*	81,323.57	520. *TOTAL REDUCTION AMOUNT DUE SELLER*	47,873.57
300. CASH AT SETTLEMENT FROM/TO BORROWER		**600. CASH AT SETTLEMENT TO/FROM SELLER**	
301. Gross amount due from borrower *(line 120)*	93,878.13	601. Gross amount due to seller *(line 420)*	90,000.00
302. Less amounts paid by/for borrower *(line 220)*	(81,323.57)	602. Less reductions in amount due seller *(line 520)*	(47,873.57)
303. CASH (☒ FROM) (☐ TO) BORROWER	12,554.56	603. CASH (☒ TO) (☐ FROM) SELLER	42,126.43

CF 3443 B (3/77) Page 1

– 2 –

L. SETTLEMENT CHARGES

	PAID FROM BORROWER'S FUNDS AT SETTLEMENT	PAID FROM SELLER'S FUNDS AT SETTLEMENT
700. TOTAL SALES/BROKER'S COMMISSION based on price $ 90,000.00 @ 6 % = 5,400		
Division of Commission (line 700) as follows:		
701. $ 5,400 to Quick Sale Realty Co.		
702. $ to		
703. Commission paid at Settlement		$5,400.00
704.		
800. ITEMS PAYABLE IN CONNECTION WITH LOAN		
801. Loan Origination Fee %		
802. Loan Discount 3 %	2,100.00	
803. Appraisal Fee 200 to Butts	200.00	
804. Credit Report 40 to Equitable	40.00	
805. Lender's Inspection Fee		
806. Mortgage Insurance Application Fee to		
807. Assumption Fee		
808. Documents	45.00	
809.		
810.		
811.		
900. ITEMS REQUIRED BY LENDER TO BE PAID IN ADVANCE		
901. Interest from 4/15 to 4/31 @ $18.00 /day	288.00	
902. Mortgage Insurance Premium for months to		
903. Hazard Insurance Premium for years to		
904. years to		
905.		
1000. RESERVES DEPOSITED WITH LENDER		
1001. Hazard insurance 3 months @ $ 65.50 per month	196.50	
1002. Mortgage insurance months @ $ per month		
1003. City property taxes months @ $ per month		
1004. County property taxes 2.5 months @ $ 92.25 per month	230.63	
1005. Annual assessments months @ $ per month		
1006. months @ $ per month		
1007. months @ $ per month		
1008. months @ $ per month		
1100. TITLE CHARGES		
1101. Settlement or closing fee to		
1102. Abstract or title search to		
1103. Title examination to		
1104. Title insurance binder to		
1105. Document preparation to		
1106. Notary fees to		
1107. Attorney's fees to		
(includes above items numbers;		
1108. Title insurance to AC Title Company	768.00	
(includes above items numbers;		
1109. Lender's coverage $ 72,000		
1110. Owner's coverage $ 90,000		
1111.		
1112.		
1113.		
1200. GOVERNMENT RECORDING AND TRANSFER CHARGES		
1201. Recording fees: Deed $ 5.00 ; Mortgage $ 5.00 ; Releases $	10.00	
1202. City/county tax/stamps: Deed $; Mortgage $		
1203. State tax/stamps: Deed $; Mortgage $		
1204.		
1205.		
1300. ADDITIONAL SETTLEMENT CHARGES		
1301. Survey to		
1302. Pest inspection to Rose		50.00
1303.		
1304.		
1305.		
1400. TOTAL SETTLEMENT CHARGES *(enter on lines 103, Section J and 502, Section K)*	$3,878.13	$5,450.00

CF 3443 B (3/77) Page 2   HUD-1 Rev. 5/76

Source: U.S. Department of Housing and Urban Development, "Settlement Statement," Form CF 3443 B (3/77), revised May 1976, pp. 1–2.

One day prior to the actual closing, the buyer may request a completed copy of the standard settlement form. At settlement, both buyers and sellers are entitled to receive an itemized statement of what each paid.

Abusive Practices Under RESPA, certain **abusive practices** are prohibited. These include kickbacks and referral fees, such as those previously paid by lenders or title companies to brokers or others for sending them business. The provision that the seller cannot designate the title company avoids a practice whereby title companies gave many free services to developers in order to ensure themselves of the final business. Excessively large escrow accounts also are not permitted.

Truth in Lending

The *Consumer Credit Protection Act of 1968* is usually spoken of as the **truth in lending law.** It applies to most types of consumer loans. In real estate finance, real property loans of over $25,000 to individuals are included, provided they are made by creditors who make loans frequently. Under the act, the Federal Reserve was assigned the duty of drafting the regulations. They appear in the Fed's ***Regulation Z***; consequently, this name is often applied to the act. Enforcement is by the lender's normal regulator or the Federal Trade Commission.

The act does not regulate the terms or conditions of loans; it merely requires that all interest and finance charges be specified clearly to the borrower, and that an **annual percentage rate (APR)** of interest be calculated. This is an estimate of the effective rate. The borrower must also be supplied with a disclosure statement that lists total finance charges and the APR. The statement must also specify when payments begin, their total number, their due dates, the security, any late charges, and prepayment penalties. On adjustable-rate mortgages, the lender must furnish the borrower with complete loan information including the index, change dates, caps, and similar significant factors, and must offer the borrower the opportunity to receive an itemization of the amount charged for financing.

The annual percentage rate is higher than the interest rate on a mortgage because the finance charge used to calculate the APR includes charges over and above interest. Furthermore, the amount financed is often less than the loan amount.

Calculating the APR Three separate payments can be included in the **finance charge** on a mortgage: the total interest payments, the prepaid finance charges, and any mortgage insurance payment required by the lender. The truth in lending law considers all of these as part of the borrowing cost. **Prepaid finance charges** are those charges made by the lender in addition to regular interest payments. They include points (origination and discount fees), any charges for processing the loan or payments, and prepaid interest.

The **amount financed** is the total loan minus the prepaid finance charges collected by the lender. This corrects for the fact that some of the mortgage principal goes immediately to the lender. It is not available for the borrower to use in payment for the purchase.

The annual percentage rate is the calculated rate of interest paid rather than the stated interest. It uses the total finance charge (rather than the interest rate) and the amount financed (rather than the contract principal). The lender knows what payments will be received over the period of the loan and the amount actually lent (the amount financed). The APR is the interest rate that makes the present value of the future receipts (these form an annuity) exactly equal to the amount actually financed. If the amount financed is $72,000 and the mortgage calls for monthly payments of $768 per month over the next 30 years, a calculator or interest factor table will show that the APR is 12.5 percent.

SUMMARY

The largest losses on mortgages come from loans with high loan-to-value ratios or those for which buyers put up only a small amount of money because of junior financing. Accurate appraisals are vital on high loan-to-value loans. If overvaluations occur, buyers have no real equity. They are unlikely to pay for selling costs from their own pockets merely to prevent a loss to the lender.

The ratio of housing expense to the buyer's future income is another key factor. Losses occur if the expense ratio is too high or if income drops because of the loss of a job, sickness, or divorce. Nonowner-occupied houses have a higher loss ratio, as do unusual properties that appeal to a limited market.

In qualifying borrowers, lenders make an overall judgment that their chances of defaulting are low. This means balancing a borrower's expenses, income, assets, and the down payment as well as past credit record. Even with other factors favorable, however, many lenders set maximum housing and expense-to-income ratios that borrowers may not exceed. Lower maximums apply if down payments are low or rates are adjustable.

Appraisal is the process of estimating the market value of a property. How much a property is worth depends on its location, its site, and its improvements. The best valuations are reached by comparisons with actual sales in an active market, supplemented for new houses by accurate cost data on houses of a type that is selling currently.

The sales comparison approach arrives at a valuation by comparing the property being appraised with recent sales of similar units. Since houses are not identical, adjustments must be made between the houses being compared for the value of differences in improvements, location and site, and time of sale. Although several houses are compared, the appraiser places most weight in the final estimate on those houses with the fewest differences from the subject property.

Cost and income are additional approaches to valuation. Except for new units, they are less useful for single-family houses. Even using these approaches, sales comparisons are necessary for land values and to check features in demand. The appraiser uses data from these other approaches to confirm his or her judgment, which is based primarily on knowledge of what is happening to demand as reflected in current housing sales.

The underwriting process ends in a recommendation to accept the loan application and issue a commitment, or to reject it. Both the terms of the loan and a rejection may be negotiable if the applicant can offer additional information or security.

The process of closing differs greatly among localities, depending on local customs. Settlement may take place through escrow agents, lawyers, title companies, or brokers. Who pays what varies, as does the amount of the charges. However, all loans must meet the requirements of the Real Estate Settlement Procedures Act and of the truth in lending law. Lenders must also comply with the Equal Credit Opportunity Act and the Fair Credit Reporting Act, as well as with numerous specific state requirements.

KEY TERMS

abusive practices	**location**
amount financed	**market value**
annual percentage rate (APR)	**physical depreciation**
appraisal	**prepaid finance charges**
closing	**prorate**
comparable properties	**qualified borrower**
cost approach	**Real Estate Settlement**
depreciation	**Procedures Act (RESPA)**
Equal Credit Opportunity Act	**Regulation Z**
escrow accounts	**replacement costs**
Fair Credit Reporting Act	**reproduction costs**
federally related mortgage loan	**reserves**
finance charge	**sales comparison**
functional obsolescence	**approach**
gross rent multiplier (GRM)	**settlement**
impounds	**settlement statement**
income capitalization approach	**stable monthly income**
loan application	**substitution**
loan commitment	**truth in lending law**
loan committees	**underwriting**

QUESTIONS

1. What are the key factors that a lender's underwriter should consider in deciding whether or not to recommend a loan?

2. Explain the potential trade-offs that lenders must examine between loan-to-value ratio, housing expense-to-income ratio, and a borrower's balance sheet when determining whether to recommend making a loan.
3. Discuss the importance of location in valuing a real property.
4. In deciding whether a property will support a loan, what do lenders usually consider?
5. Discuss the advantages and disadvantages of the sales comparison approach.
6. Discuss the advantages and disadvantages of the cost approach.
7. Briefly describe the procedure a prospective borrower must go through in order to obtain a loan.
8. What purpose do impounds serve?
9. What is the difference between the annual percentage rate and the stated interest rate?
10. Explain the concept of underwriting a loan.
11. Explain the procedure of settlement and the role of the Real Estate Settlement Procedures Act.
12. What is "truth in lending"?

Analysis for Financing Income Properties

14 Decisions to Invest and Lend on Income Properties

OBJECTIVES

When you finish this chapter, you should be able to:

- discuss the decision process for lending and investing on income properties.

- point out some of the difficulties of analyzing income properties.

- identify factors that can make real estate investments profitable.

- describe how financial statements are projected.

- recognize that different approaches to value are based on individual sections of the cash flow statements.

- distinguish between market value and price and understand how shifts in ownership and lending relationships alter prices and investment values.

DECISIONS TO INVEST and to lend are the driving forces in the real estate markets. Developers do not act unless they are convinced that a new property will be profitable and will meet their investment objectives. When existing properties change hands, both the buyer and the seller must decide that the price, even with the inclusion of transaction costs, fits their goals. Lenders do not put up money unless they believe that their chances of being repaid, either by the borrower or through foreclosure, are reasonably high.

Part 4 analyzes the decisions required to finance income properties successfully. This chapter introduces key elements common to the various types of decisions discussed in later chapters.

The financing process includes three main participants. The critical decisions are made and the integration of the financing plan is done by the *equity investors.* Their ability to put together a deal depends on the *lenders,* who are investors in the debt. They are also strongly influenced by *local, state,* and *federal governments,* which control the use of land and buildings and provide necessary services for them. Even more basic are the effects on profitability of federal and state governments through the internal revenue code.

This chapter first discusses some of the main factors that influence the success or failure of real estate investments. It then examines the projection of revenues and expenses, which are the basis of the cash flow estimates underlying most investment decisions. Finally, it emphasizes the importance of the way in which ownership rights and financing are structured. Actual profitability to investors depends heavily on this structuring process. The cash flows to the investor and lender are affected by leverage as well as by revenues and expenses.

INVESTING IN INCOME PROPERTIES

Investors who own capital search constantly for profitable investment opportunities. They may act as principals, or as developers or promoters who put deals together and offer shares to more passive investors. The field of real estate offers many possibilities for investment, but it may also involve a great deal of effort and high risks. Those desiring to invest in income property must seek out offerings that might meet their needs and then analyze them to determine potential risks and rewards. Finally, on the basis of their examination, the investors must decide whether or not these offerings meet the needs of their own portfolios.

The Investment Process

The task of finding, financing, and buying worthwhile properties can be a complex one. The investor must make an initial choice between buying an existing building and seeking a development opportunity. If the investor finds a property that appears desirable, he or she must screen the offer to see that it is suitable and likely to be profitable. It may be necessary for the investor to enter preliminary negotiations to retain rights to the property during the period in which more detailed and expensive analysis is under way.

Real estate investment decisions are based on projections of potential returns, which must be high enough to cover the risk-free real interest rate plus (a) a premium to cover expected inflation and such costs as (b) management, (c) illiquidity, and (d) transactions, as well as (e) the probability that the actual return will differ from those projected. Income projections involve a large measure of uncertainty. High values for each of these components have always contributed high anticipated returns on income real estate, and especially on development projects.

Real estate deals cannot be completed quickly. A large amount of information must be collected and analyzed. Arranging financing can be a complex matter in itself. Moreover, markets shift rapidly; since properties tend to be illiquid, it may take time and money to market them. Anyone who must sell under time pressure may be forced to accept a considerably reduced price.

Effective management is required to get the most out of property. Books on how to make millions on real estate sell well because they emphasize the fact that, in a market that lacks good information, returns to exceptional personal effort can be high. Furthermore, because leverage can be great, individuals can enter the real estate investment market without much capital.

Variations in potential returns are huge, especially in highly leveraged situations. Small changes in revenues or costs bring about larger movements in net operating income and still greater fluctuations in the amount of cash available after necessary debt payments. To pay for the dangers arising from variable returns, yields for real estate investments must include substantial risk premiums.

Estimating profitability can be as complicated as estimating returns. For a standard apartment building or one of a number of office buildings, there may be enough information available to permit the prospective investor to arrive at a purchase decision rapidly. If the prospective investment is a new development, a redevelopment, or in an area in transition (changing uses or quality), the investor may need a long time in which to gauge the future market for the project. In 1986, one of San Francisco's most prominent sites had been under option to a number of potential developers for over ten years. In many cities, empty redevelopment sites have been under continuous scrutiny and negotiation for even longer periods.

If the property looks worthwhile after a preliminary screening, the investor must find financing and must determine the forms of ownership and sources of equity capital. The investor's tax situation can be extremely important in this process. A key factor may be the proper tailoring of the investment and its financing to the needs of potential lenders and investors. The better it fits their profitability and risk requirements, the higher will be the property's value to them, and the easier will be the financing negotiations. If financing is available and a profitable deal is projected, a sale and a closing can then take place.

Feasibility

The critical factor for any investment is making certain that the return will be worth the time and money committed as well as the risks involved. Will it pay off? A great deal depends on the correct projection of future revenues. Unless the property meets long-term market demands, a profitable investment in unlikely.

Feasibility, or the ability of a project to generate enough income to meet its debt payments and profit goals, is critical for both the investor and the lender. Determining feasibility requires an economic analysis of the project that answers such questions as the following: What will the market be like? How much revenue and expenses can be expected? Are the location and improvements suitable for present and future use? In the development process, governmental approvals often determine whether or not a project can work. The necessary construction and land-use permits must be secured in a reasonable time period, and they must authorize the level of improvements desired.

The Projections

In order to make the best use of the investment information available, techniques have gradually developed to organize it in logical form. The focus in income properties is on *expected future cash flows*. Both investors and lenders must be certain that a property will continue to find and meet a market demand. They should feel confident that revenues sufficient to cover future financing and other expenses will be received. Moreover, the cash flow must assure the desired level of profit.

Risks are high among properties because markets are imperfect and the amount of information available tends to be inadequate. Each building is unique in some respects. Although the number of informed investors has grown tremendously, it is still not large. The level of analytical skills remains low relative to that in many other investment markets. Exact information about other transactions is difficult to obtain. Investors with good information and the ability to analyze it well often have a relative advantage over others in the market.

Projections of demand and supply are often faulty for income properties. Because of the length of time required to develop a property, many decisions are made on facts that are out of date. Developers and lenders, seeing rising rents and a lack of supply, rush to fill the need. Too many see the same gap. By the time all have acted to meet the same shortage—often three to five years later—the market may be oversupplied. It can take several years for an excess supply to be absorbed. Meanwhile, high vacancies and rents lower than expected cause losses instead of gains. Numerous failures may occur.

Still, this same market diversity may lead to large potential profits for investors. More fortunes have been made in real estate than in any other market. Some simply reflect the luck of being in the right place at the right time. Yet the number of investors with sufficient management skills to stay successful throughout ups and downs of the market has been far smaller. Everyone with knowledge of local scenes can recount tales of investors who burst on the scene like meteors, rising to great successes and then disappearing almost as rapidly. They can also point out a much smaller number who were able to prosper and retain their gains.

PROFIT POSSIBILITIES

The wide variety of financing arrangements, differences in potential taxes among investors, and opportunities for creative management all lead to major profit possibilities. How much a property will yield depends on four separate factors:

1. the price paid
2. future cash flows, including those from operations and from a sale or refinancing
3. the financing availability and terms
4. tax costs

Success frequently depends on buying a property at the right price. It is much easier to profit if the price is low enough. Paying too much may mean a constant struggle to break even.

Cash Flows

Profits depend on the difference between the amounts received as rents and the amounts paid to others. For real property, net income is usually only a small part of the gross. As a result, any increase in gross revenues with a lesser change in expenses will cause a large percentage rise in profits.

EXAMPLE: Typically, a creative new owner might find a property with $100,000 in gross income and $98,000 in expenses. If, through better management and new ideas, the owner could raise the amount collected in rent to $125,000 while expenses rose only to $105,000 (not an improbable change), actual net income would be multiplied tenfold.

$$\frac{\$125,000 - \$105,000}{\$100,000 - \$98,000} = \frac{\$20,000}{\$2,000} = 10$$

Such a change in income is likely to cause an equivalent increase in the selling price. How much a building sells for depends on the amount of its net income times its *net income multiplier.* If the market continues to pay the same price for each dollar of earnings, any increase in earnings leads to an equivalent increase in the selling price of a property. But the amount that the market pays for earnings is not constant. If the net income multiplier rises, so will the income from a sale; if its falls, a loss may occur.

A large part of the projected profitability of properties purchased in the mid-1980s came from the cash proceeds that buyers expected to receive upon sale. In turn, a major share of higher expected selling prices and of potential profits arose from a belief that inflation would continue to raise revenues.

The rapid rise in prices in the 1970s was due primarily to inflationary increases in earnings multiplied by a rise in the price-to-income ratio. At the start of this period, a building with a net operating income of $500,000 might have sold with a net income multiplier (price ÷ net operating income) of 8, or for $4 million. A few years later its income could have climbed to $800,000, while the market net income multiplier rose to 12. Its price would have jumped to $9.6 million. Less than half of the 140 percent increase in price would have been due to the increase (including inflation) in earnings; the largest share would have resulted from the change in the net income multiplier.

On the other hand, when inflation slowed in this period, the net earnings of many buildings dropped. Furthermore, between 1980 and 1982 net income multipliers on office buildings fell by 20 percent. Even buildings for which net operating income remained constant thereby experienced a drop in value of 20 percent.

Financing and Taxes

Chapter 3 introduced the concept of *leverage*—the idea that differential yields on debt and equity cause the rates of return to investors to fluctuate more widely than movements in income. Leverage means that the amount and terms of financing play a crucial role in most real estate investment decisions. When good financing is available, investors can own and control a sizable amount of property for little cash. When the amount of equity per dollar investment is low, large percentage gains and losses are possible. Taxes also play a role in many real estate investments. A reduction in taxes paid can significantly increase an investor's profits. (Chapter 16 will analyze these effects in detail.)

RISKS AND PERSONAL FACTORS

Investors who locate potentially profitable properties must still decide whether they want them in their portfolios. Will the property meet their risk criteria and personal needs? Yields are high on real property because risks are great. Leverage works both ways; small movements in income can rapidly swing a building from profit to loss. In the example, if expenses increased to $105,000 from $98,000 but income rose only to $103,000, a net profit would turn into a loss of $2,000. Many factors can cause such shifts:

- Rents and other income fluctuate.
- Buildings or whole neighborhoods deteriorate or become obsolete.
- Wages and other costs rise.

- Competition intensifies.
- Interest rates, taxes, and other financial costs may rise sharply.

Investors' risks are of two types: loss of value of individual properties and loss of value of an entire portfolio. Chapter 3 discussed *portfolio risk,* pointing out that it is a function of the interrelationship among various types of loans and investments. It is determined both by the riskiness of individual investments and by the covariances or correlations among all those contained in a portfolio.

Many investors have added real estate to their portfolios because the timing of its returns differs from that on stocks and bonds. Inflation has been favorable to real estate and unfavorable to investments in financial instruments. This negative correlation of the returns on the two types of investments reduces portfolio risks and enhances the overall value of investing in real property.

The Investor's Personal Factors

Even a brief consideration of the many forces influencing successful real estate loans and investments shows why personal factors are so significant. Investors differ in their knowledge and management skills. The net income from a building can vary widely depending on the talent, insight, and ability of the owner.

Real estate tends to be illiquid. Its purchase and operation may engender complex legal problems. Many successful investments depend on the ability to manipulate government approvals and regulations. Some take large amounts of individual effort and time; others can be kept locked in the safety deposit box with minimal concern. Two different projects may call for vastly different amounts of wealth or assets needed to participate. The attitudes of individuals and of different institutions toward risk make certain properties desirable as investments and others not.

Investors seeking real estate investments must take their time, talent, assets, and needs into account before actively pursuing a property or a real estate security. They must make decisions about how well it meets their own investment objectives. They must have the requisite wealth and be willing to take the risks involved. One type of property will be worth more to an owner whose needs or skills it matches than will another. People with limited capital will use as little money as possible and search for units requiring hands-on management and sweat equity. Active executives will invest through partnerships that require minimum attention on their part. Pension funds may seek properties with a minimum value, such as $1 million or $5 million.

To recapitulate, investors search for real estate that will be feasible to own. They may make money by buying properties with (a) a high potential for increased operating income. They may raise both their risks and their returns through (b) leverage, using borrowed money with a yield below the rate of return on the property. (c) Favorable tax consequences may also be available. And just as they hope the operating income will rise they also hope that will sell the property with (d) a more favorable income multiplier, so that profits will rise still more.

While all these possibilities exist, they do not necessarily make an investment logical. Investors should seek properties on which returns will be acceptable without relying on inflation or a change in income multipliers. Investors will be far safer if they depend on a good operating income available at the time they invest. If, in addition to a favorable income outlook, some or all of the other possibilities result from a single deal, returns may be spectacular.

THE DECISION PROCESS

Prospective investors are offered a real estate asset—buildings and land—at a proposed price. They must determine whether and under what conditions a purchase makes sense. The basic decisions depend on projections of cash flows required to estimate the net present value of the investment and its expected yield or rate of return.

Figure 14-1 outlines the flow of analysis necessary for evaluating a prospective real estate investment. Decisions about these subjects for analysis are usually made in the order shown in the figure, and they will be discussed in that order in this chapter and the next.

In the figure, the first box under the offer of property is divided to show revenues and expenses plus the structuring of financing and ownership. Both are included because returns to the equity owners and the lenders depend on each of them. Projected revenues and expenses determine net operating income. How this is divided among the claims of equity and debt holders and of taxes depends on how the investment is structured.

Structuring

The value of a property to investors and its safety for lenders depend on the amount of leverage and on the ways in which rights to all or parts of the income stream are split. One of the basic skills of a successful real estate promoter or investor is the ability to structure an investment so that its value to the owners and lenders surpasses the amount that must be paid. **Structuring** divides the security, risks, and taxes of a property so as to enhance their values or to convince lenders and investors to commit the necessary funds. Suppliers of money have different objectives, needs, risk preferences, and tax positions. Tailoring an investment to the particular requirements of those with funds to lend or invest generates higher values for each individual than does lumping all potential investors into a single group. In a properly structured arrangement, each investor finds a slice or claim on the property that fits his or her desires and for which he or she is willing to pay.

Structuring for income properties is similar to creative financing in the home market, but the possible variations are much greater:

- For an income property, the land can be separated from the building in the deal.
- The rights to rents (leases) can be sold and borrowed upon.

Figure 14-1
The Flow of Analysis of Real Estate Investments

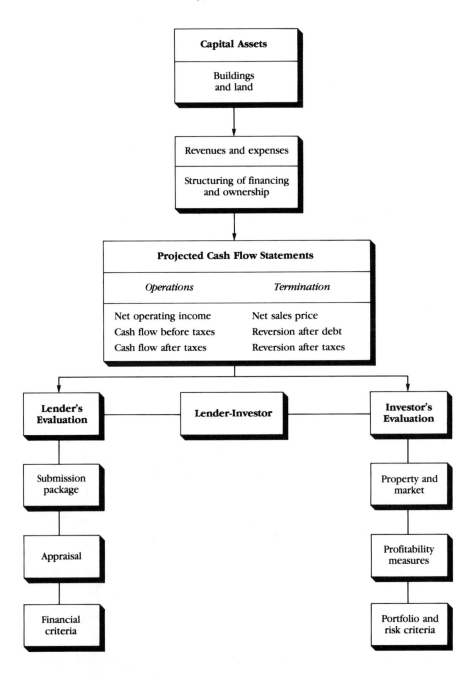

- There can be participations in income and shared appreciation.
- Tenants can become part owners.
- A number of junior mortgages can be created.

The figure emphasizes the need to make structural decisions *before* the lenders and the investors complete their evaluations.

Cash Flow Statements

The third box shows the projected cash flow statements that enter into the valuation process. No single or simple cash flow exists. Some cash is generated by operations—that is, net operating income. Some comes from the termination of an investment—its sale or its refinancing. These amounts are shown under net sales price. Each is further divided into amounts going to the debt holders and to taxes, with the rest belonging to the equity owners. (The next section discusses these statements in greater detail.)

The Lenders' and Investors' Evaluations

The projected cash flows for the prospective property make up part of the raw material upon which lenders and investors make their decisions. (Chapter 15 will discuss the lender's evaluation.) The lender receives the necessary data in the form of a loan application and submission package. It uses this information to appraise or estimate the value of the property and to determine whether it meets financial criteria for making the loan.

Chapter 17 analyzes the investor's evaluation. As the rest of this chapter and Chapter 16 on taxes make clear, a key task of the prospective investor is to analyze the property and the market to determine potential cash flows and to decide on the specific ownership and debt structure that appears optimum.* Who receives the cash flows determines both profitability and risks. Profitability can be estimated for each potential financing structure. Investors must then decide whether these meet their portfolio and risk desires. With such evaluations, they can negotiate different aspects of the project so that it fits the criteria of the lenders, the governments, and investors, and can move forward.

Lender-Investors

Between the boxes for the lender's and the investor's evaluation in the figure appears a box labeled "Lender-Investor." It emphasizes the point—analyzed in detail in Chapter 19—that the line between lenders and investors has become fuzzy; there is no longer a clear-cut distinction between the two categories. In many arrangements, lenders also gain the right to participate in a property's cash flow in addition to the fixed debt service.

---

*Here an investor is a principal or promoter who retains a share of the investment.

During the period of high inflation from 1973 to 1982, long-term fixed-rate mortgages virtually disappeared from the market for income properties. Lenders realized that rapid property appreciation was creating large profits for investors, while rising interest rates sharply reduced the value of their fixed-rate mortgages. They demanded so high a premium for long-term fixed-rate loans that investors had trouble putting together feasible packages.

Alternative financing techniques increased in popularity. Some traditional lenders continued to make fixed-rate loans by charging a large number of points up front. At the same time, they reduced the borrower's prepayment options by insisting that the loan be closed for a minimum period (5 or 10 years) and that prepayment penalties be high.

Other lenders preferred to be participants in the profits of a property. Numerous forms of participation developed, among them joint ventures, convertible mortgages, sales and leasebacks, participation in rents or profits, and shared appreciation mortgages. (Each of these will be discussed in later chapters.)

Secondary financing also became far more popular during this inflationary period. With high interest rates, if traditional loan-to-value ratios were used, the amount of required debt service often exceeded the expected cash flow. To solve this problem, borrowers reduced the amount of debt that required regular monthly cash payments and made up the difference by establishing funds (reserves) to meet shortfalls of operating income and by negotiating second and third mortgages that accrued interest until the loan was due. These negative amortization loans tended to be for short periods, such as 3 to 5 years.

Since such funds carried far higher risk, with less equity and dangerous balloon payments, more money came from nontraditional lenders and carried rates usually far above those from traditional sources. The most usual source was the seller carry-back. Other important sources were foreign lenders, mortgage investment trusts, and more speculative individuals. This secondary lending tended to carry high interest rates (which sellers often converted into a higher sales price) or to include participation agreements, most frequently through shared appreciation, but also through shared revenues.

When inflation slowed down, the percentage of loans and investments carrying participations and related features dropped. Lenders continued, however, to emphasize policies that reduce risks of unexpected inflation by insisting on adjustable interest rates or mortgages that become due and require that rates be renegotiated after a limited number of years (3, 5, or 10).

PRO FORMA FINANCIAL STATEMENTS

Accurate projections of future cash flows are the key to successful lending and investment. Although common sense, good judgment, and a proper consideration of alternatives are valuable, good results depend on correct estimates of future revenues and expenses. Future projections commonly take the form of fairly standard **pro forma financial statements.** These are estimated or illustrative statements, in contrast to those that report actual facts. A complete cash flow projection usually consists of two statements, one covering the operating period, the other the *termination,* or sale.

A correct projection of future cash flows through these statements lies at the heart of the decisions necessary for both successful investing and lending. The investor and the lender each must project the amount of money needed and how much will be received back in each period after netting revenues and expenditures. The projections must estimate both the cash flow and the after-tax consequences of the proposals. Good analysis also requires a recognition of the risks that the projections will be wrong.

The usefulness of pro forma statements hinges on the care with which they are prepared. The amount of time and effort spent on projections varies greatly with the size and complexity of a particular commitment. Many shortcuts may be taken in smaller investments. Those who lack the necessary analytical skills tend to use rough rules of thumb.

Statements for existing property can be developed from past data projected into the future. Those for new developments depend on the knowledge of the developers about existing conditions, on the skill of market analysis, and on the accuracy of assumptions about future rents and how rapidly the property will rent up.

Investors, developers, lenders, and appraisers use information from comparable properties to check the logic of their assumptions. An estimate based on a rent of $25 a year per square foot makes no sense if similar properties are renting for only $18 a year. Estimated expenses of 25 percent of gross potential income will lead to far too high a projected value if actual expenses run at 35 percent.

The Underlying Assumptions

EXAMPLE: Because operating and sales projections are central to the analysis performed by lenders and investors, we illustrate how they are constructed using Tables 14-1 to 14-4. These projections reflect information for a typical income property. The data apply to Plaza Square, a central city office building with retail space. Plaza Square has 104,300 square feet of office space, of which 87,614 are net rentable areas. Retail space consists of 17,400 square feet. There are 200 parking spaces.

Table 14-1 shows the basic data used in the tables that follow. The property is purchased for $15,154,000, which includes all acquisition costs. The mortgage covers 80 percent of the entire purchase price. The interest rate is 10.5 percent, and the mortgage is amortized over 360 monthly payments, resulting in a mortgage constant of 0.0091. The mortgage must be paid through a balloon payment in year 7. Other key variables are listed in the table and are discussed as they are used in the tables that follow.

Table 14-1
Background Data for Plaza Square's Financial Statements

Item	Amount
Purchase price, including closing	$15,154,000
Vacancies and collection losses	13%, 9%, 5%, 5%, 5%
Mortgage	80% of price; 10.5% interest; amortization monthly over 30 years; payable at end of year 7. Mortgage constant (K) = 0.0091.
Reserves	$200,000 upon purchase
Depreciation (straight line, 31.5 years)	3.04%, 3.17%, 3.17%, 3.17%, 3.17%
Depreciable basis	$13,144,000
Holding period	5 years
Expected sales price (NOI ÷ 9.7)	$20,678,335
Selling expenses	6% of sales price
Investors' marginal tax rate	33% (28% federal + 5% net state and local)
Income	Potential rents increase 5% per year; operating expenses increase 4% per year.

Cash Flows, Debt Service, Tax Payments

The type of information contained in a typical operating period cash flow statement is included in Table 14-2. Such accounts reflect best estimates of the amount of income as well as when it will be received. For purposes of analysis, such statements divide into three parts:

1. The first seven lines of the table project the **net operating income (NOI),** which is also called the free-and-clear return or the cash flow before debt service (see Chapter 4). The first five lines calculate the actual revenues to be received, or the **effective gross income.** Next, operating expenses are subtracted from effective gross income to yield the NOI. Information on net operating income forms the basis for traditional appraisals. Lenders tend to emphasize the NOI, since it determines whether cash is adequate to meet the debt service as well as for other purposes.
2. In the next four lines debt service and reserves are subtracted from net operating income, resulting in an estimate of the **before-tax cash flow (BTCF):**

$$BTCF = NOI - \text{debt service} - \text{reserves}$$

Table 14-2
Plaza Square Income Statement

	1986	1987	1988	1989	1990
Gross potential rent	$2,145,407	$2,252,677	$2,365,311	$2,483,577	$2,607,756
Less vacancies and collection losses	(278,903)	(202,741)	(118,266)	(124,179)	(130,388)
Net rent	$1,866,504	$2,049,936	$2,247,046	$2,359,398	$2,477,368
Other income*	290,178	299,687	309,772	320,470	331,825
Effective gross income	$2,156,683	$2,349,624	$2,556,817	$2,679,868	$2,809,193
Less operating expenses	(686,745)	(714,215)	(742,783)	(772,494)	(803,394)
Net operating income (NOI)	$1,469,938	$1,635,409	$1,814,034	$1,907,374	$2,005,798
Less interest	(1,272,936)	(1,266,866)	(1,260,158)	(1,252,746)	(1,244,556)
Less amortization of principal	(57,812)	(63,882)	(70,590)	(78,002)	(86,192)
Less reserves	0	0	0	0	0
Before-tax cash flow (BTCF)	$139,190	$304,661	$483,286	$576,626	$675,050
Less taxes (33% marginal tax rate)	0	0	0	(40,378)	(113,511)
After-tax cash flow (ATCF)	$139,190	$304,661	$483,286	$536,248	$561,539

*Other income = 7% of gross rent + parking income ($120,000) + 10% interest on reserves.

Debt service forms the priority claim against income. Either it must be met from operating income or, if NOI falls short, reserves must be available or additional equity must be paid in to meet the required payments of principal and interest. Reserves cover shortfalls in the cash flow and make funds available for major maintenance and refurbishment. The amounts set aside for reserves are part of taxable income. In this case reserves were established at the time of purchase from equity, and since they were not used, no additional reserves need to be set aside from income.

3. The final two lines project the **after-tax cash flow (ATCF).** Taxes depend on the amount of taxable income and an owner's tax rate. Taxable income equals net operating income minus interest minus depreciation. Taxes (calculated in Table 16-1 in Chapter 16) equal the taxable income times the tax rate. Thus:

$$\text{ATCF} = \text{BTCF} - (\text{taxable income} \times \text{tax rate})$$

If taxable income is less than the before-tax cash flow, as in this example, a tax shelter is said to exist. In a **tax shelter,** owners receive cash on which they do not have to pay current taxes. Taxable income can be negative if the amount of depreciation plus interest exceeds net operating income. Until 1987, tax losses on properties could also be used to reduce taxes on other income.

As Chapter 16 explains, however, the Tax Reform Act of 1986 drastically reduced such advantages from real estate investments.

PROJECTING THE OPERATING STATEMENT

The heart of the pro forma income statement is an accurate projection of revenues and expenses. For existing buildings, revenue projections begin with the current rent rolls. For proposed developments, a market study is necessary. In neither case will a potential rent schedule alone suffice. What lenders need is a projection of the revenues that can actually be expected with some certainty. For Plaza Square, estimated current rents are $21 annually per square foot for office space, $16 annually per square foot for retail space, and $50 per month for parking space. These projections are based on an analysis of existing leases and a detailed study of the market. They are not simply taken from current asking prices or recent leases; they are based on a complete analysis of the market supply and demand.

Supply and Demand

Comparable and competitive buildings must be studied in detail to produce an accurate market study. An economic feasibility study is also needed to determine the trend in construction and vacancies. Too many projects go bad because of failure to recognize the impact of supply and demand on rents. For new developments, leasing will not start for several years. The critical question in such studies should be what rents will be three years from now, not what they were last year.

Projections may be prepared by an independent consultant. Outside experts carry more weight in convincing lenders and investors that the projections have used disciplined analysis based on reasonable assumptions taken from actual field investigations.

Revenues

The amount of the *gross potential rents* hinges on the amount of space and the level of rent the market is expected to pay for each unit. What rents can be charged while maintaining vacancies at a desirably low level is controlled by market demand and competition. When excess space exists, potential rents fall because of the landlord's need to make concessions. **Concessions** are ways of reducing actual rents without cutting the quoted rent charge. For example, in the mid-1980s, when vacancies rose to high levels in many cities, free rent for the first year on a 3- or 5-year lease became common. Other concessions may take the form of the landlord's paying moving costs, or making a larger than normal share of tenant improvements, or taking over existing leases. Because moving is expensive for tenants, landlords hope they can strike a better bargain when the first lease terminates.

Vacancies may be regulated by adjusting rents to demand. Rent levels and expected vacancies trade off to establish both the amount of vacancies and the *net rent* collected. In Table 14-2 the first year's losses from projected vacancies are 13 percent, falling to 9 percent and then to 5 percent of potential rents. A vacancy rate of 5 percent is commonly used as an ideal figure in the industry even though such a generalization is frequently wrong. During the mid-1980s many good projections showed vacancy estimates of 20 to 25 percent, declining to 5 percent only over a period of several years. Some types of properties never achieve a vacancy rate as low as 5 percent.

Other income, the next item in Table 14-2, can come from several sources. For Plaza Square, it includes parking revenue, interest on reserves, and **escalations,** which are payments received from tenants to cover all or part of any increase in operating expenses. Landlords want escalations written into the lease to protect themselves against inflation. How much tenants agree to pay depends on the market and on individual negotiation. The estimates of potential income less the amount that will be lost through vacancies, collection losses, and concessions equal the projected effective gross income.

Operating Expenses

The amount it costs to service the tenants and manage and maintain the property varies with the kind of building, the level of property taxes in the area, and the effectiveness of the property management. Accounting packages and studies by the Building Owners and Managers Association (BOMA) divide expenses into a hundred or more categories. For projection purposes, however, they are usually combined to a handful. Table 14-3 breaks down operating expenses for the Plaza Square building into administrative costs, utilities, maintenance, property taxes, and a miscellaneous category. Note that depreciation (which will be discussed in Chapter 16) is listed separately. It is not part of the cash flow statement used to calculate net operating income, since depreciation is a book, rather than a cash, transaction.

An examination of expenses for different buildings and cities reveals wide variations. Office building expenses may vary from 25 percent to 50 percent of gross potential rents, depending on a building's age, type, and location. On the basis of the expected performance in the first year for Plaza Square, shown in Table 14-3, expenses are estimated at about 32 percent of gross potential rents. They are expected to rise at a rate of 4 percent per year (from Table 14-1), which is slightly less than the projected rate of increase in rents. Taxes and other fixed costs tend to lag slightly behind revenues.

Projections for existing buildings can be based on past operating statements, but each must be analyzed carefully. Many techniques are used to manipulate both revenues and expenses. Free rents up front, postponement of maintenance, and use of cheap, substandard materials and workmanship may all result in a high apparent net revenue. When these artificial influences are removed, future net income may be considerably lower.

Table 14-3
Combined Operating Expense Statement
of Plaza Square Office Building

	First Year Only
Administrative expenses	
Management fees	$68,092
Accounting and professional	15,510
Advertising and miscellaneous	20,730
Insurance	42,704
Utilities	144,909
Maintenance	
Janitorial and gardening	113,773
Repairs	25,243
Property taxes	237,846
Miscellaneous	17,938
Total operating expenses	$686,745
As a percentage of	
gross potential rent	32.00%
Depreciation	$399,884

The largest share of expenses is fixed, or it varies only slightly with the actual occupancy of a building. As a result, because nearly constant expenses are being subtracted, any movements in effective income will have a magnified impact on net income. Since a gap exists between gross effecive income and expenses, equal-percentage increases in both will cause actual cash flow to rise. This is an example of operating leverage. A high rate of inflation can quickly increase a building's returns, depending on how fast leases turn over and on escalation clauses. Landlords like short leases when rapid inflation is projected. The opposite is true for stable periods or those in which supply outruns demand.

The Cash Flow before Taxes

Most of the emphasis in projecting cash flows is properly placed on net operating income. The most difficult to estimate accurately, it forms the basis for the remaining data in the operating statement and frequently for the sales projection as well (see again Table 14-2). Although the remaining lines of the operating statements are extremely significant for individual investors, they are often not even considered by many lenders and some types of investors. The estimates of before- and after-tax flows depend on specific negotiations and individual characteristics. Therefore, they differ greatly depending on the amount of debt, the interest rate, and the amortization agreement. They also differ with the tax situation and marginal tax rate of each potential investor.

The before-tax cash flow line estimates the amount of cash available for payment to the investors. Debt service and the amount put aside for reserves are subtracted from net operating income to find the amounts available for distribution.

How much goes to debt service depends on the financing agreements. In the Plaza Square example, mortgage payments are constant. On the other hand, some agreements may not require any interest payments (they accrue) for a period. Others demand a balloon payment, which really means a refinancing, in a fairly short time.

As shown in Table 14-1, the mortgage constant (k) for Plaza Square is based on an interest rate of 10.5 percent, with the principal amortized over 360 monthly payments (30 years). This results in a monthly mortgage constant of 0.0091, or an annual payment of $1,330,748. The amount credited to principal rises steadily but slowly during the five-year holding period.

This contract required that $200,000 be placed in reserves initially and that they be maintained at that level. No transfers to the reserve fund are shown in the operating statement because the initial reserves did not have to be called upon.

The After-Tax Cash Flow

The final section of Table 14-2 shows the taxes to be paid and the amount of cash available for the investors. As Chapter 16 will make clear, taxes or benefits depend on the marginal tax rate of each investor. The rates are affected by how much other income investors have and by the amount of taxes or benefits arising from the investment under investigation. To illustrate the tax effects, salespeople select a rate they believe would be typical of an interested investor. (They usually assume a maximum tax bracket to improve the investment's comparative yield.) Some investments that appear uninteresting on preliminary analysis may be quite attractive when viewed on an after-tax basis. In other cases, investors may make a poor choice through failure to realize that they will not earn as much as in the projection. If their marginal tax rate differs from that used in the pro forma statement, their after-tax rate of return will also differ.

The marginal tax rate for each of the Plaza Square investors is assumed to be 33 percent, based on a federal income tax rate of 28 percent and net state and local income tax rates of 5 percent. The last two lines of Table 14-2 show that, under the Tax Reform Act of 1986, the tax shelter aspects of real estate investments still exist, but in a form greatly diminished from those under the previous law. In the first three years, all of the cash flow goes to the investors without any tax payments. Chapter 16 explains how this happens. Tax losses are occurring, but they cannot be used (as was formerly the case) to offset other types of income, such as wages and salaries. By year 5, taxes are being paid, but the taxes in that year are only 22.8 percent of BTCF, even though the investor is assumed to be subject to a normal tax rate of 33 percent.

PROJECTING THE TERMINATION STATEMENT

As Figure 14-1 made clear, two different types of financial statements must be estimated to analyze the yield of an investment. Depending on how long a property is held, the cash flow received from appreciation at the time it is sold may well exceed in present value all the benefits received during the operating period. In many investments, a projected increase in the selling over the purchase price accounts for most of the hoped-for profits. As a result, even though the projections may have even less reliability than those for operations, they are a necessary part of investment analysis.

The Statement

Table 14-4 presents the kind of pro forma statement used to analyze the cash flow or the reversion to be received upon sale. It is called a **termination statement** because investments can end without a sale, and receipts may continue after a sale. The termination statement has three parts, equivalent to those of the operating statement.

1. The first part is a net sales price. This is the selling price less selling and closing expenses paid by the seller.
2. The second part projects the before-tax cash flow, which in this case is called the **before-tax cash on sale** (reversion). It consists of the net sales price less any mortgage payments plus any cash reserves.
3. The third part measures the **after-tax cash on sale** or the **after-tax reversion.** How large a return an investment yields may be strongly influenced by the taxes on sale. In some cases the after-tax cash flow can be negative; investors must pay more in taxes than they receive in cash. The need to put up additional funds occurs when depreciation allowances during operation have been large, resulting in high termination taxes.

The Projections

Virtually no independent information exists for estimating future prices beyond what is known about the current market. Most estimates simply assume that the market will continue to pay the same amount per dollar of net operating income as it is paying now. If a dollar of NOI sells for $10, the same 10-to-1 ratio is used as a basis for estimating selling prices. Minor adjustments may be made— for example, in the range of 9-to-1 to 11-to-1—based on an analysis of under- or oversupply, but such adjustments tend to be extremely subjective.

Under this technique, when a future price-to-earnings ratio (or its equivalent, the capitalization rate) has been chosen, the projected selling price depends completely on the estimated net operating income in the year of the sale. In Table 14-4, for example, the selling price of $20,678,335 is derived directly from the estimated NOI of $2,005,798 in year 5 of Table 14-2. This operating income has been capitalized at the initial year's capitalization rate of 9.7 percent or,

Table 14-4
Termination Statement

1. Sales price	$20,678,335
Less selling cost	(1,240,700)
2. Net sales price	$19,437,635
Less mortgage balance	(11,766,722)
Plus reserves	200,000
Before-tax cash on sale (reversion)	$7,870,913
3. Taxable income	$6,352,598
Tax rate	33.00%
Total tax	$2,096,357
After-tax cash on sale (reversion)	$5,774,556

equivalently, it has been multiplied by 10.31, the price of a dollar of earnings when the capitalization rate is 9.7 percent. The importance of making estimates of projected revenues and expenses as accurate as possible becomes even greater because both the current cash flows and the reversion depend on them.

The net sales price also depends on how expensive it is to sell the property. Commissions and closing costs—lawyers' fees, title fees, and any financing points paid by the seller—all must be subtracted from the gross sales price.

Before- and After-Tax Reversions

The projected before-tax cash flow is the net selling price minus the outstanding debt plus any reserve funds. Again, almost all errors arise in the projected selling price, since variations in the outstanding principal and reserves are minor.

The estimated after-tax reversion is more likely to vary. First, the tax code changes frequently, especially for real estate. Tax rates and the treatment of capital gains and of depreciation allowances are likely to alter. Second, the reversion depends on the individual investor's marginal tax bracket, which can shift from year to year and may well change radically prior to the final termination of a property. How taxable income at termination is found for such cases as the Plaza Square building in Table 14-4 is explained in Chapter 16 on taxes, in Table 16-4.

APPROACHES TO VALUATION

The pro forma operating statements form the basis for valuing a property from both a lender's and an investor's point of view. However, many different methods are used to transform the income and selling price data into value estimates. There is no agreement on how to classify the numerous approaches to valuation. Sometimes the differences are spoken of as a contrast between traditional and modern methods.* Others emphasize the contrasts between appraisal and investment analysis.

An investment may be judged differently by investors such as pension funds, which do not have to pay income or profits taxes, and by individuals, who do. Using still another classification, a distinction can be made between techniques that estimate the net present value of a property given a required rate of return, and those that calculate the rate of return or yield given the amount of an investment.

Cash Flows and Income

Valuation methods may be classified in two ways: by type of income estimate and by the treatment of cash flows. The horizontal division of Table 14-5 considers three distinct types of income estimates: NOI, BTCF, and ATCF. The three vertical columns divide the estimates by the period over which the cash flows are received. Vertical column 2, "One-time Cash Flow," includes the techniques that primarily take into account only operating cash flows. These techniques estimate the income of a single period and assume that it reflects the cash flows for the entire holding period.

The techniques in this column are the more traditional ones. The single-period cash flows used for the valuation may be either the next year's projected income or a stabilized income taking account of expected market adjustments and the need to average unusual expenses over a longer period.

Column 3, "One-time Cash Flow and Appreciation or Depreciation," includes techniques that recognize that the property's cash flow will not remain constant. At the end of a holding period the value of a property may have appreciated or depreciated. These valuations assume a regular progression in incomes and a final selling price that differs from the purchase price.

The more modern techniques in column 4, "Holding Period (Including Reversion)," are based mainly on discounted cash flows that include estimates for each year's income, including the cash to be received or paid upon a sale.

Even this simple method of classifying valuation techniques creates nine cells. Each cell includes at least one possible method for judging the value and suitability of a loan or an investment. Chapter 15 discusses the techniques, such as capitalization and discounted cash flows, that are most commonly used in the appraisal process and in a lender's analysis of what constitutes a suitable loan. Chapter 17 covers many of the remaining methods frequently used in decision making by investors, such as net present value and internal rates of return.

---

*For a good discussion of the approaches to valuation, see S. A. Pyhrr and J. R. Cooper, *Real Estate Investment* (New York: Wiley, 1982), chs. 3, 10, and 11.

Table 14-5
Valuation Techniques Using the Income Approach

Type of Income	Type of Cash Flow Estimate		
	One-time Cash Flow	One-time Cash Flow and Appreciation or Depreciation	Holding Period (Including Reversion)
Cash Flow before Debt Service and Taxes (NOI)	Capitalized (investment) value Capitalization rates Gross income multipliers Free-and-clear rate of return	Capitalization rates Recapture	Discounted cash flow Internal rate of return
Cash Flow before Taxes (BTCF)	Equity rate of return Band of investment	Mortgage-equity	Payback
Cash Flow after Taxes (ATCF)	Equity rate of return	Equity rate of return	Net present value Internal rate of return Modified internal rate of return

VALUES TO INVESTORS

Investment analysis is complicated by the different methods of valuing cash flows and the fact that structuring can alter the actual flows as well as the shares going to investors and to lenders. Chapter 19 presents examples of financing alternatives that drastically alter the risks and the expected rates of return. Imagination in structuring ownership and the ability to find lenders and investors who desire particular features of the investment can lead to sharp increases in prices and investment yields. The fact that such large rises are possible is a key factor making real estate such an attractive field for so many investors.

For example, returns have been increased by investors taking advantage of potential tax preferences. Pension funds do not need depreciation deductions, which may be the chief attraction for high-income investors (in Chapter 16). Splitting these deductions correctly can mean lower payments to the tax collector, resulting in higher after-tax cash flows. Similarly, retired people may want security of returns, while younger investors may primarily seek high profit possibilities. Structuring ownership rights can increase income or lower discount rates, thereby enhancing the amount and value of future cash flows and raising the value of a property to its owners. The needs of each type of investor can be better matched by reshaping benefit flows. The average risk premium falls, while prices and the value to those supplying funds to the project rise.

Prices and Market Values

Market value is an estimate made by appraisers or analysts of the most probable price at which a property will sell in a competitive market with prudent, knowledgeable buyers and sellers who are not acting under duress. Estimates of market value assume that a property is being sold in a competitive, efficient market with good information available to all. In fact, most observers agree that most real estate markets are inefficient.*

As a result, large variations in prices and in the values received by lenders and investors occur because individuals recognize and implement creative ways of treating properties. They may see opportunities for changing a property's use, leading to greater demand; they may introduce better management or more profitable financing alternatives. The big payoffs are achieved for real estate investments when such opportunities are seized. Analysis helps in finding such prospects and in calculating the amounts of potential returns.

In studying the techniques for estimating values and prices in the rest of this book, keep two points in mind:

1. If the real estate market were completely efficient, differences in real values would not occur. The number of knowledgeable lenders and investors would be large enough so that a property would sell at its true value.
2. Even if only a single price existed, the division between loans and equity could differ, as would discount rates. Changing leverage would cause variations in risks. Investors who bought with very thin equities would expect a higher rate of return because their risks would be larger; but because the higher yields are on a lower base, their total cash flow might be less.

In an efficient market, the number of lenders and investors who recognized all the circumstances of possible arrangements and who based their decisions on the same estimated risk-adjusted returns would be so great that only a single value and price would prevail. Even though the debt-to-equity ratios and risks differed, if price were different, competition would lead to a single optimum market price. However, the real estate market does not work that way. Information is too poor; the number of knowledgeable participants is limited; some lenders and investors will make or accept less than optimum terms. Those who

---

*For an excellent discussion of this point, see *The Appraisal of Real Estate,* 8th ed. (Chicago: American Institute of Real Estate Appraisers, 1983), ch. 4.

have a better understanding of the market and of financing methods, and who structure and negotiate more favorable arrangements, will increase their real risk-adjusted returns.

SUMMARY

Potential investors and lenders must decide whether a property offer or loan request promises a yield commensurate with its risks. General techniques described in later chapters assist in making such decisions on a logical basis.

Real estate investments can be profitable if they meet an investor's portfolio needs. Profitability can be increased—and may rise to high levels—if improved management or unanticipated inflation raises revenues faster than expenses. A shift in income multipliers can add to gains or losses. A successful structuring of financing and the use of leverage can also improve profits.

Since the value of an income property depends on future cash flows, projecting them accurately is critical to proper investment decisions. Decision makers need both operating and termination projections, divided into sections for before and after debt service and taxes. The specific sections used for valuation of a property depend on the available information, on an analyst's skill, and sometimes on the particular use to which the property will be put.

Skilled analysts can raise values or tailor ownership rights to the desires of investors. A property can be financed in innumerable ways. Selection of the right ingredients will mean that all owners and lenders are better off. Good information remains scarce, however; sometimes money can be made by increasing demand through showing potential investors previously unperceived advantages.

KEY TERMS

after-tax cash flow (ATCF)	**escalations**
after-tax cash on sale	**feasibility**
after-tax reversion	**net operating income (NOI)**
before-tax cash flow (BTCF)	**pro forma financial statement**
before-tax cash on sale	**structuring**
concessions	**tax shelter**
effective gross income	**termination statement**

QUESTIONS

1. Real estate practitioners believe that income property offers unusual profit opportunities. Do you agree? Explain your answer.
2. The Sunday newspaper offers a small office building for sale for $400,000. What kind of information would you seek to help you decide whether this was a fair price?

3. What are the chief factors that determine whether or not an investment in an income property will have an adequate yield?
4. Explain the difference between the risks in individual investments and in a portfolio.
5. What is meant by structuring an investment?
6. Give some examples of how owners can increase the profitability of a property.
7. What is a tax shelter?
8. Produce a first-year pro forma statement for net operating income for an office building, given the following data:

    Rentable area: 100,000 square feet at $20 per square foot

    Parking area: 200 spaces at $700 per year

    Vacancies and collection losses percentage: 5 percent (for both office and parking space)

    Operating expense: $5 per square foot of office space; $150 per parking space

9. Suppose the net operating income of the above office building rises at 5 percent a year. At the end of year 5 the building is sold at a price ten times its NOI in year 5. The selling cost is 6 percent of the selling price. Produce a pro forma before-tax termination statement.
10. Should an investor look at the NOI, the before-tax flows, or the after-tax flows in valuing a building? Explain.

15 The Lender's Evaluation

OBJECTIVES

When you finish this chapter, you should be able to:

- describe the type of procedures lenders use in arriving at decisions to lend.

- know what kind of information lenders want.

- discuss appraisals for income properties and particularly how values are estimated through capitalizing income.

- explain the difference between direct and yield capitalization methods.

- analyze the various techniques for obtaining capitalization rates and their use in value estimates.

- list the main criteria used by lenders in their decisions, and explain their logic and utility.

LENDERS INVEST IN mortgage loans by advancing a sum of money (the loan) to obtain a future stream of cash consisting of the interest and amortization payments plus payment of the balance, if any (a balloon or reversion). In deciding whether or not to invest in a particular loan, lenders seek as much assurance as possible that the future payments will be made on time and with minimum collection costs.

A major element in evaluating loans on income properties is their projected cash flows. However, a great deal of supplementary information is also required. Some is needed to check the soundness of the investment project, the location and suitability of the building, and the reliability of the income estimates. More data are also required to qualify the applicant in terms of experience, financial assets, and trustworthiness.

Most institutional lenders are required to use an appraisal of a property in order to assure themselves that their decisions are based on current estimates of its market value. These appraisals place most emphasis on the income approach to valuation, but the estimates based on cash flows are reconciled with values established through the sales comparison and cost approaches.

The projection and evaluation of cash flows is additionally important because lenders may also participate in the cash flow over and above the amount pledged to their debt service. As a result, some of the lenders' return often depends on the growth of the property's income or its final sales price. In participations— also called *kickers*—lenders must perform analysis identical to that of other investors in order to judge their potential returns and risks.

When we think of commercial lenders as a group, we usually think first of conventional lenders, such as insurance companies, pension funds, or bankers. However, a great deal of mortgage money is advanced on junior mortgages by sellers, foreign sources, and less risk-averse lenders. In these cases also, judgment is likely to be based on a complete analysis of the investment potential of the property.

THE SUBMISSION PROCESS

Decisions to lend depend on an orderly organization of the data needed to find the profitability and risk of each proposal. Most lenders specify the information they require from prospective borrowers in the form of a **submission package** before they will consider a loan. A good deal of information is filled in on prepared forms that call for detailed financial data. Prospective borrowers must also furnish supplemental information aimed at showing that the market will accept the project and that the cost and revenue projections are reasonable.

Lenders have related internal forms that their underwriters use to summarize the pertinent information from the submission package, to adjust it to more reasonable estimates, and to make a recommendation to the loan committee. When loans go bad, it is often because key data were not analyzed before the loan was made.

The Submission Package

The details of each submission package vary with the size of the loan and on whether it covers an existing building or a proposed development. Submissions range in length from a few pages to hundreds, but all must contain the background needed for the lender to decide whether the projected income will be sufficient to make the loan and investment sensible. The economic factors that influence success must be carefully evaluated. To prosper, the borrower must have both necessary skills and capital. Design and construction must conform to current and future market needs and tastes. Cost and revenue projections must be sound.

Submission packages include at least eight types of information:

1. the loan and its security
2. the location of the project
3. the details of the property
4. an evaluation of the market
5. the borrower's background and financial responsibility
6. pro forma projected financial statements and feasibility analysis
7. an appraisal
8. a summary of the prospects for the project

Each of these items is discussed in more detail below.

The Loan and its Security

Submissions usually begin with a statement about the specifics of the loan requested, its security, and the applicant. Important in consideration of the loan are its amount, interest rate, the payment constant, the maturity, fees, and any participation agreements. The commitment to make the loan includes a number of provisos, such as the time within which the loan must be closed, other financing on the property, and required legal opinions.

The property is briefly described, showing its selling price and estimated value, its type, size, and special features. The borrower is named, but it may be a shell corporation or a general partner with few assets. What borrower is listed depends on the legal structure believed most advantageous. In the section covering the borrower's background, whatever organizational form is named is backed up by information about the actual persons involved.

In addition to describing the loan requested and its terms, the submission shows how these relate to the security. It catalogs the loan-to-value ratio, the mortgage per square foot, and similar general items such as debt coverage and the break-even point.

Location, Property, and Market

The second, third, and fourth items in the submission package describe in detail the location, the project, and its market. Information on location begins in general terms and becomes specific. Included is information on the economic viability of the city, a more detailed study of the neighborhood, and very specific information on the site including soil conditions, utilities, and zoning. The economic and statistical data are supplemented with photos of the neighborhood and the city.

The project itself must be completely delineated in the submission. A detailed description of the project, its design, its cost, and its potential or expected revenues should be included. Submissions contain a general description as well as specific plans and specifications. Information on such factors as the number of rooms, the number of apartments, space, amenities, parking, and rent range is needed for the final decision. This information must be thorough enough to show the lender that the cost estimates are accurate and that the building will be able to generate the required revenue.

The location and property descriptions lead into a very specific projection of the market for the project. It is not sufficient simply to know what the potential rent schedule will be; lenders want estimates of actual revenues. Economic and statistical information on the location and its market are supplemented by photographs of the neighborhood and city. Since lenders and investors are concerned with cash flows over a 5- to 10-year holding period, during which many changes can occur, consideration of possible competition as well as the market's relative strength are especially significant.

Information about the Borrower

Of special importance are facts about the applicant and the other principals involved in the venture, including the contractors and professionals providing supporting service. Lenders often have a minimum requirement for the number of projects that applicants have successfully completed and rented out or sold. Lenders are concerned with both the personal and corporate financial condition of the applicants. Information on the principals must include all financial guarantees and contingent obligations. Any past problems should be revealed in the submission package, since they will surface during the credit check. Increasingly lenders insist on a verification that basic legal conditions and requirements are being adhered to. The lender also wants—and may make the approval contingent on—relevent title insurance documents, guarantees, bonds, or letters of credit and other documents supporting the venture.

Pro Forma Financial Statements and Appraisals

Because inflation and disinflation have so altered traditional income analysis and because estimates of financial feasibility from both the lender's and the borrower's points of view require detailed knowledge, the submission package is likely to contain complete projected pro forma cash flow statements, an analysis of the project's feasibility, and an appraisal report, the latter usually prepared by an independent fee appraiser. How much credence is given one type of financial presentation over the other depends on the skills of the lenders' underwriters, and on those of the loan committee. In any case, the lender needs the type of information contained in the submission package to arrive at an independent judgment about whether or not to grant the loan.

The Summary

Finally, the submission package must contain an analysis showing that the project's cash flow should be able to meet the debt service requirements. If debt payments cannot be met, the lender wants to be as certain as possible that the mortgage security is large enough to protect the lender against most dangers of loss upon foreclosure or sale. These "bottom line" estimates use both the traditional mortgage appraisal and an analysis of the pro forma financial statements.

The information required for the submission is clearly similar to that needed by developers for their own decision making. Although they might modify assumptions about certain costs, revenues, and profitability for their own purposes, and although they may be far more concerned about their personal tax condition and ultimate risk and profitability, the planning performed by developers parallels that required of lenders. They cannot proceed either to development or to negotiate a purchase until they receive a commitment from a lender.

THE APPRAISAL

Although all of the information in the submission package is used in the lender's underwriting process, customarily lenders have paid most attention to the market value estimated through the appraisal process. The regulations governing financial institutions frequently require that an adequate appraisal be performed. The appraisal must be considered before a loan is made and must remain in every loan file. Consequently, we must now examine the appraisal process in some detail before returning to the underwriting process lenders apply to the loan submission package.

The appraisal is an attempt to assemble all the elements that affect a property's present and future benefits so the amount the market is willing to pay now and will be willing to pay in the future can be estimated and a value assigned. How well the task is accomplished depends on the extent and accuracy of the facts gathered and on the skill of the appraiser.

Every time lenders have suffered large losses on income properties, appraisals have come under attack. Critics of appraisers claim that their basic techniques are flawed; that they depend too much on judgment and can be distorted by overly optimistic expectations. They say that appraisers put too much weight on borrowers' projections of the future. If buyers are paying prices higher than those that will be supported by future revenues, the appraisal process tends to accept their valuations. Estimated values exceed those that will prevail when buyers take a more realistic approach to the future.

THE INCOME APPROACH TO VALUE

Chapter 13 described how appraisers attempt to reconcile estimates of value obtained through three separate techniques—sales comparison, cost analysis, and the income approach—before arriving at their value estimate. Because the income approach is the least useful for valuing single-family houses, we delayed discussing it until now.

The **income approach** (also called the economic approach) assumes that the value of a property equals the present value of all future benefits that will flow from it. There are four steps involved in finding this value:

1. The particular income or benefits to be valued is selected.
2. Either a current value or future values of this income is estimated. As Table 14-5 in Chapter 14 made clear, different valuation techniques may be applied depending on the time periods and types of benefits included in the analysis.
3. A specific capitalization or discount rate is chosen. The **capitalization rate** relates the property's income to its value. Rates vary with time, with the kind of property, and with location.
4. The appraiser uses the process of capitalization to translate the expected income into an estimate of present value.

Capitalization

In the most general case, **capitalization** estimates the present value of a property by discounting at a selected interest rate the future benefits it is expected to provide:

$$\text{value} = \frac{\text{expected income}}{\text{interest rate}} \qquad V = \frac{I}{i} \tag{15.1}$$

Appraisers speak of two capitalization methods: direct and yield capitalization.

Direct capitalization converts, in one step, a projection of a single year's income into value. Thus it follows directly from Equation 15.1. First, the net operating income for a year is estimated. Then a capitalization rate is chosen that reflects observations of the relationship between income and value. In this technique, the capitalization rate (R) is usually found directly from the market. The next section describes methods used to extract the capitalization rate from sales data by dividing the net income of comparable properties by the price each sold for, and then adjusting the comparable data to provide a capitalization rate for the property being appraised.

$$\text{Capitalization rate} = \frac{\text{net operating income}}{\text{sales price}} \qquad \textbf{(15.2)}$$

$$R = \frac{\text{NOI}}{\text{SP}}$$

On the basis of such estimated capitalization (or "cap") rates and a projected income, the process of capitalization results in an estimated value for the property being appraised.

$$\text{Value} = \frac{\text{net operating income}}{\text{capitalization rate}} \qquad \textbf{(15.3)}$$

$$V = \frac{\text{NOI}}{R}$$

Yield capitalization converts a stream of future benefits to present value through discounting by a yield or rate of return estimated as that required to obtain capital of the type being valued. After the future cash flows have been projected and the correct yield or discount rate has been estimated, the data are inserted in Equation 3.3:

$$PV = \frac{CF_1}{1+i} + \frac{CF_2}{(1+i)^2} + \frac{CF_3}{(1+i)^3} + \cdots + \frac{CF_n}{(1+i)^n} \qquad \textbf{(15.4)}$$

Before the widespread use of financial calculators and personal computers, solving such problems by hand or with the use of interest factor tables was quite arduous and led to the development of a number of specialized methods for this purpose. Now it is usually simpler to solve for present values directly than to use what were designed as shortcut methods.

Estimating Income

The initial job of the appraiser is to project the cash flows or income benefits that must be capitalized to find the value of a property. The previous chapter (especially Tables 14-2 and 14.4) examined in detail the forms that such income estimates take and some of the methods and difficulties in finding good information. Depending on the method used, the income estimate may cover only a single year or the entire holding period.

The amount of detail in an appraisal is determined by how much time the appraiser has available and the complexity of the problem. Appraisers usually complain that their fees are inadequate for them to spend the time to obtain all the information they should have. Although not stated as such, their estimates of market value should be recognized as having a rather wide range of probabilities.

Appraisals differ in the income flows they project and, therefore, in the capitalization rate which is applied. In the following section we discuss four different approaches to selecting the income to be estimated and the capitalization rate to be used in the valuation. In theory, even though the estimate of cash flow for each approach may differ greatly from the others, the value estimates of all the approaches should be the same if the proper capitalization rate for each flow is found. The rate for each income flow will differ by exactly the amount needed to give the proper value. Appraisers often use two or three separate techniques as a check against the others.

In fact, appraisers use different income capitalization techniques because they believe one or another is more likely to be accurate in a particular set of circumstances. The amount of information they can obtain about income flows or the independent knowledge they have to choose a correct capitalization rate differs from time to time and by type of property.

DIRECT CAPITALIZATION

In direct capitalization techniques, capitalization rates are found by use of market data for comparable sales or yields. Information from these comparables is gathered and the capitalization rate to be applied is extracted from it. It is assumed that the data from the market correctly reflects the valuation that investors place on income and, therefore, that the relationships of the data show a correct capitalization rate. Before agreeing to the price they pay, rational investors project their total return to include cash flows both from operations and from capital appreciation or depreciation, and they make certain that they are not paying more than the capitalized values of the projected cash flows. As a result, market transactions reflect a yield or discount rate that equals or exceeds investors' minimum requirements. If the market was capitalizing at a higher rate (a lower value), they would not buy. A number of techniques can be used to extract the desired rate, of which three—comparable sales, gross income multiplier, and band of investment—are analyzed in the sections that follow.

An Overall Capitalization Rate

The simplest technique estimates the net operating income of a property for a year and then capitalizes it at a single **overall capitalization rate.** This rate does not distinguish between possible separate returns to land and buildings or to mortgages and equity. The income period may be last year's, next year's, or the projected first fully rented year.

EXAMPLE: An office building whose current year's net operating income (NOI) is $868,300 is to be valued. By examining comparable sales (as discussed next) the appraiser finds that a proper overall capitalization rate (R) is 9.7 per-cent. The value (V) of the property is estimated at $8.95 million (rounded) by applying Equation 15.3.

$$\text{Value} = \frac{\text{net operating income}}{\text{overall capitalization rate}}$$

$$V = \frac{\text{NOI}}{R}$$

$$V = \frac{\$868,300}{.097} = \$8,951,546$$

Comparable Sales

One of the easiest techniques of selecting capitalization rates is through market comparisons. The *comparable sales* or **market extraction method** finds a set of rates actually paid in the market by dividing each property's net operating income by its sales price. The appraiser lists the comparables and, using his or her judgment, adds any adjustments necessary due to differences in timing, financing, or attributes of the property such as size. In selecting com-parables and picking a specific rate, the appraiser makes certain that the income estimates and quoted prices are consistent with those of the property being valued.

This method makes no assumptions about income changes or reversions. It assumes that the market correctly defines an overall capitalization rate; that this rate can be extracted by market comparisons; and that it can be applied to the subject property's estimated net operating income.

EXAMPLE: Table 15-1 gives information taken from an appraiser's report used in the solution of Equation 15.3 in the previous example. The appraiser was asked to estimate the value of the office building with retail space, the stabilized net operating income of which he projected at $868,300. He found no other sales in the city comparable to the subject property, but he did find five sales spread over the previous 14 months in the wider metropolitan area. In all but one case, the size of the comparables was less than half that of the property being appraised and the information on their financing was inexact.

In deriving his estimate of the capitalization rate, he noted that the market cap rates varied from a low of 8.6 percent to a high of 10.3 percent. On the basis of a more detailed comparison of individual features, he concluded that the proper capitalization rate for the subject property was 9.7 percent. Therefore, the property was worth $8.95 million.

Note that this method sweeps many of the valuation problems under the table. It does not attempt to account for depreciation, for tax benefits, or for

Table 15-1
Obtaining the Capitalization Rate from Market Data

Comparable	Sale Date	Net Operating Income (I)	Sale Price (V)	Capitalization Rate (R)
1	3/86	$926,916	$10,200,000	0.091
2	10/85	300,873	3,500,000	0.086
3	10/85	154,800	1,600,000	0.097
4	2/85	436,900	4,250,000	0.103
5	2/85	290,856	2,960,000	0.098
Subject property	4/86	$868,300		

appreciation. It simply assumes that all of these factors have been properly taken into account by the market when the buyers of the other buildings decided how much to pay for a dollar of current net operating income. It then assumes that the time pattern, financing, and other variables for the subject building are close to the market average. A capitalization rate (R) is extracted from the other sales by dividing their sales price (SP) into their income (NOI):

$$R = \frac{\text{NOI}}{\text{SP}}$$

When this cap rate is divided into the estimated stabilized NOI for the subject property, the result, it is assumed, will be an adequate measure of current market value.

Gross Income Multipliers

Another simple method of converting projections of income into estimates of market value uses a **gross income multiplier (GIM)**. It is found by dividing the known sales prices of comparable properties by their gross incomes and adjusting for differences between the property being appraised and the others. To find the value of the property, the appraiser estimates its gross income (vacancies and operating expenses are not subtracted). This income is then multiplied by the multiplier estimated from the market, or:

$$V = I \times \text{GIM} \tag{15.5}$$

$$\text{where GIM} = \frac{\text{sales price}}{\text{gross income}}$$

Note that an income multiplier is the inverse of a cap rate. Rather than dividing income by price, the price is divided by income. Appraisers speak of multipliers or factors in contrast to the cap rate. Income multipliers can be based on net or other forms of income, but in the most common cases—as in this chapter— they use gross income not corrected for expenses.

EXAMPLE: An appraiser is asked to value an apartment house with an annual rent roll of $760,000. In a city of 100,000, she finds six somewhat comparable sales occurring over the preceding three months. Their calculated gross income multipliers range from 7.6 to 9.7 and are spread fairly evenly over that range. After adjustments, she estimates the gross income multiplier to be 8. The value of the apartment is $6,080,000, since

$$V = I \times GIM \qquad V = \$760,000 \times 8 = \$6,080,000$$

Apartment houses frequently sell on this basis. However, the knowledge gained in this manner has a considerable probable variance. For an exact estimate of the GIM to apply, corrections would have to be made for time, financing terms, size of buildings, age, prior maintenance, location, management, and normal vacancies, plus a number of other significant factors. The final estimated GIM of 8 and the resulting estimated value can be no more than an approximation.

The Band of Investment

Another method of deriving a capitalization rate is called the **band of investment.** The net operating income of a property is divided into two or more cash flows to cover the payments due the lender or lenders and the investors. Each of these flows, when discounted at its proper rate, determines the total value of the property. Each participant in financing a project expects to earn at a separate rate. If net operating income is capitalized by a rate equal to the weighted average of each source of financing times its required yield, the correct value of the property will result.

One application of this method, the **mortgage-equity method,** divides the capital for a property into that supplied by mortgages and that by equity holders. Their weighted average rate of return is the cost of capital for the property. It meets the current yields demanded by lenders and investors for the type of property being valued.

In using this method, appraisers find the mortgage constant (which is the lender's cash flow) demanded in the market. They also estimate from the market the yield that investors require in order to invest in similar properties. They then form a composite overall rate by weighting each return by the share of debt and equity required to purchase the property. Thus, the capitalization rate equals the loan-to-value ratio (L ÷ V) times the mortgage constant (K) plus the share of equity, which is the amount not financed by the mortgage $(1 - [L \div V])$, times the return on equity (ROE).

$$R = K\left(\frac{L}{V}\right) + \left(1 - \frac{L}{V}\right)(\text{ROE}) \tag{15.6}$$

Note that the yield on the equity (ROE) is the cash-on-cash return. It is also called the equity dividend rate.

EXAMPLE: Consider a property with next year's net operating income estimated at $100,000. It will be financed by a mortgage with an 80 percent loan-to-value ratio at 10 percent interest for 360 monthly payments, together with 20 percent of equity. The annual mortgage constant for a mortgage at 10 percent interest is .1053. This is the discount rate that makes the debt service payments equal to the mortgage's present value. The current first year's return on equity (ROE) is 12 percent. Inserting these data in equation 15.6, we find the capitalization rate to be .1082.

$$R = .1053(.80) + (1 - .80).12 = .1082$$

This cap rate is then used to capitalize the projected income, resulting in an estimated value of $924,000 (rounded):

$$V = \frac{\text{NOI}}{R} \qquad V = \frac{\$100,000}{.1082} = \$924,214$$

Problems in Estimating Capitalization Rates

The need for obtaining the proper capitalization or discount rates is obvious from the large errors that creep in if the capitalization rate is incorrect. Small variations in capitalization rates make big differences in estimated value. Consider a building in which the stabilized net operating income has been properly estimated at $100,000 but the appraiser must choose between capitalization rates of 8 percent and 9 percent—a smaller difference than is commonly found in the market. Depending on which rate is selected, the estimated value will differ by 12.5 percent, or $138,889 in this example:

$$V = \frac{\text{NOI}}{R} \qquad V = \frac{\$100,000}{.08} = \$1,250,000, \text{ or}$$

$$V = \frac{\$100,000}{.09} = \$1,111,111$$

Causes of Differences between Cap Rates   At least four major difficulties
are encountered in selecting capitalization rates.

1. Accurate market information that is applicable to the subject property is
   hard to find. The number of sales of similar types of income property in
   an area is limited. Each has a unique price-to-income ratio, depending on
   the reasons for selling, the financing available, the location, the building's
   age and its tenants. The appraiser must make ad hoc adjustments for each
   of these factors plus many similar ones.
2. We do not expect most properties to maintain their income flows forever.
   Buildings gradually lose their ability to earn the same income. They are a
   wasting asset. For this reason part of the investment must be recaptured
   from annual income. Some of the return must be set aside to maintain the
   value of the initial investment. This use or claim against the income to
   maintain the initial value of the investment is called **recapture.**

   The capitalization rate is the sum of the return *on* the investment
   and *of* the investment. The **return *on* investment** is the investor's
   equity yield; the **return *of* investment** is called the *recapture rate.* It
   measures the amount needed to maintain the investment at its original
   value.

   > **EXAMPLE:** Consider an investment of $100 in an oil well that prom-
   > ises to pay out $20 a year. What is the investor's return? If the well will be
   > depleted and worth nothing at the end of five years, the investment's yield
   > is zero. All of the cash flow is required to recapture the amount originally
   > invested. But if at the end of five years the investment in the well would
   > sell for $100, its yield is 20 percent, since none of the $20-a-year payments
   > would be needed for recapture. The entire cash flow is a return on the
   > investment.

3. As a result of inflation or improved markets, the income of a building may
   be expected to rise, as may its final selling price. Tables 14-2 and 14-4, for
   example, pictured a steady increase in income, which also resulted in a
   selling price well above cost. These potential changes in cash flow must
   be accounted for either in the estimated income (I) or in the capitalization rate (R).
4. We saw in Tables 14-2 and 14-4 that the pro forma statements gave at least
   six different estimates of future cash flows—net operating income and
   before- and after-tax flows with or without reversions on sale. Although by
   definition a proper capitalization rate exists to relate each type of income
   estimate to a building's value, finding the correct rate may be difficult.
   Each uses or neglects information that the others take into account. Moreover, incomplete techniques may leave out significant facts that make
   arriving at the correct capitalized value more difficult.

A key point is that the simple direct capitalization methods consider future income and appreciation as well as tax benefits only indirectly. It is not clear from the comparable data what assumptions purchasers are making about future income and prices nor what tax brackets marginal purchasers fall into. Yet these may be critical elements in the determination of both market value and the price specific investors are willing to pay.

In the pro forma cash flow income statements for Plaza Square in the last chapter (Tables 14-2 and 14-4), note the unevenness of the projected cash flows and the large expected reversion. The techniques that capitalize current income use this additional information only in an elementary fashion. As a result, other techniques have developed to conserve some of this additional knowledge.

YIELD CAPITALIZATION

The potential errors in direct capitalization have increased the use of yield capitalization. These methods (shown in the last two columns of Table 14-5) use the income flow for a property's holding period. Yield capitalization identifies all future cash flows, fixes an appropriate discount (yield) rate, and then discounts each future benefit so as to find the property's present value.

A number of complex procedures have been developed to take into account particular assumptions as to future patterns of cash flows, appreciation or depreciation, and changes in financing. Because of their complexity and degree of specialization, such techniques can be found in most appraisal texts and will not be detailed here. They include formulas for handling **recapture rates,** or the division of income into that part which is a return *of* investment, in contrast to the yield or the return *on* investment. Other methods, such as Ellwood formulas, which use mortgage-equity relationships, also take the various factors into account.

The Discounted Cash Flow Method

One of the most common techniques used in yield capitalization is the **discounted cash flow method.** As its name implies, this method is an application of the general procedures for estimating present values through discounting future cash flows. The discount rate can be the internal rate of return from comparable sales, or one constructed from the mortgage-equity, or other techniques.

In using this procedure, an appraiser, lender, or investor must project net operating income for each year of an estimated holding period. In addition, the final year's NOI is used to project a sales price that determines the final cash flow (reversion). The sales price is often derived by capitalizing the last year's NOI either by applying the current market cap rate (the method used for the Plaza Square building in Table 14-4) or by some rate considered to be the long-term normal cap rate (such as 10 percent).

The estimated discount rate (i) is applied to the cash flows. The discount factors for i are found in interest factor tables. The factors are multiplied by each year's projected cash flow, and the resulting products are summed to obtain an estimated present value.

EXAMPLE: An appraiser is given the cash flow projections for Plaza Square contained in Tables 14-2 and 14-4. From them, she abstracts the expected net operating incomes for each year of the holding period, as well as the expected cash flow upon sale. These data are shown in columns 2 and 3 of Table 15-2. Using the techniques discussed in the next paragraph, the appraiser concludes that a proper discount rate is 14 percent. From an interest factor table, she obtains and lists in column 4 the present-value factors (IFPV) needed to discount each year's expected cash flow. Column 5, the product of the preceding columns, shows the present value of each year's flow. Their sum, or $10,031,454, is the estimated value of the property. Rather than using the form shown in the table, the appraiser can insert the data (in thousands) directly into Equation 3.3 and solve rapidly with either a financial calculator or a computer:

$$PV = \frac{1470}{1.14} + \frac{1635}{1.14^2} + \frac{1814}{1.14^3} + \frac{1907}{1.14^4} + \frac{9877}{1.14^5} = 10,031 = \$10,031,454$$

Finding the Discount Rate

A basic problem in the discounted cash flow method is picking the proper discount rate. As in single-period capitalization techniques, estimated values are sensitive to small errors in the discount factor.

One method is to find the rate of return investors are asking in the market for investments with similar risks. For example, rates may be built up from either the risk-free (T-bill) or mortgage interest rates. Thus, in the Plaza Square example in Table 15-2, one method of finding a proper rate would be to build it up from a base equal to the mortgage rate of 10.5 percent. Then a further 3.5 percent could be added to this to account for added risks for owning the entire property as opposed to lending on a mortgage.

Appraisers also derive the discount rate from market comparisons. They have or can obtain pro forma statements for comparable buildings that have recently been sold. From the sales prices and the net operating income statements, they can solve for the buyers' internal rate of return. These IRRs can be adjusted in the same way used in the direct market comparison or capitalization approach. Since the market should discount cash flows from the subject property at the same rate, the IRR estimated from the market forms the correct discount rate. However, a comparison of the purchase price of the Plaza Square building in Table 14-1 and the value estimated in Table 15-2 demonstrates again the vast differences in values that result from minor changes in estimated cap rates.

Table 15-2
The Discounted Cash Flow Method
Plaza Square Building

Year	Net Operating Income	Reversion	Present Value Factor at 14%	Present Value
1	$1,469,938		0.8772	$1,289,419
2	1,635,409		0.7695	1,258,394
3	1,814,034		0.6750	1,224,421
4	1,907,374		0.5921	1,129,319
5	2,005,798		0.5194	1,041,749
5		$7,870,913	0.5194	4,088,152
Total present (market) value				$10,031,454

The discounted cash flow is the last of four different techniques we have illustrated. Each reflects a separate procedure used by appraisers to determine market value under the income approach. Each one, as well as innumerable similar possibilities, differs somewhat from the others either in estimating the cash flows to be capitalized or in the method of determining the capitalization rate. Since all of them find the value by applying the general equations of 15.1 and 3.3, any one can be used successfully if the appraiser projects the cash flows correctly and selects the appropriate discount factor.

Whether the estimate of the market value of a property turns out to be highly useful or nearly disastrous to the lender and investor depends on the appraiser's skill and judgment. Which technique offers the best chance for success depends on the availability of information, on the time available to analyze it, and on the ability of the user. The best procedures are those that enable the analyst to find the most complete and accurate data and to use them with the least chance of error. Because so many possibilities exist of making large errors from small differences in discount rates or income projections, appraisers usually check against the other approaches to value and may use several of the techniques available to convert income projections into value estimates.

UNDERWRITING STANDARDS

The loan application, the appraisal, and the related information submitted by the potential borrower form the basis used by the lenders' underwriters to analyze the request. The underwriter makes a recommendation to the loan committee to approve, to reject, or to negotiate new or additional conditions. Typically, lenders use a fairly standard set of criteria for their analysis. Figure

Figure 15-1
Typical Lender's Underwriting Criteria

- Borrowers' track record
- Location and improvements
- Market conditions
- Maximum loan-to-value ratio
- Minimum break-even ratio
- Maximum loan per unit
- Feasible vacancy losses
- Logical operating expense ratio
- Accuracy of appraisal
- Potential profitability
- Acceptable loan terms

15-1 presents a list of items taken from the summary sheet used by a large savings and loan in making decisions on requests for loans on income properties.

The Borrower and the Property

Even before proceeding to an economic analysis, the lender decides whether the request meets minimal standards. Do the borrowers have a good enough track record for the firm to be willing to deal with them? Is the property of an acceptable kind? The underwriter examines the property's location and the design, quality, and maintenance of the improvements. Many projects fail because of poor design or the failure of the owners to make repairs. On the other hand, some buildings may carry low prices because of poor prior management, which the prospective buyer could cure.

Current and prospective market conditions are important. Many loan requests show projected revenues far higher than the market can support. An expensive building in a run-down neighborhood will not be able to command top rents. A high rate of occupancy is not likely to last if the city as a whole has a high vacancy rate.

Maximum Loans

Several factors determine whether or not the amount requested is too high. The loan-to-value ratio is the first hurdle. As we have seen, this ratio is the amount of the loan divided by the market value or sales price of the property. For some lenders, a maximum ratio is set by government regulations. Others set their own, and they vary by type of property and market demand. In the example of Plaza Square (Table 14-1) the investors request a $12,123,200 mortgage for a building appraised at $15,154,000. The loan-to-value ratio is 80 percent—just about at many lenders' limits, which rarely are above 80 percent of value.

Debt Service Coverage Ratio   In many cases, the maximum loan is set by the **debt service coverage ratio** which is the ratio of net operating income over debt service. It measures a margin of error available to borrowers in projected NOI before they run a negative cash flow. As a result, it is a rough measure of risk. It shows how much income could fall while still covering the debt service payments.

In the case of Plaza Square, the first year's NOI is projected to be $1,469,938 (see Table 15-2). The first year's debt service, based on a loan request of $12,123,200, is $1,330,748. Thus the debt service coverage ratio is:

$$\text{Debt coverage ratio} = \frac{\text{NOI}}{\text{debt payment}} = \frac{\$1,469,938}{\$1,330,748} = 1.10 \qquad (15.7)$$

The ratio of 1.10 is below 1.25, which is the ratio many lenders have traditionally set as the minimum ratio they will accept. This means that the initial ratio of NOI to debt service is too risky for many lenders.

If the lender believes the projected first year's income but will lend only when the coverage ratio is 1.25, we can calculate how much the loan would have to be reduced or the terms of the loan altered to make it conform to the 1.25 ratio. Dividing the NOI by the minimum debt service coverage ratio, we obtain the maximum amount of debt payment the income can support:

$$\text{Maximum debt payment} = \frac{\text{NOI}}{\text{minimum debt coverage ratio}} \qquad (15.8)$$
$$= \frac{\$1,469,938}{1.25} = \$1,175,950$$

The annual mortgage constant for a 10.5 percent 30-year loan is .10977. It can be used with the maximum supportable debt service to solve for the maximum loan. By putting the information into the necessary equation, we find the answer:

$$\text{Maximum loan} = \frac{\text{maximum debt payment}}{\text{mortgage constant}} \qquad (15.9)$$
$$= \frac{\$1,175,950}{.10977} = \$10,712,854$$

If the mortgage request exceeds the maximum loan calculated in this way, the lender might insist on a reduction of the amount requested. If investors were not able to come up with the additional cash, they could suggest alternatives. Either the mortgage constant could be reduced or the investor might be allowed to put up some percentage of the difference in the form of a cash reserve that could be used only with permission of the lender.

To find how much the mortgage constant would have to be reduced, we can divide the desired mortgage into the maximum debt payment (given the NOI and minimum coverage ratio). The result shows a maximum annual mortgage constant of .097.

$$\text{Maximum mortgage constant} = \frac{\text{maximum debt payment}}{\text{desired mortgage}} \qquad (15.10)$$
$$= \frac{\$1,175,950}{\$12,123,200} = .097$$

If the lender would reduce the interest rate to 9 percent or allow negative amortization, the loan could be granted even if the 1.25 coverage ratio was considered inviolable.

One good argument for allowing a lower initial coverage ratio can be made by calculating the coverage ratio for later years. It surpasses 1.35 in the third year and reaches 1.50 by the fifth year. Similar arguments based on an expected inflationary increase in revenues leads many lenders to accept lower initial year ratios. In some cases they may be even lower than 1.00, provided that the initial reserves are considered adequate.

The Break-even Ratio   A third limit on the amount lent is frequently the requirement that the break-even ratio be below a maximum. Lenders want to know how far income can fall below its projected amount without endangering loan repayments. The **break-even ratio** is a measure of their safety. It is constructed by dividing the amount of payments needed to meet the building's expenses and debt service payments by the gross possible income. The ratio and its calculation for the Plaza Square building are:

$$\text{Break-even ratio} = \frac{\text{operating expenses} + \text{debt service}}{\text{gross possible income}} \qquad (15.11)$$
$$= \frac{\$686,745 + \$1,330,748}{\$2,435,585} = 82.8\%$$

As this ratio indicates, the building must be 82.8 percent occupied to meet its minimum cash flow requirements. If the vacancies rise above 17.2 percent, the building will not break even. Its ratio is below the 84 percent level that many lenders in the past considered a maximum break-even ratio. They would not lend if the ratio exceeded this maximum. However, assumptions that inflation would bring about a faster rise in revenues than debt service caused many lenders to shade this as well as other maximums.

Loan per Unit   A final limit on the size of loans is often the requirement that the amount lent per unit (per square foot in commercial buildings or per apartment in residential buildings) not exceed a maximum derived from standard costs in the locality. In the Plaza Square case, the underwriter finds that the cost per square foot is $91 plus $20,400 per parking unit. Since the loan is 80 percent of value, the loan is $72.80 per square foot and $16,320 per parking space. Depending on other costs in the locality, these could be above or below the lender's maximum.

The logic of limiting the loan per square foot is to make sure that the building is competitive. A building with a loan that is higher than average per unit will have trouble earning the necessary debt service. For example, office buildings rent per square foot. A property's rents are limited by those of its neighbors. If a property's costs and **loan per unit** exceed those of its neighbors, the revenue collected will be less per dollar of loan, and thus the capacity to meet payments if reverses occur is less. A ratio that is too high alerts the underwriters to this potential danger.

The Economic Rationale

If the amount of loan requested seems reasonable, the underwriter must decide whether the entire proposal makes economic sense. Will the property carry the loan? This primarily means checking the projections contained in the appraisal and pro forma operating and termination statements.

Vacancy and Collection Losses   An obvious starting point is with the **vacancy and collection loss ratio.** It measures the amount of projected losses in revenue from vacancies and collection losses divided by gross rents. It may be too high or too low. The market usually assumes that this ratio will be 5 percent and projects operating revenues on that basis.

But certain types of property, such as apartments with high seasonal turnovers, have vacancies that are rarely that low. A high turnover means that the ratio will be considerably larger than 5 percent. The underwriter must check that this fact is included in the projection of gross effective income. In other cases, weak markets may result in 15 percent to 20 percent vacancies throughout the area. If the market has many other buildings with high vacancies, an underwriter must be suspicious of projections showing a 5 percent vacancy ratio. This holds true even if the property shows low vacancies currently.

The Operating Expense Ratio   To find the **operating expense ratio,** the total operating expenses are divided by effective gross income, which includes both gross rents and other income. Both must be taken for a stabilized year; in the project's first year or in an oversupplied market, higher than normal vacancies will lower effective income and balloon this ratio.

In the Plaza Square case, the operating expense ratio is calculated as follows:

$$\text{Operating expense ratio} = \frac{\text{operating expense}}{\text{gross rents} + \text{other income}} \qquad (15.12)$$

$$= \frac{\$686,745}{\$2,145,407 + \$290,178} = 28.2\%$$

Again, the underwriters compare this ratio with those of competitive buildings. It should be neither much higher nor much lower than comparable ratios. If it is too low, it creates suspicion that some expenses have been omitted. If it is too high, it raises questions about the efficiency of the building. Was it jerry-built or poorly planned so that its maintenance costs run above normal? If the ratio is too high, less revenue will be left after maintenance to meet debt payments and profits.

The Lender's Economic Forecast   These simple ratio tests give the underwriter some feel for the accuracy of the operating statements and the appraisal. However, more critical analysis must be applied to the income projections and the capitalization rates. The underwriter asks whether the projections and the techniques used by the appraiser meet the lender's standards. The lender needs independent market information. It must check the appraisal against its own knowledge and data about the market. Then the lender must decide whether it trusts the current market or feels the need to adopt less exuberant expectations.

The lender knows that in a competitive lending atmosphere it will lose the loan to another lender if it insists that the value of the property is less than that estimated by other appraisers and underwriters. It must decide whether it wants to make the loan badly enough to accept the risks of a market in which buildings are being valued and appraised higher on the basis, as British economist John Maynard Keynes put it, of "animal spirits." The lender knows from experience how often markets become carried away, and the record shows that in such periods many lenders assume risks that are far too great.

Even though the appraisal and maximum loan may meet the lender's criteria, the lender must still analyze the project from the investor's point of view as well. The amount of secondary loans and their terms are significant. If the cash flow left after the lender's debt service must go to meet other debt payments, the safety margin is reduced. If interest is accrued and a large balloon payment must be met after a year or two, the success of the project may be too dependent on the accuracy of the income projections and the assumptions as to the future sale and loan market.

If the lender plans to participate in the project, the profit possibilities are even more critical, as are the exact terms. Many lenders have found that borrowers are unwilling to terminate unprofitable ventures because they have nothing to lose by delay if all of the funds at risk belong to the lenders. Kickers may look fine on paper, but they are worth nothing unless the project is economically viable.

The Loan Terms

Some lenders have firm criteria that they insist must be met; a loan that does not measure up is rejected. Others recognize that some feaures may be negotiable. Standard loans are more likely to have to pass a single pass-or-fail test, whereas secondary loans made by sellers may be completely reworked. Falling between these extremes are loans in which the lender makes adjustments in return for fees, a higher interest rate, and participation.

Mortgage bankers and brokers become specialists in shaping terms to particular situations. They often work with a variety of lenders, each of whom has somewhat different criteria. Part of their function is to show prospective borrowers the types of terms possible and how they can be obtained. The rest of the book explains how the borrowing problem appears to investors and presents some common solutions.

SUMMARY

Loan submission packages are planned to provide lenders with the information they need for profitable decisions. The package includes a loan application and the specifics of the requested loan.

Independent appraisals have traditionally been central to lenders' analyses. The appraisals contain cost and market comparisons, but for income properties emphasis has been placed on the income approach. Projected incomes are capitalized or discounted to arrive at an estimated value.

There are a number of different techniques used in the income approach to valuation. They differ in the income (cash flow) periods covered, in the use of information on potential appreciation and depreciation (recapture), and in their treatment of financing and debt service. Which one works best depends on available information and on the analyst's skills. The advantage to using more detailed approaches is that important information is less likely to be neglected.

In all the methods of appraising income property, it is important that the appraisers include all the necessary factors in projecting cash flows and selecting capitalization rates. Small errors in rates lead to large variations in values. Because data are so prone to error, appraisers are likely to check their valuations by using more than one technique.

Lenders usually consider a broad set of criteria in deciding whether and how much to lend. They are interested primarily in the soundness of the project and the ability of the borrower to make it pay off. However, they also apply various ratio tests: debt coverage, loan-to-value, break-even, and vacancy and operating expense ratios. The loan limits set in these tests have been proven by experience to be safe on average. If a loan request fails a particular test, it must either have major offsetting advantages or be restructured to meet the standards.

KEY TERMS

band of investment

break-even ratio

capitalization

capitalization rate

debt service coverage ratio

direct capitalization

discounted cash flow method

gross income multiplier (GIM)

income approach

loan per unit

market extraction method

mortgage-equity method

operating expense ratio

overall capitalization rate

recapture

recapture rate

return *of* investment

return *on* investment

submission package

vacancy and collection loss ratio

yield capitalization

QUESTIONS

1. What is the most important information lenders look for in the submission package?
2. Describe the income approach to valuation.
3. Why is it so difficult to obtain accurate cap rate estimates?
4. Among those appraisal techniques using direct capitalization, which appears most logical? Why?
5. Explain the differences between direct and yield capitalization.
6. The NOI of an office building is estimated to be $150,000. The market yield on equity is 15 percent, while the mortgage associated with the building is for 30 years at 13 percent. The mortgage covers 80 percent of the value. Apply the band of investment technique to find the value of the property.
7. The NOI of a property is $500,000 in year 1 and it appreciates at 5 percent per year. It is sold in year 5 with a cap rate of 9.5 percent applying to the NOI of year 5. The discount rate investors use is 15 percent. Find the value of the property using the discounted cash flow method.
8. What are the main factors determining whether the loan amount requested is too high?
9. Calculate the maximum debt payments for the properties in questions 6 and 7, assuming first a maximum debt coverage ratio 1.25 and then 1.10 for each.
10. Define and explain the logic underlying the following ratios:
    break-even ratio
    loan per unit
    vacancy and collection loss ratio
    operating expense ratio

16 Taxes and the Investment Decision

OBJECTIVES

When you finish this chapter, you should be able to:

- explain the background for and the treatment of real estate investments under tax reform.

- describe the factors that enter into a decision about what form of ownership to use in holding property.

- discuss the features in the ownership of real property that can yield tax benefits not usually available in other investments.

- show how depreciation deductions larger than actual losses in value can reduce tax liabilities.

- explain the concept of passive income and the special relief granted to active participants in rental real estate.

- describe the tax credits available for certain real estate investments.

- outline methods of postponing taxes on sale.

Beginning in the 1970s—and especially after the large increase in tax benefits in 1981—real estate decision making was dominated by tax considerations. One of the objectives of the Tax Reform Act of 1986 was to reverse this situation in the hope that taxes would once again be only one of many factors determining the economic feasibility and profitability of real estate investments.

Before tax reform, tax considerations had become predominant because of high marginal tax rates. Investing in real estate was a way of sharply reducing the impact of these high rates. As a result, innumerable real estate investments were sold based not on the economic feasibility of the underlying property, but rather on the promise that all of the required equity could be paid for at the expense of the government through reduced tax payments. This was possible because, if ownership was properly structured, tax losses flowing through to the investor would reduce taxable income from other sources—such as salary or dividends—and, therefore, the amount the investor paid in taxes.

Tax savings were large enough to pay for the real estate investment from which the savings flowed. Tens of thousands of properties were sold because the amounts owed the government in income taxes could be reduced by a change in ownership. The Tax Reform Act of 1986 attempted to curtail this practice by defining income from real estate investments as income from **passive activities.** These were defined as (1) trade or business activities in which the taxpayer (or spouse) does not materially participate by being involved on a regular, continuous, and substantial basis, and (2) rental activities where payments are primarily for the use of tangible property.

Under the Tax Reform Act (and after a transition period for previously owned property), income from passive activities can no longer be used to offset other types of income, with certain exceptions discussed later. Instead, passive income must be separated from other income. Losses from such income can be used only to offset income or gains from other passive activities, or carried forward to offset such positive income in future years. This change in the tax law, together with lower marginal tax brackets, shifts the emphasis in real estate investment analysis from tax avoidance to economic feasibility.

THE MOVEMENT FOR TAX REFORM

There were at least six major objectives of the tax reform movement:*

1. Simplify reporting for taxes and make it unnecessary for most families to itemize deductions.

*See *Newsweek,* August 25, 1986, especially the articles by Senator Daniel P. Moynihan and Robert Samuelson.

2. Reduce the number of tax brackets.
3. Reduce individual tax rates and tax payments. It was estimated that only 20 percent to 25 percent of families would have income above the 15 percent tax bracket.
4. Remove completely most low-income families from the tax rolls.
5. Remove tax considerations from their preeminent role in determining where and when investments would be made.
6. Increase fairness and raise revenues by reducing the major tax shelters, especially the ownership of real estate through limited partnerships.

The drive for tax reform was fueled by a belief that the tax system had become increasingly complex and unfair. Too many decisions were primarily tax-driven. Complex tax preferences hindered overall economic performance more than they helped. Because so much income escaped from the tax net, people with high incomes were able to pay few if any taxes, while the average taxpayer paid too much. By making the system more equitable, the amount collected from the individual tax could be reduced and marginal tax rates could be drastically cut.

Because there had been a large glut of income properties throughout the country, and high vacancy rates, these changes encountered far less opposition from owners of real estate than might have been predicted. Perhaps many believed that when the excess capacity of such property disappeared and shortages existed once again, it would be possible to remove the more restrictive clauses from the tax code. Many recognized that after such a drastic revision there was likely to be a long period during which numerous amendments would be enacted.

The Major Changes

Although the Tax Reform Act to change the revenue code was far from simple (it measured well over a thousand pages), only a few basic techniques were used to accomplish its purpose.

- The amount of income exempted from taxation for each taxpayer, spouse, and dependent was raised to $2,000.
- The standard deduction—the amount that can be subtracted from gross income by those taxpayers not itemizing specific deductions—was raised to $3,000 on individual returns and to $5,000 on joint returns.
- The number of tax brackets was reduced from 15 to 3 (0, 15 percent, and 28 percent) plus some additional surcharges for upper-income families (those with family incomes above $71,900).
- A number of authorized deductions from taxable income, as well as tax credits, were either reduced or removed completely. These included such deductions as those for two-earner families, state and local sales taxes, interest, some charitable contributions, and a portion of employee business expenses.

- Some tax shelters were abolished. The most significant tax shelter that was changed for real estate investors eliminated the use of tax losses from most passive activities to reduce taxable income from other sources.
- The investment tax credit was abolished and the period over which real property could be depreciated was lengthened.
- Tax benefits for low-income, rehabilitated, and historic properties were reduced.
- The right to exclude a percentage of capital gains from taxable income was removed.

Changes in the tax code are made almost every year, and major revisions take place every two or three years. Therefore, any description of the tax code more than a few months old is likely to be out of date. Furthermore, the Tax Reform Act of 1986 contained numerous phase-in or transition rules as well as ambiguities that could only be resolved by regulations and interpretations from the Internal Revenue Service (IRS). Any description of how the tax system works becomes rapidly dated. Investors contemplating a specific transaction should check the current rules with a tax lawyer or an accountant.

Regardless of the exact provisions of the tax code at any particular time, those involved in real estate finance cannot understand many financing techniques unless they themselves recognize how their decisions are influenced by tax considerations.

A basic knowledge of how the tax system affects property values and the advantages of particular financing methods is necessary for the analysis of most real estate transactions. Armed with such knowledge, investors can judge the significance of tax issues in specific proposals, foresee how they would be affected by changes in the tax laws, and decide how to incorporate such changes into their investment decisions.

Tax rates and the amount of taxes owed depend on the form of ownership used to hold property. Therefore, one of the earliest decisions in planning an investment in real estate is how the property should be held. This decision also influences risks and other factors in addition to taxes. This chapter examines ten different methods of owning real estate; it then details the general theory of how tax considerations can make real estate investments more favorable than other types of investment.

SELECTING THE FORM OF OWNERSHIP

Early in the investment decision process, an investor must decide how a particular proposal should be structured, both in terms of the amount of debt and equity and also how the equity should be raised and owned. The form of ownership and the relationships among those who furnish various amounts of debt and equity affect taxes, profits, and risks. In addition, there are also a number of mixed relationships based on leases, as well as different forms of participation agreements and options that must be incorporated into the investment decision.

Property can be owned in a variety of legal forms. Each may differ somewhat from the others in the following ways:

- the amount of income taxes to be paid
- the amount of personal liability
- the ease of transferring ownership rights
- the continuity of the enterprise
- how much personal management is demanded or possible
- the amount of regulation, tax preparation, and public reporting
- to a minor extent, the permissible activities of the owners

Furthermore, ownership agreements often spell out rights to compensation, and they may disproportionately allocate certain charges and benefits to one owner over another.

Individual Ownership, Joint Tenancy, and Tenancy in Common

The simplest and most common way of holding property is through **individual ownership.** Although most profits or losses from individual ownership of businesses and trades are reported as part of the owner's income, special provisions apply (as later sections make clear) if income comes primarily from renting property. Moreover, the owner is liable *without limit* for any debts, injury, or similar claims of persons damaged through the property. Furthermore, the property will be subject to liens for any of the owner's other debts.

Joint tenancies and tenancies in common are similar to individual ownership but are based on ownership by two or more persons. They differ from each other primarily with respect to the share of ownership, the rights of survivorship, and potential liabilities for federal estate taxes. In a **joint tenancy,** the ownership interests are equal for all the owners and the survivor or survivors own the property. In a **tenancy in common,** the owners may have unequal shares in the property and the ownership interest of the deceased becomes part of his or her estate. Taxes and liability basically follow the rules of individual ownership. Problems with tenancies in common arise when there is disagreement about the management or sale of the property; all owners must agree to the terms and conditions before a sale is possible.

Corporations

Among businesses that have grown to sufficient size, the **corporation** becomes the most widely used form of ownership. This is as true in real estate as it is in other fields. Corporations are creatures of the state and must be chartered by it; what a corporation can or cannot do is limited by its charter. Many states have special rules and taxes that apply only to real estate corporations.

The disadvantages of the corporation form are primarily in taxation and recordkeeping:

- Since it is a legal entity, the corporation's profits are taxable.
- The corporation pays the state special fees for its charter. Chartering also involves special legal advice and expenses.
- Certain taxes must be paid simply for the corporation to continue in existence, whether the firm is profitable or not.
- The records of major actions requiring approval by corporate directors must be kept in a specified form.
- Other taxes must be paid in order to transfer stock.

The most important influence on the decision whether or not to use this form of ownership is the tax on corporate profits. Corporations are usually double-taxation entities. The corporation must pay a tax on its profits, and then the stockholders are taxed on its dividends when they receive them. On the other hand, many publicly traded real estate corporations have a record of paying few if any taxes. Their depreciation allowances and interest write-offs are so large that they are able to make decisions as though they were tax-exempt.

A major advantage of this form is that the corporation has limited liability; its stockholders are not responsible for corporate debts, and losses are limited to the invested capital. Further, the corporation has a life of its own, and its stocks are easily transferred from one shareholder to another. Finally, a corporation can hide its ownership, thereby affording considerable privacy to its stockholders.

General Partnerships and Joint Ventures

The partnership is the usual and traditional form of holding property among several individuals if they wish to remain unincorporated. The role of the partnership has become far more important in recent years. To gather large amounts of investment capital, partnerships with thousands of individual partners have been formed. This development has caused basic changes in the entire field of real estate investing and lending.

The problem with partnerships lies in terms of liability. In **general partnerships,** normally each partner can bind the group, and an act of the firm is the responsibility of all. Each partner is usually liable for the entire debt and any personal liabilities created by the property owned by the partnership. The advantage of holding property in a partnership is that the partnership pays no income tax in and of itself, even though it files its own return for information purposes. Instead, each partner picks up his or her own share of the total return and includes it on his or her personal income tax return.

General partnerships have great flexibility. The ownership and compensation shares and responsibilities are spelled out in the partnership agreements. These can be drafted to match each investor's risk-to-return objectives. Management responsibilities, tax benefits, and cash flows can be allocated in any way the partners wish. The rights of each investor are established, preferably in the partnership agreement.

A **joint venture** is a partnership formed for a single purpose. It is most common in real estate and construction, and its purpose is usually the purchase, development, or ownership of a single property.

Limited Partnerships and Syndicates

Limited partnerships have been one of the fastest growing forms of real estate ownership. One of the objectives of the tax-reform movement was to reduce some of their advantages. In a **limited partnership,** the control and liability of certain of the partners are curtailed by the division of the partnership into general and limited partners. The general partners are subject to the usual rules of liability and have a voice in management and control. The limited partners may have no voice in management; their liability is usually limited to their initial capital contribution. The partnership need not dissolve because of the death of a limited partner, as it must by the death of a general partner. Transferability of ownership interests in a limited partnership is curtailed and may not even be possible.

Limited partnerships frequently take the form of public or private syndicates. A **syndicate** is a group of investors gathered together to invest in one or more properties. The promoter usually designates the general partner and attracts investors through securities brokers. Promoters often receive up-front compensation for their efforts. In addition, through the general partnership the promoters may receive extra allocations of cash flows, both in the operating and termination periods.

The importance of limited partnerships prior to the Tax Reform Act was such that over $14.9 billion was raised through offerings of limited partnerships in 1985. About 46 percent of this sum was raised through public offerings (registered with the Securities and Exchange Commission); the remainder was raised through unregistered private offerings sold to wealthier and more sophisticated investors.

Master Limited Partnerships

The **master limited partnership (MLP)** is a specialized form that unites into a single overall limited partnership a number of limited partnerships plus direct ownership of assets and the ability to create debt. There are two major advantages of the master limited partnership:

1. The shares may be publicly traded; consequently, they have additional liquidity. Many MLPs are traded on the stock exchanges or over the counter.
2. MLPs can offset the passive losses of some partnerships against the gains from others. As a result of this "netting," losses that otherwise could not be used until years later can serve to shelter current income.

Frequently MLPs have resulted when syndicators exchanged several existing limited partnerships for those of a new MLP in order to consolidate their management and financing and to increase their liquidity. Others have come about as a result of corporate spin-offs of properties.

Problems for MLPs arise primarily because the market has trouble valuing the partnerships, since their ownership rights cover many individual properties, each of which may have a market value that differs greatly from that shown on their books. In addition, it is difficult to value their shares for tax purposes because the costs and prior losses vary among new and old owners.

Real Estate Investment Trusts

Chapter 6 described the history and operations of *real estate investment trusts (REITs)*. They have grown because they offer tax advantages, limited liability, greater transferability, and professional management. They are slightly limited in their activities and must have at least 100 owners, with no more than 50 percent held by any five individuals. Over $3.5 billion were raised by REITs in 1985.

REITs are single-taxed, not double-taxed, provided that they distribute 95 percent or more of their income in a year and that their income comes mainly from specified passive real estate sources. Although they cannot pass through tax losses to their owners, the losses can be carried forward to offset future earnings. Furthermore, REITs can distribute dividends from capital, which are not taxable. Such dividends are common when their cash flow exceeds their taxable income.

Real Estate Mortgage Investment Companies

The 1986 Tax Reform Act established a new ownership entity called a **real estate mortgage investment company (REMIC).** This is a new type of conduit established primarily to hold a pool of mortgages. In contrast to previous tax regulations, even when the mortgages are actively managed, the REMIC will not be taxed as such; it is another form of single-tax entity.

The REMIC form was established as an aid to the securitization of mortgages. Under previous rules, the issuance of multiple classes of interests in order to split the risks and time to maturity of a mortgage pool among different types of securities and owners could cause the firm to be subject to the double taxation of the corporate tax. Use of a REMIC avoids this problem.

Tax-exempt Entities

A good deal of real estate is bought by trusts or other entities that pay no taxes. In the 1980s pension trusts have been large entrants into the market as they seek to diversify their portfolios. **Individual retirement accounts (IRAs)** and **Keogh plans** have also become more significant. These are primarily trusts through which individuals accumulate funds for retirement. Taxes need not be paid on current earnings. Since in theory such investments need not be liquid, real estate makes a logical use for such accumulations.

TAX BURDENS AND BENEFITS

The amount of taxes paid lowers the final after-tax income of investors. To the degree that real estate investments pay few or no taxes, when yields are compared on an after-tax basis, real property has decided advantages over many other forms of investment. This section explains how such tax savings arise.

Tax shelters are extra deductions or credits against income available only to taxpayers whose income is generated through such vehicles. Traditionally, real estate has benefited from a number of special tax rules. They may permit some cash flow to be received without a current tax payment, and they served in the past to reduce taxes payable on other income. The tax code requires a special registration and treatment of certain tax shelters.

The treatment of income from property has changed with nearly every new tax bill. Most battles over tax legislation have featured major confrontations between those wanting to reduce real estate tax preferences and those wnting to increase them. Good investment and financing decisions must take into account both the way in which taxes affect real estate values and how they may change in response to possible alterations in the Internal Revenue Code.

Taxes on Income and Sale

The basic idea behind an income tax is simple. Taypayers report their income by including all current ordinary and capital gains income. To arrive at their taxable income, they then subtract their costs of producing that income and, on individual returns, certain authorized deductions and exemptions. According to their tax status—which varies with the individual and with the form of ownership—they then find the tax rate that applies in their particular marginal tax bracket. Multiplying their taxable income by their correct tax rate, they find the taxes they owe. Although the description sounds straightforward, the proper execution is extremely complex.

The Tax Rate

Under the tax system, the amount of taxes paid depends on the bracket in which income falls. One of the purposes of tax reform was to simplify the tax code and reduce the number of tax brackets. Table 16-1 shows that this was accomplished for most families (those with taxable incomes under $71,900). However, the situation is more complex for families with higher incomes and for individuals with taxable incomes of over $41,000—brackets that include the owners of most income real estate.

In studying the table, note first that in calculating its taxable income a family of four would subtract a minimum of $13,000 from its adjusted gross

Table 16-1
Individual Income Tax Rates
Under Tax Revision

From: Adjusted gross income

Subtract: Personal exemptions of $2,000 for self, spouse, and each other dependent, and the standard deduction: $3,000 for single filer, $5,000 for joint. Or, instead of the standard deduction, subtract itemized deductions

Equals: Taxable income

Tax is calculated from tax table plus surcharges.

	If Taxable Income Is over This Bracket	A Base Tax of:	Plus This Percent of Income over the Bracket
Single filer:			
	0	0	15%
	$17,850	$2,678	28%
Joint filer:			
	0	0	15%
	$29,750	$4,463	28%

Note that from $41,000 to approximately $127,000 for single filer, and from $71,900 to $185,000 for joint filer, surcharge raises marginal tax rate to 33 percent. Brackets are indexed for inflation.

income. This would include $2,000 of personal exemptions for each family member plus a $5,000 standard deduction. The first bracket of taxable income runs to $29,750 and is taxed at a 15 percent rate. With $13,000 of exemptions and deductions, gross income would have to be over $42,750 ($13,000 + $29,750) before the 28 percent rate applied. Furthermore, these brackets are indexed and therefore will move upward with future increases in the Consumer Price Index.

The Tax Surcharge Calculations of tax rates become more complex for filers in higher income brackets. The 1986 tax bill granted far larger percentage decreases in rates to upper-income families than to those in middle-income brackets. As a result, Congress determined that when adjusted gross income exceeds a certain level, *all* taxable income—not just that above the first two brackets—is subject to the flat 28 percent rate.

This is accomplished by placing a **surcharge**—an additional tax above the regular rate in a bracket—on income until the desired result is obtained. For joint filers, the surcharge starts at $71,900. Income in the bracket from approximately $71,900 to $145,000 is taxed at a 33 percent rate, or until the 15 percent rate on income in the first bracket has all been offset. Then, in a similar manner, a surcharge is collected until the tax-reducing effects of personal exemptions are phased out. After the surcharges have raised the tax on *all* adjusted gross income to a flat 28 percent (which occurs at approximately $127,400 for single and from $185,300 to $200,000 for joint filers), the flat rate of 28 percent is applied to all additional income.

However, the surcharges are not the only effect on the higher income brackets. As we shall see, still more complex and higher rates apply for landlords actively managing rental properties and eligible to use up to $25,000 in losses to offset other income. This right is phased out for those with adjusted gross incomes between $100,000 and $150,000. In the discussion of this regulation later, we shall see that this results in a marginal tax rate of 49.5 percent for those in this group and in this bracket. A similar phaseout applies to the use of tax credits for investing in low-income housing for those who have incomes between $200,000 and $250,000.

In addition to the federal income tax, most states and many localities have income taxes. Although their rates and regulations differ widely, most by far have rate tables, exemptions, and deductions similar to the federal ones. State and local income taxes are deductible from adjusted gross income on the federal return. In the tables of this book, we often use 33 percent as the marginal tax rate that applies. This can be thought of either as a federal tax in the bracket from $71,900 to $145,000 or as a combined federal tax rate of 28 percent plus state and local rates of 5 percent.

The Alternative Minimum Tax

Another complication of the tax law is that persons who receive a fair amount of tax benefits from tax preferences, such as extra deductions and exclusions from taxable income, must calculate their potential taxes by a second method. The **alternative minimum tax (AMT)** requires adding back certain tax preference items to taxable income and then applying a different tax rate. **Tax preference items** are those that allow for lower tax rates, specified deductions, and exclusions from taxable income.

The decrease in tax shelters and authorized miscellaneous deductions greatly reduced the importance of the alternative minimum tax. However, it may still snare some real estate investors, particularly if the use of transition rules reduces their ordinary taxable income.

REAL ESTATE TAX SHELTERS

The purpose of tax shelters is to reduce the amount of reported taxable income and, therefore, the amount of taxes that must be paid currently. How do tax shelters shield cash flows from the payment of current taxes? In real estate investments, potential tax savings have arisen in four principal ways:

■ Some tax payments may be **deferred**—that is, delayed—until a future date. This occurs when taxable income is reduced by allowable deductions. Since the delayed payment is discounted to obtain its present value, the present value of the delayed payment is always less than that of an equal payment made today.

■ Certain types of expenditures for real property receive **tax credits.** Tax credits are sums, granted for engaging in particular activities, that may be subtracted from taxes owed. Since a tax credit allows a dollar-for-dollar reduction in taxes, it is obviously worth more than a deduction that reduces taxes only by the marginal tax rate to which it would be subjected. Credits are available for the rehabilitation of old and historic buildings and for providing low-income housing.

■ The rate at which deferred taxes may be paid may be lower than current rates. Prior to the Tax Reform Act of 1986, a large share of capital gains could be excluded from taxable income. Thus, if the law allowed a 50 percent capital gains exclusion and the tax rate was 28 percent, the actual tax on capital gains would be only 14 percent. Many observers believe that special treatment for capital gains is likely to be reintroduced into the tax system.

■ Real estate benefits from **tax leverage**—the ability to claim expenses for the entire property even though the equity may cover only a small share of the value. An investor with only a 10 percent equity in a property (the remaining 90 percent financed with a qualified nonrecourse loan) can claim all the depreciation and other benefits of the property. (Nonrecourse loans are discussed in the next section; tax leverage is covered later, under "Deferred and Reduced Taxes.")

In addition to these types of shelters, as previous chapters have discussed, investors have the ability to use tax-exempt bonds for the construction of rental housing and to fund certain kinds of mortgages. The history of the revenue code reveals a constant fight by lawyers and accountants to devise new types of tax shelters and by lobbying associations to introduce others into the code. Few would be surprised by the appearance or reappearance of additional tax shelters.

The Remaining Shelters

Although one of the objectives of tax reform was to reduce the ability to shield taxes by use of these methods, at least five important shelters were left in the real estate field.

1. Owners may deduct payments of mortgage interest and all property taxes on first and second homes.
2. Owners who sell their principal residence may delay reporting the capital gain if they buy another. If they are over 55 years of age, they need not report the first $125,000 of their gain on a single sale.
3. Taxes may be delayed on cash flows received from owning income property.

4. Individuals who actively participate in rental real estate activities may sub-tract a limited amount of their losses from current taxable income from other sources.
5. Investors may receive tax credits by investing in low-income housing or by rehabilitating old or historic buildings.

Although some of these shelters were greatly curtailed compared to the "good old days" of 1982 to 1984, when they were at a peak, they remain significant in the analysis of many real estate purchases.

THE DEDUCTION OF MORTGAGE INTEREST AND PROPERTY TAXES

The deductions for mortgage interest and property taxes on homes were hardly changed in the Tax Reform Act of 1986. Although President Reagan had proposed curtailing them, the tax preferences were too popular. Only two major changes were made:

1. The deduction for mortgage interest was limited to a principal home and one second home.
2. The size of the mortgage for which interest could be deducted was limited.

Other kinds of consumer interest were made nondeductible. The press seized on this fact to point out that consumers could continue to obtain this tax benefit by taking out mortgage equity loans on their homes in order to finance other types of consumer purchases, such as automobiles. Through the use of the mortgage interest deduction, interest payments on these other purchases would be deductible for tax purposes. The limit on the size of home mortgages for which interest could be deducted was enacted to prevent some of this shift-ing; no eligible mortgage can exceed the fair market value of its property. Interest can be subtracted only to the extent that a loan does not exceed the original purchase price of a house plus any expenditures for home improvements or for necessary educational or medical expenses. This means that owners whose equity increases because the value of their house appreciates are limited in the amount they can borrow on a deductible basis.

The Increase in Ownership Costs

Lowering tax rates lessened the advantages of homeownership compared to renting. Although the impact was not great for middle-income families, costs of ownership rose drastically for high-income families. How the changes occurred is demonstrated in Tables 16-2 and 16-3.

Table 16-2 examines the reduction in ownership costs for a family with $42,500 in adjusted gross income who bought a house for $120,000 and has

Table 16-2
The Effect of Lower Tax Rates on the
Tax Preference Subsidy

	1986 Law	1985 Law
Family income less $1,000 in deductions	$41,500	$41,500
Less personal exemptions*	8,000	4,320
Taxable income before housing and remaining standard deduction	$33,500	$37,180
Deductions for mortgage interest and property tax†	$15,120	$15,120
Loss in standard deduction	4,000	2,670
Reduction in taxable income	$11,120	$12,450
Reduction in taxes owed	$1,668	$3,245

*Four exemptions.

†$120,000 house with charges of 12.6% covering opportunity costs and a mortgage at 11 percent and annual property taxes at 1.6% of value.

$1,000 of non-housing-related deductions. Three factors enter into their total benefit:

1. In this example, the ability to deduct mortgage interest payments plus the reduction in income (opportunity costs) due to the down payment reduce taxable income by $13,200, assuming that interest rates and equity earnings are 11 percent annually.
2. Property taxes are another deduction resulting from ownership, and this is estimated at $1,920, based on an assumed property tax rate of 1.6 percent of the price. These first two factors result in a combined deduction from taxable income of $15,120.
3. In contrast, most middle-income families will lose part of their standard deduction when they have to itemize in order to obtain the mortgage interest and property tax deductions. In the example, it is assumed that this loss in standard deduction is $2,670 before tax reform and $4,000 after. (The standard deduction was raised by the 1986 act, causing a larger loss.)

When all of these adjustments are taken into account, the net decrease in taxable income under the 1986 bill is $11,120, and with the new tax rate of 15 percent for families in this bracket, the total tax saving from ownership in contrast to renting is $1,668. The net decrease in taxable income under the 1985 tax law was $12,450. This sum falls into several marginal tax brackets, but the average tax rate was 26.1 percent, so that the total tax saving in this case is $3,245. As a result of the decrease in tax rates, tax savings for this middle-income family are cut by almost 50 percent.

Table 16-3
The Impact on After-Tax Housing Costs
of the 1986 Tax Reform Bill

	$300,000 House and $150,000 Income	$120,000 House and $42,500 Income
1985 Tax Law		
Pretax annual ownership cost	$30,000	$12,000
Tax saving	18,900*	3,245
After-tax cost	$11,100	$8,755
1986 Tax Law		
Pretax annual ownership cost	$30,000	$12,000
Tax saving	12,474†	1,668
After-tax cost	$17,526	$10,332

*50% marginal tax bracket.

†33% marginal tax bracket.

Costs Rise More for High-Income Families

Table 16-3 points out some other special factors resulting from the tax cut. In the discussion of the costs of ownership in Chapter 10, we saw that because expected appreciation and mortgage interest rates are related, the costs of ownership must be adjusted for potential appreciation. For this example, we assume that the pretax costs of ownership are 10 percent of the price of a house. The estimated pretax ownership costs of $30,000 and $12,000 are derived by multiplying the price of the house by this 10 percent.

The tax saving for the more expensive house is calculated following the same technique as in Table 16-2. The result is a projected saving of $18,900 under the 1985 law and of $12,474 under the 1986 act. The after-tax cost of ownership rises from $11,100 to $17,526.

Note that while the percentage decrease in the tax benefit is larger for the middle-income family, the increase in the after-tax cost for the higher-income family is much greater. The real projected after-tax costs for owning the $120,000 house rise about 18 percent, while the increase for the $300,000 house is over 55 percent. This difference primarily reflects the much larger benefit the upper-income family secures when taxes are higher. The way the preference works is also reflected in the fact that the after-tax cost for the middle-income family rises from 7.3 percent of the price of the house to 8.6 percent, while that for the upper-income family rises from 3.7 percent to 5.8 percent. (This point is also discussed in Chapters 7 and 10.)

Table 16-3 illustrates dramatically how a reduction in marginal tax rates serves to raise the costs of homeownership because the value of the tax preference (subsidy) is reduced. How this cut in tax effects would influence the demand for housing could not be determined in advance, but most observers expected that the result would be a gradual decrease in the percentage of home-ownership and pressure on the market prices of more expensive homes, where the percentage increase is much more significant.

The precise effects could not be projected because the various influences move in opposite ways and because many houses are bought for primarily noneconomic reasons. When the marginal tax rate is lowered, the value of a tax deduction becomes less, and thus demand falls. On the other hand, demand for ownership will rise to the extent that the changes raise after-tax family income, lower interest rates, and raise rents. The net effect is a result of the combination of the separate impacts.

POSTPONING OR REDUCING TAXES UPON SALE OF A HOME

Another important tax shelter for homeowners is the ability to postpone or avoid entirely the tax normally due upon any capital gain resulting from the sale of a property. The tax on part or all of the gain from the sale of a principal residence can be postponed if a new house is bought or built and lived in as a principal residence within two years before or two years after a home is sold. A **principal residence** is usually the home in which one lives.

If the purchase price for the new home is at least as high as the selling price of the old house, the entire gain may be postponed. (The gain depends on the price paid and improvements made for the house sold, less the price received, which is adjusted for selling costs, including financing costs, and for costs incurred in fixing up the property within 90 days of the sale). If the pur-chase price of the new home is less than the sales price of the old, the gain taxed in the year of sale is either the gain on the sale or the amount by which the adjusted sales price exceeds the purchase price of the new home, whichever is less.

Sellers who are 55 years of age or older may exclude $125,000 of a gain from the sale of their principal home if they meet certain other conditions. They must have lived in the property sold for three out of the last five years and they may never have claimed the exclusion previously. This is a one-time-only exclu-sion. If a house is owned jointly, only one of the pair must meet the age quali-fication. In effect, the gain is forgiven; it is not merely a postponement of the tax liability.

In both types of exclusion from current gross income, the sale and its details as well as the amount of gain must be reported to the Internal Revenue Service (IRS) on a special form.

DEFERRED AND REDUCED TAXES

Prior to tax reform, by far the most important tax shelter was the ability to defer current tax payments and to pay them at lower rates when they were finally due. Although the special treatment of passive income and the removal of the special treatment of capital gains have greatly diminished the importance of this feature, it remains significant. Even though owning real estate no longer allows for much reduction of income from other sources, current taxes on the cash flow from a property are likely to be low or zero.

Deferred Taxes

If payment of taxes on cash received from an investment or from other sources can be delayed, an investor has more money to spend or invest. Because of interest, money received today has a greater present value than that to be received in the future. As a corollary, even if the same amount of taxes must be paid later as now, the cost of a deferred tax is less than that paid today. The tax deferral is sometimes called an interest-free loan from the government, which must be paid when taxable income is received in the future.

EXAMPLE: A piece of real estate pays out $1,000 in current tax-sheltered income. It might have a before-tax cash flow (BTCF) of $1,000, on which no taxes were due, making its after-tax cash flow (ATCF) also $1,000. Consider investors who are in a 33 percent marginal tax bracket. If they must pay taxes when the $1,000 is received, they would have only $670 (their ATCF) left after taxes. With a tax shelter, however, they retain the full amount.

Assume that the investors hold the property for 10 years and must pay the $330 deferred taxes when it is sold, and that they earn 10 percent on their funds in the interim. At a 10 percent discount rate, the present value of a $330 payment to be made in 10 years is $128 today. Thus, the value of the tax deferral is $202 (the $330 not paid today less the $128 present value of the future payment). How much shelter is realized from a transaction depends on the amount of tax deferred, the length of time before the tax is paid, and the discount rate.

Lower Future Tax Rates

Deferring taxes is worthwhile even if the amount of taxes paid later is the same. If, in addition, the amount of taxes is reduced, the gain will be even larger. Several things can reduce future tax rates:

1. A person may retire or have less income. Gains may be taken in years when losses are large or other income low.
2. The entire tax schedule may be reduced. (Of course, it may also be raised.)
3. Special rules may apply, of which the capital gains exclusion has been the most important. However, when Congress reduced the top marginal tax rates in the 1986 Tax Reform Act, it also ended the special capital gains exclusion, making capital gains subject to the same rates as other income. Because this was recognized as extremely controversial, the code sections

for calculating and treating capital gains were retained. Many observers assumed that special capital gains treatment would be reintroduced in the future.

The After-Tax Cash Flow

Three principal factors permit the deferral of current income taxes. They cause the current after-tax cash flow from real property to be higher than it would be if all the income were subject to normal taxation.

- Depreciation, which is a cost of producing income and which therefore reduces taxable income, is not a cash payment. Taxable income declines, but no payment must be set aside. Cash is available for current distribution.
- The cash flow can be increased without payment of current taxes if books can be kept by the **accrual method of accounting.** Under the accrual method, expenses are deducted when they are incurred, whether or not they are paid in the same year. The amount of the deduction may, however, be limited by complex IRS regulations drafted in an effort to avoid misuse of this privilege.
- *Tax leverage*—that is, the concentration of all the tax losses for the equity holders—increases the amount of taxes that can be deferred. (Tax leverage is discussed next.)

The amount of taxes that can be deferred compared to the cash flow also depends on the amount of passive income and losses. In addition, as discussed in a following section, if the income arises from active participation in a rental property, up to $25,000 of losses may be used to offset income from other sources.

Tax Leverage

The existence of tax leverage concentrates all of the tax benefits for the equity-holders. Even if the benefits are not a large percentage of the total property value, they may be high compared to the equity. Thus, if the cash flow is 5 percent of a property's value, it can equal 50 percent of an investor's equity if the equity is 10 percent and the debt is 90 percent.

EXAMPLE: Investors buy a $100,000 building with a $10,000 down payment. Their tax bracket is 33 percent. The property has a cash flow of $10,000 a year but reports no taxable income because of depreciation and other authorized deductions. The investors receive $10,000 a year in cash. If this were taxable, they would have to pay $3,300 in taxes and would have only $6,700 to spend. As a result of the tax shelter, they increase their spendable income by $3,300 a year. At the end of year 3, they have saved $9,900 through reduced tax payments.

The ability of tax leverage to shelter income is closely related to the special treatment of interest owed on qualified real estate loans under the **at-risk rule.** This rule states that, in general, the amount of a taxpayer's loss deductions cannot exceed the amount the taxpayer has at risk in an activity—that is, losses are limited to the amount of equity plus any additional debt guaranteed by the borrower. These are **recourse loans,** in which the borrower puts his or her other income and property at risk. In contrast, most mortgages on income property are specifically not guaranteed by the borrower. If the borrower cannot repay the loan, the lender is limited to a claim against the property itself. Such loans are called **nonrecourse loans.**

However, by special exemptions in the tax code, the at-risk rule does not apply to nonrecourse loans on real estate from **qualified lenders**—that is, those actively and regularly engaged in the business of lending money, excluding in most cases, seller and promoter financing. Instead, even though financed by such nonrecourse loans, an owner of real estate can claim all the interest paid on the whole property. How much value the additional loss will be to the investor, of course, will depend on the amount of taxable income from other passive investments that is available to be offset.

The Depreciation Deduction

The **depreciation deduction** is an allowance for the wasting of assets used in producing income. The assets must have a life of more than one year. Since it is assumed that land does not depreciate, the value of any investment in a property must be divided between land, to which depreciation does not apply, and the building, to which it does.

Property serves as a tax shelter to the degree that the depreciation deduction exceeds the actual loss in value. In practice, buildings have lost value at a far slower pace than that allowed in the tax codes for the recovery of an investment. (In fact, many have actually appreciated.) This is a main factor enabling real estate to serve as a tax shelter.

However, another factor enters into the picture: inflation, which causes the costs of replacing a building to rise. Should depreciation allowances take into account only the original value of a building or should they consider its replacement costs? Because of inflation, if depreciation allowances are based only on the original capital investment, the deductions from income for tax purposes might fall far short of current replacement costs. The need to compensate for inflation has been the basis for those advocating more rapid depreciation allowances and reduced capital gains taxes. Prior to 1986 this reasoning was accepted, and the depreciation allowances were increased. However, the U.S. Treasury and many economists pointed out that the increases were arbitrary. This method of correcting for inflation caused wide divergences among different types of investments; taxes on land and buildings were much higher than those on other types of investments. One of the purposes of tax reform was to remove some of these inequities by making the depreciation deductions come closer to mirroring the actual cost of replacement.

Calculating the Depreciation Deduction

The amount of depreciation that can be deducted depends on (1) the depreciable basis, (2) the depreciation method, and (3) the *useful life* or *recovery period*—the number of years over which depreciation is spread.

The Depreciable Basis   A **basis** is a measure of the investment in a property. The *original* or *initial basis* is the amount paid for a property plus closing costs, such as commissions, recording, legal fees, and title insurance. The **depreciable basis** is the amount against which the depreciation rates are applied in order to calculate the annual depreciation deductions after the value of the nondepreciable land is subtracted. Properties can be acquired in many ways other than by purchase; therefore, the IRS has complex regulations for determining the correct basis for a wide variety of ownership transfer conditions, such as when the property is acquired by exchange.

The **adjusted basis** includes all additions and subtractions from the original basis due to such factors as improvements, casualty losses, and the amount of claimed depreciation.

Straight-line Depreciation   The basic depreciation method has been the straight-line method. Under **straight-line depreciation** the amount of depreciation allowed each year is a certain percentage of the original basis. The allowed percentage is obtained by dividing 1 by the useful life or recovery period. If the useful life is 31.5, the allowed percentage is 3.17 percent, or $1 \div 31.5$. If the useful life is 27.5, the allowed percentage is 3.64, or $1 \div 27.5$. For ease of application and to account for property bought at different times during the year, the IRS issues tables with rounded percentages to show the exact rate that may be deducted each year.*

Many of the congressional battles over taxes have centered around the size of each year's deduction, which is based on the authorized length of the recovery period. In the recent past, the authorized useful life for real estate properties has varied between 15 and 40 years. The 1986 Tax Reform Act uses a 27.5-year life for residential property and 31.5 years for nonresidential real estate. Since the actual useful life of most properties is over 60 years, any of these choices provides some tax shelter. Clearly, the shorter the recovery period for

---

*Amortization for tax purposes is similar to straight-line depreciation. It applies to certain expenses not included in the depreciation basis, such as interest and taxes during the construction period, and certain financing and organization charges. Some amortization periods are shorter and some longer than those for depreciation. In the example of operating statements, such charges are included with depreciation to simplify presentation.

tax purposes, the greater the advantage to the taxpayer. Other major debates have been over how to correct for inflation and whether to substitute other techniques for the straight-line method.

The Accelerated Cost Recovery System

The **accelerated cost recovery system (ACRS)** allows taxpayers to recover the unadjusted basis of property over a designated period. The code fixes for each class of property a recovery percentage to be deducted each year. One method of classification is to differentiate between personal and real property. **Personal property** is property that is not real estate, such as furniture or equipment. **Real property** is land and, generally, anything that is erected on, growing on, or attached to the land.

The 1986 act divided personal property into six cost-recovery classes from 3 to 20 years. The first four (3–10 years) could be depreciated by use of the 200 percent declining-balance method. The 15- and 20-year classes could use a 150 percent declining-balance method.

Real property was divided into two classes. Residential rental property was allowed only straight-line depreciation over a 27.5-year period, while nonresidential real property was placed in a 31.5-year class and also was allowed to use only the straight-line technique.

The Declining-balance Method

Under the **declining balance** method, the amount of depreciation taken each year is subtracted from the remaining adjusted balance before the following year's depreciation is computed. How this works can be illustrated by examining the annual depreciation deductions for equipment in the 10-year, 200 percent declining-balance class. The depreciation charges in each year are 200 percent of the remaining undepreciated book value (BV) divided by the number (n) of years over which the property is being depreciated:

$$\text{Depreciation charge} = 2.00 \left(\frac{\text{BV}}{n} \right) \tag{16.1}$$

For a 10-year property, n is 10. Because this formula would never exhaust the property's basis, the system switches (the *crossover point*) to the straight-line method in the year when the formula would yield rates too low to depreciate the entire basis over the remaining years in the class life. The IRS issues specific tables for each class, allowing for rounding, the switch, and other factors.

EXAMPLE: A $10,000 piece of equipment falls in the 10-year, 200 percent class. In year 1, under the general rule and applying equation 16.1, the first year's depreciation would be 20 percent or $2,000, since 2.00 ($10,000 ÷ 10) = $2,000. In year 2, applying the formula again to the undepreciated balance of $8,000

($10,000 − $2,000) results in a depreciation rate of 16 percent or $1,600: 2.00 ($8,000 ÷ 10) = $1,600. In year 3, the rate and amount would be 12.8 percent and $1,280: 2.00 ($6,400 ÷ 10) = $1,280. The write-offs would continue according to the formula until year 6, when the declining-balance procedure shifts to the straight-line. As a result, the depreciation rates for each of the last five years are 6.6 percent. Putting them all together, the declining-balance technique yields a schedule of 20 percent, 16 percent, 12.8 percent, 9.8 percent, 8.4 percent, 6.6 percent, 6.6 percent, 6.6 percent, 6.6 percent, 6.6 percent, totaling 100 percent. (As noted earlier, the schedule published by the IRS may differ somewhat from this.)

If the declining-balance method were not authorized, deductions at the straight-line rate of 10 percent per year would allow a 50 percent write-off in the first five years, in contrast to the 67 percent authorized under the declining-balance method. This more rapid write-off of the depreciation allowance is called **accelerated depreciation.**

Deduction for Interest

Another significant method of deferring taxes has been through the interest channel and the suspension of the at-risk rule for real estate. Under previous tax law, purchasers used large borrowings and the right to accrue interest to defer taxes and to shift ordinary income into the capital gains category. A running battle has been going on between tax lawyers on one hand and Congress and the IRS on the other in this sphere. The result has been a complex set of rules and regulations setting limits on what interest may be deducted from current taxable income.

The Tax Reform Act was meant to reduce the importance of this issue through the special treatment of passive income and by setting the same tax rate for capital gains as for ordinary income. However, most tax experts believe that the contest between the IRS and investors is likely to continue in this area. As a result, the amount of taxes that can be postponed will become clear only after numerous additional rulings.

Example of Operating Period Tax Calculations

Table 16-4 demonstrates how excess depreciation and interest operate to provide a tax shelter. For this purpose, the table uses the Plaza Square example from Chapter 14, based on the same background data found in Table 14-1 on page 374. The top line of Table 16-4 shows the net operating income (NOI) carried forward from the Plaza Square income statement in Table 14-2 on page 375. From this income, taxpayers deduct depreciation and mortgage interest—both authorized expense deductions. When these are deducted, the property shows a loss for tax purposes in the first two years.

Next, Table 16-4 shows the effect of the passive loss rule on the treatment of losses. It assumes that the property is held in a limited partnership and that

Table 16-4
Calculation of Taxes and Tax Benefits
Plaza Square

	Year 1	Year 2	Year 3	Year 4	Year 5
Net operating income	$1,469,938	$1,635,409	$1,814,034	$1,907,374	$2,005,798
Less interest	(1,272,936)	(1,266,866)	(1,260,158)	(1,252,746)	(1,244,556)
Less depreciation	(399,884)	(417,270)	(417,270)	(417,270)	(417,270)
Income or (loss) before tax	($202,882)	($48,726)	$136,606	$237,358	$343,972
Tax loss carryforward	0	(202,882)	(251,608)	(115,002)	0
Taxable income	0	0	0	122,356	343,972
Times marginal tax rate	33%	33%	33%	33%	33%
Taxes	$0	$0	$0	$40,378	$113,511
Taxable income or (loss)	(202,882)	(48,726)	136,606	237,358	343,972
Plus depreciation	399,884	417,270	417,270	417,270	417,270
Less amortization of principal	(57,812)	(63,882)	(70,590)	(78,002)	(86,192)
Before tax cash flow (BTCF)	$139,190	$304,661	$483,286	$576,626	$675,050
Less tax	0	0	0	40,378	113,511
After tax cash flow (ATCF)	$139,190	$304,661	$483,286	$536,248	$561,539

Note: The assumptions are those shown in Table 14-1 and net operating income is from Table 14-2. Real property depreciation: 3.04%, 3.17%, 3.17%, 3.17%, 3.17%.

the individual partners are subject to a 33 percent marginal tax rate and that they have no other passive gains that can be offset by these losses.

Look at lines 4 through 8 for year 1. Even though a taxable loss occurs, an investor for whom this is passive income cannot use the loss to reduce nonpassive taxable income. On the other hand, no taxes need be paid in the first year. The tax loss of $202,882 is carried forward, as shown in line 5 for year 2. The loss in the second year is added to the previous amount and the total is carried forward to year 3. That year is different; the property has taxable income. Still, no tax need be paid. Instead, the income is subtracted from the loss carryforward. In year 4, the amount of positive income exceeds the loss carried forward, so that a tax payment is necessary.

The bottom half of the table illustrates the significant differences between cash flows and taxable income and between the before- and after-tax cash flows. To obtain the before-tax cash flow, depreciation deductions are added back to taxable income because they require no cash, even though they are deductible in calculating taxable income. With the opposite effect, amortization of principal must be subtracted because it is not an expense for tax purposes.

The result is a sizable cash flow that is not subject to taxes. Thus, in year 1 the investors receive $139,190 in tax-deferred income. The first year in which taxes must be paid is year 4. (The remaining chapters give examples in which no taxes are paid for the entire operating period.) The early receipt of cash even when the building is unprofitable on a book income basis can significantly raise the effective yield. However, because the depreciation allowance deduction is larger than the actual depreciation of the property, gains are occurring that will be taxed upon sale. Consequently, the total tax effect on the internal rate of return of this property cannot be calculated until the taxes on sale are taken into account. Taxes are only deferred, not avoided.

THE NET CASH FLOW (REVERSION) AT TERMINATION

The value of the tax deferral and the profitability and value of real property depend to a great extent on the cash flow received upon sale (the *reversion*). How much cash an investor gets back is, in turn, highly influenced by the amount of taxes due. This aspect of feasibility analysis was altered much more by the 1986 Tax Reform Act than was the operating period analysis.

The Tax on Capital Gains

Under the previous tax law, with capital gains taxed at a lower rate than ordinary income, a great deal of effort had to be devoted to assuring that as large a part of the sales price as possible could be treated as a long-term capital gain, to which a lower rate of taxes applied. In addition, taxes could be further reduced by delaying the time at which the tax had to be paid. As a result, many different tax considerations entered into the planning of a sale and into the calculation of potential taxes. If the tax rate on ordinary income and that on capital gains is the same, as under the 1986 Tax Reform Act, only the first two of the following factors remain pertinent and tax considerations play a more minor role.

- The first item in calculating the taxable income and the tax on a sale is to figure the actual gain. A **capital gain** is the difference between the investors' adjusted basis and the property's sales price less selling costs.
- Second, the taxable gain reported in a year may be reduced, as we shall see shortly, by exchanges or installment sales. This factor, too, requires careful analysis and planning.
- Third, under earlier tax law it was necessary to determine whether a gain could be treated as a long-term gain subject to a **capital gains deduction.** If so, a certain percentage of the gain could be excluded from taxable income (60 percent under the 1985 code). To qualify for this treatment, a gain had to be long term, which was defined as an investment held more than six months. Further, the seller had to qualify as an investor, not a dealer. Dealers hold a property for sale; investors hold property for long-term investment or use it as an asset in operating their trade or business. The amount of gain that could be excluded from

current taxable income had to be reported as a tax preference item, subject to the alternative minimum tax.

■ Fourth, another calculation estimated the amount of gain subject to **depreciation recapture**—that is, the amount of a gain that would be treated as ordinary income rather than as capital gains income. Depending on the type of property, the use of accelerated depreciation could mean that some of the gain was taxed as ordinary income.

■ Finally, the actual amount of gain to be excluded was subtracted and the top marginal tax rate was then applied to the remaining amount.

Since the 1986 Tax Reform Act removed the special deduction for long term or other capital gains and applied the ordinary income rate to the total gain, the last three steps will not be required after 1987 unless some form of preference for gains is returned to the system.

Cash Flow and Taxes on Termination

How the taxes and actual cash to be received on sale are projected is illustrated in Table 16-5. It uses the sales information from Plaza Square presented in Table 14-4. The projected sales price is $20,678,335. Of this amount, $1,240,700 is required to cover selling costs, leaving a net sales price of $19,437,635.

The initial basis for the property (including land) was $15,154,000. Total deductions for depreciation have been $2,068,963, leaving a remaining adjusted basis of $13,085,037. If improvements had been made or casualty losses taken, the adjusted basis would include these events also. The capital gain on sale is the difference between the net sales price and the adjusted basis, or a difference of $6,352,598.

The line under the calculated gain shows that, in this case, the tax loss carryforward is zero. The previous table showed that all the losses had been used up in year 4. However, if an investor had a tax loss carryforward remaining at the time of sale, it would be subtracted from the gain in calculating the taxes due. In this example, when a 33 percent marginal tax rate is applied to the gain, the total tax due is seen to be $2,096,357.

The final six lines of Table 16-5 show the projected cash flow on reversion after taxes. Cash from the net sale is increased by the cash reserve and is reduced by the need to pay off the outstanding mortgage. Total before-tax cash on sale is $7,870,913. From this is subtracted the estimated tax to obtain the projected after-tax cash on sale.

Table 16-3 exemplified how the costs of homeownership were affected by tax reform. A similar type of calculation can be performed for income property.

THE INCREASE IN TAXES

One of the stated purposes of the tax reforms submitted by President Reagan in 1985 and reworked by Congress was to reduce the tax advantages

Table 16-5
Pro Forma Termination Statement
Plaza Square

Gross sales price	$20,678,335
Less selling costs	(1,240,700)
Net sales price	$19,437,635
Adjusted basis	(13,085,037)
Gain	$6,352,598
Less tax loss carryforward	0
Taxable income	$6,352,598
Total tax due (33%)	($2,096,357)
Net sales price	$19,437,635
Plus reserves	200,000
Less outstanding mortgage	(11,766,721)
Cash from sales	$7,870,913
Less total tax due	(2,096,357)
Net cash flow on sale	$5,774,556

provided by real estate as opposed to other investments. The three most critical changes were:

1. The segregation of income from rental properties and limited partnerships into a class whose losses could not be used to offset income from other types of sources.
2. A decrease in authorized depreciation deductions. The period over which residential property could be depreciated was extended from 19 years to 27.5 years, and the right to use the 175 percent declining-balance method was dropped. The period for nonresidential property was extended from 19 to 31.5 years.
3. The right to exclude part of capital gains from taxable income was abolished.

Numerous other changes were also enacted, but except for the decrease in marginal tax rates, these three caused the greatest impact. Lower tax rates worked to increase after-tax cash flow, thus partially offsetting the increases from the other alterations.

Estimating the Change in Taxes Due

Table 16-6 makes clear, in actual and present-value terms, the total tax impact of the various changes. The table compares the projected taxes and tax

Table 16-6
Comparisons of Taxes for an
Income Property

Year	1985 Law* Taxable Income	1985 Law* Tax Saving (or Tax) (50% Tax Bracket)	1986 Tax Reform† Taxable Income	1986 Tax Reform† (Tax) (33% Tax Bracket)	Tax Reform Increase in Tax or (Tax Saving) Amount (Column 3 Minus Column 5)	Tax Reform Increase in Tax or (Tax Saving) Present Value at 14% Discount
1	$(622,933)	$311,467	$0	$0	$311,467	$273,216
2	(306,025)	153,013	0	0	153,013	117,738
3	(6,734)	3,367	0	0	3,367	2,273
4	94,017	(47,009)	122,356	(40,377)	(6,631)	(3,926)
5	200,632	(100,316)	343,973	(113,511)	13,195	6,853
On sale	3,213,929	(1,606,965)	6,352,598	(2,096,357)	489,393	254,175

Total decrease in PV $650,330

*All assumptions are identical to those of Table 16-4 except for the impact of taxes. These columns apply the 1985 law with a 19-year depreciation period and the ability to reduce taxes from other income.

†These columns are taken directly from Tables 16-4 and 16-5.

benefits of the Plaza Square data under the 1985 and 1986 tax laws. It assumes that the building is owned by a limited partnership and that passive losses cannot be used to reduce taxable income. The owners fall into the 50 percent tax bracket under the 1985 law and into the 33 percent bracket for the 1986 act.

Columns 2 and 3 reflect the large tax benefits that existed under the earlier act. The losses that could reduce income were larger under the earlier act; the 1986 act increased the class life for the depreciation allowances by 66 percent, thus reducing the deductions by 40 percent. Even more important was the ability under the 1985 act to offset other income with the tax losses from real estate. Thus, in year 1, this privilege led to tax benefits from operations of over $310,000, although by year 5 taxes were over $100,000.

Columns 4 and 5 reflect the tax results under the 1986 act. The rule disallowing the use of passive losses to reduce other types of income prevents taxable income from falling below zero. Because of the smaller depreciation deductions, taxable income also rises more rapidly than in the 1985 case. At sale, the loss of the ability to exclude part of a long-term capital gain means that taxes are considerably higher. This occurs even though the actual capital gain is larger under the 1985 law, since at the time of sale the property has a lower *adjusted basis,* due to the faster prior write-offs.

The final two columns show the differences in the tax burdens for each year. Column 6 lists the higher taxes paid under tax reform; column 7 reports their present values using a 14 percent discount rate. The total tax burden increases by $650,330, or about 20 percent of the equity contribution for the property. Of course, how much taxes rise varies somewhat among investors and among properties. Specific amounts depend on leverage, the tax basis, the taxpayers' positive passive income (if any), tax brackets, and similar considerations. However, this example reflects the major thrust of the changes for typical cases.

ACTIVE PARTICIPATION IN RENTAL REAL ESTATE

In addition to the deduction of interest and the postponement of capital gains on individuals' homes and the continued deferral of some of the taxes on the cash flow from income properties, the 1986 act allows a special relief from the general inability to deduct passive losses from other income. If an investor actively participates in a rental investment and meets a limitation on his or her adjusted gross income, the investor may offset up to $25,000 of other income— such as from wages, salaries and dividends—by using losses occurring in this specially treated activity.

Although this relief seems unimportant compared with the large amounts previously deductible through passive participation in limited partnerships, projections disclosed that it would bring relief to a large number of families. Estimates showed that from 60 percent to 80 percent of residential housing is owned by individuals who hold only one or a limited number of units. Many families rent out their old home. Others possess duplexes, triplexes, and quadriplexes, in which they may occupy one unit while renting out the others. Most small apartment houses are owned by individuals or small general partnerships. Partly for political reasons—to avoid antagonizing a large number of voters in order to collect a limited amount of revenue—and partly based on the view that such rentals are legitimate business activities not primarily pursued for tax avoidance, Congress included this special relief in the 1986 tax code. To be eligible for the relief, a taxpayer must own at least 10 percent (by value) of all interests in such activity.

In addition to allowing as little as 10 percent ownership, the definition of active participation was made quite broad. There were suggestions that if owners of second homes and small apartments used full-time managers or realty agents, they might not be eligible for this deduction. Under the congressional interpretation, **active participation in rental activities** does *not* require regular, continuous, and substantial involvement in operations. The taxpayer must simply participate in the making of management decisions or arranging for others to provide services in a significant and *bona fide* sense.

Furthermore, certain types of partnership income were specifically excluded from the definition of passive income. These exclusions cover such activities as operating a hotel or other real estate in which the profits depend on business activities as well as on the value of the property. Also excluded were portfolio income from a partnership and contracts with limited partners for personal services.

On the other hand, specifically defined as passive income and not eligible for this relief is all other limited partners' income, on the basis that limited partners are generally precluded from participating in the partnership's business if they want to retain their limited liability status. Similarly, income under long term rentals and leases is generally defined as passive income and is not eligible for relief.

This provision permits an investor to offset $25,000 of nonpassive income. However, the specific applications tend to be complex, particularly if the taxpayer has income, losses, and credits from a number of properties. This $25,000 relief is phased out at a rate of 50 percent (one dollar of relief lost for each two dollars of income), starting at an adjusted gross income of $100,000. The ability to use this special deduction is lost altogether when adjusted gross income reaches $150,000. Consequently, as noted earlier, the real tax rate in this bracket may run as high as 49.5 percent.

EXAMPLE: Why the marginal tax rate is so high can be demonstrated in a simplified case. A taxpayer actively manages a rental property that has losses totaling $25,000. As a result of the special provision, these losses are used to offset income from wages and dividends, thereby reducing taxable income by $25,000.

The taxpayer's adjusted gross income is $100,000. What happens if the family earns an extra $10,000? Because of the phaseout provision, this increase in adjusted gross income means that only $20,000 of the rental loss can now be used to offset their active income. (The remaining $5,000 loss, plus any other, would be suspended and carried forward.) The taxpayer's taxable income rises by $15,000, consisting of the $10,000 of additional earnings plus the $5,000 that can no longer be offset because of the phaseout provision. At a marginal tax rate of 33 percent, applied to the $15,000 increase in taxable income, taxes paid rise by $4,950. This sum is 49.5 percent of the $10,000 increase in income actually earned.

The tax rate might be somewhat less, depending on other deductions and on whether taxable income is actually in the surcharge brackets. Because such a high *de facto* marginal rate appears excessive in light of the underlying reasoning behind the 1986 act, this seems an obvious area in which some special tax relief would be expected.

SPECIAL REAL ESTATE TAX CREDITS

Prior to the Tax Reform Act of 1986, investors willing to develop and construct low-income housing or to rehabilitate historic and other old buildings were offered a number of incentives through additional tax deferrals or through tax credits. The incentives varied depending on the use and age of the building and on whether new construction or rehabilitation was involved. Some properties received accelerated depreciation; others were allowed to amortize construction period interest and taxes more rapidly; still others were granted a special rehabilitation investment tax credit, or the use of tax-exempt bond financing.

The Tax Reform Act abolished the special depreciation allowances, altered the amounts and requirements for the rehabilitation investment credit, and added credits for the construction, rehabilitation, or acquisition of certain low-income rental housing units.

Tax Credits for Rehabilitation Expenditures

Tax credits were continued for the rehabilitation of older nonresidential buildings and for the rehabilitation and preservation of certified historic structures, whether residential or nonresidential. For an investor to obtain these credits, the Secretary of the Interior must certify that the rehabilitation is consistent with the historic character of the building or the historic district in which it is located. Older buildings are defined as those originally placed in service before 1936.

The rehabilitation must meet certain criteria based on the amount of expenditures, the amount of the original building retained, and the specific types of expenditures. If the investor complies with these and similar regulations, he or she becomes eligible for one of two tiers of credits: (1) Older buildings not certified as historic can receive a 10 percent tax credit, while (2) historic buildings can receive a 20 percent credit. These tax credits can be deducted directly from taxes owed.

Lawmakers felt that these special credits had a beneficial impact on maintaining and restoring the older sections of many cities that had deteriorated under competition from outlying shopping malls and business parks specifically designed to attract an automobile-oriented public. This was one area of the 1986 law in which tax benefits were actually increased on a relative basis, since with lower marginal taxes the value of a credit rises compared to a deduction from taxable income.

Tax Credits for Low-Income Rental Housing

Credits similar to rehabilitation tax credits were authorized in the 1986 act for the construction and rehabilitation of low-income rental units. Such credits can be taken each year for ten years, provided that the property is maintained in its low-income use. Three separate credits are authorized:

1. A maximum credit of 9 percent every year for ten years on expenditures for new construction and rehabilitation of each qualifying low-income housing unit. This credit is indexed to remain at a present value of 80 percent of the expenditures on the unit.

2. A maximum credit of 4 percent each year for similar expenditures if the property is financed with tax-exempt bonds or similar subsidies. The indexing in this case is to maintain a present value of 30 percent of the expenditures.
3. A maximum credit of 4 percent for each year on the cost of acquisition of each existing low-income housing unit. This is a special credit to permit the transfer of such units from public ownership.

These credits apply only to specific low-income units, not to the building or project as a whole. The project must maintain a minimum number of these units, and they must be rented to low-income families and at reasonable rents determined in accordance with procedures similar to those described in Chapter 7. Annual reports are required, and prior credits can be recaptured. The share of costs eligible for the credit is based on the number and square feet in the eligible low-income units compared with the the total space in the project.

In addition to the specific criteria determining an investor's right to qualify for the low-income rental housing credits, there are more general criteria: (1) The rights to the credits must be received from the state in which the project is located. (2) The volume of rights that can be issued by any state is limited on a per-capita basis. (3) Ten percent of a state's volume must be reserved for projects that are developed by certain types of nonprofit organizations.

Basically, taxpayers may claim tax credits up to an amount equal to the $25,000 special deduction for those actively participating in property rental. However, these credits are available to the limited partners of partnerships, even though they do not actively participate but only receive passive limited partnership income. The regulations establishing the ways in which the tax credits interact with the limitations and relief from passive income are extremely complex. As a result of these regulations, those continuing to use these special incentives will find that the 1986 act failed to simplify the preparation of their tax returns.

As with the relief for active participants, the right to claim tax credits in a year is phased out as adjusted gross income rises. However, for these tax credits, the phaseout starts when adjusted gross income reaches $200,000 and is completed when it reaches $250,000.

DELAYING THE TAX LIABILITY

With lower marginal tax rates, it is less worthwhile for an investor to spend a great deal of effort and funds to delay the payment of taxes that would normally be due on the sale of a property. Still, as we have just seen, marginal rates can vary greatly from year to year and a tax delayed is a tax that costs less. Consequently, some investors will continue to delay the time at which taxes on sale are due.

There are various methods for deferring taxes due upon termination. A significant but unpredictable one results from the way property is treated for tax purposes when its owner dies. In such cases, the depreciable basis is raised to the value shown for estate taxes. Elderly people often delay selling investments to avoid paying the tax on capital gains.

More predictable and more subject to decision analysis is the deferral of taxes through the use of exchanges and installment sales.

Tax-deferred Exchanges

A **tax-deferred exchange** takes place when owners exchange their equity in one property for that in another without the need to pay taxes. Because legal requirements are complex, such deals frequently call for specialists in the field. To qualify as a tax-deferred exchange, assets must be of "like kind"—that is, considered similar under the tax code. All real property is treated as essentially alike.

An exchange must be planned in advance and be labeled as such. Upon exchange, the new basis for depreciation is that of the property given up plus any added equity. If equities are not exactly equal, which is usually the case, the party with the smaller equity balances the trade by adding cash, or a mortgage, or other unlike property. This added balance is called **boot.** The recipient of the boot pays capital gains taxes on it.

In considering a trade, investors must recognize that they sacrifice future depreciation deductions when they avoid a current tax upon sale. As in other tax decisions, the degree to which this is worthwhile depends on the length of deferral, the discount rate, and on current compared with expected tax rates. Who gives the boot and who receives it are extremely important details to be considered. To determine the basis of his or her new property, the investor giving the boot adds it to the basis of the property he or she gave up.

EXAMPLE: Investor A owns an apartment house with a market value of $80,000 and an adjusted basis of $30,000. He exchanges this building for Investor B's apartment house, which has a market value of $90,000, giving his building plus $10,000 in cash. Investor A's basis for the newly acquired building is the $10,000 cash boot given, plus the $30,000 adjusted basis of the building he traded. Thus his new basis is $40,000.

The situation for Investor B is different. Assume that the $90,000 building this investor traded had an adjusted basis of $50,000. In return, she received from Investor A a building worth $80,000 and a $10,000 boot in the form of cash. If she had received all cash, she would have had a $40,000 capital gain. Instead, she recognizes as a capital gain and pays taxes on only the $10,000 in cash. She retains the same cost basis of $50,000 on her new building as on the one exchanged. This basis is not reduced by the cash received because she has paid a capital gains tax on this additional sum.

Installment Sales

An **installment sale** occurs when a seller accepts a note or other loan contract rather than cash for part of the selling price. The seller receives the amount owed as a series of future installment payments. Such sales are extremely common on income properties in order to both postpone taxes and furnish partial financing for the sale. Sellers frequently accept a junior mortgage (often in the form of a *wraparound*), thus maintaining the existing loans and reducing the buyer's cash requirements. The seller gains because taxes on the sale become due only as each installment payment is received. For tax purposes, each payment is divided between the part that is a taxable profit and the remainder that is the return of the original investment.

When at least one payment will be received after the tax year in which the sale took place, the installment method is required, although the taxpayer may "elect out"—that is, treat the transaction as a normal sale. To figure how much of a payment is income in an installment sale, the seller calculates the gain on the sale and its percentage (the gross profit percentage) of the contract price. The **contract price** is the total amount of all payments to be received by the seller. It includes any portion of assumed mortgages to third parties that exceeds the property's adjusted basis. The **gross profit percentage** is the gain (gross profit) divided by the contract price. The gain is treated as a long-term capital gain.

Under the Tax Reform Act of 1986, special provisions apply to installment sales of rental real property whose value exceeds $150,000. The changes are complex, but generally the provisions deny the use of the installment method for a portion of the sales price. They do this by requiring that a portion of the outstanding debts be treated for tax purposes as a payment in the year the property is sold. The greater the debt in relation to the value of the asset, the less attractive is the use of the installment method.

EXAMPLE: An investor sells her property for $150,000 and receives $25,000 in cash plus a second mortgage of $50,000 payable in four installments of $12,500 each plus interest at 10 percent. The buyer assumes a $75,000 first mortgage. This means that the seller's contract price is $75,000, consisting of the cash payment and the second mortgage. By subtracting the adjusted basis from the selling price, she finds that she has a $37,500 long-term gain. In the year of sale, she can elect to report on an installment basis. Her gross profit percentage is 50 percent ($37,500 ÷ $75,000), which she must apply to each part of the taxable income she receives. Thus she reports $5,000 (.5 × $10,000) as taxable income the first year and $2,500 (.5 × $5,000) as she receives each of the four additional installments (see columns 2 and 5 in Table 16-7). She reports the interest separately.

Table 16-7 also clarifies the advantages of the installment sale. It compares the present value of the tax payments with the amount that would have to be paid if the installment sales option were not elected. Columns 2, 3, and 4 show

Table 16-7
Value of the Tax Deferral

Year	Taxable Income	Tax at 33 Percent	Present Value of Tax	Taxable Income	Tax at 33 Percent	Present Value of Tax at 14 Percent Discount Rate
0	$15,000	$4,950	$4,950	$5,000	$1,650	$1,650
1				2,500	825	724
2				2,500	825	635
3				2,500	825	557
4				2,500	825	488
Total			$4,950			$4,054

the taxes due on a regular sale. The next three columns show the present value of the taxes due under an installment sale. The delay lowers the present value or cost of the tax, thereby saving in this case about 18 percent of the taxes due. Savings increase the higher the tax rate and the lower the discount rate. If dividing the gain by spreading over time reduces the applicable tax bracket, delaying payment may be especially valuable. The cost of the delay depends on the risks of not receiving the cash at the time of sale, on the amount of interest received relative to its cost to the seller, and on how the additional financing affects the selling price.

SUMMARY

The Tax Reform Act of 1986 drastically decreased the tax shelters available through real estate investing. It increased the importance of the economic feasibility of an investment, in contrast to the primacy of tax considerations under previous tax law.

Property can be owned in several forms, which differ somewhat with respect to taxes, personal liability, ease of transfer, management, and other features. Which form of ownership is used depends on the size of the property, the number of investors, and their objectives.

The significant tax shelters available through homeownership were left intact under the reforms. Owners can deduct their mortgage interest and property tax payments from their taxable income. They can postpone payment of capital gains if they buy another principal residence within a specified period, and they need not pay taxes on up to $125,000 in gains if they are over 55 years of age.

Taxes are deferred to later periods when the depreciation deduction exceeds the actual loss in value. Current taxes are reduced even though higher taxes may have to be paid at the time of sale. The accrual method of accounting may also delay taxes due by reducing current taxable income and not the cash flow.

Income from most real estate investment and that of limited partners falls into a special category called income from passive activities. In general, losses from passive activities can be offset only against income or gains from other passive activities. If the losses cannot be used in a year, they can be carried forward. They cannot be deducted from (or shield) taxable income from other sources such as salaries or dividends. One major exception is that owners who actively participate in the management of rental real estate can use up to $25,000 in such losses to reduce other taxable income. However, this relief is phased out as adjusted gross income grows from $100,000 to $150,000.

Special tax credits are available for investors who rehabilitate older non-residential or historic buildings or who construct or rehabilitate low-income rental housing units. The right to use these credits is also limited and is phased out as gross adjusted income rises above $200,000.

Taxes upon sale can be reduced by tax-deferred exchanges and by the use of installment sales. Exchanges are complex, particularly because exchanged properties have a lower depreciable basis than regular purchases. Although installment sales delay taxes, they also increase collection risks.

KEY TERMS

accelerated cost recovery
   system (ACRS)
accelerated depreciation
accrual method of accounting
active participation in rental
   activities
adjusted basis
alternative minimum tax
   (AMT)
at-risk rule
basis
boot
capital gain
capital gains deduction
contract price
corporation
declining balance
deferred tax payments
depreciable basis
depreciation deduction
depreciation recapture
general partnership
gross profit percentage

individual ownership
individual retirement account
   (IRA)
installment sale
joint tenancy
joint venture
Keogh plan
limited partnership
master limited partnership (MLP)
nonrecourse loan
passive activities
personal property
principal residence
qualified lender
real estate mortgage investment
   company (REMIC)
real property
recourse loan
straight-line depreciation
surcharge
syndicate
tax credits
tax-deferred exchange

tax leverage   **tax shelter**
tax preference item   **tenancy in common**

QUESTIONS

1. Explain what is meant by income from passive activities and its importance for tax planning.
2. How do tax shelters work?
3. What is a master limited partnership, and why has its use increased?
4. What is a tax surcharge?
5. Explain the tax advantages of homeownership.
6. What is the logic of the depreciation deduction? Why may it serve as a tax shelter?
7. How is a capital gain calculated?
8. Explain the relationship of the at-risk rule to real estate investments.
9. Calculate the annual depreciation deductions for equipment that costs $100,000 and falls in the 7-year, 200 percent declining-balance class.
10. What is meant by the $25,000 relief for an active participant in rental real estate? How would it reduce an investor's taxes?
11. What are the major real estate tax credits, and how are they used by investors?

17 The Investor's Evaluation

OBJECTIVES

When you finish this chapter, you should be able to:

- outline the kinds of processes investors use in making their decisions.

- explain traditional measures of profitability such as the gross rent multiplier, the free-and-clear rate of return, and cash-on-cash equity returns.

- use net present values and internal rates of return to evaluate offerings of investment real estate.

- discuss the pros and cons of the different measures and indexes of profitability.

- discuss some methods of measuring risk.

- describe what syndicates are and how they work.

- know the difference between public and private placements of real estate securities.

- recognize some of the key factors needed to analyze syndication offerings.

THE FINANCING OF real estate requires decisions by both lenders and investors. Chapter 15 examined many of the factors lenders take into account in deciding whether and how much to lend. Now we survey the other side of the picture—decisions investors must make. They want to find the expected profitability and risks of proposed property purchases so as to be able to compare them with alternative investments.

THE PRINCIPAL DECISION FACTORS

There are several types of considerations that enter into investors' judgments about a prospective investment (see Figure 17-1). To decide whether potential risks and returns are worthwhile relative to other investment opportunities, investors must project prospective profits and risks. They do this by measuring the equity yields or the amounts of profit contained in the pro forma operating and sales statements.

The cash flow to the investors depends on their choice of leverage—the debt-to-equity ratio—and on the amount of taxes or tax benefits. The form of ownership selected helps determine both taxes and risks. As Figure 17-1 indicates, there is a feedback relationship between leverage-ownership decisions and profitability. Leverage determines how the net operating income is split between debt service and returns to equity. Preliminary unsatisfactory returns to either investors or lenders can often be improved by restructuring the financial and ownership organization, by changing the amounts each side puts up, or by altering the relationships between the partners in a deal.

Cash flow projections are translated into rates of return and profitability indexes. Comparative profitability-to-risk measures enable investors to decide what to do about offers they receive. Do the proposals as they stand meet their objectives? If not, can the terms be negotiated to make them better and more acceptable? Most proposals offered to a typical investor are rejected. In some cases only a brief perusal makes it clear that the investor's objectives cannot be met. In other cases analysis and negotiations may extend over long periods while more and more facts are developed and alternatives are explored.

This chapter begins by showing how investors develop profitability measures. Then we consider how structuring the investment differently can shift potential risks and returns. We conclude by discussing syndications, a special form of ownership that has become extremely important.

INDEXES OF PROFITABILITY

Profitability analysis consists of translating pro forma cash flow statements into **profitability indexes (PIs)**, which measure expected profits or yields

Figure 17-1
The Investment Decision

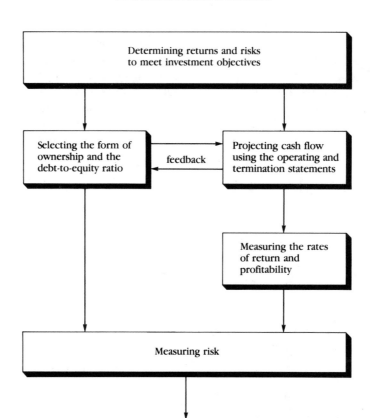

that the investor can compare with each other and with experience. Each index summarizes the data on an individual project. Rules can be formulated that tell the investor whether a proposal should be accepted, rejected, or negotiated.

The advent of the computer has made it possible to calculate many possible indexes, each based on a different set of assumptions about the future. In fact, separate indexes are often calculated for a wide number of assumptions about the economy and the particular structuring of an investment. Separate calculations are also made using different assumptions about the length of the holding period before the investment is sold.

Consequently, the field of investment analysis has seen a rapid increase in the number of available profitability indexes. In the construction of these measures, there is usually a trade-off between the simplicity of calculation and ease of understanding and the total volume of information furnished. Each investor can decide whether the minimal information obtainable through simple procedures will suffice or whether it is worth spending the additional effort to assemble and use more complete information.

The desirability of an investment depends on many things, some of which require projecting estimates into the future. Income properties have a cash flow, certain tax benefits, and potential income at termination. Analysis of the profitability of a purchase requires balancing these expected benefits against the initial and all future money payments.

TRADITIONAL MEASURES

The simplest profitability measures are those confined to only a single period flow of income. They may use an estimate of stabilized income, or income for the first year, or an average income over a number of years. A major shortcoming of such measures is that they fail to take into account the time value of money.

Gross Rent Multipliers and Rates of Return

Earlier chapters introduced several measures of this single-income type— gross rent multipliers, rate of return on assets (ROR), and rate of return on equity (ROE). These are the measures found on most brokers' offering sheets. Apparently because of their comparative simplicity, they continue to be used despite obvious disadvantages.

Tables 17-1 and 17-2 contain data that make it possible to review their contents and to compare them with other methods of measuring profitability. Table 17-1 recapitulates the data on the Plaza Square building example used in the previous chapters. Table 17-2 repeats the equations for the gross rent

Table 17-1
Recapitulation of Data on the Plaza Square Building

Price of building:	$15,154,000					
Equity:	3,230,800*					
			(in thousands)			
						Cash Flow
	1986	1987	1988	1989	1990	on Sale
Gross rent†	$2,415	$2,511	$2,609	$2,711	$2,818	
Net operating income	1,470	1,635	1,814	1,907	2,006	$19,438
Before-tax cash flow	139	305	483	577	675	7,871
After-tax cash flow	139	305	483	536	561	5,775

*Equity equals down payment of $3,030,800 plus reserve of $200,000.
†Includes other income and parking income, but not interest on reserves.

Table 17-2
Traditional Measures of Profitability
(in thousands)

Measure	Equation	First Year	Five-Year Average
Gross rent multiplier (GRM)	Gross rent × GRM = price	$2,415 × 6.27 = $15,154	$2,613 × 5.80 = $15,154
Return on assets (ROR)	$ROR = \dfrac{NOI}{price}$	$9.70\% = \dfrac{\$1,470}{\$15,154}$	$11.65\% = \dfrac{\$1,766}{\$15,154}$
Return on equity (BTCF)	$ROE\,(1) = \dfrac{BTCF}{E}$	$4.30\% = \dfrac{\$139}{\$3,231}$	$13.49\% = \dfrac{\$436}{\$3,231}$
Return on equity (ATCF)	$ROE\,(2) = \dfrac{ATCF}{E}$	$4.30\% = \dfrac{\$139}{\$3,231}$	$12.53\% = \dfrac{\$405}{\$3,231}$

multiplier, the return on assets (ROR), and for two versions of return on equity (ROE). It also shows the results of calculating these indexes based on income projected either for the first year or for five years.

The amount of detail required for each index—and therefore the information it contains—expands as one moves down the table. The gross rent multiplier fails to include information on vacancies, expenses, debt service, and taxes. Each of these can differ greatly among properties and, therefore, interpreting GRMs requires more insight into these absent factors.

In the discussion of capitalization rates and the free-and-clear return (ROR) in Chapter 15, we noted that some defend their use on the assumption that market values should not depend on financing and, therefore, that the free-and-clear return is in some ways a better and truer measure of value than those that include financing. Yet since the returns to investors do vary with leverage and debt service, most investors prefer to include such data in their decision process.

The return on equity (ROE)—also called the cash-on-cash and the *equity dividend rate*—has been in the past the most popular technique. With the advent of the computer, the more modern methods have replaced it among most professionals. Table 17-2 makes clear that after-tax rates differ from those based on pretax data. But because the results of this analysis depend so heavily on the accuracy of the projections and on stability in the tax laws, and because both of them vary so widely, these measures can vary greatly from the projections to the actual outcomes. Any measure of profitability is only as good as the information and intuition with which it is crafted.

Other facts that stand out in the table and that apply to all measures are the variations between the indexes based on five-year averages and those using only the first year. Although the latter are used most commonly, such results may conceal more than they reveal. Since rents in Table 17-2 are projected to rise by

5 percent a year, the relationship between the first-year indexes and the five-year indexes is slight.

The main reason for using any of these measures is availability of data, minimum use of future expectations, and simplicity. If an investor has enough experience in the market, a quick perusal of these measures gives some indication of how a property compares with others in the market. However, when future increases in income and in selling price are significant, data on a single year or even a few years do not contribute much to making a good decision.

Payback Period

The **payback period** for an investment is the number of years required to recover the original cash investment. It is the ratio of the initial investment to the annual cash flows for the recovery period. The payback period depends on whether or not tax effects are taken into account.

EXAMPLE: An investor is offered a property for an equity investment of $100,000. The annual cash flow before taxes and after debt service is projected at $10,000 and the after-tax cash flow is $8,500. The payback period using the BTCF is estimated as:

$$\text{Payback period} = \frac{\text{equity}}{\text{before-tax cash flow}} = \frac{E}{BTCF} = \frac{\$100,000}{\$10,000} = 10 \text{ years} \quad \textbf{(17.1)}$$

On the other hand, if we consider the tax effects, we find:

$$\text{Payback period} = \frac{\text{equity}}{\text{after-tax cash flow}} = \frac{E}{ATCF} = \frac{\$100,000}{\$8,500} = 11.8 \text{ years} \quad \textbf{(17.2)}$$

To increase accuracy, the projected cash flows must include year-by-year projected changes in income.

The payback period method usefully identifies the period of time over which invested funds are at risk. However, investors want to receive a profit beyond the mere recovery of their investment. Using a criterion of choosing investments with the shortest payback period, we might select an investment that brings back the invested funds rapidly but generates no profit. On the other hand, the payback period criterion can lead to rejection of an investment that returns funds more slowly but generates substantial profits through continued payments extending well beyond the payback of the initial investment.

All of the above profitability measures are easy to calculate and understand. Yet they leave out much information that might lead to better decisions. With the widespread use of calculators and computer spreadsheets to track many variables simultaneously, simplicity is no longer as great a virtue as it once was. Other indexes that provide all of the detail of the pro forma statements, including debt service, appreciation, shifts in income, taxes, and projected sales prices, can be calculated with little more effort and supply much more useful data.

DISCOUNTED CASH FLOW METHODS

Discounted cash flow methods use the information on projected cash flows from the pro forma operating and termination statements in a sophisticated manner. They can include the different factors neglected in the traditional techniques, enabling an analyst to test the impact of separate assumptions and scenarios. Their chief drawback arises from the fact that their results look so definitive that investors tend to forget how much they depend on the data and assumptions on which they are built. If these are weak, the whole structure can crumble.

Net Present Values and the Investment Decision

Although the concepts of net present value (NPV) were introduced in Chapter 3 (Equation 3.3) and have been used to find present value in a number of cash flow comparisons, we have not considered in detail how this technique is used to select among a number of competing investments. The key idea is that only those investments should be selected that are likely to yield a minimum **required rate of return,** also called the *cutoff* or *hurdle rate.* The required rate must include a sufficient risk premium so that its risk-adjusted results will be profitable and will equal or surpass those of alternatives.

In the present value method, all projected cash flows, including the reversion, are discounted to present values using this required rate of return. The difference between all positive and negative values is the **net present value (NPV)**. The technique can be used for every type of cash flow, but usually it is applied to net operating income or to the after-tax cash flow. The discount rate selected must differ depending on which concept of cash flow is employed, since the risk and risk premium differ with the amount of leverage.

Choosing the required rate of return can be accomplished in several ways. Some investors pick a minimum cutoff rate; they will not invest in a real property unless they can earn some minimum (such as 16 percent) after taxes on their equity. Others, figuring the marginal yield they are earning in other fields, might then decide that if they can earn the same rate of return from real estate, it will be worthwhile because of the diversification offered. Still others may build up to the desired discount rate by adding to the rate they pay on borrowings an additional sum (say 5 percent) to cover the cost of management and added risks.

EXAMPLE: Table 17-3 illustrates how net present values are calculated from the data for the Plaza Square building offer found in Table 17-1. Column

Table 17-3
Calculating Net Present Values

Year	Investment	After-Tax Cash Flow	Discount Factor at 16%	Present Value of Negative Payments at 16%	Present Value of Positive Payments at 16%
0	($1,938,480)		1.0000	($1,938,480)	
1	(723,699)	$ 139,190	0.8621	(623,879)	$ 119,991
2	(810,543)	304,661	0.7432	(602,366)	226,413
3		483,286	0.6407		309,621
4		536,248	0.5523		296,165
5		561,539	0.4761		267,356
5	(Reversion)	5,774,556	0.4761		2,749,341
		Total present value		($3,164,724)	$3,968,887
		Net present value			$ 804,163

2 shows the amount invested. The total equity is initially $3,230,800. However, the investment is spread over three years. The investors agree to make a down payment of slightly over 60 percent of the required equity and then to pay 20 percent of the equity plus 12 percent a year interest on the outstanding balance in each of the next two years. (Such phasing-in of investments has become very common.) The table also shows the expected incomes and reversion.

The analyst chooses 16 percent as the minimum desired rate of return. The discount factor for each year is multiplied by that year's cash flow. (It is assumed that all flows occur at year end.) All present values are summed to find that the net present value of the investment is $804,163. This is the total projected profit.

Rather than finding the net present value of all expenditures and income combined, as in Table 17-3, analysts often compute the present values of the equity investment and of the cash income flows separately. In such cases, the net present value is obtained by subtracting the present value of the investments from that of the projected cash flows. As an example from the table we can calculate:

Present value of income and reversion	$3,968,887
Present value of the investment	$3,164,724
Net present value	$ 804,163

This purchase may be deemed worthwhile because the net present value is positive. If the projections are correct, the investor expects to make money.

Table 17-4
Calculating a Present Value
Profitability Index

$$\text{Profitability index (PI)} = \frac{\text{present value of positive payments}}{\text{present value of negative payments}}$$

$$\text{PI} = \frac{\$3,968,887}{\$3,164,724} = 1.25$$

The Present Value Profitability Index

Present value data are often translated into **present value profitability index** by dividing the present value of all positive flows by all negative flows. If cash outlays occur only in the first year, this benefit-to-cost ratio can also be calculated as the present value of future returns over the initial cash outlay.

EXAMPLE: An actual profitability calculation is presented in Table 17-4. The present values of income in the previous table are added together and are then divided by the present values of the equity investments. The ratio of profitability is 1.25, reflecting the fact that the investment is profitable at a 16 percent discount rate. An index below 1.00 would mean that the investment would not be earning the desired discount rate.

Profitability indexes (PIs) can be used to compare different investments, but they run into problems if the cash outlays are of different sizes. Normally, one would select an investment with a PI of 1.2 over one with an index of 1.1. But what if the net present value of the projected profits of the first property was $18,000 with outlays of $15,000, while that of the second was $110,000 with outlays of $100,000? In both cases, profits exceed the 16 percent discount rate required for the investment. But we can easily calculate that the dollar profit in the first case is $3,000 ($18,000 ÷ $15,000 = PI of 1.2), while in the second it is $10,000 ($110,000 ÷ $100,000 = PI of 1.1). When conflicts of this sort exist, the choice depends on the investor's capital position and general investment strategy rather than on a simple comparison of profitability indexes.

Internal Rate of Return

In Chapter 4 the internal rate of return was defined as that rate of return at which the present value of all future positive inflows equals the present value of all outflows. In other words, it equates the initial capital investment and the future cash flows. The formula for its solution is given in Equation 4.3.

EXAMPLE: We can calculate the internal rate of return that an investor would receive from the Plaza Square building on an after-tax basis. The equity investment is $3,230,800. Although the investors use three payments rather than cash for the down payment, and therefore pay additional interest, it is the present value of the payments that is used in finding the IRR, on the assumption that the interest rate charged equals the investors' discount rate. The after-tax cash flows from operations and sale (in Table 14-2) are inserted in the equation. The internal rate of return, found with a calculator, is 21.49 percent:

$$\text{Equity} = \frac{\text{ATCF}_1}{1 + \text{IRR}} + \frac{\text{ATCF}_2}{(1 + \text{IRR})^2} + \frac{\text{ATCF}_3}{(1 + \text{IRR})^3} + \cdots$$
$$+ \frac{\text{ATCF}_n}{(1 + \text{IRR})^n} + \frac{\text{REV}}{(1 + \text{IRR})^n} \quad (17.3)$$

$$\$3{,}230{,}800 = \frac{139{,}190}{1 + \text{IRR}} + \frac{304{,}661}{(1 + \text{IRR})^2} + \frac{483{,}286}{(1 + \text{IRR})^3} + \frac{536{,}284}{(1 + \text{IRR})^4}$$
$$+ \frac{561{,}539}{(1 + \text{IRR})^5} + \frac{5{,}774{,}556}{(1 + \text{IRR})^5}$$

$$\text{IRR} = 21.49\%$$

Investors will accept those proposals with IRRs that exceed the minimum discount rate they believe is necessary to compensate them for the particular risks involved. In discussing present values, we assumed that the minimal acceptable rate of return for an investment of this type was 16 percent. If the IRR falls short of this cutoff rate, an effort could be made to raise the IRR by renegotiation or by restructuring the financing.

Sometimes it is suggested that a good rule to guide decisions is to rank all proposals by their IRRs, then take them in turn from the highest to the lowest until all funds are used up. However, this approach neglects several points:

- Comparisons among IRRs should be made after they have been corrected for differential risks.
- As with the NPV, the amount of actual profits is significant. An investor might prefer a $15,000 investment with an IRR of 18 percent to a $5,000 one with an IRR of 20 percent, especially if he or she could choose only one.
- An investor might also want to choose on the basis of the payback period. How fast the investor gets his or her funds back may be more important than small differences in IRRs.
- In addition to specific risk, the investor should also consider how an investment affects the overall portfolio. If there was a big difference in their covariances, three properties, each with a return of 18 percent, might be preferable to three, each of which promised a 20 percent yield but whose risks were highly correlated. The reduction in risk from the greater portfolio diversification would make the sacrifice of a 2 percent potential return worthwhile.

Comparison of Present Value and Rate of Return

Arguments often arise among analysts as to whether it is better to make choices based on present values or on internal rates of return. In most cases it makes little difference. Comparison of two properties using either method usually leads to the identical choice. But differences are occasionally found. The two measures can lead to opposite conclusions, particularly if the cash flows are uneven or the internal rate of return is considerably removed from the discount factor used in present value calculations. In Table 17.5, for example, both property 1 and property 2 sell for $100,000. If we calculate net present values at a 10 percent discount rate, columns 3 and 5 demonstrate that the first property has a net present value of $31,958, compared with the second property's NPV of $26,795. It appears that an investor should certainly invest in property 1 in preference to 2. But the IRR of property 2 is nearly 3 percent higher. Using this profitability criterion, the investor should pick 2.

If an investor could choose only one property, which should be picked— the one with the higher present value or the one with the higher internal rate of return? To answer, we must first recognize what causes this difference. The internal rate of return assumes that the cash flow received in any year can be reinvested at the calculated rate of return until the end of the investment period. The present value procedure, on the other hand, implies either that the funds received as cash flow will be used elsewhere at the then-existing market rate or that, if they are reinvested in the project, it will be at the selected rate used to discount the future cash flows.

Thus the present value procedure in the table assumes that the reinvestment rate would be at 10 percent for both projects. On the other hand, the internal rate of return calculation results in the use of a 19 percent reinvestment rate for the first investment and 22 percent for the second. Uneven flows arising

Table 17-5
Comparisons of Net Present Value
and Internal Rate of Return

Year	Property 1	Present Value at 10%	Property 2	Present Value at 10%
Investment 0	($100,000)	($100,000)	($100,000)	($100,000)
1	0	0	40,000	36,364
2	20,000	16,529	40,000	33,058
3	40,000	30,053	40,000	30,053
4	125,000	85,377	40,000	27,321
Present value		$31,958		$26,795
Internal rate of return	19.07%		21.86%	

at different points in the future cause the conflict that makes the two criteria suggest opposite choices.

If some of the returns are negative during the operating period and the cash flows change from negative to positive and vice versa more than once, *multiple* internal rates of return may result. Although this is a disconcerting and commonly recognized problem, when it occurs the ability to select returns is not too difficult in practice. The rates differ because the investor is borrowing money in some periods and reinvesting in others. The investor can make logical decisions in such cases by separating the IRRs by period and relating them to his or her portfolio and objectives.

However, the problem raised by the separate reinvestment assumptions may require a modification of the profitability measure. At times, the implied reinvestment rates from the IRRs are much higher than would appear logical. An investor receiving a cash flow at the rate of 25 percent may find that the only possible reinvestments pay no more than 10 percent. The investor will be earning 25 percent for the period the funds are actually invested but will not be able to keep the funds fully invested at the 25 percent rate of return for the entire period. As a result, the investor might prefer a 22 percent IRR if the cash flow were delayed, since the reinvestment problem would be reduced.

Although such examples call attention to the need to consider the timing of cash flows in using IRRs for decision purposes, some analysts argue that one should not really be concerned about the reinvestment issue.* The IRR correctly measures the return on cash for the period funds are tied up in the investment. What the funds will return when reinvested can be thought of as a separate problem. At times, a faster cash flow and the need to reinvest is desirable. Future yields may be projected above current ones, or the cash flow may be desired for liquidity purposes.

The Modified Internal Rate of Return

If the projections result in an IRR with a reinvestment rate that seems too high, one method investors frequently use is to calculate the **modified internal rate of return (MIRR).** Under this procedure, a reinvestment rate that appears logical is picked—such as 14 percent. Cash flows are then compounded forward at this rate until the terminal period. At that point all of the compounded cash flows plus the termination cash are added together. This value is then discounted back to equate to the initial investment. The result is the modified internal rate of return. In it, if the IRR exceeds the selected reinvestment rate, the reinvestment occurs at a lower rate.

EXAMPLE: An investment is offered at $100,000 which will pay $50,000 at the end of each of the next 3 years, and then will be worthless. Its internal rate

---

*For example, see J. C. Van Horne, *Financial Management and Policy,* 7th ed. (Englewood Cliffs, N.J.: Prentice-Hall, 1986), 153.

Table 17-6
Calculating a Modified Internal Rate of Return
With a Reinvestment Rate of 12 Percent

Year	Investment	Cash Flow	Compounding Factor at 12% IFFV	Value at End of Period
0	$100,000			
1		$50,000	1.2544	$62,720
2		50,000	1.12	56,000
3		50,000	1	50,000
Total				$168,720

$$\text{Investment} = \frac{\text{end of period values}}{(1 + \text{MIRR})^3}$$

$$\$100,000 = \frac{\$168,720}{(1 + \text{MIRR})^3}$$

$$\text{MIRR} = 19.05\%$$

$$\text{Regular IRR} = 23.38\%$$

of return is 23.38 percent. The investor believes that, because the current economic situation is unusual, when she receives the $50,000 cash flows at the end of each year, she will only be able to reinvest them at 12 percent.

Table 17-6 shows a calculation of the MIRR. Column 4 gives the compound interest rate factors (IFFV) needed to calculate the value of each cash flow at the end of the period if they are reinvested at 12 percent. When all of the reinvested cash flows are summed at the end of the period, they equal $168,720. The IRR required to equate this to the initial investment of $100,000 is 19.05 percent.

Unless this modification is used, many investors reject IRRs on the assumption that they will not be able to reinvest at its rate. They therefore believe that the present value calculations are preferable. They consider it unlikely that current rates of return will continue unchanged in the future.

If the amount of equity required is small but the effort required is high, the internal rate of return is also a poor measure. For example, most developers use mainly their own efforts; their actual cash investment is practically nothing. To find their most profitable approach to a problem, they must use the net present value method. As we shall see in Chapter 19, IRRs in such cases may be extremely high, but their base and cash flows are so small that they are virtually meaningless.

A major advantage of the internal rate of return, on the other hand, is that it does not require specifying a discount rate in advance. The rate of return arises in the course of the investment analysis of each project. Because rates of return are comparable, it is simpler to compute and compare them for all possible projects. Furthermore, they provide an index of how much better off the investor will be as a result of renegotiation or restructuring. The fact that they are in a percent form makes IRRs easier to compare with yields from other investments. Many investors find it difficult intuitively to relate the excess NPVs, which are in dollars, to yields.

MEASURING RISK

After measuring potential profitability, investors must adjust for possible risks in order to decide whether to accept a particular real estate proposal in competition either with another property or with an alternative investment elsewhere. They must first decide how large a risk premium is included in the projected returns. Investment real estate offerings show high rates of return because risks are great. Investors want to compare yields that have been corrected for risks.

Risk Premiums

A risk premium compensates for the probability that the projected yields will be off the mark. The variability of returns for properties is large because so many things can go wrong. The economy may turn down. Projected inflation and appreciation may not materialize. The information used may be incorrect. The local market may fall off sharply because of excess competition or a failure to grow. Expenses may be higher than projected. All of these possibilities are sometimes termed *business risk*.

The use of leverage in real estate finance adds further financial risks. If the cash flow from a property is inadequate for a period, a foreclosure will occur unless income from other sources is called upon to cover payments. When most of NOI is set aside to meet a large debt service, a single year's bad results can end in default. Many frustrated investors grind their teeth when they see successful projects that they had to give up because they could not find the funds to ride out comparatively short loss periods.

A smaller debt service means a lower break-even point, which may allow a property to be retained through a period with large vacancies and the failure of rents to rise. If the debt payments can be met, returns will depend on the full holding period, rather than being cut off early by loss of the property through a failure to meet debt payments.*

---

*For more detailed discussion of risks, see S. J. Maisel, ed., *Risk and Capital Adequacy in Commercial Banks* (Chicago: University of Chicago Press, 1981), 6–8, Ch. 2; also S. A. Pyhrr and J. R. Cooper, *Real Estate Investment* (New York: Wiley, 1982), Ch. 12.

Correcting for Risks

Investors deal with risk in various ways. The simplest is to be conservative. They add a large risk premium in calculating discounted cash flows or subtract it from projected rates of return. If their premiums are too far above the market, they will never make a purchase because most net present values they calculate will be negative.

Sensitivity Analysis   With the advent of personal computers, **sensitivity analysis** to measure the danger from incorrect assumptions has become widespread. Using financial spreadsheets—the most popular use of personal computers—the investor can see quickly and simply how IRRs and discounted values change as a result of altering assumptions. The investor can run a model with three appreciation rates, three leverage ratios, and three revenue assumptions in an hour or two. He or she then compares the results to see how sensitive the promised returns are to the assumptions.

In some cases, analysts weight each calculation by assigning it a probability similar to the example for adjustable-rate loans in Table 12-2. The results of the different assumptions can then be averaged and the decision based on the weighted probability average. More commonly, decision makers examine the worst-case possibility in some detail and assign it a subjective probability in their mind. They then decide whether they are willing to take the indicated risk.

Simulations   A more complex and formal procedure uses **Monte Carlo risk simulations** to calculate expected rates of return and their variances. Both the Maisel and the Phyrr and Cooper books referred to in the footnote on page 459 contain examples of this technique. The analyst assigns probability distributions to each of a limited set of assumptions that are expected to vary and to affect the project's return. A computer model then selects randomly (the *Monte Carlo simulation*) from each distribution and calculates potential returns. The average expected return, its variance, and the pertinent statistics are calculated and used to arrive at a proper risk premium.

Partitioning

A somewhat less formal technique examines the forces underlying the projected rates of return in more detail. **Partitioning**—dividing up a return into its components—enables the investor to see how much of the expected return comes from inflation, from improved management, from tax saving, or from other factors.

EXAMPLE: Table 17-7 is a simple three-way partition of the projected increase in net present value in the Plaza Square case. Columns 2 and 3 divide the after-tax cash flow from operations into tax saving from depreciation deductions and all other. The final column reflects the after-tax gain from the difference between the cost at purchase and the net sales price.

Table 17-7
Partition of Net Present Value by Its Components
At 14% Discount Rate

Present Value of Investment in Plaza Square: $4,290,999

Year	After-Tax Cash Flow Excluding Depreciation Deduction	Tax Savings from Depreciation Deduction	After-Tax Appreciation
1	$7,228	$131,962	
2	166,962	137,699	
3	345,587	137,699	
4	398,549	137,699	
5	423,840	137,699	
Reversion			$5,774,556
Total	$1,342,166	$682,758	$5,774,556
Present value at 14%	824,176	467,699	2,999,123
Percent of total present value	19.21%	10.90%	69.89%

The final rows in each column show the total cash from each source and their present values discounted at 14 percent. They also show the share of each in the total gain in value. We see that 19.21 percent came from improved operating income, 10.90 percent from the tax savings, and 69.89 percent from expected appreciation.

The decision maker gets a feeling for risks by seeing the share of each in the total. The larger the share from operations, the safer the projection, especially if the increased revenue projections are conservative. The present value of the tax savings from different depreciation methods can be compared to see how much difference accelerated depreciation would make. This technique can be used in greater detail to analyze more of the assumptions and to compare particular investments to match investors' objectives and constraints.

The Final Decision

The analyses of profitability and risk usually lead the investor to a decision to reject an offer or to make a counteroffer. The analyses can show how returns can be increased or risks reduced, either by restructuring the debt-to-equity relationships or by altering prices or the debt service. (Chapter 19 contains examples of how this works.) In any case, the investor must also consider how a property will fit into his or her holdings. A lower return can be accepted if it adds diversification to the portfolio.

SYNDICATIONS

Before proceeding to a discussion of more specialized forms of borrowing and lending, this section examines one especially popular form of ownership: limited partnership syndications. This also serves as another example of how to calculate profitability.

A critical problem in financing many real estate projects has been finding capital. A logical solution was to interest several people—friends, clients, or acquaintances—in the joint purchase of a property. The investment economics could be explained to a few key people, who often would then bring in additional money from friends and relatives. This type of partnership has existed throughout the real estate industry. It is only in the past 30 years, however, that the concept has gone far beyond this simple relationship.

The growth of a broader interest in real estate, the development of limited partnerships, the possibility of high gains through leverage, and the sales of tax benefits led to rapid expansion in the field of real estate syndication. The field has undergone—and probably will continue to undergo—major ups and downs because the values offered have often depended too heavily on everything's "going right" for the project. When the economy has weakened or ventures have drifted too far from economic reality, many syndicates have experienced plummeting values. Moreover, limited partnerships have been a particular target of tax reform. The bankruptcy of a number of prominent syndication firms in 1986 also caused a slowdown and a major set-back to their activities.

What Is a Real Estate Syndicate?

A **syndicate** is usually a group of investors gathered together to invest in one or more real estate activities. They may own through a partnership, corporation, or trust. Frequently joint ventures have been set up in which a promoter contributes entrepreneurial activities and management expertise, while passive investors put up the money. In many cases, the ventures have one or a few general partners and many limited ones. Real estate ownership through this normally burdensome form is possible on the assumption that management problems are small, income distribution simple, and liability coverable by insurance.

Many people think of real estate syndication as analogous to fractionalizing the ownership of real estate into individual shares, just as common stock represents a fractionalized ownership of the company. The investors contribute money without management responsibilities and with limited liability, while the sponsor or promoter assumes the responsibilities of management.

How Syndicates Work

At first, most syndications were individual projects. Today, the idea for the syndicate usually originates with promoters who have an idea for a new development or see an existing property that they feel is a good buy. They put together a proposal which requires more capital than they have available. They must then decide what their relationship should be to the proposed syndicate. In many cases promoters have thought of the syndicate primarily as a way of selling property. For a new development, the syndicate makes construction possible and ensures the promoters a profit.

Since 1970, however, the largest volume of syndications has come from firms for which syndication is a primary business. For example, the largest firm, Balcor/American Express, has sold over $3 billion worth of syndications. Close to ten firms have each sold more than $1 billion. The fifteen largest firms have done about 75 percent of the total volume.

The firms search for properties, buy them, form the syndicate, prepare the offering of its shares to the public, manage the property, and finally sell it. They profit from their charges for each of these activities and from their participation in both operating income and any appreciation. Sales of real estate syndicates totaled about $15 billion in 1985.

Many syndicators have their own distribution systems. Most of the largest, however, distribute through traditional securities firms; in fact, many of the largest brokerage houses have affiliated real estate syndicators. Anyone who deals with a stock brokerage firm can call his or her account executive, who will be happy to send copies of the prospectuses of syndications that the firm is promoting. Investors can then buy the partnership shares through the broker.

The Factors Causing Growth

Although syndications have primarily been sold, not bought, the selling has been possible because they possess a genuine underlying economic advantage. When people want to invest in real estate, a syndication may well be a logical form. The principal economic advantages are of four types:

1. Syndicates and joint ventures are single-tax entities. They have offered sizable tax shelters, and this has been the primary feature used by promoters and salesmen to sell syndications. Without the tax shelter, it is probable that real estate syndication would have remained a fairly small-scale, local enterprise, appealing mainly to groups of friends and acquaintances. The reduction in tax advantages as a result of the 1986 Tax Reform Act will test the importance of syndicates.

2. Investment expertise and independent judgment are available to the investor. One of the major promises of syndication is that by purchasing a small investment, one becomes a partner with skilled real estate operators. Although this is not often the case, it can occur. Many of the nation's

largest and most prominent real estate professionals use joint venture relationships extensively. An individual who properly selects his or her investment can become a partner with some of the major financial institutions or most prominent real estate entrepreneurs.

Clearly, the possibility of obtaining such expertise is critical for many potential investors who simply do not have the time or skills to analyze individual properties. They can put their time to better use by analyzing their potential partners and then putting their trust in the expertise of the promoters with whom they have decided to invest. Given the fractionalization and poor information in real estate markets, participation by professionals is especially important.

3. The investor has an opportunity to realize economies of scale in buying and managing properties. Small properties, even if they can be bought at a good price, are at a competitive disadvantage to larger properties. Their operating expenses are proportionately greater. Recreational facilities and special features are higher on a per-unit basis. Property management—for both the on-site resident manager and the off-site executive manager—is more efficient and cheaper when spread over a larger number of units.

    The same types of scale economies apply to acquisition activities. The costs of evaluating the market area, arranging financing, negotiating purchase terms, and obtaining legal documentation do not vary directly with the size of a property. Similar analysis and work are required for each purchase, regardless of size. The *relative* costs of these activities are greater for small properties.

4. Through syndications, investors can achieve improved diversification and "staying power." The partnership can buy multiple properties, thereby lessening dependence on any one property. The problem of risks tied to a particular location or property type, which plagues individual buyers of real estate, can be avoided. Similarly, it may be easier for a partnership to raise and maintain the reserves necessary to avoid a complete failure due to temporarily impeded cash flows. The amount of reserves for a number of properties will be proportionally less if the properties have sufficient diversification. As a result, the risks through diversified partnerships may be considerably less than those through investment in one or two properties.

The Hazards of Syndication Offers   As with all investments that appear sound on the surface, the prospective investor must probe each syndication carefully. Many syndicators make most of their profits from the selling process. They need products to sell and can become careless in selecting the properties they choose. This is especially true in an inflationary climate. If the syndicator overpays, obtaining competitive profits becomes difficult.

Many syndicators' projections in the 1980s became far too optimistic. The fact that they usually contain a separate opinion from a fee appraiser is far from a guarantee of accuracy. As syndications became more popular, promoters raised their fees. Smaller percentages of the funds raised actually went into the property.

Although it is possible to find diversified syndications, many offerings contain only a single property. Investors must manage their own diversification by investing less in more offerings. Furthermore, a form of reverse diversification can occur. Syndicators can also speculate by becoming general partners for more and more limited partnerships, thereby spreading their limited capital too far. If one property defaults, they may not have the funds to save it. This can lead to cash shortages and bankruptcies in other properties that, standing alone, would be safe. Instead, foreclosures and losses hit all of their partnerships.

Many cases of questionable practices or outright fraud have also occurred. As in any investments, careful investigation and analysis are essential. The fact that a certain type of investment may have advantages is no guarantee of success for individual endeavors. Risks due to incompetence, poor projections, and the cyclical nature of real estate and credit remain high.

Types of Syndications

Syndicates can take any of the forms of real estate ownership—corporations, joint ventures, joint ownership, REITs, general partnerships, or limited partnerships. One of the largest syndications—that of Rockefeller Center Property in 1985 for $750 million—took the form of a REIT. However, most syndicates are formed as limited partnerships. This is so often the case that many observers use the terms "limited partnership" and "syndication" synonymously.

Syndicates can differ in other ways than in forms of ownership:

- Investments can be made through a private or public offering.
- The syndicate can hold single or multiple properties.
- Offering documents may specify the exact property or properties to be purchased. Or they may leave the selection of the property to the sponsor after the partnership has been formed.

These latter unspecified offerings are called **blind pools.** Investors purchase on the strength of the general objectives and characteristics of the pool as described by its promoters. Investors do not know what property will be owned but depend, instead, on the reputation of the promoters. Frequently such offerings include the right of **rescission;** that is, investors can ask for their money back for a short period after the properties have been bought, if they do not like what has been accumulated.

Syndications as Securities

The shares offered by promoters in a syndicate usually qualify legally as securities. A **security** is an investment contract in which investors buy a property for a profit rather than for their own personal use and in which the purchase is made on the basis of continuing third-party management.

Sales of securities require full disclosure of a wide variety of information:

- a discussion of possible risks
- earnings projections on a per-share basis
- the sponsor's past track record
- a full explanation of compensation and fees
- specifics on the partnership agreements and any arrangements for or lack of transferability
- a detailed discussion of tax considerations
- complete information on the individual properties to be acquired or a statement of principles that will be followed for a blind pool

This information is necessary whether the securities are registered with the Securities and Exchange Commission (SEC) or a state securities commission, or not registered at all.

Public and Private Offerings

As a general rule, securities offered for sale must meet the standards of the SEC and thus are **public offerings.** However, if they qualify for a specific exemption they need not be registered. The two most common exemptions are:

- **Intrastate exemptions,** in which everyone involved with the syndicate lives and operates within the boundaries of a single state. (But such syndicates may be subject to state regulations and registration under so-called blue sky laws.)
- The **private placement exemption,** which applies if the offering goes only to investors capable of bearing the economic risks of the investment and who personally have enough knowledge and experience in financial and business matters to be capable of evaluating the merits and risks of investing in the security. This exemption was limited initially to a maximum of 35 investors, but it has since expanded greatly.

Subscribers to private placements are required to sign investor qualification letters detailing their knowledge and experience and their ability to take the risks. Typically, investors might qualify to bear the risk (a) if they are in the top federal income tax bracket and the investment does not exceed 20 percent of their net worth excluding their house and personal property; (b) if they have a net worth exceeding $1 million and the investment does not exceed 10 percent of their net worth; or (c) if their income exceeds $200,000 a year and the subscription does not exceed 10 percent of their net worth.

Although these qualifications seem strict, the number of people who can qualify is surprisingly large. The total amount raised through private placements usually equals or exceeds that of public placements. In 1985, over $8 billion were raised through private placements.

Classes of Syndications

As a practical matter, securities offerings can be divided into three groups:

1. Some private placements are limited to a small group of friends and acquaintances. The promoters call on individuals to explain the investment and sell the securities personally. Although these are not necessarily small projects—some include properties worth $50 million or more—most are smaller, and the selling is restricted to a limited group.
2. In terms of value, most private placements are made through securities dealers. Brokers receive offerings from the promoters and sell them to their customers. The main difference from a public offering is that the securities are not registered and that the purchaser must be able to bear the risk. Nonregistration saves expenses and time.
3. The final group is made up of public offerings, in which the securities have been registered with the SEC. These may be sold directly by sponsors qualifying as broker-dealers, or they may be sold through a network of regular stockbrokers.

Choosing an Investment

The choice of a particular security is similar to that of other real estate investments. Investors are offered a share in a property or properties. Depending on the promoter, they may receive detailed pro forma operating and sales statements with complete justifications for each, or they may receive mainly pretty pictures, with a ringing declaration of how good an investment real estate has been.

Whatever other documentation is provided, complete **due diligence** reports are always available. These are the disclosures required by law. They disclose how the funds are to be used and usually contain a projection of after-tax returns, together with a listing of the assumptions included in the projections. With sufficiently detailed information, investors can reshape the data in accordance with their own assumptions so as to arrive at personal estimates of risks and returns. However, in many cases brokers offer only a summary of the statement to their clients.

A great deal of any hoped-for return depends on the ability of the sponsors. Prudent investors want to know what the sponsor's track record is. How large and stable is the organization? Does it have adequate credit to meet cash flow shortages? What is its general reputation? Answers to these questions are critical. The best-looking pro forma statement means nothing if those who prepared it are inept or dishonest.

The Partnership Agreement and Compensation

Important in any choice is the specific partnership agreement, which spells out the rights of all participants. The agreement must make clear that the limited partners are not involved in management but are to be kept fully informed. Since the limited partnership is not a taxable entity, its income or losses flow through to the partners. The most frustrating experience for syndicate members is to find on April 15 that the general partner has not prepared the necessary partnership tax returns.

Another important item in the agreement is any obligation to pay future **assessments,** which are additional contributions to the partnership capital required of all limited partners. Some agreements specify no future required assessments; others may allow 10 percent or 15 percent of the original amount to be assessed in case of need. Still others may require or allow even larger amounts. Clearly, how much an investor can be assessed is an important criterion for deciding how large an investment to make.

Many real estate partnerships permit some *phased investments,* for three main reasons: because developments take time, because critically negative cash flows may result from repairing and improving properties, or because it is assumed that rents will rise. For example, the partners might agree to invest $50,000 but to pay $20,000 initially and then $15,000 on each of the next two anniversaries of the first payment. Usually promissory notes are signed. If a partner does not pay the amount due, the note allows the partnership to sue in court or, usually, to repurchase the shares at their original value less all book losses. The notes may or may not require interest payments.

Many kinds of compensation agreements exist. The sponsors may take sizable fees up front. They may also collect real estate brokerage and refinancing commissions. Securities brokers may be paid 10 percent of the money raised for their efforts. Fees for managing the property and the partnership are charged. The sponsors usually participate in the cash flow from operations, and the amounts required vary from case to case. For example, they might take 20 percent of all cash, or 50 percent of all cash above a 6 percent guaranteed return to the limited partners, or perhaps 10 percent above a 10 percent return to the investors. Similarly, the amount that the sponsor receives upon a sale or refinancing can vary widely. How much an investor profits is influenced by the sponsor's share. In many cases during the period of inflation, sponsors raised their compensation levels to such heights that investors received minimal returns.

A study by Steven Roulac and Company in the 1985 *Questor Real Estate Securities Year Book* showed that only 63 percent of the total dollars raised in equity public limited partnerships actually went to buy properties. Partnership formation costs (underwriting commissions, organization and distribution fees) took 11 percent. Acquisition and financing charges accounted for 19 percent. After another 7 percent was set aside for reserves, the remaining 63 percent was used to purchase properties.* The more of an investment that does not go into

Questor's Strategic Real Estate Letter 7, no. 11 (November 1985):1.

the property, the lower one's profit prospects should be. Therefore, a comparison of how much actually goes to buy property and how the income from the property will be split is vital in choosing among potential syndications.

AN EXAMPLE OF A SYNDICATION

The Biltmore apartment building was a private placement offering made toward the end of 1984 (see Table 17-8). The promoters held an option on the 88-unit apartment house built in 1976. The purchase price was $3.1 million. Of this amount, $350,000 was attributed to land and the remainder was the depreciable basis. Two outstanding mortgages existed on the property, both assumable. The first was at 9 percent with an annual constant of .096555. The second was at 11 percent with no requirement for current interest or amortization

Table 17-8
Investment in Biltmore Apartments
Private Placement Statement
Offering Summary January 1, 1985

Property: 88-unit, 8-building garden apartment building built in 1976.

Purchase price	$3,100,000	
Depreciable basis	$2,750,000	
Financing		
First mortgage	9% (annual constant = .096555)	$1,600,000
Second mortgage	11% interest to accrue for 5 years	600,000
Down payment		900,000
Proceeds of Equity Offering		
Down payment	$900,000	
Operating reserves	50,000	
Acquisition fee	160,000	
Offering expenses	30,000	
Security sales commission	110,000	
Total equity	$1,250,000	

- 25 units of $50,000 each, payable $20,000 down and $15,000 at first anniversary and $15,000 at second. Promissory note required.

- General partner to purchase three units; 22 limited partnership units.

- Down payment and acquisition costs payable in three annual installments.

- All operating cash flow and tax benefits to be distributed equally per unit.

- At sale: First priority of cash distribution—return of initial invested capital; second priority—10% (noncompounded) per year preferred return to investors on capital; third priority—remaining cash split 80% to unit holders, 20% to general partners.

payments; interest would accrue until the interest and principal were due at the end of 5 years.

The seller, who had a large potential profit, agreed to take the $900,000 down payment in three equal annual installments. No interest would be charged, but he demanded that promissory notes be required from each of the future partners and that they be pledged to insure the second and third payments. The promoters also agreed to spread their acquisition fee over this 3-year period.

The Partnership Agreement

The total amount of equity to be raised was $1.25 million. It was divided into 25 shares of $50,000 each. The general partners agreed to take three units and, through their securities affiliate, sold the remaining 22 shares to limited partners. The syndicators received a 10 percent commission on each unit sold.

Limited partners had to be qualified before they could buy. They could show either that their last two years' income and this year's prospective income was over $200,000 a year, or that they had a net worth of over $1 million. In neither case could the investment exceed 10 percent of their net worth.

All of the 25 partnership units sold would share equally in any cash flow and any losses or gains during the operating period. Upon the sale of the property, any cash left after repayment of the mortgages and payment of selling expenses would be divided as follows:

1. The partners would receive back the amount of their capital investment or as much as could be paid from the available funds.
2. The partners would receive, as a second priority, payments equal to 10 percent a year (noncompounded) of their initial investment.
3. Any additional cash would be divided, with 20 percent going to the general partner and the remaining 80 percent split among the limited partners in accordance with the number of units owned. All partners would be liable for any taxes on recapture or capital gains in accordance with their share of the funds paid out.

Shares could be purchased for an initial payment of $20,000, plus $15,000 required on each of the next two anniversaries. Individual promissory notes had to be signed for the amounts due. No additional assessments were required.

The general partners receive a management fee for managing the property and an additional fee for managing the partnership. The general partners have the right to consent or not to consent to transfers of units and to approve purchases of additional properties or refinancing. The consent of the general partners and of limited partners holding over 50 percent of contributed capital is required to approve a sale of the property, the appointment of a new general partner, amendments to the agreement, acquisition of more property, and dissolution of the partnership.

The Pro Forma Statements

Tables 17-9 and 17-10 show the pro forma statements presented in the statement for the Biltmore private placement offering. They assumed that the transfer would occur at the start of 1985. The data for operations at purchase were based on the existing rent roll and on operating expenses, except that operating expenses were raised to include two additional fees to the general partners—an off-site property management fee of 6 percent of gross income and $12,000 a year for a partnership management fee.

The level of rents was projected to increase at a rate of 9 percent a year. This was based on an assumption of 5 percent a year inflation and rents rising at a rate of 4 percent a year faster than inflation. The Biltmore is located in Concord, California—a town experiencing rapid growth and an apartment shortage. The apartments had a 98 percent occupancy level for the previous year, but the pro forma statement assumed a 5 percent vacancy and collection loss. The marginal tax rate for partners was projected at 50 percent, somewhat below the California maximum of 55.5 percent, which included both federal and state income taxes.

The prices for both the purchase and the sale were based on a gross rent multiplier of 8.6. Thus the entire projected appreciation was based on the

Table 17-9
Projected Operating Statement for the Biltmore Partnership
(in thousands, rounded)

		Year				
	At Purchase	1985	1986	1987	1988	1989
Income	$360	$392	$428	$466	$508	$554
Less operating expenses	(130)	(135)	(141)	(146)	(152)	(158)
Net operating income	$230	$257	$287	$320	$356	$396
Less debt service		(154)	(154)	(154)	(154)	(154)
Before-tax cash flow		$103	$133	$165	$202	$241
Net operating income		$257	$287	$320	$356	$396
Less interest		(210)	(209)	(208)	(207)	(206)
Less depreciation		(248)	(248)	(220)	(193)	(193)
Taxable income		($200)	($169)	($108)	($43)	($2)
Tax savings (or tax)(50% tax rate)		100	85	54	22	1
Before-tax cash flow		$103	$133	$165	$202	$241
Plus tax savings (or minus tax)		100	85	54	22	1
After-tax cash flow		$203	$217	$220	$223	$242

Depreciable basis: $2,750,000, uses 18 years ACRS or 9, 9, 8, 7, 7, 7%.

Table 17-10
Termination Statement of the
Biltmore Partnership
(in thousands, rounded)

Description	Amount
Gross sales price	$5,192
Less selling costs	(312)
Net sales price	$4,881
Adjusted basis	(1,808)
Gain	$3,073
Taxable income	
Recapture	330
40% of long-term gain	1,097
Total	$1,427
Tax due (50% tax bracket)	$714
Net sales price	$4,881
Plus reserves	160
Less outstanding mortgage	(2,132)
Less accrued interest	(396)
Cash from sales	$2,513

Note: Recapture based on additional depreciation of ACRS of $1,292,500 minus straight line of $962,500.

assumption that rents would rise. Accelerated depreciation, using the 175 percent declining balance, would be adopted. Since this is a residential property only, recapture of the excess deduction over the straight line was included. Taxable income would be reduced by the ability to exclude 60 percent of the long-term capital gain. This assumption, and that for the tax rate, were based on the view that the tax code would not change—an assumption that experience has shown is always dubious.

Calculating the Rate of Return

Tables 17-11 and 17-12 contain the offering statement's projection of the rates of return that could be expected by a purchaser of a share in the limited partnership who had tax obligations in the 50 percent bracket. Table 17-11 details the actual cash flow that a partner would expect upon sale, based on the division of the final cash provided in the partnership agreement. Although the extra percent paid to the general partners for managing a successful project is not large, it gives them an active incentive to manage well.

Table 17-12 supplies the data used in calculating the 29 percent internal rate of return projected by the offering. Column 2 shows the investment phased

Table 17-11
Final Cash Flow from the Biltmore Partnership
(in thousands, rounded)

Cash from sale	$2,513	
Return of capital	(1,250)	
10% preferred return	(625)	
Remainder	$638	
20% to general partner	128	Per Share
80% to investors	511	(in dollars)
Investors' before-tax cash flow	$2,386	$95,422
Investors' tax*	(677)	(27,096)
Investors' after-tax cash flow	$1,708	$68,325

*Investors' tax is based on $\dfrac{\text{cash flow to limited partners}}{\text{cash from sale}} \times$ tax due (from Table 17-10).

Table 17-12
Investor's Internal Rate of Return on the Biltmore Partnership
$50,000 Share

Year	Investment	Cash Flow	Benefits or (Taxes) (50% Bracket)	Total Costs or Benefits	Present Value at 16% Discount	Present Value at 29% Discount
Initial	($20,000)			($20,000)	($20,000)	($20,000)
1985	(15,000)	$4,108	$4,006	(6,886)	(5,936)	(5,336)
1986	(15,000)	5,305	3,389	(6,306)	(4,687)	(3,788)
1987		6,620	2,161	8,781	5,625	4,087
1988		8,064	866	8,930	4,932	3,222
1989		9,650	49	9,699	4,618	2,712
Sale 1989		95,422	(27,096)	68,325	32,531	19,103
Total					$17,084	($0)
Internal rate of return = 29%						

in with three separate payments. Columns 3 and 4 list the expected cash flow and tax benefits. Column 5 summarizes the total inflow or outflow of benefits in each year. Column 6 shows that with a required rate of return of 16 percent, the net present value of the proposal is $17,084. (The final column merely demonstrates that the present values of each year's benefits discounted at the IRR of 29 percent add up to zero, which is the definition of a correct internal rate of return.)

Partitioning the projected yield to find what it is based on makes clear that most of the expected gain comes from the assumption that the rate of inflation during this period will average 5 percent, and that the rents of this apartment will rise by an additional 4 percent a year because of high demand in the local area.

The higher rent roll, multiplied by the same gross rent multiplier, leads to a large gain upon sale. Even though the discount rate greatly reduces the present values of future flows, expected appreciation is the main cause of the projected profits. An investor who realizes the importance of the projected rent increase can use other information sources to check the key assumptions leading to this increase. An independent confirmation that the major assumptions are logical together with careful scrutiny of how much the promoters are taking for themselves can be major criteria for deciding whether or not this syndication makes sense.

The Biltmore example also demonstrates the dramatic changes a projection can undergo before its final realization. In 1987, it appeared that the projected rate of return would not be achieved. The slowdown in inflation and a spurt of new apartment construction meant that the growth in both rents and income was falling well behind projections. Instead of approximately breaking even at the end of 1989, new projections showed a loss of $60,000 in that year.

Tax reform also lowered returns. Prior to the Tax Reform Act of 1986, losses could be used to shelter other income, resulting in a saving of taxes. Since limited partnerships are passive activities, this right to shield other income was phased out, thereby reducing the after-tax flow. The special treatment of capital gains was also abolished. On the other hand, partners' marginal tax rates fell to either 28 percent or 33 percent. In addition, the full tax benefits were received for the first two years. The reductions affected primarily the later years, which carried less weight because of the high discount rates shown in the initial projections.

Since so much of the return depended on the final selling price, how much the investment would suffer remained uncertain. If interest rates remained low, the capitalization rate for net operating income would also be lower, raising the final selling price. Lower tax benefits might reduce new construction and cause rents to rise. On the other hand, smaller tax benefits would also reduce the sales price. Altogether, it now seemed likely that projected returns would at least be cut in half. Still, these might be satisfactory when compared with other investments.

SUMMARY

Investors need techniques to evaluate proposals in order to determine their potential profitability and risks. These methods can also indicate how proposals may be restructured to improve potential risk-to-return relationships.

Traditional measures of profitability, like traditional appraisal methods, use limited periods and fail to account for future possibilities in the income estimates they employ. They also do not consider the time value of money.

More modern techniques of measuring profitability emphasize discounted cash flows. Projected income and sales statements are used to calculate either the net present value of a property or its actual or modified internal rates of return. Although decisions based on these criteria are usually similar, each may be advantageous in particular circumstances.

Syndicates composed of limited partnerships are one of the important ways in which individuals invest in real estate. Partnership shares are securities, subject to the disclosure rules of the Securities and Exchange Commission and to state "blue sky" laws, even though they may not require registration.

The terms of the partnership agreements and the projected profits provide the information needed to make investment decisions. An examination of the prospectuses of various offerings shows a wide variety of terms, of risks, and of profit possibilities.

The initial profitability measures for many real estate investments are high because the amount of risk may be large. Investors must measure, even if only roughly, the differences in risks, both in general and with respect to their own portfolios. Decisions to reject, to purchase, or to negotiate a new price or structure result from the detailed analysis of potential risks and profitability.

KEY TERMS

assessments
blind pool
due diligence
intrastate exemptions
modified internal rate of return (MIRR)
Monte Carlo risk simulation
net present value (NPV)
partitioning
payback period
present value profitability index

private placement
   exemption
profitability indexes
   (PIs)
public offerings
required rate of return
rescission
security
sensitivity analysis
syndicate

QUESTIONS

1. Compute the GRM and free-and-clear rate of return for the following two buildings. Which is a better buy?

	Building 1	Building 2
Gross rent	$10,000	$12,000
Price	$120,000	$120,000
Vacancy and collection loss	5% of gross rent	4% of gross rent
Operating expense	$5,000	$6,500

2. What are the advantages of the modern profitability techniques over the old ones?

3. Explain why in certain cases IRRs may not be useful indexes of profitability.

4. Sometimes present value profitability indexes will not give accurate evaluations of different investment opportunities. What are such cases?
5. What are the similarities and differences between NPV and IRR in measuring profits?
6. Do you think NPV is a better technique than IRR and MIRR? What is the major problem associated with the application of NPV?
7. Are the securities resulting from real estate syndication analogous to common stocks? Why or why not?
8. Explain briefly how a syndication works.
9. What are some advantages of investing in syndications?
10. Are blind pools much more risky than other forms of syndications?
11. How can investors make use of partitioning to measure risk?
12. Partition the investor's results in Table 17-12 into those resulting from the after-tax cash flow from operations and that from the sale.
13. A limited partnership is offered which requires an initial payment of $25,000 and $25,000 at the end of year 1. Its expected after-tax cash flow from operations is $7,000 in year 1, $8,000 in year 2, $10,000 in year 3. At the end of year 4 the final cash flow from operations and from the sale of the property is projected as $60,000.
    a. If the required rate of return is 16 percent, what is the net present value of the partnership? Is it acceptable?
    b. What would be the NPV with a required rate of return of 12 percent?
    c. What is the property's payback period?
    d. What is its internal rate of return?

18 Loans for Land Development and Construction

OBJECTIVES

When you finish this chapter, you should be able to:

- describe the basic features of land development and construction loans.

- discuss the risks in these loans and the degree to which they are reduced by take-out commitments.

- explain permanent and standby financing.

- understand the relationships between front money and the rate of disbursements on the loans.

- be able to calculate the net present value to the borrower and the rate of return to the lender of these loans.

T HE MOST DYNAMIC, skillful, risky, and profitable sector of the real estate market has been the development of land and the construction of buildings. Developers start with raw land and may end up with whole new cities. They make the basic decisions as to what land should be used and how to use it. They decide how to organize and finance a project and then carry it through the planning and, frequently, the construction processes. They may sell the completed project, or own and manage it, or be general partners in a syndicate or joint venture.

A wide variety of firms perform the development function. Some are individual developers and promoters. Others may be large firms specializing in this work. Builders and real estate companies are also active in the development process. Financial analysis for both investors and lenders follows the fundamental procedures detailed in the last four chapters. Differences arise primarily because the loan disbursements and repayments are phased over a considerable period of time and because of the extra caution required as a result of greater risks.

The success of both land development and construction loans depends on the creation of future values. The developer acquires land that must then be improved. It may be sold as individual lots or end up as an industrial park, or it may be developed into some form of income property. The job of developers is complex and often frustrating. They must combine and hold together the land, the architect, and the general design of the development. They must see that the market analysis is adequate, obtain government approvals, secure financing, and supervise the construction and marketing of the project. None of these steps is simple; few will be accomplished smoothly. Developers always seem to be rushing and then waiting, expediting and then trying to be patient as one stage is held up by others who can be motivated and hurried only with difficulty.

CHARACTERISTICS OF DEVELOPMENT AND CONSTRUCTION LOANS

Land development and construction loans are closely related. **Land development loans** finance the installation of streets, sewers, utilities, and the other on-site and off-site improvements necessary to make raw land suitable for building. **Construction loans** finance the costs required for a building or buildings. When the loan is made to the developer of a new project such as a subdivision, industrial park, or large income property, it may be termed more generally a *loan for development.*

Both land development and construction loans are usually short-term, **open-end mortgages.** These are mortgages that contain clauses allowing the borrower to receive additional advances of money without rewriting the original mortgage. The mortgages are secured by the land and work in progress. An amount agreed to beforehand is paid out in phases. Disbursements are made to cover purchases of land, material, and labor after these production factors have been incorporated into the property. Sometimes the two types of loans go to a single builder-developer, but if each function is handled by a different party, the loans are separate. In a few rare cases in which the borrower has a very strong credit rating, regular commercial loans may be made for land development and construction purposes.

Rates

Land development and construction loans customarily last from 6 months to 3 years, depending on the projected time until completion. They are expensive, with up-front fees of 2 to 3 points plus transaction and supervision expenses. Interest rates are commonly variable, set at 2 percent to 5 percent above a bank's prime lending rate. Such rates, which move with the prime, are called **floating rates.** The **prime rate** is that charged to a bank's largest and best customers. Since, on average, the outstanding loan is only about half of the loan amount (because the loan is disbursed over the entire period and not all at the start), the points up front can raise the actual interest rates by a considerable amount, depending on the length of the loan.

As a rule, the necessary interest on a construction loan is included in the borrower's budget and is paid out to the lender monthly. In other cases, the interest accrues during the loan period and is simply added to the outstanding loan balance. In either case, setting up part of the loan as a reserve for interest is necessary because the builder-developer has no income from the project to use for interest payments until revenues from sales come in or until the building is refinanced. The final loan balance includes both the amounts the borrower has used for other expenses and all financial costs. The delay in payments to the lender greatly increases risks. Lenders have little knowledge about whether the project is succeeding until the first payment is due. At that point they are trapped; their money has been paid out and their prime remedy is to take over any failed projects. Foreclosure delays may be lengthy, especially if a borrower declares bankruptcy.

Risks to the Developer and the Lender

Land, development, and construction loans and investments are extremely risky. In fact, holding raw land carries such great dangers that few institutional lenders make loans on it unless other income—for example, from farming, other businesses, or sale of assets—is available to cover the negative cash flow. Institutions do lend on development projects, but generally only when all plans are approved and construction is about to start.

The long duration of the development process represents a basic danger. The decision maker must commit major resources today on the basis of projections of future costs and market acceptability. Increasingly, developers find that by the time they are ready to contract for work, costs have shifted dramatically and some materials or labor may be in short supply. Prices may be higher and the potential delays great. A market that is strong when a job is planned may soften significantly if other projects, begun after the proposal reached the negotiation stage, are completed sooner.

Construction problems may also be underestimated. Delays may arise due to strikes, weather, and labor or material shortages. It may take much longer than expected to get approvals or financing. The market analysis may have failed in its projection of market demands and competition, so that tenants are difficult to find and rents are lower than expected. The location may not be as good as projected. For these and similar reasons, the finished building may be worth far less than projected from the plans, even though its costs may be as high or higher.

The lenders' risks are nearly as great; studies of banks show construction loans to be among their riskiest, with the largest losses. This occurs because the possible sources of error are so numerous. Management may be poor, the costs underestimated, or the demand weak. Lenders must depend on the pro forma projected cash flow statements, which are only as accurate as the skills that go into their development and the desire and ability of the developer to finish the project within budget.

Financing the Project

Developers must solve three problems in obtaining the necessary financing for a project:

1. The first and greatest difficulty is obtaining the actual equity money, called **front money.** This term is used to describe the money developers or promoters must put up prior to the time they can draw on financing through a mortgage. It also includes the amount needed to supplement the funds received through lenders.
2. Developers must obtain take-out commitments (see Chapter 6). These are promises from lenders that they will fund the project when it is completed. Lenders will make long-term, permanent loans to qualified buyers or to developers if they retain ownership. The commitment makes certain that funds will be available to repay the construction loan.
3. If the developers have take-out commitments in hand, they can borrow for the development and construction process. These short-term loans are paid out as the work progresses and are to be repaid upon completion.

OBTAINING FRONT MONEY

Financing the development of construction projects is difficult because the risks are so high. At this stage many things can go wrong. Indeed, the riskiest period in any project is when the proposals are completely fluid. Anyone putting up front money during this period expects a high reward because of the risks. Developers need capital for their preliminary plans, to make the necessary studies for their presentation, and to control the land they will develop. These expenditures must be made before they can arrange debt financing. As the number of approvals to be obtained and requirements to be met has proliferated, the amount of front money developers need has risen rapidly.

Front money is also needed during the actual process of land development and construction. Even though some loans are available during this period, developers must find enough money to bridge the gaps between the phases or times at which the financing becomes available.

Sources of Funds

Developers look to several sources for their front money. One is their own capital, which provides the maximum discretion and fewest restrictions. But only a limited number of developers enjoy the luxury of having substantial financing of their own.

In addition to their own funds, developers can turn to several other sources of front money. One may be a regular credit line from their banks. Another is to obtain as much credit as possible from their suppliers or consultants. It is common to find that the lawyer, the architect, and even the market analyst delay their billing in return for a share of the potential profits.

During the construction phase suppliers often act in the role of lenders. Even though they may not be compensated for it, they find that their bills are simply paid late. This whole problem of loans during the construction process is one of the factors raising the cost of construction. Suppliers who find themselves with debts continually owed to them reflect this in their prices. Suppliers who must anticipate waiting to be paid for their work will very likely charge higher prices. They add an extra increment both for the time they must wait and—more importantly—for the uncertainty associated with collecting the account at all.

Of greater concern is that the developers' dependence on suppliers for credit may influence the quality of the goods or services the suppliers provide. If payment is not immediately forthcoming, suppliers may be motivated to furnish less than top-quality materials. In the case of consultants providing professional services, their objectivity may be noticeably influenced by what form the payments take. Clearly, consultants whose payments depend on the successful availability of financing will be highly motivated to make sure that such funds become available. Consequently, the soundness of their advice may be impaired.

Joint Ventures

Because of the enormous difficulties of coming up with the needed front money, developers often turn to the joint venture in order to find financial partners who can assume the major burden for these expenditures. This is one reason why some of the largest developers have gone into partnerships with insurance companies or pension funds.

If the venture is to be a form of limited partnership, the developer must provide prospective partners with considerable amounts of information before they can be admitted. Therefore, a good deal of the planning must have already taken place. The dimensions of the project must be defined, possible economic benefits must be identified, and there must be a projected set of financial statements. Without considerable detailed information of this type, joint venture partners cannot know whether they ought to become involved.

This means again that substantial resources are required even before a developer is in a position to admit financial partners. Even if the developer seeks to minimize front-money requirements through finding a buyer (preselling) for the project before it becomes necessary to incur capital expenditures, a fair amount of up-front work must have been done, and payments made, to move the venture to the point at which it can be considered by a potential purchaser.

Land Development and Subdividing Options

Probably the prime source of front money is through a favorable deal with landowners. Essentially, developers seek to have landowners allow them to defer the time when the money must be put up for the land. One frequent method of ensuring the availability of the land during the planning period is through a series of options. These might include a lease of the land with an option to buy at some later time. The first lease payments could be small or payments might be deferred until the property is completed and income is being produced. In other cases, developers may buy the land on an extended purchase contract with only small early payments required. Developers usually insist that there be no recourse if they fail to meet the remainder of the contract. The entire security will be the land itself.

In another procedure, the owner retains title while the land is being developed and may even furnish part of the capital for improvements. As individual lots are sold, the owner transfers title to the purchaser. Part of the income from the sale is paid to the owner for his or her land and risk, while part goes as a return to the developer.

In still another method, the builder buys the land but the original owner retains a large purchase-money mortgage against the property. The lien is usually a **blanket mortgage**—that is, one that covers a number of parcels or the entire parcel of land. When an individual lot is sold, the mortgage holder receives payment for somewhat more than the amount of land involved, so that the debt owed becomes an ever-smaller percentage of the value of the still unsold land. Upon receipt of payment, the mortgage holder releases his or her claim and the purchaser receives a clear title.

The Release Price

The amount that the developer must pay to be able to grant a clear title to a specific parcel is called the **release price.** Typically, release prices range from 110 percent to 120 percent of the actual cost of the land or of the average loan per lot (including interest) from a lender. The owners and lenders may specify the order in which parcels of the subdivision may be started and sold in order to avoid being stuck with all the bad lots if the project does not sell out.

EXAMPLE: Assume that 25 acres of land are purchased for $12,000 an acre with a down payment of 10 percent. The total land is worth $300,000, and the buyer puts up $30,000, with the seller retaining a blanket mortgage for $270,000. The land is divided into 100 lots, which means that the land cost for each lot is $2,700. Every time a lot is sold, the developer pays 115 percent of the mortgage amount per lot, or $3,105, to the mortgage holder, who releases the lot to the new owner. The amount owed on the mortgage becomes a decreasing percentage of the value of the unsold land. Depending on whether the contract requires interest and how much has accrued, the $270,000 mortgage will have been completely paid off when 87 lots have been sold; the developer retains all amounts after that point.

Although this example covers the lots for a housing subdivision, the same system of sales and releases applies to industrial parks, mixed-use developments, redevelopment projects, and other types of land development.

Credit for Improvements

If the land is to be built upon or improved before sale, the firm making a construction loan usually requires a subordination agreement. Under such an agreement, the holder of the blanket mortgage agrees to allow his or her claim to be junior, or second, to the construction loan even though it was recorded first in time. The conditions of such subordination clauses and the release clause that specifies the conditions for transferring titles on individual lots are an important part of the bargaining in land sales. Such conditions, as well as the use of options and developing on others' land, are usually paid for through the fact that the price of the land becomes higher than it would be in a cash sale. For example, in the case of land bought for $300,000 including a subordinated mortgage, the cash price might be only $225,000.

Credit for construction of land improvements is expensive, but not quite as difficult to obtain as credit for purchasing raw land. Developers who have used their own capital to buy the land or who have received financing through the owner or another land investor are often able to borrow the money needed for streets, lights, and other improvements from a combination of financial institutions, material suppliers, and subcontractors, in a system similar to that used for the construction of the house. In fact, in much tract development the construction of the house and land improvements proceed and are financed together.

STANDBY AND PERMANENT FINANCING

Lenders attempt to share part of the risk of making construction loans by insisting that the developer have a **take-out commitment** before they lend. Such commitments provide that a permanent loan will be made by the take-out lender if the project is completed according to plan and it is owned by a qualified borrower. They must be from a recognized lender (making them "bankable"), and they must be drawn so that the construction lender feels they are ironclad.

In some cases, the construction lender also agrees to make the final loan if the building is sold to a suitable buyer. We saw in Chapter 6 that these are called *combination loans.* They are efficient because one set of transaction costs is avoided. Most take-outs are based on a promise of a permanent loan. These are the usual long-term market loans. In some cases, however, developers take **standby loans** instead. These are short-term interim loans made under an assumption that they will shortly be refinanced.

Development Risks

Construction and development lenders face two types of risks:

1. *Construction risks* are risks that a developer will run out of money or will fail to complete the project. Builders may experience cost overruns, strikes, inspection problems, or they may lose their money elsewhere. These risks are assumed by the construction lenders. The take-out commitment does not offer protection in these cases because its promise does not take effect if the builder fails to complete the project.
2. *Economic risks* also exist. When the building is finished, perhaps it will not be sold or rented. Interest rates may rise so as to make the project uneconomic. Some of these risks are borne by the take-out lender.

Floor-to-ceiling Commitments

To reduce their risk, lenders now offer so-called **floor-to-ceiling commitments.** The permanent lender agrees to advance a certain sum (the floor) upon completion, but other amounts sufficient to fund a complete building (the ceiling) are advanced only if the building is occupied by suitable tenants. The construction lender will usually advance amounts only equal to the floor of the take-out.

EXAMPLE: A permanent commitment (the ceiling) is made to fund a building for $2 million. However, different amounts of money are advanced in three stages. The floor amount of $1.4 million will be advanced upon completion. An additional $300,000 will be made available when the revenues of the building equal 60 percent of the projected initial rent roll. The final $300,000 will be paid when rents equal 80 percent of the initial projection. The uncovered gap between the floor, or the funds available upon completion, and the ceiling of 80 percent occupancy is $600,000.

Standby Financing

In cases where builders feel they can get better terms by delaying their permanent arrangements, they can obtain a construction loan against a standby commitment. Standby financing is money available to carry a project after it has been completed but before a permanent loan has been obtained. To construction lenders, no difference exists between a standby and a permanent loan; they are assured a take-out upon completion.

Standby lenders plan *not* to make loans; they are disappointed if they must. They charge sizable commitment fees—for example, 2 percent for the first year, payable in advance, and 1 percent in advance each additional 6 months. They gamble that the developer will be able to get permanent financing elsewhere. If they have to make a loan, it is written at a high interest rate and with penalties that build up the longer it takes to find money elsewhere. The idea is to force the builder to take permanent loans from traditional lenders, even if they are expensive.

Developers may take standby loans in the hope that interest rates will drop. Some use them to cover the gap on a take-out commitment during the rent-up period. They know that if they can show lenders a successfully operating project, they can negotiate much better terms and not have to give up as much of their equity. The loan can be made based on actualities rather than projections. Construction lenders do not care, provided they are protected. The standby lenders are in the business of accepting high risks for the added reward, and the developer is willing to pay it in the hope that it will reduce his future borrowing costs.

THE DEVELOPMENT LOAN

The submission package for a land development loan is similar to those for permanent or construction loans. Lenders must be convinced that the completed lots will sell, since they are repaid only when this occurs. Therefore, they want to see feasibility and market studies. They are also concerned with the site planning, physical surveys, and soil reports; the funds will not be forthcoming until all permits are granted.

The amount of the loan depends on the specific cost estimates. Lenders also want a financial statement from the borrower and frequently require a performance bond or guarantee that the work will be completed. They need an appraisal to show that the lots are being priced competitively. Lenders often require that projects be constructed in phases. They want to limit the inventory of unsold lots to a three- or four-month absorption rate in case the market projections turn out to be wrong or the market dries up suddenly.

An Example of a Development Loan

A fairly typical case is one in which the developer buys the land but the sellers retain a large purchase-money mortgage. The sellers are willing to subordinate their mortgage to a loan for the construction necessary to develop salable lots. In this example, the developer, John Mason, prepares a proposed development called Fair Oaks. He approaches the DeRosa family to purchase a 22-acre tract from their farm, which lies in the path of the city's development. Roads, sewers, and water are available at the edge of the tract. Mason has already drawn up a budget (see Table 18-1). He can afford to pay $47,000 per acre, or $1,034,000 for the tract, if the DeRosas are willing to accept a $34,000 down payment with a $1 million mortgage.

Table 18-1
Budget
Fair Oaks Project

Expenditure	Amount
Land, 22 acres at $47,000 per acre	$1,034,000
Development	
hard costs	355,500
soft costs	60,500
Developer's overhead and profit	290,000
Gross sales of 60 lots at $29,000 each	$1,740,000

First mortgage loan $416,000, including interest, at 3 points and 3 percent over bank prime

Distribution of Cash Flow from Sales

60 lots at $29,000 each	$1,740,000
To landowner: $19,000 per lot × 52.63 lots	$1,000,000
To lender: $7,700 per lot × 54.03 lots	$416,000
To developer: $2,300 per lot × 53 + $29,000 × 7	$324,000

The mortgage would be due in 2 years and would be subordinated to a first mortgage loan from a savings bank, needed to cover the cost of development. Mason plans to subdivide the tract into 60 lots, believing he could sell each lot at an average price of $29,000. He offers the DeRosas a release price of $19,000 per lot, or 114 percent of the land mortgage on each one.

The DeRosas would receive $20,000 for a 1-year option to be applied as part of the down payment. Closing would occur and the remainder of the down payment would be due as soon as Mason received the necessary planning approvals and permits for construction. On the basis of independent estimates that the cash value of their property was about $850,000, the DeRosas agree to the arrangement.

Remainder of the Budget

Mason next approaches Farmer's Savings Bank for a land development loan of $416,000. Of this amount, $39,500 is to cover the lender's interest and points. He submits a complete construction budget, including clearing, excavation, grading and paving, as well as costs for utilities, sewers, and water distribution. Since these costs cover the actual "bricks and mortar," they are sometimes referred to as **hard costs.** The estimated hard costs of $355,000, shown in Table 18-1, include on-site expenses of management and supervision. Also included in the budget are the indirect or **soft costs,** such as loan fees, interest, and legal fees.

The bank agrees to the loan provided that Mason can show them he has $80,000 of his own funds available. Its lending criteria require him to have at least 20 percent of the total construction expenditures in cash to cover working capital and possible cost overruns. The bank's initial fee is 3 points and the interest rate is variable at 3 percent over the Bank of America's prime lending rate. Interest will accrue on all advances. The bank will make disbursements (advances) monthly based on the developer's requisitions and certification of the work accomplished, sums paid out, and waivers of liens by subcontractors and material suppliers. The bank has the right to inspect the development, in order to make sure that the work is being performed in a workmanlike manner, according to plan, and with the necessary government permits and inspections.

The bank also requires a detailed budget showing the projected expenses for each phase. It specifies that any cost overruns must be met by funds from the developer. The bank's release price is $7,700 per lot, or 111 percent of the average estimated expenses per lot. It views this as a safe loan because it calculates that its outstanding loan will never exceed 35 percent of the real value of the land and improvements, given the fact the DeRosas' loan is subordinated to the bank's mortgage. At the time of the loan, the prime rate is 11 percent, so the bank will receive 14 percent interest on the outstanding debt. Furthermore, since money will be outstanding for less than six months on average, the 3 points received at the start will raise the bank's yield on the loan to over 20 percent, minus the risk premium and handling costs.

The Repayment Schedule

In Mason's projected disbursements under the loan and repayment schedule for the project, he estimates that he would have to put up about $31,000 before closing and add about $15,000 to the bank's initial advance in order to make the remainder of the down payment on the land (see Table 18-2). He hopes he can limit his cash costs to an additional $19,000 available as working capital. This would leave about $15,000 of the $80,000 in the front money required by the bank available for overruns. He also knows from experience that if necessary he can delay some material and subcontractor payments.

Under the plan, the first lots are to be ready for sale at the end of the fifth month. They will be sold either to builders or to homeowners at a rate of seven lots per month and at an average selling price of $29,000 per lot. As Table 18-1 reflects, the combined release prices to the bank and to the DeRosas total $26,700. If all goes well, Mason expects to get back $2,300 of his front money for each lot sold until they are paid off. Since he projects using about $66,000 of his own money, at that rate about 30 lots will have to be sold before he gets his own money back. Most of his profits will be concentrated in the last seven lots, after his debt to the bank and to the DeRosas has been repaid.

The Present Value of the Project

In the process of developing the project, Mason had compared the proposal with other alternatives he had available, estimating the net present value of the Fair Oaks project (see Table 18-3). He assumed that all expenditures would be made at the start of a quarter and all receipts would come at the quarter's

Table 18-2
Schedule of Monthly
Draws and Repayments
Fair Oaks Project

Months	Sales in Units	Draws*	Lender		Landowner	
			Repayment	Balance	Repayment	Balance
Closing	—	$24,300	—	$24,300	—	$1,000,000
1–3	—	188,700	—	213,000	—	1,000,000
4–6	7	129,000	$53,900	288,100	$133,000	867,000
7–9	23	70,700	177,100	181,700	437,000	430,000
10–12	21	2,800	161,700	22,800	399,000	31,000
13–14	9	500	23,300	—	31,000	—
Total	60	$416,000	$416,000	—	$1,000,000	—

*Includes points and interest accruals.

Table 18-3
Net Present Value
Fair Oaks Project

		Discount Factors	
Months	Cash Flows	IFPV at 20%	Present Values
1–3	($25,000)	1.0000	($25,000)
4–6	(6,000)	0.9516	(5,710)
Closing	(15,000)	0.9056	(13,584)
7–9	(11,000)	0.9056	(9,961)
10–12	(8,000)	0.8618	(6,894)
13–15	52,900	0.7804	41,284
16–18	48,300	0.7427	35,870
19–20	207,000	0.7185	148,730
Total	$243,200		$164,735

end. This simplified the calculation and was slightly conservative. Because of the high risk of land development, Mason set the required discount rate at 20 percent. The table shows that at this rate the net present value of the project was $164,735.

Mason's internal rate of return (IRR) can be calculated as 35.3 percent. This is a good example of a case in which it is better to use net present value (NPV) rather than IRR to evaluate a proposal. Both techniques show Fair Oaks to be a very profitable endeavor. However, because the investment is small, even minor changes in the estimated cash requirements will cause large fluctuations in the IRR. Most of the return is really payment for the developer's knowledge and skills, not for his capital. By using NPV with a sufficiently high discount rate to cover risks, Mason can get a better estimate of whether this project is a good use of his time or whether he would be better off trying something else. When he examines the projected returns on other projects, he can use the same discount rate, thereby enabling him to compare their net present values to find how much he can net for his personal efforts.

CONSTRUCTION FINANCING

Lending on construction projects requires specialized skills. The amount of detail is enormous. Money tends to disappear if not closely controlled. Lenders must make sure that they do not pay for work not in place and that what has been completed is free of prior liens to workers, subcontractors, or material suppliers. Money is usually held back until releases are received or the period for **mechanics' liens** has run out. Mechanics' liens are claims against property to secure debts owed to those performing work or furnishing material to a project.

Lenders try to ascertain that the value in place and that of the land exceeds the total they have advanced. They also want to be certain that the contractor and the developer have enough remaining funds to finish the project. If lenders must take over an unfinished project, losses can rarely be avoided. The job will stand unfinished and deteriorating before it can be restarted. New contractors must be found, and they are likely to be expensive. In many cities, it is not uncommon to see half-completed buildings standing for two or three years with no progress having been made. This reflects the fact that builders can go into bankruptcy to delay foreclosure.

Sources of Construction Loans

Loans for the construction process are needed in addition to those for land development. As noted earlier, construction financing is a specialized part of the market, especially on large income properties. Commercial banks furnish by far the largest share of construction money. Next come savings institutions, which tend to concentrate on residential properties, particularly ones on which they make the permanent loan.

In certain localities, the main lenders may differ in their practices from the national norm depending on the legal situation and regional traditions. Other potential sources of funds are mortgage companies and real estate investment trusts (REITs). The latter played a large part in the early 1970s but, after a disastrous period in which they lent too much money for poorly conceived projects, many of which failed, they fled the field. Recently they have been reentering the field of development loans. In 1983 and 1984 a number of savings institutions expanded rapidly into income properties, using their newfound de-regulated freedom. Many discovered that the skills required exceeded their capacity, and they failed as a result of making bad construction loans.

The Submission Package

Although most lenders insist on a take-out commitment even before they agree to a construction loan, they still require a submission package resembling that of the final lender. They want detailed information on the project and its cost. And they require an appraiser's judgment as to the value of the completed building in order to determine a maximum loan. Even so, they normally do not lend more than the floor of the take-out commitment.

Of particular concern is the contractor's ability to complete the job. Lenders demand a sound track record to show that the builder has the necessary man-agement skills. They also check the builder's financial statements. As with land development loans, lenders may insist on guarantees from financially sound principals or require performance bonds, perhaps even a bank line of credit guaranteeing adequate financial support to finish the job.

Disbursement of Funds

A natural tension arises between the builder—who is probably short of cash and eager to use a minimum of front money—and the lender, who wants to be certain that no funds are advanced unless they represent at least an equal increase in the value of the building.

The usual procedure for paying out construction loans is through a system of payments made at certain stages of the building process. These systems of **advances**—or **draws,** as they are commonly called—have the purpose of making capital available to builders to replenish most of the amount they have had to pay from their own capital or borrow from suppliers to bring the building to a certain stage of completion.

The construction mortgage is recorded prior to the start of building. The note specifies the manner in which disbursements are to be made. Many possible payment methods and rates of advance exist. In contracts to build houses for individuals, it is common to require a deposit by the owners contracting for the construction of sufficient funds to cover the difference between the contract and the loan. The lender or his agent then reimburses the builder for receipted bills as they are presented. In other cases, the owner may certify the bills, which are then paid directly by the lender.

Stage-of-completion Agreements Far more common, and particularly applicable to *operative* (or speculative) building, are **stage-of-completion agreements** by the lender to furnish funds when certain amounts of work have been completed or certain stages of construction have been reached. In the most flexible system—but one commonly used only on large construction projects—lenders advance each month the interest payment due for the previous month's interest plus a percentage of the total cost of the work that they and the builder agree went into the structure during the previous period. More usual, particularly for house building, is an agreement to pay a certain percentage of the loan at specific stages of construction.

Schedules for disbursements are negotiated between the builder and the lender. Many different forms of agreement are employed, calling for anywhere from three to fifteen payments as the work progresses. A typical agreement based on five advances calls for the bank to pay the builder 20 percent of the contract price at each of five stages of construction: (1) at completion of foundation and rough flooring; (2) at completion of roofing; (3) at completion of plastering; (4) at completion and acceptance of the job; and (5) after the end of the mechanics' lien period.

Under such systems, the builder usually calls the lender to report that a specific stage has been reached. The lender then sends an inspector to the site to see that the work has been accomplished and to check both its quantity and quality. The lender ascertains that the plans are being followed and sometimes asks to see receipted bills for the materials included in the work. The degree of care used in checking depends on the credit standing of the builder, on the lien laws, and on the general health of the construction market.

The Timing of Disbursements

In theory, under this five-stage system, builders may be required to invest personal capital in the project up to 20 percent of the value of the building. When their investment approaches that amount, they reach the next stage and should be able to draw against the mortgage. Their work in progress should be limited to five times their working capital; otherwise, there will be periods when they cannot meet their bills because their investment in work in progress exceeds their available capital. They may be solvent but illiquid. Builders should have some additional, but not necessarily liquid, capital to pay for unpredictable setbacks that could cause losses on the property.

The available amount of working capital, however, often falls short. Builders are frequently the beneficiaries of an average of two or three weeks' credit from their workers, trade contractors, and material dealers. At any stage there is likely to be considerable completed work for which they receive an advance from lenders but for which they have not paid their suppliers. Although this enables builders to double the work they can undertake with a given amount of capital, it is one of the factors that makes construction lending so risky.

These complex relationships mean that it is not only the builder and the lender who are concerned with the rate of disbursements; all parties to the venture are interested in minimizing their risk and financial exposure. Consequently, the various contracting parties—the general contractor who manages the entire job, the subcontractors, material supply houses, and individual construction workers—all endeavor to avoid having any other party "get ahead of them" by drawing funds for work not yet accomplished or paid for.

Holdbacks

Lenders try to avoid disbursing funds in excess of the value of work done to date through a system of **holdbacks,** in which they retain an amount such as 5 percent to 10 percent of all work completed in a period. When the project is finished, they continue to hold such a percentage of the loan in order to protect their position against future liens that might be filed against the job until the lien period has passed. The amount of holdback is often a matter of bitter debate.

With developers trying to minimize their cash involvement while lenders attempt to keep their advances below the value of work done, a delicate balance of timing obviously prevails, and accounting systems and control measures are therefore very important. The nature of the construction industry, however, is such that record-keeping capabilities and the number of good accounting systems are limited. The amount of paperwork involved is tremendous, with the builder bearing the responsibility for dealing with schedules, bills, books, and inspections. The plans, specifications, contracts, agreements, and related documents for a job may fill many file cabinets. The general contractor works through numerous subcontractors and may have a dozen or more for each job, receiving several bids for each subcontract awarded. The problem of simply keeping track of all the paper, let alone that of trying to set up effective systems for control, is monumental.

Because the problems are so difficult and control is so hard to establish—and also because many contractors start as skilled workers and have limited capital—the building industry has one of the highest bankruptcy rates of all industries in the United States. This puts even more pressure on the lender to ensure that the money disbursed to the builder on the construction loan is, in fact, spent on the job for which it is paid.

Schemes are constantly being advanced to try to solve the industry's many difficulties. Thus far, however, none has been successful. The lender's best method of avoiding defaults is to make sure that the initial budgets are proper and adequate and that the actual progress of the job is checked carefully as disbursements are made.

AN EXAMPLE OF CONSTRUCTION LENDING

A medium-sized developer, A to Z Builders, has applied to Western State Bank for a construction loan on the Washington Square building. The developer submits a duplicate of the package used to obtain a permanent loan commitment from the Western State Insurance Company. The commitment is for $5,510,000, or 75 percent of its estimate of the cost of the completed project.

Underwriting

The bank's underwriters examine the proposal in detail. They note from the budget (Table 18-4) that the project has estimated hard costs of $5,106,000. Funds for the contractor's overhead are included. (In this case, A to Z plans to act as the general contractor as well as developer.)

The soft costs are estimated at $1,347,000. They include financial costs, insurance, architects' and engineers' charges, legal and title fees, permits, and the developer's overhead and profit. The submission package also contains pro forma statements, an independent appraisal, background on the developer, and corporate and personal financial statements.

The bank's underwriters find the borrower's track record to be suitable and agree with the design, economic projections, and the appraisal. They recommend a construction loan commitment up to the $5,510,000 promised by the take-out lender. (The Washington Square building and its construction budget are also used as examples in Chapter 19.)

Conditions

The loan is to be secured by a note and deed of trust, which must be recorded before any construction commences. The developer must post a performance bond for the amount of the loan and assign the take-out commitment

Table 18-4
Proposed Construction Budget
of A to Z Builders
Washington Square Office Building

Hard costs	
Building	$4,255,000
Tenant improvements	601,000
Contingencies	250,000
Subtotal	$5,106,000
Land cost	$905,000
Soft costs	
Legal and tax	$168,000
Loan fees	170,000
Construction interest	449,000
Architects/engineers	140,000
Other costs and overhead	345,000
Contingencies	75,000
Subtotal	$1,347,000
Total project cost	$7,358,000
Developer's contribution, land, overhead, and profits	$1,848,000
Construction loan	5,510,000
Total project cost	$7,358,000

to the bank. The bank's attorneys will carefully check the commitment to make sure it is usable and can be enforced when construction is completed.

The bank charges 3 points plus costs for loan processing and inspection, for a total loan fee of $170,000. The interest rate is variable at 3 percent above the bank's prime rate—12 percent at this time. Thus, interest charges are projected at 15 percent compounded monthly, based on a 360-day year.

Before starting construction, the developer must submit approved building permits and independent opinions as to soil suitability, zoning, compliance with earthquake and other government regulations, as well as a hazard insurance policy. Detailed plans and cost breakdowns must be furnished and at least 70 percent of the cost must be covered by firm bids. The lender has the right to review and approve all subcontractors. A title insurance policy that continues and covers each additional advance is necessary, and it will have to be updated prior to each advance to prove an absence of outstanding claims or liens.

The developer must present satisfactory evidence to the bank that it has the required equity funds to complete the project. If at any time cost overruns occur, A to Z must deposit extra funds to cover these costs. The developer must also agree not to make any substantial change in plans or to order extra work without the prior approval of the lender.

Disbursements

The construction loan is to be disbursed monthly on the basis of a signed requisition from the developer. Each draw covers only the labor and material actually put in place in the building in the previous month plus the interest for the lender. The lender will inspect the work in progress prior to each advance in order to verify that the work is actually in place, that it is progressing according to schedule, that the plans are being followed, and that the workmanship is acceptable.

Each payment covers only 90 percent of the work actually accomplished; the lender holds back the remaining 10 percent to cover contingencies. The amount held back will be paid when all the work is properly completed, certified for occupancy, and the time period for liens has expired. If extra work or expenses over the schedule are incurred, A to Z must show that they have been paid for from equity funds.

Table 18-5 shows the planned schedule of the construction draws on the Washington Square building. At closing, the bank advances to A to Z a sum to cover prior soft costs. In addition, the bank credits itself with the loan fee. Column 2 of the table shows the projected monthly disbursements to the developer. Column 4 lists the interest accrued during the month on the outstanding amounts of the loan, shown in the final column. The total increase in the developer's debt in each month is carried in column 5. When the project is completed, the developer is paid the sums previously held back. The bank receives the amount it is owed—$5,510,000—when A to Z issues a mortgage for this amount to Western State Insurance Company against the permanent loan commitment it entered into before construction began.

The Cost of the Loan

Construction loans are expensive, as noted earlier. Risks are high and the costs of inspections and paperwork are substantial. What is the rate of return to lenders (the cost to developers) on such loans? To calculate a lender's yield, the actual payments made to the developer (not including the financing fee and the interest paid out and received back immediately in a bookkeeping transaction) must be compared with the amount the lender receives back when the loan is paid off.

Looking at it from the developer's point of view, it receives only the cash shown in column 2 of Table 18-5. Yet at the end it owes $5,510,000 shown at the bottom of the final column, which includes the interest payments for the loan.

Table 18-5
Schedule of Disbursements
Washington Square Office Building

Developer's contribution	$1,848,000
Construction loan	5,510,000
Total project cost	$7,358,000

Month	Builder's Draw	Financing Fees	Interest Payment*	Total Advanced in Month	Cumulative Loan Balance
Closing	$255,000	$170,000	$0	$425,000	$425,000
1	0	0	5,313	5,313	430,313
2	676,000	0	5,379	681,379	1,111,692
3	721,000	0	13,896	734,896	1,846,588
4	532,000	0	23,082	555,082	2,401,670
5	393,000	0	30,021	423,021	2,824,691
6	346,000	0	35,309	381,309	3,206,000
7	345,000	0	40,075	385,075	3,591,075
8	332,000	0	44,888	376,888	3,967,963
9	309,000	0	49,596	358,596	4,326,559
10	269,000	0	54,082	323,082	4,649,641
11	253,000	0	58,121	311,121	4,960,762
12	487,228	0	62,010	549,238	5,510,000
Total	$4,918,288	$170,000	$421,772	$5,510,000	$5,510,000

*Calculated as 1.25 percent of the balance outstanding at end of previous month.

The monthly outflows from the bank are also the amounts in column 2, and the bank receives back the $5,510,000 repayment of the outstanding balance, which is paid for through the take-out loan. Equation 4.3 made clear that the effective interest rate or yield to a lender is the discount rate (IRR) needed to equate the present value of all future outflows (P) and inflows (the receipt, REC). Thus, the lenders can find its expected return by solving for the internal rate of return.

EXAMPLE: In the Washington Square building, the bank receives its repayment from the take-out lender at the end of month 12. Therefore, to find its effective yield, the bank must discount this receipt back from the final period in order to obtain its present value. Similarly, all the bank's advances must be discounted back to the present. Since the cash flows occur by the month, the IRR will be at a monthly rate that must be annualized:

$$\frac{REC}{(1 + IRR)^n} = P_0 + \frac{P_1}{1 + IRR} + \frac{P_2}{(1 + IRR)^2} + \cdots + \frac{P_n}{(1 + IRR)^n} \qquad \textbf{(18.1)}$$

$$\frac{\$5,510,000}{(1 + IRR)^{12}} = \$255,000 + 0 + \frac{\$676,000}{(1 + IRR)^{2}} + \ldots + \frac{\$487,228}{(1 + IRR)^{12}}$$

The annualized IRR is 22.1 percent. Because of the initial fee, the lender receives and the developer pays a rate higher than the coupon rate of 15 percent. The rate seems high, but this is not pure interest because it covers the risk premium and the transaction costs. Lenders specializing in development and construction loans are able to reduce both expenses and risks through the skills they develop over time.

SUMMARY

Land development and construction loans are made for short terms. They are secured by open-end mortgages. The total agreed amount is disbursed in partial payments, or draws, in accordance with a schedule that reflects the actual amount of work accomplished and paid for by the developer.

These are among the riskiest of all loans. Many things can go wrong, and frequently do. If costs are underestimated, or if they rise because of unanticipated events, developers can run out of money with which to finish construction, and the lender can be saddled with an unfinished project. Therefore, lenders attempt to protect themselves by insisting that developers have enough funds of their own (front money) which, when added to the amount of the construction or development loan, will be sufficient to finish the project with some safety factor. They plan to disburse funds only in accordance with economic values actually incorporated in the job. Lenders try to insist that the developers add their own funds if cost overruns occur. They protect themselves against changes in the market value of the project by insisting on a take-out commitment.

The take-out commitments must come from recognizable, bankable financial institutions. These lenders commit to making a standby or permanent loan when the project is completed according to plan.

Land development loans are especially risky. They can be paid off only if the lots actually sell. Lenders (including sellers who subordinate their interest) insist on receiving a higher percentage of the price of each lot sold (the release price) than they have lent; they want their investment back before the last lots are sold. The construction lenders usually insist that projects be started in phases, limiting the unsold lots under construction to an agreed-upon number.

The yield to the lender calculated on the amount lent may appear excessive. However, the lender's return covers significant costs plus high risks. Skilled construction lenders make high profits; poor ones frequently end up with high losses.

KEY TERMS

advances

blanket mortgage

construction loans

draws

floating rates
floor-to-ceiling commitments
front money
hard costs
holdbacks
land development loans
mechanics' liens

open-end mortgage
prime rate
release price
soft costs
stage-of-completion agreements
standby loans
take-out commitment

QUESTIONS

1. What are the basic characteristics of development and construction loans?
2. Why are land, development, and construction loans so risky? To what degree is the risk reduced by the existence of a take-out commitment?
3. What are the main sources of front money?
4. What are common methods used by developers to secure land?
5. Assume that a developer buys 30 acres of land for $10,000 an acre, paying 15 percent down, with the remaining balance being financed by a mortgage at no interest. The release price is 120 percent of the mortgage amount per lot.
   a. If the land is divided into 50 lots, how many lots must be sold to pay off the mortgage?
   b. If the mortgage is paid off after 50 lots have been sold, into how many lots does the developer divide the land?
6. Explain what floor-to-ceiling commitments are. Why are they used?
7. What is standby financing? When would it be most prevalent?
8. What are the main sources of construction loans?
9. Give an example of a stage-of-completion agreement (agreement for draws) and describe how it works.
10. A to Z Builders brings another project to Western State Bank. It has a take-out commitment for $2 million and the following schedule of required funds by months:

Closing	$100,000			
Month 1	20,000	7	$120,000
2	280,000	8	60,000
3	270,000	9	40,000
4	200,000	10	20,000
5	140,000	11	10,000
6	140,000	12	100,000

The bank agrees to make a construction loan for up to $2 million in accordance with actual expenditures. Disbursements are to be made monthly. A loan fee of 3 points ($60,000) is payable upon closing. The interest rate will float at 3 percent above the prime rate. Interest is to be computed monthly on the previous month's ending balance, and is to accrue. The prime rate is 9 percent, and it is assumed that it will remain so for the entire period.

Prepare a table for this loan similar to Table 18-5. Calculate the effective yield to the lender (cost to the borrower) under the assumption that the draws follow the projections and the loan is paid off at the end of the twelfth month.

19 An Examination of Selected Financing Alternatives

OBJECTIVES

When you finish this chapter, you should be able to:

- discuss the risks faced by lenders and methods used to try to reduce them.

- explain some methods of sharing tax benefits.

- know that a wide variety of financing alternatives exists, and understand how and why they cause risks and returns to change.

- understand how a joint venture differs from traditional financing and why it is used.

- describe the uses of options and convertible mortgages in financing income properties.

- explain how leasebacks and leasehold mortgages work.

- recognize the role played in financing by participations in income and appreciation.

- compare the advantages and disadvantages of various financing techniques.

T HE EMPHASIS in Part 4 has been on the analysis lenders and investors use in deciding whether and how much to lend or invest on income property. Tax structuring and lender participations are two significant concepts that have caused drastic changes in financing. Both have become popular because they make financing easier to obtain and raise property values by dividing risks and tax benefits in a more logical way. When ownership rights and loans fit participants' individual needs more closely, everyone may be better off.

PROTECTING AGAINST RISKS

A lender or investor faces a variety of risks, prominent among which are business, financial, purchasing-power, and interest rate risks. In recent years loans and ownership rights have undergone changes that reduce or offset such risks or make them more measurable and acceptable.

New Lender–Investor Relationships

The risks in lending on an income property depend on how well net income has been projected, on the ability of the property's managers, and on whether or not other shifts in the business environment occur, such as high interest rates or unexpected inflation or recession. Risks are increased because values are affected not only by overall economic conditions, but also by conditions in the locality and in the neighborhoods within it.

A local recession, such as those that hit Detroit, Silicon Valley (the high-technology area near San Jose, California), Denver, and Texas, can cause vacancies, the bankruptcy of numerous developers, and foreclosures of buildings. Errors can be made in selecting a particular site within an area. The lenders' risks are heightened because most loans on income property are without recourse; the properties are owned by shell corporations without other assets.

The traditional responses of lenders to these dangers were to use the underwriting criteria explained in Chapter 15. But in the late 1970s and mid-1980s these techniques became unsatisfactory as a result of inflation, soaring interest rates, and then local surpluses of space. Traditional lending criteria failed to protect against the increased risks. Furthermore, as long as inflationary expectations resulted in projections of rising income and appreciation, few if any loans met the traditional criteria, such as a 1.25 debt coverage ratio. Both lenders and investors found that to make a loan or purchase, they had to base prices on future cash flows, not current ones. Investors became willing to accept initial negative cash flows, and, consequently, they needed additional credit to fund them.

Lenders became convinced that they were carrying too much of the risk without adequate compensation, and they began to use various techniques to protect themselves. Some loans were made for short, fixed periods. More loans carried variable (floating) rates. Joint ventures and *sale-leasebacks* (to be discussed shortly) became more common. Mortgages more often included the right to participate in future revenues or selling prices.

The particular tactics lenders adopt to minimize risks vary with the overall availability of funds and the competition for loans. When funds are available and desirable loans are scarce, lenders make *straight loans* or *bullet loans*— those written with fixed rates and amortization requirements that may range from no principal repayments to complete amortization in short periods such as 15 years, or to balloon payments of the entire principal due in 5 to 15 years. The terms on loans differ with the borrower's record, the desirability of the property, and the competitive situation. Lenders try to protect themselves by tying the size of the loan to signed leases and rent revenues, by keeping the loans closed for longer periods, and by demanding high prepayment penalties.

In periods when money has been tight and when lending to those with weaker credit, lenders have been able to increase their potential yield and their projected risk-adjusted returns by obtaining participations in the property's income or appreciation. Developers and borrowers almost always prefer not to share profits if they can help it. How much of potential profits they are willing to give up depends on several factors:

- How tight the funds market is
- How much capital the developer has relative to what must be borrowed
- How willing the lender is to share risks, either by increasing the amount of the loan or by reducing the fixed interest and debt service burden
- How much the lender will relax other criteria, such as the debt service coverage, the amount of amortization (zero or negative), reporting requirements, and freedom of management

Other Methods of Protection

Participations and underwriting criteria are two methods of trying to assure future payments, but there are other ways of influencing expected risks and returns. One of the oldest techniques bases the amount lent and the interest rate on the credit of the tenants and the length of their leases. Loans for shopping centers frequently require that a certain percentage of the space and rent roll be leased to national retailers with high credit ratings. In the cases of single-occupancy office buildings, supermarkets, department stores, and many others, the amount lent may be based almost entirely on the leases.

In some cases, buildings carry a hierarchy of loans and leases, each with different risks and interest rates. A first and second mortgage may be considered safe because they cover only a relatively small share of the value. Third and fourth mortgages or loans on land subordinated to building loans are far riskier and carry higher rates.

Another method of trying to protect revenues (discussed in Chapter 14) is the inclusion of *escalations,* or the obligation of tenants to share any increases in operating expenses. Such protection is desired by owners for obvious reasons, but escalations also help to assure a better mortgage loan.

Purchasing-power and Interest Rate Risk

Purchasing-power risk is the danger that inflation will have been under-estimated. **Interest rate risk** is the danger that interest rates will rise more than expected. Interest rates contain premiums to protect against both of these dangers, but from experience we know that the market expectations that become embodied in interest rates may be far off the mark. In the early 1980s, many lenders were still collecting 6 percent or 7 percent interest on mortgages while market rates were at 14 or 15 percent. They consequently experienced large losses in current income compared with that available on new loans. If they were forced to sell the mortgages, they suffered large capital losses. Such interest movements were due both to unexpected changes in inflation and to movements in real interest rates. In the mid-1980s real interest rates were 3 percent to 4 percent higher than they had been over the previous 20 years.

Lenders look upon either variable-rate mortgages or participations as ways of offsetting such risks. Many borrowers prefer participations because the amounts they must pay are tied to actual revenues or earnings, and thus they carry less risk than variable interest rates, which may not be earned. Lenders share in profits, but defaults can be avoided if inflation fails to bring about additional revenues or profits.

SHARING TAX BENEFITS

In addition to changing risks, alternative financing methods may increase tax benefits and shift them among investors and lenders. How a property is financed can change when taxes must be paid as well as the amount of tax due.

Time of Receipt of Income

Many ways are available to shift the time at which income is received. These techniques transfer both taxes and risks. For example, developers may sell a property as soon as it is completed. If they receive cash, their risk is ended. However, they must pay taxes on the gain. In contrast, if they borrow on the property or sell it on an installment basis, they retain the risk but defer some or all of their tax liability.

Similarly, as Chapter 16 discussed, if one party to a transaction maintains its books on a cash basis while the other uses the accrual method, the latter can claim taxes as a current expense, thereby gaining an immediate tax write-off. On the other hand, the lender or investor on a cash basis delays any tax payment until the money is actually received. If interest accrues for five years, the difference in delayed taxes and in the value of the property can be considerable.

Allocating Tax Benefits

In cases where the tax brackets of the investors differ, taxes can be reduced by shifting ownership rights—for example, substituting leases or financing for outright ownership—so as to maximize depreciation deductions from taxable income. Thus pension funds, as a rule, do not pay taxes on their income. As a result, if these funds hold land or nondepreciable property and lease it to a taxable entity, the renter has a deductible expense that reduces taxes, while the fund is not obliged to pay taxes on its receipts. In the opposite case, care is taken not to transfer ownership of depreciable property to a nontaxable entity, which would eliminate the value of the available depreciation deductions. Full advantage of these deductions remains with the investor.

In another example, many sales are timed to maximize the depreciation deduction. A sale by an owner whose depreciable basis is low is taxed as a capital gain. He or she may spread the tax payments over several years through an installment sale that also serves to help finance the purchase. On the other hand, the new owner will receive a stepped-up basis, with a consequent reduction in the total taxes collected by the IRS.

METHODS OF FINANCING

Various methods have been developed to take advantage of such differences in taxes and risks. In order to describe and contrast them in more detail, we divide them into the general categories of traditional mortgages, joint ventures, lender participations, leaseholds, multi-class ownership, and contingent payments.

Traditional Mortgages   Traditional fixed-rate mortgage loans meet the standard underwriting criteria discussed in Chapter 15. Lenders consider them safe, with a high probability of repayment. Safety is guarded by careful underwriting, by limiting the loan-to-value ratio, and by insisting on a maximum debt coverage ratio that is believed adequate to compensate for errors in the projections or for a downturn in demand. The mortgages may have fixed or variable interest rates. Amortization schedules may cover anywhere from 15 to 35 years. Interest rate risk and purchasing-power risk may be reduced by requiring repayment (balloon payments) or the setting of a new interest rate at shorter intervals—for example, at the end of five to ten years.

Joint Ventures   At the opposite end from traditional loans are joint ventures in which the lender and developer become partners. In many cases, the lender-investor puts up all or nearly all of the money. The developer furnishes management and construction skills and frequently a personal guarantee to put up money if cost overruns occur. Numerous ways of splitting income between the partners can be worked out. Usually the lender-investor receives a preferred return on the funds it puts up; the remaining income is split with the developer-borrower according to terms set forth in the partnership agreement.

Lender Participations   Other types of agreements allow the lender to share in the cash flow expected from the property. Such **kickers** take a variety of forms. Among them are (a) direct sharing in the total revenue collected or in the net cash flow after payment of operating expenses and debt service; (b) participation in revenues or operating income after a certain threshold level of income has been achieved; (c) an escalating participation in revenues or rental income over time; (d) "free equity," in which the lender conditions the granting of the loan on the developer's assigning to the lender a certain percentage ownership in the project; (e) a division of the before-tax profits; (f) shared appreciation mortgages (SAMs); and (g) options, warrants, or convertible mortgages, all of which give the lender the right to buy some or all of the property at a fixed price after a period of time has elapsed.

Leaseholds   Leaseholds, or split-level financing, change the form of ownership and allow a developer, tenant, or the seller of an existing property to retain rights through a long-term lease. Such agreements are entered into in order to alter the risks, to allow more leverage, or to shift the tax benefits.

Among special lease arrangements are so-called **sandwich leases,** in which a tenant who has a long-term or master lease on a building may sublease it to a wide variety of other tenants. Since the original lessee is both landlord and tenant, she holds a sandwich lease. If the difference between the amount paid and the amount received is great enough, she may borrow against her sandwich lease.

Such situations may make sense in tailoring risks because of the tremendous importance of management in assuring a property's value. An individual, a pension fund, or a trustee may find that instead of paying a straight management fee, it is worthwhile to turn over temporary control through a lease in order to receive a guaranteed fixed return, even though the manager-lessee makes extra profits.

Multiclass Ownership   Tax and cash flow benefits can be separated and sold to those who can best use them. But unless a legitimate economic justification exists for the split, it is likely to be contested by the Internal Revenue Service (IRS) and may be difficult to defend.

In this category, separate partnerships may own different rights in a property or supply loans that carry rights to future income. Thus, partnership A might own a property and lease it to partnership B for rents just sufficient to meet the debt service. The A owners receive no current cash flow; their return consists essentially of tax deductions and the right to a possible future gain. The B owners may have made a profit on the sale of the property to A, or may receive a high cash return from being in charge of current operations. On the other hand, B may have made the investment worthwhile for A by giving up rights to any tax shelter and by a large participation in any increase in the value of the property.

For example, sales of this kind have been very common for new apartment houses with assured rights to convert them into condominiums. It is assumed that the conversions will occur and the properties will be sold after five years. In the interim, the purchasers (the class A partners) would receive large tax deductions even though their prospects of any cash income from operations or sale are virtually nil. These are the types of arrangements the movement for tax reform sought to abolish. Multiclass ownership is also popular with foreign investors not interested in current cash flow or tax benefits, but seeking safety for their principal and eventual capital gains.

Contingent Payments   In many agreements, the amount of funds to be paid and their timing may be made contingent on events that will occur in the future. **Contingent payment agreements** are another form of shifting the risks between borrowers and lenders. Some common forms of such agreements include the following:

- Sellers, in order to make a sale, or new borrowers agree to furnish funds from other sources to insure that loan payments can be met if occupancy or rents drop below projected levels for periods up to two to five years.
- Sellers agree that payment of the final portion of the total consideration need not be made until a designated level of occupancy or receipts is reached (the floor-to-ceiling arrangement).
- Sellers sign leases (sale-leasebacks, to be discussed shortly) sufficient to guarantee all debt payments.
- Lenders agree to give up any claims to payments beyond those that can be received from the sale price of the property.
- Buyers and lenders agree to split future profits with the sellers.

In all of these cases, the risks are shared because the price or payment depends on the property's achieving or failing to achieve some future cash flow.

The remaining sections of this chapter analyze and provide examples of some of the most common of these techniques. Almost all of them require skilled advice in drafting, since the results achieved follow directly from the clauses included in the agreements, which can vary widely.

FINANCING ALTERNATIVES

To illustrate the differences among major types of financing alternatives, we examine methods by which a developer might finance a particular project. We consider in more detail the Washington Square building described in

Table 18-4. This is the property with the construction loan to A to Z Builders, the builder and developer of the project, that was analyzed in Table 18-5.

The Project

The previous tables, summarized in Table 19-1, reflected that land and construction costs for the project are estimated at $7,358,000. Included in this amount is $1,848,000 to cover the land, overhead, and profits on the construction work done by A to Z, but not those from the development process. The developer calculates that its actual investment in the building and land would total $1,400,000. This includes $495,000 in front money to cover options on the land, the detailed plans, permits, working capital, overhead, and reserves, plus $905,000 to buy the land at the closing prior to construction. The remaining $448,000 will be earned during construction on the basis of the builder's profits and expenses in this period. The builder's estimated actual cost to completion, subtracting this profit from the estimated cost of $7,358,000 is $6,910,000.

In this case, A to Z may be putting more than the normal amount into the project; it is buying the land and making payments that could be delayed. In a more typical example, the developer might be able to arrange such a project with only $50,000 to $100,000 of its own money.

Of the construction budget, $5,510,000 is funded by the construction loan based on a firm take-out commitment. In this case, because the project is deemed to be one with excellent prospects, Western State Insurance, after the construction budget was reworked, agreed to a long-term mortgage of $5,510,000 when the building is complete. This is the *floor,* or minimum take-out loan. Table 19-1 also shows an estimated market value based on an appraisal for the building of $9,520,000 if it were fully (80 percent) leased at the estimated level of rents projected for two years after the start of construction. This market value was arrived at by capitalizing the first rental year's projected net operating income (NOI) of $856,800 at a capitalization rate of .09 percent ($856,800 ÷ .09 = $9,520,000).

The difference between the capitalized value of $9,520,000 and the construction budget of $7,358,000 is the developer's profit—the reward A to Z Builders expects for putting the project together, devising the concept, supervising the design, obtaining the permits and the financing, and taking the risk that the cost of the project will not meet the budget. The amount the developer actually receives in profits depends on its costs, on the amount of future benefits it creates, and on how the benefits and risks are shared between the developer and the potential lender-investor.

The Pro Forma Statements

The value of income properties like the Washington Square building depends on the projected cash flows and the level at which the market capitalizes these

Table 19-1
Pro Forma Operating and Sales Statement
Washington Square Office Building

Developer's investment at year zero	$1,400,000
Total construction budget	$7,358,000
Developer's actual cost	$6,910,000
Long-term commitment (floor) and construction mortgage	$5,510,000

Value when leased $\qquad V = \dfrac{NOI}{R} \qquad = \dfrac{\$856,800}{.09} = \$9,520,000$

Selling price at end of year 6 $\qquad SP = \dfrac{NOI}{R} \qquad = \dfrac{\$1,146,592}{.09} = \$12,739,907$

Net selling price (94% of gross) NSP = $11,975,513

Net Operating Income
Year

Income	1	2	3	4	5	6
Gross income	$1,157,835	$1,215,727	$1,276,513	$1,340,339	$1,407,356	$1,447,723
Less 5% vacancy	(57,892)	(60,786)	(63,826)	(67,017)	(70,368)	(73,886)
Effective gross income	$1,099,943	$1,154,940	$1,212,687	$1,273,322	$1,336,988	$1,403,837
Less operating expenses	(243,143)	(246,732)	(249,987)	(252,859)	(255,298)	(257,246)
Net operating income	$856,800	$908,208	$962,700	$1,020,463	$1,081,690	$1,146,592

Internal Rate of Return

$$V = \frac{NOI_1}{(1 + IRR)} + \frac{NOI_2}{(1 + IRR)^2} + \ldots + \frac{NOI_n + Net\,SP}{(1 + IRR)^n} \qquad \textbf{(4.3)}$$

Year 0	1	2	5	6

$$\$9,520,000 = \frac{\$856,000}{(1 + IRR)} + \frac{\$908,208}{(1 + IRR)^2} + \ldots + \frac{\$1,081,690}{(1 + IRR)^5} + \frac{\$1,146,592 + \$11,975,513}{(1 + IRR)^6}$$

Internal rate of return = 13.32%

future flows. Included in Table 19-1 are the projected net operating income before debt service and taxes for the building.

Because the market is active, it is assumed that the building can be pre-leased. The first year's projected income is based on normal occupancy. As noted, this results in expected net operating income for year 1 of $856,800. By year 6, the NOI is projected as increasing to $1,146,592. This assumes a rate of inflation of about 5 percent, with revenues rising faster than expenses.

When the project was under development, office buildings of this type were selling in the market at capitalization rates of 9 percent. Therefore, the market value of the building based on capitalizing the first year's projected NOI gives the estimate of $9,520,000. If successfully completed and leased, the value of the building is $2,162,000 above its projected construction budget. Under the assumption that the NOI in year 6 would be $1,146,592 and that the building would sell at the end of that year with the same 9 percent capitalization as at the beginning, the projected selling price for the building at that time is $12,739,907. The operating income and net selling price together for the sixth year are $13,122,105. The expected yield to a buyer paying initially $9,520,000 in cash and receiving back $11,975,513 after sales expenses is at an annual rate of 13.3 percent over the six-year holding period.

The Financing Alternatives

By approaching a mortgage banker after it had roughed out its costs and expected income, A to Z Builders was able to get a listing of a number of financing alternatives, each differing somewhat in risk and returns. From the list, it and the mortgage banker selected seven alternatives to be analyzed in more detail. They were able to work out the net present values and rates of return for each of them. To show how this works, the rest of this chapter examines in detail each alternative to illustrate some major differences among financing techniques.*

The examples include:

1. a presale of the building
2. a fixed-rate mortgage
3. a joint venture
4. a mortgage either convertible or with options or warrants
5. split-level financing with the sale of land and a leaseback with a leasehold mortgage
6. a mortgage with contingent interest
7. a shared-appreciation mortgage (SAM)

*This method of comparing alternatives and their potential returns has been developed for classroom use from an initial presentation prepared by the BA Mortgage and International Realty Corporation, a BankAmerica company. The estimates are based on the 1985 tax code; therefore, the relative returns would be somewhat different if the 1987 code were applied. However, the analysis remains the same. Applying the lower depreciation deductions and higher capital gains taxes makes an interesting exercise that can serve to check whether the basic principles are understood.

The basic operating income, cost of development, and projected selling price are identical in all seven cases. The differences in yield and profits are due entirely to the method by which the debt service, rights to income and appreciation, and tax benefits are structured. The risks borne by the lender and developer also differ from case to case, so the risk-adjusted yields may be much closer together.

Since the lenders are also investors in several cases, we call them lender-investors. How much they are willing to lend or invest depends on their appraisal of the value of the building, on the debt coverage ratio, and on the other underwriting criteria discussed in Chapter 15. However, the degree to which they are willing to lower the fixed interest rate and alter the loan-to-value and debt coverage ratios depends also on the amount of gain they expect from a particular form of participation. The developer's profits depend on when it puts up money and receives its cash flows, on the amount it borrows, and on what rights it must give up. The total of cash flows to the lender and developer together is also influenced by the amount of tax benefits.

As Table 19-10 will show in its summary of the different financing alternatives, depending on the technique adopted the developer's internal rate of return can vary between 29 percent and over 124 percent. Using a single discount rate of 12 percent, the net present value of A to Z's profits could range from $772,545 to $1,974,135. No clear relationship exists between the size of the internal rates of return (IRRs), which depend heavily on the amount invested by the developer, and the amount of profits.

A SALE UPON COMPLETION, OR A FIXED-RATE MORTGAGE

Presale

The developer finds that it can sell the Washington Square building prior to the start of construction. A pension fund would offer a commitment with a floor of $5,510,000, equivalent to its estimate of 75 percent of the total cost of land and construction. The ceiling or final price offered is expected to be $9,520,000. This price is based on reaching a net operating income of $856,800 in year 1, as projected in the pro forma statements. The pension fund capitalizes this income at a 9 percent rate. If the pro forma projection is accurate, the fund's internal rate of return based on the ceiling price will be 13.3 percent (see Table 19-1). Given the current market and the fund's desire to diversify its portfolio with some real estate investments, the fund is willing to accept a 13.3 percent projected IRR. The agreement is bankable and suitable for A to Z to obtain a construction loan. Since the fund is an all-cash investor, many analysts would treat this 13.3 percent as the benchmark rate of return in the market. It does not contain any premiums for leverage risks or tax considerations.

Table 19-2 reflects A to Z's basic analysis. It estimates that its $1.4 million investment will be tied up for two years. Most of this amount must be paid out

Table 19-2
Developer's Net Present Value
and Internal Rate of Return on a Presale
Washington Square Office Building

Developer's investment at year zero	$ 1,400,000
Tax calculation	
Receipt at end of first operating year (94% of SP)	$ 8,948,800
Less cost of construction	(6,910,000)
Gain	$ 2,038,800
Tax (at 35% rate)	(713,580)
After-tax cash flow	
Net selling price (NSP)	$ 8,948,800
Less construction mortgage	(5,510,000)
Less tax	(713,580)
After-tax cash flow (ATCF)	$ 2,275,220
Calculation of net present value at 12%	
Present value of $2,725,220 × .7972	$ 2,172,545
Less initial present value $1,400,000	(1,400,000)
Net present value	$772,545
Internal rate of return of developer	39.52%

at the start of construction. Some will be used before construction begins and some after; therefore, assuming that the funds are all invested at the start of construction, A to Z estimates that using $1.4 million as the amount of its investment for two years will be about right, on average, and will provide accurate estimates of rates of returns and yields.

Construction, which will take a year, will be financed by a bank loan that includes interest. Upon completion, the pension fund will advance the floor amount to pay off the construction loan. At the end of the first year of operation, the building will have reached 80 percent occupancy and A to Z will receive the remainder of the net sales price of $8,948,800. (Selling and closing costs are estimated at 6 percent.) A to Z also calculates its potential cash flow from the first year's operations. However, the developer decides that because the amount from operations depends so much on future events, it will not include it in the projections of net values and IRRs.

After A to Z has paid its taxes and the construction loan, it will have a net cash flow of $2,725,220. For purposes of comparison with respect to this and A to Z's other alternatives, it decides to estimate net present values by discounting all receipts at 12 percent. The net present value of the project under the presale option is $772,545 (see Table 19-2). The internal rate of return based on the initial investment of $1.4 million is 39.5 percent.

A Fixed-Rate Mortgage

Straight mortgages—especially those with fixed rates—are hard to obtain at the time A to Z is comparing its alternatives, but the mortgage bankers believe that they can get a 12 percent fixed mortgage for 360 months with an annual mortgage constant of .1234. Although in theory the lender would advance up to 75 percent of the value of the property, in fact, at this time, the maximum straight loan available is for $5,554,619, or slightly less than 60 percent of the appraised value of the completed project. The lender would charge 2 points. The limit on the loan is set because, in this tight market, lenders stick to a debt coverage ratio of 1.25. In periods with more available funds, they might cut the ratio to 1.15 or even less. A lower ratio and a lower mortgage constant would make possible loans of 75 or even 80 percent of value. The lender includes a 2 percent pre-payment penalty and an agreement that the loan cannot be assumed. It believes that the loan is safe and that, since it is for a below-normal share of the project's current market value, it is likely to be paid off soon after the building develops an operating record.

Table 19-3 shows the details of this arrangement. The developer's actual cost to completion is projected at $6,910,000. Because the loan it receives on completion is $5,443,527 after paying points, its total investment is $1,466,473 at the beginning of the first year of operations. The table also shows the details of its after-tax cash flow. As in all the cases, A to Z's net sales price for the building is $11,975,513. After paying off the mortgage and taxes, its after-tax cash flow at the end of year 6 is $5,137,627.

To calculate the internal rate of return and the net present value for each of the alternatives, it is important that similar assumptions be made as to when investments are made and income is received. The time line used for the developer in each case is pictured in Table 19-4. It is assumed that the developer must spend its initial investment of $1.4 million at the start of construction, which is year zero on the time line. Construction is completed at the end of a year, at which time permanent financing begins. In this case, the loan is for $5,443,527 after paying points, so the developer's investment increases by $66,473 to $1,466,473 ($6,910,000 − $5,443,527). The developer's after-tax cash flows (from Table 19-3), shown in column 4, are assumed to be received at year end. Thus, the after-tax cash flow for the first year of operations is shown on the time line two years after the start of construction. (End-of-year receipts are common in most presentations, since they greatly simplify calculations.) The cash flow on sale of $5,137,627 is received at the end of the sixth year of operations, which is seven years from the start of the investment. Column 7 shows the details of how the developer's internal rate of return is figured. The net present value is $1,974,135 and the IRR is 29.3 percent.

Table 19-3
The Fixed-Rate Mortgage Alternative
Washington Square Office Building

Developer's investment at year zero		$1,400,000

Loan
Income available for debt service (1.25 ×) = $\frac{\$856,800}{1.25}$ = $685,440

Loan amount (12%, 30 years, .1234K) = $\frac{\$685,440}{.1234}$ = $5,554,619

Developer's investment at completion		
Developer's cost of building		$6,910,000
Loan amount	$ 5,554,619	
Less mortgage fee (2%)	$ (111,092)	
Cash from mortgage		$5,443,527
Developer's investment at completion		$1,466,473

Operating Period Cash Flow

Year

Income	1	2	3	4	5	6
Net operating income	$856,800	$908,208	$962,700	$1,020,463	$1,081,690	$1,146,592
Less interest	(666,554)	(664,266)	(661,702)	(658,832)	(655,616)	(652,015)
Less depreciation*	(322,650)	(342,009)	(342,009)	(342,009)	(342,009)	(342,009)
Taxable income	(132,404)	(98,067)	(41,011)	19,622	84,065	152,568
Taxable income (or loss)	(132,404)	(98,067)	(41,011)	19,622	84,065	152,568
Plus depreciation	322,650	342,009	342,009	342,009	342,009	342,009
Less amortization	(19,072)	(21,360)	(23,924)	(26,795)	(30,010)	(33,611)
Less (tax) or plus saving	66,202	49,033	20,505	(9,811)	(42,033)	(76,284)
After-tax cash flow	$237,376	$271,615	$297,580	$ 325,025	$ 354,032	$ 384,682

After-Tax Cash Flow at Sale

Tax calculation	
Receipt at end of sixth operating year (94% of SP)	$11,975,513
Less adjusted basis	(5,325,305)
Gain	$6,650,208
Tax	(1,330,042)
After-tax cash flow	
Net selling price (NSP)	$11,975,513
Less mortgage repayment	(5,507,844)
Less tax	(1,330,042)
After-tax cash flow (ATCF)	$5,137,627

*Depreciation based on 19-year straight line: 5.0, 5.3, 5.3, 5.3, 5.3, 5.3.

Table 19-4
Calculation of Net Present Value and Internal Rate of Return
Washington Square Office Building

Year	Time	Expenditure	After-Tax Cash Flow	Present Value Factor At 12%	Present Value	Internal Rate of Return Factor
0	Start of construction	($1,400,000)		1.0000	($1,400,000)	$\dfrac{(\$1,400,000)}{(1 + IRR)^0}$
1	Completion	(66,473)		0.8929	(59,351)	$\dfrac{(66,473)}{(1 + IRR)^1}$
2	First year ATCF		$237,376	0.7972	189,235	$\dfrac{237,376}{(1 + IRR)^2}$
3	Second year ATCF		271,615	0.7118	193,330	$\dfrac{271,615}{(1 + IRR)^3}$
4	Third year ATCF		297,580	0.6355	189,117	$\dfrac{297,580}{(1 + IRR)^4}$
5	Fourth year ATCF		325,025	0.5674	184,428	$\dfrac{325,025}{(1 + IRR)^5}$
6	Fifth year ATCF		354,032	0.5066	179,363	$\dfrac{354,032}{(1 + IRR)^6}$
7	Sixth year ATCF		384,682	0.4523	174,010	$\dfrac{384,682}{(1 + IRR)^7}$
7	Net cash on sale		$5,137,627	0.4523	$2,324,002	$\dfrac{5,137,627}{(1 + IRR)^7}$

Net present value of developer's return at 12% discount $1,974,135
Internal rate of return of developer's investment   29.28%

Investor-Lender's Yield or Internal Rate of Return

Year 0	1	2	5	6	6

$$\$5,443,527 = \frac{\$685,626}{(1 + IRR)} + \frac{\$685,626}{(1 + IRR)^2} + \ldots + \frac{\$685,626}{(1 + IRR)^5} + \frac{\$685,626}{(1 + IRR)^6} + \frac{\$5,507,844}{(1 + IRR)^6}$$

Internal rate of return of investors 12.74%

The lender-investors' time line may differ from that of the developers. If they put up money at the start of construction, their time line (as in Tables 19-5 and 19-7) will be the same as the developer's. On the other hand, if they lend only at completion, which is the start of the first operating year, their time line will start one year later. In this case (Table 19-4), their loan is made upon completion, and their debt service receipts are shown at the end of each year. The last year's debt service and mortgage repayment come at the end of the sixth year of operations. The lender-investors' yield of 12.74 percent exceeds their coupon interest rate of 12 percent; the difference arises because of the 2 points they earn for making the loan, and the prepayment penalty.

THE JOINT VENTURE

The second major type of financing suggested by the mortgage banker was a joint venture. Rather than acting as passive lenders when money was tight or with reputable developers short of capital, many savings and loans, savings banks, insurance companies, real estate investment trusts (REITs), and other traditional mortgage servicers decided they would prefer to be partners right from the start of a project. Recognizing the risks they take in conventional loans, lenders may want to share fully in the profits. Joint ventures are partnerships established to handle a single project that may last until the project is sold.

All kinds of joint venture agreements are possible. In a typical situation, the developer contributes expertise, a concept, and the risk of spending time without profit. The lender-investor contributes the equity. Developers may act as the general contractor and as manager of the completed project. The lender usually wants an agent on-site to see that the money is spent properly, that the construction conforms to specifications and the budget, and to take action if the project is not meeting the agreed-upon time schedule and the financial plan.

Because the developer has so little invested in a project, it is vital that the investor have some way of terminating an unsatisfactory arrangement. Many developers want to keep going as long as possible in the hope that some lucky circumstance will turn an unprofitable venture around. Investors should insist that if certain projections are not met, they can dissolve the partnership through a *buy-sell* agreement. If the agreement is triggered, they could offer to buy or be willing to sell at a certain price.

By entering as a partner, lender-investors gain a larger say over the design, construction, and operations than they would have as mere lenders. At the same time, their risks are magnified. In the mid-1980s many savings and loans that entered into joint ventures without the requisite skills to handle them had disastrous experiences. The failure of a number of large associations demonstrated that joint ventures are much more difficult to manage than conventional loans.

The Joint Venture Alternative for the Washington Square Building

A savings and loan association is a probable investor for the Washington Square building project. It agrees to put up the total actual cost to the developer of $6,910,000, except for $100,000, which it insists that the developer supply to show its good faith. For its contribution of $100,000 and its development of a plan, A to Z Builders is granted, on completion, an imputed capital account equal to 10 percent of that of the savings and loan, or $691,000.

The cash flow from the project will go first to provide the savings and loan an 8.5 percent preferred return on its capital contribution. The next call on the cash flow will be an 8.5 percent preferred return to the developer on its capital account. After that, all of the cash flow will be divided, 50 percent going to each of the two partners. Similarly, upon sale the investors' equity will be returned first, plus any shortfall in their preferred return. Then the developer will have a similar claim for its imputed account. Any remaining funds will be split evenly between the partners, half going to the investors and half going to the developer.

The Investors' and Developer's Return

Table 19-5 shows the way the net operating income from the property would be divided. The preferred returns are fully earned even in the first year of operations. If the property took several years to rent up, the right to a preferred return would be significant. In the first year, in addition to the preferred returns, $210,715 is available to be split 50-50. It is clear that, with time, the developer experiences a faster percentage growth in its share than do the investors, even though the absolute increases are the same.

In calculating the investor-lenders' rate of return, it is assumed that they put up half of their investment at the start and the remainder at completion; this would average about the same as funding throughout the construction period. Their IRR is 13.1 percent, compared with the mortgage return of 12 percent. The investors have much more at risk, since they have put up almost the entire cost of the project. Still, if the estimates are correct, they are putting up only 74 percent of the projected initial value. In this arrangement, the developer gains because it has a much smaller investment. Thus its IRR goes to 125 percent. Where capital contributions are minimal, use of the IRR makes little or no sense because it is based on such a small capital base and does not take into account the developer's effort and risk. What is more relevant is a comparison of net present values. Under this arrangement, its NPV at $1,496,837 is well below that from a fixed-rate mortgage. The developer must trade off its much smaller need for capital for a somewhat lower NPV. How much expected profit to sacrifice depends on other prospects, on how much capital it has or can obtain, and on what risks it wants to take.

OPTIONS AND CONVERTIBLE MORTGAGES

Options are an increasingly popular instrument in the field of finance. *Options* are contracts that grant one party the right—but not the obligation—to take a particular action. When options are used as part of a financing arrangement, they usually grant the lender the right to buy a property at a fixed price after a certain time has elapsed. A clause is often included which grants the seller the right to continue to use the property under a long-term lease.

Table 19-5
The Joint Venture Alternative
Washington Square Office Building

Investors' cost	$6,910,000

Developer's imputed capital account	$691,000
Developer's investment at year zero	$100,000
Developer's investment at completion	$100,000

	Cash Flow Projection					Combined Return Preferred + 50-50 Split
		Preferred Return				
Year	Net Operating Income	Investors' at 8.5%	Developer's at 8.5%	Net Remaining	Investors'	Developer's After-Tax Cash Flow
1	$856,800	$587,350	$58,735	$210,715	$692,708	$243,371
2	908,208	587,350	58,735	262,123	718,412	288,488
3	962,700	587,350	58,735	316,615	745,658	302,111
4	1,020,463	587,350	58,735	374,378	774,539	316,552
5	1,081,690	587,350	58,735	435,605	805,153	331,859
6	1,146,592	587,350	58,735	500,507	837,603	348,084
Sale	$11,975,513	$6,910,000	$691,000	$4,374,513	$9,097,257	$1,503,044

Sale	Net sales price	$11,975,513
	Less investors' equity	(6,910,000)
	Less developer's imputed equity	(691,000)
	Remainder to be divided 50-50	$4,374,513
Net present value of developer's return at 12% discount		$1,496,837
Internal rate of return of developer's investment		124.69%

Investor-Lenders' Yield or Internal Rate of Return

Year 0	1	2	3	7	7

$$\$3,455,000 + \frac{\$3,455,000}{(1 + \text{IRR})} = \frac{\$692,708}{(1 + \text{IRR})^2} + \frac{\$718,412}{(1 + \text{IRR})^3} + \dots + \frac{\$837,603}{(1 + \text{IRR})^7} + \frac{\$9,097,257}{(1 + \text{IRR})^7}$$

Internal rate of return of investors 13.05%

EXAMPLE: The Golden Rule department store can borrow $5 million on its building from the Universal Insurance Company. Golden Rule grants Universal an option to buy the building at the end of five years for $8 million. If the option is taken up, the outstanding mortgage will be paid off from the amount due under the option. Universal agrees that if it exercises its option, it will lease the building to Golden Rule under specified terms. The option might give the right to purchase as of a certain date, or that right might extend over a period, or perhaps be exercisable on the first day of any year from years 5 to 8.

A **convertible mortgage** is a mortgage that contains an option to convert the mortgage into a certain share of the equity. In the above example, instead of a separate option, Universal's mortgage could contain the right to be converted into 60 percent (or any other percent) of the equity at the end of five years. If Universal converts, the mortgage is wiped out in payment for its equity interest.

Convertible second mortgages are especially popular with foreign investors. Typically, they allow interest to accrue so that no income is received until the end. In this way they give the developer the extra tax advantage of taking an interest deduction without needing to make a cash payment. At the end of a period—such as five years—the lender has the right either to be paid the amount due or to convert the mortgage into an ownership share.

The Advantages

Convertible mortgages or loans with options usually carry a higher loan-to-value ratio and a lower interest rate than conventional mortgages. Frequently the loan is large enough so that the developer receives more cash (on which taxes are not due, since the payment is in the form of a loan) than it invested. The developer retains 100 percent ownership of the property during the option period, taking all of the depreciation deductions and all operating profits or losses.

The terms are more generous than those of a conventional loan because the lender has the right to share in the appreciation. Although the loan is somewhat riskier, it is still protected by the mortgage. If the project is a success, the lenders can purchase equity by converting or exercising their option. They gain the benefits made possible by their loan. They take the future potential benefits into account when they determine the amount and interest rate on the convertible mortgage.

One possible drawback for developer-borrowers is that taxes will be due at the time of conversion because it is equivalent to a sale of equity. They must make certain that they obtain some cash to pay the taxes.

The Convertible-mortgage Alternative for the Washington Square Building

A to Z Builders could finance its Washington Square building project with a convertible mortgage (see Table 19-6). In this case, the lender is willing to

Table 19-6
The Convertible Mortgage Alternative
Washington Square Office Building

Loan amount (10%, 30 years, .1053 K, 1.06 ×,	$7,616,000
plus 20% of all increases in NOI over $856,000)	
Developer's cost of building	$6,910,000
Developer's investment at year zero	$1,400,000
Developer's investment at completion	($706,000)

Cash Flow Projection

Year	Net Operating Income	Annual Debt Service	Investors' 20% of NOI Increases	Investors' Total Return	Developer's After-Tax Cash Flow
1	$ 856,800	$802,030	$ 0	$ 802,030	$168,495
2	908,208	802,030	10,282	812,312	191,575
3	962,700	802,030	21,180	823,210	205,699
4	1,020,463	802,030	32,733	834,763	220,582
5	1,081,690	802,030	44,978	847,008	236,260
6	1,146,592	802,030	57,958	859,989	252,770
Sale	$11,975,513			$11,041,222	$606,233

Sale	Net sales price	$11,975,513
	Less mortgage payment	(7,304,056)
	Remaining balance	$4,671,457
	80% to investor	3,737,165
	20% to developer	934,291
	Developer's cash withdrawal	706,000
	Developer's gain	1,640,291
	Tax at sale	(328,058)
	ATCF (934,291 − 328,058)	$606,233

Net present value of developer's return at 12% discount $1,352,853
Internal rate of return of developer's investment   70.65%

Investor-Lenders' Yield or Internal Rate of Return

Year 0	1	2	5	6	6

$$\$7,616,000 = \frac{\$802,030}{(1 + IRR)} + \frac{\$812,312}{(1 + IRR)^2} + \cdots + \frac{\$847,008}{(1 + IRR)^5} + \frac{\$859,989}{(1 + IRR)^6} + \frac{\$11,041,222}{(1 + IRR)^6}$$

Internal rate of return of investors   15.86%

make a loan for 80 percent of the building's estimated value of $9,520,000. The convertible mortgage will be for $7,616,000 with an interest rate of 10 percent and a mortgage constant of .1053. Additional interest will be paid equal to 20 percent of all increases in net operating income above the base rate of $856,800. After six years, the mortgage is convertible into an 80 percent ownership of the property.

From the developer's point of view, the convertible mortgage granted upon completion pays off the construction loan and all of its investment and leaves it with an immediate tax-free loan of $706,000 ($7,616,000 − $6,910,000), money it can use elsewhere. The developer has the right to operate the building for six years with a below-market interest rate. It retains the full depreciation deduction. At the end of year 6, if the property has been profitable, the mortgage is converted and the building is sold. The developer still retains 20 percent of the net cash on sale. If the property is unprofitable, its risks are greatly reduced. The developer has made money on the development, while the lower fixed interest rate increases its ability to fund a period with less-than-expected operating income.

The table shows that by increasing their risk somewhat, lenders are able to increase their yield on the mortgage to about 15.9 percent. The developer has reduced its risk greatly, since it has *financed out* (received more than its cash investment from the mortgage financing). The net present value of the developer's investment is $1,352,853. Because its investment is paid off upon completion (year 1 of the time line shown in Table 19-4), its internal rate of return is extremely high at 71 percent; but, again, the IRR has little meaning.

LEASEBACKS

A **lease** is a contract between an owner (the **lessor**) and a tenant (the **lessee**) setting forth conditions upon which the tenant may occupy and use the properties, as well as specifying the terms of the occupancy. The lessee (tenant) agrees to pay the owner (landlord-lessor) rent according to terms set forth in the lease.

Leases can be used as a financing technique competitive with mortgage financing. For this purpose, two important types of leases are:

■ **Sale-leasebacks,** in which a property is purchased and simultaneously leased back to the seller or another party upon previously agreed-upon terms.
■ **Land sale-leasebacks,** in which the purchaser buys only the land and leases it back to the developer. Arrangements to finance the improvements built on the leasehold through a mortgage are often made simultaneously. Such arrangements are called *split-level financing,* since the terms of the lease and the mortgage may differ considerably.

Sale-Leasebacks

Leasebacks have become an extremely important financing tool. Major retail chains, such as department and food stores, have traditionally used this technique. Large banks and corporations have recently entered into arrangements to finance their headquarters or plants in this way. For example, the Bank of America sold its world headquarters in San Francisco for $660 million in 1985, with a partial leaseback; that is, it guaranteed to lease its existing space, but its commitment decreased over time. At the time, this was believed to be the highest sales price ever paid for a single office building. Many cities sold their city halls, their auditoriums, and even their museums, but a subsequent change in tax regulations made this basically no longer profitable.

Typically, in such arrangements the seller agrees to lease the property on a net-net lease—the tenant pays all expenses, including property taxes—for a long period, such as 15 to 30 years, with a series of options to renew, perhaps at lower rates or on the basis of reappraisals. However, in cases such as the Bank of America sale, the seller simply agrees to rent a certain amount of space for a number of years. The new owner operates the building and gains any appreciation.

There are a number of reasons why owners prefer to sell and lease back the property:

- The former owner continues to use the property with the equivalent of 100 percent financing. In contrast, if the firm retains ownership and finances it on a mortgage, it will have to furnish 25 to 35 percent of equity funds above the mortgage. Capital-short firms like sale-leasebacks.
- By using its real estate, a company can improve its balance sheet. In many cases, appreciated property is worth far more than is shown on the corporation's books. When the property is sold, a capital gain results. The amount of gain minus any taxes becomes an addition to the firm's capital. A major reason so many banks have sold their buildings is that they were under regulatory pressure to increase their capital. They did so by taking the capital gains that had accrued on their real estate.
- By selling, companies get out of the real estate business. Many firms find that their comparative advantage is greater in their own line of endeavor than in real estate. It is more profitable to invest their time and capital where their skills count for more than they do when investing in real estate.
- If a firm can lease back for only five or ten years, it gains flexibility in choosing future locations. A great many older Safeway or A & P supermarkets stand empty because the food chains gave up leases on them, even though in some cases they were designed and built specifically for them.
- There are tax advantages to sale-leasebacks. Rent on a lease is fully deductible as a business expense, whereas land is not depreciable, and the

available deductions for the building may have been used up. Instead, under a leaseback, a high-bracket taxpayer pays rent to a pension fund or other landlord with a negligible or low tax rate. The lessees reduce their taxes, since all rents are a deductible expense, while the lessors pay no taxes on their added income.

Lender-investors gain because their return (including appreciation) is usually somewhat above what could be charged on a straight mortgage. If the lessee has a high credit rating, a long-term lease will carry a rate close to what the firm would have to pay in the bond market. For poorer credit risks, lender-investors often take a participation agreement. In either case, lender-investors may have a lower discount rate than the seller-lessee, and thus place a higher value on the residual appreciation they will receive when the lease runs out. This additional net present value to the investor may make the transaction worthwhile.

Land Sale-Leasebacks

Developers may sell the *land,* which cannot be depreciated, and simultaneously lease it back. In the lease, they may obtain the right to mortgage a building to be erected on the land and also arrange to have the rights of the landowner subordinated to the claims of the mortgage lender. Mortgages on such buildings are called **leasehold mortgages.** If they are foreclosed, the landowners' rights on their subordinated ground leases are equivalent to those of a second mortgage holder. The investor can either pay off the building's mortgage or give up the claim to the land.

Since the risks to the lessors (the landowners) are larger than on a first mortgage, they demand a higher return, either in the form of a higher lease payment, or through agreements for contingent payments, or by sharing in any enhanced values of the property.

The Leaseback Alternative for the Washington Square Building

A to Z Builders finds that it can obtain a contract for a land sale-leaseback and a leasehold mortgage (see Table 19-7). The lender-investors will buy the land at its price of $905,000 and will also lend on a leasehold mortgage. They add together the lease rent and mortgage debt payments and determine the size of the mortgage by accepting an initial debt coverage ratio of 1.15 times this total. As a result, they would grant a mortgage of $5,960,000 as well as paying $905,000 for the land, leaving the developers with a final investment of $45,000.

The mortgage loan would be written at 10.5 percent for 30 years, or with a constant of .1098. The rent on the land will be 10 percent of the land's price plus 50 percent of all increases in net operating income over the $856,800 base. Upon sale, the mortgage must be paid off and the land repurchased. The land price will be determined by capitalizing at a 9 percent rate the land rent being

Table 19-7
The Land Sale-Leaseback Alternative
Washington Square Office Building

Investors' purchase of land	$905,000
Rent on land 10% (plus 50% of increases in NOI)	$90,500
Net operating income for rent and debt	$856,800
Income for mortgage and rent (1.15 ×)	$745,043
Available for mortgage	$654,500
Loan amount (10.5%, 30 years, .1098K)	$5,960,000
Developer's investment at year zero	$1,400,000
Developer's investment at completion	$45,000

Cash Flow Projection

Year	Net Operating Income	Mortgage Debt Service	Land Rent	50% of NOI Increases (Overage)	Lenders' Cash Flow	Developer's After-Tax Cash Flow
1	$ 856,800	$654,222	$90,500	$ 0	$ 744,722	$ 112,078
2	908,208	654,222	90,500	25,704	770,426	137,782
3	962,700	654,222	90,500	52,950	797,672	165,029
4	1,020,463	654,222	90,500	81,831	826,553	193,910
5	1,081,690	654,222	90,500	112,445	857,167	224,524
6	1,146,592	654,222	90,500	144,896	889,617	256,974
Sale	$11,975,513				$7,347,879	$3,619,583

Repayment to lenders: Mortgage	$5,737,925
Last year overage capitalized at 9%	1,609,954
Total	$7,347,879

Developer's net sales price	$10,365,559
Developer's after-tax cash flow	$3,619,583

Net present value of developer's return at 12% discount	$1,868,683
Internal rate of return of developer's investment	45.61%

Investor-Lender's Yield or Internal Rate of Return

Year 0	1	2	3	7	7

$$\$905,000 \; + \; \frac{\$5,960,000}{(1 + IRR)} \; = \; \frac{\$744,722}{(1 + IRR)^2} + \frac{\$770,426}{(1 + IRR)^3} + \cdots + \frac{\$889,617}{(1 + IRR)^7} + \frac{\$7,347,879}{(1 + IRR)^7}$$

Internal rate of return of investors   12.19%

received at that time. Thus, the lender-investor pays $905,000 for the land and receives $1,609,954 upon sale. The mortgage is to be closed for six years to give the property a chance to build up excess rents needed to make the arrangements profitable. The projected results for both the landlord-investor and the developer are shown in Table 19-7. The developer's NPV of $1,868,683 with virtually no investment after completion makes this one of the most attractive alternatives.

MORTGAGES WITH CONTINGENT INTEREST

One of the most common types of mortgages with kickers gives the lender the right to participate in the income from a property. Lenders make a loan under conventional underwriting standards but at a somewhat below-market interest rate in order to obtain the right to participate in future income. As we have seen, reducing the mortgage constant with a given debt-coverage ratio raises the amount that can be lent.

Contingent Interest

Such mortgage contracts provide that in addition to an agreed-upon debt service payment, the lender will receive a sum contingent on the earning level a property achieves. This **contingent interest** can be based either on gross income or on net income after operating expenses have been subtracted. Payments may be a percentage either of the total defined income or of increases in income over some projected initial starting point.

As a rule, lenders would prefer payments based on gross revenues. They are easier to measure, and lenders do not have to worry about a borrower's padding expense accounts. Even with projections that are too high, the lender will receive some contingent interest. Borrowers' desires are just the opposite; they prefer paying a percentage of net income over an initial base. If there are unavoidable increases in operating expenses, they want to avoid increased debt service. They do not want to pay out additional interest unless the property's income reaches some break-even point.

The Advantages

Borrowers see several advantages in contingent interest agreements. Since they reduce the initial debt service on which the debt coverage ratio is figured, they can borrow more and tie up less of their own capital. If the property fails to meet its earnings expectations, they can carry it for a longer period because of the reduced fixed-debt service requirements. Tax advantages can develop if they trade lower amortization payments for contingent interest. Since interest— including the contingent interest—is deducted for tax purposes while principal payments are not, their after-tax cash flow rises even if total debt service payments remain the same. Most important, by giving up some future benefits, they may be able to borrow in tight money markets when credit would otherwise be unavailable.

Lenders are more willing to lend because they have built-in protection against inflation. If inflation raises the property's rents, their income tied to revenues goes up also. More flexible payments may save a certain number of properties from foreclosure since lenders need not shade their underwriting standards to allow for higher interest rates. Because the fixed-debt payments conform to a normal break-even ratio, borrowers are likely to meet payments even if revenues fall somewhat below expectations.

Lenders trade off the cut in the initial fixed rate for the expected receipts of contingent interest. They plan so that the blended yield from the two sources exceeds that of a conventional mortgage. If revenues fall below projections, they will not get their expected interest, but they know that if the shortfall occurs because of disinflation, they would have trouble collecting in any case.

The Mortgage with Contingent Interest Alternative for the Washington Square Building

A to Z Builders finds that it can obtain a loan with lender participation (see Table 19-8). The loan would be for $5,996,850, with a basic interest rate of 11 percent, or 100 basis points under the fixed-rate mortgage for that period. This would enable A to Z to borrow an additional $541,000. (Compare this with Table 19-3.) As in the sale-leaseback alternative, A to Z gives up 50 percent of any increase in net operating income plus the capitalized value of the rental overages. An **overage** is the additional rent resulting from higher revenues.

At first, the lenders' fixed interest rate is below market, but they receive 50 percent of any increase in net operating income. The lenders insist that the loan be *locked in* (closed) for a minimum of six years to give appreciation time to work. The developer must also agree to a 5 percent prepayment penalty and to pay an added sum based on the contingent interest payment in the year just prior to sale. When sold, this contingent interest is capitalized at 9 percent to determine the amount of this payment to the lenders. The table indicates that this sum is projected at $1,609,954.

The final figures in the table show that lenders project a net yield of 15.6 percent, compared to 12 percent on conventional loans. Furthermore, they have an inflationary hedge. The developer's net present value is $1,267,384, since it gives up a rather large sum at the time of sale. Its IRR is 31 percent.

SHARED APPRECIATION MORTGAGES

Shared appreciation mortgages (SAMs) are used in creative financing for homes (see Chapter 11). The same principles apply in the market for income property. To reduce the required monthly payments and increase the size of the loan, borrowers agree to share with lenders any increase in the value of the property. As an extra inducement, they may also agree to share part of any rise

Table 19-8
The Mortgage with Contingent Interest Alternative
Washington Square Office Building

Income available for debt service $(1.25 \times) = \dfrac{\$856,800}{1.25} = \$685,440$

Loan amount (11%, 30 years, .1143K, $= \dfrac{\$685,440}{.1143} = \$5,996,850$
plus 50% of all increases in NOI)

Developer's investment at year zero $1,400,000
Developer's investment at completion $910,000

Cash Flow Projection

Year	Net Operating Income	Annual Debt Service	50% of NOI Increases (Overage)	Lenders' Cash Flow	Developer's After-Tax Cash Flow
1	$ 856,800	$685,313	$ 0	$ 685,313	$ 234,239
2	908,208	685,313	25,704	711,017	242,507
3	962,700	685,313	52,950	738,263	240,941
4	1,020,463	685,313	81,831	767,144	239,202
5	1,081,690	685,313	112,445	797,758	237,272
6	1,146,592	685,313	144,896	830,209	235,129
Sale	$11,975,513			$7,693,455	$3,331,945

Sale	Net sales price	$11,975,513
	Less mortgage repayment	(5,793,811)
	Less contingent interest capitalized at 9%	(1,609,954)
	Less 5% prepayment penalty	(289,691)
	Developer's net cash flow (before tax)	$4,282,058
	Lenders' net cash flow	$7,693,455

Net present value of developer's return at 12% discount $1,267,384
Internal rate of return of developer's investment   29.83%

Investor-Lenders' Yield or Internal Rate of Return

Year 0	1	2	5	6	6

$$\$5,996,850 = \frac{\$685,313}{(1 + IRR)} + \frac{\$711,017}{(1 + IRR)^2} + \cdots + \frac{\$797,758}{(1 + IRR)^5} + \frac{\$830,209}{(1 + IRR)^6} + \frac{\$7,693,455}{(1 + IRR)^6}$$

Internal rate of return of investors   15.57%

in net operating income (as in the previous section). Appreciation can be measured in several ways—for example, as the sales price above the estimated initial value, as the net cash flow upon sale, or as any amount above an arbitrary level.

Interest and Equity

Since shared appreciation mortgages trade lower interest rates and a larger loan for a share of the appreciation, they make sense only if the lender is convinced that appreciation will occur. Many SAMs made in the early 1980s and based on expectations of high inflation turned out to be "duds" from the lender's point of view. The developer financed out, but the lender found that no appreciation was being shared. On the other hand, disinflation lowered interest rates so that, while the fixed rates may have been below market when made, they may have ended up above the market rates of a year or two later.

Lenders on SAMs want to be certain that the arrangement will last long enough for the property to appreciate. On the other hand, they do not want to be locked into a situation with a low fixed interest rate after appreciation slows. To meet these opposing desires, contracts set a minimum lock-in period but also require that the property be sold or refinanced by a specific time. Thus the mortgage may be closed for five years but may contain a clause requiring that the property be sold or refinanced by the end of year 10.

In many SAMs, lenders shape loans to be almost equivalent to those of a joint venture. They reduce the debt coverage ratio to as low as 1.10 to cover all of the actual land and construction costs. How low they cut the fixed interest rate depends on their assumptions as to future appreciation. Lenders use pro forma operating and termination statements to estimate how much the shared appreciations will increase their rate of return.

Problems in Sharing

As with home mortgages, problems arise because so much of appreciation depends on a developer's management skills, maintenance, repairs, and improvements. In many of the creative arrangements discussed in this chapter, a lender's return depends as much on the developer's performance as on the property and the economy. In periods of rapid inflation, the impact of the economy may overwhelm the developer's performance, but in more stable periods lenders need to exercise extreme caution in choosing partners as well as in drafting the sharing agreements. Track records, integrity, and the developer's financial resources must be weighed carefully for successful choices.

The SAM Alternative and the Washington Square Building

A shared appreciation mortgage is the final financing alternative considered by A to Z Builders. Under a contract of this type, the developer would expect the loan to reimburse it for all of its expenses. A to Z would have no money of its own invested when the building was completed. Furthermore, it would obtain the lowest fixed interest rate of all the alternatives considered, together with a reasonable debt service.

The fixed interest rate for the SAM has been lowered to 9.5 percent, which means that the loan can cover all of the developer's costs at completion of $6,910,000, even with a debt coverage ratio of 1.25 (see Table 19-9). The share of future income and appreciation has been set high enough so that the lenders' actual expected yield is 14.4 percent. In estimating yield, lenders must feel confident in the estimates of both the rate of increase in net operating income and the capitalization rate at which the properties will sell.

The developer would be giving up a 20 percent share of any increase in net operating income and 50 percent of any appreciation. The net present value of the developer's position would be $1,470,262, and its IRR would be 46 percent. The developer reduces its risks greatly and, consequently, accepts a lower NPV than it would under several other alternatives.

THE FINANCING DECISION

The Washington Square example outlines the type of financing arrangements that successful developers with a good track record and an adequate amount of front money may find in the market. The methods proposed for the Washington Square building project are summarized in Table 19-10. The amount of loans made available could range from $5,444,000 to $7,616,000. The fixed interest rates would vary between 9.5 percent and 12 percent. The developer's own investment at the conclusion of the project could range from $1,466,000 to an ability to withdraw $706,000. Most of these arrangements require giving up certain rights to future income and appreciation.

The Potential Returns

In examining the developer's potential return, note that the net present value of A to Z's position at the start of construction is projected to vary from $773,000 to $1,974,000. Its IRRs cover a much wider range, but such comparisons are not particularly useful because they reflect major differences in the amount of capital investment and they do not reflect the return for the developer's initiative and skill.

For many reasons, the developer's decision about which financing alternative to seek cannot be based on the expected net present values alone. The estimates hinge on the projected pro forma statements. What actually occurs will be influenced by the skill with which market estimates are made, by whether the project can be brought in at or below budget, by how well the market develops in a specific location, and by what happens to the economy, especially with respect to real demand and inflation.

Table 19-9
The Shared Appreciation Mortgage Alternative
Washington Square Office Building

Loan amount (9.5%, 30 years, .1009 K, 1.23 ×, plus 20% of NOI, plus 50% of appreciation)	$6,910,000	

Developer's investment at year zero	$1,400,000	
Developer's investment at completion	$0	

Cash Flow Projection

Year	Net Operating Income	Mortgage Debt Service	Investors' 20% of NOI Increases	Investors' Total Return	Developer's After-Tax Cash Flow
1	$ 856,800	$697,236	$ 0	$ 697,236	$ 159,564
2	908,208	697,236	10,282	707,518	200,690
3	962,700	697,236	21,180	718,416	244,284
4	1,020,463	697,236	32,733	729,969	290,494
5	1,081,690	697,236	44,978	742,214	339,476
6	1,146,592	697,236	57,958	755,195	391,397
Sale	$11,975,513			$9,287,384	$1,895,713

Sale	Net sales price	$11,975,513
	Repayment of mortgage	(6,599,255)
	Net cash flow	$5,376,258
	50% to investors	$2,688,129
	50% to developer	$2,688,129

Net present value of developer's return at 12% discount	$1,470,262	
Internal rate of return of developer's investment	45.65%	

Investor-Lenders' Yield or Internal Rate of Return

Year 0	1	2	5	6	6

$$\$6,910,000 = \frac{\$697,236}{(1 + IRR)} + \frac{\$707,518}{(1 + IRR)^2} + \ldots + \frac{\$742,214}{(1 + IRR)^5} + \frac{\$755,195}{(1 + IRR)^6} + \frac{\$9,287,384}{(1 + IRR)^6}$$

Internal rate of return of investors 14.42%

Table19-10
Summary of Financing Alternatives
Washington Square Office Building

Cost and income projections

Total construction budget	$7,358,000
Developer's actual cost	$6,910,000
First-year net operating income	$856,800
Market value capitalized at 9%	$9,520,000
Sixth-year net operating income	$1,146,592
Sale price in sixth year at 9%	$12,739,907

	Lender-Investors			Developer		
Financing Alternative	Loan ($000)	Investment ($000)	IRR	Investment at Completion ($000)	NPV ($000)	IRR
Presale	n/a	9,520	13.3%	1,400	773	40%
Fixed-rate mortgage	5,444	n/a	12.7%	1,466	1,974	29%
Joint venture	n/a	6,910	13.1%	100	1,497	125%
Convertible mortgage	7,616	n/a	15.9%	(706)	1,353	71%
Land sale-leaseback	5,960	905	12.2%	45	1,869	46%
Mortgage with contingent interest	5,997	n/a	15.6%	910	1,267	30%
Shared appreciation mortgage	6,910	n/a	14.4%	0	1,470	46%

Note: Figures are rounded; n/a = not applicable.

The Decision to Negotiate

In deciding which financing to seek, A to Z Builders must consider, among other factors, its own risk preferences, income, possible tax changes and marginal tax brackets, the amount of capital it has available, and possible alternative uses for its capital. At times A to Z may prefer to act as a merchant builder, primarily building for sale. At other times its objective may be to add to its own portfolio. A to Z may want maximum flexibility in the loan terms so as to be able to take advantage of new opportunities.

Either because it believes the market will turn down or because it needs capital for other projects, A to Z may decide it wants to get out as much money up front as possible. On the other hand, if it believes that the prospects for the project are extremely good or if it wants a major inflation hedge, the builder may instead take a conventional mortgage that contains a maximum risk exposure but also has the greatest upside potential.

In any case, A to Z Builders recognizes that the alternatives sketched out by the mortgage banker are only the beginning of actual negotiations. Whether it can obtain any loan and under what specific conditions depends on which lenders are in the market when it completes its submission package, and on how the lenders evaluate the project based on its submission, skills, and reputation. A good deal of bargaining and adjustment of terms may be necessary before the developer finds the funds it wants.

When the project is actually ready for submission, A to Z or its mortgage banker may simulate various economic scenarios to help A to Z identify the potential risks and returns and, therefore, which type of loan has the greatest appeal. It knows, too, that given very volatile financial markets, terms and conditions change frequently. What promises to be a very profitable endeavor when the developer embarks on its detailed plan may not work at all if the money market becomes too tight.

In any case, by understanding how changes in interest and discount rates affect the present values of future expected benefits, A to Z can make better plans and decisions. It can see the degree to which any project depends on its particular developmental skills and ability, how much depends on the market, and how much is influenced by financing terms and availability.

In its planning, the developer must take into account the major factors at work in real estate and finance. Supply of and demand for funds shift market interest and discount rates, resulting in changes in the affordability and demand for properties and in their prospective cash flows. At the same time, the shifting interest rates and the availability of mortgage and equity capital cause the market to change the values it gives to these flows. The prices of properties change, as do their expected risks and returns.

SUMMARY

New techniques of financing income properties arose for a number of reasons. Conventional underwriting methods did not work well during periods of inflation; the possibility of sharing tax benefits led to different ownership forms and to some lenders believing that they should participate in the returns to compensate for their risk.

Fixed-rate mortgages based on traditional standards protect lenders against default, but they do not guard against the risks of inflation and changes in interest rates. The amount lent will require large equity investments if sales prices are based on assumptions of increased income and appreciation, whereas loan-to-value and debt coverage ratios are based on appraisals that use only the first year's or stabilized income.

Interest rate risks can be reduced for lenders but are raised for borrowers by including variable interest rates in mortgages. They can also be lowered by making payments contingent on specified events.

In joint ventures, investor-lenders put up most of the cash. They receive more control over the project, a preferred claim against income, and a share in the income from a sale or refinancing, plus a share in all additional income. Their risks can be high because they put up more money and they face the risks inherent in any partnership relationship. Developers reduce their capital risks but may give up more of any upside potential.

Initially, options and convertible mortgages are similar to conventional mortgages. After a period, the lender has the right to convert the mortgage or to use an option to obtain a share of the equity. If not converted, the mortgage is due in the usual way. To obtain the conversion privilege, the lender may lower the fixed interest rate and be more willing to lend as well as to make more money available than on a conventional loan.

In leasebacks, investor-lenders purchase some or all of the property, but the original owner retains rights in the form of a lease. A wide variety of arrangements allow this technique to be used as a substitute for other forms of financing. The sellers need less of their own money and may substitute rent—a deductible expense—for property with few or no depreciation deductions. They give up rights to future appreciation.

Lenders can participate in future income from operating revenues or sales. A variety of sharing arrangements can be worked out. How the risks and returns are shared depends on how badly owners need a loan, on the amount they need, on the availability of loanable funds, and on what risks lenders are willing to assume.

Both lenders and borrowers can use projected pro forma income and termination statements to calculate what they are giving up and what they may gain from any specific arrangement. How well they actually do depends on the accuracy of the projections or on income above that expected initially. However, they can also test to see how sensitive the projected results are to a change in any of the basic assumptions.

KEY TERMS

bullet loan	leasehold mortgages
contingent interest	lessee
contingent payment agreements	lessor
convertible mortgage	overage
interest rate risk	purchasing-power risk
kickers	sale-leasebacks
land sale-leasebacks	sandwich leases
lease	

QUESTIONS

1. The Golden Rule department store built its building 25 years ago. On its books, the building has been almost completely depreciated. What are some of the advantages of selling the building and leasing back the right to occupy it?

2. Many developers want to "finance out." What does this mean?
3. Why have balloon payments become more common in the financing of income properties?
4. What are some advantages to a developer of entering into a joint venture with a lender?
5. What are some advantages to a lender of entering into a joint venture with a developer?
6. Explain why the level of interest rates influences the use of traditional underwriting standards.
7. Describe four forms of lender participation.
8. How does a floor-to-ceiling commitment to lend work?
9. Explain the position of purchasers of land who lease back the land and subordinate their rights to the lender on a leasehold mortgage.
10. Best-Built Developers approaches Universal Life Insurance Company with the following submission: It proposes to build a $3 million free-standing office building. It estimates the first year's rent roll at $320,000, vacancies at 5 percent, and operating expenses at 30 percent. Capitalization rates are not expected to change. Rents and expenses are projected to rise 4 percent per year. Interest rates for mortgages on equivalent buildings are 10 percent with an annual mortgage constant of .1061. Best-Built asks for a mortgage loan of $2.25 million. Universal requires a debt coverage ratio of 1.20.
    a. Construct a before-tax pro forma operating and termination statement (5 percent sales costs) for a five-year holding period.
    b. How much would Universal be willing to lend?
    c. Assume that Universal is willing to reduce the interest rate to 9 percent with a .0970 constant, provided that it receives 20 percent of all increases in net operating income and 50 percent of any difference between the net sales price and $3 million. It will lend $2.25 million. Show Universal's receipts and calculate its yield for the five-year holding period.

GLOSSARY

abusive practices Kickbacks, referral fees, and other conflicts of interest prohibited by the Real Estate Settlement Procedures Act. **13***

accelerated cost recovery system (ACRS) A system of accelerated depreciation for tax purposes that prescribes depreciation rates by asset classifications. **16**

accelerated depreciation A depreciation allowance in which the initial deductions exceed those authorized under the straight-line method. **16**

acceleration The process based on a provision in a mortgage allowing a lender to declare the entire principal immediately due and payable in the event of a default. **2**

accrual method of accounting An accounting system whereby revenue and expenses are recognized in a period, whether or not actually received or paid out. **16**

active participation in rental activities Internal Revenue Service designation for taxpayers who participate in the making of management decisions or arranging for others to provide services in a significant sense for properties they own and rent to others. **16**

actual economic costs The amount of income sacrificed in owning a house. In addition to cash costs, it takes into account opportunity and transaction costs as well as appreciation or depreciation. **10**

advances In construction lending, the partial disbursement of funds under a note. **18**

adjustable-rate mortgage (ARM) A mortgage in which the contract interest rate adjusts periodically. **1, 11**

adjusted basis The changed basis resulting from adjustments through events such as improvements, casualty losses, and prior depreciation deductions. **16**

affordability The ability of a family to meet the cash payments required to purchase a home. **2, 10**

affordability index An index that measures the percentage of families with incomes sufficient to purchase a home. **10**

after-tax cash flow (ATCF) The net amount of any receipt or payment during the operating period that includes the effect of income taxes. **14**

after-tax (reversion) cash-on-sale The net amount of any receipt or payment at the time of termination that includes the effect of income taxes. **14**

alternative minimum tax An alternative tax the base of which includes types of income and special deductions not fully taxed by the regular income tax. **16**

amortization The liquidation of a financial obligation on an installment basis. **2**

amount financed The amount of the loan minus finance charges collected by the lender. **13**

annual (or monthly) payments The payments on the mortgage and/or payments for property taxes, insurance, maintenance, and repairs. **10**

annual percentage rate (APR) The effective interest rate required under the Truth in Lending Act. **13**

annuity A series of payments for a specified period. **3**

---

*Numbers in boldface denote chapters in which these terms are discussed.

534

appraisal   An estimate and opinion of value.   **13**

appreciation   An increase in value, in contrast to *Depreciation.*   **10**

assessments   The right to require additional payments from partners.   **17**

asset to liability management   A procedure to measure risks due to interest rate mismatches in a portfolio and to act in order to reduce them.   **9**

assumption   An agreement whereby the purchaser agrees to make the payments on the mortgage debt. The original borrower remains secondarily liable unless specifically released.   **2**

at-risk rule   The rule limiting deduction of losses for tax purposes to the amount at risk and that can be lost in an activity.   **16**

automated teller machines (ATMs)   Machines used by financial institutions for issuing cash and accepting deposits and payments.   **9**

balloon payment   The final installment payment on a note, which is greater than the preceding installments and which pays the note in full.   **2**

band of investment   A method of finding a capitalization rate by adding the required return on mortgage debt to the required return on equity, each weighted by the proportion it makes up of the total price.   **15**

basis   The measure of an investment in property for tax purposes.   **16**

basis point   One-hundredth of one percent.   **3**

before-tax cash flow (BTCF)   The residual cash return to the equity holder before income taxes. Net operating income minus debt service payments and amounts set aside for reserves.   **4, 14**

before-tax (reversion) cash-on-sale   The amount available for equity holders from a sale prior to income tax payments. Net sales price minus mortgage repayment plus cash reserves.   **14**

beneficiary   The lender on a deed of trust.   **2**

blanket mortgage   A single mortgage that covers more than one piece of real estate.   **18**

blind pool   A syndication in which the properties to be purchased are not specified at the time the funds are raised.   **17**

boot   The cash or unlike property in an exchange.   **16**

break-even ratio   The ratio of total operating expenses plus debt service to the gross potential income. It measures the percent of occupancy necessary to cover the debt service and operating expenses.   **15**

builders' bonds   Mortgage-backed securities issued by builders based on mortgages accumulated from their sales of houses.   **8**

bullet loan   Loans primarily on income properties, for fixed periods (5 to 15 years) with large balloon payments.   **19**

buy-down   A loan in which someone other than the borrower—usually the seller—puts up money to reduce the borrower's monthly payments.   **11**

call option   The right to prepay a mortgage. The value of the right to prepay.   **4**

capital gains   Gains (or losses) from the sale or exchange of capital assets which meet tests for capital gains established in the tax code.   **16**

capital gains deduction   That part of a net long-term capital gain that can be deducted from the total and is not subject to the regular income tax.   **16**

capital stock associations   Savings and loan institutions organized with common stockholders in contrast to mutual ownership.   **6**

capitalization   Determining the value of a property by discounting expected future income payments that are summed to give present value.   **15**

capitalization rate   The ratio of income to price, or the rate of interest considered a reasonable return on the investment, which when divided into net income yields a present value for the property.   **15**

caps   The maximum in a period of either interest rates or payments on an adjustable-rate mortgage.   **11**

cash payments   The total cash cost to own a house. Payments for the mortgage, property taxes, insurance, and maintenance, less any tax saving.   **10**

cash-on-cash return   The annual cash flow, NOI after debt service, divided by the investor's equity; also known as return on equity and the equity dividend rate.   **4**

certificate of eligibility   A certificate certifying that a veteran is eligible to participate in the loan guarantee program.   **8**

certificate of deposit   A fixed-term saving instrument that earns a higher rate of interest than a passbook account.   **6**

certificate of reasonable value   A certificate stating the value of a property for loan purposes, as determined by the Veterans Administration.   **8**

closed mortgage   A mortgage that does not allow prepayment for a period.   **2**

closing   The arrangements under which all payments are settled and title is transferred.   **13**

closing costs   The expenses incurred at the time a property is transferred upon sale.   **8**

co-insurance   An insurance policy that shares the risk between the insurer and the insured.   **8**

collateralization   The pledging of mortgages, bonds, or other marketable properties as security for a loan.   **8**

collateralized mortgage obligations (CMOs)   A special form of mortgage-backed security in which repayments of one class of security are completed before any principal payments are made on the following class.   **8**

combination loans   Construction mortgage loans that can be assumed by the home buyer.   **6**

commitment   A pledge or firm agreement to make a loan.   **7**

comparable properties   Properties reasonably similar to the one being valued and whose prices are known through recent sales; therefore, they can be used for comparative purposes in the appraisal process.   **13**

compound interest   Interest paid on the original principal and also on the accrued and unpaid interest that has accumulated.   **3**

concessions   Free rent or other payments from a landlord to a tenant for signing a lease.   **14**

conditional commitment   A promise from the FHA that it will issue mortgage insurance if the borrower meets the necessary credit conditions.   **8**

construction loan   A loan made to finance the actual construction of a property.   **18**

constructive notice   A notice to the public, communicated through the public recording of a document, that an action has taken place.   **2**

contingent financing clause   A clause in the purchase agreement (sales contract) specifying the financing terms that must be available if the sale is to go through.   **12**

contingent interest   Interest payments based on a property's income.   **19**

contingent payments   Payments the amount and timing of which depend on the occurrence of future events.   **19**

contract of sale   An agreement to transfer title after certain payments and conditions have been met.   **11**

contract interest rate   *See* face interest rate, nominal interest rate.

contract price In an exchange, the total value of all benefits received by the seller. **16**

conventional loan A mortgage loan made by a financial institution without insurance or guarantee by a government agency. **6**

convertible mortgage A mortgage for which the lender has the right to demand a share of the equity as repayment of the principal. **19**

corporation A group or body of persons established and treated by law as an individual or unit with both rights and liabilities distinct and apart from those of the persons composing it. **16**

cost approach A technique of appraisal that establishes value by estimating the cost to reproduce the improvements, subtracts depreciation, and then adds in the fair market value of the land. **13**

coupon interest rate The contract interest rate on a mortgage specified in the note or bond. **3**

covariance A measure of the degree to which movements of assets are related. **3**

covenants Promises made in mortgages or deeds of trust to perform or not to perform certain duties. **2**

creative financing In its broadest form, any financing other than the standard, level-payment interest mortgage. In some cases, it is defined as any money advanced by other than a financial institution. **1, 11**

credit The net borrowing in the economy. **5**

credit crunch A period in which the supply of credit falls far short of the demand at prevailing interest rates. **5**

credit cycles The oscillation of credit between periods of expansion and contraction. **5**

credit enhancement The use of third-party guarantees, such as bank letters of credit, bonding by insurance companies, or pledges of other assets, to assure a minimum level of income or cash flow needed to make debt payments. **8**

cut-off rate *See* required rate of return.

debt The sum of money owed as specified in an express agreement. **1**

debt service The required periodic payments on interest and principal established by the mortgage note. **4**

debt service coverage ratio The ratio of annual net operating income before debt service and taxes divided by the annual debt service. **15**

declining balance A form of accelerated depreciation in which a set percentage of depreciation is applied to the declining balance of the asset value that results when previous depreciation is deducted from the original asset value. The depreciation is deducted from the original asset value. The depreciation percentage is usually established as a certain percentage of straight-line depreciation. **16**

deed in lieu of foreclosure The conveyance of the title by an owner-borrower to a lender when the loan is in default, for the purpose of avoiding foreclosure costs and the stigma of foreclosure. **2**

deed of trust A conveyance of the title to land to a trustee as collateral security for the payment of a debt. It includes conditions requiring the trustee to reconvey the title upon the payment of the debt and granting the trustee the power to sell the land to pay the debt in the event of a default on the part of the debtor. **2**

default Failure to fulfill a duty or a promise or to discharge an obligation. **2**

default premium The difference between the expected return and the contract return arising from the risk of probability of a loss through default. It makes up part of the gross or face interest note. **3**

deferred taxes   A tax payment delayed until a future date.   **16**

deficiency judgment   A judgment issued by a court to pay the balance owed on a loan if, after a default, the security pledged does not satisfy the debt.   **2**

depreciable basis   The basis against which the depreciation rates are applied in order to calculate the depreciation deduction.   **16**

depreciation   The loss of value in real property brought about by age, physical deterioration, or functional or economic obsolescence. Broadly, a loss in value from any cause, in contrast to appreciation.   **13**

depreciation deduction   A subtraction from taxable income allowed to cover depreciation expenses.   **3**

depreciation recapture   The requirement that additional depreciation resulting from an accelerated depreciation allowance be treated as ordinary income rather than as a capital gain in calculating income taxes due upon the sale of a property.   **16**

direct capitalization   The estimate of the value of an income stream to be received indefinitely (in perpetuity), obtained by dividing the stream by an appropriate capitalization rate.   **15**

direct subsidy   The amount paid directly by a government to reduce a family's rent or housing expense.   **7**

discount factor   The amount by which a future payment is multiplied in order to calculate its present value.   **3**

discount rate   The interest rate a bank must pay to borrow from a Federal Reserve bank.   **5**

discounted cash flow method   A procedure for estimating value by discounting all projected future cash flows in order to obtain their present values.   **15**

discounting   The process of multiplying future values by a discount factor in order to obtain their present values.   **3**

disintermediation   The process in which savers replace their savings accounts at financial institutions with money market instruments that they purchase directly.   **5, 6**

diversification   The process of selecting assets that are expected to react to future events in a dissimilar manner in order to reduce the risks in a portfolio.   **3**

draws   In construction lending, the advances or payments made for the completed portions of a work in progress.   **18**

dual interest-rate mortgage (DIM)   A mortgage that has both graduated payments and adjustable interest rates.   **11**

due diligence   The requirement that those offering securities to the public take care that there be no material misstatements or omissions of facts in the description of the security.   **17**

due-on-sale   A clause in mortgages stipulating that the entire balance comes due when the property is sold.   **2**

duration   The weighted average of the times when the payments on a mortgage are expected. The weights are proportional to the present value of a payment as a share of the present value of the mortgage.   **9**

economies of scale   A reduction in average costs arising from the increased size of a firm.   **9**

economies of scope   A reduction in average costs arising when a firm expands its line of products.   **9**

effective gross income   The projected revenues expected to be collected in operating an income property. It consists of gross potential income less allowances for vacancies and collection losses.   **14**

effective interest rate   The actual rate of return or yield to the lender. The rate of interest charged on an adjustable-rate mortgage; the value of the index plus a specified margin.   **4, 11**

effective yield   The true cost of a loan. The interest rate that equates the present value of future payments with the current market price.   **4**

Employee Retirement Income Security Act (ERISA)   An act defining the pension rights of employees and the duties of pension trustees.   **6**

equitable ownership   The rights of purchasers under a contract of sale. Their interest in the property can be sold or borrowed against.   **11**

Equal Credit Opportunity Act   A federal law forbidding discrimination of various kinds in the granting of credit.   **13**

equity   The interest or value an owner has in real estate over and above the liens against it.   **1**

equity loans   Junior mortgages made by lending institutions against the equity in homes.   **6**

equity of redemption   The right to redeem property during the foreclosure period, such as a mortgagor's right to redeem within a year after foreclosure sale.   **2**

equity sharing   An arrangement under which two parties jointly purchase a house. The occupier pays rent to the other party to cover his or her share.   **11**

escalations   Amounts required by leases to cover upward movements in operating costs.   **14**

escrow accounts   Impounds or accounts maintained for borrowers in order to hold monies until payments are due.   **13**

escrows   The deposit of instruments and funds with instructions to a neutral, third party to carry out the provisions of an agreement or contract.   **2**

Eurodollars   Dollar deposits held at banks outside of the United States.   **9**

expansion   That period of a credit or business cycle when output and the demand for credit are growing.   **5**

expense-to-income ratio   The ratio of housing expenses (see P.I.T.I.) to a family's gross monthly income.   **10**

externalities   The values of a property dependant on its neighborhood, public services, or other factors outside the owner's control.   **7**

FHLB advances   Loans made by Federal Home Loan Banks to their members.   **7**

face interest rate   The rate of interest specified on the note or loan; also known as the contract or nominal interest rate.   **3**

Farmers Home Administration (FmHA)   An agency of the federal government that makes, participates in, and insures loans for rural housing and other purposes.   **7**

feasibility   The ability of a property to generate sufficient income to meet its debt payments and profit goals.   **14**

federal funds rate   The interest rate charged by financial institutions for lending funds to each other, primarily on an overnight basis.   **5**

Federal Home Loan Bank System (FHLBS)   The Federal Home Loan Bank Board and the 12 federally chartered regional banks as well as the member associations. The Board and the banks are responsible for regulating member thrift institutions and supplying credit to them.   **7**

Federal Home Loan Mortgage Corporation (FHLMC)   A secondary market facility of the Federal Home Loan Bank system that buys and sells mortgage loans and issues mortgage participations and other types of mortgage-backed securities.   **7**

Federal Housing Administration (FHA)   A part of the Department of Housing and Urban Development that insures loans made by approved lenders to qualified borrowers.   **7**

Federal Land Banks (FLB)   A part of the Farm Credit Administration. They are the major lender on farm properties.   **7**

Federal National Mortgage Association (FNMA, also called "Fannie Mae")   A government-sponsored corporation that supplements private mortgage funds by buying and selling mortgages in the secondary market and by issuing its own securities as well as mortgage-backed securities.   **7**

Federal Reserve System   The Board of Governors and the 12 district banks, which act as the central bank of the United States. The governors and the district bank presidents are responsible for formulating and operating monetary policy.   **5**

Federal Savings and Loan Insurance Corporation (FSLIC)   An instrumentality of the federal government that insures the savings accounts in member institutions.   **6**

federally related mortgage   A loan made by any lender insured or regulated by a federal agency, or a loan to be insured, guaranteed, or sold to a government agency.   **13**

finance charge   Payments for financing a mortgage, including interest, finance charges, and required mortgage insurance payments.   **13**

financial intermediaries   Financial institutions that act as intermediaries between savers and borrowers by selling their own obligations for money and, in turn, lending accumulated funds to borrowers.   **5**

financial leverage   The leverage arising from debt financing.   **4**

fixed-rate mortgage (FRM)   A mortgage loan with a constant interest rate for the life of the loan.   **2**

float   Funds credited to an institution's reserves before the paying institution is charged; a source of the monetary base.   **8**

floating rates   Interest rates tied to an index, such as the banks' prime rate.   **18**

floor-to-ceiling commitment   A commitment to advance some minimum amount upon completion, together with a maximum amount that will be lent if the project meets a specified occupancy ratio.   **18**

flow of funds account   A set of accounts issued by the Federal Reserve that measures the flows between borrowers and lenders and between savers and investors.   **5**

forbearance   Agreement by a lender to delay foreclosure or to refrain from taking other similar action when the borrower defaults on a loan.   **2, 8**

foreclosure   A procedure whereby property pledged as security for a debt is sold to pay the debt in the event of default in payments or other terms.   **2**

free-and-clear return   The rate of return on assets. Their net operating income divided by their price or value. Also called the overall capitalization rate and the rate of return on assets (ROR).   **4**

front money   Funds necessary to start a development, generally required from the developer or equity owner, before a lender will agree to a loan.   **18**

functional obsolescence   The loss in value resulting when a property cannot render a given service as well as new property designed for that purpose.   **13**

fungible   Having the ability to substitute one part for another in a financial transaction (said of money); the close relationships among markets for loans.   **3**

future value   The value at some specified later date of a deposit or cash flow invested at compound interest.   **3**

general partnership   A partnership in which all partners share in the management responsibilities and have unlimited liability for losses.   **16**

Government National Mortgage Association (GNMA, also called "Ginnie Mae")   A government corporation, part of the Department of Housing and Urban Development, that provides special assistance for certain FHA and VA loans. It also guarantees securities backed by mortgage loans.   **7**

graduated payment adjustable mortgage (GPAM)   A loan that combines the features of a graduated payment mortgage and an adjustable-rate mortgage.   **11**

graduated payment mortgage (GPM)   A loan in which the debt service payments begin at one level and increase by a certain amount each year until they reach a predetermined level.   **11**

gross income multiplier (GIM)   The factor calculated by dividing the sales price by the annual gross income; used with similar information from recent sales of comparable properties in estimating a property's value.   **15**

gross profit percentage   The gain from a sale divided by its contract price.   **16**

gross rent multiplier (GRM)   The gross potential rental income from a property divided by its sales price.   **13**

growing equity mortgage (GEM)   A fixed-rate mortgage on which monthly payments increase according to an index or some predetermined amount in order to shorten its period of amortization.   **11**

hard costs   The direct costs for a development or construction project, as distinguished from legal, financing, architects', and similar fees required for the project.   **18**

high-powered money   The monetary base controlled by the Federal Reserve. Its movements are a prime ingredient in causing changes in the amount of credit.   **5**

holdback   That portion of a loan not funded until some additional requirement is satisfied. In construction lending, it is a percentage of the work completed but not paid for until the project is finished.   **18**

housing expenses   The payments for debt service, property taxes, and hazard insurance (P.I.T.I.)   **10**

housing vouchers   Vouchers for rent given directly to eligible families who may spend them on units of their choice.   **7**

hurdle rate   *See* required rate of return.

impounds   *See* escrows.

income approach   An appraisal procedure that capitalizes the projected future income of a property in order to estimate its market value.   **15**

income capitalization approach   *See* income approach.

index   In adjustable-rate mortgages, the measure upon which the effective interest rate changes are based.   **11**

individual ownership   The form of property ownership in which the title is held by an individual.   **16**

individual retirement account (IRA)   A savings account that, under specified conditions, allows for the deferment of a limited amount of taxes.   **16**

initial expenditures   In purchasing a house, the down payment and other charges at closing, including financing charges.   **10**

initial index rate   On an adjustable-rate mortgage, the interest rate paid until the first change date.   **11**

installment sale   A sale in which part or all of the selling price is paid for in a later year.   **16**

interest   The amount charged for the use of a sum of money, usually expressed as a percentage of the sum.   **2, 3**

interest factors   A quantity that, when multiplied by a number, yields the compound value of the initial number.   **3**

interest rate risk   The risk that interest rates will rise and cause a decline in the market value of an asset.   **19**

interest rate structure   The relationship among interest rates that results from the variations in their individual characteristics.   **3**

interest rate swap   A contract under which institutions exchange payment streams arising from loans with different terms.   **9**

internal rate of return (IRR)   The yield or discount rate that equates the present value of all positive and negative cash flows for an investment.   **4**

intrastate exemption   One of a series of exemptions that allows issuers of securities not to register them with the Securities and Exchange Commission; here, they can avoid registering if all concerned live in the same state.   **17**

investment   In the Gross National Product and the Flow of Funds Accounts the purchase of goods produced in a period that lasts more than one year.   **5**

investment property   Under the tax laws, most real properties--but not those used in a trade or business or held mainly for sale to customers--are capital assets that qualify for capital gains treatment. Special rules apply to the excluded items.   **16**

joint tenancy   Joint ownership by two or more persons with right of survivorship; all joint tenants own equal interest and have equal rights in the property.   **16**

joint venture   An arrangement between two or more parties to own or develop real estate.   **19**

judicial sale   A sale through foreclosure of the collateral security, conducted under the auspices of a court.   **2**

junior mortgage   A lien that is subsequent to that of the holder of a prior mortgage.   **2**

Keogh plan   A voluntary savings plan for self-employed individuals on which taxes on the interest are deferred.   **16**

kicker   A benefit lenders receive over and above the ordinary interest payment.   **19**

land development loan   A loan used to finance the development of land, such as for the installation of streets, utilities, and other site improvements.   **18**

land sale-leaseback   A sale in which a seller deeds property to a buyer who simultaneously leases the property back to the seller, usually on a long-term basis.   **19**

lease-option   An agreement that gives a tenant the right to occupy a property and requires him or her to purchase it within a specified time period.   **11**

lease purchase   An agreement that gives a tenant the right to occupy a property and to purchase it within a specified time period.   **11**

leasehold   The rights of a tenant (lessee) in real property acquired as the result of a lease or rental agreement.   **19**

leasehold mortgage   A loan secured by the tenant's interest, as in a leasehold.   **19**

legal reserve requirement   The amount of reserves (deposits) that a financial institution must maintain at a Federal Reserve Bank. It is a specified percentage of the deposits an institution accepts.   **5**

lessee   One who contracts to rent property under a lease contract.   **19**

lessor   An owner who enters into a lease with a tenant.   **19**

leverage   The use of debt for investment purposes.   **4**

liability   Debt for which one is legally obligated.   **2**

lien   A form of encumbrance that usually makes property security for the payment of a debt or discharge of an obligation. Examples are for judgements, taxes, mortgages, and deeds of trust.   **2**

limited partnership   A partnership consisting of general partners, who manage and are fully liable, and of limited partners, who do not manage and are liable only for the amount they have invested.   **16**

liquidity premium   The amount in an interest rate that covers the lender's risk due to the illiquidity of the funds lent.   **3**

liquidity risk   The danger that one will not be able to raise the cash necessary to meet one's obligations.   **9**

loan application   A form that states the amount requested for a loan and its terms, identifies the borrower and the property to be pledged, and provides other necessary information about the borrower and the property.   **13**

loan commitment   A promise, usually in writing, to make a future loan if specified conditions are met.   **13**

loan committee   The group in a financial institution responsible for approving loans.   **13**

loan fee   The charge made at the granting of a loan in addition to the required interest.   **2**

loan per unit   The amount of a loan divided by the number of units of a specified type such as apartments, square feet of office space, or parking spaces.   **15**

loan-to-value ratio   The percentage of the selling price or appraised value of a property that a lending institution will grant to a borrower.   **2**

location   The effect of the place in which a property is located on its market value.   **13**

market extraction method   The use of comparable sales of similar properties to estimate the market value of a property.   **15**

market failure   The inability of the free-market forces of demand and supply to bring about a desired goal.   **7**

market value   The price at which a willing seller would sell and a willing buyer would buy, neither being under abnormal pressure.   **13**

master limited partnership   The ownership of shares in a number of limited partnerships through a single overall limited partnership. Frequently, shares are saleable on a listed exchange or in the over-the-counter market.   **16**

maturity date   The date on which a loan or a mortgage becomes due and must be paid in full.   **2**

mechanic's lien   A claim existing in favor of mechanics or other persons who have performed work in or furnished materials for the erection or repair of a building.   **18**

minimum property standards   Minimum standards that a property must meet to be eligible for Federal Housing Administration mortgage insurance.   **8**

modified internal rate of return (MIRR)   A method of calculating rates of return in which the user supplies the assumed interest rate at which the cash flows will be reinvested.   **17**

modified pass-through   One type of mortgage-backed security guaranteed by the Government National Mortgage Association. The lender is responsible for sending scheduled payments to the investor, whether or not the borrower makes the payments.   **8**

monetary base   The amount of high-powered money that determines the maximum amount of the nation's money supply.   **5**

monetary policy   The use by the Federal Reserve Board of its controls over the nation's money supply and interest rates to help achieve the nation's economic goals.   **5**

money   The claims of individuals and firms against the government and financial institutions that serve as a medium of exchange and as a standard and store of value.   **5**

money market certificates   Savings certificates issued by financial institutions on which the interest rates are related to those in the overall money market.   **6**

Monte Carlo simulation   A method of estimating risks by drawing a large number of events from probability distributions.   **17**

mortgage   An instrument that pledges property as security for a debt or obligation.   **1**

mortgage-backed securities   Securities collateralized by a pool of mortgage loans.   **1, 8**

mortgage constant   The percentage of a loan required to cover the necessary payments on principal and interest.   **2**

mortgage-equity method   A system of estimating the capitalization rate for property valuation based on the weighted expected returns of all lenders and equity-holders in the property.   **15**

mortgage guarantee   A promise by the Veterans Administration to reimburse lenders up to a maximum amount on mortgages that it guarantees against losses from defaults.   **8**

mortgage insurance   The insurance of a mortgage lender against losses caused by the default of a mortgagor.   **8**

mortgage payment   The per-period sum of interest and any amortization promised on a mortgage.   **10**

mortgage pool   A group of mortgages used to collateralize a mortgage security.   **4**

mortgage tilt   Term describing the high nominal mortgage payments required in the early life of a mortgage when nominal interest rates include a large inflation premium.   **10**

mortgagee   One to whom a mortgagor gives a mortgage; a lender.   **2**

mortgagor   One who gives a mortgage on his or her property in order to secure a loan or the performance of an obligation; a borrower.   **2**

municipals   Tax-exempt municipal bonds. Recipients of income from such bonds need not include the interest payments in reported taxable income.   **7**

mutual   A form of organization in which the firm is owned by its members.   **6**

national housing policy   The stated goal of the U.S. government to insure that every household has the opportunity to live in a decent house, in a suitable environment, at a cost that leaves sufficient income available for other needs.   **7**

negative amortization   A condition in which the principal of a loan increases over time because payments are less than the amount of interest due in the period.   **1, 2**

negative leverage   A condition in which the debt service for a property exceeds the rate of return.   **4**

net operating income   The difference between the effective gross income and operating expenses.   **4**

net present value   The difference between the present value of all projected cash inflows and outflows.   **17**

nominal interest rate   The interest rate specified on the face of an agreement and not corrected for price changes.   **3**

nonrecourse loan   A loan for which the borrower does not assume personal liability in case of nonpayment.   **16**

NOW accounts   Accounts on which funds can be drawn by negotiable orders of withdrawal. They are equivalent to checking accounts that bear interest.   **6**

open market operations   The use by the Federal Reserve System of the purchase and sale of notes and bonds for the purpose of regulating the money supply and influencing interest rates.   **5**

open mortgage   A mortgage that permits prepayments.   **2**

open-end mortgage   A mortgage that states the intention of the borrower and the lender to allow the property to stand as security, not only for an original loan, but also for future advances.   **18**

operating expense ratio   The ratio obtained by dividing total operating expenses by effective gross income.   **15**

opportunity cost   The amount of income foregone as a result of making a down payment on a house rather than investing the amount of the down payment elsewhere.   **10**

option premium   The premium paid for a right to purchase or lease a property on specified terms within a given period of time.   **3**

over-the-counter market   A type of market in which financial assets are sold by telephone or computer links rather than through an organized exchange such as the New York Stock Exchange.   **1**

overage   The additional rents or interest a landlord or lender receives as a result of an agreement to participate in all revenues above a certain level.   **19**

overall capitalization rate   The capitalization rate obtained by dividing projected annual net operating income by the value or sales price of a property.   **15**

P.I.T.I.   The payments covering principal, interest, property taxes, and insurance.   **10**

participation   The sharing by two or more lenders of ownership in a mortgage loan.   **8**

participation certificate   A form of mortgage-backed security. Each certificate holder has the right to a specified share of any payments on interest and principal.   **8**

partitioning   The division of an investment's yield into the components on which it is based.   **17**

partnership   *See* general partnership, limited partnership, master limited partnership.

passive activities   Activities in which a partner neither materially participates in management nor provides personal services.   **16**

pass-through certificate   A mortgage-backed security in which the payments received, including prepayments, are passed through to the holders of the securities.   **8**

payback period   The time over which the amount of an investment is paid off. The equity divided by the cash flow to an investor.   **17**

personal property   Property such as furniture or equipment that is not real property.   **16**

physical depreciation   The loss in value of a property through physical deterioration.   **13**

points   The amount of a discount stated as a percentage. Each point equals 1 percent of the loan amount.   **4**

portfolio risk   The risk of receiving less than the expected rate of return on a portfolio. Usually, the total portfolio risk is less than the sum of the risks on individual assets in the portfolio.   **3**

positive carry   The income earned from holding a financial instrument when the interest it pays exceeds the interest required on the amounts borrowed to hold the instrument in inventory.   **8**

power of sale   The right of a mortgagee or trustee to sell property in default without court proceedings.   **2**

premium   Amounts included in interest rates to cover the possibility of losses based on the probability of events such as default, prepayments, or shifts in interest rates (the term structure premium).   **3**

prepaid finance charges   Charges by a lender, in addition to interest, to make a loan. Under the Truth in Lending Act, these charges must be included in calculating the annual percentage rate.   **13**

prepayment privilege   The right of a borrower to pay a mortgage in advance of its scheduled due date.   **2**

present value   The current value of an amount to be received in the future.   **3**

present-value profitability index   The profitability index obtained by dividing the present value of the expected cash flow from an investment by its price.   **17**

price-level adjusted mortgage (PLAM)   A mortgage whose interest rate is fixed at an agreed-upon real rate but whose principal adjusts each year in accordance with a price index.   **11**

primary market   A market in which loans are originated.   **6**

prime rate   The publicly announced interest rate that banks charge certain of their better customers.   **18**

principal   The outstanding amount of a loan.   **2**

principal residence   Usually, the home in which one lives.   **16**

private placement exemption   Rules that allow securities to be issued without being registered with the Securities and Exchange Commission.   **17**

pro forma financial statement   A projection of expected income and expenses plus reversion for a specified property.   **14**

profitability indexes   Estimates of the expected profits or rates of return from a property in a form suitable for comparison with other estimates.   **17**

promissory note   A promise signed by a borrower acknowledging a debt and the terms under which the debt is to be repaid.   **2**

proration   A division of certain expenses at the time of closing, so that the buyer and seller each pay the portion of the expenses for his or her period of ownership.   **13**

public offerings   Securities that have been registered with the Securities and Exchange Commission.   **17**

purchase-money mortgage   A trust deed or mortgage given as part or all of the consideration for property at the time of purchase.   **2**

purchasing-power risk   The risk that inflation will cause the dollars received back in the future in payment of a debt to buy less than they do at the time the loan is made.   **19**

qualification   The process through which a lender determines that a borrower can be expected to meet monthly payments promptly.   **12**

qualified buyer   One who can reasonably be expected to meet monthly mortgage payments without servicing difficulties.   **13**

qualified lenders   Those actively and regularly engaged in the business of lending money, usually excluding seller and promoter financing.   **16**

rate of return on assets (ROR)   The net operating income of a property divided by the total value of the assets (its price). Also called the free-and-clear return and the overall capitalization rate.   **4**

real estate investment trust (REIT)   A special arrangement under federal law whereby investors may pool funds for investments in real estate and mortgages and yet escape corporation taxes.   **6**

real estate mortgage investment company (REMIC)   A special conduit for actively managing and securitizing mortgages. It is a single-tax entity.   **16**

Real Estate Settlement Procedures Act (RESPA)   Federal legislation that regulates certain aspects of real estate settlements. It requires the disclosure of settlement costs, the use of uniform statements, and prohibits kickbacks.   **13**

real interest rate   The nominal interest rate corrected for changes in the price level.   **3**

real property   Land and, generally, anything that is erected on, growing on, or attached to land.   **16**

recapture rate   The portion of the return from an investment that covers its loss in value over time from depreciation.   **15**

recession   A period of underemployment and lower than normal output.   **5**

recording   The placing of legal documents on the public record in the registrar's office.   **2**

recourse loan   A mortgage for which the borrower is personally liable.   **16**

refinance   To repay a debt from the proceeds of a new loan, using the same property as security.   **12**

Regulation Q   The regulation of the Federal Reserve establishing maximum interest rates on deposits. Almost all such ceilings had been removed by 1986.   **9**

Regulation Z   The regulation of the Federal Reserve implementing the Truth in Lending Act.   **13**

release   The instrument that discharges property used as security from a lien.   **2**

release price   The amount of a development loan that must be repaid when each property under a blanket mortgage is sold.   **18**

replacement cost   The cost of replacing a property with one having equivalent utility and amenities, but not identical improvements.   **13**

reproduction cost   The cost of faithfully reproducing the improvements on a property to duplicate the original ones.   **13**

required rate of return   The rate of return required by an investor; the discount rate used in calculating net present value. Also called the cut-off or hurdle rate.   **17**

rescission   The right to cancel a purchase or agreement.   **17**

reserves   1. Those portions of earnings or of initial payments set aside to take care of possible losses or shortfalls in the cash flow. 2. Amounts required to be maintained as deposits at Federal Reserve banks based on an institution's own deposits.   **5, 13**

return   Any income derived from an investment in a period plus any change in its market value.   **3**

return of investment   That part of an investment's return considered as paying back the initial capital investment.   **15**

return on equity (ROE)   The ratio of cash flow after debt service to the equity; also called the cash-on-cash return.   **4**

return on investment   That part of an investment's return which is in addition to the return of the investment's capital.   **15**

reverse annuity mortgage (RAM)   An agreement in which the amount of a loan is paid out in monthly payments rather than as a lump-sum amount.   **11**

reversion   The amount received back at the end of an investment holding period.   **3**

right to reinstate   The right of a borrower to halt enforcement of a lien by paying all sums owed prior to the time the mortgage accelerated plus expenses while curing all defaults.   **2**

risk   The probability of a future loss.   **3**

risk-averse   The reluctance of an investor or lender to incur the risk of a loss or of a fluctuating return.   **3**

risk-free rate   The basic interest rate that includes no risk premium; often thought of as the rate on a 3-month U.S. Treasury bill.   **3**

rollover mortgage   A mortgage whose interest rate is subject to change at agreed-upon intervals.   **11**

sale-leaseback   A transaction in which the owner of a property sells it but retains occupancy by leasing it from the buyer.   **11, 19**

sales comparison approach   A method of appraising in which the market value is estimated from actual prices paid for comparable properties sold in the recent past.   **13**

sandwich lease   A situation in which a tenant with a master lease subleases in turn to other tenants, thus becoming both a landlord and a tenant.   **19**

saving   In the Gross National Product and Flow of Funds Accounts, income that is not spent on consumption or by the government.   **5**

Savings and Loan Cost of Funds Index   An index, published by the Federal Home Loan Banks, of the average cost paid by savings and loan associations on their liabilities in a period. It is a major index used in adjustable-rate mortgages.   **12**

secondary mortgage market   The mortgage market in which existing mortgages are traded and sold.   **1, 6**

Section 8 Program   A government subsidy program under which landlords are guaranteed a certain level of rents, even when an eligible family has insufficient income to meet the specified rent level.   **7**

securitization   The process of converting mortgage loans into securities with a wider market acceptance by using them as collateral behind these securities.   **8**

security   A deposit of pledge made to secure the fulfillment of an obligation or payment of a debt.   **2, 17**

selective credit controls   The power of the Federal Reserve Board to set credit terms on particular types of loans.   **5**

seller carry-back   A seller's providing some or all of the financing on a sale of real estate by accepting a mortgage for part of the sales price.   **11**

sensitivity analysis   A method of measuring risk by estimating the changes in returns and the chances of default that arise if the pro forma assumptions are altered.   **17**

service corporations   Subsidiaries through which savings and loan associations are authorized to perform nontraditional functions such as joint ventures and ownership of income property.   **16**

servicing   The collection of payments on a mortgage plus the related actions of a lender, including accounting, bookkeeping, follow-up on delinquent loans, and similar procedures.   **8**

settlement statement   A closing statement summarizing the charges and credits to the borrower and the seller.   **13**

shared appreciation mortgage (SAM)   A loan on which the lender accepts a lower interest rate in return for a portion of any increase in the value of the property.   **1, 11**

shortage of funds   A situation in which potential borrowers either cannot afford market interest rates or cannot obtain loans even though willing to pay the going rate.   **9**

soft costs   Financial, architectural, legal, and similar fees, as distinguished from hard costs (the actual construction of an improvement).   **18**

sponsored agencies   Federal agencies, such as the Federal National Mortgage Association and the Federal Home Loan Mortgage Corporation, established by the government but owned and operated by private individuals, which have special governmental rights and duties.   **7**

spot loans   Mortgages made to individuals but then pooled for sale in the secondary market.   **8**

spread   The amount of interest received by a lender to cover processing and servicing costs plus the default premium and the lender's profits.   **3**

stable monthly income   The adjusted level of income of a borrower that is expected to remain available for meeting mortgage and other payments.   **13**

stage of completion agreement   An agreement on the amount of the proceeds of a construction loan to be advanced when a certain level of progress is achieved in the construction of a structure.   **18**

standard deviation   The weighted probable deviation from the mean; used in measures of risk.   **3**

standby loan   A commitment to make a take-out loan in which both the potential borrower and lender assume that the standby loan will not be used.   **18**

statutory right of redemption   The right given to mortgagors who default to repay the outstanding mortgage debt plus accumulated interest and court costs, and thus to retain their property.   **2**

straight-line depreciation   A method of depreciation in which the same amount is deducted for tax purposes each year.   **16**

structuring   The division of ownership rights and financing so as to increase values through savings on tax payments and through meeting more exactly the portfolio needs of lenders and investors.   **14**

submission package   The application, reports, and projections required by lenders of prospective borrowers seeking a loan.   **15**

subordination clause   A clause in a mortgage or deed of trust permitting it to become junior to or subordinated to subsequent liens.   **2**

surcharge   An additional tax above the regular rate in a bracket.   **16**

swap   A trade by the Federal National Mortgage Association and the Federal Home Loan Mortgage Corporation of their securities for mortgages held by a lender.   **7**

syndicate   A group of persons combining to conduct business and make investments in real estate.   **16, 17**

syndicators   The firms that put together, manage, and sell investments in the form of syndicates.   **1**

T-accounts   The balance sheets used to explain Federal Reserve policy and the creation of the money supply.   **5**

take-out (permanent loan commitment)   A promise by a lender to make a permanent loan to pay off a construction loan.   **6, 18**

tandem plan   A government-subsidized mortgage plan in which the Government National Mortgage Association buys mortgages at a price above their market value in order to give an interest rate subsidy.   **7**

tax credits   Sums, granted for engaging in particular activities, that may be subtracted from taxes owed.   **16**

tax-deferred exchange   An exchange of real property through which some or all of the capital gains taxes normally due upon a sale may be deferred.   **16**

tax expenditures   The amount of reduction in taxes contained in the tax code for the purpose of accomplishing specific governmental objectives.   **7**

tax leverage   The ability of an equity holder to use the entire tax benefits from a property, even though it may be partially financed with nonrecourse loans.   **16**

tax preference items   Items that result in reduced regular taxes but that must be reported and are potentially taxable under the alternative minimum tax.   **16**

tax shelter   A means of reducing taxes currently due by using noncash expenses, such as depreciation, to reduce taxable income.   **14, 16**

teaser   A low initial interest rate on an adjustable-rate mortgage that is well below the interest rate that will prevail if the index remains stable.   **11**

tenancy in common   Ownership by two or more persons who hold undivided interest, without right of survivorship. Interests need not be equal.   **16**

term The life of a loan or an agreement. **2**

term structure of interest rates The relationships among the interest rates on loans of different maturities. **3**

term structure premium The premium paid to lenders who agree to tie up their money for longer periods of time. **3**

termination statement A pro forma statement showing the expected cash flow from a property upon sale, refinancing, or other ending of an investment. **14**

thrift industry The name applied to financial intermediaries that specialize in gathering the savings of individuals; savings and loan associations, savings banks, and (at times) credit unions. **1**

tight money Periods in the credit cycle when borrowers find it more difficult to obtain loans and when interest rates are higher than normal. **5**

time to maturity The time until a loan is paid off. **3**

time value of money The relationship of the value of money at one time compared with another because of discounting or compounding at a given interest rate. **3**

title theory The theory of mortgage law that views a mortgage as a transfer of title to the lender and gives the lender the right of possession on default. **2**

transaction costs Payments arising from the transfer of title of a property or of a loan. **10**

Truth in Lending Law A federal law requiring disclosure of the terms of a loan and, in particular, the effective annual percentage interest rate (APR). **13**

underwriting The analysis of a loan to make certain that its interest rate is appropriate to its risk and maturity. **13**

upturn The time in a credit or business cycle when contraction ends and expansion begins. **5**

usury Charging a rate of interest on a loan higher than that permitted by law. **5**

vacancy and collection loss ratio The ratio of projected vacancies and collection losses to the gross potential rent. **15**

variable-rate mortgage A loan whose interest rate fluctuates in accordance with an index over which the lender has no control. **11**

warehousing The borrowing by a mortgage banker of short-term funds from a commercial bank, using permanent loans as collateral. **6**

wraparound mortgage A junior mortgage that includes the balances due on an existing senior mortgage. **2**

yield capitalization The method of estimating value by discounting (capitalizing) the entire cash flow, in contrast to a single year or amount. **15**

zero coupon bond A bond on which the entire interest is payable only upon maturity. No payments or coupons are received until the entire principal and interest become due and payable. **3**

SELECTED REFERENCES

Part 1

Beaton, W. R. *Real Estate Finance,* 2nd ed. Englewood Cliffs, N.J.: Prentice-Hall, 1982.

Bergfeld, P. B. *Principles of Real Estate Law.* New York: McGraw-Hill, 1979.

Brueggeman, W., and L. Stone. *Real Estate Finance,* 7th ed. Homewood, Ill.: Irwin, 1981.

Buser, S. A., and P. H. Hendershott. "Pricing Default-Free Fixed-Rate Mortgages," *Housing Finance Review* 3, no.4 (1984): 405–430.

Dasso, J., and G. W. Kuhn. *Real Estate Finance.* Englewood Cliffs, N.J.: Prentice-Hall, 1983.

Dennis, M. W. *Mortgage Lending,* 2nd ed. Reston, Va.: Reston, 1983.

Downs, A. *The Revolution in Real Estate Finance.* Washington D.C.: The Brookings Institution, 1985.

Foster, C., and R. van Order. "FHA Terminations: A Prelude to Rational Mortgage Pricing," *AREUEA Journal* 13, no. 3 (1985): 273–291.

Hall, A. R. "Valuing the Mortgage Borrower's Prepayment Option," *AREUEA Journal* 13, no. 3 (1985): 229–247.

Heller, E. H. "An Institutional View of Foreign Investment in the United States," *The Real Estate Finance Journal* (Winter 1986): 62–66.

Hendershott, P. H., and S. A. Buser. "Spotting Prepayment Premiums," *Secondary Mortgage Market* 1, no.3 (1984): 21–25.

——— , S. Hu, and K. E. Villani. " The Economics of Mortgage Terminations: Implications for Mortgage Lenders and Mortgage Terms," *Housing Finance Review* 2, no. 2 (April 1983).

——— , J. D. Shelling, and K. E. Villani. "Measurement of the Spreads between Yields on Various Mortgage Contracts and Treasury Securities," *AREUEA Journal* 1, no. 4 (1984): 476–490.

Henszey, B. N., and R. M. Friedman. *Real Estate Law,* 2nd ed. New York: Wiley, 1984.

Kratovil, R., and R. Werner. *Real Estate Law,* 8th ed. Englewood Cliffs, N.J.: Prentice-Hall, 1983.

Peters, H. F., S. M. Pinkus, and D. J. Askin. "Prepayment Patterns of Conventional Mortgages: Experience from the Freddie Mac Portfolio," *Secondary Mortgage Markets* 1, no. 1 (1984): 6–11.

Salomon Brothers. *Real Estate Market Review.* New York.

Sharpe, W. F. *Investments,* 3rd ed. Englewood Cliffs, N.J.: Prentice Hall, 1985.

Sirmans, C. F. *Real Estate Finance.* New York: McGraw-Hill, 1985.

Van Horne, J. C. *Financial Management and Policy,* 7th ed. Englewood Cliffs, N.J.: Prentice-Hall, 1986.

Villani, K. E. *Pricing Mortgage Credit.* Washington D.C.: Federal Home Loan Mortgage Company, 1983, Working Paper Series No. 1.

Part 2

Baer, H. "Thrift Dominance and Specialization in Housing Finance: The Role of Taxation," *Housing Finance Review* 2, no. 4 (1983): 353–367.

Balderson, F. E. *Thrifts in Crisis.* Cambridge: Ballinger, 1985.

Biederman, K. R., and J. A. Tuccillo. *Taxation and Regulation of the Savings and Loan Industry.* Lexington, Mass.: Lexington, 1975.

Brennan, M. J., and E. S. Schwartz. "Determinants of GNMA Mortgage Prices," *AREUEA Journal* 13, no. 3 (1985): 209–228.

Carron, A. S. *The Plight of the Thrift Institutions.* Washington D.C.: The Brookings Institution, 1982.

Eisenbeis, R. A. "New Investment Powers: Diversification or Specialization," *Strategic Planning for Economic and Technological Change in the Financial Services Industry.* San Francisco: Federal Home Loan Bank of San Francisco, 1983.

Federal Home Loan Bank Board. *Agenda for Reform.* Washington D.C.: Federal Home Loan Bank Board, 1983.

Guttentag, J. M. "Recent Changes in the Primary Home Mortgage Market," *Housing Finance Review* 3, no. 3 (1984): 221–254.

Hendershott, P. H., and K. E. Villani. "Residential Mortgage Markets and the Cost of Mortgage Funds," *AREUEA Journal* 8, no. 1 (1980): 50–76.

Jaffee, D. M., and K. T. Rosen. "Mortgage Credit Availability and Residential Construction," *Brookings Papers on Economic Activity,* no. 2 (1979: 333–376.

Kane, E. J. "Change and Progress in Contemporary Mortgage Markets," *Housing Finance Review* 3, no. 3 (1984): 257–282.

———. *The Gathering Crisis in Federal Deposit Insurance.* Cambridge, Mass.: Massachusetts Institute of Technology, 1985.

Kaplan, M. A. "Deregulation and New Powers in the Savings and Loan Industry: What This Portends," *Housing Finance Review* 2, no. 2 (1983): 145–156.

Kaufman, G. G. "The Role of Traditional Mortgage Lenders in Future Mortgage Lending: Problems and Prospects," *Housing Finance Review* 3, no. 3 (1984): 285–316.

Kolb, R. W., J. B. Corgel, and R. Chiang. "Effective Hedging of Mortgage Interest Rate Risk," *Housing Finance Review* 1, no. 2 (1983): 135–146.

Meador, M. "The Effects of Federally Sponsored Credit on Housing Markets: Some Evidence from Multivariate Exogeneity Tests," *Housing Finance Review* 4, no. 1 (1985): 505–515.

Moran, M. J. "The Federally Sponsored Credit Agencies: An Overview," *Federal Reserve Bulletin* 71, no. 6 (1985): 373–388.

Ochs, M. A. "Creative Hedging," *Real Estate Finance* 2, no. 2 (1986).

Quigley, J. M., and D. L. Rubinfeld, eds. *American Domestic Priorities.* Berkeley: University of California, 1985.

Seiders, D. F. "The Future of Secondary Mortgage Markets: Economic Forces and Federal Policies," *Housing Finance Review* 3, no. 3 (1984): 319–348.

Standard and Poor's. "Securitizing Commercial Real Estate," *Credit Week* (Feb. 24, 1986): 13–14.

Struyk, R. J., N. Mayer, and J. A. Tuccillo. *Federal Housing Policy at President Reagan's Midterm.* Washington D.C.: Urban Institute, 1983.

Tuccillo, J. A., R. van Order, and K. E. Villani. "Homeownership Policies and Mortgage Markets, 1960 to 1980," *Housing Finance Review* 1, no. 1 (1982) 1–22.

U.S. Council of Economic Advisers. *Economic Report of the President,* 1986. Washington D.C.: Government Printing Office, 1986.

U.S. Office of Management and Budget. *Special Analyses, Budget of the United States Government, FY* 1987. Washington D.C.: Government Printing Ofiice, 1986.

U.S. President's Commission on Housing. *The Report of the President's Commission on Housing.* Washington D.C.: Government Printing Office, 1982.

Villani, K. E. "The Secondary Mortgage Markets: What They Are, What They Do, and How to Measure Them," *Secondary Mortgage Markets* 1, no. 1 (1984): 24–44.

Zumpano, L. V., P. M. Rudolph, and D. C. Cheng. "The Demand and Supply of Mortgage Funds and Mortgage Loan Terms," *AREUEA Journal* 14, no.1 (1986): 91–109.

Part 3

Alm, J., and J. R. Follain, Jr. "Alternative Mortgage Instruments: The Tilt Problem and Consumer Welfare," *Journal of Financial and Quantitative Analysis* 19, no. 1 (1984): 113–126.

———. "Alternative Mortgage Instruments: Their Effects on Consumer Housing Choices in an Inflationary Environment," *Public Finance Quarterly* 10, no. 2 (1982): 134–157.

Buser, S. A., P. H. Hendershott, and A. B. Sanders. "Pricing Life of Loan Rate Caps on Default-Free Adjustable-Rate Mortgages," *AREUEA Journal* 13, no. 3 (1985): 248–260.

Campbell, T. S., and J. K. Dietrich. "The Determinants of Default on Insured Conventional Residential Mortgage Loans," *Journal of Finance* 38, no. 5 (1983): 1569–1581.

Diamond, D. B., Jr. "Taxes, Inflation, Speculation and the Cost of Homeownership," *AREUEA Journal* 3 (1980): 281–298.

Epperson, J. F., et al. "Pricing Default Risk in Mortgages," *AREUEA Journal* 13, no. 3 (1985): 261–272.

Foster, C., and R. van Order. "An Option-Based Model of Mortgage Default," *Housing Finance Review* 3, no. 4 (1984): 351–372.

Gillingham, R. "Measuring the Cost of Shelter for Homeowners: Theoretical and Empirical Considerations," *Review of Economics and Statistics* 65, no. 2 (1983): 254–265.

Guttentag, J. M. "Solving the Mortgage Menu Problem," *Housing Finance Review* 2, no. 3 (1983): 227–252.

Hendershott, P. H. "Valuing ARM Rate Caps: Implications of 1970–1984 Interest Rate Behavior," *AREUEA Journal* 13, no. 3 (1985): 317–332.

Jaffee, D. M. "Creative Finance: Measures, Sources, and Tests," *Housing Finance Review* 3, no. 11 (1984): 1–18.

Kau, J. B. *A Model for Pricing Adjustable-Rate Mortgages.* Federal Home Loan Bank of San Francisco, Research Report (May 1986).

Lea, M. J. "An Empirical Analysis of the Value of ARM Features," *Housing Finance Review* 4, no.1 (1985): 467–481.

Lessard, D., and F. Modigliani, eds. *New Designs for Stable Housing in an Inflationary Environment.* Boston: Federal Reserve Bank of Boston, 1975.

Manchester, J. "Evidence on Possible Default under Three Mortgage Contracts," *Housing Finance Review* 4, no. 1 (1985) 517–536.

O'Mara, W. P., et al. *Rental Housing.* Washington D.C.: Urban Land Institute, 1984.

Peters, H. F., S. M. Pinkus, and D. J. Askin. "Default: The Last Resort," *Secondary Mortgage Market* 1, no. 3 (1984): 16–20.

Pyhrr, S. A., and J. R. Cooper. *Real Estate Investment: Strategy, Analysis, Decisions.* New York: Wiley, 1982.

Rosen, K. T. *Affordable Housing.* Cambridge: Ballinger, 1984.

———. *California Housing Markets in the 1980s: Demand, Affordability, and Policies.* Cambridge: Oelgeschlager, Gunn, and Hain, 1984.

Schnidman, F., and J. A. Silverman, eds. *Housing: Supply and Affordability.* Washington D.C.: Urban Land Institute, 1983.

Vandell, K. D., and T. Thibodeau. "Estimation of Mortgage Defaults Using Disaggregate Loan History Data," *AREUEA Journal* 13, no. 3 (1985): 292–316.

Part 4

Aaron, H. J., and H. Galper. *Assessing Tax Reform.* Washington D.C.: The Brookings Institution, 1985.

Bible, D. S., and S. E. Celec. "Real Estate Investment Analysis: New Developments in Traditional Leverage Concepts," *AREUEA Journal* 8, no. 2 (1980): 198–206.

Boyce, B. N., and W. N. Kinnard, Jr. *Appraising Real Property.* Lexington, MA: Lexington Books, 1984.

Cohen, A. C. "Extracting Cap Rates 'From the Market': Beware!" *The Appraisal Journal* 47, no. 3 (1979): 370–373.

Diamond, D. B. *The Impacts on Housing of the House Tax Reform Bill and the Packwood Proposal.* Washington D.C.: National Association of Home Builders, 1986.

Findlay III, M. C., S. D. Messner, and R. A. Tarantello, eds. *Real Estate Portfolio Analysis.* Lexington, Mass.: Lexington Books, 1983.

Fogler, H. R., M. R. Granito, and L. R. Smith. "A Theoretical Analysis for Real Estate Returns," *Journal of Finance* 40, no. 3 (1985): 711–719.

Friedman, J., et al. *Real Estate Appraisal.* Reston, Va.: Reston, 1985.

Greer, G. E. *Real Estate Investor and the Federal Income Tax,* 2nd ed. New York: Wiley, 1982.

Hekman, J. S. "Rental Price Adjustment and Investment in the Office Market," *AREUEA Journal* 13, no. 1 (1985): 32–47.

Hornick, P. "Applications of Portfolio Theory to Real Estate," *Real Estate Review* 13, no. 2 (1983): 88–92.

Kau, J. B., and C. F. Sirmans. *Tax Planning for Real Estate Investors.* Englewood Cliffs, N.J.: Prentice-Hall, 1985.

Kearl, J. R. "Inflation, Mortgages and Housing," *Journal of Political Economy* 87, no. 5 (1979): 1115–1138.

Kelly, H. F. "Forecasting Office Space Demand in Urban Areas," *Real Estate Review* 13, no. 3 (1983): 87–95.

Laventhol and Horwath. *Hotel/Motel Development.* Washington D.C.: Urban Land Institute, 1984.

Maisel, S. J., and J. M. Quigley. "Tax Reform and Real Estate," *California Management Review* 28, no. 1 (1985): 155–168.

Messner, S. D., and M. C. Findlay III. "Real Estate Analysis: IRR versus FMRR," *Real Estate Appraiser and Analyst* 51, no. 2 (1985) 5–20.

Miles, M., ed. "International Real Estate Investment," special edition, *AREUEA Journal* 12, no. 3 (1984).

Nourse, H. O. "Improve Investment Decisions by Breaking the DCF Habit," *Real Estate Review* 15, no. 4 (1986): 75–80.

Ochs, M. A. "Interest Rate Protection for the Real Estate Developer," *Real Estate Finance* 1, no. 4 (1985): 8–17.

Sirmans, C. F., and A. J. Jaffe. *The Complete Real Estate Investment Handbook,* 2nd ed. Englewood Cliffs, N.J.: Prentice-Hall, 1984.

Steuerle, C. E. *Taxes, Loans, and Inflation.* Washington D.C.: The Brookings Institution, 1985.

Urban Land Institute. *Dollars & Cents of Shopping Centers.* Washington D.C.: Urban Land Institute, 1985.

——— . *Shopping Center Development Handbook,* 2nd ed. Washington D.C.: Urban Land Institute, 1985.

Urdang, S. "Participating Mortgages: Determining True Returns," *Mortgage Banking* 46, no. 7 (1986): 91–93.

Walters, D. W. *Real Estate Exchanges.* New York: Wiley, 1982.

Webb, J. R. "Real Estate Investment Acquisition Rules for Life Insurance Companies and Pension Funds: A Survey," *AREUEA Journal* 12, no. 4 (1984): 495–520.

Young, M. S. "FMRR: A Clever Hoax?" *The Appraisal Journal,* 47, no. 3 (1979): 359–369.

INDEX

Page numbers in italics refer to terms appearing in the Glossary.